Potter County Pennsylvania Potpourri

Genealogical
and Historical News
from
The Potter Enterprise

Volume I
1880-1884

Maureen M. Lee

HERITAGE BOOKS
2007

HERITAGE BOOKS
AN IMPRINT OF HERITAGE BOOKS, INC.

Books, CDs, and more—Worldwide

For our listing of thousands of titles see our website
at
www.HeritageBooks.com

Published 2007 by
HERITAGE BOOKS, INC.
Publishing Division
65 East Main Street
Westminster, Maryland 21157-5026

Copyright © 2007 Maureen M. Lee

Other books by the author:

Township Tidings, from Potter County, Pennsylvania: News from All of the Valleys, Creeks and Hollows in the County; Volume 1, The Years 1880-1884

Wayne County, Nebraska Newspaper Abstracts, 1876-1899

All rights reserved. No part of this book may be reproduced or transmitted in any form or by any means, electronic or mechanical, including photocopying, recording or by any information storage and retrieval system without written permission from the author, except for the inclusion of brief quotations in a review.

International Standard Book Number: 978-0-7884-4103-5

TABLE OF CONTENTS

Introduction v

The Potter Enterprise Abstracts 1

Index 477

INTRODUCTION

Pick up any newspaper from the nineteenth century and you are bound to be, initially, taken aback at the bluntness of the news. It seems the publishers and editors of the day had little fear of lawsuits and took the First Amendment to heart, and print. The news, whether scandalous, gory or borderline truth, was put out there for all to read.

The *Potpourri* series was created using *The Potter Enterprise*, the leading newspaper of the county in the late 1800s. Due to the vast amount of material available, the volumes have been broken into four five-year increments; 1880-1884, 1885-1889, 1890-1894 and 1895-1899.

The *Potpourri* works cover a wide variety of items: births, marriages and divorces, deaths (including suicides and homicides), crimes and court minutes, disasters such as fires and floods, real estate transactions, politics and township elections, holidays and celebrations, military and soldier news, education, fraternal events, farming and agriculture, lumbering, merchants and businesses and advertising. Soldier lists, school reports, jury lists, advertised letters, township statistics and a variety of other items will also be found herein.

For a more intimate and "neighborly" read, I would refer you to the *Township Tidings* series, which contains correspondents' reports from nearly every valley and hollow in the county – who's moving in and who's moving out, who is building, local business, those taken ill, who's visiting, church activities and events, the harvest, the weather, &c.

Potter County, which celebrated its bicentennial in 2004, has a rich history, and while these works cover only a twenty-year span, or a mere one-tenth of the county's history, they greatly detail those twenty years.

Maureen M. Lee
www.happeningsinthehills.com
September 2005

Potter County, Pennsylvania Potpourri – Volume I
1880 through 1884

The Potter Enterprise
Thursday Evening, May 12, 1880 – Vol. VII, No. 1

OFFICIAL DIRECTORY.

PROTHONOTARY – O. H. Crosby.
REGISTER AND RECORDER – O. J. Rees.
TREASURER – M. V. Larrabee.
SHERIFF – J. M. Covey.
DISTRICT ATTORNEY – J. L. Knox.
COUNTY COMMISSIONERS – A. B. Crowell, Dana Drake, William R. Greenman.
COUNTY CLERK – George W. Pearsoll.
AUDITORS – Thomas Coulston, Robert McDowell, D. C. Chase.
COUNTY SUPERINTENDENT – A. F. Hollenbeck.
COUNTY SURVEYOR – W. A. Crosby.
COUNTY CORONER – D. Chas. Meine.
JUDICIARY – PRESIDENT JUDGE – H. W. Williams; ADDITIONAL LAW JUDGE – S. F. Wilson.
ASSOCIATE JUDGES – N. C. Hammond, E. W. Chappel.
TIME OF HOLDING COURT – First Monday in March, Second Monday in June, Third Monday in September and the Second Monday in December.

Coudersport Church Directory.

PRESBYTERIAN – Corner of Main and Fourth streets.
METHODIST EPISCOPAL – Third street, between Main and East streets, Rev. T. R. Stratton, Pastor services every Sunday at 10:30 a.m., and 7:30 p.m.
BAPTIST – Market St., south side of the river, Episcopal Services every Sunday morning by Rev. J. McBride Sterrett.

BUSINESS DIRECTORY.

ATTORNEYS.

ISAAC BENSON. **C. L. PECK**
Benson & Peck, Attorneys-at-Law.
With power to retain M. F. Elliott to assist in the trial of causes. Collections promptly attended to.
OFFICE NORTH SIDE OF SECOND ST., BETWEEN EAST ST., AND THE RIVER, COUDERSPORT, PA.

F. W. KNOX & SON, Attorneys-at-Law,
Will attend the several Courts of Potter, McKean and Cameron counties.
OFFICE, CORNER OF MAIN & FIRST ST., COUDERSPORT, PA.

B. RENNELLS & SON,
BLACKSMITHS, Corner of West and Second Streets, Coudersport, Penn'a.
Horse Shoeing, Carriage Ironing and Custom work in all its branches.

PHYSICIANS.

DR. F. BUCK,
PHYSICIAN AND OPERATIVE SURGEON.
COUDERSPORT, PA.
All calls promptly attended to.

MATTISON & SWETLAND.
Dr. E. S. MATTISON, Physician and Surgeon, Office on West Street, between Second and Third. All calls promptly attended, night or day.

HOTELS.

THE BAKER HOUSE,
M. L. GRIDLEY, Proprietor.
Corner Second and East Streets,
COUDERSPORT, PA.
Refitted and refurnished. Good rooms, good table, good sample room for commercial travelers and good appointments all around.

OLEONA HOTEL.
J. O. EDGCOMB, LESSEE,
KETTLE CREEK, PA.
A Pleasant resort for summer visitors, being situated in the heart of the best fishing and hunting grounds of Northern Pennsylvania. Terms moderate.

COUDERSPORT HOTEL,
MILES WHITE, Proprietor. Corner Main and Second Sts., Coudersport, Pa. All stages stop at this house for passengers. Terms reasonable.

MAJOR J. M. KILBOURNE, PROPRIETOR OF
KILBOURNE'S HOTEL,
PIKE MILLS, Potter County, Pa.
Having completed a new and commodious house on the site of the old hotel, lately destroyed by fire, would say to the public that he is ready to provide good accommodations for the weary traveler and a pleasant home for all who call. This Hotel is near the BEST FISHING GROUNDS in Northern Pennsylvania. Mercantile travelers invited to call. Old and new patrons will find us at the old site, at the new bridge over Pine Creek. Good stables and good care taken of teams. Charges down to cheap times. Fishing season from April 1st to August 15th.

MACHINERY.
LEWIS A. GLACE,
AGENT FOR THE BODINE JONVAL TURBINE Water Wheel, of Mt. Morris, N.Y., is now prepared to put them in on fair terms. The power of this Turbine is equal to any wheel, and it is cheaper. When desired plans and estimates will be carefully prepared for persons about to erect mills.

LEWIS A. GLACE,
Coudersport, Pa., March 31, 1875.

STAGE LINE.
COUDERSPORT (via Oswayo) to WELLSVILLE and return, three times per week, leaving Coudersport Mondays, Wednesdays and Fridays, arriving in Wellsville same afternoon. Leave Wellsville Tuesdays, Thursday and Saturday, arriving in Coudersport same evening. Special attention given to passengers and the carrying of small packages. Charges very low.

J. O. MERRILL, Prop'r.

SURVEYING & CONVEYANCING.
ORLANDO J. REES,
SURVEYOR, CONVEYANCER AND DRAUGHTSMAN, Prothonotary's office, Court House, COUDERSPORT, Pa. Business promptly attended to in any part of the county.

> **C. H. ARMSTRONG,**
> DEALER IN GROCERIES, PROVISIONS, CROCKERY
> Glassware, Woodenware, Boots and Shoes.
> Second street, nearly opposite the Court House.
> Coudersport, Pa.

> **Teeth Extracted,   Comparatively**
> **PAINLESS.**
> By a perfectly safe and pleasant process. No gas or chloroform used, both are dangerous. Filling and orders for plates promptly attended to, work, cheaper than the cheapest.
> S. A. PHILLIPS, Dentist.
> Office over French's drug store, Coudersport, Pa.

> **RESTAURANT.**
> **THAD. KELLY,**
> WARM MEALS of LUNCH at all hours. Oysters, in their season, served on short notice. Families supplied at reasonable rates. Good beds for lodgers, when desired.
> Second Street, COUDERSPORT, PA.
Nearly opposite Court House.

> **MEAT MARKET.**
> **K. ZIMMERMAN.**
> SECOND STREET, COUDERSPORT, PA.
> Keeps on hand the best quality of Fresh Meats, Smoked Hams and Shoulders, Dried Beef, Smoked Halibut, Herring, Codfish, Mackerel, Lard, Tallow, etc. After May 1st will run a meat wagon to the surrounding country.

> **F. B. McNAMARA, TAILOR,**
> Wishes to inform the citizens of Coudersport and vicinity that he has moved to the village and is ready to do all kinds of work in his line, and hopes by attention to business to have a fair share of public patronage. All work entrusted to his care will be made neat and substantial and at prices to suit the times. NEW YORK and PHILADELPHIS FASHIONS received every three months; I do not make work on a machine; it will keep its shape, and a fit every time; all kinds of farm produce taken in exchange for work; all kinds of garments cut, from boys clothes to a lady's riding habit. Place of business, upper end of Main street, inquire of anyone – everybody knows me.
> F. B. McNAMARA.

ON HAND
For Spring's Work
A. C. PERKINS,
INTENDS TO CONTINUE THE
Blacksmithing Business
AT THE OLD STAND.
Everything in his line will receive careful attention. Special attention paid to
HORSE SHOEING.
and long experience in the business warrants us in guaranteeing satisfaction.
COUNTRY PRODUCE
of all kinds taken at the market price.
GIVE US A CALL.
A. C. PERKINS.
SOUTH SIDE OF SECOND STREET,
COUDERSPORT, PA.

ESTABLISHED IN 1867
ARTHUR B. MANN,
FIRE, LIFE & ACCIDENT INSURANCE AGENT.
COUDERSPORT, PENNA.
Policies in RELIABLE Companies written at STANDARD RATES.
Will visit any part of the Country promptly, on request.

EXPRESS LINE.
Daily Stage and Express Line
Good Coaches and Fast Time
FROM
Coudersport to Port Allegany,
AND INTERMEDIATE POINTS.
Stages will leave Coudersport at 7:30 a.m., arriving in Port Allegany in time for all trains.
Leaves Port Allegany after trains arrive reaching Coudersport at 6:30 p.m.
Best Horses, Best Coaches and Best Time.
EXPRESS MATTER
will receive prompt attention.
D. F. GLASSMIRE, PROPRIETOR.

JOHN B. PEARSALL,
PRACTICAL HOUSE PAINTER,
Coudersport, Pa.,

Having commenced business for the Painting season for 1876, I hold myself in readiness to do

House Painting, Paper Hanging,
COLORING WALLS AND CEILINGS

in oil or kalsomine colors.

All work entrusted to my care will receive PROMPT ATTENTION, and warranted to give satisfaction. A share of the public patronage is respectfully solicited. Work done in all parts of the County, and charges reasonable.

JOHN B. PEARSALL.

COUDERSPORT GRADED SCHOOL.
ANNOUNCEMENT FOR 1879-80.
Prof. JOHN R. GROVES, A.M., Principal.
FRANCIS M. BENNETT, Grammar School Department.
HELEN M. BROOKS, Primary Department.

Fall Term begins,	August 25, 1879
Fall Term ends,	November 21, 1879
Winter Term begins,	November 26, 1879
Winter Term ends,	March 4, 1880
Spring Term begins,	March 8, 1880
Spring Term ends,	May 6, 1880

RATES OF TUITION

To be paid or secured at commencement of the term.

Primary Department, per term	$3.00
Intermediate Department, per term	4.00
High School Department, per term	5.00

Spring Term $1 less each Department.

Classes in "Elocution" and for instruction in the "Theory and Practice of Teaching" will be formed when necessary.

Rooms can be secured at reasonable rates by those desiring to board themselves, and boarding at from $2.00 to $3.00 per week.

D. C. LARRABEE, Secretary   H. J. OLMSTED, President

> **Stage Lines.**
> Stages will leave Coudersport as follows:
> PORT ALLEGANY, daily except Sunday.
> WELLSVILLE, via Colesburg, and Ellisburg, Tuesday, Thursday and Saturday.
> WELLSVILLE, via Oswayo, Monday, Wednesday and Friday.
> WESTFIELD, via Brookland and Ulysses, Tuesday, Thursday and Saturday.
> WESTFIELD, via Raymond and Ulysses, Monday, Wednesday and Friday.
> CERES, Monday, Wednesday and Friday.
> KETTLE CREEK, Tuesday and Friday.
> SINNEMAHONING, Wednesday and Saturday.

Fishing Creek. It is Mr. Otis Lyman that can be seen applying the persuader to hose mules, and says, "Get along there for I don't care a darn, it's a girl."

MARRIED.

NORTON – FULTZ – At the residence of Dr. A. French, May 5, 1880, by Rev. T. R. Stratton, Mr. F. J. Norton and Miss Laura Fultz, all of Coudersport, Pa.

CHESBRO – LYMAN – At the residence of Jasper Spafford, May 5, 1880, by Rev. T. R. Stratton, Mr. Warren C. Chesbro of Homer, Pa., and Miss Hattie Lyman of Sweden, Pa.

- Joseph M'Chesney, who a short time ago was married to Miss Mary Kernan of Coudersport, had the misfortune to lose his dwelling house in the Rixford fire. He also had several derricks and a quantity of oil destroyed.

DIED.

FURMAN – In Sweden, May 8, 1880, Clara, daughter of Andrew and Maria Furman, aged 13 years.

Harrison Valley. Still another death from diphtheria. Mr. John J. Jones lost his only daughter on Saturday last.

Ulysses. There is a gloom cast over the people of this vicinity, Dr. Eaton's little girl was buried May 2d, after much suffering. The Doctor himself was then stricken down with the same disease, diphtheria, but hopes are entertained of his recovery.

- Mrs. M'Cormick of this place received a dispatch Monday evening announcing the death of her husband, in New York. For a number of years Mr. M'Cormick has spent most of his time in South America, and but a short time ago left this place to go to Brazil, but owing to ill health was unable to get farther than New York. The deceased leaves a wife and several children to mourn his loss.

Isaac Baker Killed.

Last Friday afternoon about five o'clock, at Dr. O. T. Ellison's saw mill, a short distance above town, Isaac Baker of Eulalia township, was almost instantly killed by the large circular saw used in sawing lumber.

For a short time past Mr. Baker had been at work in the mill attending a small cut-off saw and occasionally assisting in jacking-in logs from the pond. Less than an hour before his death he had a very narrow escape, while putting on a belt that had slipped from its wheel, and he would have doubtless been drawn between the belt and wheel in such a manner that it would have resulted in his death but for the interference of some of the mill hands who were better acquainted with machinery.

After this he returned to the cut-off saw, where he was at work but a few moments when Joe Brown drove into the mill yard for a load of plank, as the plank had to be sorted, the man tail-sawing left to assist Joe, and Mr. Baker took his place.

The first slab that dropped from the saw as Mr. Baker took his place was a very heavy one, and instead of carrying it back and across the carriage track, he attempted to lift it over the saw, but in some manner the slab near the end caught the saw, and before he could let go, he was drawn upon the saw and thrown some eight or nine feet back, a mangled, quivering, old man, with just life enough to gasp, "Oh, my God, take me off from here." A few gasps and his spirit returned to its Maker. When thrown from the saw, Mr. Baker struck upon the log carriage, which had been gigged back as soon as the slab fell from the log, his head striking against some of the iron work, cutting a large gash in the top of his head and right temple.

He was quickly removed from the carriage to the mill floor, but never spoke again, and was dead almost as soon as the hands could reach him.

Our reporter found the body lying on the mill floor, upon a blanket, with a pillow placed under his head, and the body partially covered, but still presenting a most horrible sight. He was lying on the left side, the left boot heel was torn off, the calf of the right leg was ragged where the saw teeth had cut almost to the bone, the clothes were more than half torn from the body. The saw had struck at the upper part of the hips, cutting through, at the small of the back, rather more on the right than on the left side, and passing up a little more than half way to the shoulders, leaving the internal organs exposed to view, somewhat lascerated by the saw. At the top of the head the scalp was torn loose, perhaps four or five inches square; the right temple was covered with blood and had the appearance of being crushed in, and was caused when thrown from the saw. The skull was doubtless fractured at the temple and the top of the head. Spots of blood and shreds of flesh were scattered about the carriage and later a small piece of the back bone was found at the rear of the mill, where it had been thrown by the saw.

Potter County, Pennsylvania Potpourri – Volume I
1880 through 1884

The body was placed in a neat coffin and removed to his former residence, and on Saturday was interred in the Crandall Hill burying ground.

The deceased was about sixty years of age, he leaves a wife who has been sick for some time and at the time of the accident was still unable to leave her bed, and several children, one or two grown up and the youngest we are informed about fourteen years of age.

It would seem that the deceased had a presentament of his untimely end. Thursday he came very near drowning while working at the logs on the pond, and Friday as he was leaving the house he said to his wife, "I came very near being drowned yesterday. I suppose to-day will finish me."

The deceased served some time in the army during the late war, doing his duty as a soldier and has been a hard working, honest man. The family is left in destitute circumstances.

Close of School.

We print below the programme of exercises which were performed in connection with the close of school, in the Graded School Building in this village, Wednesday evening, May 5th. Miss Haskell and Miss Hollenbeck, who were expected, were not present. All who took part acquitted themselves creditably, and were benefitted, besides giving pleasure to others. Mr. Chas. Nelson was the committee on music. To him and to the ladies and gentlemen who so kindly assisted in the preparation of the music, especial thanks are due.

Music
Prayer

A Lesson in Good Manners,	Anna Boyer
Going to District School,	Isabella Crane
The Second Guests	Lavinia Dingee
A Dream	Mable Dingman
A Sermon for Young Folks	Celia Gillon
Essay	Edith Haskell
Essay	F. Hollenbeck
Grandmothers	Jay Lewis
A Legend of Bregenz	Carrie Larrabee
What is Life?	Lula Millard

Music

Pyramus and Thisbe	May Nelson
Defense of Hofer	Wm. Norton
Success in Life – Oration	Chas. Nelson
The Vagabonds	Homer White
Attire – Essay	E. Witter

Music
Adjournment

On Thursday evening, the 6th, Prof. A. N. Raub, Principal of the Central State Normal School, Lock Haven, delivered an interesting and instructive address on Reforms in Education. Every person that has any interest in the cause of education, should, if possible, have heard that address.

Forster
Money saved by purchasing at the
BOSS
GROCERY
Examine my goods before purchasing else where and you will admit that I keep the very best that the market affords, and the largest stock of Groceries and Provisions,
TEAS, COFFEES, SPICES, SOAPS, SALT DRIED BEEF,
HAMS, AND PORK, SALT FISH, CROCKERY, WOODEN WARE, YANKEE NOTIONS,
&C., &C.
CIGARS AND TOBACCO Of the Best Brands.
THORNTON & CHESTER'S FLOUR
I desire especially to call attention to my large stock of Men and Boys
FINE & HEAVY BOOTS.
Boss Grocery Store.
Edward Forster.

E. O. REES,
Watchmaker and Jeweler
COUDERSPORT, PA.
Watches,
Clocks,
Jewelry,
Plated Ware,
Spectacles,
Glasses,
Fire Arms,
Ammunition, &c.,
KEPT CONSTANTLY ON HAND.
REPAIRING
Of all kinds prompt attendance.
FISHING TACKLE.
A large assortment of rods, lines, reels, hooks and the celebrated McBRIDE FLIES.
AGENT FOR THE CELEBRATED
ESTEY COTTAGE ORGAN
E. O. Rees.

L. B. COLE & SON,
LIFE, FIRE AND ACCIDENT
Insurance Agents,
COUDERSPORT, PA.
Office – In building formerly occupied by
Mack Gillon.
Reliable Companies Represented,
Policies Written at Low Rates.
Will attend in business in any part of the County.

The best place in Potter County to exchange
FARM PRODUCE, LUMBER or SHINGLES for
DRY GOODS, GROCERIES,
Hats, Caps,
Boots and Shoes,
HARDWARE, RUBBER
GOODS, ETC., ETC.,
IS AT
JONES & DODGE'S.
Having a Branch Store at RIXFORD enables
us to pay the highest market prices for all
kinds of
MERCHANTABLE PRODUCE
and at the same time compete in prices with
any business concern in Potter County.
Give us a call.
JONES & DODGE,
SHINGLE HOUSE, PA.

HIGH CLASS
POULTRY
PLYMOUTH ROCKS,
BROWN LEGHORNS,
BLACK RED GAMES,
AND
ROWEN DUCKS.
Eggs after February 20th, from my best
stock, fresh and carefully packed at $2.00
per sitting of 13. Chickens for sale in the fall.
THOMAS R. SHEAR.
Coudersport. Pa.

CORNER STORE   CORNER STORE
P. A. STEBBINS, JR. & BRO.,
Have just received direct from
NEW YORK and PHILADELPHIA
Markets, the most complete stock
of GOODS ever brought into
this place. We have an ELEGANT line of
FANCY GOODS,
DRESS FABRICS, SUITINGS, ETC.,
A FULL LINE OF
DRESS GOODS,
HOSIERY, NOTIONS,
CARPETS, HATS, ETC.,
A VERY NICE STOCK OF
LADIES', MISSES', &
CHILDREN'S SHOES, ETC.
A LARGE STOCK OF
MEN'S, YOUTHS' & BOYS'
CLOTHING, purchased direct
A FINE AND CHOICE STOCK
OF GROCERIES,
Replenished every week.
We invite a careful inspection of our
GOODS and PRICES.
We make a SPECIALTY in keeping good
GOODS and sell at POPULAR PRICES.
Corner Main Street, Coudersport.
P. A. STEBBINS, JR. & BRO.

LOOK, TO YOUR CLAIMS.
The Tide Water Pipe Line is running many
thousand barrels of oil, and so is
George Brahmer
Going to do many dollars worth of work in his
NEW BLACKSMITH SHOP.
You will find him in the building formerly occupied
as a Cooper Shop. So
GIVE HIM A CALL
and see if you can
GET SATISFACTION
Come on
WITH YOUR WORK
All Kinds of Produce taken in exchange for Work.
GEO. BRAHMER.

THE ARK.
NEW GOODS
are received at this STORE every 30 days. Consisting of
DRY GOODS,
NOTIONS,
CLOTHING
HATS AND CAPS,
BOOTS AND SHOES,
CROCKERY, AND
GLASS WARE,
GROCERIES AND
PROVISIONS.
Highest CASH price paid for
PRODUCE
in exchange.
HAY PRESSES.
I am manufacturing hay presses of my own invention,
that are light in comparison with other presses, which
I can sell for about one-third the price asked for
any other good press. It is light, durable, and cheap.
Just the thing for every farmer who hauls hay.
For particulars call on or address
N. W. HERRING,
MILLPORT, PA.

STOVES.
We are now ready for the Fall and
Winter trade with a large new stock of
HEATING AND COOKING
STOVES.
New and Handsome Designs and Latest Improvements.
Although stoves are advancing in price
we are still selling at
ROCK BOTTOM
Please call and examine our stoves and compare
prices, whether you want to buy or not.
We have as usual a large and well
selected stock of Heavy and Shelf Hard
ware, Building Materials, etc. Now is
the time to Buy Hardware, as prices are
still low but rapidly advancing.
H. J. OLMSTED & Sons.
H. J. OLMSTED, H. C. OLMSTED, A. C. OLMSTED.

LOOK HERE.
If you want to buy First-class Goods, and buy them Cheap, call on
D. F. GLASSMIRE.
Corner of Main and Second Streets,
Coudersport, Pa.,
Where you will find a large assortment of
Dry Goods,
Dress Goods,
Ready-Made Clothing,
Hats and Caps,
GROCERIES and PROVISIONS.
Boots and Shoes,
Field and Garden Seeds
etc., etc.,
Which will be sold cheap for cash
Quick Sales and Small Profits.
Is his Motto.
HAY SCALES.
D. F. Glassmire has put in a set of Hay
Scales from the BUFFALO SCALE WORKS
which are warranted to give
Correct Weight Every time.
He has a 'UNITED STATES TEST WEIGHT'
to regulate his Scales by, and as the Bar is inside
the store, they are not apt to get out of order.
A Record kept of all loads, &c., weighed on these Scales.
D. F. GLASSMIRE, Proprietor.
Coudersport, Pa., May 21, 1874.

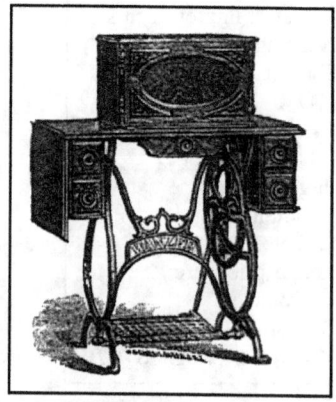

**THE
WANZER
SEWING MACHINE**
A NEW
SHUTTLE LOCK
STITCH MACHINE.

FOR SALE AT
"THE ARK"
E. N. STEBBINS,
Agent.

Potter County, Pennsylvania Potpourri – Volume I
1880 through 1884

The Potter Enterprise
Thursday Evening, May 19, 1880 – Vol. VII, No. 2

We shall have to crave the indulgence of our subscribers for a few weeks. Our printing office is a thing of the past. All we saved was a quantity of paper stock, office desk and paper cases; our Gordon was taken out but badly broken, our hand press was dumped through the side of the building, the track was broken and the press otherwise injured, can be repaired. Our subscription book, and we believe all accounts are saved.

Could the fire have been kept from the building ten minutes longer it would have been saved, but a sudden gust of wind carried the flames to the eaves and then there was no salvation.

We return our thanks to the gentlemen and ladies who did all that could possibly be done to save the building. Never was more earnest workers.

This paper is issued from the Journal office, the proprietors and publisher having tendered us all the accommodations possible. The Journal office force assisted us at the fire and since in every way possible.

Mr. Hughes and Mr. Gould have tendered us assistance in the loan of material, for which we are very grateful.

The *Enterprise* will be issued regularly, but just how or in what shape we are yet unable to say. As soon as possible we shall put in a new office. The office has gone up in smoke and down in melted metal, but will come to the front again in due time. Not dead but sleeping. Our business office will be at the residence of Z. J. Thompson until further notice.

Coudersport in Ashes.
The Entire Business Portion of the Town Destroyed.
The Post Office, the Bank, the Enterprise Office, all the
Dry Goods and Grocery Stores Destroyed.

On Tuesday afternoon about three p.m. the cry of fire startled the people of Coudersport, carrying with it terror to every heart, as the fate of Rew City, Rixford and Milton swept like a flash of lightning across the brain. The fire started in a small building on Second street between the store of P. A. Stebbins, Jr., and the furniture store of C. Reissman. Our reporter was one of the first to reach the fire, and it was apparent at a glance that its course could not be stayed until the frame row which lined Main street from Second to Third should go. Efforts to save the contents of the buildings were made and very many goods were removed to the Court House square and other places. The wind blew gently from the southwest, and it was feared that the residence of Mrs. Mann, north of Third street, on west side of Main must burn, but suddenly the wind veered and blew from the north west, and by a gallant fight the house of Mrs. Mann and the dwelling of C. Reissman, on the northwest corner of the square, bounded by Second and Third and Main and West streets were saved and thanks to the heroic efforts of a few men, who stood on the dome of the steeple and the roof of the building, and in spite of a scorching smoke and flame, saved it from destruction. The building north of the Court House square got pretty warm at times, and once it looked as though the Baker House must burn, but it stands, the only hotel in the place. Many of the goods taken out of the stores and piled in the streets and on the square caught fire and burned, and to their disgrace be it written, some people seemed bent upon plunder, quietly picking up any article which might possibly be of value to them and making off with it.

ORIGIN OF THE FIRE.

It is easy enough to tell pretty near where the fire started but how it started no one knows. The idea of spontaneous combustion is advanced by some, others think the ashes from a cigar or pipe might have been the start. However, it is useless to speculate. The fire came and the business portion of Coudersport is gone.

POLICE.

The town council held a special meeting last evening and appointed a number of special police men to keep watch and ward over the exposed goods.

INSURANCES.

The following is a partial list of losses and insurance: P. A. Stebbins Jr. & Bro.'s store building, $3000, contents $12000. Insurance $4500.

The Bank Building, loss $600. No insurance.

W. K. Jones, Coudersport Bank, saved all his cash. Bills Receivable and Bank Ledgers. Loss on safes, bank furniture &c.

Rosa Anton, millinery, 2d floor of Bank building, loss ---, insurance $500.

Dr. Amos French, store and contents, loss $3,500. No insurance.

Dr. E. S. Phillips, dentist, 2d floor of French's building, loss above insurance, $75, mostly on smaller tools.

Edward Forster, store and contents, loss $5,000, insurance $2,000.

Ignatz Grisel was putting up a new building; loss perhaps $1,500, no insurance.

C. S. Jones' store and contents; loss 20,000, insurance 5,000.

F. E. Lyon's building, occupied by Andrews & Olmsted, loss 1,800, covered by insurance. Andrews and Olmsted's stock of goods, loss from 1,000 to 2,000, insurance.

H. J. Olmsted and sons loss on building and goods 10,000, insurance 4,000.

L. H. Cobb's law office, second floor of Olmsted building, loss 500, no insurance.

Eulalia Lodge, F.A.M., loss 800, insurance 500.

Mary R. Jones, executrix, store building, loss 2,000, insurance 1,500.

E. N. Stebbins goods therein loss 1,000, covered by insurance.

Reymond Bendel, household goods and tailor shop. Loss perhaps $200. No insurance.

M. S. Thompson, Postoffice building and store. Loss $2500. Covered by insurance.

L. B. Cole & Son, Insurance office on Third street. Loss $1000. No insurance.

C. Reissman's old house on Third street and cabinet shop and stock on Second street. $3000 above insurance.

W. B. Gordnier's building on Second street and $3000. No insurance.

Potter County, Pennsylvania Potpourri – Volume I
1880 through 1884

E. S. Mattison, office furniture. Loss small. No insurance.
D. F. Glassmire Jr. Livery stable, saved horses and buggies. Loss on sleighs, papers, etc. $1000. No insurance.
Z. J. Thompson, wagon shop. Loss on building and stock $2000. No insurance.
Geo. Brehmer, blacksmith shop. Loss $50. No insurance.
F. E. Neefe, wagon shop. Loss $500. No insurance.
A. C. Perkins, blacksmith shop. Loss $1000. No insurance.
D. F. Glassmire, Coudersport Hotel and barn, store and barn. Loss $13000. Insurance 3500.
Miles White, keeping Coudersport Hotel. Loss 1500. Insurance 700.
J. A. Haynes, book agent stopping at Hotel. Loss 70. No insurance.
John Scott, boarder. Loss on clothing and money 100. No insurance.
George Green, barber in basement of hotel, loss, 50. No insurance.
M. L. Stevenson, suit of clothes.
Engineer's office, J.S., P.C. and B.R.R., in second floor of Glassmire's store building. Loss 500. No insurance.
Singer Sewing Machine company. Loss not stated. No insurance.
Isaac Benson, Dike block. Loss 800.
E. O. Rees, jeweler. Loss 600 to 800. Insurance 500.
Pierce and Lovel, furniture dealers. Loss 500. No insurance.
R. W. Niles household goods. Loss 300. No insurance.
C. H. Armstrong, brick store and grocery. Loss 6000. Insurance 1500.
Abram Jones, restaurant and bowling alley building. Loss 600. Covered by insurance.
Thad Kelley restaurant, loss 500, no insurance.
Olmsted and Larrabee's law office, saved all valuable books, papers and safe, loss on building 800, no insurance; books and furniture 100, covered by insurance.
Carl Zimmerman, butcher shop and building, loss 1500, insurance 1000.
Enterprise building owned by F. W. Knox, loss 3,200, no insurance.
Norton and Doane, hardware, loss 500, covered by insurance.
Enterprise office, loss 4,000, insurance 2,000.
Mrs. A. C. Haven, house, household goods and barn, loss 1,000, insurance unknown. Mrs. Belle Ross loss on household goods, covered by insurance.
At this early hour we can not write so fully as we could wish. Incidents and accidents worthy of mention are numerous enough, but lack of space forbids their recital.
Charles Kernan a clerk for E. N. Stebbins, had a stroke very similar to sunstroke, and was in a critical condition last evening.
The Post Office is located in the office of A. B. Mann for the present.
Thirty-eight buildings were burned. Loss probably $200,000; insurance, $75,000, at a very rough estimate.
All the mail matter was saved, but the fellow that saved it left the mail keys, and patrons had to wait until Postmaster Thompson sent to Roulet for a key.
Cyrenus Jones, the artist, lost $50 in goods; no insurance.

TELEGRAPH OFFICE.

Will be in the law office of F. W. Knox and Son at present.

Wednesday Morning.

The Bank is located in the land office of John S. Ross, at the upper end of Main street.

M. S. Thompson & Co., Drugs and Books and the Postoffice, in the basement of the M.E. church.

E. N. Stebbins' general store is in Benson's brick store, on Second street, east of the river.

H. J. Olmsted & Sons hardware store in the Hallauer building on East street.

Norton & Doane's hardware in the Kline building on East street.

C. H. Armstrong, grocer, in his building formerly occupied by A. S. Armstrong as shoe shop, on Third street.

P. A. Stebbins, Jr. & Bro. will put up a temporary building, so will E. O. Rees, jeweler.

All the safes except the large bank safe were put into the streets.

The court house was saved by the most strenuous exertions, of a few men.

A strong breeze from the south came up Wednesday morning and fanned the embers into a blaze, and the flying sparks endangered the building on the north side of Third street, and a large number of men worked for two hours to extinguish the fire on the ruins of Tuesday.

Very many goods were stolen.

Born.

LYON – May 16th, 1880, to Mary, wife of F. E. Lyon, of Sweden, a son, weight nine pounds.

Sudden Death.

On Saturday last the wife of William Snyder, of Sweden, *nee* Mary Neefe, was taken with a chill, and on Sunday morning at nine o'clock she died. She leaves several children, one of them a babe but eight months old.

Died.

CRITTENDEN – May 7th, 1880, at her residence in Marathon, Cortland county, N.Y., Nancy Jones, wife of Leroy Crittenden, aged 37 years.

The deceased was a niece of the late Captain Arch F. Jones. She was for many years a resident of this borough, and she leaves many friends in this vicinity who mourn her early death. The sorrowing husband and children have the sympathy of their friends and former neighbors in Coudersport.

JOHNSON – At his residence in Roulet, on Wednesday, May 12th, 1880, Washington Johnson, of Bright's disease of the kidneys.

- Miss Charlotte S. Huntington died on Tuesday at the residence of Mr. E. A. Heseltine, just south of the village. Deceased was a daughter of Rev. E. P. Huntington, who was a pastor of the M.E. Church during the war. Her home was at Bingham, Potter county, Pa., and she was visiting at the home of Mr.

Heseltine at the time of her death. The remains were taken to Bingham for burial. – *Hornellsville Times.*

- On Wednesday of last week Patrick Fitz Stephens of Potter county came to this place and delivered himself up to M. Bullard, Revenue Collector. There is strong evidence against him for running an illicit distillery in Potter county, near Wellsville, N.Y. Office Bullard has been working on this case for some time, and has such a sure thing of it, as reported, that the suspected party seems to have voluntarily surrendered himself. Fitz Stephens gave bail for his appearance at Williamsport at the next term of the District Court. – *Wellsboro Gazette.*

- By every road come tidings of disastrous forest fires. E. O. Rees informed us on Monday that the Kettle Creek country was being badly scorched by fire, and that H. H. Guernsey, of Ulysses, had to fight fire for three days to save his buildings.

Census Enumerator.

The following appointments have been made by the Supervisor for the several districts in this county:
99. John Bodler, Abbott and Stewardson.
100. Charles Coats, Allegany.
101. J. H. Chase, Bingham.
102. D. W. Butterworth, Coudersport and Eulalia.
103. Fayette Lewis, Harrison.
104. W. C. Reynolds, Hebron.
105. B. F. Mulford, Hector.
106. E. O. Austin, Homer, Sylvania, Portage and Wharton.
107. B. F. Sherman, Oswayo and Genesee.
108. J. Q. Merrick, Pike and West Branch.
109. Clinton McDowell, Pleasant Valley and Clara.
110. Wm. S. Brine, Roulet and Keating.
111. F. N. Newton, Sharon.
112. J. W. Pearsall, Sweden and Summit.
113. Burton Lewis, Ulysses and Lewisville.

MEMORIAL DAY.
PROGRAM OF EXERCISES.

Decoration Day will be observed in Coudersport on Saturday, May 29th, 1880.

Services will begin at the monument at one o'clock p.m.

Hon. Horace Bemis, of Hornellsville, N.Y., will deliver the address.

At the conclusion of the services on the square a procession will be formed to march to the cemetery, under the direction of the Marshall (W. B. Gordnier) and will be composed of Bands of Music, the different Lodges of Knights of Honor, Sunday Schools, Committees, etc.

All are expected to join in the procession, and those that are unable to walk will be provided with carriages. By Order of Committee.

Potter Enterprise
Thursday Evening, May 27, 1880 – Vol. 7, No. 3

THE FIRE. NO HEAD LINES NEEDED. READ FOR YOURSELVES.

The smoke has cleared away and we all more fully appreciate the terrible disaster that has overtaken, what we once boasted was the handsomest little village in the State of Pennsylvania.

Previous to the blaze of Tuesday of last week one could not believe that the wiping out of the three squares would make the whole town look so desolate. Now nearly the whole town is on "Main street" and the ruins are too plainly visible from all points.

Of the origin of the fire no more is known to-day than at first. When first discovered there was a thin wreath of smoke arising from a small building back of P. A. Stebbins, Jr. & Bro.'s store, used as a wood shed, and store room for salt, oil, &c. Before any one could reach this point, notwithstanding several persons were less than half a dozen rods away and saw the first smoke, before the blaze broke through the sides or roof, the whole building was in flames, and the flames were rapidly crawling up the rear of the store, and the sides of Charles Reissman's furniture store just across the alley from the building in which the fire started.

Everything was as dry as a tinder and although it was comparatively still, the flames created a breeze that drove the fire in a northeasterly direction, up through the block built entirely of wood, filled with stores, offices and other business enterprises.

One of the singular things of the day was the fact that during the continuance of the fire, at different times, the wind came from every point of the compass, and the greater part of the time was a strong wind.

It was evident from the start that the block of stores on Main street and the buildings on the south side of Second street must go, and everybody labored to save the goods in the stores. Every store in the block had recently stocked up for the spring trade, and many of our merchants find their losses much heavier than they reported the night of the fire.

Most of the goods were carried and thrown into the Court House square, where a large portion afterwards burned because the heat was too great to permit of their removal.

Aristocratic silks and plebian calico were alike trailed through the dust of the street, and dumped in one promiscuous pile, with boots and shoes, groceries and provisions. A conglomerate mass, representing the stock in trade of our merchants.

Building after building caught fire, north and west from the starting point, and as the flames followed the block on, this square, they also leaped across Second street, catching almost simultaneously the whole length from the Coudersport Hotel to Z. J. Thompson's wagon shop.

An attempt was made to save the hotel and men were throwing water on Perkins' shop but it proved useless, and the men were driven from their posts in less time that it takes to write it.

Before the front of Stebbins' store fell in, every building on that square, except the dwelling house of Charles Reisman and every building on the square south, except Mrs. Havens' barn was in a blaze. The dark clouds of smoke, the fiery blaze and the crackling flames making a horrid picture of destruction, the like of which we hope Coudersport will never again witness.

After the fire got well under way on the south side of Second street, the wind changed, coming from the north and but for this change the northern part of the town would also have been burned. On every building, north of Third street willing hands were at work, and this change in the wind made their work effective. Charles Reissman's house, the only building left on the square where the fire originated was on fire a number of times, and was only saved by the most persistent work. Had this building burned it is highly probable that the Journal printing office would also have burned and on, on, and none can tell where the path of destruction would have led.

From the Coudersport Hotel the flames crossed to the store of D. F. Glassmire, breaking out simultaneously along the whole side and on the barn attached, not inch by inch, but yard by yard, it jumped from one building to another, until the whole street to the *Enterprise* building was a sheet of flame. Here was some of the most persistent fighting of the whole fire. Men, women and children carried water until ready to drop with exhaustion. But for a sudden gust of wind which carried the flame from the Zimmerman building full against the cornice at the southwest corner this building would have been saved. In ten minutes more the Zimmerman building had spent its force, but those ten minutes marked the doom of the *Enterprise* building, and with it nearly every thing in the printing office line therein. Until the roof was in flames it was believed the limit had been reached. The next and last hard fight was on the Hallauer building, which with the aid of carpets and a liberal supply of water was saved. The Baker House was in considerable danger, but it was covered with carpets, and kept wet, and was easily saved, by taking time by the forelock, and being prepared.

For ten or fifteen minutes after Mrs. Havens' barn caught fire, from falling cinders, it could have been saved by a man or two carrying water upon it, but at that time, there was no one in that section, all being on other streets, too busy putting out fires that caught on their own property. In this barn Mrs. Isabelle Ross had a large quantity of valuable household goods, nearly all of which burned.

EMBERS.

Ellison's barn and house were saved by carpets and men from his mill.

For a time Z. J. Thompson's dwelling was in imminent danger from falling cinders. R. L. Nichols' two houses were in like danger. B. Rennells' blacksmith shop was on fire several times, and his house is badly scorched, both were saved with difficulty.

The house occupied by James Johnston also shows the effects of the fire.

A. B. Mann's house was further away and escaped with slight damage, owing to the vigilance of those watching the falling cinders.

Mrs. Mary W. Mann's house was in great danger. The large balsam trees on the south, materially assisted by keeping off the heat. They are badly scorched, and their beauty has probably departed forever. If killed, it can truthfully be said "they died in a good cause."

Clinton Olmsted's, A. S. Armstrong's, Miss C. A. Metzger's millinery store and dwellings, the M.E. Church, and other buildings were in great danger, and but for the change in the wind would have been food for the flames in spite of all the efforts to save them.

Through all the smoke and flame the steeple of the Court House could occasionally be seen looming up like a beacon of hope, and by hard work our temple of justice is intact, but grimed with smoke. While at work on this building, W. B. Rees slipped, sliding some ten or a dozen feet ere he regained his footing. A few feet more and a sheer fall of about seventy feet would have resulted in his death.

D. F. Glassmire was out of town at the time. His safe was thrown out, but his account books lying on the desk were burned. In his stable, one of his gray stage horses, in a box stall, was overlooked, and burned to death.

Charles Reissmann had two hogs burned and a number of chickens. He still has several hens shorn of a portion of their feathers by the fire.

In Cole's shop, James Pearsall, wagon maker, lost all his tools, and a quantity of paints, varnishes, etc. A. Kiehle, blacksmith, also lost some tools and his day book.

A. C. Perkins lost his books. Z. J. Thompson had ten wagon gearings, sleighs and cutters burned. Most of the wagon woods were thrown out, but the fire was so hot they could not be removed and they were burned where they laid.

Nearly all the safes in the Main street block were tumbled out upon the sidewalk. Those left in the buildings stood the test and no papers were lost. Here after our merchants will use canvas covered ledgers, as these passed through scarcely soiled, while those bound in leather were wrinkled and drawn out of shape.

Thieves were unusually plenty on Tuesday. Some of our merchants claim that more goods were stolen than burned. A piece of valuable dress goods belonging to P. A. Stebbins, Jr. & Bro., was found on the road near Colesburg, Wednesday morning.

After Andrews & Olmsted's show case had been carried out, a man was seen to kick the top in and help himself to the contents. This firm had 3,500 cigars stolen.

Olmsted & Sons had a quantity of hardware stolen, after it had been taken across the river near the tannery.

C. S. Jones was on his way to Chicago when the fire occurred. He returned Saturday evening.

Miles White, landlord of the Coudersport Hotel, lost his books.

Olmsted and Larrabee saved their fine law library, with scarcely any damage.

The Masons removed their regalia, jewels, and a portion of the furniture. Their loss above insurance is less than $200.

Several small fires started near the river and even south of the river from burning shingles.

Charley Stebbins' bird dog, "Sharpe," the best woodcock dog in this section, burned in the store.

Charred shingles were found above Lymansville and partially burned paper on Ayer's Hill.

J. O. Merrill had a stage wagon burned in the Coudersport Hotel barn. Mr. Corsaw also lost a buggy in hotel yard.

J. T. Jackson, William Sherwood, J. W. Allen, Dr. Post and Albert Rennells, had wagons totally or partially destroyed in Thompson's wagon shop.

On Tuesday there were more of our citizens out of town than upon any one day in the past year.

Friendly dispatches were received by many of our citizens, offering aid in provisions and clothing, if necessary.

The town council have fixed fire limits. Will be published next week.

Fifteen special constables were put on duty Tuesday night. No arrests were found necessary, and their duty consisted chiefly in watching goods piled about town, and the dying fires of fire-scorched Coudersport.

For a time it was impossible to get any thing in the merchandise line, but on Thursday new goods began to arrive, and with them the omnipresent drummer, who reaped a rich harvest of orders. Many of our merchants ordered goods by telegraph Wednesday morning.

L. R. Bliss, the Photographer, lost about $100 worth of chemicals and fixtures.

Of the many accounts of the fire telegraphed from this place, that of C. L. Peck, Esq., to the Bradford *Era* was the nearest correct.

On Wednesday everybody complained of aches and pains, the result of hard labor at the big blaze.

Very little drunkenness was observed either Tuesday or Wednesday, notwithstanding the excitement at the number of people on the streets, and the temptation to revive drooping spirits.

The Baker House is crowded with guests.

On Thursday the music of the hammer and saw was started and has continued service on temporary buildings. No one is idle who is willing to work.

Within an hour after the collapse of the *Enterprise* building, the *Journal* and *Enterprise* printers were at the case crying "copy," (though it must be owned in rather a weak voice, for they were nearly all tired out.) for the *Journal-Enterprise* Extra, the demand for which exceeded the supply. Extra copies of the papers were also called for until the editions including half sheets were exhausted.

Temporary quarters are being occupied and business will soon be progressing. The postoffice has been moved to the M.E. Church basement, and now

Many go to church who never went before

And those who did go, now go the more.

The postoffice will soon be removed to a new building just east of the jail yard, at the corner.

E. N. Stebbins has occupied the brick store belonging to Isaac Benson, east of the river. Ed says he has safely landed the "Ark," not on top but at the foot of Mt. -----.

Olmsted & Sons, hardware, will occupy the Davidson building, which W. K. Jones had partially demolished to give place to the bank building.

Andrews and Olmsted, groceries, occupy the Hallauer building and have hung their banner on the outer wall.

C. S. Jones and Son, may be found next to the M.E. Church, in Miss C. A. Metzgar's building. They are putting up a temporary structure on the jail lot.

I. Grisel, harness maker, is putting up quarters on East street, below Kline's shoe shop.

Dr. French has not resumed, but we understand intends building with brick at an early day.

Dr. Phillips, dentist, has secured rooms on second floor of Hallauer building.

The Coudersport Bank has removed to the Fox and Ross land office.

Miss Anton, milliner, we are informed, will not continue business.

P. A. Stebbins, Jr. and Bro., have a large temporary building east of jail, which they will occupy in a day or two.

Charles Reissman has turned his house into a furniture store.

Mr. Keihle and James Pearsall, in Cole's shop, have not yet located. The shop will not be rebuilt, we are informed.

D. F. Glassmire, Jr., has moved his livery to B. Rennell's barn. He is preparing to put up a stable on First street between Main and East.

Z. J. Thompson, wagon shop, not yet located.

George Brehmer, blacksmith, has put up a shop on First street, nearly north of C. H. Armstrong's dwelling.

A. C. Perkins will occupy a building with F. E. Neefe.

The Coudersport Hotel is not likely to be rebuilt at present. Miles White and family are stopping with Henry Nelson.

D. F. Glassmire will not rebuild his store.

N. M. Glassmire, Agent for Singer Sewing Machine Company, is putting up a building in connection with I. Grisel on East street.

The telegraph office has been removed to R.L. Nichols' office on West street.

The Engineer's office at Ross' land office.

E. O. Rees occupies, or will, a portion of C. S. Jones' "new store" on the jail yard.

A. L. Pierce has not yet located.

The family of Robert Niles has removed to Oswayo.

Abram Jones building will not be built at present. Thad Kelley is occupying a part of the Stevens' house on West street.

Olmsted & Larrabee now occupy the Sheriff's office in the Court House.

Potter County, Pennsylvania Potpourri – Volume I
1880 through 1884

Zimmerman, commenced business Wednesday morning in the basement of the Baker House. Has since removed to his new shop, next to the Hallauer building.

George Green, barber, has set up his chair at the Baker House.

Norton & Doane occupy the Kline building. They will put up a temporary building on the jail lot.

C. S. Jones, artist, is taking matters very easy and has gone fishing.

The Stockholders of the Enterprise Printing Association met on Monday afternoon, nearly all the stock being represented, and arrangements made whereby the publisher, W. W. Thompson, is to continue the publication as soon as possible as publisher and proprietor. He will have to build an office, just where is not yet fully settled. The *Enterprise* building, owned by F. W. Knox, is not to be rebuilt this year.

Mrs. A. C. Haven is stopping with friends in Lymansville. Her case is a peculiarly trying one, losing the house in which she was raised and had lived so long, and nearly all the household goods.

L. H. Cobb, attorney, may be found at Court House.

Dr. E. S. Mattison is at present stopping with L. B. Cole. Expects soon to occupy the Stevens house on West street.

Mr. Brine informs us that he will immediately put in a brick machine that will enable him to turn out 12,000 per day. The shed for his first kiln was raised on Monday last.

Mrs. C. Reissman lost a child's brown straw hat, trimmed with brown ribbon and wreath, belonging to a little daughter who died a few years since and consequently of more than money value. Any one having the hat will confer a great favor by returning it.

The publisher of the *Enterprise* lost a turkey morocco diary of 1878, containing memorandums and a quantity of postage stamps. He will be glad to present to any one returning it the stamps and a book equally as valuable.

LOSSES AND INSURANCE.

The following is a corrected list of losses and insurances: P. A. Stebbins, Jr. & Bro.'s store building, $3500, contents $12000. Insurance $4500.

The Bank Building, loss $600. No insurance.

W. K. Jones, Coudersport Bank, saved all his cash. Bills Receivable and Bank Ledgers. Loss on safes, bank furniture &c., small, with no insurance.

Rosa Anton, millinery, 2d floor of Bank building, probably covered by insurance.

Dr. Amos French, store and contents, loss $3,500. No insurance.

Dr. S. A. Phillips, dentist, 2d floor of French's building, loss above insurance, $75, mostly on smaller tool.

Edward Forster, store and contents, loss $5,000. Insurance $2,000.

Ignatz Grisel was putting up a new building; loss perhaps $1,500, no insurance.

C. S. Jones' store and contents, loss 12,000, insurance 3,000.

F. E. Lyon's building, occupied by Andrews & Olmsted, loss 1,200, insurance $1000. Andrews and Olmsted's stock of goods, loss about 950; insurance 800.

H. J. Olmsted and sons loss on building and goods 8000; insurance 4,000.

L. H. Cobb's law office, second floor of Olmsted building, loss 500, no insurance.

Eulalia Lodge F.A.M., loss 673, insurance 500. This was one of the handsomest furnished lodge rooms in the country.

Mary R. Jones, executrix, store building, loss 2,400, insurance 1,500. E. N. Stebbins' goods therein, loss 3,200, covered by insurance.

Reymond Bendel, household goods and tailor shop. Loss perhaps $200. No insurance.

M. S. Thompson, Postoffice building and store. Loss $3,500. Insurance, $2,600.

L. B. Cole & Son, Insurance office on Third street, and wagon and blacksmith shop on Second Street. Loss, $1000. No insurance.

C. Reissman's old house on Third Street and cabinet shop and stock on Second street. $3000 above insurance.

W. B. Gordnier's building on Second street and West, $3000. No insurance.

E. S. Mattison, office furniture. Loss small. No insurance.

D. F. Glassmire Jr. Livery stable, saved horses and buggies. Loss on sleighs, papers, etc. $1000. No insurance.

Z. J. Thompson, wagon shop. Loss on building and stock $2000. No insurance.

Geo. Brehmer, blacksmith shop. Loss $50. No insurance.

F. E. Neefe, wagon shop. Loss $500. No insurance.

A. C. Perins, blacksmith shop. Loss $1000. No insurance.

D. F. Glassmire, Coudersport Hotel and barn, store and barn and stage fixtures states his loss at 10,500. Insurance 4200.

Miles White, keeping Coudersport Hotel. Loss 1500. No insurance.

J. A. Haynes, book agent stopping at Hotel. Loss 70. No insurance.

John Scott, boarder. Loss on clothing and money 100. No insurance.

George Green, barber in basement of hotel, loss, 50. No insurance.

M. L. Stevenson, suit of clothes.

Engineer's office, J.S., P.C. and B.R.R., in second floor of Glassmire's store building. Loss 500. No insurance.

Singer Sewing Machine company. Loss 450. No insurance. N. M. Glassmire, Loss 125. No insurance.

Isaac Benson, Dike block. Loss 800. No insurance.

E. O. Rees, jeweler. Loss 600 to 800. Insurance 189.

A. L. Pierce, furniture dealer. Loss 500. No insurance.

R. W. Niles household goods. Loss 300. No insurance.

C. H. Armstrong, brick store and grocery. Loss 6000. Insurance 1500.

Abram Jones, restaurant and bowling alley building. Loss 600. Insurance 400.

Thad Kelley restaurant, loss 500, no insurance.

Olmsted and Larrabee's law office, saved all valuable books, papers and safe, loss on building 800, no insurance; books and furniture 200, covered by insurance.

Carl Zimmerman, butcher shop and building, loss 1500, insurance 1000.
Enterprise building owned by F. W. Knox, loss 3,200, no insurance.
Norton and Doane, hardware, loss 4,130, covered by insurance.
Enterprise office, loss 3,500, insurance 1,800.
Cyrenus Jones, the artist, lost $50 in goods, no insurance.
A. Kiehle, blacksmith tools and books, 150; no insurance.
L. R. Bliss, photographic tools, etc., loss, 100; no insurance.
James W. Pearsoll, wagon making tools, etc.; loss 150; no insurance.
Mrs. A. Haven, house, household goods and barn, loss 1,000. Mrs. Belle Ross loss on household goods three thousand, insurance 1,000.

A. B. Mann, Insurance Agent, did not wait for notice of loss, but at once telegraphed the different companies represented by him. A good share of his policies were adjusted and paid before night, Friday.

L. B. Cole and Son also had adjusters on the spot as soon as possible, and all losses were promptly adjusted on Thursday.

Both our Insurance Agencies were prompt and deserve the thanks of the insured.

Coudersport Business Directory.

Below we give the new locations so far as known of the burned out business men. If any one has been overlooked it is unintentional, and we will gladly make any needed corrections:

Andrews & Olmsted, groceries, etc., in the Hallauer building, on East street.
Anton, R. L., Milliner, Out of business.
Armstrong, C. H., Grocer, in his store on north of Court House square.
Bank of Coudersport, in land office of John S. Ross.
Bendel, Reymond, tailor, 2d floor of brick store, east of river, on Second street.
Bliss, L. R., photographer, will soon occupy a portion of a new building now going up on First street.
Cobb, L. H., law office in Court House, over the Prothonotary's office.
Cole, L. B. & Son, insurance, with L. H. Cobb.
Doane, Norton and, hardware, Kline building, East street.
Enterprise, W. W. Thompson, business office at residence of Z. J. Thompson, West street.
Forster, Edward, Grocer, out of business for the present.
French, Amos, drugs and groceries, out of business for the present.
Grisel, Ignatz, harness maker, now building on First street.
Glassmire, D. F., Jr., livery, in barn of B. Rennells on Second street.
Glassmire, D. F., stage office at his residence on Main street.
Glassmire, N. M., agent Singer Sewing Machine Company, temporary building on First street.
Green, George, barber, in the basement of the Baker House.

Jones, C. S., dry goods, drugs and groceries, next door to M.E. church, on Third street. Will have temporary building in jail yard soon.

Jones, W. K., Bank in land office of J. S. Ross, Main street.

Kiehle, A., blacksmith.

Kelly, Thad., boarding house, Fifth and West streets.

Larrabee, Olmsted and, law office, Court House, over the Commissioner's office.

Norton & Doane, hardware, in Klein building, on East street, will build temporarily in the jail yard.

Olmsted & Larrabe, law office, Court House, over Commissioner's office.

Olmsted, H. J. and Sons, hardware, east side of Court House Square.

Pierce, A. L., furniture, no location yet.

Pearsoll, James, wagon maker.

Reissman, Charles, furniture at his dwelling, 3d and West streets.

Rees, E. O., jeweler, at his dwelling on Main street, at present, will have temporary building up soon in jail yard.

Stebbins, P. A., Jr. & Bro., general store, temporary building on 2d, east of East, south side.

Stebbins, E. N., general store in brick building, north side of 2d, east of river.

Singer Sewing Machine, N. M. Glassmire, agent, temporary building at East and First streets.

Thompson, M. S. & Co., drugs, books and postoffice in basement of M.E. church, will occupy temporary building on 2d street in a few days.

Thompson, W. W., *Enterprise*, business office in dwelling of Z. J. Thompson, on West street.

Thompson, Z. J., wagon maker, will probably rebuild on the old lot at 2d and West.

Telegraph office in office of R. L. Nichols', south side of 2d street.

White, Miles, Coudersport Hotel, out of business for the present.

Western Union Telegraph office in office of R. L. Nichols, on West street.

Zimmerman, Karl, meat market, temporary.

Married.

FRENCH – WARNER – In Emporium, Pa., May 18th, 1880, by Rev. J. Vroosman, A.M., C. S. French, M.D., of Coudersport, and Miss Eva Warner, of Emporium.

Harrison Valley. The diphtheria is again raging here, and people are becoming panic stricken. Mr. H. White lost his youngest two daughters. Mr. Leonard his youngest son, and others are sick with the same dreadful disease.

Died.

BURT – At her residence on Trout Brook, May 25, 1880, Winifred, wife of Alfred Burt, aged 18 years, 9 months and 5 days.

Potter County, Pennsylvania Potpourri – Volume I
1880 through 1884

Memorial Day.

Owing to the fire the preparations for the observance of Memorial Day in Coudersport have ceased. Mr. Bemis has been notified not to come and no public observance of the day will be had here.

Notice to Jurors.

All Jurors summoned to serve at the June Term of Court are requested not to report. All causes for trial at that Term having been continued. All persons who are bound by recognizance must appear and renew the same.

O. H. Crosby, Prothonotary.
Coudersport, Pa., May 26, 1880.

Baker House
Corner Second and East St.
Coudersport, Pa.
M. L. GRIDLEY, Proprietor.

Potter Enterprise
Thursday Evening, June 3, 1880 – Vol. 7, No. 4

Married.

BERFIELD – WOOD – At the M.E. parsonage, June 1st, 1880, by Rev. T. R. Stratton, Mr. G. W. Berfield, of Homer, and Mrs. Irene Wood, of Coudersport.

WAGONER – MEAD – At Ulysses, May 25th, by the Rev. Thomas Perry, Mr. Charles E. Wagoner, of Ulysses, to Miss Laura Mead, of same place.

Died.

DODGE – At Harrison Valley, May 28th, of diphtheria, Edna, only daughter of Vincent and Hannah Dodge, aged 10 years and 20 days.

Edna was beloved by all who knew her. She was the idol of her parents, and they in this hour of trouble have the sympathy of neighbors and friends. Edna will be missed by her many young playmates, as she was of a kind disposition and ever ready to assist her young friends.

LEONARD – At Harrison Valley, May 24, of diphtheria, Bertie Leonard, aged 5 years, 7 months and 64 days.

Bertie was a brother to the one who died last month. Since a week ago last Thursday four children of this place have died with this terrible disease.

Coudersport Town Council.

1880, May 19th. Council met at the Prothonotary's office in the Court House. Present W. K. Jones, Burgess, and O. H. Crosby, C. H. Armstrong, P. A. Stebbins, Jr., and M. L. Gridley, Town Council.

The reading of the minutes of the preceding meeting was dispensed with.

On motion the following ordinance was adopted. Messrs. Armstrong, Stebbins, Gridley and Crosby, voting in favor thereof.

ORDINANCE NO 54.

Be it ordained by the Burgess and Town Council of the Borough of Coudersport and it is hereby ordained, That the fire limits of the Borough of Coudersport be and they are hereby defined to be the northern one-half of the square south of Second Street between Main and East Streets, the north-east quarter of the square bounded by Main and West and First and Second Streets, and all of the square bounded by Main and West and Second and Third Streets, within which limits it shall be unlawful to erect any building or buildings of any description, except the same be built of stone or brick with tin or slate roofs. And no person shall begin the erection of any building within the limits above described without obtaining a permit from the Town Council, and the Fire Marshal is hereby instructed to prevent the construction of any building within said limits without said permit.

On motion the Burgess was authorized to employ special policemen as in his discretion they may be needed, and his action in employing special policemen on the night of the 18th of May, 1880, is hereby ratified and confirmed.

On motion P. A. Stebbins, Jr., was appointed Fire Marshall.

Adjourned.   Arthur B. Mann, Clerk.

1880, May 24. Council met. Present, W. K. Jones, Burgess, and H. J. Olmsted, C. H. Armstrong and P. A. Stebbins, Jr., Town Council.

The minutes of the meetings of May 14th and 19th, 1880, were read and approved.

On motion the Fire Marshall was instructed to examine the Metzgar steam mill and take such steps to render property exposed by it safe from fire as he may deem necessary.

Adjourned to meet the 25th of May.   A. B. Mann, Clerk.

1880, May 25. Council met. Present, W. K. Jones, Burgess, and O. H. Crosby, C. H. Armstrong and P. A. Stebbins, Jr., Town Council.

The minutes of the meeting of May 24, 1880, were read and approved.

On motion the Street Commissioner was instructed to put in a crossing from the north-east corner of the Court House Square to Mrs. Ives' corner opposite.

Adjourned.   A. B. Mann, Clerk.

1880, May 29th. Council met. Present, W. K. Jones, Burgess, and O. H. Crosby, H. J. Olmsted, C. H. Armstrong, and P. A. Stebbins, Jr., Town Council.

The minutes of the meeting of May 25th, 1880, were read and approved.

The methods of construction of the Main street sewer were discussed at considerable length.

On motion, the Clerk was instructed to look up the records and ascertain and report to the Council the number of feet of land deeded on the West side of Main street, between Second and Third streets.

On motion, the Borough Surveyor was instructed to locate and establish the northwest corner of Main and Second streets, the southeast corner of West and Second streets, and the southwest corner of Main and Third streets, and report such establishment to the council.

Teacher's Association.

The next session of the Potter County Teacher's Association will be held at Oswayo, commencing at 2 p.m., July 1st, and closing at 12 m., July 3d.

PROGRAM.

Afternoon session – Music; address, James Dexter; reply, Henry Kies; son, Fannie Brown; What is the best for Teachers to read?, T. M. Greenman; Question box, Jasper Card; music.

Evening session – Music; Select Reading, Lillie Doyle; What are the Quincy Methods and can we use them?, Helen Brooks; Debate, Affirmative, L. D. Estes and James Dexter; negative, Samuel Beebee and Wm. Jones; question, resolved, that public money should be appropriated to support institutions of learning of a higher grade than the common school; music.

July 2 – Morning session – Music; select reading, Mrs. Jasper Card; is object teaching worth while?, Warren Brightman; essay, Jennie Pawson; new methods of teaching spelling, Emma Adams; literature, Anna Buckbee; recitation, May Pearsall.

Afternoon session – Music; select reading, Jessie Newton; relation of Normal graduates to the teacher's profession, W. W. Harvey; drawing, A. D. Howe; address, A. F. Hollenbeck.

Evening session – Music; incentives to study, H. L. Pearsall; essay, Jennie Newton; oration, Fred Leonard; song, Jennie Pawson; address, George Pearsall; select reading, Marintha Goodell; song, H. H. Hall.

July 3 – Morning session – Music; method of teaching writing, John C. French; local institute, C. M. Stillman; address, L. A. Hollenbeck; essay, Hattie Chesbro; Grammar, D. H. Cobb; adjournment.

THE EUREKA MOWER.
W. B. GORDNIER,
Coudersport, Pa., June 1st, 1880.

Potter Enterprise
Thursday Evening, June 10, 1880 – Vol. 7, No. 5

Oswayo. A china wedding at Leander Stillson's, the 1st inst., resulted in a goodly number of presents and a happy time, generally. Also a crystal wedding at Franklin Gales, the 28th ult. The house was filled to overflowing with people, over sixty pieces were presented. Solomon Hawley made the presentation speech; the Oswayo Cornet Band played some fine music and all were merry as you please.

- Mrs. Ruth Gibbs, of this village, is the widow of Samuel Gibbs, who was a member of the New York militia in the war of 1812, and as such she draws a pension from the United States. She will be 81 years of age on the 5th of August next, and she walked half a mile on Friday last to the office of a magistrate to execute her voucher. Her eyesight is impaired and she had two little girls for guides, and she is cheerful and contented.

Improvements in Coudersport.

A row of four new stores for temporary use has been put up on Second street, east of the jail. The first, 20x46 feet in size, is occupied by Norton & Doane's hardware store, the next 20x80 by C. S. Jones' general store and E. O. Rees, jeweler, the next 20x60 by M. S. Thompson & Co., drugs and books and the postoffice. The one further east 20x80 by P. A. Stebbins, Jr., & Brother, general store. The buildings are each one story high and built of hemlock, but have a good appearance.

W. W. Thompson has begun the erection of a building to be occupied as the *Enterprise* office. It is to be located where the wagon shop of Z. J. Thompson formerly stood. Will be one story high and 20x40 feet in size.

C. H. Armstrong has his new brick store under way. It will occupy his old location and will be one story high, and 22x96 feet in size. He expects to have it ready for occupancy in sixty days.

The work of the new bank building on the old site of Olmsted & Larrabee's law office, is being pushed with vigor.

The sidewalks and fences around the Court House square, which were burned, have been replaced.

D. F. Glassmire has his new stage and express office and hay scales on Second street ready for business, and is building a large barn directly in rear of his office.

D. F. Glassmire, Jr., will build a livery stable on north side of First street, west of the alley.

George H. Brehmer has his new blacksmith shop, _____ street, east of the alley.

Adjoining him on the east is the new wagon shop and blacksmith shop of F. E. Neefe and A. C. Perkins.

N. M. Glassmire is building on the northwest corner of First and East streets a building to be occupied by himself with the Singer Sewing Machine Agency.

Directly adjoining him on the north is the new photograph gallery of L. R. Bliss, which will soon be ready for occupancy. Next north on East street is a double building, the southern half of which is taken up by Ignatz Griesel with his harness shop and the north half by George H. Green, barber shop and billiard room.

Preparations for building within the fire limits on Main street are being made. P. A. Stebbins, Jr., and Brother will build on the old corner.

Edward Forster informs us that he will rebuild on his lot, intending to rent the building when completed.

C. S. Jones, general store, H. J. Olmsted & Sons, hardware, and M. S. Thompson & Co., drugs and books, will rebuild at once and probably others will conclude to build ere the season passes.

W. B. Gordnier has a nice lot on the north east corner of West and Second streets, and he puts talks of putting up a block of six stores thereon.

> **S. A. PHILLIPS, Dentist.**
> Office over Olmsted & Andrews grocery store, Hallauer building.
> TEETH EXTRACTED,
> COMPARATIVELY P A I N L E S S
> By a perfectly safe and pleasant process. No gas or chloroform used, both are dangerous. Filling and orders for plates promptly attended to, cheaper than the cheapest.

Potter Enterprise
Thursday Evening, June 17, 1880 – Vol. 7, No. 6

- Art Lewis, of Ulysses, is happy. A boy, weight nine pounds, and promises to weigh more as it grows older.

Married.

DENHOFF – ERNST – At the residence of Mr. Edward Frouk, in Sweden, by Rev. T. R. Stratton, Mr. Adam Denhoff, of Coudersport, and Mrs. Katharina Sophia Elizabeth Ernst, of Sweden.

Mr. Frouk received the invited guests with great courtesy. The groom was pleasant to his friends and attentive to his spouse. The minister arrived in the midst of a drenching rain and was thoroughly wet, which deferred the wedding ceremonies until 5 p.m. The affair was a very pleasant one and will be remembered for years by those who were present.

- The funeral services of Mr. C. H. Judd, an old and respected citizen of Harrison, aged 74 years, were largely attended at his late residence, last Monday. Rev. Peck, of this place, officiated, basing his remarks on Eccl. 7:1. – *Westfield Free Press*, June 10, 1880.

- Last week Wm. Hornsby, of Millport, purchased a revolver, and in trying it to see how it would shoot, a ball, after passing through a fence board, struck a tree, and then glancing struck Willie Lewis, a boy aged about ten years, in the cheek, making an ugly wound that will leave a bad scar. Mr. Hornsby and the boy were both badly scared, but the result is not likely to prove serious.

- Last Saturday morning Charles Neefe, of Sweden, while going to a raising bee on a neighboring farm noticed a smoke arising in the woods a short distance from the road. Prompt by curiosity he turned aside to learn the cause. He soon reached a large maple which had been struck by lightning and set on fire; at the foot of the tree he found nine old sheep and three lambs, all killed by the stroke that set fire to the tree. The sheep belonged to Mr. Neefe.

Potter County, Pennsylvania Potpourri – Volume I
1880 through 1884

Potter Enterprise
Thursday Evening, June 24, 1880 – Vol. 7, No. 7

Married.

BAKER – KIBBE – At Elkland, May 31, by Rev. W. B. Taylor, J. M. Baker, of Brookfield, and Mary Kibee, of Harrison Valley, Pa.

- Last Sunday afternoon a sad case of drowning occurred near Yeoman's mill, in Eulalia. John Gibson, living near the mill, started to go to a field a short distance from the house. His little son, aged two years, followed a short distance, but was sent back by his father. The little one returned to the house, saying he was going to see his grandmother, who lives near the tannery. He had been gone but a short time when search was made for him. To reach the road the child had to cross Dingman run upon a log, the water beneath being quite deep and at the time roily. In searching for him the parents, fearful that he might have fallen into the stream, examined this spot hurriedly and were about passing beyond to search in the brush, feeling sure the child had passed over safely, when another person passing by asked what they were looking for. On being told of the missing child he looked across the stream and near the bank he saw the body of the child face-down in the water. It is believed the child was in the water less than ten minutes, but all efforts to bring it back to life proved fruitless, and on Monday it was consigned to the grave.

Court Proceedings.

1880, June 14. Court called – Present – full bench.

The constables of all the townships appeared in court and made returns.

The defendants in all the Commonwealth cases renewed their bail to September term.

In the matter of the estate of James Scott, deceased, Arthur B. Mann was appointed Auditor to distribute funds in the hands of C. W. Beach, administrator.

In D. L. Raymond vs. J. E. Hendryx, with summons to Thomas Gilliland, garnishee. Rule on plaintiff to show cause why the judgment in this case should not be marked of record to the use of Electa Hendryx.

In Electa Hendryx, for use of J. E. Hendryx vs. Thomas Gilliland. Rule on plaintiffs to appear and show cause why the judgment in this case should not be marked to the use of Electa Hendryx.

In the matter of the appeal of A. G. Olmsted from the decision of the County Commissioners fixing the valuation of the unseated lands, the first day of next term at 2 o'clock p.m., was fixed for the hearing. Same time fixed for hearing in three other suits for appeals.

In C. W. Gorham vs. The Township of Hebron. Rule on Supervisors of Hebron township to show cause why the should not levy a special tax to pay this and other debts, returnable forthwith. Rule absolute – tax of ten mills ordered.

Albert Newman was appointed guardian of Floyd and Justus Scott, minor children of James Scott, deceased.

D. C. Larrabee was appointed guardian *ad litem* for Lewis Yentzer, Rosetta Yentzer, Nettie Dehn, Eunice Dehn and Mary Dehn, minor children and heirs of Augusta Dehn, deceased.

Mary Nicklaus was appointed guardian of Sophia Meissner, minor child of Charles A. Meissner, deceased.

A. B. Mann was appointed Auditor to examine, restate and adjust the account of Sophia L. Snyder, guardian of Addie Worden, by her administrator, Michael Snyder.

In F. W. Knox vs. D. P. Reed, R. L.White and A. V. Lyman. Rule to show cause why the above judgment should not be opened and defendants let into a defence.

Almond A. Pearsall, S. E. Cheeseman, Ole Snyder and Edson Hyde were admitted to practice law in the several courts of Potter county.

In G. W. Pearce and John Q. Pearce vs. E. E. Tooker and Byron Hurd. Rule on defendant E. E. Tooker to appear and plead (to be published as provided by Act of Assembly,) or judgment will be entered by default against him. Returnable on first day of next term.

The inventory and appraisal of goods set apart to Ann Burns, widow of James Burns, deceased, was approved.

Divorces were granted in the following cases: Rosina Braitling vs. Jacob Braitling; Gracia Grodevant vs. W. H. Grodevant.

In Lyman Clinton vs. Benjamin Clinton. Rule to show cause why Fi. Fa. should not be set aside. Returnable next term. Proceedings to stay meantime.

In J. C. Simons et al, vs. A. Thetge. Rule on H. J. Sanders, Sheriff of Tioga county, to show cause why the money raised by the sale of personal property in this case should not be paid into court. Returnable to next term.

In C. W. Beach vs. Pike Township. Rule on Supervisors of Pike township to lay a special tax to pay debt of said township. Rule made absolute and a tax of one per cent ordered.

In Willis Clark vs. V. D. White. Rule to show cause why judgment should not be opened. Rule made absolute and cause to be put at trial by plea of payment, lien of Fi Fa to remain.

In the matter of the estate of A. C. Woodcock. Administrators and their bail discharged.

John Maginnis was appointed guardian of the minor children of Matthew Moran, deceased.

L. B. Seibert was appointed Commissioner to take testimony in the case of Benjamin Cole vs. Hannah Cole.

L. B. Seibert was appointed Commissioner to take testimony in the case of Augustus Green vs. Miranda Green.

In the matter of the appointment of guardian of minor children of Albert Scott, deceased. Citation to Albert Newman to show cause why his appointment as guardian of Justus Scott and Floyd Scott should not be vacated, and also to show cause why he should not increase his bail. Returnable to next term.

Charles Marvin vs. Alice Marvin. Answer withdrawn.

Eliza Baker vs. Alanson Baker. *Als sub* ordered.

Potter County, Pennsylvania Potpourri – Volume I
1880 through 1884

In the matter of the estate of Wm. L. Reed, deceased. Administrator and his bail discharged.

The petition of Mary A. Lamonte to enjoy the benefits of the Act of Assembly approved April 2d, 1872, was granted.

The usual venires were issued.

Judgments for want of appearance affidavit of defence please, etc., were taken in the following cases. Henry Andressen, use of F. W. Knox, vs. Stewardson Township; E. D. Loveridge, now for the use of L. W. Crawford, vs. Charles Westerman; H. H. Lowell, now for use of F. W. Knox vs. Christian Gorg; C. W. Beach vs. West Branch Township; Nicholas Blackman, use of D. Coderman, vs. Genesee Township; Wm. F. Burt, use of D. Coderman, vs. Pike Township; Wm. Ansley, use of Annette Smith, vs. Pike Township; J. Richardson vs. F. Simpier; C. W. Gorman vs. Hebron township, two cases; Colwell & Chase vs. W. L. Campbell, with notice to John Glace as terre tenant; B. Smith and Adelaide Smith, devisees of C. Smith, vs. W. T. Jones; Daniel Clark vs. F. B. Nichols, and Sala Stevens, doing business under the name of Nichols & Stevens; Wm. Cobb vs. George Townsend.

C. M. Allen was appointed a Commissioner to take testimony in the case of Alice Vanhorn vs. P. Vanhorn.

M. S. Thompson was appointed guardian of Wm. W. Rossiter and Orpha Rossiter, minor children of George Rossiter, deceased.

J. M. Covey, High Sheriff of Potter county, came into court and acknowledged the following deeds: To S. F. Wilson, for the undivided one-half interest in 75 acres of land in Pike township, Potter county, Pa., sold as the property of Isaac Greenwood, for the sum of $25; to Wm. Cobb, for four hundred acres of land in Oswayo township, part of warrants Nos. 1866 and 1869, sold as the property of Anthony W. Jones, for the sum of $500; to Daniel Yentzer, for 58.5 acres of land in Pleasant Valley township, part of warrants Nos. 2170 and 2209, with the exception of 25 acres, lying in south part and school house lot, sold as the property of Benjamin Haynes and Charles Haynes, for the sum of $25; to Peter Works, for three acres of land in Hector township, sold as the property of A. A. Streeter, for the sum of $25; to Marcus Handwork for 50 acres of land in Abbott township, sold as the property of August Siebenhahiner, for the sum of $25.

M. V. Larrabee, Esq., Treasurer of Potter county, came into court and acknowledged 35 deeds to purchasers of land sold for taxes.

Potter Enterprise
Thursday Evening, July 1, 1880 – Vol. 7, No. 8

Married.

ELDERKIN – CRISTIE – At the residence of R. Ellsworth, in Bingham, Potter county, Pa., by A. A. Johnson, Esq., Mr. Nelson Elderkin, of Potter county, Pa., and Mrs. Phoebe Ann Cristie, of Bingham, Pa.

Died.

RYON – At her home in Ulysses, Sunday evening, June 20th, 1880, Mrs. Abagail Ryon, wife of Deacon Ebenezer Ryon, aged 76 years.

DIMON – At Genesee Forks, Pa., of diphtheria, June 26, 1880, Nellie, only daughter of Mr. and Mrs. Jerome Dimon, aged 5 years.

Nellie, thou hast left us,
We they loss do deeply feel;
But 'tis God that has bereft us,
He will all our sorrows heal.

LEETE – At Adkinsville, Wayne Co., West Virginia, May 25th, of consumption, J. R. Leete, M.D., aged 42 years, formerly a resident of Bingham, Potter Co., Pa.

Mr. Leete leaves a wife and six children, besides many relatives to mourn his loss. He has been a kind husband, tender father, a sincere Christian and respected by all who knew him.

Fatal Accident.

On Monday morning as the painters were about to commence work on the Second street front of the Court House the scaffolding owing to increased weight from the rains of the night before, yielded enough to throw a step ladder on which Mr. G. H. Watts was just stepping, off its perch and Mr. Watts fell to the ground. His back was broken as were each of his arms by the fall, and although every attention was paid him and everything done for him which could be done, he died in about one hour. His home was in Knoxville, Tioga county, where he leaves a wife and three children, and to which place his remains were taken by his employer, Mr. A. M. Dunham.

The step ladder in its descent, struck the Prothonotary, O. H. Crosby, Esq., on the head, cutting a serious gash several inches long therein, but happily with no more serious result than a painful wound.

Mr. A. M. Dunham, who was on the scaffold with Mr. Watts when it gave way, saved himself by grasping a post and hanging on for dear life.

This is the second fatal accident which has occurred in this borough with in a few weeks. Isaac B. Baker having came to his death by falling upon a circular saw at the mill of O. T. Ellison on the evening of Friday, May 7th.

Potter Enterprise
Thursday Evening, July 8, 1880 – Vol. 7, No. 9

Olmsted Station. Mr. and Mrs. B. Watson have had an addition to their family – a son, weight 8 pounds. All doing well.

Married.

PATTERSON – BURDIC – At Bingham, June 27th, 1880, by A. A. Johnson, Esq., Edgar Patterson and Fendora Burdic, both of Bingham, Potter county, Pa.

Potter County, Pennsylvania Potpourri – Volume I
1880 through 1884

Died.
HENDRICKSON – At Philadelphia, Pa., June 25th, 1880, of consumption, Orvis Hendrickson, formerly of Lewisville, in this county.

Tannery at North Wharton.
Indications now very favorable for the erection of a tannery at the mouth of Freeman Run by the Messrs. Costello, of Oswayo. They have secured the refuse of a large body of Hemlock lands, and express themselves well satisfied with the location. A large tannery over there means an extended boom for that portion of the county.

A Narrow Escape.
What came very near being a terrible accident occurred at the house of Mr. Oscar McNeil, near the Lane school house, Honeoye, Pa., last Thursday night. A child was sick and so a lamp was left burning during the night, standing on the table close to the head of the bed. About eleven o'clock Mrs. McNeil awoke and found the lamp all ablaze.

Mr. McNeil had just time to get it from the bed room when it exploded, throwing the burning oil on his wife and setting fire to the house, but which they were enabled to extinguish. The husband was quite badly burned tearing the burned clothes from his wife, while she escaped with a severe burn on the arm and the loss of some hair.

But for the lucky awakening, they would undoubtedly have been burned in their bed, and the accident is a reminder of what all are liable to who are in the habit of leaving the ordinary lamp burning at night. – *Reporter.*

Potter Enterprise
Thursday Evening, July 15, 1880 – Vol. 7, No. 10

- Will Bassett, the mason, is excusable for all those queer freaks last week. It is a girl weighing three and one half pounds, and all doing well.

Married.
BEEBEE – HACKETT – On Saturday, July 3d, 1880, by P. A. McDonald, Esq., Mr. E. J. Beebee, of Oswayo, and Miss Alice Hackett, of Coudersport.

ALLIS – HAMILTON – By Rev. E. A. Rice, at the Howell House, Wellsville, July 3d, Mr. Frank M. Allis, of Ellisburg, and Miss Ettie Hamilton, of Scio, N.Y.

- Mr. Nye who lived by himself last summer, just out of the village on the Niles road, and who had somehow come by the title of "the hermit," and who has been sick for several months at the house of Mr. Toles, died on Monday.

- Borough ordinance No. 55 has gone into effect. There have been two arrests, two lodgings in jail, and two fines paid, and the ordinance will probably be kept in constant use unless our laws against the sale of liquor are enforced. There are two or three hell holes in town where drunkards are turned out every day and night in utter contempt of the decent portion of the community, and yet no attempt is made by law abiding people to end the disgrace to our town.

MURDER OF DAVID INGRAHAM.
THE DASTARDLY DEED COMMITTED IN
STODDARD COUNTY, MISSOURI, LAST MONTH.

In April last, David Ingraham, of Coudersport, and William Petrie, of Eldred, McKean county, started down the Allegany river in a small boat, their intention being as stated by Ingraham, to visit the western country and perhaps to cross the Rocky Mountains and visit the Pacific coast, or if inclination led that way they might go to the Black Hills. Petrie had a stock of jewelry, which he intended to peddle out and Ingraham had $600 or $800 in ready money, to invest in any speculation which might promise a good return on the investment. But two letters have been received by Ingraham's friends in this vicinity since his departure, but a couple of weeks ago Petrie returned to Eldred, and in response to inquiries concerning Ingraham, said that they had parted at Memphis, Tennessee, and that Ingraham had gone to Leadville. This story might have passed current through all time, but last week news was received that the dead body of Ingraham had been found in a stream in Liberty township, Stoddard county, Missouri. He had evidently been shot and afterwards beaten with an ax. The murderer had then filled a meal bag with wet sand from the river bed, strapped it to the body of Ingraham, towed it half a mile down the stream and sunk it, where he thought it would never rise to confront him. A jury held an inquest on the body and rendered a verdict that Ingraham came to his death at the hands of his partner or supposed partner, who by the way, went by the name of William Prentiss, instead of his right name Petrie out there. On Thursday Petrie was arrested and locked up at Olean and word sent to the authorities of Stoddard county, Missouri, that he was so held. He will doubtless be taken to that State for trial. So far, circumstances appear to be strongly against him, but he may be able to give a satisfactory account of himself. David Ingraham was a resident and property owner in this village, being the owner of the house and lot at West and Fifth streets, at present occupied by George W. Pearsoll, the Commissioner's clerk. He was a widower, his wife having been a sister of Isaac C. Staysa, of Millport. Ingraham was also a connection to Petrie, his alleged murderer, as Petrie and Staysa married sisters. Ingraham had kept a diary of each day's events from the time he left Eldred in April, until the 16th day of June, when the entry was commenced but left unfinished, the diary being spattered with blood. This is the day on which doubtless the murder took place. The diary recorded each day's travel down the Allegany river into the Ohio, down the Mississippi to the mouth of the St. Francis, and up that stream to the mouth of Second Creek about one mile above the line between Stoddard and Durklin counties, where they encamped on the night of the 15th of June. On the morning of the 16th, Petrie took his double barreled gun and went to W. W. Dranes and brought bread, as he said for himself and partner, whom he had left with the boat at the river, and said that they were going above to the railroad to work and that he would be glad if Drane would take charge of the things until they returned. On the morning of the 17th, Petrie came again to Drane's and said that his partner had left him on the day before, and gone to Ash Hill, and that he was on his way to Dexter to take the train, and that he had left the boat and other things at the river for Drane, and for him to take charge of them until Petrie came back. On the 23d of June, Drane and Bud Nobles, while fishing, found Ingraham's dead body as above described. The body was interred on the bank of the stream.

SUDDEN DEATH. ORLANDO CHAPMAN GOES OUT OF THE WORLD UNDER SUSPICIOUS CIRCUMSTANCES.
His Wife Held by the Verdict of a Coroner's Jury and Committed to the County Jail for the Crime.

On Saturday last Orlando Chapman, of this village, died from, as the Coroner's Jury find, narcotic poison. The deceased had been a resident of this place for about two years and had lately been engaged in peeling bark for the tannery. Thursday evening he returned from the woods apparently in his usual health, ate his supper as usual, and until some hours after was apparently was apparently well and feeling as well as any one would after working out in the woods all day. Friday morning about three o'clock his wife aroused one of the boarders to go for a doctor. At that time Mr. Chapman was unconscious and the whole system seemed paralyzed. No doctor could be obtained until about eight o'clock when Dr. Post was secured. Afterwards Drs. Buck and Ellison visited the sick man, but found him as stated and frothing at the mouth. No medicine was given as it was found to be impossible for the man to swallow. Mr. Chapman lingered until three o'clock Saturday afternoon, remaining unconscious to the last.

The case seemed to demand legal investigation, and L. B. Cole, Esq., summoned a jury the same afternoon and a few witnesses were examined.

On Sunday morning Drs. Buck, Mattison, Ellison and Post held a post mortem examination in the presence of a number of witnesses. The brain was removed and thoroughly examined; the body opened, and the heart, lungs, kidneys and the whole internal organization subjected to a rigid examination. The stomach and liver were removed and sealed in glass jars for chemical analysis.

After the post mortem the witnesses were again questioned and the doctors gave their testimony. Below we give the main facts brought out in addition to that above.

When Dr. Post first saw the patient he told those in attendance that the man was suffering from poison. Thursday night or a night or two before Mrs. Chapman sent out by Mr. Baker, a boarder, to Thompson & Co.'s drug store and purchased 25 cents worth of morphine. The morphine was delivered to Mr. Chapman in presence of his wife. Thursday night after supper Mrs. Chapman gave him camphor and water. One witness testified that shortly after he complained of feeling numb and he had to be helped to bed, his clothes being removed by Mrs. C. When he stepped into his bed room was the last time he was seen in a conscious state by any on except his wife. A bottle containing morphine was found in a stand drawer. Mr. and Mrs. Chapman had occasional quarrels. "Mr. C. being jealous, and not without cause." Mrs. C. made a statement before the jury, stating that she had given Chapman morphine, a small dose; that she was in the habit of giving and using morphine; that Mr. Chapman was more affectionate that night than usual, kissing her and laying plans for the future.

Dr. Buck. – Found congestion of brain and other organs, such as might have been produced by narcotic poison; congestion of blood veins, brain, liver, lungs and kidneys show a complete paralysis of the whole system. Found evidence of no other poison except narcotic; don't think congestion could have been produced except by some narcotic; think from appearance before and examination after death, that death was produced by narcotic poison; Mrs. Chapman said she gave him a dose of morphine before he went to bed; gave what she could take out on the bow of a hair pin.

Dr. E. S. Mattison. – Found congestion of brains, lungs, and kidneys enough to produce death; could have been produced by narcotic poison or sunstroke; do not think sunstroke would have produced so complete congestion. Any narcotic would produce this effect.

Dr. O. T. Ellison. – He died from congestion of the brain; the system and condition of the patient before death showed he had received some narcotic poison; could not have been sunstricken in afternoon and have been as well as he was in the evening; I think from the appearance of the patient before death and from the examination since, that death was produced from some narcotic poison.

Dr. R. V. Post. – Brain was congested; think it was caused by poison; think it caused by morphine or opium; sunstroke would have produced the effect, but would have operated sooner.

VERDICT OF THE CORONER'S JURY.

Commonwealth of Pennsylvania, Potter County, ss:

An inquisition indented and taken at the house of Orlando Chapman, in Coudersport, County of Potter, the 10th day of July, 1880, before me, L. B. Cole, a Justice of the Peace in and for the county of Potter, upon the view of the body of Orlando Chapman, then and there lying dead, upon the oath of O. J. Rees, W. A. Crosby, George Pearsall, L. B. Cole, Jr., Daniel Monroe and A. H. Owen, good and lawful men of the county aforesaid, who being sworn to duly inquire on the part of the Commonwealth, when, where, how and after what manner the said Orlando Chapman came to his death, do say upon their oaths that the said Orlando Chapman died July 10, 1880, in Coudersport, said county, of congestion of the brain, produced by an overdose of morphine, maliciously, willfully and feloniously administered by Theresa Chapman, wife of said Orlando Chapman.

In witness whereof, as well the aforesaid Coroner, as the jurors aforesaid, have to this inquisition put their hands and seals on the 11th day of July, A.D. 1880, at the place first above mentioned.

L. B. Cole, J.P.

Orlando J. Rees, W. A. Crosby, Geo. W. Pearsall, L. B. Cole, Jr., Daniel Monroe, A. H. Owen.

The Jury came to an agreement about 11 o'clock on Sunday, and about one o'clock Constable Bassett arrested Mrs. Chapman and delivered her to the custody of the Sheriff.

The funeral of Mr. Chapman took place at 4 o'clock. The remains were followed to the grave by Leander Chapman, of Harrison, a brother of the deceased, and Daniel Chapman, aged about ten years, the only child of the dead man, as mourners.

It is stated that at the trial evidence will be produced that there had been a previous attempt on the life of Mr. Chapman. We give this rumor for what it is worth. It will be brought out that Mrs. Chapman about one year ago attempted to get poison, "poison that would kill a man."

At present only the worst side of the story can be obtained, and it will be well to take such stories with a liberal allowance for exaggeration. With the exception of the statement that evidence will be produced to show that he had been poisoned before the above is correct taken from the evidence produced or what we know can and will be produced.

K. ZIMMERMAN
Dealer in
FRESH and SALT MEATS.
Ham, Lard, Eggs, Etc.
Always on hand, AT LOW PRICES.

PHOTOGRAPHY
IN ALL ITS BRANCHES
COPYING and ENLARGING OLD PICTURES
Of Every Kind A SPECIALTY.
Also FRAMES, STEREOSCOPES and STEREO
COPIC VIEWS FOR SALE.
Views of Residences made to order.
Satisfaction guaranteed or no pay.
Gallery on East Street, South of 3d.
L. R. BLISS,
PHOTOGRAPH ARTIST.
COUDERSPORT, PA.
J. A. Haynes, authorized agent for taking
Order for copying and enlarging.

Potter County, Pennsylvania Potpourri – Volume I
1880 through 1884

Potter Enterprise
Thursday Evening, July 22, 1880 – Vol. 7, No. 11

Married.

REED – ROSSITER – At the M.E. parsonage, June 10th, 1880, by Rev. T. R. Stratton, Mr. Wm. B. Reed to Miss Orpha Rossiter, both of Homer, Pa.

BARTHOLOMEW – CHURCH – At the same place, by the same, June 11th, 1880, Mr. David Bartholomew to Miss Adell A. Church, both of Roulet.

OBITUARY.

Thomas R. Shear, the subject of this sketch, and son of Hon. William Shear, of this Borough, died at the residence of his father at 4 a.m., on Tuesday, the 20th instant, of consumption. He was born at Duffin's Creek, Pickering Twp., Ontario, Canada, October 19, 1856. Came to Coudersport with his father when quite a small boy, and has resided her ever since. From early boyhood Thomas gave promise of a useful and successful manhood, studious, quiet and industrious. He was successful in whatever he undertook, and his broad, generous principles won for him a host of affectionate friends. With always a kind word for every one he had not an enemy in the world, and there is none among us whose loss will be more universally felt and sincerely mourned than that of "Tom" Shear. Ever since his sickness in the winter of 1878 his lungs have been affected, but hopes had been entertained of his recovery; but at the great fire in Coudersport in May last over-exertion produced prostration and a relapse of his disease, and from that time on he continued to grow worse until Tuesday, when with the dawning of the day, fit symbol of his opening manhood, his spirit took its final leave of earth.

Stop, dear reader, stop just here,
And drop for him one farewell tear.

- The death of Thomas R. Shear has cast a gloom over our whole community. Though young in years he had won the respect of all who knew him. The sorrowing relatives have the sympathy of us all. He died on Tuesday morning about four o'clock, of consumption. His last illness was of several weeks duration, and was very painful, but he bore all his trials and sufferings without a murmur.

THE MURDER OF DAVID INGRAHAM.

From the Olean *Times* of Saturday, 17th instant:

Yesterday afternoon a certified copy of the Coroner's inquest of Stoddard county, Mo., having arrived, the examination of the Petrie case was called, District Attorney Smith, of McKean county, Pa., and Thomas Storrs appeared for the people and Carey and Jewell for the prisoner, Mr. Smith waived the fact that no witnesses had arrived and the examination proceeded with. Much debate was had as to admitting of the copy of the Coroner's inquest, but it was finally decided that it was not admissible and was therefore thrown out. This done there was no evidence of which to make a commitment and the prisoner was discharged.

As soon as the prisoner was liberated Constable Johnson, of Hinsdale, stepped up and served a warrant upon him. The crowd, who were strongly in favor of the prisoner, surged forward as though they would tear Petrie from the clutches of the law, but there was no leader and the movement fell through. Petrie was taken to the residence of John King and given his supper. While Petrie was eating a movement was set on foot by some hot headed fellows to liberate him, but when the carriage drove down to King's for the prisoner there was only a small crowd followed and they were as peaceful as could be desired.

Public opinion, as represented in the court room, was strong in Petrie's favor, so much so that many feared a riot should he again be held.

This morning N. W. Cobb, an officer from Missouri, arrived on train 8 on the Erie road. He was escorted up town by officer King, who hitched up his team and took him to Hinsdale, where Petrie is now held. An examination will doubtless be held this afternoon which will determine whether Petrie is to be held for a requisition or not.

Lost.
A brown and yellow canary bird – might answer to the name of Dick. The finder will be liberally rewarded by returning it to Mrs. D. F. Glassmire, Jr.

Accident.
One night last week James White, of this place, the miller at the Crittenden Mills, on the way to his farm in Sharon township, was thrown from a sulky, receiving injuries which were at first thought to be very serious, but which happily turned out not to be as bad as first supposed to be. He was brought home the next day after the accident and is able to be up and around.

Advertised Letters.
The following is a list of letters remaining uncalled for at the Coudersport post office July 1st, 1880: Crawford, Eugene; Fitzgerald, Nicholas; Haven, Miss Mary; Marsh, N. L.; Woelen, William.

Potter Enterprise
Thursday Evening, July 29, 1880 – Vol. 7, No. 12

- The infant child of Wm. Basset died on Sunday. It was but a few weeks old.

- Benjamin Fait who was hostler at the Baker House in this borough for several months last year, was drowned at Emporium on Monday. He was working for Major Seibert of the Shives House and was sent to the creek to wash a wagon and was found lying on the bottom of the creek with a bruise on his forehead, dead. Three of the traces to the wagon had been loosened and he had probably been kicked by one of the horses while about them and falling sense in the water was drowned.

Died.

STEPHENS – July 14th, 1880, at Silver Cliff, Custer county, Colorado, Rev. F. G. Stephens, of Homer, Potter county, Pa., aged 50 years.

NICHOLS – July 27th, 1880, of cholera infantum, Dutton, son of R. L. and Jennie Nichols, of Coudersport, aged 356 days.

MERCHANT – In Guilford, Chenango county, on the 28th day of June, 1880, after a long and painful illness, Mrs. Emma H. Merchant, in the 59th year of her age.

She was a sister to Pliny Harris, and spent some time at his home in Ulysses many years ago.

THE MURDER OF DAVID INGRAHAM.

Salamanca, July 22. – Much indignation is felt over release of Petrie, the Missouri murderer, which occurred at Ellicottville yesterday. It appears Petrie's lawyers succeeded in taking him out of the hands of Hinsdale authorities on a habeas corpus and before Judge Scott, in Ellicottville, where examination was held Tuesday. Meantime William Drain, the farmer who sold the bread to Petrie and who found the body of his murdered companion, David Ingraham, and who was needed to identify the prisoner as the same man, arrived in Hinsdale. Information to this effect was telegraphed to Judge Scott, who adjourned the case until yesterday morning at 8 o'clock. Unable, it is claimed, to hold him any longer, he released Petrie at 8:45. Witness Drain arrived at 11. Petrie immediately got into a buggy, which was waiting, accompanied by his lawyer, Cotter, of Smethport, and another man and drove rapidly away in the direction of Pennsylvania – the direction, by the way, in which all rogues in this locality point for when in danger of arrest. The party passed through Great Valley at 10:15 and were driving fast. Warrants for arrest of Petrie were issued here and telegrams for his arrest were sent to Limestone, Bradford and other points. It is hoped his arrest will follow, as there is no doubt but he is the murderer. From W. W. Drain of Liberty township, Stoddard county, Mo., we learn the following details of the dastardly deed, which has filled the people of Stoddard county, with indignation, and they will do all in their power to bring the villain to a just account. On the 16th of June, while Mr. Drane was at work in the field some distance from his home and the St. Francis river he was approached by a man bearing the description of Petrie, who asked where he was. Mr. Drane informed him as to his location, when the man asked how far it was to the nearest house, stating that he and a companion had got lodged on a flood jam and would want to procure bread once in a while. Drane replied that his home was the nearest, and that it was three miles from the river, and that the nearest residence on the opposite was four miles distant. The questioner then wanted to know the distance to the nearest highway and was told it was seven miles. Then the man from the boat enquired the distance to the nearest railroad and the nearest station, and was informed that it was about twenty miles. The man then accompanied Drane to his home where Mrs. Drane supplied him with bread, and he started off toward the boat. On the 17th Drane went to see his son-in-law, J. W. Nobles, seven miles from Dexter and along in the afternoon he noticed a man coming along the road which passed Mr. Nobles and he thought it was the man whom he had supplied with bread on the previous day. He stepped into the road as the man approached and asked him if he was not the man, to which he received reply in the affirmative. Drane asked him where his partner was and was told that he had gone to Ashhill, and that he, himself, was going away and would not be back for two weeks, may be not till fall, and perhaps never, and that he wanted to leave his boat in care of Drane, at the same time handing him a bunch of keys. Drane inquired about the shot gun which the man had carried the previous day. The man told him it was in the boat, which had a small cabin on it. On the 18th, Drane accompanied by a friend, went to the boat and took an inventory of its contents, which consisted as follows: One buffalo robe, two hand saws, two planes, a tape line, a hand saw set, spirit level, three comforts, two overcoats, one pair of pants, one glass hand lamp and about fifty dollars worth of spices, etc. On the opposite corner of the buffalo robe the name, "Mrs. William Petrie" was inscribed, and the name of "Wm. Petrie" adorned the handle of one of the hand saws. The shotgun was gone but a powder flask and dull hatchet were found on board. There was a bag on the boat marked "A. Prentiss." There was no blood found on the boat. After the inventory was completed the boat was locked up and but little thought of the matter.

On the 23d Mr. Drane and J. W. Noble were fishing in the river something like a quarter of a mile below the boat when they spied what seemed to be the shoulder of a man sticking out of the water. They immediately gave an alarm when citizens came to the spot and succeeded in bringing the mangled body of a man to the shore. His head was horribly mutilated, being jammed to a pumice down to the lower jaw making identification impossible.

A coroner's jury was summoned who from the evidence produced gave it as their opinion that the deceased was David Ingraham and that he came to his death at the hands of his partner, Wm. Prentiss; which they were led to suppose was the man's name from the inscription on the bag, that being the only article produced before the jury.

When found Ingraham was securely strapped to a two bushel bag, containing sand, with his hands pinioned to his sides. It appears that when the deed was committed the water was high, and when the body was consigned to the dark waters of the St. Francis, it lodged on a snag in the river, which was then covered by water, which, receding, left the body exposed. On making examination of the bank along the stream, two pieces of human skull, with the hair clotted with gore were found, and the marks on the sandy beach where the body was dragged after the murder were plainly visible.

The diary of the murdered man was found in his inside vest pocket and his hat, containing two slits was carefully stowed away in the sand bag. On the fly leaf of the diary was the following address: "David Ingraham, Bentons Mills, Pa." The entries through the diary was made "bought by Wm." and "bought by D." and from this the coroner's jury drewth conclusion that the murderer must be Wm. instead of "A. Prentiss" as was recorded on the bag. We have been shown pictures which Mr. Thomas Storrs who has acted in the prosecution from the beginning to the close, has taken of the person, and which have been identified by Mr. Drane was the man with whom he met in Missouri. – *Olean Times.*

NOTICE.

Whereas my wife, Phebe Tuttle, having left my bed and board without just cause or provocation, any one is hereby forbidden to trust her on my account, as I will not pay any debts of her contracting.

Joseph N. Tuttle, Sylvania, Pa., July 25th, 1880.

– The drunkenness and disorder on our streets at night has got to be almost unbearable by the decent people of our community. On Saturday Matthias Schmidt, who sells hard cider at a place on East street, was arrested for keeping a disorderly house and for selling intoxicating liquor, and gave bail in the sum of $100 on each charge. The uproar in the vicinity of the brewery about bed time for decent folks is terrific, and unless we are much mistaken will have to come to an end soon. We are glad to believe that the people who get "drunk and disorderly" are generally not our own citizens but are of those who have been brought in by the greatly increased demand for labor.

Population of Potter County.

We give below the official statement of the population of this county, by townships and boroughs, as shown by the census taken last month and by the census of 1870. It will be seen that taking the county through there has been a healthy increase, the gain since 1870 being about 21 per cent. Only a few of the townships, Stewardson, Ulysses, Sylvania and West Branch have lost in population, and the loss in Sylvania is accounted for by the formation of Portage being taken out of Sylvania since 1870:

TOWNSHIPS.	1880	1870
Abbott	624	534
Allegany	672	625
Bingham	832	773
Clara	238	171
Coudersport Boro	679	954
Eulalia	456	353
Genesee	886	767
Harrison	1165	1052
Hebron	835	754
Hector	958	651
Homer	190	160
Jackson, now Ulysses		49
Keating	204	78
Lewisville Boro	365	226
Oswayo	884	629
Pike	327	184
Pleasant Valley	212	140

Portage, formed since 1870	120	
Roulet	651	525
Sharon	1056	978
Sweden	420	357
Stewardson	196	210
Summit	202	145
Sylvania	217	267
Ulysses	638	789
West Branch	350	287
Total	13,658	11,265

The Potter Enterprise
Thursday Evening, August 12, 1880 – Vol. VII, No. 13

– Petrie, the murderer of David Ingraham, of Stoddard county, Mo., who was arrested in Cattaraugus county, N.Y., and then let go on technicalities, is still at large in Pennsylvania. Warrants were issued for his arrest directly after his release, but the officers have not been able to find him. – Miner.

Coudersport Town Council.

1880, July 26. – Council met. Present – W. K. Jones, Burgess, and O. H. Crosby, C. H. Armstrong, H. J. Olmsted, P. A. Stebbins, Jr., and M. L. Gridley, Town Council.

The minutes of the meeting of June 21, 1880, were read and approved.

On motion, an order was drawn in favor of E. D. Lewis, High Constable, for services as policeman to this date, for the sum of ten dollars, and the pay of the said E. D. Lewis as policeman was fixed at five dollars per week aside from his legal fees. And the Burgess was authorized to appoint three special policemen, with the authority of the high constable, said special policemen to be paid one dollar per night when on duty.

On motion, D. C. Larrabee – being about to visit Buffalo, N.Y., - was requested to purchase one half dozen badges for the policemen.

On motion the following bills were ordered paid:

Wm. Dingman, work on pound, No. 14	$0.96
R. M. Niles, work on road, No. 15	5.00
W. B. Gordnier, grates for sewer and plow handles, No. 16	9.60
E. O. Rees, Auditor's fees, June 23, 1880	1.50
A. B. Mann, Auditor's fees, June 23, 1880	1.50

On motion, E. J. Fickler was appointed Collector of the Borough tax for the year 1880, to give bond with approved security in the sum of two thousand dollars.

Horse Notes.

F. W. Knox has recently purchased of R. L. Andrews a showy driving team.

C. L. Peck has traded his Morgan for a four-year old Hambletonian, out of Wood's horse. A fine, prompt stepper.

A. B. Mann sports a team, a bay and a gray, that get as far in a day as any of them. One of them was recently injured while in the barn, but under the veterinary skill of Mr. Lay, is coming out all right.

R. L. Nichols has purchased the fine black horse heretofore owned by J. C. Moffitt, of Clara, for a carriage horse.

Lon. Crosby drives a fine span of colts, a roane and steel gray, both good travelers.

Charley Hosley of Ulysses, has a fine four-year old out of the famous trotter, Judge Fullerton. Mr. Lay is training the colt on the Coudersport track, and is making excellent time. We shall hear more of this colt some day.

Lay also has a bay mare from the oil region that turns the track in a little less time than has ever been done by any horse heretofore in this section.

M. L. Gridley is driving a speedy bay owned by Frank Andrews of Duke Centre, that promises to make a good stepper this fall.

Kitty Sandbach, owned by Ed. Cornell, is being exercised daily on the track. Kitty has been out of condition for some time past, but is now on the gain.

Those interested will find the Coudersport track a very pleasant place to spend an hour each morning. Some very good stepping will be witnessed.

- The following persons have announced themselves as candidates for nomination at the Republican Convention: For Congress, W. W. Brown, of Bradford, M'Kean county; for Senator, Lewis Emery, Jr., of M'Kean county; for Representative, R. L. White of Roulet, D. D. Chapin of Harrison; for Treasurer, C. H. Armstrong of Coudersport, Edwin Haskell of Allegany; for Sheriff, Daniel Monroe of Coudersport, G. H. Cobb of Lewisville.

NOTICE.

Wheras my wife, Johanna Moser, having left my bed and board without just cause or provocation, any one is hereby forbidden to trust her on my account, as I will not pay any debts of her contracting.

Frederic Moser, Germania, Pa., August 2, 1880.

CARRIAGES!   WAGONS!

Z. J. THOMPSON,

At his shop on West Street, COUDERSPORT, PENN'A.
is prepared to furnish everything in his line on the shortest notice and of the BEST QUALITY. The BEST of timber used and work executed in the best and most workmanlike manner. REPAIRING in all its branches will receive PROMPT ATTENTION. Satisfaction Guaranteed.

Potter County, Pennsylvania Potpourri – Volume I
1880 through 1884

The Potter Enterprise
Wednesday Evening, August 18, 1880 – Vol. VII, No. 14

MARRIED.

NICHOLS – LANDON – At Clara, Aug. 7, 1880, by J. L. Allen, J.P., Mr. Dallas Nichols of Sharon Centre and Miss Maria M. Landon, of Sweden, Pa.

Genesee Fork. Died – At Genesee Fork, Pa., August 8, Ruth Fuller, aged 6 years. Daughter of Mr. and Mrs. L. Fuller, of this place.

Genesee Fork. – At West Creek, of Diphteria, August 8, Fred Miller, aged 13. August 10, Stella Miller, aged 9. August 15, Dora Miller, aged 11. All children of Mrs. Mary Miller, widow of G. W. Miller.

Allegany. Diphtheria has made its appearance at Andrews Settlement. A. C. Scoville's youngest son was the first victim; Fred, aged fourteen years, he was sick eight days.

How to Become Naturalized.

An applicant for naturalization, if he arrived in this country after he was eighteen years of age, must make declaration before the clerk of any court of record having common law jurisdiction and a seal, of his intention to become a citizen, two years at least before his admission as such. At the end of five years from the time of his arrival in the country, such declaration having been made two years before, he is entitled to his papers upon application to the court. In case the applicant arrived in the United States before he was eighteen years of age and has attained the age of twenty-one years, and has been in the country five years, he is entitled to become a citizen without the declaration two years in advance; he will then make the declaration at the time of his admission that for two years it has been his intention to become a citizen. The applicant must declare an oath that he will support the Constitution of the United States, and renounce all allegiance to foreign powers. Furthermore, the court must be satisfied by one or more witnesses that the applicant has lived in the country at least five years, and in the State in which the court is held at least one year and that he has been a man of good moral character. A man who has served in either the regular or volunteer army of the United States and has been honorably discharged can be admitted upon his petition without previous declaration. The oath of the applicant in no case allowed to prove the fact of his residence.

JURY LIST, SEPT. TERM, 1880.
TRAVERSE JURORS.

Patrick Doyle, Farmer, Oswayo; John Carpenter, Merchant, Genesee; A. F. Raymond, Farmer, Ulysses; E. O. Rees, Jeweler, Coudersport, I. H. Dingman, Farmer, Hebron; A. J. Barnes, Merchant, Sharon; George Baker, Laborer, Coudersport; H. C. Olmsted, Merchant, Coudersport; C. D. Tubbs, Farmer, Hector; William Shear, Tanner, Coudersport; J. H. Wright, Farmer, Sharon; G.

W. Francis, Farmer, Stewardson; W. B. Rees, Carpenter, Coudersport; Allen Hammond, Farmer, Oswayo; Sterling Devens, Farmer, Homer; Samuel White, Farmer, Sharon; J. C. Helfrecht, Farmer, Abbott; George Rees, Farmer, Sylvania; H. B. Whitehed, Farmer, Harrison; George English, Farmer, Eulalia; Herman Bridges, Farmer, Keating; T. J. Farnham, Farmer, Oswayo; G. W. Colvin, Farmer, Bingham; Thos. T. O'Donald, Farmer, Genesee; John Schollard, Farmer, Hebron; Benj. Johnson, Farmer, Harrison; Vint Dodge, Farmer, Harrison; J. S. Little, Farmer, Hector; Frank Stevens, Clerk, Coudersport; G. C. Lewis, Farmer, Keating; Charles Grover, Farmer, Bingham; S. H. Martin, Farmer, Pike; Lewis Hoppe, Farmer, Abbott; J. N. Crowell, Farmer, Ulysses; R. C. Hosley, Farmer, Hector; Nelson Clark, Farmer, Eulalia.

GRAND JURORS.

Henry Gnau, Farmer, Abbott; M. K. Beach, Hotel Keeper, Hector; Norman Dwight, Farmer, Hebron; F. P. Nichols, Farmer, Sharon; A. W. Carmer, Shoe Maker, Oswayo; Lyman Rooks, Farmer, Harrison; Henry Neiman, Farmer, W. Branch; L. J. Earle, Farmer, Hector; Alva Carpenter, Farmer, Ulysses; Charles Hackett, Farmer, Genesee; C. Sandbach, Hotel Keeper, Abbott; E. D. Ayers, Farmer, Hebron; Giles Allaard, Farmer, Eulalia; Michael Dwire, Farmer, Genesee; Coleman Smith, Farmer, Oswayo; James Tyler, Farmer, Clara; William Daniels, Farmer, Bingham; W. W. Dwight, Farmer, Hebron; Thos. Parker, Farmer, Lewisville; William Hill, Farmer, Genesee; Charles Burt, Farmer, Bingham; A. C. Voorhees, Farmer, Sharon; Edwin Lyman, Farmer, Sweden; Thos. Crittenden, Farmer, Oswayo.

The Potter Enterprise
Wednesday Evening, August 25, 1880 – Vol. VII, No. 15

MARRIED.

MORREY – BABICOCK – In Roulet, August 21st, 1880, by Albert Green, J.P., Mr. William Morrey and Mrs. Maria Babicock. All of Roulet, Pa.

- The infant child of Mr. and Mrs. W. A. Crosby of Coudersport, was buried on Friday afternoon last.

- The following in reference to the game laws of Pennsylvania is of great interest to sportsmen, and should be cut out as a matter of reference in disputed questions concerning the game laws: Woodcock, July 4th to January 1st; plover, July 15th to January 1st; rail bird, September 1st to December 1st; reed birds, September 1st to December 1st; squirrel, September 1st to January 1st; wild fowl, September 1st to May 15th; ruffled grouse, October 1st to January 1st; pinnated grouse, October 1st to January 1st; quail, October 15th to January 1st; rabbit, October 15th to January 1st; wild turkey, October 15th to January 1st; deer, October 1st to January 1st.

Potter County, Pennsylvania Potpourri – Volume I
1880 through 1884

The Potter Enterprise
Wednesday Evening, September 1, 1880 – Vol. VII, No. 16

- The happiest, don't care a continental, man we have seen in many a day, was George Snyder of Ayer's Hill, last week. It was, "have a smoke boys. It weighs nine pounds, and is the sweetest little girl baby you ever laid eyes on."

- Mrs. Lucas Cushing, aged seventy years, was buried on Thursday last, from the home of her daughter, Mrs. H. J. Olmsted. For the past year the deceased had been almost helpless, requiring as much care as a child. Mrs. Cushing was an old and consistent member of the Baptist church.

DIED.
BARLOW – At Genesee Forks, Pa., of diptheria, August 29th, Sammie, son of Mr. and Mrs. George Barlow. Aged 9 years.

- The fence about the cemetery needs repairing. Every day or two cattle break in and damage the shrubs and flowers with which loving hands have decked the graves of departed friends.

**OSWAYO
GRADED SCHOOL.**
ANNOUNCEMENT FOR **1880-'81.**

PROF. A. D. HOWE, M.E.,   Principal;
MISS C. E. CASE, M.E.,   Assistant.

First Term begins Sept. 1st, 1880.
  do   do ends Nov. 16th, 1880.
Second do begins Nov. 17th, 1880.

Vacation, Dec. 24th, 1880; Jan. 10th, 1880. The new buildings are completed. No pains will be spared to make the School a perfect success. Thoroughness is our motto! Not how *much*, but how *well*. A tuition of one dollar per month will be charged those attending from other townships.

G. F. ROWELL, President.
J. H. DEXTER, Secretary.
AGRICULTURAL.

The Potter Enterprise
Wednesday Evening, September 8, 1880 – Vol. VII, No. 17

- Mrs. G. W. McKinney of Sweden, was buried on Monday last.

DIED.

REED – August 28, 1880, in Summit, Potter county, Pa., Edgar C. Reed, son of Luther and Louisa Reed. Aged 5 years and 10 months.
Happy they lot, dear child, escaped from earth.
Not dead, but wakened to a nobler birth.
Thy pangs all over, rest thee, pure one, rest.
We would not call thee back since thou art blessed.

MASONIC.

The disastrous fire of May the 18th, of this year, 1880, which in a few hours destroyed the entire business portion of Coudersport, and dissolved in ashes a large portion of the wealth and resources of many citizens, the accumulations of years of well directed labor; The suddenness, celerity and completeness of the work of destruction, will long be remembered by those who witnessed the disaster and labored to stay its progress, as well as by those who shared and suffered in the heavy losses it installed. But Phoenix like Coudersport is springing from its ashes and the marks of the ravages caused by the fire will soon disappear and the lovely town will look more beautiful than ever. Fine brick structures are rapidly rising in place of the old combustible wooden ones that formerly occupied the ground. The spirit and activity manifested in the prosecution of the work of rebuilding, displays in the most striking manner the commendable zeal, energy, pluck and perseverance of the merchants and other business men of Coudersport.

Conspicuous among the buildings now commenced and in process of construction, will be that of the three-story structure, covering the sites on which formerly stood the stores of C. S. Jones and F. E. Lyon. The third story of this building will be the Masonic Hall, the exclusive property of Eulalia Lodge, No. 342, A. Y. M.

The history of the Masonic organization in Coudersport is interesting and instructive and may be related in a few paragraphs:

A charter was granted by the Right Worshipful Grand Lodge of Pennsylvania on the 4th day of March, 1861, and in the month of October following, the Lodge was fully organized. The charter members were: Timothy Ives, Master; B. S. Colwell, Senior Warden and Joseph Williams, Junior Warden, Samuel Havens, C. H. Warner, J. C. Cavanaugh, G. W. G. Judd and D. C. Larrabee. From the organization of the society up to the present time, the following named gentlemen have been duly elected Masters of the lodge and served respectfully as such, namely: Timothy Ives, B. S. Colwell, C. H. Warner, D. C. Larrabee, Wm. Shear, J. W. Allen, N. H. Goodsel, R. L. White, P. A. Stebbins, Jr., E. O. Rees, W. A. Crosby, F. E. Lyon, O. H. Crosby and Miles White. The number of members in good standing at the present time is sixty-six.

Potter County, Pennsylvania Potpourri – Volume I
1880 through 1884

Previous to the fire the Masons rented and occupied the Temperance Hall over the Olmsted block, as a Lodge room. Their losses occasioned by the fire were nearly covered by insurance, but their books, papers and records were all consumed with the exception of the Charter and minute book. They now occupy a room in the Court House, awaiting the completion of their new Masonic Hall, which is expected to be ready for their occupancy in a few months. The society has prospered and by the good management and economy of its members, will have ample resources to complete the work on hand, which when finished will be sufficient for their wants, and will be a substantial ornament to the street on which it stands.

The Potter Enterprise
Wednesday Evening, September 15, 1880 – Vol. VII, No. 18

MARRIED.

ABBOTT – WESTCOTT – In Roulet, Sept. 8, by Rev. T. R. Stratton, Mr. John Abbott and Mrs. Mettie E. Westcott, both of Roulet.

DIED.

HYLER – On Ayers Hill, Potter county, Pa., September 1, 1880, Clara, daughter of Charles and Clara Hyler. Aged 3 years, 2 months and 4 days.

BURDICK – At his home in Nortonville, Jefferson county, Kan., of diseases contracted while in the army, in the 36th year of his age, Elno E. Burdick, son of Leroy Burdick of Hebron, Pa.

- William Persing, son of Joseph and Catherine Persing, died at Sunderlinville, September 4th. Aged nine years and ten months. On the 8th of July the boy was badly bitten on the hip, by a dog belonging to Perry Filmore, and the shock brought on disease which finally caused death.

Corner Stone.

On Thursday last there was an informal Corner Stone laying at the building being erected by C. S. Jones and Farnum Lyon, the third story of which is to be put on by Eulalia Lodge No. 342 A. Y. M., and occupied for Lodge purposes.

There was no ceremony and only a few of the craft were present or even knew of it. Through the enterprise of O. J. Rees the various articles were gathered and sealed in a cavity made for the purpose, near the centre of the front wall, where the hall way is to be, and is covered with a capstone or water-table.

In the box was placed:

A copy of the Potter *Pioneer* bearing date Coudersport, February 4, 1848.

A copy of the -----, a small temperance paper published at this place in 1849.

A copy of the first issue of the Potter *Journal*, in 1849.

A copy of the Potter *Journal* dated Sept. 8, 1880.

A copy of the Potter *Enterprise* of May 26, 1880, containing a corrected report of the fire of May 18th.

A copy of the Potter *Enterprise* of Sept. 8, 1880.

A list of the names and business of the members of Eulalia Lodge No. 342 A. Y. M.
Directory of the Lodge for A. L. 5880.
Names of officers of Grand Lodge of the State of Pennsylvania.
Estimate of cost of Lodge building, names of building committee and contractors.
Number inhabitants of Potter county and of Coudersport boro; number of voters in the borough; assessed valuation of borough; and a number of papers containing matters of interest to the fraternity only.

Stage Lines.
Stages will leave Coudersport as follows:
PORT ALLEGANY, daily except Sunday.
WELLSVILLE, via. Colesburg and Ellisburg Tuesday, Thursday and Saturday.
WELLSVILLE, via. Oswayo, Monday, Wednesday and Friday.
WESTFIELD, via. Brookland and Ulysses, Tuesday, Thursday and Saturday.
WESTFIELD, via. Raymond and Ulysses, Monday, Wednesday and Friday.
CERES, Monday, Wednesday and Friday, at noon.
KETTLE CREEK, Monday and Thursday.
SINNEMAHONING, Wednesday and Saturday.

The Potter Enterprise
Wednesday Evening, September 22, 1880 – Vol. VII, No. 19

Roulet. Born – To Mr. and Mrs. John Cavenaugh, a daughter. To Mr. and Mrs. Henry Barr, a son. To Mr. and Mrs. John Badger, a son. The mothers to these little ones are all sisters.

DIED.
MATTISON – In Hebron, September 19, Mrs. Tina P. Mattison, wife of Dr. Edgar S. Mattison, aged 29 years, 1 month and 4 days.
Funeral sermon will be delivered in the M. E. Church in Coudersport on Sunday morning next, at 10:30.

Potter County, Pennsylvania Potpourri – Volume I
1880 through 1884

The Potter Enterprise
Wednesday Evening, September 29, 1880 – Vol. VII, No. 20

MARRIED.

PRESHO – PRESHO – In Allegany, Sept. 20, by Rev. J. L. Swain, A. G. Presho Esq. and Mrs. Samantha Nelson Presho.

Bingham. People generally are enjoying good health, though we hear of some cases of diphtheria. There are three more cases in E. Robbins family. The skillful treatment of Dr. Cobb could not save two of them. One died Sept. 10th, aged five years, the other Sept. 16th, aged twelve years. The other four have recovered.

DIED.

BACON – At Ellisburg, Sept. 26, of cholera infantum, Lodemia, only child of Mr. and Mrs. John Bacon, aged 7 months and 28 days.

Court Proceedings.

Court convened Sept. 20, Judge Williams presiding.

Constables from different towns made reports.

Grand Jury called and sworn. Alva Carpenter appointed foreman, and Eli Glaspy constable to attend same.

Comth vs Abram Jones, continued, bail $100.

Comth vs Eldred Wood, continued, bail $100.

Comth vs Henry Grodevant, continued, bail $300.

H. C. Hosley for use of A. F. Raymond vs C. E. & W. M. Hosley et al. Rule on pl'ff to show cause why R. C. Hosley surety shall not be subrogated to right of pl'ff.

Comth vs I. Dolley, nol pros.

Comth vs Aaron and Melville Schoonover, continued, bail $300.

Frederick Zemper, Patrick Dwire and Thomas Carn admitted to citizenship.

Comth vs Eugene Clark. It appearing that sentence heretofore imposed cannot be enforced by reason of age of defendent. He was remanded to custody of Sheriff of Potter county to await further action of the Court.

In the matter of report of A. B. Mann auditor to distribute funds in hands of Executor of James Scott dec'd, term of filing extended, and auditor continued to next term.

H. H. Nye vs John Barr, Jury find in favor of pl'ff that judgment No. 115 Sep. term 1878 is fraudulent.

Comth vs Christian Zimmerman selling liquor. Plead guilty, sentenced to pay a fine of fifty dollars and the costs of prosecution and stand convicted until sentence is complied with.

Comth vs Christian Zimmerman selling liquor to minor. Plead guilty and sentenced to undergo imprisonment in the county jail for the term of ten days, pay a fine of fifty dollars and costs of prosecution and stand convicted until sentence is complied with.

Comth vs Z. Coll, nol pros.
Comth vs Wm. Trask, nol pros.
Lewis Schmeitz admitted to citizenship.
Comth vs John Rooney; continued bail $200.
Carl Seibenheimer declared a lunatic, D. C. Larrabee appointed to take charge of Seibenheimer's estate, bail with surety $1000.
Phoebe Tuttle vs Joseph N. Tuttle, divorce granted.
Mary Jane Hurlbert vs Henry Hurlburt, divorce granted.
In the matter of estate of Jacob Reckhow dec'd, administrator and bail discharged.
Comth vs R. Clancey, nol pros.
Rose M. Clark vs Richard Clark *alias sub* in divorce to issue.
Comth vs F. E. Ball, James Ball and Abrose Ball, discharged, no prosecutor appearing Court direct capias to issue for R. C. Carpenter and M. Kenyon prosecutors.
Otto Paul admitted to citizenship.
Comth vs Christopher Dennis, rape, true bill, continued.
Comth vs Geo. Baker, arson. Continued.
Comth vs Walter Roer, open lewdness, true bill, continued. Bail $300.
Comth vs Gilbert Adams, adultery, true bill continued. Bail $300.
Comth vs John Darcey, perjury, true bill, continued, bail $50. Nol pros to enter on payment of costs.
Comth vs H. C. James, false imprisonment, not a true bill, prosecutor to pay the costs.
Mary E. Ward vs Hugh Ward, *alias sub* in divorce awarded.
Jane McNess appointed guardian of Estella Baker formerly Estella McNess, minor child of Charles McNess dec'd.
Comth vs Gilbert Glover, assault and battery, true bill, bench warrant issued.
Comth vs Hiram Graham, fornication and bastardy, true bill.
B. C. Cole vs Hannah Cole, F. J. Gear appointed commissioner to take testimony, Sheriff to make proclamation.
Charles W. Berfield vs Elizabeth Berfield, L. B. Seibert appointed commissioner to take testimony.
Augustus Green vs Miranda Green, F. J. Gear appointed commissioner to take testimony.
Comth vs Lawrence Moran, fornication and bastardy, true bill.
Comth vs J. S. Barclay, assault and battery, true bill, continued. Bail $100.
In the matter of the dissolution of the corporation of the Enterprise Printing Co. Prayer of petitioners granted, to go into effect when a certified copy of order be filed and recognized in the office of the secretary of the Commonwealth of Pennsylvania.
J. H. Bailey assignee vs Sam'l B. Woodring, motion to show cause why judg't should not be entered, returnable next term.
Geo. Herring vs Emeline Herring *alias sub* in divorce to issue.
Geo. Fox M.D. vs Amanda Crum, et al on motion, plea of not guilt, to be entered.

In the matter of estate of Joel Haskins dec'd, late of Oswayo twp, order for sale of real estate continued.

Lydia Clark vs James Clark *alias sub* in divorce to issue.

Anna Bell Seibert vs John Seibert, *alias sub* in divorce to issue.

E. Rathbone use of A. Raymond vs James Gibson, A. B. Mann appointed auditor to distribute funds arising from Sheriff's sale of real estate.

On motion, death of Pl'ff suggested, and name of Sarah M. Billings adm' be substituted in several suits.

M. V. Larrabee acknowledged deeds for 132 tracts of land sold for taxes.

Zepheniah Teed vs C. H. Rushmore, jury find for pl'ff.

W. W. Dodd vs John R. Miller, jury find for pl'ff in sum of $125.

Comth vs Peleg Burdic, plead guilty. Continued.

Comth vs Geo. W. King, perjury, true bill.

Comth vs H. K. Dean, cruelty to animals, not a true bill.

Comth vs Augustus Frabel, larceny, not a true bill.

Comth vs Jos. Butler, cruelty to animals, not a true bill.

Mary S. Macken vs J. C. Hawley, rule of Pl'ff to show why she should not give bail for costs, returnable next term.

Sentence of Eugene Clark, vacated bail for appearance at next term, $300.

Comth vs Thos. H. White, open lewdness, *nol pros* on payment of costs.

Comth vs James Drock, *nol pros*.

Charles Bailey vs Carrie Bailey, *alias sub* in divorce awarded.

Comth vs Marshal Gross, surety of the peace continued. Bail $100.

Comth vs Mathias Schmidt, keeping a disorderly house, true bill.

Comth vs W. H. Grodevant, open lewdness, not a true bill.

Comth vs Mathias Schmidt, selling liquor, not a true bill.

Comth vs Geo. King, assault and battery, continued bail $300.

Comth vs Geo. King, perjury, continued, bail $300.

Nelson Race vs James Bump, defendant granted leave to perfect bail.

H. H. Nye vs John Barr, application for new trial, returnable next term.

Charles Maynard and Nellie Maynard adopted by L. W. Cushing.

In the matter of the alleged lunacy of John Henley, order vacated, it appearing that said John Henley has recovered.

Comth vs Wm. McDevit, surety of peace, discharged, pl'ff to pay his own costs, def't to pay record costs.

Comth vs Theresa Chapman, murder, true bill, continued.

J. H. Harrison vs C. D. & J. S. Vandeboe, rule to open judgment, motion for amendment of plea granted.

Comth vs Wash. Peters, larceny, *nol pros*.

Comth vs Amos Cole, *nol pros* to enter on payment of costs.

Comth vs N. L. Hitchcock, *nol pros* on payment of costs.

Comth vs Isaac Drock, *nol pros*.

Comth vs Lawrence Moran, capias ordered in this case.

Comth vs Z. Coil, adultery, *nol pros* on payment of costs.

Comth vs Z. Coil, assault and battery, *nol pros* on payment of costs.

Comth vs Lizzie Schall, adultery, *nol pros* on payment of costs.

Ordered that twenty-four Grand Jurors and forty-eight Traverse Jurors be drawn for next term.

Comth vs Oscar Seibert recognizance forfeited.
Comth vs R. Clancey, same as above.
Comth vs Matthias Schmidt, same as above.
Comth vs Martin Heuter, same as above.
Comth vs C. Seibenhemer, continued.

John M. Covey, Sheriff of Potter county acknowledged following deeds for land sold at Sheriff's Sale:

To R. C. Hosley, for 33 perches in Lewisville for $875.
To John McGinnis for 1 acre in Genesee, for $157.
To Thomas Gale 50.8 acres in Hebron for $100.
To N. Dwight, 108.4 acres in Hebron, for $1,000.

Judg't for want of appearance: E. D. Loveridge for use L. W. Crawford vs Charles Westerman; Wm. R. McEwen and Jno. McEwen vs J. H. Reves; Joseph Mann vs Mary and A. P. Hay; G. W. Pierce & J. Q. Pierce vs E. E. Tooker and B. Howard; Geo. Fox et al vs T. Cornish et al; Alfred Scott vs Napoleon Woodcock.

Report of Grand Jury – That we have examined the county buildings and property and find that the wall enclosing the jail yard is in need of repairs, the pointing of the wall having scaled off and the stones become loose and the wall unsafe; that repairs are needed inside the jail, and that the commissioners furnish more bedding for the prisoners, as they have not sufficient to make them comfortable; that the water closets in the Court House square be either removed or cleaned and repaired; in its present condition it is a public nuisance and should not be permitted to remain so.

Sept. 25, Court adjourned to meet Oct. 1, 1880. (The session for Oct. 1st is for the purpose of perfecting naturalization papers.)

The Potter Enterprise
Wednesday Evening, October 6, 1880 – Vol. VII, No. 21

MARRIED.

HERZOG – CANNON – October 2nd, 1880, by O. J. Rees, at his residence, Conrad Herzog of Farmer's Valley, Pa., to Miss Francis Lenora Cannon of Sweden, Pa.

Oswayo. Death has again visited our midst with that fatal disease called diphtheria. Jerome Stuart has lost one child and one grand-child, Sidney Lyman two, and Elder Miller one. Our friends have the sympathy of the entire community in their trials.

The Potter Enterprise
Wednesday Evening, October 13, 1880 – Vol. VII, No. 22

MARRIED.

COLE – NEWTON – At the residence of A. F. Hollenbeck, in Coudersport, Oct. 7, 1880, by L. B. Cole, Esq., Mr. Arthur L. Cole of Clara, and Miss Jennie D. Newton of Sharon.

DIED.

HASKINS – In Summit, Potter county, Pa., Sept. 25, 1880, William W. Haskins, son of Washington and Marinda Haskins, aged 3 years, 10 months and 17 days.

LENT – In Sawyer, Bradford county, Pa., Sept. 26, 1880, of Typhoid fever, Cordelia, wife of E. B. Lent.

BREUNLE – In Eulalia, Christian Breunle, Oct. 10th, 1880, aged 60 years.

About twenty-one years ago Mr. Breunle settled on a new and unimproved farm south of this village, coming here we believe from some town on the Hudson. He was by occupation a marble cutter, a skilled mechanic in his line; a man of active and cultivated intellect. He was superintendent when our jail was built, and a few years ago when Bradford county built a new Court House, Mr. Breunle had charge of the ornamental marble and stone cutting, but with all his work away, he found time with the aid of his industrious family to clear up his farm, build buildings, plant fruit trees, etc., and he leaves to his family a very productive and attractive farm.

Mr. Breunle was a man of marked character, one whom it was a pleasure to meet, always gentlemanly and considerate, of kindly and equitable disposition, greatly loved by his family, in all of his dealings an honorable man. This community has lost one of her best citizens and his family a noble and kind hearted protector and father.

Mr. Breunle was buried on Monday last, and the funeral was largely attended by his neighbors and the business men of this place.

The members of Eulalia Lodge, No. 342 A.Y.M., living in this vicinity attended the funeral in a body, burying the deceased with masonic honors.

PREMIUMS AWARDED
At the Potter County Fair, 1880.
CLASS NO. 1.

Subdivision No. 1, Thoroughbred Shorthorns, 1st Premium, A. B. Crowell, 3 yr old Shorthorn Durham Bull.

3d Premium, M. A. Veley, 3 yr old Shorthorn Durham.

Honorable Mention, A. Kiehl, Durham Cow.

Subdivision, No 2, Thoroughbred Alderneys, 1st Premium, J. W. Allen, Yearling Alderney Bull; Mrs. Mary A. Ross, 5 yr old cow, Lady Gurnsey.

2nd Premium, Mrs. Mary A. Ross, 2 yr old Heifer, Miss Jersey.

Subdivision No 3, Thoroughbred Ayershires, 1st Premium, Thomas G. Hull, 1 yearling Ayershire Bull; 1 Ayershire Calf; William Dent, 4 yr old Ayershire Bull; Thomas G. Hull, 3 yr old Ayershire Cow.

Subdivision No 4, Grade Cattle, 1st Premium, Chris Knowlton, 2 yr old Bull; Consider Stearns, Yearling Bull, ½ Ayer. bal Holstein, (dropped June 1st 1879); Mrs. Mary A. Ross, 2 yr old Heifer, Abby; Earl G. Crane, 4 yr old Cow ½ Alderney; G. W. Johnston, Bull Calf; Almeron Nelson, Durham and Alderney Cow.

Subdivision No 4, 2nd Premium, Wallace W. Benson, 1 Yearling Bull, ½ Dur. ½ Ald'y; Nelson Woodcock, 1 Cow.

3d Premium, Fred Schadenberger, 2 yr old Bull.

Subdivision No 5, Oxen & Native Cattle, 1st Premium, A. D. Colcord, 1 pr Oxen.

2d Premium, Nelson Vanwegen, Pr 2 yr old Steers; Charles Verguson, Yearling Steers; H. S. Lent, Yoke Oxen.

3d Premium, Porter H. Clark, Yoke 3 yr old Steers.

CLASS NO. 2.

Subdivision No 1, Stallions for Draft, 1st Premium, J. W. Allen, 2 yr old Stallion, Granger Boy; 2 yr old Stallion, Allegany Boy; D. E. Lewis, 3 yr old Stallion.

2nd premium, Jacob Kimm, 4 yr old Stallion.

Subdivision No 2, Stallions for Road, 1st Premium, J. W. Allen, Stallion, Tom Tanner.

Subdivision No 3, Brood Mares and Colts, 1st premium, Jacob Kimm, 2 yr old Colt; M. L. Gridley, Mare and sucking Colt; Roscoe Stearns, Yearling Colt; Asa Downs, Sucking Colt; Adelbert L. Luce, Pr Draft Horses; Dr. Amos French, 3 yr old Colt; L. W. Baker, pr Draft Horses.

2nd premiums, E. J. Fickler, mare and colt; E. M. Bishop, 2 yr old colt; W. B. Gordnier, yearling colt; Nelson Vanwegen, draft team geldings; R. A. Campbell, 2 yr old colt.

Subdivision No 4, Horses for Farm Work, 1st Premium, Roscoe Stearns, span mules; R. H. Smith, pr 4 yr old geldings, farm team; D. H. Veley, pr mares, farm team; Dal Benson, walking team; George Burt, 2 yr old colt.

2nd premium, Consider Stearns, team farm mules; Jacob Kimm, walking team.

3d premium, Chris Knowlton, walking team.

Subdivision No 5 horses for pleasure or road, 1st premium, W. A. Crosby, 4 yr old gelding; Z. J. Thompson, mare; M. V. Larrabee, matched pr driving horses; A. B. Crowell, pr 4 yr old driving mares.

2nd premiums, J. W. Wiley, span matched 4 yr olds; Leroy Lyman, 4 yr old mare; J. L. Haughenberry, pr driving horses; Willis Carpenter, horse, single driver; Leroy Lyman, matched pr 4 yr old colts.

3d premium, Dr. S. A. Phillips, black mare, pleasure.

CLASS NO. 3.

Subdivision, No 1, Fine Wool Sheep, 1st premium; Charles Verguson, 3 ewes.

Potter County, Pennsylvania Potpourri – Volume I
1880 through 1884

Subdivision No 2, Middle Wool Sheep, 1st premium, Arthur Lyman, buck sheep, 3/8 Cotswold.

2nd premium, Wallace W. Benson, Cotswold ram.

Subdivision No 3, Long Wood Sheep, 1st premium, S. L. Burdick, 3 ewes, 3 buck lambs.

CLASS NO. 4.

Subdivision No 1 Berkshires or Chester Whites, 1st premium, Chris Knowlton, Berkshire boar; Berkshire sow; litter Berkshire pigs.

2nd premium, Wallace W. Benson, Berkshire sow and litter pigs; J. W. Allen, litter pigs, Berkshire; F. A. Nelson, Berkshire boar; Berkshire sow.

Subdivision No 2, Suffolks or Poland China, 1st premium, J. W. Allen, Suffolk sow; litter Suffolk pigs.

2nd premium, J. W. Allen, Poland China sow.

CLASS NO. 5

Poultry, 1st premium, W. C. Rennells, pr Brown Leghorns, 4 mos; Geo. Weber, pr bronze turkeys; O. J. Rose, trio Sea Bright American; Wm. Shear Jr., variety blooded fowls; F. E. Wimmer, pr Plymouth Rocks, 6 mos., Wm. Dingman, banties; Wm. Shear Jr., Rouen ducks.

2nd premium, Harlow Dingee, Rouen ducks; F. A. Nelson, coup White Leghorn chickens; W. C. Rennells, pr Plymouth Rocks.

3d premium, O. J. Rose, trio Plymouth Rocks; F. E. Wimmer, pr Plymouth Rocks, 3 mos.

CLASS NO. 6.

Subdivision No 1, Butter, Cheese & Honey, 1st premium, Orange L. Hall, tub butter; Mrs. W. W. Benson, gal maple syrup; Ezra Turner, box honey.

2nd premium, Leroy Lyman, honey; A. L. Harvey, tub butter.

3d premium, A. B. Crowell, tub butter; F. B. Nelson cheese – factory.

Subdivision No 2, Field Crops, 1st premium, Nelson Vanwegen, 3 ¼ acres corn; Leroy Lyman, ½ bushel oats, sample of 3 acres; ½ bush corn; A. B. Crowell, peas, 50 bushel on 1 ½ acres; M. A. Veley, millet.

Subdivision No 3, Grains, Seeds and Flour, 1st premium, Mrs. L. Schildberger, bush Snowflakes; Chris Schadenberger, variety potatoes; H. Baker, variety potatoes; ½ bush red Kidney beans; 25 ears popcorn; S. L. Burdick, 6 late Rose potatoes; A. B. Goodsell, seedling potatoes, 3 yrs old; H. E. Austin, sample yellow corn; sample white corn; 25 ears Lackawaxan white corn; 25 ears Dullon white corn; 25 ears 8 row yellow corn.

2nd premium, Eugene W. Dodd, 6 varieties potatoes; Nelson Woodcock, 4 varieties potatoes; E. M. Bishop, variety potatoes.

Subdivision No 4, Vegetables, 1st premium, Mrs. L. Schildberger, 6 heads cabbages; Roscoe Stearns, ½ bush onions; 1 bushel turnips; Eugene W. Dodd, 3 pumpkins; 3 squashes; 10 varieties garden vegetables; 6 cucumbers; Mrs. C. H. Armstrong, 5 beets; Jeremiah Gordon, peck onions; 7 beets; A. Marschner, parsnips; carrots; N. H. Goodsell, basket tomatoes; A. D. Colcord, 3 watermelons; E. O. Austin, sample citrons; Mrs. Isaac Benson, basket peppers; Earl G. Crane, cluster 13 tomatoes; N. H. Goodsell, 6 hubbard squashes; Miles White, 1 squash.

2nd premium, Mrs. L. Schildberger, variety of vegetables; Chris Schadenberger, turnips; Lewis Glace, variety of beets; Wallace Abson, large peppers; A. B. Goodsell, 6 cabbages; A. D. Colcord, 3 citrons.

3d premium, Nelson Woodcock, 6 heads cabbage; Mrs. L. Schildenberger, ½ bushel onions.

Subdivision No. 5, Fruits, 1st premium, Mrs. L. Schildberger, 12 varieties apples; E. J. Fickler, basket grapes; M. W. Gridley, pears; N. H. Goodsell, 6 varieties winter apples; specimen 18 peaches; Mrs. H. B. Ives basket transparent crabs.

2nd premium, Eugene W. Dodd, 8 varieties winter apples; E. M. Bishop variety apples; Sylvester Greenman, basket sweet crab apples; N. H. Goodsell, sample Pears.

3d premium, Nelson Vanwegen, 8 varieties apples.

CLASS NO. 7.

Subdivision No 2, Mowing and Reapers, R. H. Smith, Warrior mower.

Subdivision No 3, Carriages, Wagons, etc., 1st premium, James Pearsall, cutter; Consider Stearns, top buggy; Amos Veley, platform spring wagon; Messrs. Bronson & Burt, family carriage; G. H. Chapin, platform.

Subdivision No 5, Leather, Harness, Shoes, etc., 1st premium, Lane & Conley, pr boots; pr shoes; Ignatz Griesel, single harness.

Subdivision No 6, Miscellaneous, 1st premium; A. Marschner, ornamental carving; specimen statuary; Albert Rennells, spool holder; Lewis Glace, scroll saw; Fred Grom, specimen graining at Armstrong's store; A. A. Howe, cellar wall at Nelson Clark's.

Subdivision No 7, Cabinet Ware & Sewing Machines, A. Marschner, fancy cabinet ware.

CLASS NO. 8.

Subdivision No 1, Art, 1st premium, Homer Hall, 5 specimens Architectural drawing; Mrs. W. A. Crosby, oil painting – portrait; Miss Eva Dyke, 3 paintings on wood; Miss Nellie Olmsted, 2 oil paintings; J. E. Sackett, mechanical drawing.

Subdivision No 2, Domestic Manufacture, 1st premium, Mrs. J. S. Ross, worsted bed quilt; Geo. Weber, silk quilt; Mrs. Daniel Smith, bed quilt; H. Baker, pr cotton stockings; Mrs. Albert Rennells, 5 yds white flannel; 5 yds colored flannel; A. Varney, pieced quilt; Mrs. Jerome Knickerbocker, rug; Mrs. A. L. Pierce, rag carpet; Mrs. A. Rounsville, bunch stocking yarn; Mrs. Seth Lewis, log cabin quilt.

2nd premium, H. Baker, pr double woolen mittens by girl under 12 years; Mrs. H. H. Heggie, quilt; Mrs. O. Merrill, 5 yds rag carpet; Mrs. Albert Rennells, pr flannel sheets; five yds full cloth; Mrs. R. L. Nichols, patchwork; Mrs. A. Rounsville, pieced bedquilt; Miss Sallie Mehring, specimen rag carpet.

3d premium, Miss Sallie Mehring, specimen rag carpet; Mrs. P. A. Webb, rag carpet.

Subdivision No 3, Culinary Articles, 1st premium, Mrs. J. S. Ross, crab apple jelly; grape jelly; pie-plant jelly; apple jelly; peach jelly; Christian Schaudenberger, berry jelly; Mrs. N. M. Glassmire, variety pickles; Mrs. N. H.

Goodsell, fruit cake; loaf wheat bread; currant preserves; tomato catsup; Mrs. F. A. Nelson; can peaches; Mrs. E. M. Bishop, 2 plates cookies; gal maple vinegar; Mrs. N. M. Glassmire, variety canned fruits.

2nd premium, Mrs. J. S. Ross, berry jelly; Mrs. W. R. Greenman, plate sugar cookies; Mrs. F. A. Nelson, tomato catsup; Belle Reynolds, loaf hop yeast bread.

3d premium, E. M. Bishop, qt. catsup.

Subdivision No 4, Ornamental Needle Work, 1st premium, Mrs. H. B. Ives, 5 knit scarfs; Miss Nellie Olmsted, fascinator; Mrs. Francis Hammond, rug, toilet set; fancy stand; Mrs. J. L. Knox, child's crochet shawl; Mrs. N. M. Glassmire, chair seat; worsted spatter cloth; Miss Mary Olmsted, sofa pillow; Mrs. Daniel Smith, rug; Eva Dyke, point lace handkerchief; Gertrude Boyington, worsted motto; Mrs. Isaac Benson, afghan tidy; Mrs. G. H. Chapin, cotton ball tidy; Kate Reynolds, 2 book marks; Nellie Perkins, pr pillow shams; Anna Jeorg, zephyr afghan.

2nd premium, Mrs. J. L. Knox, child's carriage afghan; Mary Olmsted, 2 tidies; Mrs. H. C. Olmsted, toilet set; stand spread; Mrs. Francis Hammond, lambriquin; Mrs. R. L. Nichols, gent's scarf; Mathilda Doerner, crotchet worsted hood; Belle Reynolds, bookmark; Sallie Mehring, worsted tidy.

3d premium, Nellie Perkins, cotton canvas tidy; Mrs. W. C. Rennells, gent's scarf.

Subdivision No 5, Embroidery, 1st premium, Mrs. L. Schildberger, pillows, pillow cases and laces (handmade); Mrs. T. Benton Brown, 2 pr embroidered stockings; towel; pillow cases; 2 embr'd night dresses; Mrs. Isaac Benson, worsted and silk sofa pillow.

Subdivision No 6 Fancy Goods, 1st premium, Mrs. Mary R. Jones, needle book; dressing case; D. E. Boyington, air castle, scroll card basket; A. Marschner, collection wall brackets; Emelia Doerner, pr crochet suspenders.

2nd premium, Gertrude Boyington, slipper case; match safe.

Subdivision No 7, Flowers, 1st premium, Mrs. N. M. Glassmire, variety house plants; Mrs. C. H. Armstrong, display of cut flowers; 2 pots garden flowers; Mrs. N. M. Glassmire, hand boquet; Mrs. C. H. Armstrong, boquet cut flowers.

2nd premium, Mrs. L. Schildberger, parlor boquet; Mrs. N. M. Glassmire, table boquet; Mrs. C. H. Armstrong, double scarlet geranium.

CLASS NO. 9.

1st premium, Mrs. N. H. Goodsell, soft soap; cider vinegar; Mrs. D. C. Larrabee, 5 mock oranges; 4 gourds.

RACES.

Race No 1, for Potter county horses, Henry C. James, David Grier, 1st; L. L. Lay, Judge Fullerton; 2nd; Chas. Hosley, Old Milo, 3d.

Race No 2, for 45 Class, R. L. Dike, Hattie, 1st; Ed Cornell, Kitty Sandbach, 2nd; M. L. Gridley, Country Boy, 3d.

Race No. 3, for 3 minute Class, C. B. Whitehead, C. D. Fenton, 1st; L. L. Lay, Judge Fullerton, 2nd; Chas. Hosley, Old Milo, 3d.

Race No 5, Free for All, R. L. Dike, Hattie, 1st; Ed Cornell, Kitty Sandbach, 2nd; Henry James, David Grier, 3d.

Potter County, Pennsylvania Potpourri – Volume I
1880 through 1884

Coudersport Graded School.

Through the kindness of the Editor we are enabled to make this our first monthly Report of Scholarship for 1880 and 1881, to the patrons of our Graded School.

The chief object of the report is information; that parents may have some knowledge of the progress of their children. One hundred per cent is taken as the standard of scholarship; and seventy per cent has been taken as the lowest to be printed. If the names of some pupils do not appear, it is either because they have been absent upon examination days, or else in all of their studies they have fallen below seventy per cent. Some were absent from examination, at least in the Grammar School and in the High School, whose record, had they been present, would have been *fair*. Very few of our people realize the importance of regular attendance in order to have good scholarship. Parents send your children regularly to school.

HIGH SCHOOL.

NAMES.	Algebra	Geometry	1st Grammar	2d Grammar	U. S. History	Drawing	Writing	Civil Government
Amy White,	80				90	95		80
Rosa Crane,	95				100	90		80
Jas. Rounnseville,						80		
Mary Johnston,						90	90	
Elbert Greenman,		80				90	95	95
Jennie White,		80				95		95
Mary Aylesworth,			0		70			
Cora Bisbee,			80		70	75	75	
Laura Monroe,			90		80	75	75	
Homer White,			88			95	90	
May Nelson,				90	95	90	80	
Lydia Stearns,				75	90	85	80	
Carrie Larrabee,				99	80	90	80	

NAMES.	Reading	First Arithmetic	Second Arithmetic	Eng. Comp.	Latin	Geography	Spelling
Homer White,							84
Jas. Rounnseville,	75						
Cora Bisbee,	75	0				75	
Laura Monroe,	80		80			80	90

Potter County, Pennsylvania Potpourri – Volume I
1880 through 1884

Rosa Crane,	80	0	93			90
Mary Aylesworth,	70	0			70	77
Inez Metzger,	80					
Amy White,		0	90			
May Nelson,		0			80	80
Lydia Stearns,		0			90	
Carrie Larrabee,		0			90	
Mary Johnston,					80	
Elbert Greenman,				95	100	
Jennie White,					100	

GRAMMAR SCHOOL.

NAMES.	Reading	Arithmetic	Language	Geography	U. S. History	Spelling	Writing
Mary Armstrong,	80	73	0	0		87	0
Anna Boyer,	75	80	84	0		0	0
Isabella Crane,	80	70	83	78		97	70
Martha Dingee,	85	0	79	85	0	70	87
Celia Gillon,	70	0	82	0		97	70
Elsie Gorham,	70	0	70	0	0	76	85
Emily Johnston,	78	0	70	70		70	73
Lula Millard,	80	95	0	78	75	91	78
Inez Metzger,		75	70	0	72	0	75
Nora Metzger,	75	0	70	71	0	0	72
Nellie Perkins,	80	95	78	0	70	86	72
Kittie Swetland,	85	75	91	73		84	80
John Allen,	80	0	0	90		90	70
Orlando Chase,	75	70	75	0	0	0	75
Julius Colcord,	0	80	0	0		0	0
Chester Presho,	0	0	0	0	74		90
Mackey White,	75	0	72	78		0	80

Free Hand Drawing. – Nora Metzger, 76; Lula Millard, 78; Nellie Perkins, 75; Kittie Swetland, 78; Emily Johnston, 75; Elsie Gorham, 70; Mackey White, 75.

Potter County, Pennsylvania Potpourri – Volume I
1880 through 1884

PRIMARY SCHOOL.

NAMES.	Arithmetic	Spelling	Geography	Reading	M. Arithmetic
Maggie Metzger,	70	99	99	99	
Nelia Marble		75	0	0	70
Lily White	0	0	80	70	
Nellie Millard	0	98	0	70	
Lizzie Ryon	75	98	70	0	
Digna McCormick	75	99	70	0	
Jay Lewis		90	0	96	82
Dan'l Chapman			70	75	82
Frank French	85	100	79	90	
Arthur Buck	90	99	72	75	
Charlie Marble	95	70	75	70	
John Boyer		72	0	70	0
Nellie Buck		80		70	72
Annie Gillon		82	0	72	79
Lettie Gordnier		95		70	0
Iola Yates		93		85	75
Lizzie Johnston		79		70	75
C. Calkins		97		92	82
Carrie Tuttle		99		96	0
Theodore Metzger		75		79	70
Rose Mann		85		80	72
Stephen Gillon		79	0	75	0
Harry Millard		70		70	0
John Calkins		75		75	0
Henry Junge		95	0	70	70
Edgar Veley		82	0	70	70
Charley White		70		0	72
Bertha Neefe		75		75	70
Annie Neefe		79		75	70
Freddie Brahmer		70		70	70
Sophie Wolfanger				75	
Geo. Wolfanger				70	
Louisa Wolfanger				80	

John R. Groves, Prin.

The Potter Enterprise
Wednesday Evening, October 20, 1880 – Vol. VII, No. 23

Millport. Mr. Bert Campbell and Miss Sarah Carpenter were united in marriage on the 13th inst. They have the good wishes of their many friends for their future happiness.

Roulet. Mrs. Burton lost a little son, aged about 6 years, with diphtheria, on Thursday last.

DIED.

LYMAN – In Oswayo, Pa., Sept. 24, 1880, Lea S., aged 4 years, 3 months, and 12 days. Also, Sept. 30, 1880, Maud R., aged 12 years, 6 months and 22 days. They were the youngest son and oldest daughter of A. S. and Rachel Lyman.

BRICK
ONE HUNDRED THOUSAND
For Sale on my Yard.
W. B. GORDNIER.

The Potter Enterprise
Wednesday Evening, October 27, 1880 – Vol. VII, No. 24

- It is a boy and Art Olmsted is the happy dad.

MARRIED.

SWARTHOUT – CRAWFORD – At Wellsville, Oct. 6th, by Rev. A. Coit, at the Parsonage, Myron J. Swarthout, of Sharon, Pa., and Miss Sarah Crawford, Sharon, Pa.

CHANDLER – GOODSELL – At the residence of the bride's parents, in Coudersport, Oct. 22nd, 1880, by Rev. Wm. Marshall, Miss Emma Goodsell of Coudersport, and Mr. James Ezra Chandler of Port Allegany.

DIED.

HASKINS – In Summit, Potter Co., Pa., William W. Haskins, son of Washington and Marinda Haskins, aged 3 years, 10 months and 19 days.

Weep not dear mother for thy child,
Thy loss is but his gain;
Reposing on the Saviour's breast,
He's free from grief and pain.
So bear thy burden weary one,
The toil will soon be o'er,
Thy longing eyes their weeping done,

Shall see the Golden Shore.

Ulysses, Pa., Oct. 19. – Quite a serious accident took place in this boro last Tuesday afternoon, on Burt street. As John Jones of Harrison, Pa., was starting for home from Beuben Hawkins' place, his team started so swiftly and made so short a turn from the yard into the street, as to throw from their seat on a buckboard Mr. Jones' wife and a niece of her's, Miss Clarabel Fling, of Mansfield, Pa., the wagon running over both ladies, and breaking three of Miss Fling's ribs. Both were obliged to stay over night at Mr. Hawkins', and Miss Fling is still there, but Mrs. Jones was able to ride home the next morning, she, fortunately, having no bones broken, though a wheel passed diagonally over her abdomen, and then over an ankle.

- We learn that Messrs. W. and L. R. Gale, tanners, of Middle valley, Wayne county, Pa., have purchased Major Kilbourne's property at Pike Mills, for $4,000 in hand, and will erect thereon a large tannery. It is their desire and purpose to erect the saw mill and boarding house this fall and winter if the weather will permit, and in early spring will build the tannery buildings. It is to be a large establishment, consuming 12,000 cords of bark annually. They have purchased all the bark of F. W. Knox, William Dent and others in that locality. Pike Mills or Galeville will soon be a thriving, prosperous and important village, and the only wonder is that someone has not heretofore occupied this territory, but we regret to lose the genial Major from this locality, and hope he will soon find another pleasant home in Potter.

The Potter Enterprise
Wednesday Evening, November 3, 1880 – Vol. VII, No. 25

- Joe Moore is the happy father of a young Kanuck. Joe is a modest young man, and we regret to say that his employer played a mean trick on him the night he received the telegram announcing the advent of the youngster. Joe is given to blushing, and M. S. stood at the door and whispered to each person as he entered, "Ask Joe about the baby." No lights were lit in the post-office that night; the light of Joe's countenance furnishing an ample supply.

MARRIED.

VOSS – NOELK – At the hall of Mr. Joseph Schwarzenbach, in Germania, Oct. 23d, 1880, by Henry Theis, Esq., Mr. August Voss and Miss Lizzie Noelk, both of Germania.

DIED.

JORDEN – In Sylvania, at his residence Oct. 15, 1880, of dropsy, Mr. Jorden, aged 72 years.

He was the oldest man in our town. He was resigned to his death. Farewell Brother Jorden for a short season.

Potter County, Pennsylvania Potpourri – Volume I
1880 through 1884

TUTTLE – On the 12th of Oct., 1880, of diphtheria, Albert Tuttle. Aged 16 years.

Scarce the dawn of life began,
Ere I measured out my span.

MOORE – At Leidy, Clinton county, Pa., Johnny, only son of George and Nancy Moore, and grandson of Charles and Ellen Wykoff. Aged 3 years and 6 months.

School Report.

Report of the First, Second, Third and Fourth grades of the Lewisville Graded School, for the month ending Oct. 22, 1880.

FOURTH GRADE.

SCHOLARS.	Writing.	Mental Arithmetic	Arithmetic.	Reading.	Spelling.	Grammar.	Geography.
Clara Gridley,	95		95	100	100	95	100
Lottie Cushing,	98		98	100	100	95	100
Raymond Cobb,	95		100	100	98	100	100
Hattie Dunbar,	90		90	90	97		95
Matie Potter,	92		100	100	97	95	90
Pauline Cobb,	94		95	100	96	95	98
Gertie Mintayne,	96		90	95	96	95	100
May Henderson,	90		90	90	94	90	
Charles Bronson,	90		90	95	94	90	90
Julia Chapel,	85		80	100	90	85	90
Anson Pickett,	75		85	90	95	90	85
Mamie Millard,	80		85	90	95		90
John Bailey,	80		85	90	85		75
Althea Hopkins,	80		85	90	90		90
Ray Freeman,	80		90	90	85		80
Rosa Neal,	70		70	75	75		70
Inez Daniels,	85		90	90	94	100	100

THIRD GRADE.

	Writing.	Mental Arithmetic	Arithmetic.	Reading.	Spelling.	Grammar.	Geography.
Satie Bennitt,	80	95		88	100		
Ann Brigham,	95	98		100	100		
Eva Dunbar,	80	90		80	80		
Arthur Corey,	80	85		87	85		
Mattie Corey,	70	90		80	90		
Frank Jacobus,	75	98		85	90		
Elisha Perry,	75	80		70	70		

SECOND GRADE.

Fanny Bronson,	98	100	98	100
Eddie Marion,	95	100	95	94
Grace Perry,	84	90	80	87
Inez Ives,	80	87	90	90
Burtie Perry,	72	70	70	70
Daisy Erlbeck,			90	80
Mittie Brown,	70	90	90	85
Delbet Genung,	90	70	70	70

FIRST GRADE.

Arthur Kear,	95	98
Earnest Kear,	70	70
Roy Millon,	90	95
Wolsey Potter,	80	95
Bert D. Perry,	90	95
Otis Guinnip,	90	70
George Cobb,	70	75
May Farnsworth,	90	85
Lena Guinnip,	90	90
Anna Genung,	90	85
Lucy Henderson,	90	90
Floyd Baker,	90	90
Alta Crum,	80	80

The marking is done on the scale of one hundred; one hundred per cent being perfect, and seventy the lowest reported; a few names are not reported on account of falling below seventy per cent in all the markings.

Emma L. Adams, Teacher.

Agriculture in Northern Pa.

The farmers in Northern Pennsylvania deservedly stand high in their vocation. Year by year are they improving their farms and otherwise manifesting a lively interest in the products of the field. The late fairs held at Mansfield and Wellsboro in Tioga county, Coudersport in Potter, and Troy and Towanda in Bradford county, all show that the farmers are alive to do their own interests. There is one very important branch connected with farming that is sadly neglected. We refer to the raising of sheep. No place in the broad limits of the United States, is better adapted to the raising of sheep, than the counties embraced in the Northern tier. Connected with this branch of farming is the manufacture of wooled fabrics. In Tioga county where there is sold by our merchants annually a half million yards of flannel, not one yard is manufactured here. This state of things compels a constant expenditure of money to build up some manufacturing district remote from this locality. The farmers are doing their part in raising corn, wheat, oats, potatoes, buckwheat and fruits; and in making the best article of butter in the land, also raising fine crops of tobacco, now let them stock their farms with sheep, and try to induce some practical manufacturers to establish woolen mills, and they will thereby enhance the value of their farms and do much towards bringing prosperity and thrift to our people in general – *Blossburg Register*.

The Potter Enterprise
Wednesday Evening, November 10, 1880 – Vol. VII, No. 26

MARRIED.

WALLEY – BOYINGTON – At the residence of the bride's aunt, in Olean, N.Y., Thursday evening, November 4th, 1880, by Rev. Father J. J. Hamil, Mr. W. A. Walley of Olean, N.Y., and Miss Nellie P. J. Boyington of Roulet, Pa.

GRIDLEY – DINGMAN – At the residence of the bride's parents, Nov. 3d, 1880, by Rev. T. R. Stratton, Mr. Loren Gridley of Alfred, N.Y., and Miss Laura Dingman of Coudersport, Pa.

Roulet. On Sunday morning last, Ora Nell, youngest child and only daughter of Mr. and Mrs. Dan Reed, died of diphtheria. Two other children in the same family are sick with the same disease.

Jury List, Dec. Term, 1880.
GRAND JURORS.

W. S. Moore, Farmer, W. Branch; John Taubert, Farmer, Homer; M. A. Surdam, Farmer, Hector; Henry Kimm, Farmer, Roulet; Burt Oleson, Farmer, Stewardson; C. C. Allis, Farmer, Genesee; A. L. Harvey, Farmer, Ulysses; D. F. Glassmire, Merchant, Coudersport; Chas. Coats, Farmer, Allegany; Edward Rathbone, Farmer, Lewisville; E. E. Swift, Farmer, Hebron; Wm. Frink, Farmer, Hebron; C. S. Redner, Farmer, Hector; Rufus Corey, Farmer, Hector; J. H. Leach, Farmer, Oswayo; J. B. Parker, Farmer, Hector; L. C. Perry, Farmer, Ulysses; E. F. C. Jeorg, Farmer, Stewardson; F. P. Huntingdon, Farmer, Bingham; T. B. Abbot, Farmer, Eulalia; John Shields, Farmer, Oswayo; N. C. Newton, Farmer, Sharon; A. R. Jordon, Farmer, Sylvania; E. D. Wheaton, Farmer, Bingham.

TRAVERS JURORS.

R. L. White, Merchant, Roulet; Dallas Benson, Farmer, Eulalia; F. A. Brown, Farmer, Pike; John L. Smith, Farmer, Harrison; James Barnes, Lumberman, Hebron; C. F. Tyler, Farmer, Hebron; J. C. Bishop, Farmer, Allegany; Ira Bishop, Farmer, Allegany; H. R. Douglass, Farmer, Hector; J. T. Rathbone, Farmer, Oswayo; John Dawley, Farmer, Clara; M. P. Flinn, Farmer, Hector; Oscar Nelson, Farmer, Allegany; C. A. Neefe, Farmer, Sweden; Benjamin Burt, Farmer, Roulet; W. C. Quimby, Farmer, Roulet; Hosea Spencer, Farmer, Bingham; John Gordnier, Farmer, Homer; F. Badgener, Farmer, Harrison; J. Dickerson, Farmer, Sharon; F. P. Brooks, Farmer, Clara; Wm. Basset, Mason, Coudersport; John Moran, Farmer, Oswayo; Lester Watson, Farmer, Summit; August Bodler, Farmer, Abbott; John Brownlee, Farmer, Portage; Charles Head, Farmer, Oswayo; John Brooks, Farmer, Wharton; Alvin

Reynolds, Farmer, Summit; David Gardner, Farmer, Harrison; Frank Buck, Physician, Coudersport; A. D. Nelson, Farmer, Wharton; Dean Healy, Farmer, Oswayo; E. Crippen, Farmer, W. Branch; John Raymond, Farmer, Bingham; Charles Barr, Farmer, Sylvania; Alanson Burt, Farmer, Ulysses; N. J. Peck, Merchant; Bingham; Lewis Yentzer, Farmer, Roulet; A. J. Bailey, Farmer, Wharton; Morris Lent, Farmer, Hebron; Henry Harris, Farmer, Keating; L. H. Kinney, Farmer, Sharon; H. C. Hosley, Merchant, Lewisville; John Holbert, Farmer, Bingham; Hoxie Roberts, Farmer, Sweden; J. W. Allen, Farmer, Eulalia; Merrick Jackson, Farmer, Summit.

The Potter Enterprise
Wednesday Evening, November 17, 1880 – Vol. VII, No. 27

DIED.

BAILEY – In West Branch, Nov. 7th, 1880, at the residence of his daughter, Mrs. Lewis Osgood, Mr. David Bailey, aged 79 years and 25 days.

- Upon the night of the 14th, the barn of Henry Taubert, of Sweden was burned, together with four cows, one yoke of oxen, 300 bushels of oats, hay, straw, etc. contained therein. Insurance $1,000. Insured with L. B. Cole & Son of Coudersport. The fire was evidently the work of an incendiary.

- Hemlock Row had a narrow escape this (Tuesday) morning, from conflagration, which might have wiped out another section of Coudersport. Most of the buildings have terra cotta chimneys. The one in Rees' jewelry store became over-heated and set fire to the wood work around it. A small blaze had commenced creeping up through the roof when discovered. A pail of water extinguished the flames before any damage was done. Had the fire got fairly started, the four stores in the row, and perhaps the hotel barn opposite would have been destroyed. Brick chimneys will now be put up.

Fishing Creek. We have had one of the severest wind blows that I ever experienced on the Creek. It blew a barn on the Fred Yentzer farm, now occupied by R. Church, from the under-pining, and unroofed one-third of one-half of the barn, the building is 50 by 60 feet.

It also blew a portion of the roof off Mr. Wm. Tauscher's barn, and unroofed a log house for Mr. F. D. Weimer that was filled with hay. Next it struck a log house owned by H. Baker, blowing it down to the chamber floor. The house was used as a store and granary, it also struck a log barn which was used as a shelter for wagons and farming tools, and a portion of it was used to keep hogs in, there were four hogs in it at the time and not one of them was hurt, it struck his house at the southeast corner and blew it off the foundation, moving it to the north three feet, and to the west six feet, starting the roof and doing considerable other damage to the house.

The fences all along the creek were laid low, post and board fences not excepted.

I think there will be quite a number of the young people that will be considerably smaller on account of the wind blow, and the older ones will get gray considerably quicker.

It laid the timber in all directions, laying acres in places.

"Our Railroad."

As usual at this time of year, "our railroad" is again attracting attention, and rumors are current that it is going to be built. A fact that is and has been patent to every one for years, the question being only as to time. Whenever the Reading railroad has its affairs satisfactorily adjusted, it must seek a western connection, and the Pine Creek and Jersey Shore is the only feasible on open to them.

We see it stated that the Reading is in a fair way to have its present difficulties adjusted and be in a position to further extend its line at an early day, and we sincerely hope that such is the case, but we have had so many "false alarms" that the people of this section are rather skeptical.

The Reading road is now in the hands of three receivers, and the stock is still selling at a good price, showing that some capitalists are confident that a satisfactory settlement can and will be made.

The road is a necessity to Potter county, now more than ever before. New tanneries are being built and the county has entered upon an era of progress, that would make the road a paying one, we believe, from the local traffic alone. The road would take the butter, cheese, eggs, and no inconsiderable amount of apples, potatoes and grain from a large area of country. Then the bark and lumber from our forests would find a market. Of hemlock, this county has the finest and largest supply of any in the state, a large portion of which will be easy to access to this railroad. We have large amounts of cherry, basswood, and the finest hard maple in the world, all of which are in demand, and would be utilized if there was an outlet to market.

A new tannery has been built near Coudersport this season. Next year a large tannery will be built at Pike Mills. A great deal of the timber from which the bark is taken for these tanneries will be floated down the streams, the lumbermen paying just about the cost of delivering on the banks, and no doubt much of the timber will rot on the ground for want of purchasers at a fair price unless we get a railroad, or the price of lumber advances far beyond what we have any reason to expect.

With a railroad through this section new mills would be erected, and much of the lumber cut out near where the trees are felled, and a great portion of it would be shipped over the railroad. Bark will be as cheap here as anywhere for many years to come on account of the immense supply, and outside tanneries would purchase large quantities.

The Buffalo road would have an eastern outlet, and would more than double its freight from the lake regions. The Reading road would have an outlet west for its coal, and in return would receive a share of the freight from the far west.

Then, too, the vast beds of soft coal on the West Branch and Pine Creek could be opened and the vast mineral wealth of that section would find ready market east and west, and prove a source of revenue to the road. The coal veins on the West Branch and Pine Creek have been explored and opened, and their value proved beyond a doubt. There is no guess work about it, the thickness and extent of the seams and beds are known.

At present no line of railroad touches this county, with the exception of a few miles of the B. N. Y. & P. R. R. cutting across one corner, less than five miles in all. The Jersey Shore road would cut the county its entire length from east to west.

We believe the day is not far distant when this new territory will be opened by the railroad and brought in closer connection with the outside world.

The Potter Enterprise
Wednesday Evening, November 24, 1880 – Vol. VII, No. 28

Ulysses. Clark Crum's wife died about a month ago, though he was forty years her senior he is able to be around, but not as well as common.

- Charley Smith, one of the Smith Brothers, who kept a meat market in this place last spring, was one of the men burned at the Bordell fire. It was supposed his injuries were slight, and that he would recover, but last week he grew suddenly worse and died. He was an industrious young man, and while in this place made many friends who will regret his untimely end.

Ulysses. Charles Smith, a son of John Smith, was brought home to his father's in Ulysses and buried in the Lewisville cemetery by the side of his mother who died about ten years ago. His friends and acquaintances deeply lament his untimely death.

Genesee Forks. An imposing procession passed through this place on Wednesday, with the remains of Chas. Smith, one of the victims of the Bordell fire.

DIED.

GLASSMIRE – In Coudersport, Nov. 18, Caroline, wife of D. F. Glassmire, aged 56 years.

PHENIX – At Pike Mills, Nov. 13, 1880, of diphtheria, Vernie Bell Phenix, daughter of Joshua and Anna Phenix. Aged 3 years, 11 months and 21 days.
> Dear mother, do not think of me as in the tomb,
> For I shall not see its dark shadows and gloom,
> And I shall not fear, though the river be wide,
> For Jesus will carry me over the tide.

ABSON – At the residence of his son, Walter Abson, on Saturday, Nov. 13, of consumption, Anthony Abson, aged 56 years and 8 months.
> Closed the wearied lids, o'er the sightless eyes,
> Straightened the stiffened form, of one who lies, robed for the silent tomb.
> Speechless the closed lips, quiet the pulseless hand;
> Gone at grim Death's command, to mystery's dark gloom.

The tired brain, the troubled breast,
Sought and craved for quiet rest, when gaunt disease held sway.
He sleeps and never more shall wake,
Till Gabriel Death's fetters break, at Jehovah's judgment day.
Lay him low beneath the sod,
Leave life's record with our God, who by his own decree,
Shall be the Judge of great and small;
Shall judge the faults and failings all, more merciful than we.

- Last week we made mention of the burning of Henry Taubert's barn and contents. Since then Mr. Taubert has been arrested, charged with setting fire to the building, to defraud the insurance company. A partial examination was had before Esq. Phelps, on Monday, and continued to-day at 1 o'clock. It looks dark for Henry.

The Potter Enterprise
Wednesday Evening, December 1, 1880 – Vol. VII, No. 29

Genesee Forks. A little girl came to stay with D. Dunbar, Jr. on Thanksgiving.

MARRIED.
GROVER – PRESHO – By Rev. J. L. Swain, at his residence near Raymond, Nov. 24th, 1880, Mr. William J. Grover of Ulysses, Pa., and Mrs. Sarah A. Presho of Raymond, eldest daughter of the late Seth Conable Esq.

WILLIAMS – CRUM – At the residence of the bride's father, in Ulysses, Nov. 24, 1880, by Rev. S. D. Pickett, Mr. George E. Williams and Miss Sarah M. Crum. Both of Ulysses, Potter county, Pa.

DIED.
GREEN – At 8 A.M. on the 25th inst., Mrs. Ellen Lindsey Green, wife of Mr. Luther Green, after extreme suffering for eleven hours. Aged about 30 years.

WEBSTER – November 25th, at his home near Ellisburg, Mr. M. T. C. Webster Sen. Aged about 79.

Ulysses. Two children of Mr. and Mrs. Dell Crowell were taken from their embrace, by that terrible disease diphtheria. One was two years and a half old and the other but a few months. Those children were their parents joy and delight, and their all.

Bingham. Mr. Thompson of Bingham Centre, buried a little boy a few days ago, and Nov. 25th his only daughter was laid by the side of her brother. She was about ten years old.

Genesee Forks. The remains of T. Webster were interred in the burying ground of this place yesterday. A large procession followed. He was an old resident of this town.

Asylum Peters.

This aged colored man, so well known to the old settlers in the vicinity of Lymansville, died at the house of Walter Edgecomb, in Homer, Nov. 24th. Being one of the first settlers of Potter, a brief sketch of his life might not be out of place at this time. Mr. Peters was born in Bradford county, Pa., in the year 1793, and named after the township in which he was born. In 1806 he came to Ceres, M'Kean county, with General Bravo, a surveyor and the man who located the three warrants known as the Bravo lands. He was cook for Bravo and his party while they were surveying, and when that work was done the boy Asylum was sold to Wm. Ayers for one hundred dollars with the understanding that Mr. Ayers should give him a certain amount of schooling and his freedom when he was twenty-one years of age.

In 1808 Mr. Ayers moved into Potter county, and occupied the Keating farm, six miles east from Coudersport, coming in on what was then the only road in the county, the "old Boon road" which run north of Coudersport near where Sam Thompson now lives, passing up Prosser hollow and across which is now known as the Harris farm, to the Keating farm in Sweden township, thence in a southerly direction to the Hopper house on the Jersey Shore Turnpike, thence down the Cross Fork to the mouth, and thence to a point near Renovo.

Mr. Ayer's family consisted of wife, two sons, one daughter and the black boy Asylum, and they were the first settlers in the county.

Before his time was out Peters left Mr. Ayers and went to live at Isaac Lymans, at what is now Lymansville, where he remained until after he became of age, when he went to live with Jonathan Edgecomb and has ever since remained with the family, where he has been kindly treated and where he was always felt that he had a home.

Mr. Peters was the only man that was ever lawfully a slave in this county, and the only person who has lived here seventy-two years. By his death we are reminded that Pennsylvania was once a slave state, and some of the younger readers of the *Enterprise* will be surprised to learn that as late as 1840, more than sixty colored persons were legally held slaves in this Commonwealth.

Almeron Nelson.

Obituary.

Caroline Mills Glassmire, wife of Daniel F. Glassmire, Sr., was born in Lancaster county, Pa., January 29th, 1824, and died in Coudersport, Pa., November 18th, 1880. In early youth she consecrated herself to the service of God, and for forty years blessed the church and the world by the purity of her life, and by the constancy of her devotion to the cause of Christ, and to the best interests of her kind. While always ready to take her full share of any church work, prolific in plans, self-forgetful and tireless, she instinctively shrunk from the public gaze. As a wife, she lived to and for her husband. As a mother, she bore her children a sweet and precious burden on her heart continually.

Her religious duties and obligations were ever held paramount to all. A beautiful consistency of profession and conduct distinguished her demeanor both as a Christian and in the social circle. Many of her associates and acquaintances were not religious. Her influence even upon such inspired in them the highest respect for her christian principles and impressed them with the reality and true dignity of the christian. The words she uttered were listened to with eagerness and treasured up in the inmost recesses of the memory and of the heart. They will be repeated within the circle of those friends who knew her inner life, as oracles issuing out of the temple of God.

She was benevolent in proportion to her available means, but her charitie was unostentatious. With her own hands she labored for the poor, and her feet often bore her to their habitations on errands of mercy. Yet she did not seek to be solitary in these acts of kindness, but co-operated freely with other noble women of her church and vicinity in associations for humane and benevolent purposes. She was remarkable for a very vivid imagination, and a sensibility which heightened all her enjoyments, and made her society fascinating. Her talent for conversation could be exceeded by no one – she was always new. Love gleamed in her face and sparkled in her eye; her charity extended to all. She appeared always to be in a prayerful frame of mind. In the early part of her religious career she was sorely tempted respecting that church in which, afterward, she so often exulted in having becoming a member. Her love for souls was ardent and sincere; and none could leave her company without sharing in her prayers and being followed by her blessing. The dealings of God toward her in many things were very remarkable. But those who devote themselves to His service, as she eminently did, may hope for the guidance of His spirit. "The secret of the Lord is with the righteous." Her intercourse with God was such that she brought all her concerns, spiritual and temporal, to the Mercy Seat, and could then wait without any anxiety the issue of his will. And the answers to her prayers were so frequent that she stood strong in faith, giving glory to God.

Truly it may be said of her that she has left an example of christian piety as pure, beautiful and attractive, as the Church Militant in these latter days is wont to exhibit. Those who had the happiness of enjoying her intimate acquaintance – those who were accustomed to meet with her where the children of God spoke often one to another – know well that through the long years of her christian life, she has not rested from her labors as victor upon a conquered field. They will testify that, with no intermission, she has to the last been eminently active, watchful and self-denying; that her religious experience and utterances were ever fresh, edifying and spiritual; that she was reverent, humble, grateful, trustful, filial, quite above the examples of our current christianity. For myself, I seemed always, when in her presence, in what (for want of some more discriptive term) has often been denominated a *religious atmosphere.*

She died as she had lived, with a lively hope of immortality. Her last intelligible utterences were made up of what made up her life – earnest prayer and triumphant assurance: "My Heavenly Father is good;" "My blessed Saviour is precious;" "Everything seems so beautiful and lovely;" "My dear husband and children are all here," she cried, with eyes and hands raised toward heaven. Such a death bed. It appeared like the verge of heaven, like waiting in the Sanctuary, surmounted by angels and archangels; and above all a place which the presence of God rendered sacred. A cloud of the Divine presence rested on all; and while she could hardly be said to be an inhabitant of earth, being now speechless, and her eyes fixed, victory and glory were written on her countenance, and giving as it were on her dying lips. No language can paint what appeared in that face. The more we gazed upon it, the more we saw heaven unspeakable. Calmly she sank into her bed of rest, while her buoyant spirit rose to join the praises of the sky, and her own kindred. How much will they have to communicate; how much to enjoy. Who would forego a happy eternity for anything this sublunary world could promise or bestow?

"Thou art gone to the grave; but we will not deplore thee;
Whose God was they ransom, they guardian and guide;
He gave thee, and he will restore thee;
And death has no sting, for the Saviour has died."

T. R. Stratton.

- Last week Henry Taubert was held to bail in the sum of $1,000, on the charge of burning his own barn. He boards with Covey.

Potter County, Pa.

So it seems that the forest and streams of Potter county do contain something besides brook trout and the fleet footed deer. Mr. A. G. Lyman, on the Cross Forks, according to the *Journal*, has cut over 300,000 feet of cherry timber already this season, and expects to make it 800,000 before spring. In other localities in the same county, beech and birch are equally plentiful, and often attains a growth equal to the tallest pines, and measuring in many places from twenty to forty feet from root to branch. The completion of the proposed Jersey Shore and Pine Creek Railroad will render accessible all these vast tracts of timber, and in time, force the hills and valleys of virgin Potter to blossom as the rose. We are happy to learn from unquestioned authority that plans are working to this much desired end, and we shall not be surprised, if at an early day, the sturdy yeomanry of the Pine Creek region are startled from their day-dreams by the unexpected neighing of the iron horse. Potter county has made wonderful progress within the last ten years, and in point of culture and resources, outranks many of her more pretentious neighbors. Coudersport, the capitol of the county, lately scourged by fire, is being rebuilt in the most substantial manner, and needs only to be connected by rail with the outside world, to become one of the most prosperous young cities in Northern Pennsylvania. Already enjoying the exhilarating influence of two most excellent newspapers the *Journal* and *Enterprise* – vanguards of civilization, we predict for the town and county, unrivaled prosperity for years to come. – *Olean Times*.

The Potter Enterprise
Wednesday Evening, December 8, 1880 – Vol. VII, No. 30

Roulet. Born – To Mr. and Mrs. Earnest Keeler a daughter. Also, to Mr. and Mrs. Elisha Willoughby, a daughter.

Potter County, Pennsylvania Potpourri – Volume I
1880 through 1884

MARRIED.

WEIMER – DRAKE – At the residence of the bride's parents, by Rev. Isaac George of Fredonia, November 17, 1880, Willis D. Weimer, formerly of Pleasant Valley, Potter county, late of Coleville, M'Kean county, and Miss Eva O. Drake of Salamanca, Cattaraugus county.

DIED.

MARION – In Ulysses, Nov. 29th, 1880, of diphtheria, Carrie Marion, aged 2 years and 8 months.

Roulet. William Willoughby lost his two children by diphtheria a few weeks ago.

Allegany. Yesterday, a little boy, the youngest child of D. Carpenter, who lives in Sweden, was brought to the Ford cemetery and buried, after which the funeral was held at the school house. The child died with diphtheria, he was only sick a few days.

Roulet. Died – In Roulet, November 26, 1880, Stewart M'Dorman, aged 31 years. Mr. M'Dorman came from W. Virginia one year ago, for the purpose of working a farm for L. W. Crawford, by hard work he soon lost his health, he was taken with hemorage of the lungs, which ended in consumption. At the time of his death he was living in the tenant house of L. Lyman. As soon as his critical condition was known, willing hands did all that could be done to relieve the sufferer, but to no avail. He quietly passed away, leaving a wife and three small children. The town took charge of the remains which were interred in the Roulet cemetery, and on Monday, the 6th inst., sent the family to their friends in West Virginia.

The Potter Enterprise
Wednesday Evening, December 15, 1880 – Vol. VII, No. 31

- Mrs. Barton, widow of James Barton, at one time landlord at the Baker House in this place, was buried on Kettle Creek last Sunday. She was ill only twenty-four hours.

Coudersport.

According to promise we shall proceed to compare our new stores with the old ones that occupied the sites now built up in a palatial style, and we believe no town of its size has been so benefitted by a fire as Coudersport.

We shall begin with M. S. Thompson & Co.'s. The old store was burned in the great conflagration of May 18th, was 69x20 feet, built in the old style sixteen feet posts, two stories high, and had stood at the time of the fire for nearly fifty years, it was the oldest store building in town. It had been used as a drug store for several years with the *Journal* office overhead. However, three years before the fire, the *Journal* office had been removed to the corner of Second and West streets. The new store is 80 by 28 inside, two stories high, fourteen feet between joists, the front room is 26x60 feet, done off in Queen Anne style, a very elaborate affair with ash, cherry, black walnut, black birch, etc. In fact it is a beauty. Nine different styles or patterns of paper adorn the walls and ceilings upon the first floor. The second story is divided into offices of two rooms each with folding doors between. A gentleman from Eldred said there was not so fine a drug store in the city, and we believe him. The store is built of brick, with galvanized iron cornice and tin roof. There are five counters below, beautifully inlaid and moulded. One of these is devoted to Japanese goods, the first that was ever brought into Potter county, and so excites much comment and admiration. Entering the new "People's drug store," we are bewildered with the array of plated ware, strange woods, wrought in wonderful shapes, lacquer, etc., etc., until the head fairly swims. We will say without meaning a puff, that M. S. Thompson has wonderfully fine taste in the selection of goods for holidays.

We come next to P. A. Stebbins Jr., & Bro's new store. The old one was next in age to M. S. Thompson's, it was sixty feet in length by twenty-four in width, devoted to dry goods, boots and shoes, and the etcetras of a country store, backed by a wareroom 20x24 feet, which contained on one side three hundred feet of shelving, and on the other side two hundred feet. This was a very plain building, and was the first swept away by the fire of May 18th. The new building occupying the site of the old frame affair, is brick, with iron front and cornice, tin roof and stone entrance. Behind the store is placed a tank of gasoline from which gas is made that lights the store with twenty-six burners, rendering night, day. The store room is 33x70 feet, containing walnut topped counters, four hundred and thirty feet of shelving for dry goods, etc., etc., with a centre counter fronting two hundred feet of shelving, twenty-four drawers and forty-five feet of show case. It is unnecessary to say that four clerks are kept on the hop from early morn to dewy eve.

Thompson and Stebbins' stores are ornaments to our place, and we are willing to affirm that no other place of the size is so liberally endowed with substantial business buildings. – *Zypholite in Northern Tier Reporter.*

- Statement of the stock and produce raised in the township of Ulysses, Potter county, Pa., taken November, 1880.

Horses	167
3 yr. old Colts	24
2 yr. old Colts	35
1 yr. old Colts	23
Sucklings	20
Dogs	79
Mules	2
Oxen	24
Cows	592
3 yr. old cattle	150
2 yr. old cattle	126
1 yr. old cattle	191

Calves	257
Sheep	1192
Shoats	240
Hay, Tons	2488
Wheat, bu.	1139
Barley, bu.	159
Rye, bu.	36
Buckwheat, bu.	3023
Oats, bu.	24638
Corn, bu.	6617
Peas, bu.	532
Potatoes, bu.	8346
Apples, bu.	7971
Butter, pounds	76895
Maple Sugar, pounds	20940

Average age of voters, 47 years.

R. L. Clark, Assessor.

The Potter Enterprise
Wednesday Evening, December 22, 1880 – Vol. VII, No. 32

DIED.

CARPENTER – In Sweden, Pa., Dec. 4th, 1880, of diphtheria, David Deane, son of David D. and Susan Carpenter, aged 2 years, 5 months and 19 days.

WOOD – In Oswayo, Nov. 22d, 1880, Frankie E. Wood, aged 11 years, and Julia A. Wood, Nov. 25th, aged 7 years, of diphtheria.

- Sheriff Covey started for the Western Penitentiary Monday noon with Henry Taubert.

Allegany.

Statistics for Allegany township for the years

	1876	1877	1878	1879	1880
Horses working,	180	153	165	170	154
Oxen working,	32	22	30	28	28
Cows,	486	465	425	434	488
Dogs,	76	74	62	83	76
Colts, 3 years,	9	8	16	13	21
Colts, 2 years,	9	12	18	17	15
Colts, 1 year,	17	25	22	16	17
Colts, suckling	24	24	15	17	13
Heifers, milking, 3 yrs	92	88	92	115	188
Heifers, milking, 2 yrs	56	47	45	65	46
Heifers, not milking, 3 yrs				2	3
Heifers, not milking, 2 yrs				42	45
Steers, 3 years,				20	14

Steers, 2 years,	46	50	74	16	19
Yearlings,	135	170	199	226	243
Calves,	393	263	291	354	272
Sheep,	684	624	930	1226	1619
Shoats to winter,	179	135	141	93	114
Winter wheat, bushels	692	1242	1352	1281	611
Spring wheat, bushels		691	1073	997	336
Corn, ear, bushels	4088	6691	4732	5244	4200
Buckwheat, bushels	1966	3171	2405	3435	2751
Oats, bushels	24287	28428	20686	20674	19243
Millet, bushels	601	978	461	1074	1380
Rye, bushels	59	98	140	233	233
Peas, bushels	142	215	368	140	194
Beans, bushels	50	87	91	125	84
Potatoes, bushels	6903	13190	8129	4703	11081
Apples, bushels	7085	4470	1682	9295	7602
Turnips, bushels	985	1771	640	1481	827
Hay, tons,	3563	2087	1998	2292	2043
Pork killed, pounds	23998	45478	34806	11204	37932
Butter, pounds	61386	63925	55208	59647	60784
Cheese, pounds	20940	37438	62600	45995	48900
Maple sugar, pounds	17511	23121	21438	30183	19465
Wool, pounds	2158	3325	3040	4084	5482
Acres winter wheat sowed,		153	116	52	56
Bushels, winter wheat sowed		268	221	99	101
Acres rye sowed			19	22	7 ½
Bushels rye sowed			30	34	9 ½
No swarms bees wintered,				78	86
Young swarms,				118	103
Am't honey taken from same,				684	795

Charles Coats, Assessor.

THE CHAPMAN CASE.
Sudden Termination on Thursday Last.

Most of our readers will remember the Chapman case in which Mrs. Theresa Chapman was charged with causing the death of her husband, Norman Chapman, by administering narcotic poison, in July last, in the boro of Coudersport.

At the September Court the Grand Jury returned a true bill, and last week a second true bill was returned for murder, the bill of September Court containing a slight omission; reading near the close of the indictment, "aforesaid" without repeating the name of the defendant, a triffling omission, but in a murder case trifles are made the most of, and the attorneys for the Commonwealth thought it best to close, if possible, every loop hole for legal quibble, consequently second indictment.

The case was called on Thursday morning, the defendant being present, and the Court room well filled.

After the calling of the case, the District Attorney, James L. Knox, made a statement to the Court, the substance of which was as follows.

The evening previous he had learned of an irregularity in the Grand Jury room and upon investigation found there had been twenty-four persons present, and acting as Grand Jurors, all having been sworn, but one of the persons, I. H. Leach of Hector twp., had not been summoned, and his name did not appear on the Venire.

Mr. Knox stated the Mr. Leech said in explanation, that he had seen in the papers the Jury list and the name H. J. Leach, and supposed that he was the person meant, and that the publication was the only notice required.

This announcement caused quite a stir in Court, among the spectators. Of course the attorneys knew it before, and the attorneys, or some of them at least, were aware of the fact on Monday. As they were for the defence, they kept quiet, prepared to take advantage of the fact if necessary.

The announcement of the District Attorney required that the case be settled then and there, and A. G. Olmsted moved that the indictment found this term be quashed on account of the presence of Mr. Leach in the grand jury room. The motion was granted, leaving the September indictment still holding good. After consultation the District Attorney entered a nolle prosequi in the case of September indictment, this leaving the case in the same position it was before any indictment was found, and leaving Mrs. Chapman clear.

The case can be taken up again at any time if thought necessary or desirable. The prosecuting attorneys do not believe they could secure a conviction on the evidence they could produce, and for this reason the *nol. pros.* was entered. The defense would probably have taken no action on the jury muddle, unless their client had been convicted, in which case a new trial would have been obtained.

The how, why, and wherefore of the 24th man in the jury, has been discussed by hundreds. We cannot see why the Mr. Leach of Hector should suppose he was a juryman. He received no summons from the Sheriff, and his name did not appear in the Court Calendar, or in the list as published. As published, the list reads, commencing with the 13th name:

C. S. Redner	Farmer	Hector
Rufus Corey	"	"
J. H. Leach	"	Oswayo
J. B. Parker	"	Hector

J. H. Leach is the only Leach on the list, and his residence is printed as Oswayo. Mr. Leach of Hector has "H. I." for his initials.

Twenty-four Grand Jurors were summoned. E. D. Wheaton of Bingham, did not report, being ill. Mr. Leach of Hector was sworn, and answered at roll call to the name of Leach. In the jury room one of the Jurymen noticed twenty-four were present, but supposed the absent Juryman had reported, and that 24 instead of 23 was a legal grand jury.

We believe no advantage has been taken of this occurrance in any other than the Chapman case. But we do predict that it will be a long time before such a blunder again occurs in Potter county.

No farther action in the Chapman case is contemplated and unless some new evidence turns up, we shall hear no more of it, so far as the law is concerned.

Court Proceedings.

1880, Dec. 13th. Court called. Present a full bench.

The constables of the several boroughs and townships appeared in court and made returns.

The following commonwealth cases were continued. Vs E. M. Woodcock, for netting wild pigeons; vs John Rooney, assault and battery; vs Gilbert Adams, for adultery; vs Abraham Jones, for netting wild pigeons; vs Christopher Dennis, for rape; vs David Lewis, James Lewis and James Patterson, for riot and assault; vs Walter Reer, for open lewdness; vs R. H. Haynes, for assault and battery.

The Grand Jury was called and sworn. Charles Coats appointed foreman, and M. N. Babcock constable to attend the same. The Grand Jury was in session until the 17th, and found the following true bills: Vs Theresa Chapman, for murder; vs David Lewis, James Lewis and James Patterson, for riot and assault and battery; vs R. Haynes for assault and battery; vs Henry Taubert for burning property with intent to defraud an insurance company. To this indictment the defendant plead guilty and was sentenced to the Western Penitentiary for two years and three calendar months. Vs Henry Taubert, cruelty to animals, to this indictment the defendant plead guilty, sentence withheld; vs Thomas Garity, William Norman, John Norman and M. Millen, for riot and assault and battery; vs George King for perjury. The Grand Jury also made a presentment vs Mason Nelson for selling liquor, and they ignored the following bills: Vs Jacob P. Wambold, the prosecutor, R. H. Haynes, to pay costs; vs John E. Lee for selling liquor on Sunday and selling liquor; vs Freeman Ayres, assault and battery, the prosecutor, William T. Jones, to pay costs; vs Miles O'Higley for selling unwholesome meat, the prosecutor, James Bradley, to pay costs; vs Samuel Brown for assault and battery, the prosecutor, Charles A. Turck, to pay the costs.

In the matter of the proposed road from the cross roads near the Catholic church in Genesee township to the Ellisburg and Wellsville road; rule to show cause why exceptions should not be filed; returnable next term.

Forty-five traverse jurors answered to their names.

Motions and rules were made and taken in the following cases: In David Ingraham vs Joseph J. Carey; death of David Ingraham suggested, and Henry Ingraham, executor and sole legatee substituted. In J. Q. Merrick and Sarah Merrick vs John M. Covey, rule to show cause why appeal should not be stricken off. In W. T. Jones vs Mary Ann Jordan, rule to show cause why the mechanics lien should not be set aside. In A. D. Sterrett vs William Ansley, the death of defendant suggested. In Florian Rausch vs Samuel B. Woodring, the death of the plaintiff suggested and rule taken to show cause why judgment should not be stricken off, etc. In Mary A. McDonald vs Genesee Independent School District, rule on plaintiff to give bail for costs. In Joseph Mann and R. L.

Potter County, Pennsylvania Potpourri – Volume I
1880 through 1884

Nichols vs F. P. Brooks, court direct a plea of not guilty to be entered. In Joseph Mann and R. L. Nichols vs Luke Stevens, Justus Hickok and A. A. Mulkin, rule on defendants to appear and plead. In F. W. Knox vs William Ansley and William Putnam, the death of William Ansley suggested. In C. Hunsicker for use vs Jacob Gamble at al, court direct a plea of not guilty to be entered.

W. W. Farnsworth was appointed an overseer of the Poor of Lewisville borough.

Subpoenas and alias subpoenas in divorce were issued in the following cases: Catherine Cole vs William Cole; Chas. N. Wilber vs Mary A. Wilber; Benjamin Cole vs Hannah Cole; a decree of divorce was granted to Isaac Herring from Emeliza Herring; in Charles Bailey vs Carrie Bailey, a proclamation was ordered, and L. C. Kinner appointed a commissioner to take testimony; Mary E. Ward vs Hugh Ward, proclamation ordered and C. M. Allen appointed a commissioner to take testimony; in Lydia Clark vs James Clark, proclamation ordered and Edson Hyde appointed commissioner to take testimony; same order in Anna Belle Seibert vs John M. Seibert.

Nolle prosequis were entered in the following cases: Commonwealth vs John Brownlee and Thomas Hunt, held to bail for forcibly entry and detainer; vs John Miller assault and battery; vs Mathias Schmidt keeping disorderly house; vs Theresa Chapman murder.

In the commonwealth vs Geo. King; assault and battery; a jury returned a verdict of not guilty; the defendant to pay three-fourths of the costs, and the prosecutor, John Healey, to pay one-fourth the costs.

Honorables R. J. C. Walker and R. P. Allen, of the Lycoming county bar were admitted to practice in the several courts of this county.

Patrick Roach was appointed guardian of the minor children of George Grandier.

Mary Crosby was appointed guardian of the minor children of Abel U. Crosby, deceased.

Henry M. Gardner was appointed stenographer of the several courts of Potter county.

The appointment of Arthur B. Mann as auditor to distribute the funds in hands of administrator of the estate of James Scott, was continued. Also his appointment to distribute the funds arising from Sheriff's sale of real estate of James Gibson.

In the commonwealth vs George Baker, indicted for arson. A jury found the defendant not guilty.

Clinton A. Miller was appointed guardian of minor children of Jesse J. Carman, deceased.

A. B. Mann was appointed an auditor to audit the accounts of the Prothonotary and Register and Recorder for the year 1880.

In the commonwealth vs J. L. Barclay indicted for assault and battery. A jury found the defendant guilty and he was sentenced to pay a fine of one dollar and the costs of prosecution.

The indictment vs Theresa Chapman for murder found at this term was on motion, quashed, for the reason that one H. I. Leach was sworn as a grand juror, and acted as such grand juror during the hearing of the case, while said Leach was not summoned as a grand juror and was not upon the venire of grand jurors.

And the court ordered that H. I. Leach be withdrawn from the grand jury room and not return.

John M. Covey, High Sheriff, appeared in court and acknowledged the execution of a deed.

To Joseph Mann for 70.9 acres of land in Clara township, sold as the property of Mary Hay and Alexander P. Hay, Dec. 14th, 1880, for $205.

Judgments for want of appearance, plea, affidavit of defence, were taken in the following cases: L. Allison vs C. B. Lewis; Norman W. Keach vs S. M. Sharp, garnishee of Ashley Sanderson; Alfred Scott vs Napoleon Woodcock; George Fox, M.D. vs Henry Brown and George W. Coffin, *terre tenant*; Thomas B. French vs H. A. Avery and Miles Mitchell; J. McEwen, *et al* vs same parties; Grover and Baker Sewing Machine Co. vs John Pye; H. J. Olmsted vs Wharton township; H. Birdsall, Son & Company vs W. H. Turner; Smith Dexter, Jr. vs J. P. Randall, Jr.; Isaac Benson vs Stewardson township (three cases: E. N. Stebbins vs J. W. Clark, *et al.*).

In the commonwealth vs Thomas Garity, William Moran, John Moran and M. Millon, indicted for riot and assault and battery. The jury found Thomas Garity and M. Mellon (the only defendant arrested, the other two being supposed to be in New York State out of reach of our officers,) not guilty of riot, but guilty of assault and battery. And the court sentence M. Millen to pay a fine of $10, and undergo imprisonment in the county jail for one calendar month, and Thomas Garity to pay a fine of $50 and undergo an imprisonment of four calendar months.

M. V. Larrabee, County Treasurer, appeared in court and acknowledged two deeds for lands sold for non-payment of taxes.

Rule to show cause why special taxes should not be levied to pay debts were taken on the following named townships: West Branch, Sharon, Stewardson, Genesee, Eulalia and Abbott.

A subpoena in divorce was issued in the case of Virginia Quinnette vs Edwin Quinnette.

O. H. Crosby was appointed an auditor to restate and audit the account of Joel Bolich, administrator of the estate of Jasper Nelson.

Marshall Gross was held in the sum of $200 for his appearance at next court.

The commonwealth vs Peleg Burdick, indicted for selling liquor, was continued.

The commonwealth vs George W. King, indicted for perjury, was tried and the jury found the defendant not guilty. The prosecutor, Andy McAllister to pay $8 of the costs and the defendant to pay the balance.

Recognizances were forfeited in the following cases: Commonwealth vs Hiram Graham, fornication and bastardy; vs Aaron Schoonover and Melim Schoonover, larceny of timber; vs John D. Dorsey, perjury.

George W. King, John Healy and Andrew McAllister, gave bail to next term for payment of certain costs.

Bench warrants were issued for Chas. A. Turck, James Bradley and R. H. Haynes, prosecutors in certain cases where the indictments were ignored by the grand jury.

The court ordered that 400 names be put in the jury boxes for the coming year. The usual venires were issued and at 10:30 a.m., Saturday, court adjourned.

The Potter Enterprise
Thursday Evening, January 8, 1881 – Vol. VII, No. 33

- It is Dr. Buck who steps high this time. Weight unknown.

MARRIED.

COBB – DICKINSON – At the residence of F. W. Knox, in Coudersport, Dec. 24th, 1879, by Rev. T. R. Stratton, Mr. Lyman H. Cobb and Miss Edith M. Dickenson, all of Coudersport.

BLAUVELT – JOHNSON – At the M.E. Parsonage in Coudersport, Jan. 1, 1880, by Rev. T. R. Stratton, Mr. Delos Blauvelt, of Ayers Hill, and Miss Hattie Johnson.

CONE – STILLMAN – At the residence of the bride's parents in Hebron, by Rev. T. R. Stratton, Mr. Edward Cone and Miss May Stillman, all of Hebron, Pa.

- A little daughter of Mr. Slarrow of Yocum Hill, aged about eleven years, died a few days since, making the third from diphtheria in this family. There are no new cases in that neighborhood. Several who have had the disease are improving very slowly.

Allegany. Yesterday the gate of the grave-yard was again opened to receive the infant son of Charles Green, who died on Saturday, the 3d inst., aged two years – but I am not certain whether from diphtheria or croup as both are reported as the cause.

DIED.

STRYKER – In Allegany, of Diphtheria, on the morning of December 26, 1879, Jimmie, only remaining son of Mr. and Mrs. Marshall Stryker, aged eight years.

Also, on the same morning, their little daughter Fannie, aged three years.

With her these parents watched in hope and fear for fourteen days, while the brother was to be laid in the same little grave with her on Saturday the 27th, after being sick only six days. A solemn funeral service was conducted by Rev. J. L. Swain at the house – the mother not being able to go from home.

While these doubly afflicted parents are mourning their great loss, they remember with great thankfulness the kind offices of their neighbors, to the living, and watchful care of the little ones so suddenly taken from them.

Potter County, Pennsylvania Potpourri – Volume I
1880 through 1884

They have indeed had many trials, not only this, but a few years ago, a son aged ten years was taken from them. Much of the time since then the mother has been sick, and last spring for many weeks the father was laid up from work by a very bad hand.

    Around the throne of God in Heaven
        Thousands of children stand,
        Children whose sins are all forgiven,
    A holy, happy band.

McDOWELL – In Pleasant Valley, Pa., Dec. 21st, 1879, of typhoid fever, Mable, second daughter of Robert and Sarah McDowell, in the 15th year of her age.

SMITH – At his home in Irving, Kansas, Dec. 20, 1879, Collins Smith, after a long illness.

RETROSPECT FOR 1879.

January – Thermometer 14 degrees below zero. Oyster supper for the benefit of the Episcopal church at Coudersport Hotel, receipts $20. N. M. Glassmire buys the H. T. Nelson property on the south side. Mail blockade, Coudersport eight days without mail, owing to snow upon the railroads. Albert C. Woodcock killed near Ellisburg by a load of lumber, Jan. 6th. R. L. Nichols' residence has a narrow escape from fire by the falling of a bracket lamp. F. L. Andrews appointed postmaster at Ellisburg. Byron Wood appointed Mercantile Appraiser. Prothonotary's office has a new stove. One prisoner in jail. Dr. A. M. Reynolds removes to New York state. Fire at postoffice, half a pound of celery seed destroyed, no insurance. Masonic lodge room re-furnished. January thaw.

February – Dr. O. T. Ellison continues to improve his mill property. Dr. S. A. Phillips settles in Coudersport. Two men with frozen feet quartered on Eulalia township. Eugene Dodd of Sweden has an arm broken. St. Valentine's day. Washington's birthday with its numerous balls in various parts of the county. Thad Kelley puts a new floor in his reading room. D. F. Glassmire re-floors the reading room in the Coudersport Hotel. Croup puts in an appearance in various portions of the county. Hon. Woolsey Burtis removes to Lewisville. Telegraph in operation. A. H. Pierce sells his property in Coudersport to Joseph Mann for $1,000. 15th, thermometer 19 degrees below zero. Eleven Mile oil well down 1500 feet; engine removed. 17th, Mrs. Michael Snyder of Sweden died. Aaron Metzgar died at the residence of his sister in Coudersport on the 15th. 17th, Eugene Bishop's house in Ulysses burned, no insurance. Township election. Alanson West died in Hebron, 26th. Another snow blockade. Hauling pipe for the pipe line.

March – C. H. Armstrong opens his new store on Second street. Miss Eva Dyke returns from an extended visit in the west. Telegraph office at Coudersport goes into the hands of the Western Union. Darius Moon of Millport has two ribs broken. Court week – Hon. S. F. Wilson presiding. Death of Capt. Arch F. Jones, March 8th. A. A. Swetland of Harrison Valley rents Mrs. Wood's house on Main street. John Grover has a narrow escape from death from the effect of a fall in Millport. Mrs. Lewis, mother of Erastus Lewis, sustains severe injuries from a fall. Maple sugar. Chicken-pox. Month came in like lamb, and went out making Rome howl.

April – Plenty of snow storms. Trout fishing booming. Excitement along the pipe line, caused by anti-pipe liners. Carl Zimmerman opens a meat market on Second street. Death of Hon. John S. Mann, April 12th. W. K. Jones elected Burgess. Hon. Lewis Mann of Washington, attends the funeral of his brother, Hon. J. S. Mann. Telegraph office removed from the post-office to D. F. Glassmire's store building. Joel White of White's Corners, dies suddenly at Rixford, McKean county, Pa. Matt Gridley loses a horse by diphtheria. The little son of Fred Schwab of Germania, is scalded by upsetting a teakettle of boiling water upon himself, and dies next day. Oscar Cavanaugh dies at Duke Centre, April 16th. R. Zinnert of Germania, has a leg broken and severely bruised by a wagon passing over him at Renovo, Pa. Cattle could not be turned out to grass until the latter part of the month. House of R. L. Clark burned in Ulysses.

May – Wild flowers in bloom. Leeks up. New sidewalks going down. A. G. Olmsted thin out the shade trees before his Main street residence. Lon Crosby builds a porch around his residence. A lodge of Knights of Honor organized, with rooms over Andrews & Olmsted's. Dr. C. S. French removes to Sterling Run, Cameron county, Pa. A white deer seen near Lymansville. Frank Howell of Oswayo, goes to Nebraska. Marion Harrington injured by a railroad of McKean county, receives damages from the Railroad Company. L. B. Cole's blacksmith and wagon shop takes fire, but is saved with small damage to the roof. Extensive wood fires in Clara township. A. Chriman's barn burned in Clara. Marshall Nichols' house on Horse Run burned. James Cole of Clara, builds a new barn. A daughter of Merrit Gridley, of Ulysses, accidentally shot by her brother with a revolver. Strawberries and pine-apples put in an appearance in market. Main street bridge re-planked. Mervill Calkins compositor in the Enterprise office, removed to Minnesota. F. W. Knox removes his old residence and begins work upon his proposed villa. James Johnson has a fracas with a kicking horse, harness and buggy damaged. Decoration Day, May 30th. Mrs. Nelson Vanwegen of Hebron, falls down stairs and breaks one of the bones near the ankle. Three frosts the third week in this month. May 27th morning ice formed one-sixteenth of an inch thick. Miles White rents the Coudersport Hotel. L. Estherson arrested for selling foreign watches. Ben Turner, son of Dr. Turner of Oswayo, injured by an accidental blow from a crowbar. N. H. Goodsell accidentally severely bruised by a loose belt while engaged with his planer at his planing mill on the south side. Mr. and Mrs. Frank Wagoner of Lewisville, ran away with by a three-year old colt, and Mrs. W. badly bruised. Mrs. J. M. Hamilton badly burned about the face by a flame from the stove. Tide Water Pipe Line completed. Ice cream festival for Presbyterian church, May 30th. Peleg Burdic repairs his hotel stand at Sharon Centre. Chauncy Wilcox of Millport, injured by being thrown from a wagon.

June – Christian Zimmerman begins building his brewery. Miss Alice Swartout of Hebron, was injured on the 2d inst by falling down stairs with a pail of water, recovered. St. German's church of Germania, receives the gift of a bell. E. N. Stebbins builds an awning over his store front. Richard Van Ammon of Sweden, has a leg broken. Andy Coleman of Burtville, injured by being thrown from a wagon. Frosts, 6th and 7th. Cyrenus Rennells injured by a wagon passing over his foot. Charles Landgon killed at the mill of M. H. Johnston, Eleven Mile. Jeff Burdic of Millport, severely injured by a falling limb. Calvin Ford's team runaway on Second street. E. N. Stebbins christens his store "The Ark." C. E. Hungerford opens a photograph gallery. Miss Carrie White becomes telegraph operator at Coudersport. John Jordan dies in Wharton on the 24th inst.

July – Fourth of July. Huckleberries arrive in market. Diphtheria rages in Ulysses. West street sewer extended to and across Sixth street. John Lyman celebrated his 90th birthday. Robert Niles injured by being thrown from a wagon. Mr. and Mrs. W. B. Gordnier thrown from a buggy by the breaking of an axle. J. O. Merrill's stage wagon tipped over by his team on Main street. Dr. E. S. Mattison thrown from his buggy by the breaking of a seat. Matt Gridley's horse breaks through the bridge at Lehman's. July 29th, Maurice Saunders of Roulet was killed by a loaded hay wagon passing over him. "Little" Dan Glassmire's pet deer killed. George Baker is hurt by being thrown from his wagon. July 26th, severe rain storm, streams bank full. 24th, Mr. and Mrs. Henry Nelson's silver wedding. Young man by name of Coe, living at Oswayo, shot in the neck in a row on the South Branch.

August – Blackberries. George Brahmer opens a blacksmith shop on Second street. Norman Dwight's team run away in Wellsville, N.Y. Amos Velie hurt by his team in Port Allegany. Burt Strang of Hebron hurt by a falling limb while cutting trees. Charley Welton married. Mrs. Wm. Metzgar injured by being thrown from a buggy in Bingham township. School directors of Coudersport purchase new desks and seats for the graded school. N. M. Glassmire puts a knee out of joint. An archery club organized in Coudersport.

September – Thomas Kernan back from Michigan. Mr. Ellis, of Ellisburg, has an accident near Shongo; his team and loaded wagon falling through a bridge. James Benson leaves for Princeton, N.J. Frosts. Isaac Wykoff digs in four weeks 1900 pounds of Gensing. D. F. Glassmire erects a street lamp. Mrs. Henry Nelson is injured by falling from the steps of the Coudersport Hotel, 17th inst. Roger Swetland puts an ankle out of joint. Miss Anton opens a millinery store at Coudersport. Mr. James Bates of Bingham, died suddenly Sept. 11th, of aneurism. Charles F. Huntington is admitted to the bar of Potter county, and departs for Nebraska. Wm. Bonnywitz of Sylvania, is badly cut with a corn cutter, 17th inst. Potter County Fair, Sept. 24th, 25th, and 26th.

October – Everybody goes after chestnuts. George Weimer of Roulet, has a leg broken by the lever of a stump machine, Oct. 14th. Oct. 4th John Yentzer of Roulet, meets with an accident while pulling stumps. Wallace Burdick of Sharon Centre, has a surgical operation performed on his leg, by Dr. Freeman of Smethport, Pa. Gensing. One of J. W. Allen's colts has a runaway on Main street. Rev. Mr. Stratton appointed to fill the M.E. Church pulpit for the ensuing conference year. John Kuhn's horse falls down his well in Sweden. The Cross Fork mail route opened. Mr. and Mrs. Nelson Clark golden wedding, 12th inst. D. C. Larrabee lays more stone walk. C. J. Marble sells his meat market. Mason Nelson's son from Denver, Col., arrives 25th. Diphtheria raging at Yocum Hill and Ulysses. Rev. F. Stevens of Ayres' Hill goes to Denver, Col., for his health. Jos. Zengerle of Germania accidentally shot and killed, Oct. 25th. November – Snow. A lady clerk at the "Ark." Election, Nov. 5th. Cyrus Turner dies 2nd inst. Miss Anna Aylesworth, Roulet, injured by being run over by a lumber wagon. Thanksgiving, 27th. Ellison's grist mill undergoing repairs. Keystone Mills being repaired. M. S. Thompson's street lamp shattered by a runaway team. Winter term of graded school begins 26th. A dastardly outrage perpetrated upon the person of Mrs. James Clark of Freeman Run. Bad roads. Erastus Merrill of Ulysses has a cancerous hand amputated Nov. 12th. A small cyclone passes over Coudersport on the 12th. Elmer Aylesworth's team ranaway on Second street. Preparations steadily going forward for the building of the large tannery just below Coudersport. Nov. 26th, Chas. H. Armstrong has a narrow escape from fire.

December – Roscoe Andrews of Andrews Settlement had his hand injured by a cider mill. Temperance boom triumphant. Railroad project again agitated. The white deer killed near Lymansville. F. D. Weimer builds a blacksmith shop on Fishing Creek. J. H. Peterson of Sharon, accidentally wounds himself in the hand with a revolver. Merchants lay in holiday goods. Commission appointed by the court to inquire into the insanity of John Henley of Hebron. Over one hundred students at the graded school. On the 14th, the last child of E. Reamsch of Yocum Hill, died of diphtheria, six in all with that fell disease. The hunting season closes, hunters have had fair luck. Cyrenus Jones stuffs the skin of the white deer killed near Lymansville. Mrs. Frank Stedman of Harrison Valley, and Mr. Roger Swetland have a runaway accident on Crandall Hill. Christmas. Many Christmas trees and lots of gifts. The snow plow busy 22d. Lock boxes placed in the post office. 20th, Wm. Dodd of Sweden has a runaway accident near Coudersport and Mrs. Dodd is badly hurt. The Coudersport Cornet Band reorganized. Mr. C. Aylesworth is injured by a falling limb while chopping in the woods. L. F. Andrews kills seven turkeys that weigh 97 pounds total.

December, since our last issue. – At W. A. Crosby's appeared a fine Christmas present, a boy, weight unknown. At Owen Metzgar's a like affair took place a day or two later, and another boy is added to the population of Coudersport. Last week an heir was born to Mr. and Mrs. Zenas Byam, of Allegany. On the evening of the 24th, Oscar Seifert broke into the shop and residence of Mr. Nye, on the Niles Hill Road, ransacking the place thoroughly, and carrying away a gun. Mr. Nye found a glove on his bed where the youthful burglar had thrown the articles of wearing apparel belonging to Mr. Nye, after going through the pockets. An acquaintance of Mr. Nye took the glove the next morning and in the presence of young Seifert exhibited it as one found by him in the street. Seifert immediately claimed the glove, showing the mate to it to prove his property. He was then accused of the crime, which he denied. Mr. Nye told him if he would return the gun he would say nothing further about the matter, but still the boy denied all knowledge of the robbery. Afterwards he became frightened and left town, and then Constable Bassett was sent after him. On his return, the boy as a prisoner, stopped at the stone-quarry just below town, and from a pile of stone drew forth the stolen gun. The young lad at an examination before a justice was held for appearance at court, and for want of bail was lodged in the "Castle." As this is the second offence of the kind committed by Oscar, it will probably lead to his being committed to some reformatory institution. Since the above was entered bail has been entered.

NOTICE.

Whereas my wife, Lois S. Casterline, has left my bed and board without any just cause or provocation, this is to notify all persons not to harbor or trust her on my account as I shall pay no debts of her contracting.

Cyrus Casterline.
Sharon, December 8, 1879.

The Potter Enterprise
Wednesday Evening, January 12, 1881 – Vol. VII, No. 34

MARRIED.

BROOK – HAY – At Clara, Pa., Dec. 26, 1880, by J. L. Allen, Esq., Mr. Timothy P. Brook, of Riley, Clinton county, Mich., and Miss Cora A. Hay, of Clara, Potter county, Pa.

EDMONDS – NELSON – At the residence of W. G. Wilber, in Wharton, Pa., by B. E. Berfield, Esq., Mr. Alpha M. Edmonds, of Corry, Erie County, Pa., and Miss Nancy E. Nelson, of Wharton, Potter county, Pa.

- Invitations will be issued in a few days for the First Grand Ball of the Coudersport Cornet Band to be held in Coudersport's New Opera House. The Band boys will leave nothing undone to make it a success. This will be the first entertainment in the Opera House and we trust will be well patronized. The Band has purchased several new instruments and the boys are devoting much time to make the organization one of the best. If you do not care to dance, purchase a ticket and take your supper. Encourage the boys, they deserve it.

The Potter Enterprise
Wednesday Evening, January 19, 1881 – Vol. VII, No. 35

Golden Wedding.

Mr. and Mrs. Erastus Merrill celebrated their fiftieth marriage anniversary on the 11th of January 1881, at their home in Ulysses.

They came to this county nearly forty-five years ago, they endured the hardships and privations incident to early settlers of those days. They are now living on the same farm to which they first came. Their family consisted of seven children, five of whom are now living, and all were present except their oldest daughter, who was detained on account of sickness. Among the other guests were the more distant relatives; Rev. Thomas Perry and wife, Rev. S. D. Pickett and wife.

The presents consisted of a plain gold ring, two brooches, two sets of cuff pins, one set cuff buttons, one scarf pin, one gold dollar, one pair kid gloves, for Mrs. Merrill.

One pair gold bowed spectacles, one gold shirt stud, and last but not least, one gold headed cane for Mr. Merrill.

The dinner was a success.

The entertainment consisted of both vocal and instrumental music, and other appropriate services.

- John P. Brehmer died at his residence in Eulalia, on Sunday last, at the advance age of ninety-one years. Mr. Brehmer was born in Prussia, but for the past forty-five years has resided on the farm where he died. A good citizen and an honest man, one whose word was as good as the wheat. His wife is in a very feeble condition, and will probably not long survive the death of her husband.

Teachers' Association.

Programme of the Teachers' Association at Ellisburg, January 29th, 1881:

FORENOON SESSION.

Address, Edgar Tucker; Recitation, Lettie Palmer; Methods of teaching beginners in grammar, Anna Jones; Square and Cube Root, A. D. Howe; Educational Progress, A. F. Hollenbeck; Questions.

AFTERNOON SESSION.

Business correspondence, J. C. French; Methods of Teaching Geography, Miss H. H. Hall; Select Reading, Lottie Webster; Recitation, Oratta Potter; Music, H. H. Hall; Answering questions; Essay, William Nelson; Select Reading, Ella Hemphill.

EVENING SESSION.

Recitation, Anna Rice; How to Teach Notation and Numeration, H. H. Hall; Song, Maria Wells; Debate – Resolved, "That the school directors should be salaried officers, and the number reduced to three." Affirmative – Thomas Gilliland and Charles Nelson. Negative – Frank Bishop and Edgar Tucker. Recitation, Effie Hurd; Esay, Emma Adams; Address, D. H. Cobb; Select Reading, Nettie Bishop; Music at the discretion of the President.

The Wharton Teachers' Association will be held at the Brownlee school house, Feb'y 5, 1881.

AFTERNOON SESSION.

1 p.m. – Devotional exercises by Rev. Wm. Peck; music by the Association; essay, S. B. Haskins; school room ventilation, W. W. Harvey; method of teaching Geography, R. E. Gibson; necessary qualifications for a successful teacher, C. M. Stillman; essay, B. F. Gates; answering of questions; music.

EVENING SESSION.

Music; select reading, R. W. Swetland; essay, Miss Thompson; normal schools, M. J. Colcord; dissertation, A. L. Cole; should the annual school term be increased? E. O. Austin; music; oration, L. D. Ripple; debate: - Resolved, That the place of County Superintendent should be filled by District

Superintendents, elected every two years by the popular vote of the district. Aff., E. O. Austin, M. J. Colcord; Neg., A. L. Cole, W. W. Harvey. Committee: C. M. Stillman, L. D. Ripple, R. W. Swetland.

The Potter Enterprise
Wednesday Evening, January 26, 1881 – Vol. VII, No. 36

Lawrence Mills. Wednesday morning, January 12th, Markie, oldest son of Henry S. and Clara J. Bartoo, fell asleep in Jesus. Little Markie was a sweet child, but only for a short time was he given to cheer the hearts of those who loved him best. The bereaved parents have the heart-felt sympathy of the entire community.

DIED.

BREHMER – Jan. 16, 1881, J. P. Brehmer, aged 91 years 1 month and 11 days.

He was born near Wetzlar, Prussia, December 4, 1789, and emigrated to the United States in 1833. He moved to Eulalia, Potter county, in 1840. He had been married to his wife, who still survives him seventy-one years.

County Commissioners.

At their last meeting the County Commissioners made the following appointments: G. W. Pearsall, clerk; Benson & Peck, Attorneys; E. O. Rees to wind town clerk.

Their annual statement will be printed next week. Among other items it shows the following:

Auditors wages	$105.00
Commonwealth costs	1235.68
Bond to Jos. Mann, paid	1321.61
Int. on bonds to I. Benson	1020.00
Expenses for Insane	243.00
Election Expenses	1147.92
Grand Jury	941.80
Traverse Jury	1472.24
Boarding Prisoners	207.75
Penitentiary expenses	79.76
Road Damages	245.00
Road Views	521.60

The total expenses for the year were $13,778.69. There is due from Collectors $3,328.21, which will be cut down probably half by abatements and per centage. There is a balance in the hands of the Treasurer of $6,820.27, about $2,300.00 of which consists of uncanceled county orders.

Potter County, Pennsylvania Potpourri – Volume I
1880 through 1884

Coudersport Graded School.

Through the kindness of the editors of our county papers, we are enabled to give the report of scholarship for the first month of the Winter Term, to the patrons of the school, and to the public.

The examinations in the Grammar and High schools are mostly written, and no result below 70 per cent is published; but the place is marked by a cypher. If the student falls below 70 per cent in all of his studies, his name does not appear.

HIGH SCHOOL.

NAMES.	Algebra-Geometry	Grammar	Eng. Comp.	U. S. History	Drawing.	Writing.
Rosa Crane,	80		87	90	78	
Mary Johnston,	70	80			88	
Amos W. Colcord	91		89	90	85	85
Jas. Rounseville,	0	71		80	78	
Thomas Ross,	0				0	75
Homer White,					95	90
Laura Monroe,		0		0	0	76
May Nelson,		80		85	80	
Carrie Larrabee,						
Katie Reissman,		78		0	0	80
Fred Mitchell,		0		70	0	75

NAMES.	Reading	1st & 2d Arith.	Geography	Latin.	Spelling
Jas. Rounseville,	77			0	
Amos W. Colcord,	90			99	
Rosa Crane,	88	97	93		98
Laura Monroe,	80	70	70		70
Inez Metzgar,	80				
Homer White,		80			
Fred Mitchell,	77	90	85		0
Katie Reissman,		0	70		87
Mary Johnston,		70	90	92	
May Nelson,		0	82		87
Carrie Larrabee,					
Thomas Ross,		80	87		84

GRAMMAR SCHOOL.

NAMES.	Reading	Arithmetic	Language	Geography	U. S. History	Spelling	Writing
Mary Armstrong,	90	70	85	0		76	70
Anna Boyer,	80	70	0	76		80	70
Isabella Crane,							
Martha Dingee,	90	0	80	0	85	88	87
Celia Gillon,	0	0	70	70		80	70
Emily Johnston,							
Lula Millard,	78	95	85	70	80	84	80
Inez Metzger,		70	85	0	80	80	75
Nora Metzger,	72	79	0	71	0	0	70
Nellie Perkins,	80	93	75	0	0	84	76
Mary McCormick							
Katie Kernan,	90						
John Allen,	85	0	80	77	0	92	0
Chester Presho,	70	0	70	70	0	0	85
Mackey White,			85	80			
John Niles,	85	75	90	0		72	70
Wm. Norton,	75	80	80	85	90	0	90
Chas. Doerner,	70	0	0	0		70	75
Chas. Gordnier,	75	70	75	0	0	88	
Frank Gordnier,	72	0	75	0	70	80	80
Geo. Gillon,	70	90	80	89		92	0

Drawing. – Nora Metzger, 70; Inez Metzgar, 70; Martha Dingee, 70; Lula Millard, 75; Nellie Perkins, 72; Chas. Gordnier, 80; Wm. Norton, 75; Chas. Doerner, 75.

The names of those pupils who were absent from examination and who probably might have attained a fair standing are followed by blanks.

Potter County, Pennsylvania Potpourri – Volume I
1880 through 1884

PRIMARY SCHOOL.

NAMES.	Arithmetic	Spelling	Geography	Reading	M. Arithmetic
Maggie Metzger,	90	100	99	80	
Lizzie Ryon,	90	97	71	0	
Digna McCormick	95	100	0	71	
Annie Dingee,	90	70	77	80	
Charlie Marble,	0	76	70	70	
Frank French,	70	96	96	82	
Arthur Buck,	75	0	99	0	
Jay Lewis,		70	85	81	
Nellie Millard,	70	100	70	70	
Schuyler Dingee,	88	0	79	79	
Nora Burt,	70	92	80	70	
Nellie Ryon,	70	96	0	0	
Hettie Beebee,	70	92	0	0	
Dan'l Chapman,		80	90	73	72
Nelia Marble,		79	80	81	75
Nellie Buck,		80	85	89	99
Iola Yates,		90	79	85	70
Lizzie Johnston,		70	70	70	77
C. Calkins,		81	85	80	80
Eva Mann,		79	76	90	76
Katie Grom		82	80	89	71
Annie Gillon,		95	80	70	98
John Boyer,		76	76	70	0
Theodore Grom,		77	70	75	71
Stephen Gillon,		80	71	77	0
Jud'n Rounseville,	81	90	75	80	
Lettie Gordnier,		81	71	79	70
Henry Junge,		80	79	88	73
Edgar Veley,		70	71	0	78
Frank Marble,		79		73	72
Theodore Metzger,		72	70	82	76
Samuel Beebe,		81		79	72
Bertha Neefe,		90		82	72
Annie Neefe,		100		85	70
Harry Millard,		70		0	70
Freddie Brahmer,		80		79	90
Mary Klein,		76		78	75
Carrie Sible,		79		80	70
Frank Dingman,		70		70	80

The Potter Enterprise
Wednesday Evening, February 2, 1881 – Vol. VII, No. 37

- Albert Lyman's mill on the Cross Fork was burned on Friday last, destroying two fine saws, carriage, belts &c. The Engine and boiler were not injured. No lumber of any account was burned. It was first reported as an incendiary fire, but is now believed to have caught at the arch. Mr. Lyman will now remove the machinery to Dry Run, and expects to be cutting lumber again within four weeks.

BANK ROBBERY.
The Bank of Coudersport Robbed of $914.50.

Our people were startled Friday morning, a little after nine o'clock, by the announcement that the Bank had been robbed in open daylight, and Mr. Doerner bound, blindfolded, and put in the vault.

Since the fire last May, the Bank has occupied the Land office of the Fox & Ross estate, at the upper end of town. Mr. J. M. Hamilton has charge of the Land office. W. K. Jones owns the Bank, C. A. Doerner acting as cashier.

Friday morning Mr. Hamilton reached the Bank a few minutes after nine o'clock, found a chair or two tipped over; the vault door closed but not fastened. Inside the vault he found Mr. Doerner lying on his back, his feet tied, his hands tied behind him, and a bag or sack fastened over his head, nearly suffocated.

He was quickly released by Mr. Hamilton, and told substantially the following story:

Shortly after entering the Bank and while fixing the fire, he heard the door open, as he supposed by Mr. Hamilton, and the next instant, while his back was toward the door (the stove stands directly in front of the door and only a few feet distant) a sack was thrown over his head and drawn tight, before he could resist or even get sight of the person or persons entering. He was then tied and put in the vault. He thought he had not been in the vault over ten or fifteen minutes when released.

Examination showed $37.50 in gold and $877.00 in bills missing, no silver was taken. Two pieces of gold were found on the floor.

The sack used was made of two thicknesses of unbleached muslin, with a draw string.

Albert Lyman had been at the Bank and left. W. K. Jones had been there and left. C. A. Doerner and J. M. Hamilton had gone to the bank, all of whom were seen by parties living near. But no one was found who saw other parties go there, and the robbery yet remains a mystery.

- On Monday the Coudersport Bank was removed to its new quarters, the stone building erected for that purpose on Second street. The building is the handsomest one in the town and the inside is finished elegantly. The lower floor is occupied by the Bank and John S. Ross as business office. Two large Plate windows furnish light during the day and at night gas will be used. The vault is a large one, fire and burglar proof. The heavy iron doors have the combination lock; the walls are of sand stone two feet thick, each stone reaching clear through; inside it is fitted up with shelves and pigeon-holes, and contains besides, two small burglar proof safes. The counter is of polished walnut and other hard woods. The whole office is nicely furnished, the latest addition being a combination desk of black walnut, the finest thing of the kind we have seen, which was a present to Will from his mother. The Bank is now in a convenient place to accommodate business men, and is as conveniently arranged as one could ask for.

JURY LIST.
TRAVERSE JURORS.

Seth Drake, Farmer, Sharon; G. R. Smith, Farmer, Oswayo; E. S. Worden, Farmer, Hector; Charles Head, Farmer, Oswayo; Edwin Lyman, Farmer, Sweden; John M'Ginnis, Farmer, Genesee; A. W. Andrews, Farmer, Allegany; Wm. Foster, Farmer, Wharton; A. G. Presho, Farmer, Allegany; Charles Cronk, Farmer, Sharon; Gottleib Traub, Farmer, W. Branch; John Francis, Farmer, Ulysses; Daniel Hober, Farmer, Bingham; Addison Clark, Farmer, Bingham; B. B. Burt, Merchant, Roulet; W. B. Lent, Farmer, Hebron; John Abbott, Laborer, Roulet; N. H. Rice, Farmer, Oswayo; J. L. Douglass, Farmer, Hector; C. H. Armstrong, Merchant, Coudersport; Hugh Young, Farmer, Portage; M. D. Briggs, Farmer, Bingham; D. C. Smith, Laborer, Oswayo; A. J. Burlison, Farmer, Sylvania; John Coulston, Farmer, Genesee; I. B. Carpenter, Farmer, Bingham; J. W. Allen, Farmer, Eulalia; M. V. Larrabee, Farmer, Roulet; Josiah Webster, Farmer, Genesee; John M. Covey, Ex-Sheriff, Coudersport, F. M. Reynolds, Farmer, Allegany; Charles Grover, Farmer, Bingham; Seth Briggs, Farmer, Wharton; C. A. Pinneo, Farmer, Oswayo; L. D. Estes, Farmer, Oswayo; Orlando Kaple, Farmer, Sweden.

GRAND JURORS.

F. N. Ayers, Farmer, Hebron; H. T. Reynolds, Farmer, Ulysses; J. M. Spafford, Merchant, Eulalia; A. V. Lyman, Merchant, Roulet; J. L. Barclay, Farmer, Wharton; John Wallace, Farmer, Summit; L. B. Cole, Justice Peace, Coudersport; W. E. Gilbert, Farmer, Harrison; John Abson, Carpenter, Coudersport; A. Bisbee, Farmer, W. Branch; James Gibson, Laborer, Hector; Wm. Kimball, Farmer, Eulalia; E. D. Leet, Farmer, Ulysses; H. D. Woodard, Farmer, Hebron; O. M. Kemp, Farmer, Oswayo; Eberhart Gnau, Farmer, Abbott; E. W. Ryan, Farmer, Ulysses; Walter Wells, Merchant, Oswayo; Ira Easton, Farmer, Genesee; A. F. Dodge, Farmer, Harrison; Henry G. Hurd, Farmer, Genesee; G. W. Clinton, Farmer, Sylvania; L. D. Ripple, Farmer, Portage; Consider Stearns, Farmer, Eulalia.

The Potter Enterprise
Wednesday Evening, February 9, 1881 – Vol. VII, No. 38

- The first fatal case of diphtheria in this immediate section, was that of a Miss Wallace, who died at the residence of Walter Abson, near Lymansville, last Sunday.

Potter County, Pennsylvania Potpourri – Volume I
1880 through 1884

- Next Tuesday evening, Feb. 22d, the Coudersport Cornet Band will give their first ball in Coudersport's new Opera House. First class music has been engaged; the decorating committee are doing their part to make the hall attractive, and there is every reason to believe this will be the most successful party ever given in this place. Supper will be spread in the store room on the first floor, so there will be no risk of taking cold by going to supper from the warm ball room.

The Potter Enterprise
Wednesday Evening, February 16, 1881 – Vol. VII, No. 39

- Frank Lent is the happy father of a ten and one-half pound boy, born Monday morning.

Roulet. Died – In Roulet, Feb. 4th, the infant daughter of Mr. and Mrs. R. B. Lane. – On Saturday morning, Feb. 5th, Christian Fisher, aged 81 years. – On Sunday p.m. Feb. 13, Anna Louisa, youngest child of Mr. and Mrs. John Eckert.

Ulysses. Tim Monroe died Jan. 21st, 1881, at the residence of Perry Bingham, in Lewisville, aged twenty-one.

Ulysses. Mrs. Lydia Ann Quimby, daughter of George W. Daniels, died last month aged fifty-four.

- There was an ice gorge at the Second street bridge last Saturday, and men and boys worked all day to save that structure – it was saved.

Twenty Years of Prohibition.

Hon. H. W. Williams, President Judge of Potter county, where prohibition law prevails, says:

"For twenty years there has not been a licensed hotel or restaurant within the confines of the county. There are enough of both at all suitable places for the accommodation of the public, but in none of them is there a public bar. The sale is conducted, therefore, at great disadvantage clandestinely, and is very limited in amount. As to results, I can say that, while the country has been steadily growing in population and business, pauperism and crime have steadily decreased. For the past five years the jail has been fully one half the time without any other inmate than the keeper and his family. Twice within the past ten years I have, at the regular term of court discharged the jury on the second day of the term, without their having been called to consider a single case of any description. The effect of this system is felt in many ways; taxes are reduced, the business of the criminal courts greatly reduced, industry and sobriety take the place of idleness and dissipation, and intelligence and morality are advanced."

The above statement is certainly worthy the candid consideration of all, but especially of the tax payers and those who desire the best good of the people. To reduce taxes and elevate the condition of the people, remove the cause of crime, which is found largely in the licenses, and a very important step will have been taken in the right direction. – *Montrose Democrat.*

Diphtheria.

Ed. Enterprise: With your permission I desire for a few weeks to occupy a part of a column of your paper to call attention to that highly contagious disease, diphtheria, that has and is making desolate so many homes in this country.

I am one of those that believe that disease can be in a great measure stamped out or eradicated if the energetic and intelligent citizens will, in every district where a case is reported, act in harmony and with determination. If smallpox was to-day reported in Coudersport, Oswayo or Lewisville or any other point, every man and woman would immediately consider themselves a committee to in every way fence against the spread of that disease, out of the way hospitals would be provided, and the unfortunate sick one wold be hurried to the pest house – and no one would enter unless they had the disease. If my memory is not at fault, Lewis Mann in the winter of 1854 – then a merchant in Coudersport, contracted the disease in New York – and quite a number of persons caught the contagious disease, but none died, and for the very reason that the Borough Council and every citizen did their duty.

Now every thinking, reasoning person knows that diphtheria is just as contagious as smallpox, and the death list of the former is one hundred per cent greater than the latter, and why is this? because the people have not been educated to fear and dread diphtheria like the smallpox; and doctors and county papers are, I fear, sadly neglecting a humane duty in this regard.

The Board of Health of New York has issued a circular "How to tell Diphtheria." "Give heed," it says, "the moment you observe signs in your child of unwonted weakness, fatigue or physical debility, particularly if it is accompanied with a little fever. Make the child frequently open its mouth, so that you can observe its throat. It is in the throat that they lay observer will first observe any certain signs of diphtheria. Never mind how red or inflamed the throat may appear. That does not indicate the disease. But the instant you see a white spot and detect a bad odor run for a doctor. The white spot will grow. Other white spots will appear, and eventually they will run together in great blotches if the disease is not checked. The time to summon medical assistance is before these spots run together.

While you are "running for a doctor," there is much to do for those who are at home – as far as possible, put a room in order for your sick child, at once put it in a profuse sweat, and the best and quickest way that I know of, is to boil dry corn in the ear for say, forty minutes, wrap the hot, steaming corn in cloths or papers and place all around the patient, keep well covered and let perspiring continue for an hour, rub entirely dry and change the clothing, giving quite often a little whisky, procure tar if possible and fumigate the room at least twice a day, if this cannot be obtained, burn sulphur, procure at a drug store chloride of lime and place in your room, slack at least twice a day a small piece of lime near the bed. I know of a very skillful physician who has had a very extensive practice, who says when the patient is old enough, he burns tar in an ordinary clay pipe, has the person fumigate the mouth and blow the smoke out through the nose.

Herewith find the following important suggestions of Dr. James Crane, president of the Brooklyn Health Department, recently issued, as far as possible his suggestions should be followed:

"Diphtheria and scarlet fever are highly contagious diseases, attacking persons of all ages. They may be contracted from persons that are already affected, from the clothing they have worn and from everything which has been in the room with them. Even the walls of the room may infect persons coming into it after the patient has recovered, unless the poison is destroyed. In order to prevent their spread in a family or house where they exist and to promote the recovery of the persons attacked, the following simple measures should be conscientiously and rigidly carried out, thereby preventing much suffering and saving human life: - An upper, sunny room, provided if possible with an open fireplace, and with no other children on the same floor, should be arranged for the patient by removing everything from it which can be spared, such as books, clothing and window curtains, remembering that when once the patient has entered the room nothing can with safety be removed until disinfected or fumigated. One or two adults should take the entire charge of the patient, under no circumstances coming in contact with other persons, more especially with children. Open windows and open fireplaces, with fire in them day and night, avoiding drafts and chilly air, protect the sick and those who nurse them. Nothing should be removed from the room when the patient has once entered it, until it has been thoroughly disinfected or fumigated.

"Procure from a drug store one pound of suplhate or zinc; the price should not exceed thirty cents. Put into an ordinary water pail eight tablespoonsful of sulphate of zinc and four of common salt, and to this add one gallon of boiling water. This disinfecting solution is to be kept in the room, and into it should be placed and kept for one hour very article of soiled clothing, bedding, handkerchiefs, etc. When they are removed from this they should be placed in boiling water before being washed. The dishes and spoons used by the patient should be put into boiling water before they are permitted to leave the room. Remember that every article which is in the room can convey the disease and that nothing should go from it until the poison which it might carry is destroyed.

"See that the whole house from cellar to attic is clean. Keep the cellar dry, well ventilated and well white-washed, never allow, even for a day, garbage or other filth to be kept in it. Open the windows of sleeping rooms every day as long a time as possible, fresh air being an excellent disinfectant."

In my next I will treat of the origin and spread of this disease.

The Potter Enterprise
Wednesday Evening, February 23, 1881 – Vol. VII, No. 40

- If you want a drink of cider, call on Frank Brown, for it is a girl and weighs ten pounds.

- The following item we copy from the Shingle House *Palladium*. - Married. - At the Presbyterian parsonage at Bradford, Pa., by Rev. J. R. Findly, Feb. 8, 1881. Mr. Frank J. Newton, Junior member of the firm of Jones, Dodge & co., Rixford, Pa., and Miss Ruth Russel of Buffalo, N.Y. A useful and successful life is wished from them by their many friends.

DIED.

WALLACE – In Coudersport, at the residence of Wallace Absom, Linnie, daughter of John and Sarah (Smith) Wallace. Aged 9 years, 7 months and 18 days.

SMITH – February 18, Arthur, infant son of Wm. H. and Sophronia Smith, aged 10 months and 2 days.

Rest little Arthur, on Jesus' breast,
Where he has promised we all may find rest.

- From the annual report of the inspectors of the Western Penitentiary it appears the M'Kean county was charged during the past year with 74 prisoners, who were supported 14,965 days. The value of their labor was $3,701, and the deficiency charged on their account to the county is $897.90. No other county of the thirty-two from which prisoners were sent outside of Allegheny shows such a record as this. In crime as in wealth, M'Kean leads them all. The next highest number, thirty-six, were sent from Crawford. Potter county sends five. – *Sunday News*.

Diphtheria.

Ed. Enterprise: In last week's paper facts were presented for the consideration of the people, showing clearly and unmistakably the contagious character of this disease, and this week we promised an article on the origin and spread of the malady. But at the suggestion of a leading physician here, the following is published. As every person that reads the papers this winter knows that the city of Brooklyn, N.Y., is sorely afflicted with this scourge, and one doctor has acquired eminence in his manner of treatment. A few days ago the New York *Sun* reporter interviewed him, and this warning to parents ought to have great influence with the people of this county:

"I have had two new cases of diphtheria this morning, and I was called in so late that I have great fears as to the result of both of them. You see the great thing is to meet the disease before it has acquired strength, and I impress upon all my patients who have children the necessity of sending for me the moment any of their little ones exhibit such symptoms as lassitude, sick headache or even a sore throat, thought he latter is by no means an early indication. Of course I cannot always tell positively whether the case is one of diphtheria or not, but if I have the slightest doubt on the subject I act as though I was certain, and at once administer remedies to check the complaint. The practice of waiting for developments is, I think, a fatal one; for diphtheria once developed, is a desperately hard thing to deal with.

Potter County, Pennsylvania Potpourri – Volume I
1880 through 1884

"A few winters ago I gave up my general practice to a brother physician, and went down among the tenement houses and poor quarters where diphtheria was raging, to try to learn something about the disease. I think I succeeded. I believe I can now check it even when somewhat advanced, but it cost me far more than I anticipated. I used to carry gumdrops about in my pocket to give to the sick children, and one day after I had changed my clothing and disinfected myself, I went home to my family. I had taken the gumdrops out of the pocket of the clothes I had taken off, and I took them home with me and gave one to my little boy. Half an hour afterward I was called out again, and when I returned four hours later, my wife told me that the child was ill. The moment I looked at him I saw that he had diphtheria, and I was horrified to see the progress the disease had made. But if he had been a strange child I believe I could have stopped it. As it was, I could not bear to see his sufferings, so I entrusted the case to another physician, and within twenty-four hours from the time of his seizure he died on the sofa you are sitting on now.

"And here let me say that one of the most terrible blunders that parents of children are apt to make is in letting their little ones go our, or carelessly stray into draughts after the disease appears to be wholly eradicated. Such appearances, my experience has taught me are almost invariably deceptive. The germs of the disorder still lurk in the system, and the slightest cold or indisposition is pretty sure to bring on a relapse that no skill can cure. A little white hearse went away from a house a few yards up this street this morning. It carried to the cemetery the remains of a little boy who was stricken down with diphtheria last week. He seemed to be quite recovered, and the day before yesterday he was allowed to go out. He caught a cold, and the disease returned with a malignity that defied treatment. He died last night, and under the orders of the health board he had to be buried immediately."

TOWNSHIP ELECTIONS.
ABBOTT.

Constable, Louis Hoppe; Clerk, August Voss; Treasurer, Fred Bodler; Auditor, Henry Gnau; Supervisor, Henry Gressell; School Directors, George Rexford, 59, Eberhard Gnau, 64, John Schmantz, 29, Joel Boley, 23; Inspectors, W. Sandbach, John Hug; Judge, Isaac Bailey; Assessor, Louis Hoppe.

ALLEGANY.

Supervisor, W. A. Gardner; School Directors, J. L. Collins, 28, C. Ford, 97, E. B. Morley, 68; Constable, I. Kidney; Assessor, W. H. Mattison; Clerk, E. L. Heggie; Treasurer, E. E. Kelley; Inspectors, C. E. Tucker, E. Nelson; Judge, J. Gardner; Auditor, E. Haskell.

BINGHAM.

Supervisors, John Henry, A. N. Spencer; Constable, M. N. Babcock; Treasurer, A. N. Clark; School Directors, A. A. Johnson, 89, J. H. Holbert, 111, Joseph Daniels, 88, J. E. Harvey, 30; Assessor, D. Worden; Clerk, L. B. Lewis; Judge, Joseph Coulston; Auditor, K. H. Howe; Inspectors, C. M. Burt, R. E. Grover.

COUDERSPORT.

Burgess, F. W. Knox; Council, D. F. Glassmire, Sr., D. C. Larrabee; School Directors, O. H. Crosby, A. B. Mann; Poor Masters, H. C. Olmsted, Isaac Benson; Constable, Edson Hyde; High Constable, Erastus Lewis; Assessor, Wm. Shear; Auditor, W. C. Rennells, 3 years; Judge of Election, C. S. Jones; Inspectors, Benj. Rennells, O. H. Crosby.

CLARA.

Supervisors, G. Green, J. M. Tyler; Inspectors, Jacob Cole, G. R. Fosmer; School Directors, J. L. Allen, 32, Hiram Baker, 10, G. Green, 20; Constable, O. E. Corsaw; Auditor, B. A. Green; Clerk, James Cole; Treasurer, Jesse Burdic; Assessor, Timothy Glines; Judge, Peter Beatman.

EULALIA.

Supervisor, Justus Mehring; School Directors, Henry Ingraham, B. Clark; Auditors, J. M. Spafford, Horace Yeomans; Treasurer, Samuel Thompson; Clerk, Jacob Lehman; Assessor, C. C. Breunle; Constable, S. F. Butler; Judge, Almeron Nelson; Inspectors, Sherman Baker, A. D. Colcord.

GENESEE.

Justice of the Peace, V. M. Stannard; Supervisor, Bryan McGinnis; Inspectors, James McHale, S. Hurd; Judge, Patrick Roach; Auditor, John Coulston; Assessor, Mat Moran; Constable, Wm. Atherton; Clerk, C. W. Parker; Treasurer, John Moran; School Directors, J. J. Waterman, A. C. Race; For the cattle law, 35; against the cattle law, 72.

HARRISON.

Supervisor, M. R. Swetland, L. H. Rooks; Constable, A. E. Martin; Assessor, G. P. Badgero; Clerk, J. D. Stevens; School Directors, S. K. Stevens, 87, W. Barto, 40, A. G. Dodge, 80, D. W. Coffin, 105, C. C. Haskins, 96, E. Rooks, 56, George D. Litner, 71; Treasurer, Homer Hurlburg; Judge, E. C. Outman; Inspectors, John Olney, Samuel Stone; Auditor, J. S. Haynes.

HEBRON.

Supervisors, E. E. Swift, C. A. Estes; School Directors, John Schollard, 33, J. H. Dingman, 97, A. P. Vaughn, 75, C. D. McKee, 64; Auditor, S. P. Reynolds; Inspectors, Isaac Whittum, E. E. Swift; Judge, A. Ball; Assessor, W. B. Lent; Constable, R. M. Post; Clerk, F. N. Ayars; Treasurer, E. M. Bly.

HECTOR.

Constable, E. C. Dimon; Auditor, Geo. Larrison; Assessor, Albert Wilbur; Supervisor, E. S. Worden; Treasurer, H. R. Douglass; Clerk, E. C. Dimon; Judge, Charles Corey; Inspectors, E. J. Abbey, J. S. Little; School Directors, A. D. Rogers, 44, C. N. Kilbourne, 52, J. Waters, 51, Ross Cripen, 25.

HOMER.

Supervisor, Walter Edgcomb; Clerk, A. W. Lathrop; Constable, Eli Glasby; Treasurer, John Taubert; School Directors, A. W. Lathrop, 5, J. Gordnier, 15, J. V. Gates, 20; H. Edgcomb, 20; Judge, C. F. Younglove; Inspectors, H. M. Case, Curtis Baker; Assessor, James Bundy; Auditor, G. W. Berfield; Justice of the Peace, W. C. Chesbro.

KEATING.

Constable, E. A. Whitney; Supervisor, H. Harris; Treasurer, H. Bridges; Assessor, E. Z. Dingee; Clerk, Wm. Dingee; Judge, Frank Klein; Inspectors, Austin Crosby, 7, C. W. Dingee, 5, X. Fleshuts, 5; Auditors, G. C. Lewis, F. M. Younglove; School Directors, X. Fleshutz, G. C. Lewis.

LEWISVILLE.

Constable, A. Cady; Burgess, Perry Brigham; Council, H. A. Gridley, B. J. Cushing, C. E. Burt, B. L. Easton, James Nickerson, Charles Erlbeck; Judge, Charles Monroe; Inspectors, O. R. Bassett, David E. Hosley, W. W. Farnsworth; Assessor, C. E. Hosley; Overseers of the Poor, W. W. Farnsworth, C. E. Baker; Auditor, Wm. Daniels; High constable, S. C. Baker.

OSWAYO.

Treasurer, H. H. Munson; Supervisor, George Markham; Justice of the Peace, A. S. Lyman; Clerk, Samuel Beebe; Assessor, A. S. Lyman; Constable, J. H. Stilson; School Directors, J. T. Lockwood, J. F. Morrs; Auditor, J. B. Stewart; Judge, Romeo Estes; Inspectors, George Head, T. J. Farnum.

PIKE.

Supervisor, G. W. Sutton; Treasurer, H. M. Tice; Auditor, S. P. Merrick; Constable, Dan Crandall; Assessor, O. Blackman; Clerk, F. A. Brown; Judge, M. Impson; Inspector, E. Wheaton; School Directors, H. M. Tice, 32, M. V. Prouty, 27, James Locey, 30.

PORTAGE.

Justice of the Peace, E. O. Austin; Supervisor, D. A. Everett; Constable, D. A. Everett; School Directors, John Brownlee, 17, Jacob Peet, 9, L. D. Ripple, 2, D. A. Everett, 6; Judge, M. J. Young; Auditor, Jacob Peet; Inspectors, C. C. Burdett, Rob't Brownlee; Assessor, F. P. Austin; Clerk, E. O. Austin; Treasurer, W. L.Clark.

PLEASANT VALLEY.

Constable, J. L. Yentzer; Assessor, S. M. Beckwith; School Directors, J. L. Yentzer, 27, J. P. Reed, 15, Philander Reed, 13; Inspectors, Elmer Deming, Ransom Burt; Judge, H. D. North; Supervisor, Henry Yentzer; Clerk, Rob't McDowell; Treasurer, J. V. Reed; Auditor, Earnest Lamp.

ROULET.

Justice of the Peace, Lyman Burt; Constable, John Burt; Supervisor, D. P. Jordan; Assessor, N. French; Clerk, Milo Lyman; School Directors, D. J. Caulkins, Wm. Grosbeck; Judge, E. N. Meachum; Auditor, Wm. Wiloughby; Poor Masters, Leroy Lyman, L. B. Yentzer; Inspectors, Henry Tauscher, Joseph Sampson.

SYLVANIA.

Supervisors, A. R. Jordan and G. H. Quimby; Treasurer, Joseph Hall; Assessor, Samuel B. Haskins; Auditor, Andrew Burleson; School Directors, W. C. Quimby, Henry Wheeler, J. M. Rees, John P. Havens; Inspectors of Election, Leroy Haskins, James Glaspy; Judge of Election, Henry Rees; Constable, Andrew Haskins.

Potter County, Pennsylvania Potpourri – Volume I
1880 through 1884

SHARON.
Supervisor, James Harvey; Constable, L. A. Nichols; Town Clerk, George W. Dodge; Assessor, N. C. Newton; Treasurer, John Voorhees; Auditor, L. H. Kinney; School Directors, W. A. Nichols, Elby Holmes; Judge of Election, Andrew Bradford; Inspector of Election, G. C. Lyon.

SWEDEN.
Judge, R. Snyder; Inspector, B. N. Roberts; School Directors, M. O. Harris, 20, H. J. Neefe, 46, Lyman Toombs, 27; Constable, John Freeman; Supervisor, C. F. Neefe; Clerk, J. W. Neefe; Treasurer, C. C. Chase; Assessor, Marion Herrington; Justice of the Peace, A. Chase; Auditors, C. D. Corsaw, W. W. Benson.

SUMMIT.
Supervisor, J. H. Johnston; Clerk, C. H. Ruscher; Treasurer, Wash. Haskins; Constable, Hugh Haskins; Assessor, Lester Watson; Auditor, A. D. Ayers; Judge of Election, James Nelson; Inspector, Geo. Morton; School Directors, J. H. Terry, 19, James Watson, 32, C. W. Rennells, 13, Merrick Jackson, 14, James Reed, 13.

STEWARDSON.
Treasurer, Martin Joerg; Clerk, Henry Andresen; Auditors, George Jordan, Wm. McCoy, E. Joerg; Constable, Geo. Jordan; Justice of the Peace, Wm. G. Campbell; School Directors, Martin Joerg, Wm. Y. Campbell, Wm. McCoy; Supervisor, Wesley Allen; Assessor, Martin Joerg; Judge, W. G. Campbell; Inspectors, Martin Joerg, Wesley Allen.

ULYSSES.
Justice of the Peace, E. Carpenter; Supervisor, W. Joseph; Auditor, W. Suhr; Treasurer, A. Burt; Clerk, H. T. Reynolds; Constable, E. B. Monroe; Assessor, John Francis; Judge, E. Merrill; Inspectors, C. Gridley, V. E. Freeman; School Directors, W. R. Clark, E. O. Bennitt.

WEST BRANCH.
Constable, B. F. Burrows; Supervisors, Gottleib Traub, Henry Deisroth; Clerk, A. Bisbee; Assessor, L. F. Rice; Auditor, W. S. Moore; Treasurer, Geo. W. Fowler; School Directors, Sidney Burrows, 44, A. Bisbee, 42, Geo. Mitchell, 25, Willis Connable, 23; Inspectors, Eli Main, Charles Hehl; Judge of Election, N. K. Prouty.

WHARTON.
Treasurer, A. J. Bailey; Supervisor, C. L. Ayers; Clerk, W. G. Wilbur; Auditor, J. M. Devoll; Assessor, F. Devanport; Constable, J. M. Walker; School Directors, F. M. Berfield, Thomas Logue; Judge, S. F. Horton; Inspectors, Sam'l Card, Perry Devoll.

The Potter Enterprise
Wednesday Evening, March 2, 1881 – Vol. VII, No. 41

BORN.

COBB – In Coudersport, Feb. 25, to Mr. and Mrs. L. H.Cobb, twins – a boy and a girl.

OWEN – In Coudersport, Feb. 26, to Mr. and Mrs. A. H. Owen, a son.

MARRIED.

STORY – TILBURGH – Feb. 27, by T. R. Stratton, Jesse Story of Brookland, Pa., and Alice Tilburgh of Raymonds Corners, Pa.

School Report.

From Superintendent Hollenbeck we have received a copy of the Report of the Superintendent of Public Instruction for 1880. The report exhibits for Potter county the following:

No. of Schools, 141.
Average No. of months taught, 5.95.
No. of Male Teachers, 80.
No. of Female Teachers, 141.
Average salary of Males per month, $23.78.
Average salary of Females per month, $16.94.
No. of Male scholars, 1822.
No. of Female scholars, 1769.

Average cost per month, $1.00. The lowest being Sunderlinville Independent, .44. The highest, Stewardson $3.23. Coudersport, $1.32.

Total amount of tax levied for school purposes, $19,778.03.

- Our old and valued friend, Laroy Lyman of Potter county, paid us a visit yesterday. In answer to the question whether he had hunted any this winter he replied: "No, not much. I thought I would let the boys beat me once, but they failed to do it. I have only killed 22 deer, 17 skunks, 18 foxes, 1 bear, 2 coons and 3 mink – that's all." Mr. Lyman is unquestionably one of the greatest and most successful hunters that ever tramped through the woods of Pennsylvania. Mr. Lyman says the published reports that "Jim Jacobs, the Seneca bear hunter, had been found dead in a rude cabin in a lonely part of Potter county last week and buried near the hut," was all moonshine. He says the people of his county do not bury even Indians in the woods near their "huts." – *M'Kean Miner.*

The Potter Enterprise
Wednesday Evening, March 9, 1881 – Vol. VII, No. 42

- The heaviest snow storm of the season, Thursday evening and Friday of last week. Snow fell to the depth of twelve or fourteen inches in Coudersport, on the hills it was deeper.

Beating and Abduction of a Negro Girl.

Upon last Thursday evening, March 3d, between the hours of eight and nine o'clock, there was consummated, in this village, the last act of a social outrage which began several weeks ago. The whole transaction from first to last, brings vividly before the mind similar scenes, south of "Mason and Dixon's Line," in the palmy days of slavery. The facts of the case are substantially as follows:

On the tenth of last February, Mr. T. B. Brown, civil engineer, for years a citizen of Coudersport, and now living on West street opposite the *Journal* office, became enraged at his servant girl, Miss Minnie Barnes (colored), because she failed properly to prepare for use, some linen handkerchiefs, and beat and kicked her so brutally that her whole body, according to competent witnesses, from foot to shoulder, was a mass of cut and bruises. Mr. Brown closed the affair at that time by kicking the girl out of doors. Stunned, bewildered, the girl wandered up the hill west of the village, and in the evening made her way, benumbed and stiff, to the house of Mr. A. F. Hollenbeck, county superintendent. Mrs. Hollenbeck kindly cared for the sufferer and afterward assisted her to the house of Mr. Green, a barber, and the only colored man in the place.

Mr. Green at once called in Dr. Buck to examine Miss Barnes, and supported by the sympathy and advice of a large body of our citizens, shortly commenced legal proceedings against Brown; who waving a trial before a justice, plead guilty and gave bail for appearance at court (Mr. A. B. Mann signing his bond). Mr. Mann has, we learn, since withdrawn his bail.

Thus matters stood until last Thursday evening, when Mr. Brown assisted by Mr. Elvin Womelsdorf, enticed her from the kitchen of Mr. Erastus Lewis, whose employ she then was, by means of a colored woman, whom report calls her mother and for whom it is said Brown had sent to Philadelphia.

Immediately upon securing the girl by this strategem, they put her and the woman aboard a conveyance furnished by Chambers, a Bradford oil operator, and Mr. Hugh Kernan of this place drove them to Wellsville. There the two women took the early morning train east, and are probably now in Philadelphia.

It seems that Justice has, for the present, been robbed of her lawful prey; and that the perpetrator of these infamous acts will go unpunished except as he may feel indignation and merited condemnation of an insulted and incensed community; and these he cannot escape.

The above was written by one of the most conservative men in Coudersport, and is a correct account of what is heard on the street. We hardly believe Mr. Brown is as black as he is painted, neither would we go to the other extreme. The taking away of the girl raised a furor that was likely to lead to persecution instead of prosecution. Monday the case was settled, we are informed, by Mr. Brown paying $200. The money consideration is but a small part of the punishment. The story of the beating and abduction, probably exagerated, will be spread over a large section. And yet none can say it is not just. People must learn, or ought to learn, that the law is not to be trifled with. We have had altogether too much of that in Coudersport the past year – enough to disgrace any people.

The Potter Enterprise
Wednesday Evening, March 16, 1881 – Vol. VII, No. 43

Allegany. Geo. Reves is the happy man – a fine girl added to his family.

MARRIED.

GEE – TURNER – In Oswayo, Feb. 6, 1881, by Samuel Beebe, Esq., Mr. Frank Gee, of Allegany, and Miss Emma Turner, of Oswayo.

- Mrs. John Abson of Coudersport, died on Sunday night of diphtheria. This is the first fatal case in the borough.

Raymond. Death is doing a fearful work in the south part of Allegany township. Three deaths in less than a week; and yesterday another. Diphtheria has taken two children from the family of Anson Weaver, and two more very sick.

Shingle House. Last week Mr. Burdick and his wife, aged people, whose home was at East Sharon, died within a short time of each other, and were buried at the same time.

- Mrs. Joseph Mann of Coudersport, was buried on Sunday last. She has long been a resident of this place, and will be sadly missed by many. She was noted for a kind heart, and her charity – no case of suffering ever appealed to her in vain.

- On the 24th of February, Mr. Ray Hurd, of Genesee Forks, caught in a steel trap, a fine American Eagle, measuring seven feet eight inches from tip to tip of outstretched wings. The bird is now alive and doing well and is prized very highly by its owner.

Kate Smith.

Recently Miss Kate Smith, a daughter of Daniel Smith of Roulet, was brought home from Bradford a raving maniac. She is receiving the best care possible, but at last report her condition had not improved. The Bradford *Star* of the 7th inst., speaks of this sad case as follows:

"Kate Smith, aged thirty-two years, is confined in a small room in the City Infirmary. The poor woman is insane. The causes that led to the overthrow of her mind seems to be a disappointment in a love affair. Miss Smith formerly lived at Roulet, Potter county, and has for some time been employed as a domestic in this city. Eight years ago she met and loved Humphrey Hunt, but her parents objected to the match and Hunt some time ago was married to another and is now living at Derrick City.

"Miss Smith about two weeks ago came to the house of Charles A. Terry in Harrisburg and then for the first time showed symptoms of insanity. She talked about her lost love and raved day and night. A doctor was called and the woman, at his order, confined in a room. She escaped through a window, and boarding a

Potter County, Pennsylvania Potpourri – Volume I
1880 through 1884

train for Derrick, went to the house of her old lover, which she entered in a fury, driving the family out of doors and smashing up the furniture. She was finally captured and yesterday was brought to the city in charge of four men and placed in the Infirmary. During the day she sent for two or three clergymen. She acted rationally for a time, but her sane freaks did not last long and she always closed with a torrent of abuse. She seems to have a particular hatred of masons. Her case is indeed a sad one."

Church Notes.

"If the Lord will," Lenton services will be held in Christ Church parish, Coudersport, as follows: On Sundays, (in the Baptist Church), morning service and sermon at 10-30 o'clock; evening service and sermon at 7 o'clock. Sunday School and Bible Class immediately after the morning service.

Week day services at the Dent House, the residence of Mr. E. N. Stebbins. – On Wednesday evenings at 7-30 o'clock, service with choir practice.

On Friday evening, service with lecture or reading appropriate to the solemn season. All are cordially invited to attend.

The Ladies' Aid Society of Christ Church Parish next Thursday evening at the residence of Mrs. Miles White.

Court Minutes.

March 7th, 1881. S. F. Wilson, President Judge. Messrs. Hammond and Chappel, Associates.

Constables of different townships made returns.

Commonwealth vs George Clark and Eugene Clark. Larceny. Eugene Clark discharged.

Grand Jury called and sworn. L. B. Cole, foreman, A. Chase, constable.

Commonwealth vs T. Benton Brown. Assault and battery. *Nol pros.*

O. D. Jackson vs Effie Jackson. Amended libel ordered. C. M. Allen appointed commissioner.

H. J. Olmsted vs Homer township. Rule on Supervisors to levy special tax; returnable forthwith.

Constables elect from all the townships in the county duly qualified.

Jacob H. Elwell vs Elizabeth Elwell. Divorce awarded.

A. B. Mann appointed guardian of James Fremont Carey, Carrie May Carey and Frank Carey.

C. Hunsicker for use vs Jacob Gamble, *et al.* Jury find for plaintiff the land described, to be released on payment in thirty days of $2609.98.

Joseph Mann vs F. P. Brooks. Jury find for plaintiff the land described, to be released on payment within thirty days of $5,208.87.

Commonwealth vs Abram Jones. Netting wild pigeons. *Nol pros.*

Commonwealth vs Gilbert Adams. Bail $200 for appearance at next term.

Berick & Tapel vs Wm. Radde & Sons. Writ order published.

In matter of the estate of W. W. Brown, insolvent. Rule granted on J. M. Spafford, assignee, requiring him to appear and exhibit accounts, and show cause why full amount should not be paid the creditors.

R. & J. Doty for use vs Genesee township. Rule on Supervisors to levy a special tax.

H. H. Dent for use vs Jackson township. Rule to levy special tax.

James Clark for use vs John Eldridge. Rule to continue; proceedings to stay.

B. C. Cole vs Hannah Cole. Divorce. Sheriff to make proclamation.

Emma M. Miller vs Charles Miller. C. M. Allen appointed commissioner to take testimony.

M. E. Olmsted vs Summit township. Rule to levy special tax.

Hannah M. Stryker, administratrix vs Sylvania township. Rule to levy special tax.

Commonwealth vs Eldred Woodcock. Netting wild pigeons. *Nol pros.*

Commonwealth vs D. Lewis, James Lewis and James Patterson. Assault and battery. Indictment squashed.

Sarah E. Dunn appointed guardian of minor children of Michael Dunn, dec'd.

Commonwealth vs Hiram Graham. Adultery. Sentenced to pay a fine of $1 to the Overseers of the Poor of Hector township, and the costs of prosecution; to pay to Francis Guernsey, the mother of the child the sum of $25, lying in expenses, $75 for the support of the child to date, and to give bond for payment of $1.50 per week for the support of the child until it arrives at the age of seven years, and stand committed until sentence is complied with.

Commonwealth vs Peleg Burdic. Selling liquor; *nol pros.* Defendant and bail discharged.

Commonwealth vs Christopher Dennis. Rape. Held in sum of $500 for appearance at next term.

Commonwealth vs George Northrup, James Waters and William Fay. Assault and battery and riot. Bail $200 for appearance at next term.

John Grom appointed guardian of Theodore, Catherine and Lenora Grom.

Commonwealth vs Walter Reer. Open lewdness. Not guilty. Defendant to pay two-thirds of the costs and the prosecutor to pay one-third.

Catherine Cole vs William Cole. Divorce awarded.

Commonwealth vs N. F. Beckwith. Larceny of timber. Bail $200 for appearance at next term.

William M. Perkins vs W. H. Lewis and Linus Evans. Jury return a verdict for plaintiff in sum of $50 and costs.

Commonwealth vs Leonard King. Assault and battery. Not a true bill. Marshall Gross to pay costs.

Commonwealth vs James Kenyon. Fornication and bastardy. Bail $500 for appearance at next term.

Commonwealth vs M. Jordon. Assault and battery. Bench warrant issued.

Commonwealth vs Ed J. Russell. Larceny. Not a true bill.

Commonwealth vs Daniel Hopkins. Selling liquor; true bill; bail $200 for appearance at next term.

Commonwealth vs James Lewis, David Lewis and James Patterson. Riot and assault and battery. True bill; not guilty. Defendants to pay two-thirds of the costs, and prosecutor, Ira Grover, to pay one-third.

Potter County, Pennsylvania Potpourri – Volume I
1880 through 1884

Commonwealth vs Titus Locey. Selling liquor. True bill; bail $200 for appearance at next term.

Commonwealth vs Mathias Schmidt. Selling liquor. True bill; bail $200 for appearance at next term.

Charles N. Wilber vs Mary A. Wilber. Divorce. D. W. Haven appointed commissioner to take testimony.

Commonwealth vs Freeman Ayers. Assault and battery. Not a true bill. County to pay costs.

Commonwealth vs Leonard King. Selling liquor. True bill; bail $200 for appearance at next term.

J. H. Harrison for use of Mary M. Goodman vs C. D. & J. S. VanDeboe. Plaintiff acknowledges payment in full of judgment and costs.

Commonwealth vs Wesley McDowell. Disorderly house. True bill. Bail $200 for appearance at next term.

Commonwealth vs Mason Nelson. Selling liquor. True bill; bail $100 for appearance at next court.

W. T. Burt for use vs Pike township. Rule to levy a special tax.

C. W. Beach vs Hector township. Court order a special tax of ten mills.

William M. Eaton vs Rupert A. Rosa. Rule on plaintiff why judgment should not be opened. Returnable next term.

Alice VanHorn vs P. C. VanHorn. Divorce granted.

Commonwealth vs John Dery. Surety of the Peace. Defendant discharged.

Adoption of Lenora Moore. Court direct that said child shall assume the name of Lenora Schneider, and have all the rights of a child and heir of Wm. Schneider, and be subject to the duties of a child.

Judgment for want of appearance. John D. Merranville vs Burten Crittenden; Thomas B. French vs Avery and Mitchell; McEwen Bros. vs Avery & Mitchell; James Macken vs Genesee Independent School District; Bridget Clancey vs Patrick McHale; C. Smith vs W. T. Jones; J. G. Bennett vs C. W. Stiles and B. Dodge; same vs same; M. E. Olmsted vs West Branch township; J. S. Bartoo vs J. M. Walker; Robert Roy vs Stephen Horton; Sylvester Chesbro vs Wm. M. Earle; A. Solomon vs C. Clark Trask; White & Lyman vs Ira Bartholomew, with notice to S. B. Pomeroy, garnishee; J. G. Bennett vs E. M. and D. R. Stiles; George Fox vs Bernard Teuscher; Margaret C. Benton vs Daniel Hunter; P. A. Stebbins, Jr., vs Jacob Reed and Jacob Reed, Jr.; Eli Spencer vs Abram Goodnoe; C. S. Jones & Co. for use vs D. M. Westfall; F. W. Knox vs Stewardson township; same vs A. W. Andrews; F. H. Arnold vs D. W. Moore; C. S. Jones vs Anna Babcock; P. A. Stebbins, Jr. vs A. W. Andrews; C. S. Jones for use vs Virgil Jones; Wm. V. Keating vs D. P. Reed; Lucas Cushing for use vs Peter Thatcher.

Joseph Mann vs Luke Stevens. Court direct this case to be put at issue by entry of plea of not guilty.

Mary A. McDonald vs Genesee Independent School District. Jury find for plaintiff in sum of $49.68.

Anna Belle Seibert vs John Seibert. Divorce awarded.

Lydia M. Clark vs James Clark. Divorce granted.

Hiram Knickerbacker vs Lucy Ann Knickerbacker. Divorce granted.

Daniel Monroe, Sheriff of Potter county, acknowledged deeds for property sold at Sheriff's sale to

Charles Willing, 132 5-10 acres in Hector township, for $25, sold as the property of William Loucks.

Methodist Episcopal church of Harrison Valley incorporated.

Virginia Quinnette vs Edwin Quinnette. Alias subpoena in divorce ordered.

Bail forfeited and respited in commonwealth vs R. H. Haynes; vs Miles Higley; vs Marshall Gross; vs George W. King.

Veniries issued for 36 traverse jurors and 24 grand jurors for June term next.

The Potter Enterprise
Wednesday Evening, March 23, 1881 – Vol. VII, No. 44

- Nelson Monroe, Sweden, lost a child with diphtheria, last Sunday.

- Wm. J. Latta, one of the oldest residents of Harrison township, died March __, aged 88 years, six months and five days.

- A home in Allegany made desolate by diphtheria in seven days. The four little boys of Anson Weaver have died as follows: On Friday, March 4th, Charles, aged 6 years, 8 months and 8 days; on March 7th, Fred, aged 9 months and 24 days; March 9th, Clinton, aged 2 years, 7 months and 5 days and March 9th, Lewis, aged 4 years, 8 months and eight days.

Oswayo. A few days since occurred the first fatal accident at the tannery. Mr. John Manning, working as a night hand, (it is supposed, for no one was present when the accident occurred) discovered that a large thirty-inch belt was slipping and attempted to scatter tan dust upon it to make it stick. In some manner he was caught in the belt – either caught by some article of clothing, which hardly seems probably, or fell into the belt, and before he could recover himself was drawn to the wheel. His head was literally crushed, and he sustained other bruises about the shoulders. The large belt was broken by the strain. The accident occurred about eight o'clock, and although everything was done for him that friends could do, and prompt medical skill employed, he breathed his last about midnight, leaving a wife and one child to mourn his untimely end.

DIED.

ROGERS – At Raymond, February 27, 1881, of consumption, Herbert E., son of John W. and Almira Rogers, aged 22 years, 6 months and 18 days.

At this time when the dark winged angel seems commissioned to fly swiftly through the land, sending his fatal arrows thick and fast, to so many dwellings, it might seem almost intrusive to burden your columns with more than the above notice. But the peculiar circumstances, the high esteem in which our young friend was held by the people generally, and especially by the students of the school from which he was so abruptly taken, together with the sadness of my own heart, at the loss of a member of my own school, and Bible class, urge me to ask room to notice some incidents connected with this early close of life.

For several years his health has been failing, but he has prepared for teaching, and with a strong ambition fired by the desire to do great good in the world, and thus cause his parents to be justly proud of their only son – had found that deceitful and relentless foe, consumption to the last day of his life. His parents, knowing his frail condition, would gladly have kept him at home the past winter, to care for him tenderly; but nothing could induce him to lay down the care and cease teaching.

For some weeks he had been preparing for a spelling exercise and exhibition which was held on February 18, which in addition to his school work was too much. On Sunday, February 20th, he was with us in Church and Sunday School for the last time; cheerful, but going to his home and a sick bed, never to return to the work that was waiting for him – disease was now fast doing its fatal work, but he sent several messages to his pupils, that he should "be with them on Monday." Mr. Smith, one of the directors, called to see him, he expressed regrets that he was not able to go on with the school, and wished to engage it for the summer term. Through the week, as his strength failed and his sufferings increased, he manifested strong desires to live to do good to others, and thus make his parents happy and to enjoy the home so dear to him; pleading with his mother to relieve and save him, as she had always before been able by care and gentle nursing to do.

When told that no earthly power could save him, as the cold damp of death was on his brow, he replied: "God can if 'tis best, if not all is right." Although clinging to life to the last hour, when fully convinced that his time to die had come, he was calm, and expressed regrets for unfaithfulness.

As his eyes were growing dim, he asked that the lamps be made brighter, that he might "see us the last," and wished us to "stand by him until all is over. All has been done for me that could be. Tell my scholars all good bye, thank them for their kindness the past winter. Good bye, my parents – don't be afraid to work for God. My sufferings are almost over." And soon he gently fell asleep.

On Monday, February 28, he was indeed "with his scholars," not in the school room to teach from books, but in the church to teach from the silent coffin – a touching sight it was, those six young men slowly bearing the remains of their late friend, and a still more touching sight those pupils, wearing the badge of mourning, and taking their places near the relatives; and many were the moist eyes, as those children and youth with tears and sobs stood around the coffin. And as a last parting act those six young pallbearers, at the grave, carefully deposited a shovelful of earth on the lowered coffin, and sadly turned away.

In the Spring of 1878, Herbert united with the Presbyterian Church at Raymond, of which he has since been a consistent member, and although his walk was not always been sinless or perfect, we trust his faults may all be forgiven and his good example emulated by all his young friends, and especially his fellow members of the Bible class; and may his bereaved parents ever remember his injunction and "never be afraid to work for God."

Potter County, Pennsylvania Potpourri – Volume I
1880 through 1884

A. G. Presho, Sup't. Raymond S.S.

White Wash.

The following receipt for making whitewash is the best known, combining excellence and durability. Take a barrel and slack one bushel of freshly burned lime in it, by covering it with boiling water. After it is slacked add cold water enough to bring it to the consistency of good white-wash. Then disolve in water, and add one pound of white vitrol, (sulphate of zinc) and one quart of fine salt. To give this wash a cream color, add one-half pound of yellow ochre in powder. To give it a fawn color, add a pound of yellow ochre, and one-fourth of a pound of Indian red.

Coudersport Borough Ordinance No. 56.
An Ordinance establishing a Health Officer, and prescribing his duties and for other Purposes.

BE IT ORDAINED by the Burgess, *pro tem*, and Town Council of the Borough of Coudersport, and it is hereby ordained: -

THAT hereafter whenever any person within the limits of the said Borough of Coudersport, shall be ill with scarlet fever or typhoid fever, small-pox or diphtheria or any other disease which shall be declared by the Health Officer of the Borough to be contagious, infectious and dangerous, it shall be unlawful for any person except the necessary physician, nurse or nurses to visit the house wherein such person shall be ill of such disease, under a penalty of Five Dollars for each and every such visit by an unauthorized person, to be recovered as like amounts are now by law recoverable before the Burgess or any Justice of the Peace of said Borough. – And in the case of the death of any such person from such disease the body must be interred within twenty-four hours of the death of such person, and the funeral must be private, no person being permitted to attend such funeral except the immediate adult members of the family of the deceased and such other persons as may be necessary for the proper burial of the body.

And it is further ordained that the office of Health Officer be established and that his duties are prescribed to be as follows:

In case of the illness of any person from any of the aforementioned diseases or any other disease which in the opinion of the Health Officer shall be infectious or contagious, the Health Officer shall notify all persons, by printed notices to be posted on the premises where such person shall be ill, that there is a case of infectious disease on said premises and that all persons are warned not to enter therein under the penalty prescribed in the first section of this ordinance. And in case of the death of such person ill from such disease it shall be the duty of the Health Officer to see that the funeral is conducted according to the methods hereinbefore prescribed in this ordinance.

And that the clothing worn by the deceased and the bedding on which the deceased has lain shall be buried or burned, and that the house be thoroughly fumigated and the excrement and vomit from the deceased be buried at the depth of at least two feet. And the Health Officer is hereby empowered to enter the house wherein any such person is or may be ill or deceased of any such disease as is hereinbefore mentioned and enforce the provisions of this ordinance. Any and person hindering him in the discharge of his duties shall be liable to a fine of twenty-five dollars for each and every offence, to be recovered before the Burgess or any Justice of the Peace of said borough as like amounts are now by law recoverable.

And the Health Officer is hereby empowered at his discretion to abate any nuisance within the limits of the said borough of Coudersport on the written application of three citizens of said borough setting forth that said nuisance is dangerous to the health of the community of said borough.

H. J. Olmsted, Burgess, pro. tem.
Attest: Arthur B. Mann, Clerk.

The Potter Enterprise
Wednesday Evening, March 30, 1881 – Vol. VII, No. 45

BORN.
GRABE – In Coudersport, March 25th, to Mr. and Mrs. ___ Grabe, a son.

West Pike. Orm Blackman is the happy man this time – the first daughter – why shouldn't he be? Georgie says it is nicer than the twin lambs.

MARRIED.
CLARK – GROVER – At Bingham, on March 23, 1881, by Rev. Thomas L. Perry, William J. Clark and Miss Jennie A. Grover, both of Bingham.

ANDREWS – OLMSTED – At the home of the bride, Thursday morning, March 24th, by Rev. T. R. Stratton, Frank L. Andrews of Duke Centre, and Miss Mary W. Olmsted, of Coudersport.

West Pike. Two of Wm. Smith's children were buried in this burying ground last week – one Friday night and one Saturday night, both after dark, something which never happened here before. They died with diphtheria. Others are sick in the same family with it, but hopes are entertained that they will recover.

Frank Jones.
On Thursday last Frank Jones departed this life, aged about 23, after an illness of about two months. Frank was first taken with spinal meningitis, but the immediate cause of his death was Bright's disease.

Frank had spent his life in Coudersport, received a liberal education, and was a graduate of Poughkeepsie Business College. For a few years past he has been connected with his father in the mercantile business, showing rare business qualifications, and making friends of all whom he met.

On Monday last he was buried, followed to the grave by a large number of our citizens – old and young. The Coudersport Cornet Band, of which he was a member, marched to the grave, with instruments draped, at the cemetery gate playing a funeral march, and at the grave a dirge.

The parents receive the sympathy of the entire community. Five years ago they followed an only daughter, Mary, to the grave; three years ago Storrs, the youngest of the family, was laid beside Mary, and now Frank, the last of the children, sleeps beside them, leaving the aged parents childless and alone. Their's is indeed a sad case, one that appeals to the hearts of all.

Agricultural Society.

At the meeting of the Board of Directors of the Agricultural Society last week an important step was taken, and one which we think will tend to the benefit of the county fairs. It was dividing the board into heads of departments – each director to take charge of one department, to see that the exhibits are properly placed and that all are brought to the notice of the judges, that exact justice may be meted to all.

Each director will doubtless take enough pride in his department to give it the necessary time and attention, and will have an interest in seeing it well filled and properly displayed. Instead of one or two men doing two-thirds of the work, each man will have his work allotted and for that department will be responsible.

The Committee on Premiums are now engaged and will soon have the list complete.

The time for the Fair has not been definitely fixed, but will likely be fixed for September 28th, 29th and 30th – the next week after September court.

The officers are assigned to eight departments, as follows:

First, President, W. B. Gordnier.

Second, Secretary, John S. Ross, with W. A. Crosby and George W. Pearsall, assistants.

Third, Treasurer, C. H. Armstrong.

The duties of the above are indicated by their office.

Department Fourth, Benj. Rennells, superintendent, will have charge of live stock and all matters pertaining thereto, including

Class 1, Cattle.

Class 2, Horses.

Class 3, Sheep.

Class 4, Hogs, etc.

Department Fifth, J. M. Covey, superintendent, farms and gardens, and their products.

Class 5, Grain, flour, seeds, grass and hay.

Class 6, Roots and vines.

Class 7, Orchard and small fruits.

Class 8, Dairy.

Class 9, Maple sugar, beet sugar, molasses, honey, etc.

Department Sixth, Thomas G. Hull, superintendent, poultry, etc.

Class 10, Fowls of the farm and park.

Class 11, Water fowls, wild fowls, birds and animals.

Department Seventh, L. A. Glace, superintendent, manufactures and mechanics.

Class 12, Of or for the farm or shop.

Class 13, General.
Class 14, Manufactured goods.
Department Eighth, R. L. Nichols, superintendent, arts and household.
Class 15, Drawing, painting, cabinet collection.
Class 16, Silk, cotton, wool, embroidery, etc.
Class 18, Canned fruits and kitchen department.
Class 19, Floral hall, decorations, etc.

The Potter Enterprise
Thursday Evening, April 8, 1881 – Vol. VII, No. 46

- Hugh Young is the man who steps high now – it's a boy.

Millport. Mr. and Mrs. Jasper Card have a son, weight eight pounds. The mother is doing well as can be expected. Jasper's smile is broader than usual.

MARRIED.

MATTISON – JOHNSON – In Germania, April 6th, by Henry Theis, Esq., Dr. Edgar S. Mattison and Miss Edith M. Johnson, both of Coudersport.

Oswayo. Mrs. Coleman Smith, who has been sick with rheumatism for the past few weeks, died very suddenly Monday about one o'clock. She left many friends to mourn her loss, besides her husband and two children. She was loved by all who knew her, but we feel our loss to be her gain.

North Bingham. Mrs. John White, of White's Corners, died last Sunday afternoon, at a very advance age. The funeral was on Tuesday.

North Bingham. Mrs. Coleman Smith was buried at Oswayo on Tuesday last. Deceased had relatives in Bingham township.

Millport. An old gentleman by the name of Potter died a few days since at the place known as the Wildcat district. He was poor and old, and ill treated by those who should have used him with respect.

Genesee Forks, April 11, 1881.
Hall of Genesee Forks Lodge K. of H. No. 2016.
We had the pleasure of meeting at our lodge room on Saturday evening, April 9th, N. H. Roe, the father of the late Dr. L. E. Roe, in whose behalf the appeal for aid was made, and we had the pleasure of passing into his hands the sum of $216.00, which was very thankfully received by him. We have the very best of evidence that Mr. Roe is very needy and depends upon his own efforts for his support since the death of his son. Upon the receipt of the money, the old gentleman was completely broken down, but as soon as he could control himself he made a very appropriate address, which would have melted the stoutest heart.

He thanked us over and over again, and as he passed out of the room his last words were, "God bless you, and my the order prosper."

Yours in O.M.A.,
Ira E. Easton, Dictator.

Dr. L. E. Roe was one of those signing the petition for the Genesee Forks Lodge. The night the lodge was organized he was at the bedside of a diphtheria patient, and would not leave to take the degrees, and before another meeting the doctor was a corpse, his death resulting from diphtheria contracted at the bedside of the patient he was called to see the night the lodge was instituted. A statement of the case was recently sent to sister lodges, and the response will be learned from the above.

ABOUT THE 18TH OF THIS MONTH, MR. LEVY HARRIS Will open a Heavy and well selected stock of Clothing and Gents' Furnishing goods, Boots, Shoes, Etc., in the Forster Block, Coudersport. He will astonish you with low prices.

The Potter Enterprise
Wednesday Evening, April 20, 1881 – Vol. VII, No. 48

DIED.

WHITE – In Harrison, April 3d, Sally, wife of John White, aged 77 years, 1 month and 26 days.

The deceased was a devoted wife and mother, a kind neighbor and a sincere christian.

STEWART – In West Branch, April 11th, of Diphtheria, Fredelena, infant daughter of Frank and Alice S. Stewart, aged about 11 months.

LONGEE – In West Branch, April 12th, of diphtheria, John G., son of A. A. and Eveline Longee, aged about 3 years and five months.

The two children whose deaths are recorded above were grandchildren of S. M. Conable of West Branch.

- Coudersport has five church organizations, Methodist, Presbyterian, Baptist, Episcopal and Catholic – only the three first are supplied with church buildings; has one Masonic lodge, Knights of Honor, Equitable Aid; the ladies keep up a temperance society, foreign missions and two aid societies; we have a graded school and most of the time one select school, the two employing four teachers; nine stage lines are in operation; two printing offices, both supplied with power presses, run by steam; one bank; one land office; the legal fraternity number ten, while four physicians find plenty of business; two insurance offices; three drygoods and grocery stores; four groceries; two hardwares; one drugs and books; one drugs and jewelry; three millinery; two meat markets; one telegraph office; one express office; one furniture store and cabinet shop; three wagon shops, five blacksmith shops; two gun shops; three saw mills; three planing mills; one book bindery; one harness shop; one photograph gallery; one sewing machine store; one barber shop and billiard saloon; two grist mills; one tannery in the borough and one just below town, with a general store; one foundry; one livery stable; two shoe shops; one hotel; one restaurant; several boarding houses, besides a small army of carpenters, painters, masons, laborers, etc., etc.

The Potter Enterprise
Wednesday Evening, April 27, 1881 – Vol. VII, No. 49

Freeman's Run. I believe that Frank Austin had adopted the little stranger who came to his house a few days since – it's a girl.

Ulysses. Diphtheria is still in the land; Alonzo Mustoe buried a little girl last week who died from this terrible disease.

Costelloville. Ellis Moore, who has of late been a resident of this place, was drowned at Moccason Falls, near Keating, Clinton county, the 19th. He had been employed by David Pursley since last Fall cutting logs, and went on the drive when the logs went out. He was working with the teamsters, and when the Falls were reached he with three other men were going over in a boat in which they carried their tools. As the boat touched the water below the Falls it filled with water and sank, leaving its occupants to swim ashore through the rapids. The other three men reached the shore all right, but Moore became exhausted, and his body sank. It has not yet been found, but they are searching each day, hoping they may some day find the lifeless form. It is a great bereavement for his mother to bear, he being her only child. He was drowned within four miles of where they came from. His mother starts this morning for the place where he was drowned.

DIED.

STEUART – In West Branch, April 18, 1881, of Diphtheria, Ella Francis, daughter of Frank and Alice M. Steuart, aged 4 years and about 5 months.

YALE – At his home in Willing, N.Y.
April 7, 1881, H. O. Yale, aged 47 years.

Deceased was an active member of the M.E. Church, and a local preacher of the same. For years he was in poor health, but able to attend to his business, which was farming, until seven months ago, since when he has gradually failed. His wife, formerly Jennie M. Lyman, of Oswayo, and two daughters survive him. Funeral services were held on Sunday, the 10th inst., at Stannards Corners Church. Rev. W. Miller and Presiding Elder Stevens officiated. A touching tribute from the Sunday School of which he was Superintendent, was in the form of an anchor and cross of large size, made of beautiful sweet scented flowers in great variety.

The Potter Enterprise
Wednesday Evening, May 4, 1881 – Vol. VII, No. 50

DIED.

BARTHOLEMEW – In Roulet, April 21st, Davie Bartholemew, aged 30 years.

HAMMOND – In West Branch, April 23d, Ralph Edward, infant son of Mr. and Mrs. David Hammond, aged six months and nine days.

- Last week Tuesday, Patrick McNulty had his left arm broken by the kick of a horse. He was at work pulling stumps on the brick yard of the Brine Brothers, at Roulet, when the accident happened. He was just behind one of the horses, known to be a kicker, and had hooked the chain. Just as he was straightening up, the horse kicked, striking him on the left arm between the elbow and wrist, and the kick knocking him over backward and over the stump he had just hitched to. He will now carry his arm in a sling for several weeks.

- The house on East street occupied by Harlow Dingee, caught fire on Saturday afternoon last, on the roof, from the saw mill. A space two or three feet square was blazing when discovered. In a short time more it would have been beyond control, and in all probability, several other buildings wold have fallen a victim to the flames, as there was a strong wind blowing from the north. The fire marshal, it would seem, might find something to look after there, as this is the second time the house has caught fire in less than a year.

DECORATION DAY.
Arrangements for its Observance in Coudersport.
COMMITTEE OF ARRANGEMENTS.

M. S. Thompson, Chairman; Mr. and Mrs. R. L. Nichols, Mr. and Mrs. E. N. Stebbins, Mr. and Mrs. W. B. Gordnier, Mr. and Mrs. J. L. Knox.

COMMITTEE ON DECORATIONS.

Mr. and Mrs. A. B. Mann, Mr. and Mrs. J. S. Ross, Mr. and Mrs. N. M. Glassmire, Mr. and Mrs. A. S. Olmsted, Eva Dyke, Flora Gordnier, Amy Armstrong, L. F. Andrews, W. W. Thompson, S. A. Phillips.

COMMITTEE ON VOCAL MUSIC.

H. J. Olmsted, Mrs. Francis Hammond, Mr. and Mrs. F. J. Norton, Mrs. R. L. Nichols, Mrs. M. L. Gridley, Mrs. E. N. Stebbins.

PROGRAM ADOPTED.

Decoration Day Services will be held in Coudersport, on Monday, May 30th, 1881, according the following program and order of exercises:

Marshal of the Day, W. B. Gordnier, assisted by H. T. Reynolds, M. L. Gridley, and J. M. Covey.

The procession will form on the public square at one o'clock, p.m., in the following order.

Speaker and Clergymen,
Burgess and Council,

Decorating Committee,
The different Posts of the Grand Army of the Republic,
and other Soldiers and Sailors of the late war,
Eulalia Lodge, No. 342 F. & A. M.
The different lodges of the Knights of Honor,
Coudersport Cornet Band,
Judicial, State and County officers, and
Visitors,
Citizens,
Carriages.
Line of March, down Main street to Water Street, thence to Cemetery.
EXERCISES AT THE CEMETERY.
Music by Ulysses Cornet Band,
Decorating Soldiers' Graves by the Committee,
Vocal Music,
Prayer by Rev. Wm. Marshall.

After the exercises the Procession will reform and march in reverse order, to the Soldiers' Monument on the public square.
EXERCISES AT THE MONUMENT.
Music by Coudersport Band,
Floral Decoration, by the Committee,
Vocal Music,
Prayer, by Rev. T. R. Stratton,
Music, Ulysses Cornet Band,
Address, by Hon. Horace Bemis,
Vocal Music,
Music by the Bands,
Benediction, Rev. Wm. Marshall.

It is earnestly requested that all offices and business places in Coudersport may be closed during the exercises that all may join in thus honoring our fallen comrades. J. L. Knox, Sec.

STUDEBAKER WAGONS.

NORTON & DOANE
are Agents for these
CELEBRATED WAGONS.
None but the very BEST MATERIALS
are used in the manufacture
of the Studebaker Wagons.
PRICES LOW.
NORTON & DOANE,
COUDERSPORT, PA.

The Potter Enterprise
Wednesday Evening, May 11, 1881 – Vol. VIII, No. 1

DIED.

BURROWS – In West Branch, April 26th, 1881, of diphtheria, Arnie, infant son of Sidney and Ester L. Burrows, aged 1 years, 10 months and 13 days. Also, May 5th, of diphtheria, Effie, daughter of Sidney and Ester L. Burrows, aged 5 years and 10 days.

- David White, of Sweden, had a top buggy badly wrecked on Sunday. His horse hitched to the buggy stood in front of E. Lyman's, when two dogs commenced fighting under the buggy. The horse broke loose and before matters could be righted the buggy was broken in a number of places.

- Last Sunday Constable Hoppe, lodged in jail a young man named Smith, for the robbery of Henry Andresen's store at Kettle Creek last week. Smith first broke into Mr. Andresen's office, but could not get into the store. He then went to the rear of the building raised a window and entered. He secured a few dollars in money and some fifty or sixty dollars worth of goods and decamped, but when he left he forgot to take his pocket knife with which he had fastened the window up, and this carelessness was the cause of his capture. The knife was recognized and officers sent in search of the owner, who was found on Slate Run, with a portion of the goods in his possession.

Jury List, June Term, 1881.
GRAND JURORS.

John Mahan, Farmer, Wharton; C. C. Breunle, Farmer, Eulalia; Allen Torsey, Farmer, Sharon; R. C. Hosley, Farmer, Hector; John W. Drake, Laborer, Sharon; Thomas Bishop, Farmer, Lewisville; J. J. Kenyon, Farmer, Sharon; John Klemm, Farmer, West Branch; James Bundy, Farmer, Homer; B. F. Mulford, Farmer, Hector; F. D. Stillman, Farmer, Hebron; Warren White, Farmer, Sweden; Allen Hammond, Farmer, Oswayo; Edwin Joerg, Farmer, Stewardson; B. F. Berfield, Farmer, Wharton; M. N. Swetland, Farmer, Harrison; F. A. Nelson, Farmer, Allegany; T. J. Kibbe, Farmer, Harrison; O. Blackman, Farmer, Pike; T. J. Surdam, Farmer, Hector; A. F. Hollenbeck, Sup't, Coudersport; Daniel Berger, Farmer, Summit; S. H. Spencer, Genesee, Hiram Lent, Farmer, Sweden.

TRAVERSE JURORS.

T. W. Burt, Farmer, Lewisville; L. B. Lewis, Farmer, Bingham; C. S. Ford, Farmer, Allegany; Chris Knowlton, Farmer, Roulet; D. P. Jordan, Farmer, Roulet; Charles Coats, Farmer, Allegany; Wm. Bassett, Mason, Coudersport; Lucius Grames, Farmer, Sharon; E. M. Bishop, Farmer, Hebron; J. J. Baldwin, Farmer, Hector; W. T. Lane, Farmer, Sharon; M. A. Eggleston, Farmer, Hebron; Casper Gross, Farmer, West Branch; M. R. Grover, Farmer, Bingham; Martin Lewis, Farmer, Ulysses; Fred Harrison, Laborer, Harrison; Henry Theis, Farmer, Abbott; Robert McDowell, Farmer, Pleas't Valley; Martin Joerg, Farmer, Stewardson; D. L. Raymond, Merchant, Allegany; E. C. Dimon, Farmer, Hector; G. W. Bennett, Farmer, Ulysses; M. V. Prouty, Farmer, Pike; Elijah Swift, Farmer, Hebron; J. T. Rathbone, Farmer, Oswayo; McK. Erway, Hotel Keeper, Harrison; Sam'l Beebe, Pension Agent, Oswayo; Ansel Joseph, Shoemaker, P. Valley; Ruben Lane, Shoemaker, Roulet; Martin Dodge, Farmer, Harrison; Vincent Martin, Farmer, Oswayo; Thomas Gilliland, Farmer, Allegany; R. M. Post, Farmer, Eulalia; Charles Cole, Farmer, Sharon; Willard Andresen, Clerk, Stewardson; L. W. Briggs, Farmer, Harrison.

The Potter Enterprise
Wednesday Evening, May 18, 1881 – Vol. VIII, No. 2

- John Gray, of Shingle House, rejoices over the advent of another heir, John scores three now.

MARRIED.

McCASLIN – BROOKS – At the hotel in Westfield, Pa., May 7th, 1881, by Rev. W. S. Jennings, Mr. Clarence M. McCaslin, of Marsh Creek, Tioga county, Pa., and Miss Maggie M. Brooks, of Hector, Potter county, Pa.

VAN HORN – WHITEMAN – In Lewisville Borough, Pa., May 1st, by Frank Fronson, Esq., Will Van Horn and Miss Imogene Whiteman, all of Ulysses.

CHILSON – FLING – In Lewisville Borough, Pa., May 2d, 1881, by Frank Bronson, Avery Chilson and Miss Claribel Fling, late of Mansfield, Tioga county, Pa.

- A sad death occurred at the tannery last Friday night. Last week Mr. Hammond brought from Castle Garden eight families of Germans who had landed but a day or two previous. Shortly after their arrival at the tannery one of the children, less than a year old, was taken ill and in a few hours was a corpse, leaving its parents to mourn its loss, in a strange land far from friends. It is natural that homesickness should be their portion, and added to this now comes the death of their last born, leaving their hearts desolate indeed.

- The managers of Eulalia Cemetery held a meeting on Thursday evening of last week at which it was decided to re-fence the cemetery grounds – a board fence along the road and barbed wire, four strands high around the rest. M. S. Thompson was appointed to superintend the work. Posts, boards and wire have been ordered and the work is to be completed at an early day. This is a move in the right direction.

- A year ago to-morrow, May 18th, Coudersport was left without a single store, and many other branches of business were partially or entirely wiped out by fire. Our town is not entirely built up, but Coudersport may well feel proud that so much has been accomplished. Main street, where the stores were burned is nearly all filled with brick buildings. On old post office site is M. S. Thompson & Co., two stories; next, the A. F. Jones store, two stories owned by M. E. Olmsted, occupied by Andrews & Olmsted; then the hardware, rebuilt two stories, by A. J. Olmsted & Sons; then F. E. Lyon building and C. S. Jones, three stories, occupied by E. N. Stebbins, and C. S. Jones; where his old one stood, second floor, opera house, third floor, masonic hall; Griesel's harness shop is vacant, but will be rebuilt; Forster's and Frenches, rebuilt one story by Edward Forster; Nelson building, occupied by the bank, brick laying commenced Monday for a two story building by Norton & Doane; Corner Store, rebuilt two stories, by P. A. Stebbins, Jr. & Bro.; C. H. Armstrong, on Second street, one story rebuilt; Zimmerman's meat market, now two story brick, to be occupied by E. O. Rees next month; Olmsted & Larrabee's law office, now two story stone, occupied by bank, land office, law office and telegraph office; with the one exception, all the above are brick. On Second street, west of Main, north side, Reissman's shop, Cole's shop, Gordnier's two buildings, still vacant, and is like to remain so this season; South side, Thompson's wagon shop, now Enterprise building, Thompson's blacksmith shop, two story frame to go up this summer; Perkins' blacksmith shop vacant; Coudersport hotel and barn, vacant, store and barn built west of hotel property; Second street, east from Main, Glassmire's buildings, Benson's, Abe Jones' and F. W. Knox's, still vacant. A number of the shops have been rebuilt on East and First streets; Stevens & Martin's butcher shop occupies nearly the site of Mrs. Haven's dwelling, burned, a new dwelling having been erected on same square, West street. The above shows pretty correctly, the state of the burned district to-day. We hope that a year from now we may be able to state that the burned district is entirely rebuilt.

The Potter Enterprise
Wednesday Evening, May 25, 1881 – Vol. VIII, No. 3

MARRIED.

BAKER – MONROE – At the residence of Eugene Baker, in Lymansville, May 22d, 1881, by Rev. T. R. Stratton, L. Clinton Baker and Miss Fidelia Monroe, all of Ulysses.

West Branch. We have been passing through the scourge of diphtheria. In this settlement of about twenty-five families, we have buried six little children since the 11th of April, and on the 12th of May we buried Mr. John Burrows, under most painful circumstances. Mr. Burrows was an old man nearly 72 years old, and buried his wife last January. On Friday, the 29th of April, he had some difficulty with his son-in-law, Sidney Burrows. Mr. Burrows told Sidney he lied, whereupon Sidney struck the old man with a pitch-fork which he had in his hand at the time, the blow took effect on the side of his head, and he fell senseless to the ground, and for a short time was supposed to be dead, but he soon came to consciousness, but did not appear to be rational until the next day. Dr. Ritter, of Gaines, was sent for, who came and attended the suffering man, and hopes were strong for a few days that he would get about again, but erysipelas set in, which made him worse, but they succeeded in subduing that and then diphtheria set it, and soon it became evident that he was passing beyond the reach of medical aid, and a few minutes past 12 o'clock on the morning of the 12th of May, he breathed his last. What makes the affair seem more painful, is the fact that on the 29th of April, Sidney Burrows buried one of his children, and on the 5th of May he buried another one.

DIED.

DINGMAN – Died in Allegany of diphtheria May 9th, 1881, Ann Vena Dingman, age 12 years and 10 months.

- On Monday last in Sweden township a quite serious affray occurred between George Butler and his father, Joseph Butler. The report is that there has been trouble between them for some time. Recently George had a yearling calf shot, and on Monday he accused his father of the deed. He claims that his father then struck him on the head with a stone (he has a lump on his head to show for it) and attacked him with a hoe. George then knocked the old man down and kicked and stamped him about the face and head, bruising him so that it was thought necessary to send for a physician. George was arrested the same evening and gave bail.

The Potter Enterprise
Wednesday Evening, June 1, 1881 – Vol. VIII, No. 4

Decoration Day in Coudersport.

Yesterday was Decoration Day, and was more generally observed in Potter county than ever before. At several points in the county services were held in memory of our fallen brave.

In Coudersport the preparations were on a larger scale than at other points and attracted more attention and more people than it had ever done before. It is believed fully two thousand people were present, and some estimate as high as three thousand.

The rain at one o'clock reversed the order of exercises. The court room was packed full. Seats aisles and all until it seemed there was not even room for one more. Capt. Kinny, of Sharon, was made Chairman of the day, and opened the services with a few remarks. Opening prayer by Rev. T. R. Stratton. The address by Mr. Bemis, listened to with attention and was generally liked. The choir and the two bands furnished music. After the services in the Court House, a procession of carriages and persons on foot marched to the cemetery and decorated the graves of the soldiers buried, and the monuments erected to the memory of several who died or were killed in battle, but whose remains were never found. After which the procession reformed and marched to the Court House where they were dismissed. About one thousand persons marched to the cemetery.

The Knights of Honor – Coudersport, Genesee Forks and Ulysses, numbered about seventy-five, and presented a very creditable display.

The monument in the square was trimmed in a beautiful but simple manner, and reflected credit upon those having it in charge. All in all, every one connected with the management of the services of Monday should feel satisfied with their efforts and the result.

The Potter Enterprise
Wednesday Evening, June 8, 1881 – Vol. VIII, No. 5

West Pike. Mr. Dan Crandall, our Constable, has in his custody a prisoner which is like to give him more trouble than any prisoner he ever captured before, it only weighs eight pounds but it is large enough so Dan ought to let us have cigars.

Roulet. Mrs. Horace Maltby, the aged lady who fell down the stairs two weeks ago died from the effects Thursday last.

Fishing Creek. Died on Fishing Creek, in Roulet, June 3d, 1881, Mrs. Horace Maltby, aged 77 years, 9 months and 21 days. She was a devoted christian and a kind mother, and a friend to the poor and needy, both with the aid of temporal and spiritual food, and always pointing the erring ones to the Lamb of God that taketh away the sins of the world. The bereaved friends have the heart felt sympathy of the community, as we shown on the fifth by the concourse of people that attended her funeral. The Rev. T. R. Stratton, of Coudersport, preached the funeral sermon.

In Limbo.

Our jail had another one added to its inmates last Sunday – Charles Cannon, of Denton Hill, charged with forgery. A few days ago, Geo. Butler, a young man living on Denton Hill, presented an order at the store of P. A. Stebbins, Jr. & Bro., for nine dollars, purporting to be from Daniel Berger, of Summit. Butler stated that he had been peeling bark for Berger, that the order was written by Mr. Berger's daughter, and was in payment for his work. He bought quite a number of articles, which he afterward said he had divided with Cannon. The order was a forgery.

Butler also hired a horse of Veelie, the charges amounting to $5 and received one dollar in money, giving Vellie a due bill, bearing the name of James Barclay of Wharton. Afterwards the one dollar was returned and the horse paid for, but the young man failed to take up the due bill which is said to be a forgery. It is reported that the boys were prepared to present a $50 order at the tannery, signed "Dan'l Berger." It is said Cannon planned the forgeries and Butler presented them. Butler is out on bail.

NEW RAILROAD!
THE OLEAN AND COUDERSPORT R.R. CHARTERED.
OVER THE HILL AND DOWN THE OSWAYO.
WHAT HAS ALREADY BEEN DONE IN THE MATTER.
THE OFFICERS AND A LIST OF THE STOCKHOLDERS.

On Wednesday last, the State of Pennsylvania granted a charter to the Olean and Coudersport Railroad Company, to build and maintain a railroad from Coudersport to the State line near Ceres, in McKean county, with a capital stock of $160,000, divided into shares of $100 each. Olean parties have already taken out a charter for the Olean and Bolivar Railroad, have surveyors at work, 250 laborers on the grade, and half the iron bought. By agreement the Olean and Bolivar road is to be consolidated with the Olean and Coudersport, the two lines meet at or near Ceres. The officers of the Olean and Bolivar road are: C. S. Cary, President; M. W. Barse, Vice-President; H. S. Ernst, Secretary and Treasurer; L. F. Lawton, R. W. Evans and George V. Foreman, Executive Committee. The Olean and Coudersport officers are: F. W. Knox, President; Directors, Charles S. Carey, L. F. Lawton and Miles W. Barse, of Olean, W. W. Weston, of Weston Mills, A. G. Olmsted, R. L. Nichols, A. B. Mann and Charles S. Jones, of Coudersport.

Quick work was made in getting the charter for the Olean and Coudersport railroad. Tuesday morning the application left Coudersport, reaching Harrisburg the next morning about four o'clock where it was taken in charge by M. E. Olmsted, and the same day Olmsted mailed the charter for Coudersport.

The whole road from Coudersport to Olean will be put under one management as soon as convenient, and it is believed the entire road will be completed in one hundred days, if they have not trouble in getting right of way, etc.

The road will be a three foot gauge, costing from three thousand to five thousand dollars per mile. It can be built very cheaply, as the route is very direct and the grade easy. From Ceres it will go up the Oswayo Creek, through the heart of Sharon township to the mouth of Whitney creek; up Whitney creek to the top of the ridge, and either down the hollow by Sandberg's and Steer Brook, to the Allegheny river, and thence down the river two and a half miles to Coudersport; or from the ridge down Dingman Run, striking the Allegheny river one mile below Coudersport. Which route will be taken can only be decided by the surveyors. Either will give a good grade, and there can be but very little difference in the distance.

A portion of the distance right of way has already been obtained, and we believe the land owners will appreciate the advantages to be gained sufficiently to aid this project in every way possible. The following are the Stockholders with the amounts subscribed as they appear in the charter:

F. W. Knox,	Coudersport,	$20,000.00
M. W. Barse,	Olean,	3,000.00
G. V. Foreman,	do	3,000.00
C. S. Carey,	do	3,000.00
L. F. Lawton,	do	3,000.00
R. O. Smith,	do	3,000.00
Weston Brothers,	Weston Mills,	3,000.00
D. C. Conklin,	Olean,	3,000.00
W. S. Morris,	do	3,000.00
A. G. Olmsted,	Coudersport,	10,000.00
R. L. Nichols,	do	3,000.00
A. B. Mann,	do	1,500.00
M. S. Thompson,	do	1,000.00
James L. Knox,	do	1,500.00
W. K. Jones,	do	500.00
H. J. Olmsted,	do	1,000.00
Charles S. Jones,	do	300.00
Franklin W. Knox,	do	3,200.00

On Monday the Engineers started from Ceres to Coudersport and we may reasonably expect to see the "dirt fly" in a short time.

We have known of this project for some time, but it was thought best to say nothing of it until matters could be satisfactorily arranged by those working for the success of the railroad. Mr. Knox informs us that the difficulties are now adjusted and assures us there is nothing premature in stating that the road will be built.

When completed, if not before, it is believed a narrow gauge will be built from Elkland to this place to connect with the Olean & Coudersport railroad, and a third rail put down on the Cowanesque road making a through line from Olean through Sharon, Hebron, Eulalia, Coudersport, Allegany, Ulysses and Harrison townships to Corning, N.Y. Of the road from Elkland we cannot speak quite as encouraging as of the road from Olean to Coudersport. Many believe it will be built if right of way can be obtained. It would prove a great blessing to Potter county, opening up the best section and connecting it more closely with the county seat.

Parties are now securing the remaining right of way for the Olean and Coudersport railroad, and every good citizen should aid them. We have a good county, and if we can only have some way of getting our products to market, every one will be benefitted in a greater or lesser degree. Sharon, which we expect will soon be the Potter county oil field, will be brought in direction connection with Coudersport, and will find use for the narrow gauge, hauling oil well supplies, etc., while from this way the produce and lumber will be brought to a ready market. It will be a glorious day for Potter when the narrow gauge train thunders along its valleys and climbs over its divides. Long before snow falls we expect to chronicle the advent of the first excursion train. Hurrah for the railroad, "right er along."

PUBLIC NOTICE.

Whereas my wife, Josephiana Allen, has left my bed and board without just cause or provocation, this is to forbid all persons trusting or harboring her on my account, as I shall pay no debts of her contracting after this date.

Nathan Allen,
Coudersport, April 6th, 1881.

The Potter Enterprise
Wednesday Evening, June 15, 1881 – Vol. VIII, No. 6

Millport. Jeff Burdick and Mrs. Matilda Hill were married by E. A. Graves, J.P., the 4th inst. Also the week before, at Ellisburg, Mr. Selden Sloat and Miss Stella Kemp, all of Millport. Good wishes for all parties concerned.

MARRIED.

FURMAN – ATKINS. – At Brookland, Pa., by Thomas G. Hull, J.P., Wilbur Furman and Nellie E. Atkins, both of Sweden, Potter county, Pa.

Tin Wedding.

The friends of Mr. and Mrs. Roscoe Stearns met at his house in Hebron on the 4th inst., to celebrate the tenth anniversary of their marriage. They were the recipients of a fine lot of presents, a bounteous feast was spread, and an enjoyable time was had by all. Ex-Sheriff S. P. Reynolds made the presentation speech. May they live to celebrate their golden wedding is the wish of all.

- Buildings are being put up rapidly at this place. J. C. Bump is having a house and barn built on his lot No. 29; C. D. Voorhees has the foundation laid for a dwelling house on lot No. 32; L. H. Bailey is building on lot No. 33; Jas. Harvey is building on Honeoye street, lot No. 17; John McNamire is getting out the lumber for his building on his lot on the Oswayo street. There is nothing being done yet on the new hotel. Nichols and Harvey have put an addition on their sash and blind factory and will have a nice place for a work shop and are now prepared to do all sorts of business in their line. – Brown's well on Horse Run, drilling is progressing very slowly. After they had cased down 245 feet, they struck a vein of salt water 80 feet below the casing, making it necessary to case down farther, they found that the drilling varied, being a part of the time in a very hard rock. Last Saturday they found that the hole was crooked and they have since been preparing to straighten it. They are now down by the best information we can obtain about 900 feet. – The Hoover & Wilson & Co.'s well on the Plank is now down about eleven hundred feet, where it will remain for a week or so unless they compromise with the Scott's, who have leased in that vicinity. – William M. Sanders has commenced his rig on the lease of A. and N. C. Newton, and will push business. – George Vancise has sold twenty acres of land to William Sanders. Consideration, $1,000; $100 spot cash and $900 the first day of September. – *Palladium*.

- Another hole has been made in our jail, and Decker, the builder, comes in for another round of left handed blessings. Some time ago Sterling Lewis was locked up in our county jail, for breaking into and robbing the store of Henry Andresen, on Kettle Creek. On Tuesday evening last, while there was no one in the prison part, he tried the arch of his cell, soon picking out brick enough to admit of his passing through into the attic, from thence he could pass to the dwelling part of the jail by means of a ladder, and he then passed out, no one happening to be in the hall at this time. Examination shows the arch of the upper cells to be composed of two thicknesses of brick, laid in a poor quality of mortar. A man could pick his way out in fifteen minutes, just as Lewis did, piling a stand and chair upon his bed, so that he could reach the arch, and a stick and his fingers would do the rest. Some time ago the furnace gave out, so that the lower cells could not be warmed. Monroe was then compelled to put prisoners in the upper cells, allowing them to occupy, during the day, what was built for a work room, where a stove was put up. In damp weather the jail is not a comfortable place unless there is a fire somewhere about. We do not see but the Sheriff used ordinary care, and it is fortunate that the upper cells were not tried before by some persons who deserve punishment even more than Lewis. The Sheriff offers $25 reward for the capture of Lewis, who is 5 feet nine inches in height, black hair cut short; black eyes, black mustache, small goatee; wore a black suit of clothes and a slouch hat.

Railroad.

The narrow gauge railroad project is progressing. The weather was very unfavorable last week for the engineers and but little work was done. The right of way has been secured most of the distance along the line. A number of men are at work on the grade east of the junction at Ceres, and the engineer corps commenced locating the line from Ceres to Shingle House on Monday. It is expected that contracts for ties and timber will be let at once.

The Jersey Shore and Pine Creek road again comes to the front with a proposition, in substance, if Port Allegany and Coudersport will subscribe $50,000 will bridge and finish the grade, and that iron can be obtained and put down at once. We are informed that Port Allegany will take half of the amount, leaving Coudersport to raise $25,000. Can it be done? Two months ago there would have been no trouble, but this town has subscribed liberally to the Coudersport and Olean Narrow Gauge road, and the business men of Coudersport feel poor. The fire last year wiped out considerable wealth, large sums have since been put into buildings and business, so that many of them do not feel like expending more at present. There are those able to make this loan, but will they do it. We hope they will examine the proposition, and if it is square, invest in it. It would prove of great advantage to the town, and every person in it. Give us the Jersey Shore and Pine Creek, and the Narrow Gauge, and Coudersport will boom. Many believe this move is made to stave off the narrow gauge, and if such is the case, and there are some things about it that look that way it should be set down on hard.

The Potter Enterprise
Wednesday Evening, June 22, 1881 – Vol. VIII, No. 7

- The infant child of Mr. and Mrs. John Gray, of Shingle House, died the 11th inst.

- The severest storm of the season came off on Thursday night last. The rain fell in torrents, filling the small streams, causing a good flood in the river. Most of the cellars in town were flooded. At the Nichols House the basement was rendered uninhabitable, and remained so on Sunday. Every body says it was awful, and as most every body was up to see, it must be so.

- The foot bridge at East street contributes two items of news for this week. The bridge has no railing, and is quite high from the water. The recent storms raised the water to a log flood, and at the foot bridge in question, it runs very swift. On Friday last Miss Nora Mann attempted to cross, but becoming dizzy, fell into the water, which was running so swift that she could not get a foothold, and she was carried some distance down stream. Robert Niles, who happened to be near, plunged in and brought Miss Nora to the bank, wet and badly frightened, but not injured. On Sunday, a little daughter of Mrs. Ann Armstrong, met with a similar accident at the same place, and was brought out of the water by Amos Hollenbeck.

Potter County, Pennsylvania Potpourri – Volume I
1880 through 1884

Court Proceedings.

1881, June 13. – Court called. Present a full bench, Hon. H. W. Williams, presiding.

The Constables of all the townships and boroughs appeared in Court and made returns.

Rules to show cause why judgements should not be opened were taken in the following cases: Willard Bacon, for use, vs. George R. Howe, James Clark, for use, vs. John Eldridge, Thos. A. Watson vs. D. C. Howe.

The grand jurors were called and sworn and B. F. Berfield appointed foreman.

Thirty-two traverse jury men answered to their names.

In commonwealth cases, J. A. Bogardus was held in $50 to keep the peace; Wesley McDowell, charged with keeping a disorderly house, gave bail of $100 for appearance at next term; Gilbert Adams was found by a jury not guilty of adultery; John Rooney, charged with assault and battery gave $100 bail for appearance; Christopher Dennis was found not guilty of rape; Daniel Hopkins, tried for selling liquor, was convicted and sentenced to pay a fine of $50 and costs; Titus Losey plead guilty to the same offense and received the same sentence; Geo. Butler and Charles Cannon were indicted for forgery and gave bail in $500; John Lewis for larceny; Leonard King plead guilty for selling liquor and gave bail for $300 to appear at next term; Mason Nelson also plead guilty to the charge of selling liquor and was sentenced to pay $50 and costs; a *nolle prosequi* was entered in the case of James Kenyon, charged with fornication and battery; George Butler, charged with assault and battery, &c., gave bail of $600 for appearance at next term; M. L. Beckwith, charged with larceny of timber, was, with his bail discharged. Mathias Schmidt, charged with selling liquor, one prosecution was discontinued, and the Court allowed the District Attorney to send before the grand jury another indictment against Mr. Schmidt, who gave bail in $100 for appearance at Court; James Larkin held for malicious mischief gave bail in the sum of $200 for appearance at next term; Mason Nelson was indicted for selling liquor, as also was Marion Hill, in which latter case bail was given in sum of $200; Marshall Gross in a surety of the peace case was sentenced to pay the record costs, he gave bail to next term; Elmer Aylesworth gave bail in surety of the peace; Leonard King, indicted for assault and battery, gave bail to next term. The grand jury returned the indictment for perjury vs. S. F. Butler, not a true bill, the prosecutor, Mason Nelson, to pay costs; A. D. Corey was indicted for selling liquor, so also were W. B. Monroe and Delos Genung; R. H. Haynes was convicted of assault and battery, and sentenced to pay a fine of $25 and costs.

The appointment of J. Harrison as auditor in John Barr vs Hiram York, and M. S. Thompson vs Wm. Shear was continued.

In the case of Hector school district vs Sunderlinville Independent school district, the first day of next term was fixed for a hearing.

Godfrey Bratz was appointed clerk of Abbott township; M. K. Beach treasurer of Hector; F. M. Stevens auditor of Coudersport; Z. O. Bacon supervisor of Bingham.

H. M. Foote, of Tioga county, J. Clark Metzgar, of Cameron county, and F. N. Newton, A. L. Cole and J. T. Gear, of Potter county, were admitted to practice in the several courts of this county.

The viewers in the matter of school house site in Roulet were instructed to amend their report.

Henry N. Gardner was appointed stenographer.

The following proceedings were had in divorce cases:

M. L. Foster was appointed commissioner to take testimony in the case of A. A. Streeter vs L. D. Streeter.

Charles N. Wilber was divorced from Mary A. Wilber.

The original libel in O. D. Jackson vs Effie Jackson was withdrawn.

Mary E. Ward was granted a divorce from Hugh Ward.

The sheriff was ordered to make proclamation in Virginia Quinette vs Edward Quinette, and A. B. Mann appointed commissioner.

In Eliza Baker vs Alanson L. Baker. Rule on respondent to show cause why an order should not be made directing him to pay libellant her just expenses and allowance.

In Thomas Musto vs Dewalt Shutt. Sheriff was permitted to amend his levy.

A jury was called and sworn in the case of George Fox, M.D. vs Amanda Crum, et al, who find for the plaintiff land the described in his writ to be released on the payment within ten days of $1,995.44 and costs.

A rule was taken on Harrison township to levy a special tax for payment of debts, also on Keating township.

In Henry Dean vs H. H. Guernsey, the jury find for the plaintiff $67.

A jury was called and sworn in the action of ejectment of Joseph Mann vs Peter Thatcher and David Thatcher, who find for the plaintiff the land described in his writ.

Venires were issued for 36 traverse and 24 grand jurors for September term.

The grand jury returned an indictment vs Titus Losey for selling liquor, and ignored a bill vs O. M. Wagoner for the same offense, county to pay the costs.

In W. T. Jones vs Mary A. Jordan, et al. Rule to show cause why lien should not be stricken off.

In H. J. Olmsted, in part for use of A. Rounseville vs Eulalia township; rule to show cause why judgment should not be marked satisfied.

An alias subpoena in divorce was awarded in O. E. Harris vs Wealthy Harris, and in Charles Rixford vs Rodilla Rixford.

J. T. Gear was appointed commissioner to take testimony in Flora Harrigan vs Theodore Harrigan.

In George Fox, M.D. vs Joseph Cooper and W. E. Ellsworth, ejectment. Court direct a plea of not guilty to be entered.

In W. B. Cutler vs F. A. Brown. Rule on defendant to appear and plead; rule to be published.

Daniel Monroe, High Sheriff of Potter county, appeared in court and acknowledged the following deeds:

To Daniel Yentzer for 50 acres, Pleasant Valley, sold June 14th, 1881, as property of Joseph Fessenden, for $25.

To William Cobb, Jr., for 50 acres, Bingham, sold June 15th, 1881, as property of W. H. Gee, for $170.

To Mathias Walter for 100 acres, Abbott, sold June 14th, 1881, as property of Lorenz Luthner for $25.

To O. R. Webb for one-half acre, Roulet, sold June 14th, 1881, as property of Levi Card, for $51.

To Bingham estate for 51.1 acres, Hector, sold June 14th, 1881, as property of Parker Bliss, for $25.

To R. L. Nichols for 70 acres, Sharon, sold June 15th, 1881, as property of W. P. Nichols, for $20.

To John S. Ross and W. K. Jones, executors, etc., for 6,480 square feet, Coudersport, sold June 14th, 1881, as property of Joseph E. Forster, for $25.

To George de B Keim for 13,951 acres in Jackson, West Branch and Wharton, sold June 14th, 1881, as property of Francis W. Hughes, for $2,750.

Judgments for want of appearances, affidavits of defence, and pleas, were taken in the following cases:

National Bank Exchange, of Auburn, N.Y., vs Benjamin Haynes and Mary A. Haynes; Joseph Mann and J. W. Beebe vs Peter Thatcher and David Thatcher; John T. Williams, administrator of estate of Wm. McDougall vs Genesee twp; same vs A. W. Andrews; Singer Manufacturing Company vs Leonard Davis; H. M. Tice vs Leonard Davis; V. M. Stannard vs S. H. Reaser; Grant and Dewaters vs J. J. Rice; J. W. Allen vs C. C. Judd; Eli Westgate vs Stephen Harton; Chas. N. Rawson vs Leonard Davis; Leroy Dallmage for use vs Chauncey Clerk; Weed Sewing Machine Company vs Tobias F. Smith; A. F. Jones & Son for use vs J. W. Rounds and G. H. Rounds; D. E. Smith vs A. Rohrabacher.

The Potter Enterprise
Wednesday Evening, June 29, 1881 – Vol. VIII, No. 8

Ulysses. The court of common pleas granted O. D. Jackson a divorce.

- P. D. Catlin, formerly a resident of this county, died at Emporium recently, aged sixty years.

Ulysses. Mrs. Minna Brown, daughter of John Smith, went to Michigan last spring to join her husband who had been there some time, was brought home to be laid by the side of her brother, Charles Smith, who was burned to death in the oil country.

- A panther was killed in the woods in Genesee township, Potter county, by James Callaghan, on Thursday. – *Wellsville Democrat*.

THE FOURTH AT COUDERSPORT.

P. A. Stebbins, Jr., President.
Vice-Presidents. – M. V. Larrabee, Roulet; Thomas G. Hull, Brookland; S. P. Reynolds, Hebron; Homer K. Lane, Ulysses; Francis Hammond, Coudersport, and Dr. Charles Meine, Germania.

Guns at sunrise.
Walking match at 9 o'clock.
Fantastic parade at 10 o'clock.
Reading Declaration at 1 o'clock, followed by orations.
Climbing grease pole for purse, sack race, etc., in the afternoon.
Music during the day by the Coudersport Cornet Band.
Large display of Fire Works.
Dances in the evening and lots of fun generally.
Let every one come.

Let every one turn out to the fantastic parade and all those who expect to take part, report to and confer with S. P. Olmsted, who will furnish masks.

Dedication.

The new Catholic church lately finished at the Irish Settlement, Genesee township, Potter county, was dedicated yesterday. The ceremonies were imposing and impressive. Bishop Mullen, of Erie, together with four priests, were present and participated in the ceremonies.

At 10 o'clock, a.m., the Bishop and the four priests, together with about 500 men and women, marched around the church once, chanting the litany. The Acolites, bearing the crucifix headed the procession, the Bishop and priests immediately behind them. Entering the church, the Bishop and priests proceeded to the sanctuary, still chanting the litany. After reciting the litany, high mass was celebrated, Rev. Father Leddy of this city, being Celebrant. After mass an able discourse was delivered by Rev. Father Coddy, of Titusville, taking for his text the following passage of scripture: "Thou art Peter, and upon this rock I shall build my church, and the gates of hell shall not prevail against her." The Bishop followed with a few remarks congratulating the congregation upon their success in erecting so fine an edifice for the worship of God; and praising them for having no church debt hanging over them. This ended the ceremonies in the forenoon.

In the afternoon, at 4 o'clock, vespers were changed, followed by an interesting lecture from the Bishop, on the history of the Bible. This ended the dedication ceremonies.

The church is an elegant one, and reflects great credit upon the parishioners. There were a large number present from Wellsville and towns surrounding the Settlement. – *Wellsville Democrat.*

Potter County, Pennsylvania Potpourri – Volume I
1880 through 1884

Potter County Census.

The following statement exhibits the results of the first count of population according to the schedules returned to the census office by enumerators of the districts concerned.

The statement of the population in relation to any township, town, city, or county is still subject to possible corrections by reason of the discovery of omissions or duplications of names in the lists of inhabitants returned.

Names of villages are indented and placed under the townships in which they are respectively situated, and the population of the township includes, in every case, that of all villages within it.

The villages marked with an asterisk (*) are unincorporated, and their population is given only approximately, as their limits cannot be sharply defined.

Abbott township, including village of Germania,		623
*Germania village,	101	
Allegany township,		672
Bingham township,		832
Clara township,		238
Coudersport borough,		677
Eulalia township,		554
Genesee township,		998
Harrison township,		1,162
Hebron township,		835
Hector township,		958
Homer township,		189
Keating township,		204
Lewisville borough,		365
Oswayo township, including village of Oswayo,		768
*Oswayo village,	321	
Pike township,		281
Pleasant Valley township,		211
Portage township,		114
Roulet township,		648
Sharon township, incl. The following villages,		1,055
*Millport village,	49	
*Sharon Centre village,	35	
Stewardson township,		223
Summit township,		202
Sweden township,		416
Sylvania township,		215
Ulysses township,		638
West Branch township,		374
Wharton township,		346

The Potter Enterprise
Wednesday Evening, July 13, 1881 – Vol. VIII, No. 9

Allegany. The relatives of Mr. and Mrs. Henry Haskell made them a surprise, it being the tenth anniversary of their marriage, or tin wedding. They were the recipients of numerous presents, and a good time was enjoyed by all.

- Ross, son of Wm. and Adda Rounseville, died in Coudersport this Tuesday morning, aged about 3 years, after an illness of only four days.

Ellisburg. Died at Ellisburg, Pa., June 30th, 1881, of consumption, Inez, wife of Orson Ellis, aged 36 years. How little yet how much is comprehended in these few lines, dead, yet living. Mrs. Ellis was taken ill January 2d, and during her long illness felt fully confident of the tender mercies of an all wise Providence. Expressing her willingness to die if it was her Heavenly Father's will. If spoken to of her sufferings, she would say it is nothing in comparison to what our Saviour suffered. Mrs. Ellis was universally respected and will be very much missed in the neighborhood, and it is a heart rending loss for her husband and friends. She was a loving wife, kind and obliging neighbor, combined with her cheerful manner, won many friends. We truly sympathize with husband and friends in their bereavement. I can point them only to one great Physician, who can heal the broken-hearted, and that is Jesus.

DIED.

CONABLE. – In West Branch, June 29th, 1881, of diphtheria, Samuel Maxwel, son of Willis and Alice Conable, aged 5 years, 2 months and 24 days.

- On Wednesday night last burglars entered Neefe's wagon shop, carrying off a brace and bit. This was only a preliminary steal. At Norton & Doane's hardware, the stolen tools were used to open a back window. The change drawer containing three or four dollars was emptied, a revolver taken, and three or four cheap pocket knives. The loss does not exceed eight dollars. The burglars, it is evident, are beginners, and are probably "home production."

- A new duty now devolves on the Prothonotaries of the counties under the act of June 8th, and physicians must each occupy a page in the register book. Every person who practices medicine or surgery must present to the Prothonotary his diploma for record, and the prothonotary must then enter his name, place of birth, residence, etc., on the record, and place a copy of the diplomas on file in the office for inspection. Provision is made for cases where diplomas have been lost, and where a person has been continually practicing for ten years one is not needed. The law, which is quite elaborate, can be seen now in the office of Prothonotary Crosby. – *Journal.*

July 4th.

The Fourth came in quietly, at least it did not make much noise in this section until day break, when a number of guns were fired, and the Coudersport Cornet Band paraded the streets, waking the sleepers.

The walking match was won by Frank McGinnis, in a little less than 50 minutes. His only competitor retiring before the close.

The speech in the Court House is said to have been good.

A large crowd was in town and all seemed to enjoy themselves. The fantastics were good, and in the evening the display of fireworks exceeded any other ever seen in Coudersport. The two dances were well patronized and the whole was a success.

The Potter Enterprise
Wednesday Evening, July 20, 1881 – Vol. VIII, No. 10

Roulet. Born – July 3rd, to Mr. and Mrs. Don Manning, a daughter. Also to Mr. and Mrs. Clarence Green, three daughters, all of which died. Their weight was two pounds a piece.

MARRIED.

AMIDON – GROVER. – At the residence of Thos. G. Hull, Esq., Brookland, Pa., July 10th, 1881, Milton Amidon, of Genesee Forks, Pa., to Miss Rozella Grover, of Gold, Pa.

HASKINS – VANWEGIN – In Hebron, July 3d, 1881, by O. J. Rees, Esq., Robert D. Haskins, and Miss Clara Vanwegin.

HERZOG – CAMERON – At the M. E. parsonage, in Coudersport, July 3d, 1881, by Rev. T. R. Stratton, Mr. George Herzog, of McKean county, and Miss Lettie Cameron, of Sweden, Pa.

Roulet. Died in this place, July 13th, Mrs. Ann Hazen. Also July 9th, Martin, youngest son of Lyman and Mary Burt.

- This Tuesday morning, Mr. William Metzger, of Coudersport, passed from life. For the past fifteen years he has suffered from rheumatism, and for several years has been perfectly helpless and blind. He was a patient sufferer, but often prayed that death would come to his relief. The deceased was about sixty years of age, and before he became an invalid was a very prominent business man.

- Last week Hugh Collins, engaged in peeling bark near Coudersport, met with quite a serious accident. In trying to avoid a falling tree top he threw himself backward, striking upon his sharp axe, making a long and deep wound, just below the right shoulder. The wound bled profusely. Had it been a trifle deeper the bleeding wold have been inwardly and probably proved fatal. Dr. Mattison dressed the wound and the patient is now getting along finely.

> **GERMANIA HOTEL.**
> Germania, Potter County, Pa.
> Having bought the above commodious house I wish to say to the public that I am ready to provide good accommodations for the traveler, and invite the public to call and see.
> *AUGUST VOSS*, Proprietor.

The Potter Enterprise
Wednesday Evening, July 27, 1881 – Vol. VIII, No. 11

MARRIED.

PETERSON – HAWLEY. – In Coudersport, July 29th, 1881, by O. J. Rees, Esq., Thomas Peterson, of Hebron, and Miss Eva Hawley, of Ceres, McKean county, Pa.

Burtville. Died July 9th, Martin, youngest child of Mary and Lyman Burt, aged 4 years and 7 days.

Little Martin was a very bright and lovely child. None knew him but to love him. May God console the parents in their affliction.

Martin we shall ever miss you,
   Friends can never fill the space
That is vacant by your absence,
   Who can fill our darling's place.
Little Martin thou hast left us,
   Here thy loss we deeply feel;
But 'tis God who hath bereft us;
   He can all our sorrow heal.

Allegany. The relatives and friends of Mrs. Alice Neefe, sister of M. W. Slaughter, were pained to hear of her death in the faraway land of Texas. The disease was measels.

DIED.

METZGER – In Coudersport, July 19th, William H. Metzger, aged 64 years.

He was born in Louisburg, Pa., but in the prime of life came into this county, where he has resided almost thirty-five years.

His active business habits, his integrity of character, his honesty of purpose and devotion to religion and active benevolence made him endeared to those about him.

As a Christian and as an active member and efficient Elder of the Presbyterian church of this place he was much respected.

His active life was arrested by disease and through a gradual decline he became an invalid, then dependant on others of the family and for the last four years was blind and helpless.

Yet he bore his trials with great firmness and delighted much in Christian conversation and in hearing the word of God read to him.

His illness of sixteen years was a long period to remain an invalid for that change which awaited him. His last message was to the little Willie who spent much time waiting on him. He said "Good-bye, God bless you! Try to live a Christian all your days."

His end was peace and his departure sudden. His beloved widow and children have the prayers of sympathizing friends in their affliction. May the children rise up to such excellence as to bring a blessing on the name of their departed parent and verify the promise of God, that He would be with His people and their children after them.

Raspberry Vinegar.

In these hot days a little raspberry vinegar added to a glass of cold water makes a most refreshing drink. When raspberries are abundant is the time to provide a supply, and the wild berries are quite as good as any – if not best. One of the simplest methods is to place the berries in a jar and cover with the best cider vinegar; set in a cool place, and the next day add as many more raspberries as the vinegar will cover. The next day set the jar in a pan or kettle of cold water, and gradually heat the water to boiling. If a glass jar is used some sticks must be placed between it and the kettle. When the berries are scalded through strain, and for every pint and a half of juice add a pound of sugar, heat to a boiling point in a porcelain kettle, remove the scum as it forms; and when the "vinegar" is cool bottle and cork securely.

- Last Sunday morning between three and four o'clock, a huge balloon passed over this place and was seen by George Green and Johnny Niles. Its course was from nearly east to a little south of west, following nearly the course of the valley. The form of the balloon was distinct, and lights were in the basket, showing that some person or persons were taking a voyage in the air ship. Mr. Robert Niles discovered the same air ship on returning from Brookland. It was moving at a very moderate rate, not much if any faster than he drove, and it was yet in his sight when he reached Coudersport. A number of persons along the road were called up by him to see the strange sight. When it passed over Coudersport it was quite low, so low, that those who saw it thought they could hear voices. Where this balloon started from is unknown here. It is a sight most of our people would gladly have been called up to see, even at the unholy hour of four o'clock Sunday morning.

The Potter Enterprise
Wednesday Evening, August 3, 1881 – Vol. VIII, No. 12

- Mrs. M. W. Mann was called to Buffalo on Monday, to attend her brother, John King, ill with typhoid fever. A short time after Mrs. Mann left a telegram was received that Mr. King was rapidly sinking. Monday afternoon a dispatch was received that Mr. King had died at 8 o'clock a.m.

- Sharon township, in the vicinity of Shingle House, was visited by a severe storm of rain, wind and hail on Monday of last week. In Gillet's photograph gallery every pane of glass was broken. Kinner's store had several windows smashed, and a number of dwellings were treated in like manner. Crops were beaten to the ground and the damage must foot up to a considerable sum. After the storm hail-stones were picked up measuring 2 ½ inches in diameter.

The Potter Enterprise
Wednesday Evening, August 10, 1881 – Vol. VIII, No. 13

Pleasant Valley. Ansil Joseph is happy – it's a boy. Weight, 8 ¾ pounds.

BORN.

TURNER – In Coudersport, Aug. 7th, to Mr. and Mrs. James Turner, a son, weight 10 ½ pounds.

- William Gray, of Shingle House, well known to many people in this vicinity, having worked here as a blacksmith, died Monday after a long and severe illness.

- The races for the Fair are: First, a walking match, 25 miles, for a purse of $75, divided; Second, running race for 3 year old colts, one-half mile, best two in three, purse $20, divided; three minute race, purse $75, divided; Free for all, $100, divided. Propositions for building a grand stand will be received until the 15th inst.

Dog Days.

With the 18th of last month began the "dog days," as the coming period of a month or six weeks is termed, a period regarded by many as the most unhealthy of the year, suppose to be a time when the human family is more apt to be affected with illness from exposure or from being imprudent in their habits. The date of its beginning is not placed by almanac makers alike, some giving an earlier date in July as the starting point. Baur's Lancaster almanac fixes the date as the 18th, and as this authority is a quoted one in this neighborhood it may just as well date from that day. A writer in the American Encyclopedia says of the dog days:

"Among the ancients the period of greatest heat in summer, so named because in the latitudes of the Mediterranean this period corresponded with that in which the dog star arose at the same time with the sun. To this conjunction all antiquity, and all the later followers of judicial astrology, ascribed a malignant influence. The heliacal rising of the dog star is a very indefinite phenomenon; its precise date cannot be determined, and owing to the precession of the equinoxes it does not now occur until about August 10th, when the greatest heat of the season is often over. So uncertain is the time that the ancients indiscriminately ascribe the evil influence to Sirius and Procyon (the largest stars respectively of Canis Major and Minor,) though there are several days difference in their risings. The modern almanac makers sometimes reckon the dog days from July 24th to August 24th, and sometimes from July 3d to August 11th."

Severe Storm.

Last Friday afternoon Coudersport was visited by two very severe storms, the first one coming from the South, and the second one from all quarters at once. The first storm was a heavy wind and a great fall of water, doing but little damage. A few fences were blown down and here and there a scuttle decking blown off. The second storm commenced about half past five, and was over in twenty minutes, by the clock, but it was one of those long twenty minutes, where a great deal is compressed into a small space.

The wind blew a hurricane and the water fell in torrents, the storm changing from one quarter to another almost like a whirlwind, and leaving in its patch overturned fences and broken trees.

At J. M. Hamilton's a large elm was uprooted and an apple tree; at Mrs. A. F. Jones' a large balsam was broken off fifteen or twenty feet from the earth, the top striking the roof and rolling to the ground; at Mrs. O. J. Rees' a fine apple tree and a pear tree were blown over; at D. F. Glassmire's two apple trees; at A. G. Olmsted's one shade tree broken; at Mrs. J. S. Mann's four or five fruit trees and limbs from a number of shade trees; at A. B. Mann's a shade tree broken; at the M. E. church one shade tree; Court House Square a balsam broken off; at the jail two trees broken; at C. L. Peck's four fruit trees down and a number broken, more or less; at J. S. Ross' one apple tree ruined; at Albert Goodsell's two heavily laden pear trees ruined; at F. W. Knox's a fine shade tree spoiled; at E. N. Stebbins' a pear tree uprooted, and trees damaged at several other places. One of the arches in C. H. Armstrong's store front was blown in, breaking the glass, damaging a show case and doing considerable damage to goods in the window. The iron roofing on the west side of the Enterprise office started from its fastenings, so that water ran in on the collar beams wetting the ceiling badly. E. O. Rees had a skylight broken, the water doing considerable damage to carpets and walls.

The storm was not an extensive one, and Coudersport seems to have taken the brunt of it. At the Schilderberger place, two or three trees were damaged, and in Homer some of the orchards were damaged, and some grain spoiled. Just below Coudersport, along the river, ten or a dozen large trees, hemlocks and maples were uprooted. Outside of the section mentioned, the storm was not extremely severe. It was decidedly the worst storm we ever witnessed in Coudersport, and for one, we breathed quite a bit easier when it was over. Perhaps the air was purer then.

The Potter Enterprise
Wednesday Evening, August 17, 1881 – Vol. VIII, No. 14

MARRIED.

LEWIS – HAMMOND – At the Fassett House, in Wellsville, August 8th, 1881, by Rev. A. F. Rumpff, Mr. George H. Lewis, of Troupsburg, N.Y, and Miss Libby Hammond, of Potter county, Pa.

Millport. H. D. Blanchard died suddenly at his home, near Sharon Centre, this morning. The deceased was advanced in years, and had been failing in health for some time.

- Charley Doerner has the first bicycle in town. He goes it alone but wabbles over considerable territory.

- Last Sunday night an attempt was made to break into the store of P. A. Stebbins, Jr. & Bro. The party or parties took out a few brick at the hall door, second floor, and attempted to loosen the iron door, between the two buildings, but failed. Had they succeeded in entering, Henry would have given them a warm reception, when they entered the lower rooms.

- Last week Morris Wheaton discovered a rattlesnake in the road near J. M. Kilbourne's. His snakeship crawled out of the road into the bushes, and Mr. Wheaton procured a club and started in pursuit. While prying in the bushes with his hands to discover the whereabouts of the reptile, the snake struck him on the finger. Three pints of whisky was given Mr. Wheaton, and as it made him dead drunk, it is expected that he will recover.

JURY LIST. – September Term.
GRAND JURY.

Perry Brigham, Manufact'er, Lewisville; W. E. Bishop, Farmer, Lewisville; Sidney Abbott, Farmer, Hector; Geo. Larrison, Laborer, Hector; Leroy Haskins, Farmer, Sylvania; D. C. McKee, Farmer, Hebron; Orson Ellis, Farmer, Genesee; A. N. Spencer, Farmer, Bingham; Franz Fengler, Farmer, Abbott; Jos. Schwartzenbach, Brewer, Abbott; Alfred Herring, Farmer, Sharon; G. C. Lewis, Farmer, Keating; James Glase, Laborer, Eulalia; J. S. Pearsall, Farmer, Sharon; A. A. Newton, Farmer, Sharon; Zalmon Barnes, Farmer, Sharon; Sidney Butler, Carpenter, Eulalia; C. N. Kilbourne, Farmer, Hector; Joseph H. Rees, Farmer, Sylvania; Leroy Knight, Laborer, Harrison; Dan Baker, Farmer, Bingham; J. W. Madison, Farmer, Hebron; C. V. Gill, Farmer, Harrison; Ira Bixby, Farmer, Sharon.

TRAVERSE JURY.

Arthur Lyman, Farmer, Sweden; Daniel Smith, Jr., Farmer, Roulet; W. C. Chesbro, Farmer, Homer; B. A. Green, Farmer, Clara; William Dent, Farmer, Ulysses; Alonzo Hawks, Farmer, Harrison; Tim Glines, Farmer, Clara; Nelson Crowell, Farmer, Ulysses; Wm. Carmer, Farmer, Hebron; F. P. Nichols,

Laborer, Sharon; A. J. Barnes, Farmer, Sharon; Roscoe Weimer, Farmer, Roulet; M. L. Gridley, Gentleman, Coudersport; Benj. Johnson, Farmer, Harrison; H. C. Olmsted, Merchant, Coudersport; J. A. Robbins, Farmer, Harrison; Ephriam Emmerson, Farmer, Hebron; R. F. Davis, Farmer, Hector; Reuben Collar, Farmer, Genesee; Truman Brizee, Farmer, Oswayo; C. S. Baker, Laborer, Lewisville; James Morley, Farmer, Allegany; C. W. Goram, Farmer, Hebron; A. W. Hickox, Farmer, Genesee; F. B. Nelson, Farmer, Eulalia; C. P. Kilbourne, Farmer, Hector; E. H. Bishop, Farmer, Ulysses; John Kibbe, Farmer, Oswayo; Lewis Jones, Farmer, Wharton; Lyman Rooks, Farmer, Harrison; N. A. Pinney, Laborer, Keating; Miles Marsh, Farmer, Roulet; Wilson McDowell, Farmer, Pl's't Valley; Adelbert Burtis, Farmer, Harrison; Frank Hand, Farmer, Harrison; F. A. Hendryx, Farmer, Allegany.

The Potter Enterprise
Wednesday Evening, August 24, 1881 – Vol. VIII, No. 15

- An heir reported itself at the residence of Mr. William Pinney, who resides near the stone quarry, last week.

- Charley Hungerford was buried at Smethport on Sunday last. Charley was for some years a resident of Coudersport, a steady, industrious young man, commanding the respect of all. For some time past he has resided in the oil country. His death was caused by fever.

- The man Wheaton, who was bitten recently by a rattlesnake, on Pine Creek, has been very low, but the last we heard he was improving and likely to get well.

- On Sunday morning last, Sheriff Monroe discovered that one of the prisoners in his care had about completed arrangements to leave his boarding place and the town, in an unceremonious manner. Some members of the Sheriff's family had heard a noise Friday night, not accounted for, and on Saturday night Dan. watched the cells from the outside hall until a late hour. He discovered that Charles Hannas had a light in his cell and seemed to be stirring around more than was necessary, after a time Hannas put out his lamp and the noise ceased. As Hannas had gone to bed, Dan. concluded he would do likewise, and make a careful examination by daylight. In the morning Monroe accused his prisoner of attempting to break the jail, which was promptly denied, but Monroe went on with his examination and soon found out what had caused the noise. At the head of the prisoner's bed was found a stone, a foot or more thick and about two feet long by a foot wide, covered with newspapers and clothes, under the bed was found a large quantity of mortar and loose stones, and in the wall a deep hole two foot square. The prisoner had worked through to the outside stone and partly around that. Two nights more would have let him into the yard. During the day prisoners have the liberty of the corridor, and Hannas had taken an iron rod from the railing of the upper corridor, and this instrument, about half an inch thick by two feet in length, was the tool used by him to make the hole in the wall. The rod was fastened at the corner of the railing and to the floor by a heavy burr, which must have fitted loosely, or he never could have got the rod out without the use of wrench. Some of the stones taken from the wall had been carried during the day to an adjoining cell and secreted; pieces of stones were found in the register, and around the iron casing of the window the plaster had been picked off. Some time ago the prisoner had pasted pictures from illustrated papers about the walls, one above the other, until he had covered the wall around the window, and after putting up the pictures he had tried the plaster and wall. Sheriff Monroe moved him to another cell, and gave him notice that if he should find the least scratch on the wall he should feel it his duty to chain him to the floor. Hannas said that when out in the yard he had noticed the wall particularly, and knew just where to strike a stone that was not bound by the ones above. Where he had started the opening the outside stone was under a larger stone that reached entirely across it. Hannas was locked up some time ago for breaking into Joseph Coulston's house and stealing a watch and some other property. Shortly before committing this burglary Hannas broke out of the Addison lockup. The cell damaged by Hannas is the same one from which a prisoner escaped when the jail was first completed, by digging through the wall. One of our citizens suggests that for additional security, the County Commissioners should put up a barbed wire fence about our County Bastile. We are not sure but the advice is good.

ANNOUNCEMENT.

I wish to announce that hereafter I shall make a specialty of the medical and surgical diseases of Women, having fully prepared myself to that branch of the profession. I will be found at my residence on West street, Coudersport, Pa., every day for the next three weeks save the following dates, for consultation at:
Oswayo, Lee House, Tuesday, Aug. 30.
Harrison Valley, Hotel, Wednesday and Thursday, Aug. 31st and Sept. 1st.
Costelloville, Saturday, Sept. 3d.

Edgar S. Mattison, M.D.
Aug. 24th, 1881.

The Potter Enterprise
Wednesday Evening, August 31, 1881 – Vol. VIII, No. 16

- A daughter was born to Mr. and Mrs. Elvin Womlesdorff on Monday last.

- Mr. and Mrs. F. M. Stevens rejoice in the possession of their first born – a daughter.

MARRIED.

JOSEPH – DUNBAR – At the residence of the bride's parents, Aug. 28th, by Rev. William Marshall, Charles Joseph, of Brookland, and Miss Fannie Dunbar, of Lewisville.

ARNOLD – THOMPSON – Aug. 24th, 1881, at the residence of the bride, by Wm. H. Diven, Prof. N. T. Arnold, of Ellisburg, Potter county, Pa., and Miss H. T. Thompson, of Cedar Springs, Clinton county, Pa.

- Mr. C. L. Peck informs us that two of his pension clients have struck it rich. Mr. Lewis Hall, of Hebron, for $1,900 arrears and $24 per month, and W. H. Fuller, of Roulet, we believe, for $1,554 arrears and $8 per month, which is not such a bad windfall.

- The first number of the Ulysses *Sentinel* is at hand, published by A. H. Owens. It is a six column eight page paper, well filled and well printed. The first number starts off with a good advertising patronage. It is Republican in politics, and makes the fourth paper now published in Potter county.

- On Saturday last, Mr. J. K. Burt, of Burtville, made the Enterprise a call. Mr. Burt was the first white male child born in the limits of Potter county. He has just passed his seventieth birthday, but is still a hale old man, has never used a cane, and is still able to do considerable work. He lives in the house built by him when he first started out a young man for himself, and the house is located on a part of the farm on which he was born. A few years ago he repaired the old house, making it comfortable, and he prefers the place in which he has lived so long to a new one which might be handsomer and more convenient, but would not be the old home.

- On Tuesday last, Sheriff Monroe had an increase of five in the number of his boarders. Three of them, from Harrison, were boys, charged with horse stealing. The boys are John Button, aged 12 years, D. Button, aged 10 years, and Joseph Barber, aged 13 years. The boys stole a team of horses from D. C. White, of Whites Corners, the Sunday morning previous and were arrested at Knoxville, Tioga county. The story the boys now tell is that two men offered to give them $200 if they would bring the team to a certain point, but when they reached the place the men were not there. The boys did not tell this story upon their examination, and now claim that the parties implicated threatened to kill them if they told the truth. It is believed the parties implicated will be caught and the truth brought to light.

The Potter Enterprise
Wednesday Evening, September 7, 1881 – Vol. VIII, No. 17

- Frank Stevens says it is a boy and not a girl, as we reported. We take it all back, Frank. Perhaps the next one will be a girl and then we will say it is a boy, and that will make it average about right.

MARRIED.

TRACY – BRIGGS – At the house of John Bacon, in Coudersport, on the 4t^h inst., by Rev. A. Cone, Clarence Tracy and Miss Susie Briggs, all of Bingham township, Pa.

Mrs. Witter, of Sharon, died at Smethport Saturday last, and on Monday was buried in the Coudersport cemetery.

Allegany. Mrs. F. Lent breathed her last Sept. 3d. She has finished her life's work in less than 20 years; leaves a little one of seven months, a husband and parents, sister and many friends to mourn her early death. She was prepared to do the will of her heavenly father without a murmur. May we all be prepared to meet her.

DIED.

COBB – On the 4th inst., of cholera infantum, the infant daughter of Mr. and Mrs. L. H. Cobb, aged six months.

YOUNG – In Ulysses, Sept. 3d, 1881, of cholera infantum, the infant twin daughter of R. H. and Carrie Young, aged about nine months.

Obituary.

Mrs. Adaline Wygant, daughter of Mr. David White and Martha J. White, died at the home of her parents, in Sweden, Aug. 27th, 1881.

A trifle more than forty years of worthy life was given her, several of which she was a child of God. Besides a very pleasant girlhood home, she had spent several years of unusual happiness in her married life with him who mourns her loss. During her sickness with consumption, something more than a year, skill and love did their best but in vain. Her joys and blessings had been so many, life was so very sweet, the coming years looked so bright, and she clung tenderly and tenaciously to those nearest her. Yet whatever earth and happiness and home, kept saying, she found grace wonderfully victorious, and the bed of death became in on common way the bed of delight. Her victory astonished her, and the marked triumph of divine grace will be to the memory of her loved ones like songs in the night. Waving trees seen through the windows of her sick room, choice flowers brought her in those beautiful July and August days, and friends so constant in their care, were precious to her, but she went gladly and grandly to he beauties and glories of the eternal summer in the better and abiding home. Friends, church and dear ones are sorrowful, but a blessed hope comforts as we mourn.

- Samuel Hull, of the East Fork, has been awarded $1,300 arrears of pension and $10 per month hereafter.

- On Tuesday last, two more prisoners were added to Sheriff Monroe's list, making eleven in all. One was William Story, of Hector, surrendered by his bail. The second one was Benjamin Chestnut, of Whites Corners, charged with scattering Paris Green over the hay in A. A. Ross' barn. Young Chestnut is about twelve years of age.

- Joseph Butler, Jr., a Potter county boy, but for the past thirteen years, residing near Crescent City, Iowa, is visiting his old home. Joe went west to grow up with the price of corn and has succeeded well. Has a good farm, a wife and six children, which shows substantial progress. Mr. Butler has left samples of his corn crop at this office.

- The storm on Thursday last was very severe in some parts of our county. In the north part it was accompanied by hail and much damage was done to growing crops. The water fell in torrents, and many small bridges were washed out. The house of J. C. Bishop, in Allegany, was struck by lightning and somewhat damaged. The inmates were considerably shocked, and the farm dog killed.

- Parties receiving large pension checks will do well to exhibit a little common sense, or we shall hear of some one being swindled. A short time ago it was announced that Lewis Hall had been awarded several hundred dollars arrears of pension. Last week a stranger called on Mr. Hall, stating that he was connected with the pension bureau, and that there was a slight mistake in the check, and he wished to obtain it that it might be corrected. Mr. Hall's pension check had not then been received, consequently the stranger did not get it. If he had secured possession of the check, it is highly probable that Mr. Hall would have been out of pocket the full amount.

The Potter Enterprise
Wednesday Evening, September 14, 1881 – Vol. VIII, No. 18

North Bingham. Ever since Sunday afternoon of Aug. 21st, 1881, we have been able to boast of having three Pecks of humanity at the Corners, formerly only two Pecks. Of our additional Peck I would respectfully say she weighs 7-6, which means seventy-six, and as that is a patriotic number, it is evidently a good sign and may be an indication of something about to happen. I sincerely hope and humbly trust that we may yet be able to boast of the possession of at least a bushel of that very acceptable commodity.

- Mrs. J. P. Wambold, of Sweden, died on Monday morning last.

- We were a little premature last week in announcing the arrival of new prisoners at the jail on Tuesday. Dan. did not get them until Saturday. On Friday Emery Davis and Jake Lamblin, hired a horse and buggy of Amos Velie and drove the rig to the State Line, below Eldred, in about four hours, without feed for the horse. They claimed to have fed the horse at State Line, then drove back to Port Allegany, and got supper, but did not feed the horse, from there they drove to Wes McDowells, where they claimed they fed again, but Mr. Velie says the horse was seen about daylight tied to the fence, and he is of the opinion they did not feed it there. On Saturday Velie went after his horse and met the parties on the way back. For want of the "wherewith" to settle, both were locked up in the county jail, Saturday evening, making thirteen prisoners under Dan's charge, from Saturday night until Monday morning, when the counterfeiters were removed, the largest number ever in our jail at one time, we believe.

The Potter Enterprise
Wednesday Evening, September 21, 1881 – Vol. VIII, No. 19

Eleven Mile. The young child of Mr. and Mrs. Virgil Spencer died on Tuesday morning, of cholera infantum.

North Bingham. Mrs. J. B. Robbins, of Spring Mills, died at 4 p.m. last Tuesday. Her maiden name was Minerva Raymond, sister of J. L. Raymond, of this place. The flower of the Raymond family has fallen. So beautifully even tempered in her ways that not one in ten thousand could successfully compete with her in that respect. She was born in Feb. A.D., 1818, and was in the sixty-fourth year of her age. She had been for many years a member of the Baptist Church.

Masonic Reception.

The Dedication Reception of Eulalia Lodge, No. 342, F. & A. M., on Wednesday last proved a success in every particular, and we have yet to find a single person who was dissatisfied.

About four o'clock the members of Eulalia Lodge and visiting brethren assembled in the Lodge room, from which place they marched, to the residence of D. C. Larrabee, where D.D.G.M. Charles L. Wheeler, of Bradford, was in waiting, to escort him to the Lodge. W. K. Jones was appointed marshal. The procession was headed by the Coudersport Cornet Band; next came the members, in regalia, followed by the officers of Lewisville Lodge, Duke Centre Lodge and the officers of Eulalia Lodge. The procession marched down Main to Second, Second to West, West to Water, Water to Main up Main to First, from First to East, up East to Third, from Third to Main and to the Hall, where the order was reversed, as the procession filed into the Lodge room.

The ceremonies in the Lodge was only witnessed by Masons and were not lengthy.

The address was D.D.G.M. Charles L. Wheeler, was delivered in the Court House, as there was not room enough to accommodate all in the Lodge. The Court room was well filled.

Mr. Wheeler's address was principally historical, commencing with the earliest authentic history of the Craft, and following its progress and advancement down to the present time. He also alluded to some of the principles of the order and paid a glowing tribute to this, the oldest institution organized by man. He explained what was expected of Masons, as citizens, and other points of interest to all, whether of the craft or not. Mr. Wheeler received the best of attention and all regretted that he did not talk longer.

From the Court House the crowd filed to Masonic Hall, for a social time in the Lodge and reception rooms, or the Opera House underneath where Billy Young's Full Band furnished the best of music for those wishing to dance.

The Opera House was festooned and wreathed until one failed to notice the brick walls, and want of plaster on the ceiling. The room showed great care and taste and a vast amount of work, for which the ladies of Coudersport, deserve praise, and for which the members of Eulalia Lodge return their sincere thanks.

In the ball room the best of order prevailed, and although the attendance was large there was no hurry and the company so good natured that it was not necessary to call on by numbers.

Up stairs a different scene was being enacted. Many of the guests, not caring to dance, assembled in the reception and Lodge rooms, which were brilliantly lighted, and well furnished, and passed away the short time before supper, in conversation, etc., as best suited each group.

The parlor was used in connection with the dining room, and was filled with tables. Both rooms were tastily trimmed – arches of evergreens over the doors and windows, and emblems of the craft over the arched doors and on the sides. Flowers in abundance, were on the tables, and the tables themselves, with the arrangements of fruits, etc., presented a beautiful appearance. A number of persons remarked that handsomer or better supplied tables, they had never seen at any gathering. And for this the ladies are entitled to thanks, and just where the thanks should end is hard to say, for the people of Coudersport, young and old, ladies and gentlemen, those whose friends were members of the lodge, and those who had no such incentive, rendered every service possible, and to their assistance is largely due the success of this reception.

Over one hundred and sixty couple were in attendance.

EULALIA LODGE.

The Lodge was chartered March 4th, 1861, and was organized in the October following, with nine members, viz.: - Timothy Ives, W.M.; B. S. Colwell, S.W.; Joseph Williams, J.W.; Samuel Haven, Sec.; Dr. Edward Joerg, Treas., G. W. G. Judd, D. C. Larrabee, C. H. Warriner and J. C. Cavanaugh. Of the charter members only D. C. Larrabee and G. W. G. Judd are now connected with the lodge.

In May, 1880, the fire destroyed the Hall occupied by the Masons, and a portion of their furniture, but it was mostly covered by insurance. The greatest loss to the lodge was the early records which were burned at that time.

After the fire the lodge met in the Court House until the completion of K. of H. Hall, since which time, they have occupied the hall in connection with that organization, pending the completion of their own hall, dedicated last Wednesday.

Since its organization the lodge has received 216 members, and now has a membership of 84, which is being rapidly increased, 16 having been added the past year, and a number of applications awaiting action.

The present officers of the lodge are D. C. Larrabee, W.M.; W. W. Thompson, S.W.; C. A. Stebbins, J.W.; Almeron Nelson, Treas.; N. H.

Goodsell, Sec.; Miles White, S.D.; D. F. Glassmire, J.D.; W. K. Jones, S.M.C.; Edward Forster, J.M.C.; O. J. Rees, Pur.; Benjamin Rennells, Tyler. The lodge occupies the entire third story over the stores built by C. S. Jones and F. E. Lyon, reached by broad stairs from Main street. At the head of the stairs is a comfortable hall, opening into the Tyler's room which is 12 x 16 feet, from this, entrance is had to the reception room 17 x 18 fronting on Main street and the public square; from the Tyler's room entrance is also had to the dining room, and other rooms used by the lodge one 9 x 12 and one 3 ½ x 6 opening into the Lodge room proper, and where regalia will be kept. All these rooms are covered with a green carpet of plain pattern. The Lodge room is 25 x 55 feet, carpeted with a blue figured ingrain carpet, with two windows in the west, and lighted by three chandeliers, containing four gas burners, with side lights for Secretary, &c. From the lodge double folding doors, arched, open into the dining room. The furniture is of black walnut and gilt, excepting the chairs, at the west, north and east, (according to points of compass) are moulded arches to correspond with arched entrance to dining room. The chandeliers depend from beautiful moulded centre pieces in the ceiling. This covers the north half of the building. The south half is, in front, a parlor, 23 x 22, with arched folding doors and a dining room 44 x 25, a kitchen 15 x 17, pantry 8 x 8 ½, closet 4 ½ x 6. The walls and ceiling are all 14 feet in height, making them light and airy. Forty-eight gas burners are used in all. The gas used is from Gasoline and is the same as that used in a number of places in town.

The entire cost of the lodge property is about $4,500, a portion of which remains a debt on the lodge, but with its present prosperity, the society will be able to meet all their obligations and in a few years will be out of debt and own one of the finest Lodge properties in Northern Pennsylvania.

The Potter Enterprise
Wednesday Evening, September 28, 1881 – Vol. VIII, No. 20

Freeman's Run. Born, Sept. 18th, to Mr. and Mrs. H. H. Beebe, a daughter, Weight, nine pound.

Roulet. Born, Sept. 6th, to Mr. Jno. Tenbrook and wife, a daughter.

MARRIED.

PLUM – COLLINS. – At the residence of C. H. Cole, in Port Allegany, on Sunday, Sept. 18, 1881, Mr. J. E. Plum, of Elmira, and Miss Nellie Collins, of Coudersport.

DIED.

YOUNG. – In Ulysses, Sept. 17th, 1881, Willis, infant twin son of R. H. and Carrie Young, aged about 10 months, from Cholera Infantum.

- On Saturday morning last, Jacob Weidman, of Allegany, found six of his sheep dead and two seriously injured, the work of two dogs. The dogs were discovered in the act, but will never do so any more.

Democratic County Convention.

The Potter Co. Democratic Convention met in the Court House, on Tuesday evening last and was called to order by Wm. Dent.

On motion, F. W. Knox was chosen Chairman and Thos. G. Hull and Henry Tice Secretaries.

LIST OF DELEGATES.

Abbott – Henry Tice, Louis Hoppe, Geo. Rexford.
Allegany – Chas. Nelson, A. W. Andrews, F. M. Reynolds.
Bingham – M. M. Babcock, Jos. Coulston, F. M. Reynolds.
Coudersport – Miles White, C. L. Peck, F. W. Knox.
Eulalia – F. A. Nelson, Wm. Furness, Frank Phelps.
Genesee – A. A. Hickox, John Coulston, Bryan McGinnis, Ira Easton.
Harrison – Benj. Davis.
Hector – R. F. Davis.
Lewisville – Fred Baker.
Oswayo – G. F. Rowley, John Morley, Edw. McGonigal.
Pike – A. H. Haxton.
Roulette – John Abbott, A. B. Lyman, Miles Marsh.
Sharon – A. A. Wright, Jasper Card, Abram Dereemer.
Sweden – D. D. Carpenter, Chas. Neefe, A. W. Rossman, A. Chase.
West Branch – L. F. Rice.
Wharton – Fred Davenport, Oran Cortwright.
Ulysses – A. B. Crowell, Wm. Dent, Thos. G. Hull.

C. L. Peck and A. A. Wright was appointed Committee on Credentials and Miles White Reading Clerk.

For Associate Judge, J. C. Bishop received 30 votes; N. H. Rice, 14 votes. The nomination of Mr. Bishop was made unanimous.

For Prothonotary, O. H. Crosby was nominated by acclamation.

For Register and Recorder, Chas. Parker was nominated by acclamation.

For Commissioners, the vote resulted as follows:

	1st.	2d.	3d.
Louis Hoppe,	25		
Bryan McGinnis,	9	10	
F. A. Nelson,	10	11	23
A. B. Crowell,	20	13	19
Marion Hemington,	9	7	
Charles Coats,	7		

Louis Hoppe and F. A. Nelson were declared nominated.

For Auditors, Jasper Card received 34 votes; N. H. Rice 15; Thos. Coulston, 23.

Mr. Card and Coulston were declared nominated.

Wm. Dent was appointed Delegate to the State Convention.

The Chairman was empowered to appoint Judicial Conferees.

The following were appointed, by the Convention, as County Committee for the ensuing year:

Lewisville, Geo. C. Marion; Genesee, John Coulston; Ulysses, Wm. Dent; Coudersport, O. H. Crosby; Abbott, Dr. Chas. Meine; Sweden, A. W. Rossman; Roulette, A. B. Lyman; Bingham, Chas. Grover; Eulalia, Almeron Nelson; Sharon, J. Wright; West Branch, Gottlieb Traub; Oswayo, G. F. Rowley; Allegany, A. W. Andrews.

The following resolution was offered and adopted by the convention:

Resolved. That while, with stricken hearts, we bow with humble resignation to the dispensation of Divine Providence; that has removed, from the Presidential chair of the United States, our beloved Chief Executive, James A. Garfield, we extend our earnest expression of sympathy to his bereaved family and friends.

Court Proceedings.

Court convened Sept. 19th. H. W. Williams, President Judge; Associates Hammond and Chappel.

J. Harrison continued as auditor in case of John Barr vs Hiram York, and M. S. Thompson vs Wm. Shear.

Grand Jury called and sworn. Dan Baker appointed foreman, and L. S. Nichols constable to attend the same.

Geo. Fox vs James Cooper, jury find for plff. The land described to be released on payment of $626.34, with interest and costs in ten days.

L. H. Cobb, for use of Daniel Cobb vs D. D. Carpenter, rule to open judgment, returnable next term.

Appeal of Allegany School District, from report of auditors settling the account of E. B. Morley, treasurer. Plaintiff and defendants to file statements.

Reuben F. Davis appointed Supervisor of Hector township.

D. W. Haven appointed Treasurer of Hector township.

Mary Davis vs Isaiah Davis. C. M. Allen appointed commissioner to take testimony.

Michael Veely vs Allegany township, tax of five mills ordered.

In the matter of alleged lunacy of Wm. Story. A. B. Mann, E. S. Mattison and L. B. Cole appointed commissioners, and rule on Ulysses Poor district certifying residence.

Patrick Clark vs John Rooney, settled.

And now, Sept. 20, 1881, the fact of the death of James A. Garfield, President of the United States, having been this day announced in open Court, it is now, in consideration thereof and as a token of respect for the memory of the late Chief Magistrate of this nation, ordered that the several Courts be adjourned.

William Hyatt admitted to citizenship, Sept. 21.

Veniries issued for 36 traverse jurors and 24 grand jurors, for December term.

Trustees of Bingham Estate vs Patrick McHale, verdict for Plaintiff in sum of $40 and costs.

A. B. Mann for use of F. B. McNamara vs S. E. Ives. D. C. Larrabee appointed to distribute money.

Mathew Moran adopted by Edward McGonigall, and to assume the name of Mathew McGonigall, with rights, etc.

The question of removing place of holding election in Keating township, ordered to be again submitted at Nov. election.

Edson G. Davidge and James Horton vs Jason Kibbee. Judgt in favor of Plff for land described in writ of ejectment, for want of appearance.

O. J. Rees for use of P. A. Stebbins, Jr. vs Genesee Independent School District. Mandatory writ ordered in this case.

Joseph Mann and R. L. Nichols vs Moses L. Kemp, et al. Rule on Nancy Lambert, formerly Nancy Kemp, and John Lambert to appear and plead &c.

Dan'l Clark vs Sala Stevens and B. F. Nichols. Liquidation of Judgment in this case against Nichols stricken off.

Ordered that Sunderlinville Independent School District pay to Hector School District the sum of $60, as the balance due from them.

The following action in Commonwealth cases; vs Mathias Smith, discharged; vs George Butler and Charles Cannon, forgery, plead guilty, held in sum of $300 for appearance at next term; vs Morris Jordan, assault and battery, $100 bail for appearance next term; vs Hiram Graham, fornication and bastardy, on presentation of statement and petition, approved by Commissioners, discharged; vs John Roony, assault and battery, guilty, bail $300 for payment of costs and appearance next term; vs Charles L. Hannahs, No. 2 Sept. session, 1881. House breaking, guilty, to undergo imprisonment in the Western Penitentiary for three years to be computed from expiration of No. 1 Sept. Sess., 1881; vs Charles L. Hannahs, No. 2 Sept. Sess., 1881, larceny, plead guilty. Sentenced to restore the property and undergo imprisonment in Western Penitentiary one year, pay costs and a fine of $10; vs George W. Meltzer, larceny, leave granted District Attorney to send up a bill on indictment, true bill rendered; vs A. D. Corey, selling liquor, bail $200 for appearance at next term; vs Deloss Genung, selling liquor, bail $200 for appearance at next term; vs John Button, Joseph Barber and Dell Button, larceny. Dell Button not guilty; Joseph Barber, aged 13 last February and John Button, aged 12 last April, sentenced to House of Refuge; vs Benj. Chestnut, aged 14 years, malicious mischief, guilty. Sentenced to House of Refuge; vs James Larkin, malicious mischief, discharged, no prosecutor appearing; vs Titus Locey, bench warrant ordered; vs Wesley McDowell, bench warrant ordered; vs S. Howard, selling liquor, true bill, bench warrant ordered; vs Wm. Story, surety of the peace, continued, bail $100; vs Daniel Hopkins, selling liquor, petition read and prisoner discharged; vs L. L. Jones, *nol pros* entered; vs Sidney Butler, bench warrant issued for Mason Nelson, prosecutor sentenced to pay costs; vs Peter McDermet, John O'Donnell and Michael O'Donnell, assault and battery, bench warrant issued; vs Henry Davis and Jake Lambert, cruelty to animals, *nol pros*; vs Marshall Gross, surety of the peace, bail $100 for appearance at next term; vs Wm. McCarn and F.

Vergason, cruelty to animals, not a true bill, the prosecutor, Dennis Hall, to pay costs; Mathew Moran, selling liquor, not a true bill, county to pay costs; vs John Brownlee, forgery, true bill.

Alias sub in divorce awarded in case of Edna Dunford vs George Dunford and Charles Roselle vs Martha J. Roselle; Emma M. Miller vs Charles Miller, divorce granted; N. W. Bice vs Meta Bice, C. M. Allen appointed commissioner to take testimony; Mary Alderman vs Chauncey Alderman, *alias sub* in divorce ordered; Harmon Lewis vs Martha Ann Lewis, F. G. Babcock appointed commissioner to take testimony; Josephene Allen vs Nathan B. Allen. Rule on respondent to show case why he should pay the sum of $100 to pay counsel fees and maintain plaintiff pending proceedings, returnable next term; Eliza Baker vs A. L. Baker, answer in this case withdrawn; Orrin E. Harris vs Hattie Harris. Sheriff to make proclamation and A. F. Hollenbeck appointed commissioner to take testimony; Caroline Johnson vs John K. Johnson, *alias sub* in divorce awarded; Josephine Allen vs Nathan B. Allen to be put on argument list for next term, to be heard on depositions.

Daniel Monroe, Sheriff of Potter county, acknowledged the following deeds for land sold at Sheriff's sale:

To R. H. Howe for 42.1 acres in Bingham, sold as property of Dewalt Shutt, for $125.

To Isaac Benson for 96.2 acres in Bingham, sold as property of Adison Atwater and Charles Howard, *terre tenants*, for $25.

To F. W. Knox for 57.8 acres in Sylvania, sold as property of Wm. Putnam for $25.

To Isaac Benson for ½ acre in Coudersport, sold as property of S. E. Ives for $425.

To W. G. Clark for 160 acres in Portage sold as property of Herman Bridges for $100.

To Abigal M. Bridges for 25.2 acres in Keating, sold as property of Herman Bridges for $10.

The Potter Enterprise
Wednesday Evening, October 5, 1881 – Vol. VIII, No. 21

G. A. R.

The Oswayo and Sharon Posts having sent word to Arch F. Jones Post of Coudersport, that they would meet with them in Coudersport on the evening of Oct. 1st, the following committee of arrangement was appointed: O. J. Rees, G. W. Pearsall, Dr. Frank Buck and George Tuttle, who were directed to procure supper and necessary refreshments. Saturday evening the following comrades were present from

ESTES POST 125 OSWAYO.

J. E. Lee, G. F. Rowley, A. S. Lyman, Geo. Brizzee, Horace Brizzee, V. R. Kenyon, G. K. Wilber, James Stilson, Hiram Chesbro, Wm. Fessenden, A. Christman.

BARNES POST 175 SHARON.

E. A. Graves, Samuel White, Dana Drake, Thos. Blauvelt, James Blauvelt, Jacob Cole, M. S. Shattuck, E. Graves, J. Failing, E. R. Crocker, W. A. Cole, W. S. Warner, W. D. Carpenter, R. B. Cole, L. Hoyt, Peleg Burdic, Frank Hallock, Garnet Fish, M. S. Hitchcock, L. H. Bailey, J. W. Dickinson, E. Rhodes, F. E. Lyon, Seth Drake.

The post was called to order by Commander Covey. After the usual business commander Lee of Estes Post was called to the chair. Senior vice commander Lyman, M. S. Hitchcock, Barnes Post, Junior vice commander, Jacob Failing chap. When the following recruits were duly mustered as comrades into A. F. Jones Post: John Earle, George F. Younglove and Emanuel Stuckey, after which the Posts adjourned to J. O. Edgcomb's and partook of a very nicely prepared oyster supper.

The comrades again repaired to the lodge room and whiled away a happy hour in recounting old memories.

Com. Lee moved a vote of thanks to A. F. Jones Post for the courtesies extended to the visiting Posts carried, it having been proposed that the several Posts of Potter County meet three weeks from Oct. 1st in Sharon, vote of the several Posts taken, carried and arrangements made for a meeting as proposed.

Jones Post then adjourned and the company dispersed after singing "Marching Through Georgia," in front of the court house. The comrades parted with many tokens of friendly feeling.

The Potter Enterprise
Wednesday Evening, October 12, 1881 – Vol. VIII, No. 22

- The infant child of Mr. and Mrs. Wm. Sherwood of Roulet, died on Sunday last.

DIED.

VANWEGEN – On Thursday evening, Oct. 6th, 1881, of inflammation on the brain, infant son of Levi and Clara Van Wegen, aged 7 weeks.

The Potter Enterprise
Wednesday Evening, October 19, 1881 – Vol. VIII, No. 23

Oswayo. Mr. and Mrs. Wm. Moyer rejoices in the birth of a fourteen pound boy, which occurred on the 10th inst.

Oswayo. Mr. Mike Kline and Miss Mary Barr were married, at Sharon Centre, on the evening of the 8th inst.

MARRIED.

KLEIN – FLASHUTZ. – On the 12th inst., at the house of John Klein, in Eulalia, by Rev. A. Cone, Mr. Joseph Klein and Miss Emma Flashutz, all of Keating township.

LYMAN – TAGGART. – At the residence of the bride's parents, by Rev. C. Strong, Oct. 10th, 1881, A. S. Lyman, of Oswayo, and Rachel Taggart, of Eulalia.

Eleven Mile. A real surprise party was gathered at the house of Mr. and Mrs. A. S. Lyman, on the 10th inst., but very pleasant nevertheless. The occasion was their twentieth wedding anniversary. They had no thought of celebrating the event, and consequently, were caught in the usual wash-day exercise, by the first arrivals, but an early adjournment of those exercises were effected, and soon the arrivals increased; then with the abundance of eatables, with which they came equipped, upon an extension table (which they left on departing) a right royal feast was spread. As evening came, the younger people appeared and soon their lively games were in progress while their elders enjoyed a social chat. Refreshments were partaken of again and, with kindly salutations, the party retired at a seasonable hour, leaving highly cherished memories of usefulness and value to host and hostess. The families present were those of Wm. Dalrymple, of Bolivar; D. Kelly, J. T. Rathbun, Mrs. C. Healy, G. F. Rowlee, B. F. Lyman and A. V. Butterfield, Eleven Mile; Walter Wells, W. W. Crittenden and Mrs. Hunt, Oswayo; Mrs. H. O. Yale, Willing, N.Y., and A. D. Colcord, Coudersport. Other friends sent lines of regret that they could not attend. Those from Mr. and Mrs. W. A. Crosby, accompanied by a set of flat-irons, closed with hoping "you will be able to keep your pathway smooth through life." Mr. and Mrs. G. K. Smith were kept home by sickness of family. They sent presents which are highly cherished by the recipients thereof, who, though sad by reason of the broken home circle, yet feel that they have cause for joy and thankfulness after twenty years of life together.

DIED.

CLARK – At Gold, Pa., Oct. 16th, 1881, of Typhoid fever, Norman Clark, aged 15 years and 6 months.

Curls of Smoke.

We note another ruin in "Hemlock Row." Thus one by one signs of our great fire are fading away. Never was Coudersport in a more prosperous condition. Never did it look so well, in spite of some gaps in the business portion. The fever for building tasty residences remains unabated. The villa style taking the lead. The new houses of Mrs. Mary Jones and Geo. F. Ross will be ornaments to our already beautiful village nestling the Allegany's side. We notice with pleasure that substantial sidewalks of flag and plank are taking the place of broken boards.

The river bed below Second street bridge resembles a logging stream, and we pray for a deluge of waters to sweep away the unsightly debris.

The hot and dry weather of the past Summer has flooded us with such a multitude of stenches that we are very much inclined to ask have we a borough board of health. If so cannot something be done to abate the varied smells that bear pestilence upon their baleful wings. Cannot vaults be dug deep, or limed, and decaying vegetables buried?

A citizen had a narrow escape from a pistol shot on the 13th. The weapon was accidentally discharged while holding the muzzle between his thumb and finger. His hand was simply burned with the powder. Another case of carelessness which brings to mind the accidental shootings that we see noted in every daily paper. Never was the rage for revolvers, in the North as great as at present. Almost every boy is the owner of a deadly weapon. And we expect that the list of sudden deaths will be frightfully augmented as the days go on.

The North Wharton Tannery.

One of the most marked results of a vigorous enterprise is to be seen by a visit to North Wharton, in this county. Where last spring nothing but logs and stumps were to be found, to-day looms up, in a nearly completed state, one of the finest and largest Tanneries in the United States, erected by Alfred Costello & Co. Every part of the institution is erected in the most substantial and perfect manner, and everywhere about it is a manifest intent on the part of the proprietors to spare no cost to make it one of the finest and most perfect tanneries in the world. The yard and sweat pits are erected together, are now five hundred and fifty feet long by eighty-two feet wide and when fully completed will be about seven hundred and fifty feet long, covered by a cement and gravel roof, fire proof. The sweat pits are made of heavy stone walls filled between with soil. The leach house contains twenty-four leaches, 16 x 24 feet, with machinery for four bark mills. The dry house, not yet erected, will be nearly 400 feet long, three stories high. The chimney or smoke stack is probably the finest specimen of its kind in the State; it is 128 feet high, 12 feet base with a 50-inch flue, and is surrounded with four mammoth ovens, heating seven thirty-foot boilers. The ovens are lined throughout with the best quality of fire brick, the whole surrounded by heavy stone mason work, and will be covered by iron roofing, making it thoroughly fire proof. The ovens are a sufficient distance from the yard and leach house to render it safe from fire. No two buildings stand within 120 feet of each other, and in the centre, between the buildings, is to be erected in a fire proof building, a powerful force pump, run by an engine used only for that purpose, and which will be able to throw several large streams of water over any portion of the tannery building and bark sheds; an ample supply of hose is to be kept for that purpose. The hides and leather are to be transported from one part of the tannery to another by means of cars and elevators, tracks and turn tables being so laid and constructed so that there will be but very little carrying by hand necessary in any part of the building. They have already in operation a large and commodious store and office connected together. The tannery is constructed double throughout, so as to practically run two tanneries under one roof. Each manufacturing an entirely different kind of leather from the other and to run entirely disconnected. The Company have already secured sufficient bark lands to supply their tannery for at least twenty years. The whole when in actual operation, will constitute the most extensive and grandest enterprise ever organized in this county.

Potter County, Pennsylvania Potpourri – Volume I
1880 through 1884

The Potter Enterprise
Wednesday Evening, October 26, 1881 – Vol. VIII, No. 24

Curls of Smoke.

The leaves have been killed so dead by the first freeze that collectors of autumn leaves will find it difficult to secure really fine specimens this year, and those who have neglected to gather ferns early have missed their opportunity.

The Seventh street bridge is sadly in need of repair. Some person, probably in authority, has nailed two planks across the end, and undoubtedly retired thinking they had done a noble deed. They may have saved some horse a broken leg. But is the bridge to remain a sealed book hereafter? If so, paint R.I.P. on the end and let us know.

The climate of the past dry season has been, without doubt, conducive to much sickness. Springs drying, then filling suddenly with surface water which bears into our water pipes the seeds of disease in the form of invisible fungi, that finds a nurturing nidus in various portions of our bodies, where they multiply and engender an abnormal action of the system, producing fevers, diarrhoeas, &c. Would it not be a good plan to have all of the drinking water boiled during such a drouth? Thus killing all vegetation it contains, after which it might be cooled with ice or by setting aside until needed.

We learn that deer are very numerous this fall. This is cheering news to the lover of venison. But we also learn from a gentleman of veracity, that upon the waters of the Sinnemahoning, deer are hounded with impunity. Those who haven't dogs of their own joining in the cruel sport and shooting the poor fagged deer in front of somebody else's hound, getting a piece of meat that is black with engorged blood and unfit to eat. Beside the well known fact of hundreds of deer being hounded to death that are never found. Why is not the game law enforced? Or why try to protect our game?

We wish that our citizens would get the hitching post mania and get it awful bad. In spite of the threatened fine, which by the by we never knew enforced, people will continue to hitch horses to shade trees.

We observe that two more holes are started in the roadbed of the Main street bridge. Are the borough dads buying cull lumber as economy?

Since the thinning out of the trees has begun the row of Main street lights may be seen, at night, from the Homer Hill road where it curves around the head of the hollow near C. C. Breunle's.

- Last week Merrick Jackson's son met with a serious accident, near the old Quimby mill on the Sinnemahoning. He was on his way to Cameron county with a load of potatoes and other farm produce. On the dugway, near the Quimby mill, a portion of the road suddenly gave way leaving one horse hanging only by the harness, the wagon nearly over the bank and the other horse barely able to keep his footing. Believing it impossible to get his horse back and fearing that the other horse and wagon must go over the bank if something was not done quickly, Mr. Jackson cut a portion of the harness loosening the poor brute who went down the bank among the rocks a distance of a hundred feet or more.

Before reaching the bottom the poor horse was dead. The other horse was saved. The team had been but recently purchased and this was their first trip. It is said the road has been in a dangerous condition for some time. The township will be asked to pay for the horse killed.

The Potter Enterprise
Wednesday Evening, November 2, 1881 – Vol. VIII, No. 25

- It was Wm. H. Rounseville who asked the boys to smoke, on Monday last, and an eleven pound boy was the especial cause of his rejoicing.

Costelloville. You may ask, "why Mr. Whitcome is so proud of late." Surely he has a right to be. It's a girl.

Costelloville. Mrs. Edward Glaspy, daughter of Miller Rees, died on the 25th inst., of fever, after an illness of about three weeks.

- We regret to announce the death of Mrs. A. H. Owen, wife of Mr. A. H. Owen, of the Ulysses *Sentinel*. But a short time ago they removed from Coudersport to Lewisville. Mrs. Owen was taken ill with typhoid fever and on Sunday morning last ceased to breathe, leaving a loving husband, and infant child besides other relatives and friends to mourn her loss. Mr. Owen has the heartfelt sympathy of this community in the loss and bereavement which he has thus sustained.

Curls of Smoke.

Geo. Brahmer is having built a very tasty porch upon his Water street residence. Speaking of George, reminds us that we have, in him, an example of the force of long habit. Only a short time ago he sold his blacksmith shop fully determined to quit the business forever. He is behind the anvil again, as we all expected he would be. After the same manner a person a person who gets Potter county mud upon his feet is stuck for life.

Chestnuts are extremely plenty this season. But it is said they are in a bad shape for gathering. The first freeze was so severe that the stems of the burs were killed and the burs fell to the ground without opening. And the weather has been so damp since that the nuts are still enclosed in their thorny walls. Parties going to the chestnut woods should supply themselves with a pair of thick strong gloves to use in forcing the burs open. It is said that the deer and bear have begun the harvest.

The leaves have fallen very rapidly this year. So that our sidewalks in some portions of town are unpleasantly heaped. As the fallen leaves furnish fine bedding for horses and cattle and a final fertilizer they should be placed under cover, and not burned.

F. M. Stevens, who has been an invalid for a number of months, expects to remove from our midst, to Southern Georgia, about the seventh of Nov., where he will take up a permanent abode if the climate agrees with him. Frank is a young man of sterling worth and while we dislike parting with him our best wishes for health and happiness go with him.

Our evenings, of late, have been very dull, from a business point of view. The stores closing before the usual time, 9 p.m. As the evenings are getting long why cannot our young people give us something in the way of amusement and instruction. Can we not have a home troupe or amateur theatricals, concerts, debates, lectures, &c.? For our part we dislike a simple vegetation that survives the winter by sheer force of hardiness. Give us something to make existence enjoyable.

Our nights are moonlit and frosty, and the days beautiful with the tints of the dying year and mellow sunshine.

The Potter Enterprise
Wednesday Evening, November 9, 1881 – Vol. VIII, No. 26

Forest House. All of the "boys" have smoked of late, and Joseph Klein (our blacksmith) was the individual who "set em up," he having taken unto himself a partner to share his joys and sorrows. We wish him all the joy and happiness attainable in this life, and trust he may not lack for help to "strike when the iron is hot."

MARRIED.

WAMBOLD – STUART. – In Cameron, Nov. 2d, by Rev. V. L. Garrett, Mr. Charles Wambold, of Coudersport, and Miss Lulu Stuart, of Cameron Co., Pa.

Allegany. Mrs. G. W. G. Judd died last Thursday, (Nov. 3,) and was carried to her last resting place yesterday in the cemetery at Coudersport. The funeral services was also held at the M. C. Church there. She has gone down to her grave fully prepared, after a long life of usefulness, both in her own family and in the community around them. In her sickness, she was a great sufferer, yet could praise God while passing under the rod. Rev. Dillenbeck, the new preacher in charge, delivered the funeral discourse. Waldo Judd and mother was in attendance at the funeral. Other relatives from Oswayo also.

DIED.

OWEN. – At Ulysses, Pa., on October 30th, 1881, Mrs. Owen, wife of A. H. Owen, (after a severe illness of three weeks, baffling the best skill of the physicians and the utmost care of experienced nurses,) in the 23d year of her age.

There is something peculiarly melancholy and touching in the death of this young woman. On April 29th, 1880, she was married to her bereaved and afflicted husband in the same place where she now lies in the silence of death. The young wife had become mother to a fine child, a bonny little fellow, now eight months old, and to whom she was attached with all the intensity of a mother's love. Towards her neighbors, she was retiring, but well disposed and peaceable. To her husband, she was a faithful, devoted, and loving wife. We trust that she rests in peace.

To the bereaved and sorrowing husband we extend our heartiest sympathy and for him offer our sincere prayers.

- Mrs. G. W. G. Judd was buried in the Coudersport Cemetery on Sunday last. Mrs. Judd was one of the early settlers in our county. Respected by all who knew her, and one who will be sadly missed and sincerely mourned by a large circle of friends and acquaintances. She has gone to her reward, so faithfully earned in the service of her Redeemer, in this world.

- Will Jackson, son of Merrick Jackson, was taken to the Insane Asylum at Warren on Monday. It is hoped that with the care he will receive there he will soon be enabled to return home, cured.

Curls of Smoke.

The weather is variable. Upon Friday last we had our first snow squall, and that from the south west, with the mud of the roads stiffening into hubs. The roads over which so much teaming has been done are rough. Notwithstanding this our roads, generally, are better than usual for the season.

Business is fair. The loaded teams drawing merchandise from the rail roads show that our merchants are full of enterprise.

It has been rather sickly of late, although, here in town we have had no serious diseases, he rumors of fevers raging are brought to our ears from every side. Let us attend to the sanitary condition of our village.

Len King is about to open a restaurant in the Kline building on East street. That location must be rather saloony.

Upon Friday physicians were called upon to inquire into the sanity of Will Jackson. We trust that his derangement may be but temporary. Mr. Jackson is a young man that is well liked by all that come in contact with him.

The squirrels are very scarce this year. Even the little red squirrels that used to be so numerous are rarely seen of late.

- A short time ago there was a family home gathering of the Daniel W. Goodsell family, at Hornby, N.Y. Mr. Goodsell was born at Cambridge, N.Y., May 14, 1788, and Dinah Barker Goodsell, in the same village, Oct. 4th, 1795. Their respective ages now being 93 and 86 years. Mrs. Goodsell is able to get about with the aid of crutches, but the old gentleman cannot walk at all. Their mental faculties are yet strong. Eight children were born to them, all living except one daughter. Their grandchildren number 19, great grand children 27. The names of the children are Mrs. Phoebe Pierce, Conneautville, Pa.; Mrs. Hannah Coyle, Hornby, N.Y.; George Goodsell, Hornby, N.Y.; Samuel P. Goodsell, Corning, N.Y.; Albert and Nelson H. Goodsell, both of Coudersport, Pa. Forty-five persons were present at the gathering, and the ages of the 32 were who were married aggregated 1373 years, the unmarried 67 years.

- The Ulysses *Sentinel* of last week contains the following: The right of way is being secured from the borough of Lewisville to the State Line for the use of the Ulysses and Wellsville Railroad. A considerable amount of the capital stock has been subscribed, and undoubtedly the full amount will soon be raised. It is expected that cars will be running between Lewisville and Wellsville within ninety days. Those residing along the route of the proposed road will undoubtedly grant the necessary right of way, and therefore place no obstruction in the way of the speedy construction of said road. The road will be of untold benefit to the people of this section of the country. Farmers along the route of the road will be enabled to secure the highest market price for the products of their farm, being enabled to ship their produce direct to market. Since the above was in type the required amount of stock necessary to procure the charter for the road has been subscribed. A meeting of the stock holders of the Ulysses and Wellsville R.R. was held this (Thursday) at two o'clock p.m. The following Board of Directors were elected: P. Brigham, President; T. W. Burt, Treasurer, C. E. Burt, Secretary; A. G. Olmsted, Seth Lewis, E. W. Chapple, E. U. Eaton, C. A. Lewis and E. C. Lewis.

JURY LIST. – December Term.
GRAND JURY.

Joel Bolich, Farmer, Abbott; A. F. Raymond, Farmer, Ulysses; B. F. Sherman, Farmer, Genesee; A. A. Howe, Mason, Lewisville; R. L. Clark, Farmer, Ulysses; Victor Harrison, Hotel Keeper, Harrison; E. B. Tracy, Clerk, Coudersport; Aaron Woolcot, Farmer, Sharon; L. W. Crawford, Lumberman, Roulet; S. B. Pomroy, Farmer, Roulet; S. B. Foster, Farmer, Sharon; Abram Chase, Farmer, Sweden; John Morley, Farmer, Oswayo; Marion Berfield, Farmer, Wharton; Hoxey Roberts, Farmer, Sweden; W. J. Brown, Farmer, Sharon; C. C. Chase, Farmer, Sweden; Jacob Failing, Farmer, Sharon; John B. Grom, Farmer, Sweden; L. F. Rice, Farmer, West Branch; E. D. Crippen, Farmer, Pike; C. L. Holcomb, Farmer, Sweden; Aaron Bice, Farmer, Bingham; Merrick Jackson, Farmer, Summit.

TRAVERSE JURY.

Leroy Witter, Farmer, Hebron; G. S. Baker, Farmer, Pike; Hiram Hunter, Farmer, Harrison; L. W. Cushing, Farmer, Ulysses; Nelson Clark, Farmer, Eulalia; David Killbourn, Farmer, Hector; Fayette Lewis, Carpenter, Lewisville; N. D. Ayres, Farmer, Summit; George L. Baker, Laborer, Coudersport; A. S. Worden, Farmer, Bingham; Andrew Jacobs, Farmer, Sharon; A. G. Lyman, Farmer, Summit; Burt Reed, Farmer, Roulet; M. A. Nichols, Farmer, Sharon; W. B. Monroe, Laborer, Hector; Jesse Burdick, Farmer, Clara; H. Dingman, Farmer, Hebron; D. D. Chapin, Manufacturer, Harrison; Barney Daniels, Farmer, Genesee; Albert Wilber, Farmer, Hector; William Jackson, Farmer, Abbott; Frank Welton, Farmer, Wharton; Eli Nelson, Farmer, Allegany; C. A. Doerner, Clerk, Coudersport; D. W. Havens, Farmer, Hector; R. H. Howe, Farmer, Bingham; William Clear, Farmer, Hebron; Harrison Koon, Laborer, Coudersport; Rufus Corey, Farmer, Hector; M. Younglove, Farmer, Keating; O. Thompson, Farmer, Bingham, W. M. Hosley, Farmer, Harrison; John Carpenter,

Merchant, Genesee; J. C. Hallet, Farmer, Hebron; Solomon Dunham, Farmer, Oswayo; John Rooney, Farmer, Genesee.

The Potter Enterprise
Wednesday Evening, November 16, 1881 – Vol. VIII, No. 27

BORN.

GILBERT – In Coudersport, Nov. 4th, to Mr. and Mrs. F. C. Gilbert, a daughter, weight 9 pounds.

Curls of Smoke.

In spite of the severe freezes of the past month, grasshoppers are still to be seen.

The weather, with the exception of a few rainy days, has been superb. A cool bracing air, with a clear sunshiny sky. It seems to be, for once, the weather that suits all.

Billious disorders still prevail. There are more cases of jaundice among our people than has been known for years. Liver is king of our section at present.

The hill roads are still fine. The valley roads, over which there is so much teaming, have their usual depth of November mud.

Cyrene Jones is the inventor of a new bear trap, that is a murderous looking affair. Matt McGuey was the first game caught, a sore hand resulting.

It is thought that the cause of Will Jackson's insanity was erysipelas. He had been suffering with the disease and had partially recovered, when he felt it coming back upon him, and by overheating his blood the sad disaster followed. Strong hopes of recovery are held forth to the sorrowing friends by the physicians of the asylum where Mr. Jackson was taken.

Fatal Accident.

And death of an old resident, who died at Kettle Creek, Nov. 10th, aged about 15 years.

Mr. Hugh Jordan, of Kettle Creek, Pa., killed the largest bear ever seen or killed on the waters of the Northern Tier counties. Mr. Jordan is a great hunter and trapper and I can safely say the best in Northern Pennsylvania, started on Thursday afternoon in company with Chas. Lenhart, to look after his bear pens and traps. After about two hours walk they arrived at his famous bear pen and, not at all surprised, found therein one of the largest bears ever seen in this country. It weighed over 500 pounds; the hide weighing the small sum of 48 pounds and he measured 12 inches between the ears. When found he was lying upon his back with his nose against the back end of the pen and his hindquarters against the door. He was so large that his body completely filled the pen, and they could hear his heart beat for quite a distance. Stepping to a convenient position, a shot was fired into him just under the ear and Mr. Bruin gave up the ghost without a struggle. They then opened the door, and with great difficulty succeeded in getting him out of the pen. This makes the *twenty-ninth* bear Mr. Jordan has killed on this mountain, and I will not attempt to say how many deer and other small game has been captured by him. Hugh is a very obliging hunter always willing to point out the good shots for you, not like some, always wanting to kill the game himself. But if you ever happen to fall into the famous hunter's company he will hand you the 16-shooter saying "Take him under the ear." Witness.

The Potter Enterprise
Wednesday Evening, November 23, 1881 – Vol. VIII, No. 28

Millport. Mr. Wallace Sloat has a new hired girl, a few days old, which he intends to keep until some young man carries her off.

Millport. Since our last writing, death has been in our midst and claimed for its own a son of Lewis Carpenter, a young man just beginning life for himself. William will be sadly missed by his sisters and brother. His parents have the sympathy of the neighbors in their affliction. His disease was fever.

The Potter Enterprise
Wednesday Evening, November 30, 1881 – Vol. VIII, No. 29

MARRIED.
KNAPP – REID – At the Mansion House, in Friendship, Nov. 10th, by Rev. F. M. Alfred, Thos. L. Knapp, of Annin Creek, Pa., to Miss Aldoretta Reid, of Williston, Potter Co., Pa.

- One of the boilers at Briggs' Saw Mill, Keating Summit, exploded last Friday morning, scalding an old man named Jerry Black, so that he died a short time thereafter. Mr. Black was old and feeble, and was in the habit of sitting on the top of the arch, where he could see all that was going on, and be out of the way. At the time of the explosion the gauge showed only 80 pounds of steam, but the boiler was old and rotten. A small break occurred, near where Mr. Black was seated, which threw him off the arch and his head was badly cut by coming in contact with some old irons. The hot steam covered Mr. Black and upon removing his clothes after being taken to his home, the skin and portions of flesh from the body came off. He lingered but a few hours after the accident.

W., C. & P. C. R. R.
At a meeting of the stockholders of the Wellsville, Coudersport and Pine Creek Railroad held in this city, last Friday evening, the following officers were elected:
President – J. J. S. Lee.
Vice-President – I. W. Fassett.
Secretary – H. K. Opp.
Treasurer – Henry Johnson.

Potter County, Pennsylvania Potpourri – Volume I
1880 through 1884

Directors – W. A. Baldwin, A. N. Cole, H. K. Opp, O. P. Taylor, H. N. Lewis, Jas. Macken, Wm. Spargur, Joseph Doty, I. W. Fassett, Henry Johnson, J. J. S. Lee, Hiram A. Coats, and Alfred D. Tingley, of New York City.

Sixty thousand dollars of the stock was taken that evening, and every dollar could have been raised at the meeting if deemed advisable.

The engineers are now in town and will commence surveying at once. Two routes are to be surveyed, both sides of the river, promising equal facilities as to grade and patronage for the road. It will be owing largely to the liberality of land owners which route will be finally decided upon. – *Wellsville Democrat, Nov. 23d.*

The Potter Enterprise
Wednesday Evening, December 7, 1881 – Vol. VIII, No. 30

Allegany. M. A. Veeley is the proudest man among us, all on account of that fine girl baby.

North Bingham. Mr. and Mrs. B. J. Baker have an addition to their family – it's a girl.

MARRIED.

CRUM – ANDREWS. – At the M.E. Parsonage, Port Allegany, Pa., Nov. 26, 1881, by the Rev. J. K. Underhill, Mr. Edgar Crum, of Ulysses, to Miss Adeliana Andrews, of State Line Mills, Pa.

STRANG – SAUNDERS – At the Wright House, Smethport, Pa., Nov. 23, by Rev. O. J. Rees, Ed. A. Strang, of Port Allegany, to Miss Carrie J. Saunders, of Roulet.

ENGLISH – STEVENS – At the residence of Jahiel English in Eulalia, on Dec. 4th, 1881, by L. B. Cole, J.P., John English to Adda Stephens, both of Eulalia township.

Roulet. On Thursday last the many friends of Mr. and Mrs. L. B. Pomeroy gathered at their residence to celebrate their China Wedding. They were the recipients of a number of useful as well as ornamental presents, of which, they were well deserving.

North Bingham. Mrs. Hamilton Weaver, of Harrison township, died recently.

Sartwell Creek. An infant child of Joel Fessenden's was buried on the 28th inst. About three weeks ago Mr. Fessenden's wife died; he has the sympathy of his many friends.

– Among the Postoffices established, reported Dec. 3d, we find "Elmer, Potter Co., Pa., Alfred F. Dodge, Postmaster."

Potter County, Pennsylvania Potpourri – Volume I
1880 through 1884

The Potter Enterprise
Wednesday Evening, December 14, 1881 – Vol. VIII, No. 31

Oswayo. Mr. Amos Cole, of Corning, N.Y., and Miss Ella Cone, of this place, were joined in the holy bonds of matrimony last week. We wish them peace and prosperity.

Oswayo. We are sorry to record the death of George Moody, of Ellisburg. The Spiritualist M.D. failed to save him.

- Sam'l Kenyon, formerly of this county, was shot dead recently in Marillan, Jackson county, Mich. No cause known for the murder of clue to the murderers.

Millport. Mr. Charles Tyler, who had been ill, for a long time, of typhoid fever, died on the 6th of Dec. He was a kind neighbor and many sorrowing friends attended his funeral, which took place at his home. His bereaved wife has the sympathy of all.

- Stephen VanGelder, of Hebron, has recently been awarded a back pension of $1,800 and is to receive $14 per month hereafter.

- At a regular meeting of G. H. Barnes Post, No. 175, G. A. R. Dep't of Pa., an election of officers for the ensuing year occurred with the following result: P.C., Capt. L. H. Kinney; S.V.C., A. Christman; J.V.C., Peleg Burdic; Chap., Jacob Failing; O.D., Frank Hallett; Surg., F. Crocker; Q.M., Dana Drake. – *Palladium*.

Election of Officers.

At a regular meeting of A. F. Jones Post, No. 204, G. A. R., Dep't of Pa., the following officers were duly elected for the ensuing year:
P.C. – John M. Covey; S.V.C. – L. C. King; J.V.C. – John D. Earl; Q.M. – Geo. N. Tuttle; Surgeon – Frank Buck; O.D. – C. J. Marble; Chap. – A. D. Colcord; C.A. – C. J. Marble, 3 yrs., Merrick Jackson, 2 years.
Adjutant, S.M. & Q.M.S. to be appointed, at the installation of officers, at the first stated meeting in January.

- The Ulysses and Pine Creek Railroad company was organized in this village on Friday last. The stock necessary to procure the charter was readily subscribed and ten per cent paid in. The charter has been applied for and will doubtless soon arrive. The following officers were elected: President, Dr. E. U. Eaton; treasurer, D. J. Chappel; secretary, C. E. Hosley; board of directors, G. C. Marion, C. E. Hosley, C. T. Freeman, D. J. Chappel, A. H. Cobb, D. H. Cobb, W. M. Hosley, Wm. Daniels. – *Ulysses Sentinel*.

NOTICE OF INCORPORATION.

Application will be made to the Court of Common Pleas, of Potter county, on Monday, December 12th, 1881, at 2 o'clock p.m., for the incorporation of the Card Creek Cemetery Association, organized for the purpose of maintaining a private cemetery in Roulet township of said county.

Nov. 5, 1881.

C. H. Barr.

NOTICE OF INCORPORATION.

Application will be made to the Court of Common Pleas, of Potter county, on Monday, December 12th, 1881, at 2 o'clock p.m., for the incorporation of a society, for the worship of God, and the erection and maintenance of a church building, to be located at North Bingham, Potter county, Pa., to be called "The Church Society of North Bingham."

Nov. 15, 1881.

J. L. Raymond.

The Potter Enterprise
Wednesday Evening, December 21, 1881 – Vol. VIII, No. 32

DIED.

BAKER – On the 17th inst., Geo. L. Baker of Coudersport, aged 33 years.

CLARK – At North Wharton, Dec. 13th, 1881, Mrs. Fayette Clark, aged 57 years.

- Dr. T. S. Hartly, of Ridgway, formerly Pastor of the M.E. Church, Coudersport, Pa., died, about ten days since, after a short illness.

Court Proceedings.

Court called. Present, a full bench. S. F. Wilson presiding.

Resignation of E. D. Lewis as Tip Staff tendered and accepted.

Commonwealth vs J. S. Bogardus. Recognizance forfeited.

Commonwealth vs Titus Locey, nol pros, on payment of costs.

Com. vs Chas. Cannon and Geo. Butler, defendants held in the sum of $300 for appearance at next term.

J. L. Barclay vs Allen Jordan, choice of referee approved.

J. B. Miller vs James VanVoorhees, appointment of Jas. L. Knox auditor continued.

Edna Danford by next friend vs Geo. Danford. Sheriff to make proclamation.

In the matter of removing the place of holding elections in Keating township. Ordered that the question be submitted to the electors, of said township, at the election to be held Tuesday, Feb. 21st, 1882; notice to be given as required by law.

Com. vs E. Vergason, Chas. Allen and John Guinas; defendants discharged.

Com. vs Christina Jonson and Wm. Guinnip, nol pros entered and defendants discharged.

Same vs W. H. Nelson, recognizance forfeited and respited until next term.

Dusenberry, Austin & Co. vs A. C. Ellis and Betsey Ellis. Rule to show cause why judgment shall not be stricken off as to Betsey Ellis.

Michael Dehn appointed Guardian of Augusta Dehn, Eunice Dehn and Mary Dehn minor children of Augusta Dehn, deceased.

Mary E. Jenkins declared feme sole trader upon filing and recording of petition.

In the matter of the incorporation of the church society of North Bingham, charter approved.

Com. vs W. H. Nelson, false pretenses, defendant held in the sum of $100 for appearance at next term.

Same vs A. D. Corey, bail forfeited – respited.

Same vs Joanna McGonigal. Prosecutor allowed to withdraw.

Same vs Mary Nichols, adultery, true bill.

And now Dec. 13th, rule requiring judgments to be taken on Thursday, suspended and judgments may be taken on Tuesday, for this term.

Com. vs Theodore Yentzer, Mary Nichols and Augusta Holt, burglary, true bill.

Same vs Nathan B. Allen, assault and battery. Not a true bill and county to pay costs.

Rule requiring Sheriff's deeds to be acknowledged on Thursday suspended, and ordered that deeds may be acknowledged on Wednesday and Thursday.

Com. vs W. W. Story, defendant held in $100 for appearance at next term and to keep the peace in the meantime.

Arthur B. Mann appointed auditor to settle with Prothonotary and Recorder.

In the matter of the report of auditor in case of J. B. Miller vs James VanVoorhees. Feigned issue framed wherein James Sloan, F. M. Younglove and J. J. Younglove shall be plaintiffs and J. B. Miller and S. Burrett, Sr., shall be defendants. Case pass to head of list.

In the case of S. Burrett, Sr., vs James VanVoorhees, feigned issue framed wherein James Sloan, F. M. Younglove and J. J. Younglove are plaintiffs and S. Burrett, Sr., defendant; case to be put at head of list.

In the case of Com. vs John Roony, John Brownlee, Mary Nichols and Theodore Yentzer, bail entered for appearance at next term.

L. W. Crawford vs Asa Ruby, rule on J. B. Davidson, J.P., to return complete record.

In Com. vs Elmer Aylesworth, Marshall Gross and Daniel O'Donnell, recognizance forfeited and bench warrants issued.

E. B. Tracy appointed tip staff, to fill vacancy caused by resignation of E. D. Lewis.

In the matter of the incorporation of Card Creek Cemetery Association, charter approved.

Com. vs Peter McDormott and Michael O'Donnell, nol pros entered.

Judgments for want of appearance were taken in the following cases:

Amos Raymond vs John F. McNeil; A. A. Raymond for use vs John F. McNeil; Dr. Geo. Fox vs Mahlon Peterson; State Bank of Olean vs Nelson

Parmenter; Thomas A. Glover for use vs Thos. A. Glover; Joseph Ward vs West Branch township; C. H. Armstrong use of M. E. Olmsted vs Sylvania township; H. B. Vincent vs C. L. Davis; James P. Farrell vs Chas. H. Ruscher; James P. Farrell vs Horace Lent; D. Ransom & Co. for use vs Genesee township, two judgments; Esther Holley, administratrix vs James McWasser, executor.

W. B. Cutler vs F. A. Brown et al, ejectment for specific performance of contract. Court directed a plea of not guilty to be entered.

Trustees of Bingham estate us of Geo. Fox vs Henry Hurd, et al, ejectment for specific performance of contract; court directed that plea of not guilty be entered.

Joseph Mann and R. L. Nichols vs Moses L. Kemp et al; ejectment for specific performance of contract; court directed that a plea of not guilty be entered for defendants personally served.

Joseph Mann and R. L. Nichols vs Moses L. Kemp et al; ejectment for specific performance of contract; rule on Nancey Lambert formerly Nancey Kemp & John Lambert to appear and plead (to be published as provided by Act of Assembly) or judgment by default.

Judgment for want of appearance in the following: David R. Gardner vs Malachi Hober; D. F. Glassmire, Jr., for use vs John Lewis; same vs same.

Mary Alderman vs Chauncey Alderman; Sheriff directed to make proclamation and L. H. Bailey appointed commissioner.

The Grand Jury found true bills in the following cases: Com. vs Thad Kelly, Edward McGonigal, and Joanna McGonigal, selling liquor, and John Brownlee, perjury.

Same vs Marcus Dual and Catharina Duel, charged with forsaking a child; grand jury return not a true bill and county to pay costs.

Same vs Joanna McGonigal, rule to show cause why the finding of the grand jury shall not be set aside; no prosecutor's name being on the indictment.

Same vs Edward McGonigal; rule to show cause why the indictment in this case shall not quashed returnable at next term.

Same vs Thad Kelly, defendant held in the sum of $200 for his appearance at next term.

Daniel Monroe, Sheriff, came into Court and acknowledged the following deeds:

To James White for 14 8-10 acres in Hebron township, sold as the property of E. E. and W. S. Sherwood, for the sum of $50.

To J. E. Terwilliger for 25 acres in Hector township, sold as the property of W. H. Sherwood, for the sum of $25.

To Geo. W. Chisholm for 76 1-10 acres in Hector township, sold as the property of Abran VanGorder, for the sum of $20.

To Horace A. Yundt for 155 acres in Wharton township, sold as the property of Augustus F. Boas, for the sum of $800.

RETROSPECT FOR 1881.
JANUARY.
Much sickness.
Rees opens his drug store.
Son of Sylvester Greenman kicked by a horse.
Sudden deaths of Horatio A. Nelson and J. H. Heggie.
Scarlet fever makes its appearance in Ulysses.
Porter Clark meets with an accident by cars that kills his team.
Wm. Tauscher has a leg fractured.
Mr. and Mrs. Merrill celebrate their Golden Wedding, in Ulysses.
H. Baker, of Fishing Creek, is injured by a falling tree.
FEBRUARY.
Albert Lyman's mill, on Cross Fork, burns.
Coudersport Bank moves to its new building on Second street.
Diphtheria in Coudersport.
Roads bare.
Christian Fisher, of Roulet, dies, aged 81 years.
Wm. McDougall, of Oswayo, dies, aged 75 years.
Ball of the Coudersport Band, the 22d.
MARCH.
Heavy snow storms.
Measles in Keating.
Sickness prevalent.
Mrs. John Abson dies, of diphtheria.
Mrs. Joseph Mann dies.
Measles in Ulysses.
Man killed at Oswayo tannery.
Diphtheria in Sweden.
Mrs. John Matteson, of Allegany, breaks an arm.
Frank Jones dies.
APRIL.
E. N. Stebbins moves into the Ark.
Bricklaying commenced on A. G. Olmsted's store.
Thomas Brownlee, of Wharton, has his hand cut by a shingle saw.
J. G. Merrill lays the foundation for a new house.
O. J. Rees' house has a narrow escape from fire.
Jeff Baily, of Wharton, kicked by a horse.
Diphtheria in Bingham.
Trout fishing.
Sugar making.
House of Columbus Rees, of Wharton, destroyed by fire.
Married, Dr. E. S. Mattison and Edith M. Johnson.
Misses Taggart & Raymond open a millinery store on Main street.
Lew Reisman fractures a collar bone.
Dr. Ashcraft locates at Ellisburg.
Sharon oil fever.

G. W. G. Judd kicked by a horse.
MAY.
D. C. Larrabee moves into his new house.
Sharon oil fever unabated.
Harlow Dingee's house has a narrow escape from fire.
Patrick McNulty, of Roulet, breaks an arm.
Miss Anna Buckbee elected County Superintendent, of Schools.
Burt Strong hurt, logging.
David White sustains a runaway loss.
Foundation for Mrs. Mary Jones' new house laid.
Norman Dwight moves to town.
Dr. C. S. French has a runaway accident at Millport.
Bendell, the tailor, erects a building on East street.
Potatoe bugs.
Geo. F. Ross prepares for building a residence on Second street.
John Burrows, aged 71 years, died, on West Branch.
Decoration Day.
JUNE.
Miss Turner, of Ulysses, gored by an ox.
Mrs. Horace Maltby, of Roulet, killed by falling down stairs.
Coudersport scooped by Emporium base ballists.
Scarlet fever in Pleasant Valley.
Narrow gauge RR boom.
A Pollander falls into a tannery vat and is scalded.
A panther killed in Genesee.
JULY.
Fourth, celebrated.
Mrs. Dunn of Allegany injured by an axe.
Wind storm on Sartwell Creek.
Neefe's wagon shop burglarized and Norton & Doane's Hardware store.
Dwight repairs tail race of Keystone Mills.
Sharon oil wells abandoned.
Hugh Collins cut in the back by an axe.
Wm. Metzger aged 64 dies in Coudersport.
Huckleberries, abundant.
Z. J. Thompson opens grocery on Second St.
A balloon passes over Coudersport.
AUGUST.
A severe hail storm visits Shingle House.
John King dies in Buffalo.
Camp meeting on Sinnemahoning.
Asher Burt, Pleasant Valley, kicked by a horse.
Severe storm of wind and rain in Coudersport, much damage done.
A new stage line to the Forest House.
An attempt made to burglarize P. A. Stebbins, Jr. & Bros. store.
O. L. Hall, Homer, thrown from a load of hay and injured.

Mrs. Geo. W. Pearsall purchases *Palladium*.
Bridge, Second St. repaired.
Mr. Wheaton bitten by rattlesnake on Pine Creek.
Carl Zimmerman purchases a lot on Main St.
Teachers' Institute at Coudersport.
Nine prisoners in jail.
Sentinel started at Lewisville.

SEPTEMBER.

Norton & Doane have 22 stoves broken on the RR.
Grabe Bros. go into their new furniture store.
Counterfeiters arrested at New Bergen.
A water spout at Genesee Forks.
G. W. Hackett of Genesee severely injured by a runaway.
Masonic Reception and Dedication of the Masonic Hall at Coudersport.
Meteor seen in Bingham.
Attempted, elopement in Oswayo.
Fair of Potter Co.
Dogs destroy sheep in Allegany.

OCTOBER.

Griesel building, Main street, nearly finished.
L. R. Bliss purchases a lot on Allegany avenue.
D. C. Larrabee builds a reservoir.
Andrew Berger, Summit, cuts his wrist with a chisel.

NOVEMBER.

Bear and deer plenty.
Death of Mrs. A. H. Owen, Ulysses.
Thanksgiving.
A dog goes through M. S. Thompson's store.
Henry Schilderberger occupies half of the Zimmerman block.
Wm. Jackson taken to the insane asylum.
D. W. Butterworth removes to New Brunswick, N.J.
Mrs. G. W. G. Judd, of Allegany, dies.
Whooping cough in Allegany.
Snow.
Roulet oil well abandoned.
A 300 lb. bear killed on Kettle Creek.
Hammond, of West Branch, catches five bears.
Skating.
Dr. S. A. Phillips returns from an extended hunt in the West.
Jerry Black killed by the bursting of a boiler at Briggs' saw mill, Keating Summit.
Announcement of narrow gauge rail road to Wellsville and Pine Creek.
Deer hunting.
James L. Knox converts the old Rees shop into a tenement house.
Diphtheria in Bingham.
Johnston Bros. sell their blacksmith shop on First St.

Law firm of Mann & Ormerod established.
Ulysses and Pine Creek railroad company organized.
Typhoid fever at Millport and on Freeman Run.
Geo. Moody dies at Ellisburg.

The Potter Enterprise
Wednesday Evening, January 4, 1882 – Vol. VIII, No. 33

OFFICIAL DIRECTORY.
PROTHONOTARY – W. A. Crosby.
REGISTER AND RECORDER – E. D. Lewis.
TREASURER – Edwin Haskell.
SHERIFF – Daniel Monroe.
DISTRICT ATTORNEY – L. H. Cobb.
COUNTY COMMISSIONERS – F. A. Nelson, Burt Oleson, S. H. Spencer.
COUNTY CLERK – George W. Pearsoll.
AUDITORS – Thomas Coulston, Dan. Baker, I. D. Ripple.
COUNTY SUPERINTENDENT – Anna Buckbee.
COUNTY SURVEYOR – Fayatte Lewis.
COUNTY CORONER – D. Chas. Meine.
JUDICIARY – PRESIDENT JUDGE – H. W. Williams;
ADDITIONAL LAW JUDGE – S. F. Wilson.
ASSOCIATE JUDGES – N. C. Hammond, E. W. Chappel.
TIME OF HOLDING COURT – First Monday in March, Second Monday in June, Third Monday in September and the Second Monday in December.

Pleasant Valley. Born – To Mr. and Mrs. John Reed, a daughter.

North Bingham. One day last week Mr. Dewit Chase of this place caught a beautiful Robbin-s at Spring Mills, N.Y. Success to the happy couple.

Pleasant Valley. Married – At the residence of the bride's parents, December 24th, 1881, by John Davison, Esq., Mr. Alva A. Thompson and Miss Julia Hanson, both of this place. A long and happy life to the couple is the wish of their many friends.

MARRIED.
HURD – KIES – On Dec. 30th, 1881, by Rev. J. L. Swain, at his residence, near Raymond, Mr. Henry G. Hurd, of Genesee, and Miss Lettie A. Kies, of Allegany.

CARPENTER – FURMAN – On Dec. 31st, 1881, by the Rev. J. L. Swain, at his residence, near Raymond, Mr. Willis Carpenter, of Ulysses, and Miss Ida I. Furman, of Sweden, Pa.

- Mrs. Porter H. Clark, of Hebron was buried on Sunday, Dec. 25th.

DIED.

SHELDON – In Hebron, Dec. 27th, Mr. Miles Sheldon, aged 21 years.

HENRY – In Bingham, Potter Co., Pa., on Tuesday, Dec. 20th, 1881, of Diptheria, infant daughter of Charles and Cynthia Henry, aged between two and three years.

May this soon meet the gaze of the father of the departed little one, and he fly to the side of his bereave companion at once, is the wish of all his friends.

- On Wednesday last Mr. Miles Sheldon, aged 21 years, of Hebron, was buried. Less than a week previous he was injured while at work in the woods with his father. The two were cutting logs and while at work a log rolled upon the elder Mr. Sheldon fastening him to the earth in a painful but not dangerous situation. The young man seized a lever and in his excitement lifted the log, which he could not possibly have done under ordinary circumstances, liberating his father. It is believed the young man received internal injuries from his over exertion. He was taken ill the same day, complaining of severe pains in his back, and lived but a few days.

Mr. Sheldon was an upright, industrious young man. He was engaged to be married, and the ceremony was to have taken place on New Year's day.

Election of Officers.

At a stated meeting of Coudersport Union, No. 294 E.A.U., held Dec. 20th, the following officers were elected for the ensuing term, ending June 30, 1882.

Pres., George W. Tuttle; Vice Pres., Mrs. C. J. Marble; Chancelor, Dr. Frank Buck; Advocate, William Shear; Treasurer, Robert H. Peet; Acct., Mrs. L. R. Bliss; Secretary, L. R. Bliss; Chap., Rev. Dillenbeck; Watchman, J. Johnston; Sentinel, R. M. Post; Warden, William Yunge; Med. Ex., Dr. Frank Buck.

Installation of officers, first Tuesday evening in January.

- The following are the officers of Lewisville Lodge No. 556 F. & A. M., for the ensuing Masonic year: G. C. Marion, W.M.; F. M. Bronson, S.W.; E. U. Eaton, J.W.; Seth Lewis, Sec.; W. Burtis, Treasurer; A. L. Harvey, S.D.; Arthur Lewis, J.D.; Lyman Perry, Pur.; R. L. Clark, S.M.C.; Charles Erlbeck, J.M.C.; E. Hovey, Tyler; H. K. Lane, Chaplain.

Probably a Swindle.

Several years ago a brother of Mr. James White, miller at the Crittenden flouring mills of Coudersport, "went west," to seek his fortune. His friends heard from his occasionally, and a short time ago Mr. James White received a letter, purporting to be from his brother in the west. The letter stated that this brother had sold out his property in British Columbia, and had taken in pay therefor a draft on New York for $2,000. That he could not get it cashed without discounting it some fifty dollars; that he was coming East and requested Mr. White to send him $150 to come home with, when he could get the draft cashed, save the $50 discount and would refund the loan. The money was sent by Postoffice Money Order and since then nothing has been heard from the missing brother, although there has been ample time. Another brother received an appeal similar to the one received by James White. He sent a draft on a Western Bank, which would require that the holder be identified. This draft has not been paid. It is now believed the letters were not written by the brother at all, but by a man named James Rutherford, who went to San Francisco last summer. This man was well acquainted with the White family, and it is thought he took this means to replenish his pocket book. It is barely possible that it may turn out all right yet, but so long a time has elapsed since the "brother" should have been heard from that it has all the appearance of a well laid scheme and successful swindle.

The Potter Enterprise
Wednesday Evening, January 11, 1882 – Vol. VIII, No. 34

Golden Wedding.

Hebron, Pa., Jan. 9, 1882.

In May 1831, Wm. H. Hydorn purchased a farm on which he now resides, and in the Spring of 1833 moved with his family, consisting of wife and one child, from Grafton, Renselaer Co., N.Y., to begin the work of making it a home.

January 1st, 1882, being the fiftieth anniversary of his marriage to Elenor Burdick, a goodly number of his neighbors assembled at his house to offer congratulations and leave tokens of regard. A bountiful dinner, prepared and served by the guests, was partaken of by about forty persons. Then reminiscences of life in the new county and the changes fifty years have wrought, were recalled by Messrs. Hydorn, Nelson, Clark and others.

The log house which sheltered the family many years, was superceded in 1855, by the house they now occupy. Of their six children but one lives to greet them at their golden wedding. Nine of their eleven grand children were present. Mr. Hydorn knows of but one couple that were married and living in Hebron, when he came here, who yet survives, viz.: Mr. and Mrs. Foster Reynolds now of Nortonville, Kansas. The day passed pleasantly with music and conversation, and the guests departed with many good wishes for the aged bride and groom. Leaving as mementos of their visit, presents of about twenty dollars value.

DIED.

MUNSON – In Oswayo, Monday, Jan. 2d, 1882, Dr. H. H. Munson, aged 76 years.

Deceased was an old and highly respected citizen. In compliance with his oft expressed wish, the services at his house and grave were brief and simple.

Millport. The funeral of Mr. Isaac Barnes, who died suddenly on the 2d inst., took place on the fourth of January. The sermon was preached by the Baptist minister of Coudersport. There was a large attendance, and the discourse was good and will long be remembered by the people here.

Very Neatly Trapped.

Until quite recently a young man named Jack McIntyre was the trusted station agent of the B., N. Y. & P. R. R. at Keating Summit. He is a capital telegraph operator, a splendid penman and discharged the duties of his position with honesty and dispatch. His monthly returns of receipts to the principal office at Buffalo were satisfactory for a while, but as time progressed his remittances fell far short of the statements rendered by him, and the railroad authorities began to suspect that their trusted agent at Keating Summit was not as honest as they had been led to believe. As the discrepancies increased the attention of Mr. McIntyre was called to them, but he treated these warnings with an air of unconcern, and finally sent in his resignation without making a settlement with the company. The general freight agent telegraphed to the detective of the road in this city, Mr. B. J. Wilmoth, informing him of McIntyre's dishonesty, and giving instructions to capture him at any cost. Mr. Wilmoth paid a visit to Keating Summit, and made inquiries that prompted him to form the acquaintances of a family which laid claim to a couple of attractive young ladies.

Gaining the confidence of the house Wilmoth learned that McIntyre had been paying attention to one of the girls, and that those attentions had been rather expensive. McIntyre was nowhere to be found, but as he had left his wardrobe behind him in his flight, it occurred to the detective that he would return for it. Returning to Bradford, Wilmoth blocked out a letter to the general agent in Buffalo, which he suggested be forwarded to McIntyre at Keating Summit, in care of the family with whom the latter was intimate. The decoy letter to McIntyre was to the effect that a telegraph operator was wanted at the O., B. & W., railroad freight office, and that upon application to Mr. Smith, the agent, he might get the position. The Buffalo agent did just as he was directed, and the bait completely captured McIntyre. For fear that he might be short of funds which would interfere with his coming on to Bradford, the Buffalo agent used the precaution to enclose a pass over the road, and one day the latter part of last week McIntyre sailed, full-rigged into the office of Mr. Smith, marshaled by an influential gentleman from Liberty, who had come to bear testimony to his honesty and capability. Detective Wilmoth had been previously informed of the coming of McIntyre, and when he arrived at the office of Mr. Smith he was on hand. The delegation introduced themselves; Wilmoth took a hand in the introducing act, and in a short time became familiar enough with McIntyre to invite him to his private office leaving the influential citizen from Liberty behind to continue his recommendations of his friend, and former agent at Keating Summit. In the office of Mr. Wilmoth the dishonesty of McIntyre was being thoroughly discussed, and the fellow after some persuasion acknowledged having embezzled something over three hundred dollars from the road.

"What do you propose doing about it?" asked Wilmoth.

"I can't do anything. I have no money, not a cent, but that don't bother me any. What I am here for is to get a position as operator at the freight depot," cooly answered the operator.

"I put up that little job on you," replied Wilmoth in cheerful tones, "and I rather thank that the next operating you do will be inside the prison walls of Allegany prison."

This information fell upon McIntyre with crushing force, and he wilted to extremely slender and nerveless proportions. He stammered and coughed in his effort to make an explanation, when in walked his friend from Liberty who had become uneasy owing to the protracted absence of the two. He was made acquainted with the defalcation of his erring charge, and at once expressed himself willing to make good the discrepancy. To secure himself and the company from any slip in the agreement Wilmoth compelled the man from Liberty to give a judgment note for double the amount embezzled, and young McIntyre went his way. It is unnecessary to say he did not get the position he solicited. – *Bradford Times.*

The Potter Enterprise
Wednesday Evening, January 18, 1882 – Vol. VIII, No. 35

- F. J. Norton set up the cigars last week because a daughter had come to bless his life and household.

MARRIED.

WOOD – LYMAN. – At the residence of A. E. Stickles, in Keating township, McKean county, Dec. 28, by Rev. E. P. Hubbell, Mr. Lewis F. Wood and Miss Jennie M. Lyman, both of Roulet, Potter county, Pa.

East Hebron. Mr. and Mrs. H. G. Booth recently celebrated the anniversary of their Wedding, twenty-five years ago. A large number of friends and relatives were present and everybody had a pleasant time. Our friends, who thus celebrated their silver wedding, received a number of presents, not all of silver, but very nice nevertheless, and as tokens of esteem and friendship, of more than money value.

Golden Wedding.

East Homer, Dec. 29, 1881.

Friends and neighbors met at the house of Charles Wykoff to join in celebrating the day. The weather was very bad for the occasion but everything passed off merrily, there being about fifty people present. Mr. and Mrs. Wykoff tender their sincere thanks for the many presents they received.

DIED.

RAYMOND. – At Lymansville, Dec. 14th, 1881, Amos Harvey, infant son of A. A. and M. M. Raymond, aged 8 months and 19 days.

Mr. and Mrs. Raymond ask the favor of expressing (through the medium of your valuable paper) their sincere thanks for the many marks of sympathy and kindness, shown them in this deep affliction, by the people of Lymansville. The bereaved parents were touched deeply by the spontaneous and unaffected generosity of their neighbors, and which they appreciate all the more on account of the afflictive circumstances that called it forth, and the fact that they were comparative strangers amongst them. They assure their friends that their great kindness, embalmed by affliction and gratitude, will ever be associated with the undying memory of their dear departed child. They desire, also, to express their hearty thanks to Dr. French for his tender and unremitting attention to their dear little sufferer during his last affliction.

FATAL ACCIDENT.
Instantly Killed while Working on a Log Slide.

Late Thursday afternoon, Ed Tyler, an old resident in this section, was instantly killed, on a log slide back of Ellison's Mills, less than a mile above this place. Mr. Tyler was engaged assisting his son who has a job of getting in logs from the Bingham lands. The mountain is a steep one and a ground slide is used for running the logs. Occasionally a log jumps from the slide and goes crashing through the brush and small timber with great rapidity, and there is no telling where a runaway log may stop. Mr. Tyler had been at work on the slide. A log was started from the top, coming down with fearful velocity. At that time he was at one side of the slide, which he had been repairing. The log jumped the trail a little above where Mr. Tyler was, he saw it coming and attempted to get out of the way, but could not do it. The log struck him on the left side of the head crushing his skull and hurling him some twenty feet down the hill, killing him instantly. The accident was only witnessed by one boy. When help arrived Mr. Tyler was found in a sitting position with his head between his knees, but life was extinct. He was removed to a house near by, and on Friday was buried. Mr. Tyler was about fifty years of age, has lived in this vicinity for over 25 years. He had a good education and had taught school in a number of districts. He was an honest law abiding citizen. He leaves a wife and one son, a young man of about 22 years of age, to mourn his loss.

Officers.

The following are the officers, elected and appointed, of Eulalia Lodge, No. 342, F. & A. M., Coudersport, Pa., for the ensuing Masonic year:

W. W. Thompson, W.M.; C. A. Stebbins, S.W.; W. K. Jones, J.W.; N. H. Goodsell, Sec.; Almeron Nelson, Treas.; D. F. Glassmire, Jr., S.D.; James L. Knox, J.D.; C. L. Peck, S.M.C.; S. A. Phillips, J.M.C.; L. F. Andrews, Pur.; N. A. Pinney, Guide; Wm. Shear, Chap.; B. Rennells, Tyler.

The Potter Enterprise
Wednesday Evening, January 25, 1882 – Vol. VIII, No. 36

GOLDEN WEDDING.
The 50th Anniversary of the Wedding Day.

On Saturday evening last, the relatives and friends of Mr. and Mrs. A. S. Armstrong, to the number of sixty, gathered at the home of the aged couple, in Coudersport, to celebrate their Golden Wedding. Everyone had a pleasant time.

Remarks were made by Rev. Cone and Rev. Dillenbeck. Refreshments were served and about 11 o'clock the company dispersed with well wishes for the host and hostess.

Abram Sheldon Armstrong, was born in Hopkinton, St. Lawrence Co., N.Y., June 4th, 1809. Mrs. Armstrong *nee* Eunice Wood, was born in Berkshire, Tioga Co., N.Y., August 12th, 1817. They were married at Saratoga Springs, Jan. 21st, 1832. In 1834 they settled in Ulysses, Potter county. At that time the county was sparsely inhabited and they had to undergo many of the privations incidental to the early settlers, in the then wilderness. There was not a single school house in the whole county. Churches, none, and religious services almost unknown, except occasionally at a private house, when some missionary preacher was traveling through the country. Mr. Armstrong was compelled to go to Jersey Shore, with a team, through a rough section of country, with no roads worthy the name, the best of them not being as good as the ordinary log road of to-day, with no bridges, for the purpose of obtaining corn for the subsistence of himself and family until he could clear and plant sufficient land to raise a crop.

They lived in Ulysses until 1853 when they removed to Coudersport, which has been their home ever since, with the exception of two years spent in Wisconsin, 1856-7. For three years Mr. Armstrong was the landlord of the old Temperance Hotel which stood on the corner now occupied by O. H. Crosby's residence. With this exception, Mr. Armstrong has been engaged in the boot and shoe business, since his removal to this place.

Eight children have been born to them, Charles H. in business in Coudersport; Ezra, who died in Sweden, in 1879; Orlando, now living in New York; Fred, now at home; Mrs. W. B. Gordinier, Mrs. O. H. Crosby and Miss Milla Living in Coudersport and Mrs. Hatfield, residing in Kansas City, Mo. There are at present living seven children, 17 grand children and two great grand children. Four generations were present at the golden wedding.

Mrs. Armstrong is still quite active but Mr. Armstrong has been almost an invalid for several years and is now quite feeble. The relatives and friends left many valuable presents including $100 in gold.

Mr. Armstrong has long been a member of Eulalia Lodge, F. & A. M. and the craft presented him with a purse containing $35 in gold, as a token of esteem from the Masons living in Coudersport, many of whom were present on this occasion, with their well wishes for the future welfare of himself and wife.

DIED.

WELTON – At Wharton, Pa., Jan. 10th, 1882, Bessie, daughter of Chas. and R. H. W. Welton, aged 3 months and 26 days.

HULL – At Wharton, Pa., Jan. 13th, 1882, Sarah A., wife of Joseph Hull.

TUTTLE – In Greensboro, Md., Jan. 18th, 1882, of consumption, Lucina M. Tuttle, aged 27 years and 5 months.

SEIBERT – In Wharton, Pa., Jan. 23d, 1882, Willie B. C. Seibert, aged 3 years, 5 months and 12 days.

YENTZER – In Roulet, Jan. 18th, 1882, Orrie Arlovine, youngest child of Lewis and Paulena Yentzer, aged one year, seven months and twenty days.

To Mr. and Mrs. Lewis Yentzer.
Accept these beautiful lines on the death of a loved and loving child. It is hard to bear, but the blow cannot be averted. The great Reaper has gathered another of his best treasures into his well filled granary, has clipped another branch from the family tree – another flower from the garden of earth – and bourn it away in triumph, leaving the parents hearts crushed and broken. But this child, this bird of Paradise that has taken Angels wing, we trust has gone to an Angels home. O beautiful, beautiful star of hope, that lights up the distant future with a golden radiance. Bless God we shall see our loved ones again. They may encamp for a season in the cold dreary grave, the dark valley of death; but they will soon hear the voice arise, and will accordingly strike their white tents on the homeward march. Earth's losses are heaven's gains. The pure and good are continually entering the celestial City. Thy fair child has but quickened her homeward steps – gone back to the Infinite source of all being – the bosom of Deity.

In the Scottish hills a shepherd strolled
   In the even with his ancient crook;
He found a lamb that was young and chilled,
   By the side of a purling brook.
And fearing the lamb might sicken and die,
   Or from its mother might roam,
He carried it up with tender care
   To a fold in his shepherd home.
'Mid the dreary night –o'er the eraggy peaks,
   Through wind and storm and cold,
The mother followed the captured lamb
   To the door of the shepherds fold.
Once we had a lamb by its mother's side,
   It was artless and pure and mild,
The only lamb that death had left,
   Was our bright little blue-eyed child.
But a Shepherd came when the sun was low,
   By a path that has long been trod;
And carried our lamb through the mists of night,
   To his fold in the mount of God.
With a tearful eye and a bleeding heart,
   We bear it and struggle on.
Must climb the mount by the Shepherd's tracks,
   To the fold where our lambs are gone.

- A letter received from a friend in Germania, under date of January 14, contains the following: "This afternoon Charles Sackman, from here, was instantly killed by the upsetting of a sleigh loaded with logs." We have no particulars.

- Fred Costello, proprietor of the tannery at North Wharton, met with quite a serious accident one day last week. He was adjusting a chain belt and in some manner the chain caught in the leg of his pants throwing him over so that one hand caught in the machinery stopping it. He was very soon relieved but one hand was severely jammed and one finger entirely cut off. Dr. Ellison rendered surgical aid.

The Potter Enterprise
Wednesday Evening, February 1, 1882 – Vol. VIII, No. 37

MARRIED.

PHENIX – MALTBY. – At the residence of the bride, in Roulet, Jan. 27th, 1882, by J. B. Davidson, Esq., Mr. E. W. Phenix to Mrs. Rosella Maltby, both of Roulet, Pa.

- Mrs. Alvin Rennells, of Ayers Hill, died on Monday.

DIED.

CONABLE. – In West Branch, Jan. 25th, 1882, Mamie, infant daughter of Mr. and Mrs. Willis Conable, aged about four months.

WATER WORKS.
The Citizens Water Works Company of Coudersport.

This company gave notice that application for a charter would be made about one year ago, but the matter was delayed owing to some difficulty about the water privilege. This difficulty has now been arranged and early next summer our town will be supplied with pure spring water for household and fire purposes.

The company now owns five acres, on the north side of the Niles road, on which there are numerous springs, which from Dent Brook, running through the north part of the borough. The company also have secured the privilege of water way and for pipes from Miss Kate Dent, the whole costing about $1,000.

Two dams are contemplated, although only one will be put in now. The lower dam will take in some additional springs and will be 130 feet higher than the foot of Main street. The upper dam, which is the one to be put in now, will give a fall of 160 feet. As the heavy timber surrounding the springs will not be cut this upper dam will supply the town, unless there should be a greater increase in population that there is any reason to expect now. This upper dam will be about sixty feet in length, and twelve feet in height. The pool will be about 150 feet across. The earth is being removed from the pool to form the dam. Will Bassett has the contract for cleaning the pool and building the dam – contract price $175. The work is about one-third completed.

From this dam a four inch main will be laid to Main street, and down Main to the Allegheny river. At Second street there will be two branch mains of three inch pipe. One running east to the river, the other west to West street, down West and Water street to Braitling's. In the woods the main will be buried three feet. After striking the streets the mains will be buried four feet, and will be laid in the middle of the street. Two hundred and eight rods of four inch main and one hundred and thirty rods of three inch mains will be required at present. Charles Kernan has the contract of burying the pipe at $1.25 per rod.

The pipe is made by the Warren Pipe Foundry, of Phillipsburg, N.J., and is manufactured expressly for water pipe and is said to be very much superior to ordinary pipe. The pipe has all been shipped and a few loads have already arrived. It requires sixty tons of 2,240 pounds for the mains and costs about $46.50 per ton delivered here.

The rates for the use of water have not yet been fixed, but we are assured that they will be put as low as possible, so that all may avail themselves of the privilege of plenty of pure spring water a thing our village is not blessed with at present. A few of our people are provided now with water from springs near by but most of the people depend on wells and three-fourths of these are not first class. In case of fire, with the head the upper dam will give, water can be thrown over any building in town with a reasonable supply of hose.

Now that we are sure of water works, a hose company and a hook and ladder company, but more especially the former, should be organized and measures taken to secure the necessary appliances for extinguishing fires. We have several sections in the village, where a fire once started would sweep a number of buildings in spite of all efforts, with nothing but buckets in untrained hands to quench the flames. With the experience of May, 1880 yet tugging at the purse strings of business, Coudersport cannot afford to run the risk that still stares our town in the face. With water works Coudersport can have very good appliances to put out fires at very slight expense. Hose company, No. 1 will be organized – very soon we hope.

The Potter Enterprise
Wednesday Evening, February 8, 1882 – Vol. VIII, No. 38

Raymond. Rumor says we have lost another Potter county boy, James Smith; gone to Michigan and got a wife.

- Mr. A. S. Armstrong died on Wednesday last and Friday was buried with Masonic honors. A few weeks ago we published an account of the Golden wedding of Mr. and Mrs. A. S. Armstrong, since that time Mr. A. has been gradually failing until his death last Wednesday.

Hebron.

If your last week's paper was an article on A. S. Armstrong's golden wedding, saying Mr. Armstrong came to Potter in 1834, and that there was not any school house in Potter county at that time. That is a mistake, I think. I came into Potter in the spring of 1833 and there was then a school house on the farm now occupied by G. W. Stillman, and was built the year before.

Yours Respectfully, W. H. Hydorn.

Potter County, Pennsylvania Potpourri – Volume I
1880 through 1884

TRAVERSE JURORS.

G. W. Hackett, Farmer, Genesee; C. S. Redner, Farmer, Hector; W. W. Carr, Farmer, Hector; C. E. Swift, Farmer, Hebron; Jerome Dimon, Hotel Keeper, Genesee; Charles Traub, Farmer, West Branch; Wm. Sahr, Farmer, Ulysses; B. S. Potter, Farmer, Harrison; Milo Kemp, Farmer, Harrison; Albert Colcord, Blacksmith, Eulalia; N. T. Worden, Farmer, Bingham; W. Y. Campbell, Farmer, Stewardson; Elymus Hacket, Lumberman, Genesee; John Marble, Farmer, Harrison; E. A. McKee, Farmer, Hebron; Timothy Glines, Farmer, Clara; Joseph Varney, Farmer, Sharon; J. C. Wilkinson, Farmer, Oswayo; Josiah Berfield, Farmer, Wharton; John Gordnier, Farmer, Homer; H. A. Avery, Hotel Keeper, Keating; Fred Baker, Farmer, Lewisville; George Dodge, Merchant, Sharon; Miles Dykeman, Farmer, Ulysses; Ransom Munger, Laborer, Sharon; Vincent Dodge, Farmer, Harrison; Bryne Moran, Farmer, Genesee; Aaron Perkins, Blacksmith, Coudersport; George Nichols, Farmer, Sharon; Nelson Chafee, Farmer, Hector; W. Cunningham, Farmer, Sweden; Wm. Thompson, Farmer, West Branch; C. A. Gilbert, Farmer, Harrison; Anson Hickox, Farmer, Genesee; John Gray, Clerk, Sharon; O. D. Hammond, Miller, Pike.

GRAND JURORS.

H. B. Hurd, Farmer, Ulysses; Calvin Rogers, Farmer, Allegany; Perry Filmore, Farmer, Hector; F. J. Norton, Merchant, Coudersport; Andrew Sanburg, Farmer, Hebron; Orin Card, Farmer, Portage; W. S. Holland, Preacher, Sylvania; James Douglass, Farmer, Hector; Dorne Lewis, Farmer, Bingham; G. W. Stillman, Farmer, Hebron; Amos Burbanks, Farmer, Sharon; F. P. Nichols, Farmer, Sharon; E. C. Colgrove, Farmer, Oswayo; G. W. Colvin, Farmer, Bingham; C. H. Farnsworth; Farmer, Bingham; Wm. F. Burt, Farmer, Lewisville; Laroy Burdick, Farmer, Hebron; Wallace Mahan, Farmer, Wharton; T. J. Farnum, Farmer, Oswayo; John Abott, Constable, Roulet; Frank Lent, Farmer, Hebron; C. A. Neffe, Farmer, Sweden; Wells Lathrop, Farmer, Homer; Abram Jones, Farmer, Wharton.

The Potter Enterprise
Wednesday Evening, February 15, 1882 – Vol. VIII, No. 39

MARRIED.

KNOWLTON – CORNELL. – At Cook's Hotel, Emporium, Pa., Feb. 3d, 1882, by Jonathan Gifford, Esq., Charles A. Knowlton and Isabella Cornell, both of Roulet, Potter county, Pa.

DIED.

BURROUS. – In West Branch, Feb. 3d, 1882, Vinnie, infant daughter of George and Rosa Burrous, aged six months and twelve days.

COLE. – In Coudersport, on Friday, February 10th, 1882, L. B. Cole, Esq., in the 76th year of his age.

He was born in Otsego, N.Y., where his youth was spent. Losing an arm in early life, he could not perform manual labor for a living. He came to this place in 1832 and spent in, and near our village, a period of fifty years. He was conversant with and took part in most of those operations and improvements that have promoted the welfare of this place. He was married in 1834 and about the same time was admitted to the Bar and practiced law in our courts for a few years. In 1839 he was chosen a member of the State Legislature, and was the first representative from Potter county, in the State Legislature. Later in life he became Commissioner's clerk, which office he held, with great acceptance, for twenty-five years. He was chosen Justice of the Peace five successive terms and filled the office twenty-two years. He will be missed by all who so often met him in his office or on the street. Of his family, only one son survives him.

Thus, one by one, our pioneer fathers pass away, but their names and deeds remain.

SPENCER. – At Genesee Forks, Feb. 12, 1882, Marinda, wife of S. H. Spencer, aged 38 years.

How often in the columns of the paper do we see this word, Died. But when in our midst death enters, then the reality is before us. Another one of our number is called. A respected neighbor and a beloved wife and mother.

Mrs. Spencer was converted under the preaching of Rev. A. Blanchard and joined the M.E.church. But now we trust she is one of those who have made their robes white in the blood of the lamb and has joined the anthems of praise in the church Emmanuel. May God sustain the stricken family and friends.

- L. B. Cole, Sr. was buried on Sunday last.

- Dan Hackett of Roulet killed a 400-ound bear last week.

SURPRISED.
How a young man walked into the Sheriff's hands.

Something like two years ago, Gilbert Glover and Frank Ellis, of Hector, were charged with assault and battery, the particulars of which we have no knowledge. Glover was arrested by the constable, but escaped. Some time afterward both were indicted by the Grand Jury, and a Bench Warrant issued. The young men worked in Tioga county and York State and spent a portion of their time in this county.

Once the Sheriff went to Hector to arrest one of the parties, but found him dangerously ill. Frank had a little personal property and recently an execution was issued against him and the property advertised to be sold. Last week Frank secured a stay of execution and walking into the Baker House, presented it to Sheriff Monroe. Frank has been in poor health for some time and the Sheriff failed to recognize him at once. The Sheriff inquired if he was the man whose name appeared in the stay of execution, and was answered in the affirmative. The Sheriff soon stepped out, secured his bench warrant, returned, and invited Frank to take up his quarters in the Hotel provided by the County. Frank walked over a surprised and disgusted young man. He is now out on bail.

Deputy Sheriff H. T. Nelson, learning that Glover was in the neighborhood of Harrison Valley took occasion to hunt him up, and he too was lodged in jail last week, where he still remains for want of bail.

The Potter Enterprise
Wednesday Evening, February 22, 1882 – Vol. VIII, No. 40

- The happiest man in seven counties if Sher Baker, of Lymansville, over the birth of a son and heir, on Saturday last weighing eight pounds. Mr. and Mrs. Baker have been married nearly twenty years and this is their first child.

Golden Wedding.

50th anniversary of wedding of Mr. and Mrs. Lyman Nelson Feb. 15th. About 50 guests present. The four sons and five daughters of the venerable couple were present, except one, with their companions and grandchildren. Rev. F. S. Parkhurst gave course to the exercises, opening with a brief address. Congratulatory letters from absent friends were read. The groom of 50 yrs. was presented with a beautiful gold-headed walking cane, exquisitely engraved. The "Bride of '32" was given a pair of gold spectacles, numerous other presents were given. The aged couple at the word arose, also Nelson and Mary Ann Clark, as groomsman and bridesmaid, who filled the same office 50 yrs. ago, and were united in the bonds of golden wedlock, by Rev. J. Latham oldest son-in-law of the groom. Refreshments were served in excellent style, after which the time was given over to chatting, stories of Potter 50 yrs. ago, advancement, struggles, etc. All together the reunion was one of great enjoyment and profit.

- Mrs. Chesbro, for many years a resident of Homer twp., was buried on Saturday last.

The Potter Enterprise
Wednesday Evening, March 1, 1882 – Vol. VIII, No. 41

MARRIED.

HOPKINS, GUERNSEY. – At the M.E. Parsonage in Coudersport, Feb. 22d, 1882, by Rev. C. Dillenbeck, Mr. Jerome Hopkins and Miss Bettie Guernsey, all of Gold, Pa.

HENDERSON, WEIDRICH. – At the residence of the bride's parents, Feb. 21st, 1882, by Rev. Brooks, Mr. William Henderson of Port Allegany, and Miss Lettie Weidrich, of Roulet, Pa.

DIED.

SYLVESTER. – In Allegany, Feb. 17th, 1882, at the house of Mrs. Hannah Woodcock, after a brief sickness, Mr. George Sylvester, aged about 68 years (Age not certainly known.).

Although living in this vicinity for many years, it is not known as he had any relatives in this State, but is supposed to have friends in Massachusetts.

- O. H. Emery, a well known Kettle Creek lumberman died on Saturday last. A short time ago he had an attack of Palsy which resulted in his death as stated above.

- Victoria A., wife of Dr. Frank Buck, of Coudersport, who has been sick for some time past, died on Wednesday morning, at 1:30, aged 38 years. She leaves five children, one of whom is quite young. Her parents and other of her relatives reside in this place, where she passed a greater portion of her life, which was one to inspire to love and friendship all with whom she associated. A gentle lady, firm friend, fond mother and loving companion are the thoughts which memory clusters around her name, and are firmly enshrined in the hearts of those who knew her best. The deceased was a consistent member of the M.E. Church. The mourning husband, parents and friends have the heartfelt sympathy of a large circle of friends and acquaintances. The funeral services were held at the M.E. Church, in this boro, on Friday morning at ten o'clock. – *Westfield Free Press.*

- The Tannery, Saw mill, at North Wharton was burned to the ground early Friday morning. One small planing machine was removed, everything else was burned. Loss about $3,000, partially insured. It is not known how the fire originated. The mill was a new one and had been erected less than a year.

ELECTION RETURNS.

Below we give the results of the election last Tuesday, scattering votes left out.

ALLEGANY.

Supervisors – Samuel Atkinson 39, E. E. Kelly 37, John Matteson 48, D. L. Raymond 55.

Constable – J. F. Kidney.

Assessor – Charles Coats 54, Calvin Rogers 33.

Assistant Assessors – A. B. Whipple, C. S. Ford.

Treasurer – Horace Peet 39, James Gardner 49.

Clerk – E. L. Heggie 44, F. M. Reynolds 42.

Auditor – F. S. Connable 46, C. W. Nelson 42, Geo. Nelson 42.

School Directors – Wm. Smith 69, J. L. Swain 29, E. E. Kelly 76, G. W. James 37, J. S. Collins 47, A. G. Scoville 37.

Judge of Election – Fred Andrews 42, Roscoe Andrews 39.

Inspectors – C. E. Tucker, James Bird.

Overseers of the Poor – N. A. Slade 45, A. C. Scoville 42, George Nelson 39, Alfred Cool 42.

BINGHAM.

Supervisors – D. F. Hauber 3 yrs 42; M. D. Briggs 2 yrs 32, Z. O. Bacon 48, Z. O. Bacon 1 yr 19, J. E. Harvey 46, J. E. Harvey 3 yrs 17.

Constable – M. N. Babcock 46, L. J. Thompson 63.

Assessor – M. R. Grover 40, D. Worden 71.

Assistant Assessors – R. H. Howe 39, R. Reed 39, M. R. Grover 71, S. S. Carpenter 75.

Treasurer – A. N. Clark.

Clerk – L. B. Lewis 56, A. E. Evans 57.

Auditor – N. W. Lewis.

School Directors – D. F. Hauber 115, L. E. McCarn 113.
Judge of Election – B. R. Grover.
Inspectors – C. E. Rathbone 43, L. W. Merrick 72.
Overseers of Poor – M. D. Briggs 36, D. F. Hauber 40, E. Luddington 58, G. W. Colvin 67.

COUDERSPORT.
Burgess – F. W. Knox.
Town Council – Isaac Benson, C. H. Armstrong.
School Directors – W. H. Rounsville, C. L. Peck.
Justice of the Peace – Miles White.
Overseers of Poor – C. S. Jones, R. L. Nichols.
Constable – L. B. Cole.
High Constable – Earl Crane.
Auditor – J. L. Knox.
Assessor – Z. J. Thompson.
Assistant Assessors – P. A. Stebbins jr, O. H. Crosby.
Judge of Election – W. K. Jones.
Inspectors – Amos French, E. J. Fickler.

EULALIA.
Justice of the Peace – Sherman Baker.
Constable – George McGowan 31; W. H. Fourness 27.
Supervisor – Nelson Clark.
Assessor – Mason Nelson.
Assistant Assessors – Chris Bremle, Amos Colcord.
School Directors – John D. Earle 57, L. A. Glace 38, Jacob Klein 20.
Judge of Election – Henry Ingraham.
Overseers of Poor – C. Stearns, J. M. Spafford.
Treasurer – Albert Colcord.
Inspectors – James Hill 11, Geo. English 29, A. L. Rennells 16.
Auditor – E. M. Baker.
Clerk – Jacob Lehman.

HEBRON.
Supervisor – N. Vanwegen.
Constable – R. M. Post.
Assessor – W. B. Lent.
Assistant Assessors – W. C. Reynolds, Squire Estes.
Treasurer – E. M. Bly.
Clerk – John Schollard.
Auditor – W. R. Greenman.
School Directors – A. P. Vaughn 57, E. M. Bishop 41, Peter Green 50.
Judge of Election – A. Ball.
Inspectors – C. D. McKee, S. P. Hemphill.
Overseers of Poor – Addison Stephens, Wm. Clair.

HOMER.
Supervisor – Walter Edgcomb.
Constable – Eli Glaspy 21, G. W. McKinney 19.

Clerk – W. C. Chesbro 17, A. W. Lathrop 24.
Treasurer – John Taubert.
Assessor – J. P. Gates 17, James Bundy 24.
Assistant Assessors – O. H. Crosby 41, John Bundy 24, Charles Vergason 17.
Poor Masters – P. McKinney 38, W. B. Reed 23, G. H. Gates 17.
School Directors – O. L. Hall 24, Sterling Devens 40, H. M. Case 18.
Judge of Election – James Wallace 23, Charles Verguson 17.
Inspectors – John Bundy, James Bundy.

KEATING.

Justice of the Peace – J. A. Dingee 30, H. Bridges 19.
Supervisor – N. E. Williams.
Constable – T. A. Glover.
Treasurer – J. W. Dingee 33, G. C. Lewis 16.
Clerk – W. H. Dingee.
Assessor – E. Z. Dingee.
Auditor – John Rinehuls.
Judge of Election – Thomas Glover.
Inspectors – Charles Glover, A. E. Williams.
School Directors – F. M. Younglove 36, T. Glober 34, Frank Klein 15.
For removing place of holding election to school house No. 2, 33; against removal 16.

OSWAYO.

Supervisor – O. M. Kemp.
Treasurer – R. H. Smith 59, Charles Head 43.
Clerk – Sam'l Beebe 93, S. B. Hawley 11.
Assessor – A. S. Lyman 63, Allen Hammond 41.
Assistant Assessors – Allen Ham 63, Abram Walker 67, N. H. Rice 39, G. F. Rowlee 38.
School Directors – Fred S. Roselle 103, Walter Wells 105.
Constable – Sam'l Stilson.
Auditor – B. F. Lyman 3 yrs 65, J. B. Stewart 2 yrs 103, Abram Walker 3 yrs 39.
Overseers of Poor – Allen Hammond 100, L. D. Estes 53, N. H. Rice 46.
Judge of Election – J. C. Wilkinson.
Inspectors – J. L. Fessenden, E. Daggett.

LEWISVILLE.

Burgess – T. W. Burt.
Council – C. E. Burt, B. J. Cushing, E. A. Burt, B. L. Easton, A. A. Howe, Charles Erlbeck.
Justice of the Peace – H. A. Gridley.
Constable – A. Cady.
School Directors – E. U. Eaton, B. J. Cushing, C. E. Hosley.
Assessor – G. A. Farnsworth.
Assistant Assessors – C. E. Hosley, E. A. Wagoner.
Judge of Election – Geo. Dunbar.

Inspectors – Fred Baker, Fred Allen.
Auditor – H. K. Lane.
High Constable – E. A. Hovey.
Overseers of Poor – W. A. Bishop, C. E. Baker.

WHARTON.

Justice of the Peace – Perry Devoll 47, Henry Nelson 18, B. F. Berfield 37, John Ward 7.
Constable – Mart. Devoll 49, J. M. Walker 10.
Supervisor – Maurice Jordan 41, Wm. Nickerson 20.
Overseers of Poor – Fred Devanport 43, B. F. Berfield 28, Josiah Berfield 28.
Treasurer – W. G. Wilbur.
Clerk – Arthur Barclay.
Assessor – Bigler Berfield.
Assistant Assessor – J. M. Walker, Fred Devanport.
Auditor – J. M. Walker.
Inspectors – Orrin Courtright, John Ward.
Judge of Election – S. F. Horton.

PORTAGE.

Supervisor – G. F. Smith.
Overseers of Poor – D. A. Everett, T. W. Brownlee.
School Directors – Orrin Card 2 yrs, F. Austin and T. W. Brownlee 3 yrs.
Auditor – Hugh Young.
Inspectors – Harvey Hurlburt, C. D. Austin.
Judge of Election – M. J. Young.
Assessor – L. D. Ripple.
Assistant Assessors – Robt. Brownlee, C. C. Burdette.
Constable – Orren Card.
Clerk – E. O. Austin.
Treasurer – F. P. Austin.

PLEASANT VALLEY.

Justice of the Peace – W. D. Weimer.
Judge of Election – Israel Burt.
Inspectors – D. T. Yentzer, Wilson McDowell.
Constable – Philander Reed.
Assessor – Robt. McDowell.
Assistant Assessors – J. L. Yentzer, Frank Judkins.
Supervisor – W. W. Austin.
Auditor – W. D. Weimer.
Treasurer – I. V. Reed.
Clerk – Ansel Joseph.
School Directors – C. P. Reed 34, Frank Judkins 29.
Overseers of Poor – S. M. Beckwith 16, B. A. Haynes 11.

ROULET.

Supervisor – Chris Knowlton 55, Michael Sullivan 19.
Constable – John Abbott.

Assessor – J. B. Davidson.
Assistant Assessors – N. C. French, W. S. Brine.
Treasurer – S. B. Pomeroy.
Clerk – A. V. Lyman.
Auditor – Burt Reed 71, W. S. Brine 36.
School Directors – Philip Brown 73, Michael Sullivan 52, D. P. Jordan 22.
Judge of Election – Miles Marsh.
Inspectors – Joseph Knowlton, J. V. Weimer.
Overseers of Poor – C. K. Crawford 56, Russel Reed 74, Wm. Hazen 14.

STEWARDSON.

Supervisor – Washington Campbell.
Constable – James Impson.
Clerk – Williard Andresen.
Assessor – Martin Joerg.
Assistant Assessors – Wesley Allen, Washington Campbell.
Auditor – James Impson.
Treasurer – Henry Andresen.
School Directors – Henry Andresen, John Smith, Samuel Pollard.
Judge of Election – Martin Joerg.
Inspectors – Ole Olson, Wesley Allen.

SYLVANIA.

Justice of the Peace – S. B Haskins.
Supervisor – Charles Haskins.
Constable – Nathan Tuttle.
Treasurer – S. B. Haskins.
Assessor – A. R. Jordan.
Assistant Assessors – R. J. Burleson, James Rees.
School Directors – A. R. Jordan, A. J. Burleson.
Clerk – George Clark.
Overseers of the Poor – A. R. Jordan, Charles Haskins.
Auditor – Pardon Haskins.
Inspectors – Oscar Rees, J. P. Hoven.
Judge of Election – James Rees.

SWEDEN.

Supervisor – Wm. Snyder 28, O. E. Harris 45, A. Chase 6.
Constable – S. O. Dodd 53, J. E. Freeman 28.
School Directors – Warren White 80, A. Chase 58, Henry Tauscher 80, J. T. Jackson 24.
Treasurer – Richard Snyder.
Judge of Election – C. D. Carsaw.
Inspectors – Walton White 57, J. S. Bird 8, Warren White 8.
Overseers of Poor – Johnson Chase, J. R. Miller.
Justice of the Peace – J. R. Miller.
Clerk – J. W. Neefe.
Assessors – Marion Herrington 78, Michael Snyder 34, M. T. Chase 70, Richard Snyder 41.

Auditor – Arthur Lyman 77, H. J. Neefe 76.
PIKE.
Supervisor – L. R. Gale 29, O. L. Blackman 7, Geo. Vincent 13.
Treasurer – H. M. Tice.
Constable – D. E. Crandall 18, C. H. Haxton 31.
Town Clerk – F. R. Brown.
Auditor – J. S. Phenix.
School Directors – Robt. Kelly 27, S. H. Martin 46, D. Sutton 49.
Inspectors – E. O. Lambert, Moses Hirsch.
Judge of Election – J. S. Phenix.
Justice of the Peace – J. Q. Merrick.
Overseers of Poor – James Losey, M. V. Prouty.
Assessor – J. M. Kilbourn.
Assistant Assessors – J. Q. Merrick, James Losey.
CLARA.
Supervisor – A. Green.
Constable – O. E. Carsaw, 16, Zanona Reed 18.
Assessor – Peter Beatman 31, W. A. Cole 26, Jesse Morey 32.
Treasurer – T. Glines.
Clerk – J. H. Cole 20, T. Glines 41.
Auditor – Lester Burton 28, W. A. Cole 11.
School Directors – Zanona Reed 17, J. Dawley 19, Mrs. John Dawley 13, Ellen Glines 16.
Judge of Election – Zanona Reed 34.
Inspectors – Oliver Edwards 14, Ira Fosmer 8, B. S. Wakely 8.
Overseers of Poor – Samuel Wakely, W. M. Morey.
SUMMIT.
Supervisor – O. D. Blauvelt.
Clerk – C. H. Ruscher.
Treasurer – Wash. Haskins 12, Alvin Rennels 16.
Auditor – C. A. McCarty.
Constable – John Wallace.
Assessor – Lester Watson.
Judge of Election – James Nelson.
School Directors – Hugh Haskins, James Reed, O. J. Jackson.
Inspectors – George Mortor, A. F. Ayars.
SHARON.
Justice of the Peace – G. W. Dodge 68, G. W. Pearsall 101.
Clerk – C. A. Wright 65, Wallace Burdic 100.
Supervisor – Jas. Dickinson 81, W. J. Brown 89.
Constable – Henry Press 63, G. W. Corwine 29, S. H. Manley 79.
Auditor – H. N. Butts 82, A. D. Wolcott 89.
School Directors – Jasper Card 71, Ira Bixby 155, W. J. Brown 95, Jacob Failing 17.
School Directors, to fill vacancy – Col. M. Gillett 66, W. Sutherland 21, Chas. Burbank 85.

Treasurer – W. S. Lane 62, J. C. Bump 26, John Livermore 84.
Assessor – N. C. Newton 83, R. N. Nichols 90.
Assistant Assessors – Jno. Kenyon 65, L. Grames 68, R. Munger 17, A. F. Smith 17, D. L. Moon 87, T. G. Torrey 89.
Overseers of Poor – Andrew Bradford 66, Andrew Jacobs 82, Manley Clark 5, L. Prince 19, J. L. Warner 88, Orlando Wells 89.
Judge of Election – R. Munger 66, J. H. Wright 14, F. E. Bailey 87.

ULYSSES.

Supervisor – John Francis.
Auditor – Martin Lewis.
Assessor – G. W. Bennitt.
Assistant Assessors – J. T. Hovey, F. B. Langdon.
Overseers of Poor – John Francis 2 yrs, W. J. Grover 1 yr.
Clerk – H. T. Reynolds.
Judge of Election – Wm. Suhr.
Inspectors – H. L. Atherton, M. F. Clark.
Treasurer – A. Burt.
Constable – E. B. Monroe.
School Directors, 3 yrs – M. Lewis 43, T. Carpenter 49, E. D. Leet 36; 1 yr E. Peasley 68, F. B. Langdon 31.

HARRISON.

Justice of the Peace – Martin Dodge.
Constable – J. H. Harrison.
Supervisor – W. B. Fox 82, A. F. Dodge 99.
Overseers of Poor – S. K. Stevens, A. F. Dodge.
School Directors – Charles Gilbert 99, S. E. Christman 101, J. N. Kane 59, Waldo Robinson 58.
Assessor – D. W. Coffin.
Assistant Assessors – Ed Statham, W. B. Jennings.
Auditor – M. R. Swetland 67, D. D. Chapin 65.
Treasurer – Lewis White.
Judge of Election – H. N. Stone.
Inspectors – S. J. Stetson, F. A. English.
Clerk – J. W. Havens.

ABBOTT.

Justice of the Peace – Emil Peltz.
Constable – Louis Hoppe.
Assessor – Louis Hoppe.
Assistant Assessors – George Rexford, Eberhard Gnau.
Clerk – Fred Wolfel.
Treasurer – Fred Bodler.
Auditor – Charles Scheibner.
Supervisor – John Zengerle.
School Directors – Charles Meine, Peter Zepp.
Inspectors – Wm. Sandbach Sr, John Hug.
Judge of Election – John Helfrecht.

Overseers of Poor – Romeo Zirmart, Franz Villetta.

GENESEE.

Supervisor – E. H. Estes.
Auditor – W. D. Atherton.
Judge of Election – Norman Chapman.
Assessor – Ira Easton.
Assistant Assessors – Pat Hard, James Ryan.
Overseers of Poor – James Hill, Pat Roach.
Constable – Wm. Atherton.
Clerk – C. W. Parker.
Treasurer – S. G. Rouse.
School Directors – Reuben Collar, John O'Donnell.

HECTOR.

Justice of the Peace – W. J. Loucks 51, George Larrison 41, D. W. Haven 75, A. Northrop 42.
Constable – E. Dimon 57, S. B. Miller 56.
Assessor – John W. Lewis 42, J. W. Swimlar 67.
Assistant Assessors – C. H. Francis 61, I. Sutton 41, J. M. Swimlar 37, A. E. Skinner 57.
Treasurer – J. L. Douglass 41, Albert Wilber 66.
Supervisor – E. J. Abbey 39, J. S. Little 46, J. F. Carling 26.
Auditor – C. H. Francis 40, J. L. Havens 59.
Clerk – F. H. Kilbourne 41, C. E. Dimon 63.
Overseers of Poor – James Gibson 39, J. F. Carling 12, G. W. Chisholm 28, J. S. Little 58, E. S. Worden 71.
Judge of Election – David S. Plank 53, R. S. Crippen 57.
Inspector of Election – Charles Corry, R. E. Davis.
School Directors – Sidney Abbott 30, Norman Whiteman 45, James Waters 41, R. S. Chisholm 44.

WEST BRANCH.

Constable – B. F. Burrows.
Supervisor – Henry Deisroth 24, Henry Sharier 17.
Clerk – A. Bisbee.
Overseers of Poor – C. Rukgaber, C. Prouty.
Assessor – L. F. Rice.
Assistant Assessors – John Klemm, A. Bisbee.
Auditor – John Klemm.
School Directors – B. F. Burrows, C. Schoemaker.
Inspectors – Eli Main 4, F. Stritz 33, Willis Connable 4.
Judge of Election – N. K. Prouty.

The Potter Enterprise
Wednesday Evening, March 8, 1882 – Vol. VIII, No. 42

Oswayo. D. M. Wheeler steps high. It's a girl. Weight six pounds.

Oswayo. One of Erin's fair daughters lately arrived at Oswayo from the mother country and became the bride of Mr. Michael Maher. Miss Lettica Rigney was the bride's name. Good wishes follow them.

CUT WITH AN AXE.
A Severe Wound in the Shoulder Terminates a Quarrel.

John Gibson with his family live on the McNamara farm, in Eulalia township, and for some time past Dick Howland has boarded with him. Dick promised to pay his board on Saturday of last week. Gibson wanted the money Wednesday and this difference in time caused a quarrel. Dick owned an accordion, and while he was out at work, Gibson hid the instrument and refused to give it up until the board bill was paid. Dick found the accordion and hid it in the woods. Between six and seven o'clock the two men went together to the place of hiding after the instrument, and after taking it from its hiding place, had another quarrel in which Dick secured an axe and struck Gibson with it. The two were about to clinch and Gibson was so close that the axe passed over his shoulder and the blade sank deep in the back part of the left shoulder near the back bone, opening a wound in the muscles about three inches long, and nearly two inches deep. The two walked to the house together, and Dr. C. S. French was summoned to render surgical aid. The wound is a painful one, but not necessarily dangerous.

Young Howland claims that he only acted in self defense, and the fact that no warrant has been issued gives Dick's story an air of probability.

The Potter Enterprise
Wednesday Evening, March 15, 1882 – Vol. VIII, No. 43

Forest House. A new shoemaker presented himself to Mr. and Mrs. Larkins on the 24th ult., and was received into partnership. His weight is ten pounds.

MARRIED.

CHAFFEE – BASSETT. – In Coudersport, on the 8th inst., by Rev. A. Cone, Mr. Charles B. Chaffee and Miss Hattie Bassett, all of Coudersport.

LYMAN – RILEY. – At Scio, February 26th, 1882, by Rev. James Hart, Jacob W. Lyman of Roulet, Potter County, Pa., and Miss Maria E. Riley of Port Allegany, McKean County, Pa.

Eleven Mile. Considerable sickness has prevailed, none fatal of late, until yesterday, when the infant child of Moses D. Kibbe, died of an affection of the lungs.

Eleven Mile. Wm. M. Rowlee, formerly of this place, who has resided for the past four years at Duke Centre, died last week at that borough. He had been in the army toward the close of the war, having been drafted.

DIED.

MERRILL. – In Ulysses, March 2d, 1882, after a protracted and severe sickness, Mr. Erastus Merrill, aged 74 years.

The deceased was one of the oldest settlers in the township, having moved on to the farm he occupied at the time of his death, 44 years ago. He died in the house he himself built. He was highly esteemed as an industrious, honest and peaceable citizen, a kind father, a loving husband and obliging neighbor. He was, earlier in life, in fellowship with the Free Will Baptists. The bereaved widow has the sympathies and prayers of a wide circle of friends.

Court Proceedings.

Court convened March 6th. Present Hon. S. F. Wilson and associates N. C. Hammond and E. W. Chappel.

F. G. Costen appointed guardian of Wm. Mascho, minor child of David Mascho, deceased.

In case of Louis Petlz, late of Abbott township, deceased, Frederick Woelfel appointed auditor.

G. W. Colvin appointed foreman of Grand Jury, and E. A. Whitney, constable. Grand Jury discharged, March 9th.

Com. vs Augusta Holt, adultery, *nol pros* on payment of costs and defendant discharged.

Com. vs Theodore Yentzer, burglary, *nol pros* on payment of costs.

Adelbert W. Smith vs Mary Smith. C. M. Allen appointed commissioner to take testimony.

In the matter of estate of Carl Seibenheimer, a lunatic, rule on Overseers of Poor of Abbott township, to show cause why the Court shall not make an order allowing a certain portion of the principal fund in hands of committee to be used for maintenance of lunatic.

Jos. Mann and R. L. Nichols vs Moses Kemp *et al.* Jury, under charge of the Court, return a verdict in favor of Plaintiff for land described, to be released on payment of $735.79, with cost and interest, within twenty days.

John G. Yaudes admitted to citizenship.

Com. vs B. F. Ellis, assault and battery, continued.

Com. vs Gilbert Glover, assault and battery, pled guilty, bail $200 for payment of costs.

W. B. Cutler vs F. A. Brown verdict for plaintiff for land described, to be released on payment of $647.10 with costs and interest within 30 days.

Com. vs J. McGonigal, selling liquor, *nol pros*.

Com. vs J. B. Farrell, selling liquor, not a true bill, prosecutor to pay costs.

Thos. G. Hull appointed guardian of Nellie E. Freeman, minor.

Com. vs John Brownlee, forgery, not guilty, prosecutor to pay costs.

Com. vs Garret Smith et al, riot. L. Carpenter and Burt Cammell, held in $200 for appearance next term.

Com. vs James Malery, larceny, bail $200 for appearance at next term.

Com. vs Wm. Story, defendant discharged.

Mary A. Douglass appointed a committee in lunacy to take charge of the estate of Henry R. Douglass.
Special tax of 10 mills ordered in Stewardson township.
Rule granted on Hector School District to make arrangements with Pike School District, returnable next term.
Com. vs Mary Nichols, adultery, bail $200 for appearance at next term.
Com. vs Theodore Yentzer, burglary, bail $100 for appearance at next term.
Com. vs Frank Ransome, larceny, discharged; no prosecutor appearing.
Union Church Association of Roulet, incorporated.
Henry Andresen and Decatur Francis, appointed overseers of the poor. Stewardson township.
Abram Jones appointed clerk of Wharton township.
Tax of 10 mills ordered in West Branch township.
Tax of 10 mills ordered in Jackson township.
Com. vs John Brownlee, perjury, no guilty; county for costs.
Com. vs Miles Hurd *et al.*, disturbing social gathering, bail of James Gibson forfeited and respited. Miles Hurd, Leroy Hurd and C. E. Williams held to bail for appearance at next term.
Veniries issued for thirty-six traverse and twenty-four grand jurors for June Term.
Lenora M. Presho appointed guardian of Chester E. Presho, minor.
Com. vs Thad Kelly, selling liquor, bail $100 for appearance at next term.
Tax of 10 mills ordered in Hector township.
Com. vs John Brownlee. Bail of $200 for the appearance of W. T. Jones at next term.
Estate of Hettie Deremer. D. C. Larrabee appointed auditor.
Tax of 10 mills ordered in Genesee, Wharton, Sylvania and Summit townships.
Estate of Wm. Shanley, A. F. Hollenbeck appointed auditor to distribute funds.
Willard Bacon vs G. R. Howe, verdict for defendant.
B. F. Bishop appointed auditor of Allegany township.
Rufus Scott vs John Rooney, judgment by agreement for the sum of $80.
Com. vs John Rooney, continued.
Hebron Cemetery Association incorporated.
A. F. Hollenbeck and George C. King admitted to practice in the several Courts of Potter county.
Divorces were granted in the following cases: Geo. Yentzer vs Malinda Yentzer; Luther Brizzee vs Mary E. Brizzee; Adelaid Haskins vs Ellery Haskins; Wm. McFall vs Adelaid McFall; Catherine Hodecamp vs John Hodecamp.
Charles Rowell vs Martha Rowell, publication ordered and Seth Lewis appointed commissioner to take testimony; Mary E. Goodrich vs Charles E. Goodrich, alias sub in divorce ordered; Caroline Johnson vs J. K. Johnson, A. H. Brewster appointed commissioner to take testimony; Sarah Quick vs J. B. Quick, alias sub in divorce awarded; Albert W. Smith vs Mary Smith. H. A. Gridley appointed commissioner to take testimony.

Daniel Monroe, Sheriff of Potter county acknowledged deeds for land sold at Sheriff's sale to

Bingham estate, 76 acres in Hector, for $50, sold as the property of E. H. Stone.

Bingham estate, 56 acres in Hector, for $50, sold as property of Chas. E. Gill.

D. J. and E. W. Chappel, 33 perches in Lewisville, for $25, sold as the property of P. M. Jacobus.

The Potter Enterprise
Wednesday Evening, March 22, 1882 – Vol. VIII, No. 44

Roulet. A. W. Johnson and Mrs. F. D. Weimer, are in Oswego, N.Y. where they were called by the death of their mother, Mrs. C. W. Johnson.

The Potter Enterprise
Wednesday Evening, March 29, 1882 – Vol. VIII, No. 45

Eleven Mile. On the 19th the children and grand-children of Mrs. M. E. Lyman met with her on the occasion of the seventy-eighth anniversary of her birth, and the 21st the family and friends of B. F. Lyman assisted him to celebrate his sixtieth anniversary of birth.

Oswayo. "Lin" Porter, having concluded that boarding out was rather expensive, sought the acquaintance of Miss Nettie Brockway, secured the services of Rev. Wm. North, rented a house in the Tannery row, and has commenced housekeeping in good style.

MARRIED.

CLINTON – REED. At the home of Mrs. Lewis, in Coudersport, March 14, 1882, by Rev. C. Dillenbeck, Mr. Henry Clinton and Miss Adelia I. Reed, all of Summit, Pa.

- Mrs. Susie A. Costello, daughter of Patrick and Mary Doyle, of Oswayo, died at Bear Butte Valley, Dakota, March 15th, aged 29 years.

- John Earle, of Eulalia, has rented his farm to J. W. Allen, and next week will start for Eureka Springs, Arkansas, near which place he expects to enter a homestead, under the Soldier's Act. John will have to occupy his homestead but one year, at the end of which time he will receive a patent from the United States. John served four years in the army.

OLMSTED STATION.
The Tide-water Station and What is Being Done There.

Olmsted Station is but little more than two miles and a half from Coudersport, as the crow flies, by the road it is nearly five, - at this time of the year with roads cut up, it is double the distance. As the crow flies it is over two ridges, through the woods and in the second hollow. From the top of the ridge you suddenly emerge in full view of a small but very busy village. Two dwellings, a large boarding house, boiler house, pump house, a stable, two large tanks, 1200 bbls. each for water which comes from a spring on the hillside, a weather stained derrick where the drill failed to find water, at a depth of 300 feet and a 2,000 barrel oil tank. Beyond the oil tank, work is progressing for a larger tank.

The Station is at the head of Lehman Hollow. Level ground there is none, except where graded by the hand of man. The view from the hill is very pleasant, and you will stop to take it in – and rest, especially the rest.

Of the boarding house and dwellings, they look neat and comfortable.

The boiler house is a large building, supplied with double boilers. Inside we found one end filled with brick, to be used in casing additional boilers soon to be put in. This will necessitate enlarging the building. Outside was piled immense quantities of wood which has been seasoning for two or three years, and if oil remains low will season for years to come, as it is now cheaper to use oil than wood for fuel. Opening the furnace doors, you have a view of the traditional hot place, mentioned in the Scriptures.

The oil is burned in spray, a three-eighths pipe conveys the oil to a larger pipe, where it is sprayed by steam and air. The first attempt to use oil was with a patent burner, but it did not give satisfaction and Superintendent Benton made a burner of his own, which works like a charm. A stop cock regulates the flow of oil, and water is supplied continually, so that the boilers require scarcely any care, and almost no labor at all.

Attached to the boiler house is the telegraph office, small but comfortable, heat with steam. Two operators are employed, and the office is open day and night. Here we found friend Stone dreaming of pigeons, and awaiting his time to take charge of the engine.

The pump house is a little below and contains three pumps. The first pump put in, now being removed, was soon found to light to do the work, a larger one was added and the building enlarged, and last winter a still larger one was put in and the building again enlarged. The new pump is of the Holly patent, is a beauty and at the same time a monster. The first pump weighs about twenty tons, the plungers are 7 ½ inches with 25 inch stroke, five revolutions of the pump forces two barrels of oil into the six inch pipe which composes the line. The engine is about one hundred and eighty horse power. The engine and pump work side and side, making but little more noise than an old style sewing machine, yet daily forcing some seven thousand barrels of oil on its way to Williamsport, a distance of eighty and a half miles. The west end of the line is about twenty-nine miles in length the line holds about 20,000 barrels of oil and when first tested required about a week to fill. The machinery is clean and bright and shows good care on the part of those having charge. The full capacity of the pump is rated at 10,000 barrels per day, but the runs average about 7,000 barrels. The pressure on the pipe is kept at 900 pounds to the square inch. On the wall is an automatic register which shows the pressure on the pipe and records each revolution of the pump. All the oil from the west enters the small iron tank below the pump house and is forced from it into the eastern part of the line.

Attached to the pump house is a small green house, about 12 x 18 feet, kept at an even temperature with steam pipes. This green house is well filled with choice plants in a thrifty condition. Olmsted Station probably has the largest collection of plants in the county, with the exception of Dr. Charles Meine of Germania. One would hardly look for such a thing in the woods, as the Station is, and surrounded by work, more for utility than beauty. Outside are the remains of last years flower beds, which will be renewed when the warm weather comes.

At present some twenty-five or thirty men and several teams are employed grading for a thirty-five thousand barrel tank. This is said to be the heaviest grade ever made for an oil tank. The lower side of the fill is about thirty-eight feet, the upper side of the cut about twenty-five feet, and a large portion is through rock. The grade is now nearly completed. The tank will be ninety feet across, height about twenty-eight feet and requires a grade of one hundred and four feet across. Nearly one hundred tons of tank iron is now on the ground. The grade and hauling of the iron has already cost $2,800 and nearly all this amount has been paid for in gold.

As soon as the grade is completed it will be studded with posts high enough to allow riveters on the under side, and the work of putting together the bottom will commence. When completed the posts are removed from the centre out until the whole bottom rests on the ground. People who object to noise will find it just as pleasant several miles away while this work is going on.

When the roads are dry visitors will find a trip to Olmsted Station very pleasant and profitable. W. O. Benton, the Superintendent, is always on hand, willing to show visitors all that is worth seeing, and ready to answer all questions. Everything is kept in good shape and he is proud of the Station. A better superintendent the Tide water will never find.

The Potter Enterprise
Wednesday Evening, April 5, 1882 – Vol. VIII, No. 46

Roulet. The friends of Mr. and Mrs. Isaac Lyman, assembled at their home, on the evening of the 25th ult., to celebrate their 30th anniversary of wedded life.

Bingham. A daughter of Wm. and Samantha Ensworth, also died of Diphtheria, March 23d, at 6 p.m., in the fifth year of her age. Also a child of Seldan Carpenter, aged about seven months, died of congestion of the stomach and lungs.

Bingham. Mr. Carpenter left home leaving his family in usual health, almost immediately thereafter the child fell sick and died in about twenty-four hours, so that when the father returned, his little darling had gone to be numbered with the angels.

Bingham. Death has again invaded our vicinity. Fayette McCarn, a man of sterling worth died recently, after a severe illness, with Bright's Disease. He was a depot master and had served in that capacity for several years. He was the eldest son of L. E. McCarn, Esq., of this place and died at his father's. He leaves a wife and children who with loving parents, brothers, other relatives, and numerous friends mourn his loss.

- Mr. Leroy Lyman the "mighty hunter" made us a call last week. He says that the past winter was dull for him, he only killed four bears and forty deer. – *Reporter*.

HAMMOND'S TANNERY.
Where it is, What it is Doing, and How it is Done.

Hammond's Tannery is located about one mile southwest of Coudersport, on the Allegany river, and is quite a village of itself. It is owned by Francis Hammond, formerly of Sullivan county, N.Y., who is also part owner, with his father, in a large tannery there, one of the largest in the state.

A little over two years ago, Mr. Hammond purchased the J. W. Allen farm, and the Charles Reissman farm, and commenced the erection of dwellings and tannery buildings. On the property purchased were two good houses and one large barn. Twenty-one tenant houses have been erected, and this coming summer, more will be built. The tenant houses are small ones, neat structures, most of them painted, all plastered, and well finished. They are occupied by tannery hands who are of many nationalities, Irish, Germans, Swedes, Polanders and others.

Mr. Hammond has just completed an elegant new house, and is now in New York purchasing new furniture etc., for it. The house if finished substantially, and is a model of convenience. It will be occupied sometime this month.

In connection with the tannery is a large store well filled with goods and intended for the especial convenience of the tannery employees, but it has a large trade out side of these; is well arranged and contains the business office of the tannery, and is also connected with the weighing room, where the bark, hides and leather is weighed, as they pass in and out, for use or sale.

Only sole leather is manufactured, and all the hides used are imported from South America. On every hide is found the mark or brand of the original owner. These brands are put upon the cattle when they are calves, with a hot iron, are ineffaceable, except by covering them over with a larger brand, which is not a safe thing to do as in cattle countries the stealing of cattle is a crime rated above murder, and more certain of punishment. The brand is proof positive of ownership, and should the cattle change hands the new owner must then put on his brand, and take a bill of sale, describing the cattle, age, ear mark and brand, and be able to show the bill of sale or he may loose his stock at any time. In many sections cattle are yet killed simply for the hides and tallow. The hides are prepared before shipment that moths or grubs will not work them and in this preparation is the poisonous substance that makes trouble for the tanners when a finger is accidentally cut during the process of the tanning. The hides are brought to various ports in this country, and then shipped to tanneries for tanning by hemlock, oak bark and acide process. At this tannery, hemlock bark furnishes the tannin.

The boiler house is of stone, with iron roof, connected with the leach room, and bark mills. The bark mills cut the bark in small pieces which fall into a long box, where it is moved by machinery to any point where it may be needed a shoot carries it to one of the leaches, where it is saturated with hot water. The liquor settles through the false bottom of the leach, and is forced to the lay away vats in another building. After the tannin in the liquor is exhausted it is pumped back to the leach room and used again, and again indefinitely. The only waste is the soakage from the hides, and there is so little of this that those who have worried over the contamination of the river from the tannery may rest their souls in peace. After the tan is spent so much as is needed for fuel is shoveled into a trough where an endless belt carries it to the room above the boilers, trap doors connect with furnace, so that the fireman has no use for a shovel, except it be to take care of the ashes. Still the fireman's situation is no sinecure. This building is capped with an immense smoke stack which required about 75,000 bricks to construct. From this place steam is distributed through the vat room and dry house to run an engine in each, and also to warm the rooms.

The sweat pits and vat room is located a hundred feet or more from the first building. The sweat pit is divided into ten rooms, or little pits. It is doubtless divided up for convenience. It seems to as that it ought to be altogether. One room full of condensed perfumes of the most condensed character might be endured, but ten of them! Let's get out. The vat room is a one story structure sixty feet wide by 350 feet long, and contains 210 vats, all of which are covered except those from which hides are being taken, or put in, or being filled with liquor. It is not a very unpleasant looking place if you enter from the lower end, but as you advance, the noise increases, and the smell also increases, for at the upper end is where the hides are scraped. The hide is first placed in the hide mill – a "kicking" machine that works both ways in a box, which with water pouring upon the hides, softens them. The hides are then split, each hide making two sides, then placed in the sweat pits, warm and dark rooms, where they hang until the hair becomes loose, again to the hide mill and then to the hands who remove any hair remaining, and the scraps of flesh that may adhere to the hide. The side then goes into the hemlock liquor, after remaining a time is taken out, turned and into other vats until the tannin has filled the hide and the hide is now leather, though far from being ready for market.

From the vat room the sides are taken to the dry house, a large structure, about fifty feet wide by three hundred feet in length. The sides are placed in a washer where they are turned by machinery and thoroughly rinsed. Each side receives a coating of grease and is hung up to dry. After the oil is absorbed, the sides are sprinkled and piled, very much after the manner that clothes are treated by the ironer. It then passes to the finishing room where it passed under a heavy roller, back and forth until made smooth and compact. Again it is hung up and dried, and again sponged, when it passes through another roller similar to the first which gives it the finishing polish, and we have the sole-leather ready for use or the market. The dry house treatment is very important and requires great skill that the leather may come out bright. The color makes quite a difference in the market price. This building is kept at an even temperature night and day. It is now filled with sides, direct from the vats and in all stages to that now ready for shipment. Sole-leather enough to furnish taps for all the boots and shoes in America, one would think after passing through. It requires from three to four months to change the South American Hide into the North American sole-leather, ready for use.

The capacity of the tannery is from 45,000 to 50,000 hides per year, or from 90,000 to 100,000 sides. New vats are to be added, an addition to the dry house, and the capacity considerably increased. At present from 250 to 300 sides per day pass through the various stages necessary to the making of leather. From four to five thousand cords of bark is required for the year's use. Good bark lands will net average over five to seven cords per acre, so it is plain to see the amount of land cleared to supply this demand. There is now on hand about six thousand cords of bark, piled in the yard. Much of this bark is bought of farmers. Mr. Hammond owns all the bark on several thousand acres of the Bingham lands in this section. All the bark offered, in good condition is bought, and fair prices paid.

The buildings are not elaborate structures, but have been built for use and convenience. They are substantial, but no extra pains or money has been put on them simply for looks. The site is naturally a convenient one. The bark yard is on high level ground, so that there is no hard pulling in carting bark to the mill. Ives run, a pure spring brook furnishes an ample supply of water, and one of the best quality.

The ashes from the burned bark is mixed with the scrapings and clippings from the hides and makes a most excellent fertilizer. Spent tan not burned is used for filling in the low places about the property, and in a few years the place will present a smooth appearance and the land not occupied in the tanning business will be very fertile and productive.

Besides the men employed in and about the tannery, quite a number with teams are employed continually hauling bark, hides and leather.

In the bark peeling season, a large number of men are employed in the woods.

The buildings of this tannery has added much to the growth and prosperity of this section and the good work will continue for many years to come.

Mr. Stephen Burr has a general superintendence of the business, keeping the books, attending to the bark, when brought for weight, and has charge of the store, a gentleman, and a thorough business man.

The foreman of the tannery is Mr. H. R. Whittaker, young in years, but a practical tanner who understands the business from beginning to end, gentlemanly, and a pleasant man to meet in any place.

The Potter Enterprise
Wednesday Evening, April 12, 1882 – Vol. VIII, No. 47

MARRIED.

HAZEN – FRENCH. – In Roulet, Pa., March 20th, 1882, by J. B. Davidson, Esq., William Hazen and Miss Esther French, both of Roulet.

The Potter Enterprise
Wednesday Evening, April 19, 1882 – Vol. VIII, No. 48

- Benjamin Roberts, of Sweden, died on Sunday morning last.

DIED.

HASKELL – In Allegany, April 2d, of Cholera Infantum, after an illness of but a few hours, Mamie, only child of Henry and Mary Haskell, aged five years and six months.

Citizens' Water Company.

A meeting of the Citizens' Water Company of Coudersport was held in the office of Olmsted & Larrabee, on Saturday last, and the following officers were elected for the ensuing year:

President, - A. G. Olmsted.
Treasurer, - R. L. Nichols.
Secretary, - J. L. Knox.
Executive Committee, - F. W. Knox, R. L. Nichols, P. A. Stebbins, Jr.

The executive committee was directed to prepare by-laws for the Company, and fix a schedule of water rate to be charged. The rates will be prepared in a few days. The contract for putting in the main calls for the completion of the work, on or before June 15th, 1882.

Mr. Simpson, who has the contract for putting in the Mains, arrived Monday, with fifteen trench diggers, to commence work this, Tuesday, morning.

COUDERSPORT & PORT ALLEGANY R. R.
The Company Organized Last Monday Afternoon.
Half the Stock Taken – List of Stockholders.
Work to be Commenced on Monday of Next Week!
Every Appearance of a Sure Thing This Time.

Ever since Vanderbilt secured control of the Jersey Shore and Pine Creek road, and decided to abandon the west end, efforts have been made to secure a railroad from Coudersport to Port Allegany. The matter was kept as quiet as possible, for prudential reasons. At last it looks as if there could be no doubt of the success of the enterprise.

The Company has been granted a charter, as the Coudersport & Port Allegany Railroad Co. Capital stock $150,000. Directors F. W. Knox, Isaac Benson and A. M. Benton, F. H. Arnold of Port Allegany, C. V. B. Barse, C. S. Cary of Olean, B. D. Hamlin of Smethport and F. H. Root of Buffalo.

On Monday the Directors met in Port Allegany, and perfected the organization by selecting the following officers.

President – F. W. Knox.
Vice President – C. V. B. Barce.
Treasurer – Miles W. Barce.
Secretary – A. B. Mann.
Executive Committee – F. W. Knox, A. M. Benton, C. S. Carey and F. H. Root.

The Stockholders are as follows:
F. W. Knox, Isaac Benson, A. G. Olmsted, C. S. Jones, J. L. Knox, W. K. Jones, A. B. Mann, M. S. Thompson, R. L. Nichols and Joseph Mann, of Coudersport.
B. D. Hamlin, and Henry Hamlin, of Smethport.
A. J. Wilcox, of Bradford.
F. H. Root, of Buffalo.
A. M. Benton and F. H. Arnold, of Port Allegany.
C. S. Carey, C. V. B. Barse, Miles W. Barse, of Olean.
M. E. Olmsted, of Harrisburg.

No person has been asked to subscribe that has refused. Books for additional stock subscription will be opened in Olean, to-morrow, where a number have expressed a desire to take stock. Several of those who have subscribed, offer to double their subscription, if necessary. So far as the money is concerned, there is no trouble. The names of the stockholders is sufficient to settle that question.

The road is run from Coudersport to Port Allegany, a distance of seventeen miles, all the way down the Allegany valley. The grade is less than eleven feet to the mile with not a single sharp curve.

Agreements have been entered into with the executive committee of the Jersey Shore & Pine Creek R.R. and the directors of that Company have ratified the agreement by resolution, whereby the Coudersport and Port Allegany road secures, the grade and right of way of the J.S.&P.C. Co. to Port Allegany at a nominal sum. About eleven miles is already graded, nearly all the culverts for that distance are in, which will leave but six miles to grade, most of that through fields, and the larger bridges to build.

The officers of the road have an appointment with the J.S.&P.C. executive committee at Corning on Thursday to sign the last papers necessary to the turning over of the west end to the new company. This could not be done until the C. & P. A. R. R. company perfected its organization.

Should everything prove satisfactory, two small gangs of men will be put at work, near Burtville, on Monday next.

There now seems no possible doubt of the completion of this line coming Summer.

The Company expect to be ready to contract ties as soon as Friday or Saturday of this week.

The Coudersport & Port Allegany road will be a narrow gauge, and will be well equipped on the start. Hemlock bark and Hemlock lumber will appreciate in price before the Summer is out.

It is not expected that the road will be completed under ninety days, and as rails are falling in price the iron will not be purchased until needed.

The Potter Enterprise
Wednesday Evening, April 26, 1882 – Vol. VIII, No. 49

- In passing through town last Wednesday evening, with a load of pigeoners, Wm. Sherwood attempted to cross Main street at Second. It was very dark at the time and William failed to discover that the trench diggers had been busy in that section. This important fact was not realized by him until both horses had their hind feet in the ditch and could not get out. After a time help arrived and with the aid of ropes the horses were extricated, somewhat bruised and marked. The team was driven on that night, so the injuries could not have been very serious. Since then lights have been put along the openings in the street to warn the traveler.

- Last week Sheriff Monroe and J. W. Allen, agent for the Bingham Estate, went to Hector for the purpose of ejecting Charles Seeley from a piece of land, claimed by the Bingham Estate, upon which he has squatted. Seeley showed fight and with a cocked rifle argued the matter for a little time. He threatened death and destruction if the parties offered to remove him. He was finally taken a little off his guard and before he could recover, the Sheriff and Mr. Allen had possession of his gun. Mr. Seeley is an old man, but gamey and wirey, and gave them a lively tussle for a short time. He was finally overcome and now occupies a cell in the County jail. It is likely he will have to answer the charge of resisting an officer.

- Last Wednesday, Albert Rennells met with an accident, which has kept him confined to the house ever since. Mr. Rennells lost a leg in the late war, and the stump is yet very tender, otherwise Mr. Rennells is a strong rugged man. He is engaged in freighting, and gets around with the aid of a crutch as spry as anyone. On Wednesday he was returning from Kettle Creek, where he had been to take a load of tank builders and tools. A few miles east of Cherry Springs he got out of his wagon, and in attempting to get in again, he fell heavily to the ground, striking upon the stump of his leg, he fell in front of the wheel and the heavy lumber wagon passed over one arm. The horses ran some distance before they were caught. Mr. Rennells was placed in a wagon and brought to his home in Eulalia. He was unable to sit up and it was feared that he had sustained injuries that might prove fatal. Dr. Buck rendered medical assistance, and we are glad to learn that Albert is improving.

Potter County, Pennsylvania Potpourri – Volume I
1880 through 1884

THE RAILROAD.
Every Prospect of a Railroad from Coudersport to Port Allegany.
Contract Signed for the right of way and grade of the old J. S. & P. C. R. R.
Dirt Throwing Commenced on Monday Last.

On Friday last the contract for the right of way and grade of the Jersey Shore & Pine Creek R.R. from Coudersport to Port Allegany, was signed in Corning, and it is now the property of the Coudersport and Port Allegany Narrow Gauge R.R. The latter road has it in the form of a lease, ten years absolute, and after that time it may be repossessed by the J.S.P.C., should it wish to put through a standard gauge, upon paying for all improvements made and as we understand it the purchase of all rolling stock etc. The price paid for the grade and right of way $7,000, a nominal price compared with what the work actually cost.

Yesterday, Monday, morning, work was commenced at Burtville and at the State road, by a small gang and the dirt is really flying. This is merely for the purpose of taking possession of the road, the actual work of SHOVING the road through has not commenced. The executive committee will take a trip over the line this week, and soon thereafter as possible it will be let to Contractors.

Some of the sanguine ones propose having the cars running clear through, by the Fourth of July. It will be built as fast as possible, consistent with economy.

As the matter now stands the road will surely be completed at an early day, and Coudersport will be connected with the outside world with iron rails.

Coudersport seems entering upon a new era of prosperity. The timber surrounding it will call for mills and factories to work it up. A furniture factory will find this a fine location. There is an abundance of beech, cherry, ash, chestnut, maple, basswood and other woods used in furniture.

A hub factory will find an abundance of first class black and yellow birch.

Saw mills will have business for years cutting out the hemlock alone and a handle factory could be supplied with all the white ash that could be used.

From information which we believe to be reliable, we state the Keating lands south of the river will be surveyed into village lots and sold at reasonable prices, enabling the poor man to secure a home for himself. We are also informed that John S. Ross contemplates putting his lands south of Mill Creek in the market, at reasonable rate and reasonable time. If these lands are sold at reasonable figures, we may look for a large addition to the town in homes. Heretofore the complaint has been, high prices for lots, and there has been good reason for it. There are but very few good building lots, in desirable locations for sale. We look for a better state of affairs the coming summer.

The Potter Enterprise
Wednesday Evening, May 3, 1882 – Vol. VIII, No. 50

West Branch. Lon Louge caught a young squab last Saturday morning. It weighed 9 ¾ lbs. when dressed. It is a hen squab, and they are going to try and raise it.

MARRIED.

ELDER – TAGGART. – In Andover, April 23d, by Rev. Mr. Williams, Mr. Andrew P. Elder and Miss Flora E. Taggart, both of Whites Corners.

WELLS – STRIKER. – At the residence of the bride's parents, in Allegany, April 26th, 1882, by Rev. C. Dillenbeck, Mr. Daniel W. Wells and Miss Eva Jane Striker, all of Allegany, Pa.

COOL – WARNER. – At the home of bride's mother in Coudersport, April 27th, 1882, by Rev. C. Dillenbeck, Mr. Walter P. Cool, and Miss Louisa Warner, all of Allegany, Pa.

CRAWFORD – BOWTISH. – At the residence of C. H. Cole, Esq., Saturday, April 22, 1882, by C. H. Cole, W. H. Crawford, of East Sharon, Pa., and Tilla Bowtish, of Brockport, Elk county, Pa.

- Rev. Maltby of Fishing Creek, died on Sunday last.

REV. KELLY.
Another Wolf in Sheep's Clothing.

Late developments go to show that the Methodist church of Lewisville has harbored a sanctimonious fraud in the person of their pastor, Rev. Kelly.

Mr. Kelly has been stationed there some time, and gave general satisfaction. Recently he commenced the publication of a church paper, in which he was assisted by a Miss Monroe, but no evil reports arose from their intimacy.

On Saturday last the Reverend rascal obtained a horse and buggy from Seth Lewis, for the purpose of attending quarterly meeting at Oswayo. The young lady went along, but they did not go to Oswayo. The horse and buggy was left at Wellsville and the preacher and the young lady are supposed to have gone west.

The Reverend Kelly leaves a wife and four children, at Lewisville, who receive the sympathy of all.

Miss Monroe is a good looking young lady of about twenty years of age, well educated, and has always borne a character above suspicion. The young lady is well connected in and around Lewisville and her conduct in leaving home carries grief to many a household. How she became so infatuated is a mystery as she was considered more than ordinarily bright and one whose moral principles were of the highest character.

Jury List, June Term, 1882.
GRAND JURORS.

Abbott – Gotlieb Bratz; Bingham – L. E. LeCarn; Clara – F. P. Brooks; Coudersport – John Carney, Williard Hickox; Hector – James Carling; Harrison – W. B. Fox, T. A. English, Geo. Whiteman, Hiram Chapin, J. J. White; Lewisville – G. C. Marion, O. R. Bassett; Oswayo – Patrick Doyle; Pike – Ed. Swartwood; Roulet – J. G. Saunders, Lewis Yentzer; Sweden – Arthur Lyman, W. Snyder, Thomas Chase; Summit – Ward Jacklin; Sharon – John Kenyon; Ulysses – E. W. Ryan.

Potter County, Pennsylvania Potpourri – Volume I
1880 through 1884

TRAVERSE JURORS.

Allegany – James Currier, Isaac Striker; Bingham – N. W. Lawrence; Coudersport – N. H. Goodsell, Gustave Grabe; Eulalia – Jahial English, Daniel Elliot; Hector – John Strait, James Greengrass, Geo. Larrison, Orville Earle; Hebron – E. D. Ayres; Lewisville – E. A. Burt; Oswayo – E. Delemater, John Davis, W. L. Lockwood; Pike – Moses Hirsch, W. Putman, Amos Baker; Pleasant Valley – John McDowell; Roulet – Henry Tauscher, Wm. Brine, Michael Sullivan; Sharon – Flo. Donovan, Samuel White, J. L. Warner, Sylvester Strait; Sweden – David Wambold; Summit – Charles Knickerbacker, C. W. Rennells; Stewardson – O. H. P. Knickerbacker; Ulysses – V. E. Freeman; West Branch – B. F. Burrows, Charles Prouty, John Klemm; Wharton – J. M. Devoll.

THE RAILROAD.
Important Meeting of Executive Committee and Directors.
The Contract for the Construction of the Road Signed Last Week.

On Wednesday evening of last week the Executive Committee and the Board of Directors of the Coudersport & Port Allegany Railroad, met in the offices of F. W. Knox & Son, in Coudersport. Nearly the entire board was present and the plan and details were discussed until a late hour.

The officers of the road passed over the line the day previous with Homer Blakeslee, of Olean, with whom a contract was finally concluded for the construction of the road.

Mr. Blakeslee is to finish the grade, build all the bridges, lay the ties and iron – everything ready for the running of trains, for, so reported on the street, the sum of $45,000. The Company to furnish the iron, and within thirty days supply the Contractor with an engine and flat cars, for the construction train. Before this reaches our readers it is probable that the engine and cars will be purchased.

Mr. Blakeslee is an experienced builder of narrow gauge railroads, and the company have assurance that the work will be first class in every respect. The contract calls for the completion of the road by September first. The contractor slated that with good weather and everything favorable, he would conclude his labors within sixty days. Men and teams are put at work as fast as they can be obtained and before the week is out, work will be lively all along the line.

By the first of June it is expected the first train (construction train) will be running on a portion of the road.

Dallas Benson, of Lymansville, will have charge of the Coudersport end and commences work at once, cleaning and grading on the south side of the river. Dal. has experience in the business, and will leave his mark day by day. Those wishing to work on this end should apply to him.

J. L. Knox has charge of the tie contracts, and has already contracted for a large number. About fifty thousand ties will be required, besides those used for switches. Those wishing to furnish or make ties should apply to J. L. Knox, Coudersport.

The road will be fenced on both sides, probably with barbed wire. This will require a large number of posts and will give some persons good jobs.

We think the facts stated above will be sufficient to convince the most skeptical, that the Coudersport & Port Allegany Railroad is one of the certainties.

The Potter Enterprise
Wednesday Evening, May 10, 1882 – Vol. IX, No. 1

Oswayo. There has been an epidemic of babies in this section, this spring the last one on record belongs to Mr. and Mrs. Frank Gee, it's a boy – nine pounds.

Allegany. A new boy baby at Cal Ford's.

- Some of the older inhabitants of Roulet township will remember Mr. and Mrs. George Raymer, who settled in the West a number of years ago. They are now residents of Rock City, Ill., and in their western home have prospered. On the 25th of March, this aged couple celebrated their golden wedding in the presence of over 100 relatives and guests. Mr. John Yentzer and Lewis Yentzer, nephews, and Lena Yentzer, a niece, all of Roulet, were present on this happy occasion.

West Branch. George Burrows died last Wednesday morning of consumption, he leaves a wife and one child. George was not quite 22 years old.

Oswayo. Herman Granes, son of E. A. Granes of Sharon Centre, was thrown from his wagon, and injured so that he died, Thursday night.

- Dr. Richard Post of Hebron, died on Monday afternoon, May 8th. His death was caused by Bright's disease. Mr. Post was born in Binghamton, N.Y. and at the time of his death was 67 years of age. For the past forty-seven years he has resided in Potter county, and for over thirty years he has practiced medicine. He was not a graduate but read medicine with an old physician. He was very successful in his profession and enjoyed an extensive practice. Dr. Post was a good citizen and many will mourn his loss. The funeral will take place at his late residence in Hebron, to-morrow, Wednesday at 1 o'clock p.m.

Decoration Day, May 30th, 1882.

The Day will be observed in Coudersport, by the A. F. Jones' Post No. 204, G. A. R., assisted by the citizens, in the following manner:
PROGRAMME.

The Post will meet at their hall at 12 o'clock m., and receive A. W. Estes' Post, of Oswayo, and Barnes' Post, of Sharon. Form in line at 1 p.m. and march to the Monument. After which Prayer will be offered by Rev. Marshall, followed with Public Exercises by G. A. R.; Music by the Choir; Exercises by A. F. Jones' Post; Music by the Band; Address by Rev. A. Cone; Benediction by Rev. C. Dillenbeck.

The procession will then form in the following order and proceed to the Cemetery:

Band; Post G. A. R. Flags; Comrades under arms; A. F. Jones' Post; Visiting Posts; Burgess and Clergymen; Town Council; Knights of Honor; Citizens on foot; Carriages.
Services at Cemetery will be opened by Prayer by Rev. Marshall; Memorial Services by G. A. R.; Benediction by Rev. Leavenworth; Posts will then form in line and march back to the Monument and be dismissed.
A cordial invitation is extended to all to be present.
In the evening the Oswayo Dramatic Troupe will give an entertainment at the Court House, for the benefit of A. F. Jones Post, entitled "The Social Glass" or "Victims of the Bottle."
Persons having flowers to contribute, will please to confer with W. K. Jones, who is chairman of the committee on flowers and vocal music.
  Mr. A. Sidney Lyman, of Estes Post, Oswayo, will be Commander for the day.
  A. D. Colcord, C. J. Marble, G. N. Tuttle, Committee.

The Potter Enterprise
Wednesday Evening, May 17, 1882 – Vol. IX, No. 2

MARRIED.
SCHAUSS – EMMERICK. – At the house of Chris Schaudenberger, by Frank Phelps, J.P., Chris Schauss and Barbara Emmerick, both of Eulalia.

DIED.
METZGER – At Coudersport, on Saturday last, of Apoplexy, Mrs. Pamilla Metzger, aged sixty-two years.

Sudden Death.
For some time past Mrs. William Metzger has been in poor health, which resulted in her death Saturday night last. Friday morning the young lady staying with her, and occupying the same bed, arose at her usual hour, leaving Mrs. Metzger sleeping, though breathing quite heavily, and as she had been troubled for sleep no attempt was made to waken her until about nine o'clock in the morning, when it was found impossible to rouse her. She remained unconscious until death. Physicians decided that her death was caused by Apoplexy.

Decoration Day at Oswayo.
PROGRAMME.
After services at the three cemeteries in jurisdiction, the G. A. R. and citizens will assemble at the village where service will be held, at some suitable place, as to weather. Addresses will be made by Revs. Miller and North. Suitable poems read, with choir singing and other music.
  The first service will be at the cemetery, at Oswayo Centre, at 9 a.m., and thence proceed to those near Oswayo village, and service, addresses &c., at village, will begin at 1 p.m. All are cordially invited to attend and assist in the duties of the occasion.   By Order of Committee.

Good Attendance in our Graded School.

High School, - During the Spring Term, at morning roll-call, Miss S. Stearns and Miss C. Hammond were not absent; Miss Minnie Hammond and Mr. Chas. Gordinier absent once; Miss Ida Faust twice.

Grammar School, - Ruby Witter, Mary Teuscher, were not absent; Celia Gillon, Ida Baker, Jessie Hammond, Fred Stoutenberg, absent once; Maggie Metzger, absent twice; Isabella Crane, three times.

Primary School, - Bertha Neefe, Annie Neefe, Annie Gillon, Theodore Grom, Geo. Rounseville were not absent; Jay Lewis, absent once; Rose Zimmerman, Judson Rounseville, twice; and Eva Rees, Tony Bendel three times.

THE RAILROAD.

The railroad is booming along at a satisfactory rate, weather taken into consideration. Last week was very unfavorable, yet much was accomplished. At present, about two hundred men are at work, cutting, grading, bridging &c.

The large bridges are now being made in Buffalo and timber for the small ones is partially on the ground.

Twenty thousand ties have been cut, and some of the contractors are already delivering along the line.

The right of way, from Coudersport to the John Earle farm, it is expected, will be cleared to-day, and work on the grade is now going on inside the boro limits. Mr. Blakeslee now has about all the men he can work, until the water subsides, as considerable of the grade is through low lands.

The first passenger coach was ordered Monday evening. Some trouble occurred in procuring an engine to be delivered as soon as wanted, but this difficulty is now believed to be settled, and No. 1 will probably be on hand in time.

It is highly probable that the iron will be ordered this week for immediate delivery. Since the first inquiry for iron, the price has fallen so that the company will save something like $10,000.

Everything is working satisfactorily and the road progressing rapidly. Good weather will aid materially.

The Potter Enterprise
Wednesday Evening, May 24, 1882 – Vol. IX, No. 3

- If any one meets Gene Baker, they want to ask him for a cigar, for it is a girl and weighs ten pounds.

- The Mansfield correspondent of the Wellsboro *Gazette*, of last week, says: "Mr. I. P. Collins, of Potter county, and Miss Delia Elliot, daughter of O. V. Elliot, of Mansfield, are to celebrate their marriage nuptials on Thursday of this week."

Whites Corners. Mrs. Hunter, mother of Stephen Edwards of this place, died on Thursday last. The funeral services were held at Jasper, N.Y. the following Sunday.

- The young lady who so recently eloped from Ulysses, has returned home. The Elder also repented, and we understand efforts are being made to reinstate him in the church, that he may continue preaching. Those who are pushing his case, it seems to us, are not true friends of the church. The people of Ulysses recently made Mrs. Kelly a donation of $107, which is very much to the credit of the people, and proves that there is christian love and charity yet left in the world.

Serious Affray.

Saturday last our citizens were startled by a report that Jerome Knickerbacker, of Lymansville had killed Westley Benson, also of Lymansville, in an affray in the pigeon woods, and that Knickerbacker had left for parts unknown. The story proves to be partially correct. Knickerbacker and Benson have been camping together in the woods, and Saturday morning had a fight in which Knickerbacker struck Benson several times on the head with a hatchet, and believing that he had killed Benson, left for parts unknown, and has not since been heard from. A small boy, ten or twelve years old, witnessed the fight. Just how the quarrel originated we are unable to say, as reports are quite contradictory, but all agree on one point that poor whiskey was at the bottom of all the trouble. Dr. Ellison was called Sunday morning and found Benson suffering from five severe cuts on the head. It is thought he will recover and soon be about again.

- At a meeting of the Patrons of Lymansville cheese factory, A. Nelson was chosen president, and J. M. Spafford, secretary.

The following officers were duly elected for the permanent organization. President, Robt. Mann; treasurer, J. M. Spafford; secretary, J. A. Glace; Salesmen, A. A. Raymond, Julius Neefe, Wm. Snyder, D. Benson and Henry Tauscher, weighers.

The following resolution was then adopted; Resolved – That any patron may take his own cheese out of the factory, by giving due notice previous to any sale.

The Potter Enterprise
Wednesday Evening, May 31, 1882 – Vol. IX, No. 4

- On Monday afternoon, P. A. Stebbins, Sr., passed peacefully from life, at the advanced age of seventy-six years. Mr. Stebbins was a native of New York, born July 8th, 1805, and in 1850 removed to Ulysses township in this county. In 1853 he removed to Coudersport, having been elected Sheriff, and since that time has resided here in active business life, until the past few years, when having acquired a competency he retired from business. For some years his health has not been good, and the past winter was an extremely hard one for him. He had made arrangement to visit relatives in the West, hoping for better health but a few days ago was taken with pneumonia, and in his enfeebled condition was unable to combat the disease. Kind friends and relatives rendered every assistance possible, but without avail. Mr. Stebbins will be missed by a large number of Potter county citizens. His hearty welcome upon all occasions and cheerful kindness to all in need, will long be remembered by many. He was a man of large heart, kind and genial, with a friendly word for each and every one. Four sons and a daughter remain of the family, and wife and mother having passed away some ten years since. The last sad ceremonies will take place at the house, at two o'clock this, Wednesday, afternoon.

Decoration Day.

Sleep, comrades, sleep and rest
    On this Field of the Grounded Arms,
Where does no more molest,
    Nor sentry's shot alarms!
Your silent tents of green
    We deck with fragrant flowers.
Yours has the suffering been,
    The memory shall be ours.

Decoration Day brings to Coudersport each year larger crowds than assemble any other time, or day. The long list of names of deceased soldiers, found upon the monument in the Court House square, attest the patriotism of Potter county and the terrible havoc made in the ranks of the brave boys who went to the defense of their country in the time of peril. Year by year the number of the dead heroes increase, and year by year the observances of Decoration Day becomes more general.

At an early hour the streets commenced filling with people, and by noon the crowd was very large. The A. F. Jones Post G. A. R. had spread rations for the Oswayo Post and other comrades, in the Opera House, and at noon the comrades were formed in line in front of the hall and marched to dinner. About one o'clock the line was again formed, and marched to the Monument, which had been tastily decorated with evergreens and flowers, and from thence to the Court room where the G.A.R. Services and a stirring address, by Rev. Cone, were listened to. The Court room was packed full, and yet the crowds on the streets seemed as large as ever. From the Court House, the procession marched, accompanied by teams to the cemetery, where the graves and monuments of deceased soldiers were decorated by their surviving comrades, and citizens.

About eighty old soldiers were in line, many in the uniform of the G.A.R. The Ulysses Band furnished most excellent music and presented a good appearance, in their uniforms.

The Potter Enterprise
Wednesday Evening, June 7, 1882 – Vol. IX, No. 5

- Born, to Mr. and Mrs. Will Eaton of Roulet, Pa., May 25th, a daughter.

MARRIED.

COLE – NEWTON. – May 27th, 1882. At the residence of the bride's parents by G. W. Pearsall, Esq., Mr. Charles Cole, and Miss Jessie A. Newton, all of Sharon, Potter county, Pa.

INSON – HEWETT. – On Decoration Day, at Coudersport, by the Rector of Christ Church, Theodore Inson, of Homer township, and Lillie Hewett, of Sylvania.

JOHNSON – JOHNSON. – In Olean, N.Y., May 24th, by Rev. David Winters, Mr. Chas. Johnson, of Owego, N.Y., and Mrs. Elnora Johnson, of Roulet, Pa.

The Railroad.

Four weeks ago Monday, Mr. Blakeslee took personal charge of the work on the Coudersport & Port Allegany R.R. Since that time there has been four floods in the Allegheny river, including the present one. The road runs along the river and much of the uncompleted grade through swamp and lowlands, yet in spite of so much water only a little over a mile of the grading remains untouched. Ten days of good weather would complete the grade, and small culverts sufficient for construction train purposes.

On Thursday the contract for the rails was signed. The contract is with T. Guilford Smith, of Buffalo, agent for the Montour Steel and Iron Company, of Danville, Pa., and calls for the delivery of 250 tons at Port Allegany by Monday next. The balance to be delivered in weekly installments before July 15th.

The spikes and plates are purchased from J. W. Hoffman & Co., Philadelphia, and are to be delivered in the same way and proportion as the rails.

An engine was purchased some time ago, and also a passenger coach. Flat and freight cars have been contracted for with the Gilbert Car works of Buffalo, and enough flat cars for the construction train, are to be delivered at Port Allegany, on or before June 15th, and the balance by the 1st of August. Another passenger car and a baggage car, it is expected, will be purchased this week.

A large number of ties are already delivered along the grade, and they are now being inspected and counted preparatory to delivering them to Mr. Blakeslee.

It is expected that the Coudersport depot will be located this week and the contract for its construction given this week or the first of next.

Considering the stormy weather everything is progressing very finely. Mr. Blakeslee deserves great credit for the vim with which he has pushed his part of the work. The officers of the road and the contractor are all doing their level best and success is attending their efforts on every hand.

Potter County, Pennsylvania Potpourri – Volume I
1880 through 1884

The Potter Enterprise
Wednesday Evening, June 14, 1882 – Vol. IX, No. 6

- Born, to Mr. and Mrs. Wm. Trask, West Branch, June 5th, a son. Weight nine and three-fourth pounds.

MARRIED.

HAXTON – TURCK. – At the M.E. Parsonage, June 12th, 1882, by Rev. C. Dillenbeck, Mr. Charles H. Haxton and Miss Hattie A. Turck, both of West Pike, Pa.

- Mrs. Dingee, mother of Mrs. Earl Crane, was buried last Sabbath.

DIED.

WOOD – At the residence of her mother in Wheeler, Steuben county, N.Y., June 2, 1882, of cancer in the stomach, Mrs. Catherine M. Wood, wife of Nelson Wood, of Lymansville, aged 51 years.

REED – In Summit township, June 5th, 1882, Maud Reed, daughter of Henry and Mary Reed, aged two years and five months.

RENNELLS – In Summit township, June 6th, 1882, Louis H. Rennells, infant son of Charles and Minnie Rennells, aged six months.

- Mrs. Jane Jackson, of Ulysses, met with quite a severe accident on Friday last. Mrs. Jackson was holding a fence post and her hired man was driving with a sledge and thinking he had done driving Mrs. Jackson placed her hand on top of the post, and it was struck by sledge hurting the hand severely. Dr. Eaton was called, who dressed the wound and thinks her hand can be saved. As Mrs. Jackson is a widow lady and superintends her own farm work she has the sympathy of her neighbors and friends. – *Sentinel.*

Fire.

Last Saturday night about ten o'clock the Court House bell was rung warning those awake and awakening those asleep to the fact that there was a fire somewhere in Coudersport. The flame lit up the heaven, (there wasn't enough to call it heavens) and there was a scampering of feet, that denoted considerable excitement, if not much danger.

The fire was soon found to be in C. A. Stebbins' ice house, and at first endangered the barn near, but a few minutes work deadened the flames and the danger was past, but the fire in the ice house was not out by any means, and before it was left for good the roof and sides were pretty much burned up. Water enough was thrown upon it to float the entire building, ice and all, and after it was considered all out would kindle again. It was carefully watched all night. Most of the ice yet remains in good condition and Charles will have sufficient for lemonade and ice cream. The fire was caused by setting ashes in the hall of the ice house some time during the afternoon.

Shoplifting Extraordinary.

The most extensive business in shoplifting we have heard of in many a day was brought to light in Coudersport last Wednesday, and resulted in the arrest of Mrs. John Denhoff. Some time since P. A. Stebbins & Bro. missed a piece of very fine lace, from which only a few yards had been cut, and that sold to a lady in town. A few days ago Henry Carsten, clerk in the store, discovered some of the lace on a hat worn by Mrs. Denhoff, but to make assurance doubly sure, the hat was borrowed and the lace compared with that previously sold. The comparison was satisfactory and a search warrant issued and a large quantity of goods was found. The next day Mrs. D. started for the west, with a large trunk (not having been placed under arrest) and constable Cole was dispatched with a warrant and arrested her near Port Allegany. The trunk was searched and in it was found quite a large quantity of goods, some of them from the store of Jones & Hodskin. The total value of the goods from Stebbins' was about forty-eight dollars, and from Jones & Hodskins' about twenty-five dollars, consisting of laces, fancy goods, calicos, shawls, spreads and one entire piece of factory. How she could take so many and such bulky articles without detection is a mystery. When asked why she stole the goods she said the devil made her do it, and no doubt her answer was correct. Mrs. D. has long been a resident of Coudersport, and never before has there been a question of her honesty. She seems to have been possessed with a mania, as she took many things she did not need and could not use. She gave bail in the sum of $200 for her appearance at Court, and since then, has, we are informed, left for the west where her husband resides, doubtless securing her bail against loss. This is a sad blow for her children who are considered honorable and upright.

The Potter Enterprise
Wednesday Evening, June 21, 1882 – Vol. IX, No. 7

- Our farmers who are so much annoyed by crows in destroying their corn, had better try the following very simple remedy, which is said by one who has tried it to be very effective. The barrel is suspended by a cord from a cross bar, which rests upon the ends of two stakes driven in the ground. The length of the parts are as follows: Upright stakes, 6 feet high; cross bar, 6 feet long; the barrel being so hung that it will be 2 feet from the ground. The heads of the barrels both removed, and by being hung by the cord exactly in the middle of one side, or so it balances, it turns easily with a slight wind; in fact, a barrel thus suspended is seldom still. This constant motion of so huge an object as a barrel has an alarming effect upon the corn loving crows. One barrel will answer for four of five acres. Pieces of tin and other objects, as bright colored cloth may be attached to the suspended barrel, but they are not essential to the barrel scarecrow.

Potter County, Pennsylvania Potpourri – Volume I
1880 through 1884

In the Market.

Monday the Keating Estate put four squares of land, south of the river, in the market.

One square is held in a block for $1600.

J. M. Covey bought of A. B. Mann, agent, lots 5, 6, 7, 8, in square 38, south of Mrs. Fickler's for $500.

Mrs. A. A. Hodskins, lot No. 1 in same square for $225.

J. D. Hodskins lot, No. 2, in same square, $150.

George H. Green bought lot No. 6, square 35, east of Gillons, for $225.

J. L. Knox has the refusal for a day or two of lot 1 and 2, square 35. In case he does not take it the Presbyterian church will buy them for a parsonage, if he does take them the church will take lots 3 and 4 in same square.

The lots on the river, south of the bridge are also offered at prices ranging to as high as $500. These lots will be convenient to the railroad depot, and are considered as business locations.

James Turner has purchased two of these lots.

Other squares will be put in the market as soon as the depot and sidings are located finally.

The Keatings expect to put a deep ditch through the swamp, so that it will be drained, making good lots. The timber will be estimated and sold, probably next week, and then other squares will be offered for sale.

The price of the lots now offered are very reasonable, and gives the poor man opportunity to make a home. This will largely increase the dwellings in Coudersport, as heretofore building lots could not be obtained at figures that would warrant a day laborer in purchasing and building.

Court Minutes.

June 12, 1882; present, full bench; Hon. H. W. Williams presiding.

Constables of various townships made returns.

George C. Colegrove appointed Constable of Sylvania township.

Orvilla White appointed guardian of Ellery and Ella Mascho.

Grand Jury called and sworn. S. E. McCarn foreman, Wm. Atherton Constable. Grand Jury discharged, June 14th.

George Fox M.D. vs Harry Hurd. Jury find for pl'ff the land described to be released on payment, within 15 days $83.80 and costs and interest.

A. B. Mann appointed auditor to examine and report upon the application of Ann Lincoln, guardian for confirmation of sale of real estate to Henry Hurlburt.

Estate of Wm. Seifert, late of Abbott Twp, rule on administrators to show cause why real estate should not be sold to pay debts, returnable next term.

James Scott vs George and Jacob Snyder, rule to open Judgment, returnable next term.

J. W. Stevens vs Harrison township, rule on Twp to levy a special tax, returnable forthwith.

J. M. Frech vs George Mahon, Judg't for pl'ff for the sum of $600, and costs.

H. J. Mills vs Catherine Mix, rule to return vend ex, returnable next term.

A. B. Mann appointed auditor to distribute funds arising from sale of real estate of W. S. Moore and Polly Ann Smith.

In matter of estate of Augusta S. Whipple, dec'd, administrators and bail discharged.

Annie Henry appointed guardian of Lottie, Harry and William Ellis, minor children of William Ellis, dec'd.

H. J. Olmsted vs Homer twp, special tax of ten mills ordered.

G. C. Lyon appointed trustee in the case of Anthony Jones, bail $1,000.

Jacob Knechtel, a native of Germany, admitted to citizenship.

Willie Kelley adopted by Llewellyn Whitmarsh as his child and heir.

Sam C. Hyde, of Emporium, admitted to practice in the several courts of Potter county.

Charles L. Schrader admitted to citizenship.

Ernest Remsch appointed guardian of Charles, Emil, John, Ottilier, Herman, George and William Rugg, minors.

Porter H. Clark vs the B. N. Y. & P. R. R. Co., jury find for pl'ff in the sum of $270.

Estate of Randolph P. Olmsted, late of Ulysses, citation to issue to D. E. Lewis and Ann P. Olmsted to appear and contest.

G. W. Witter appointed Supervisor of Pleasant Valley.

Norman Sherwood appointed guardian of Francis, Jennie and Willie Larkin, minor children of J. H. Larkin, dec'd.

The resignation as Jury Commissioner of Wm. Shear tendered and Columbus Rees, appointed.

H. S. Lent appointed Supervisor of Sweden twp.

J. Percy Keating, of Philadelphia, admitted to practice in the several courts of Potter county.

E. Haskell, treasurer of Potter county, acknowledged twenty-five deeds for lands sold for non payment of taxes.

Porter H. Clark vs the B. N. Y. & P. R. R. Co., rule on pl'ff to show cause why the verdict, in this case, should not be set aside; returnable next term.

L. H. Cobb appointed auditor in the case of guardian of Floyd Scott and Justus Scott.

A. F. Hollenbeck appointed auditor, estate of Jasper Nelson.

W. Bassett, for use vs Henry Baker, *et al.* John Ormerod appointed auditor to distribute funds.

Commonwealth vs Zael and Wm. Lawton, bail $200 for appearance at next term; vs Frank Ellis, bail $200 for appearance at next term; vs James Mallory, larceny, verdict of not guilty; vs Miles Hurd, Leroy Hurd, C. D. Williams, and James Gibson, forfeited and respited till next term; vs Frederick Lehman, fornication and bastardy, *nol pros*; vs Nelson Clark, F. B. Nelson and Justus Mehring, supervisors of Eulalia twp not repairing roads, not a true bill, county to pay costs; vs Andrew Springer and Anton Weiss, assault and battery, plead guilty, sentenced to pay a fine of $10 each and costs; vs Abram Nelson, stealing child, *nol pros*; vs Gilbert Glover, assault and battery, bail $100 for appearance at next term; vs Lawrence S. Moran, fornication and bastardy, *nol pros*; vs Thad

Kelley, bail forfeited and respited; vs Henry Baker, false pretenses true bill; Charles Seeley, pointing a gun at J. W. Allen, resisting an officer etc., guilty, sentenced to pay a fine of $100 to the Commonwealth, costs of prosecution, and to undergo imprisonment in the county jail for the term of five calendar months; vs M. Spencer, assault and battery, true bill, bail $100, for appearance at next term; vs Luke Sherwood, stealing timber, *nol pros*; vs Luther Tolls, assault and battery, *nol pros*; vs E. Denhoff, larceny, defendant discharged, no prosecutor appearing; vs Willis Connable, selling liquor, bench warrant issued; vs Edwin Sikes, fornication and bastardy, bench warrant issued; vs G. R. Wilber, larceny, bail $100, for appearance at next term; vs Marvin and Irwin Cory, catching pigeons, *nol pros*, on payment of costs; vs John Rooney, discharged, having paid costs; vs Charles Seeley, rule to show cause why a new trial should not be granted, refused; vs Wm. Waters, surety of the peace, bail $200; vs John Brownlee, W. T. Jones prosecutor held to bail in $200 for appearance at next term and to pay the costs; vs Mary Nichols, adultery, continued.

Divorces granted: Adelbert W. Smith vs Mary Smith; T. J. Walden vs Emma J. Walden; James E. Rutherford vs Fannie Rutherford; Caroline Johnson vs John K. Johnson.

Mary Alderman vs Chauncey Alderman; desertion added to petition in this case, subpoena awarded.

D. D. Ross vs Sarah A. Ross; D. W. Haven appointed commissioner to take testimony.

L. Hizer vs Daniel Hizer, divorce granted.

Benjamin C. Cole vs Hannah J. Cole, divorce granted.

Esther Baker vs John S. Baker, *alias sub.* in divorce to issue.

Sarah Quick vs Jonathan Quick, Edson Hyde appointed commissioner to take testimony.

Anthony Belanski, a native of Germany, admitted to citizenship.

Veniries issued for 36 traverse and 24 grand jurors for September term.

Daniel Monroe, Sheriff of Potter county acknowledged deeds as follows, for land sold at Sheriff's sale:

To F. W. Knox for 41 acres in Roulet, for $200; sold as the property of C. J. Tubbs.

To Bingham Estate for 88 4-10 acres in Genesee, for $25; sold as property of Ward Burrows.

To Bingham Estate for 65 acres in Bingham, for $25; sold as property of Mark Newcomb.

To J. W. Williams and B. F. Hilligas for 83 acres in Allegany, for $500; sold as property of George Townsend.

To H. D. Dwight and A. J. Piler for 82 acres in Oswayo, for $25; sold as property of Selah A. Porter.

To Sarah M. Billings for 130 acres in West Branch, for $1,120; sold as property of W. S. Moore and Polly Ann Smith.

The Grand Jury made the following report after examining the public buildings:

That the ceilings in the upper cells in the jail building be made more secure by planking overhead the said cells, between the ceiling and roof, or otherwise as the Commissioners may determine, as there is now but two courses of brick overlaying said cells.

That the inside of the walls surrounding the jail yard be repointed with cement or mortar.

That the Commissioners procure a supply of water from the Coudersport Water Company, necessary to be used in and about the jail building, provided it can be obtained from said company at reasonable rates.

That the plastering and painting be repaired in the Sheriff's and Prothonotary's offices in the Court House building.

The Potter Enterprise
Wednesday Evening, June 28, 1882 – Vol. IX, No. 8

Allegany. And now H. Veeley is expected to bring on the cigars, owing to that fine boy baby.

MARRIED.

BOX – JOHNSON. – In Ulysses, June 14, by Rev. W. C. Tanson, Mr. J. D. Box, of Wayne Co., Pa., and Miss Marency Johnson, of Ulysses.

LEONARD – PICKETT. – In Hector, June 20, by Rev. S. D. Pickett, Mr. Joseph Leonard and Mrs. P. Pickett.

- N. L. Dike, of Goodland, Indiana, died last week, aged sixty-three years. Many of our readers will remember the deceased, as he was for some years a resident of Coudersport in partnership with Hon. T. Ives, whose daughter he married. His son Watson T. Dike now resides in Coudersport.

DIED.

CARD. – In Roulet, Pa., June 18th, 1882, after a long and painful illness, of nearly three years, Levi Card, aged about 33 years.

Asleep in Jesus! Blessed sleep
From which none ever wake to weep
A clam and undisturbed repose,
Unbroken by the last of foes.

- Coudersport water works in running order in a portion of the town and connections are being made daily. The work is not fully completed, but enough to guarantee its success. Several fire plugs are to be put in my individuals, and the borough should put in several more.

- Seymour Norton, employed at Albert Lyman's Sweden Valley Mill, is laid up for repairs. A few days since, while edging some cherry boards his assistant allowed a stick to catch on the saw, which threw it back violently and the stick striking Mr. Norton on the right hand, broke his thumb and little finger. Mr.

Norton set the injured member himself without waiting for a doctor, and before the numbness caused by the blow had passed away. A few days before he had a very narrow escape in the same mill. He was engaged in fitting a saw at the end of the mill, when a two-inch square stick several feet in length was thrown from a running saw. The stick just grazed the side of his face, sufficiently hard to break the skin, passed on and split a thick board at the end of the mill. Two inches to one side would have struck him in the forehead and doubtless crushed his skull.

Railroad.

The railroad is progressing steadily and surely, if not quite as fast as hoped for and expected by the Company. A number of disappointments have occurred in one way and another that has caused the delay, the last one being the non arrival of spikes. The spikes and plates were delivered for shipment ten days ago, but owing to the strike of freight handlers only the plates reached Port Allegany. It is expected the spikes will reach the Company in a day or two.

The rails are now being delivered at Port Allegany. Ties are being laid and perhaps ere this reaches our readers the "iron band" will be commenced.

The bridges are making in Buffalo and will be ready as soon as needed. Mr. Wright, of Port Allegany, is driving piles for the bridges.

The engine and cars are about ready for shipment and will be dispatched to Port Allegany as soon as track can be prepared for them. It will probably be two weeks before a construction train will be a necessity.

The depot at Coudersport has been located on the corner of the square opposite the residence of A. A. Hodskin, about thirty-five rods south of the river bridge. The track will extend almost to Mrs. Warner's house, and may finally run to the river. The line runs through the lot purchased by James Turner, and upon which he intended to erect a hotel, a portion of the lumber for which he has already on the ground.

A good depot will be erected at this point, one that will be a credit to the town and ample for the business to be transacted.

About twenty-five thousand ties have already been delivered and counted, and the delivery and counting is going on daily. We will soon be "out of the woods."

FOURTH OF JULY!
COUDERSPORT.

The following is the Programme for Tuesday, July 4th, 1882:

A salute of thirteen guns as the orb of day appears in the eastern horizon.

At 11 o'clock a.m., parade of Fantastics – the most amusing and exciting ever seen in the borough.

In the procession will be seen the most noted men of our own, ancient, or future times; a varied and gorgeous representation of the Wonders of the World and by special permission of

P. T. DARNEM,

On a triumphal car, securely chained and perfectly safe,

Jumbo! JUMBO!! JUMBO!!!

Ladies and children will remain at least one square distant from Jumbo.

Want of space prevents even bare mention of the 1001 rare, marvelous, beautiful and aesthetic attractions to be witnessed in the parade of the Fantastics.

At 1:30 p.m., ten minute speeches will be delivered, in the Court House, by Hon. A. G. Olmsted and F. W. Knox, Esq., and others.

In the evening a most magnificent display of fire-works will take place on the Court House square.

The German Cornet Band will discourse sweet music at frequent intervals during the day.

A grand platform dance will be in progress in the evening in full sight of the fireworks.

There will be numerous other attractive specialties which we can not enumerate.

The committee will provide a man to read the Declaration of Independence to any one who can not read it for himself.

LEWISVILLE.

Thirteen guns at sunrise. At one o'clock p.m., the procession, headed by the Ulysses Cornet Band, will form and march to the grove, where orations will be delivered by prominent speakers. After which the rare and curious Fantastics will appear, followed by Balloon ascensions and the grandest display of fireworks ever seen in Ulysses.

HARRISON VALLEY.

Thirteen guns at sunrise. Rope walk at 10 a.m. by the celebrated Mons. Edwards. Procession will form at one o'clock and march to the grove headed by the Westfield cornet band, where orations will be delivered by Rev. Thomas L. Perry of Lewisville and Rev. Bovier of Tioga county. Foot race at four o'clock, distance one mile, purse $6, $3 to first, $2 to second, and $1 to third. Fantastics at five p.m. Balloon ascension and grand fire-works in the evening. President D. D. Chapin, Marshal McKinney Erway, assisted by George Stevens.

**The Potter Enterprise
Wednesday Evening, July 5, 1882 – Vol. IX, No. 9**

- No paper will be issued from this office next week, in accordance with our usual custom of giving the printers a holiday at this time of year.

- W. T. Hosley, of Lewisville, recently received a draft for $1,275 arrears of pension.

- James Turner, we are informed, will put up his hotel a little north of where he intended to before the narrow gauge interfered with his calculations.

Lock Haven,

June 29th, 1882.

Our State Examination took place at the Central State Normal this week, commencing the 26th and ending the 29th. The result of which, was the largest class that ever graduated in the State. The whole number being seventy-eight, not one excluded.

Among the Potter county representatives were Orisa R. Hurd, Addie C. Douglass, Edith M. Haskell, Seymour C. White, Orson Card, Eber Card and Jasper Card. Some of which stood at the head of the class.

Railroad.

Work on the railroad is progressing steadily. It is a *Railroad* now, the track being laid to the red house, a little this side of Port Allegany.

D. W. Vanwegen has the contract for erecting the depot at Coudersport. The building will be 75 feet long by 22 feet in width; a fourteen foot platform surrounding it; 14 foot posts, projection of 7 feet supported by heavy brackets; it will be battened and painted. The waiting room will be 20x22 feet; office 10x22, both wainscoted 8 feet high with hard wood, and lathed and plastered. The baggage room will be 10x22 feet; freight room 22x35 feet. To be completed by the 15th of September, at a cost of $1,150.

Notice.

The exclusive privilege to keep an eating house, and refreshment stands to sell tobacco, cigars, fruit, etc., on the grounds of the Potter County Agricultural & Horticultural Society, near Coudersport, during the annual fair, to be held Sept. 26, 27 and 28th, 1882, will be sold to the highest bidder. Bids will be received up to Saturday, August 12th, 1882, at 7 o'clock p.m. The accepted bidder will be notified on or before August 19th, 1882. Security for payment of bid, if accepted must be filed with bid. The Society reserves the right to reject any and all of the bids.

Address,
J. M. Covey, sec'y.
Coudersport, Potter Co., Pa.

P.S. The law prohibits the sale of spirituous or malt liquors in Potter Co.

NEW!
Large Stock of Furniture
Just Received at
GRABE BROS.
DEALERS IN
F U R N I T U R E,
MAIN ST., COUDERSPORT, PA.

The Potter Enterprise
Wednesday Evening, July 19, 1882 – Vol. IX, No. 10

- Mr. and Mrs. Frank Andrews are happy over the advent of a fine girl baby.

Roulet. Born – to Mr. and Mrs. Lewis Yentzer, a son. Weight twelve and three-fourth pounds.

MARRIED.
COATS – BYAM. – At the house of the bride's parents, by Rev. N. L. Campbell, Mr. Frederick J. Coats and Miss Ester E. Byam, all of Allegany, Pa.
REES – WHITNEY – At the residence of Mrs. Lewis, of Coudersport, July 4th, 1882, by Rev. C. Dillenbeck, pastor of the M. E. Church, Mr. Arthur S. Rees, of Sylvania, Pa., and Miss Hattie Whitney, of Keating, Pa.
PAGE – LEONARD – At Shingle House, Pa., July 3d, 1882, by G. W. Pearsall Esq., Mr. Charles A. Page, of Coudersport, Pa., and Miss Jennie M. Leonard, of Scio, N.Y.
STEVENS – SMITH – At Shingle House, July 3d, 1882, by G. W. Pearsall Esq., Mr. Will Stevens and Miss Abbie Smith, all of Shingle House, Pa.

Sartwell Creek. Mr. Larkin died, at the residence of his son-in-law, W. H. Slocum, on the 9th inst., at an advanced age.

- On Thursday morning, July 6th, Mortimer and Otto, two little boys aged about 3 and 4 years, sons of B. F. Burrows, attempted to cross the West Branch Creek on a foot log, when they fell into the water, their screams attracted Mr. Burrows' people, who hastened to the creek, and succeeded in saving Otto, the oldest, but the swift current carried Mortimer out of reach and out of sight, and it was four or five hours before his lifeless body was found. Every effort was made to save him by brave men who did not cease their efforts until the body was found.

- The Fireworks purchased for the Fourth of July, and not used on account of too much "heavy fog" will be made use of to celebrate the advent of the railroad. Due notice will be given and everybody invited.

- Germania is ahead for dances. Although it rained for three successive days, including the Fourth, the crowd of people gathered at that place was beyond all expectations. The Germania Hall was crowded to its utmost capacity all night, and dancing was kept until 7 o'clock the next morning. Dances were also held at the two breweries the same evening, and all were very largely attended, and no fighting or even wrangling was heard whatever. Such is what we call an enjoyable occasion. – *Free Press.*

- A charter has been granted for a railroad called the Pine Creek and Tioga R.R., to run from Pike Mills *down* Pine Creek. If all the projected roads to Pike Mills are built, the mountains will have to be leveled to give room for the rails.

- Charters have been granted for the State Line, Brookland and Pine Creek railroad to connect with the Wellsville & Ulysses narrow gauge; for the Sinnemahoning and Pine creek R.R., from Pike Mills to Wharton Mills, for the Pike and Kettle Creek R.R., from Pike Mills to Westport.

Badly Injured.

On Monday last while assisting in raising the frame of the Goodyear mill [recently burned] at the Four Mile, on the Portage, Mr. L. Taggart fell from the structure to the ground striking on a pile of stones and other rubbish, breaking a bone of the upper jaw, knocking out four teeth, breaking a cheek bone and also a bone over one of his eyes. In falling one of his legs struck a bolt head which was protruding several inches, penetrating the fleshy part of his leg making a deep and ugly wound. He was picked up senseless, revived and brought to his home in Emporium, in an unconscious condition and remained unconscious until the next day. It was a terrible fall and a narrow escape from instant death. Thanks to skillful treatment and a strong constitution, he is rapidly recovering and will soon be on his feet again. – *Emporium Independent.*

The Railroad.

The railroad is progressing slowly but surely and the iron rails are daily reaching out toward Coudersport. About three miles of track has been laid with

Potter County, Pennsylvania Potpourri – Volume I
1880 through 1884

push cars and the road balasted as fast as laid. Work will progress much faster now, as six flat cars have been received and the engine is on hand to pull them.

The Burtville bridge is about ready to put up, the two other bridges are being built and will be ready as soon as the piles are driven. The number of workmen has been largely increased.

At this point, grading is going on for the extension north of the depot and for switches. The foundation for the depot is up, and this, Monday morning, the carpenters have commenced work. A good job of grading has been done about the depot and the street commissioner has graded the road in front and north, making a great improvement in the street.

Wool Carding.

I have repaired the carding machine, making it first class, and am now ready to receive wool. Wool sent by state will receive careful attention and will be promptly returned. Wool taken in exchange for carding, if desired.

C. J. Marble,
Coudersport, June 20, 1882.

The Potter Enterprise
Wednesday Evening, July 26, 1882 – Vol. IX, No. 11

MARRIED.

PRINCE – WHITE. – In Bolivar, N.Y., July 9th, by H. H. Pratt, Justice of the Peace, at his house, Mr. Alfred B. Prince and Miss Gertrude White, all of Sharon, Pa.

- The County Commissioners are putting in attachments to the Second St. main for the purpose of introducing water into the Court House.

- Charles Shaw, of Harrison Valley, Pa., was in town on Sunday night, and so was the whisky he was carrying in his abdominal reservoir. During the evening he got hilarious and imagined he was the English navy bombarding Alexandria. He got so noisy that officer Hubertus requested him to keep quiet. He opened on the officer with an entire squadron, when the officer attempted to arrest him. He resisted the officer and a general scrimmage ensued in which Shaw pummeled Hubertus and the officer brought his club into play. Shaw got away and run to the Clinton House, where he was stopping. The officer followed him and found him in his room, where he again attempted to arrest him. Shaw raised a chair and struck at the officer, but with rare military strategy Hubertus dodged and the chair was broken by striking the door-casing. Shaw then jumped into bed and the officer succeeded in getting a handcuff on his left wrist. Then the prisoner got out of bed and fled, and the officer failed to find him until about five o'clock on Monday morning, when he discovered him in front of W. F. Jones' residence on Main street. He went toward him and attempted to arrest him, when Shaw struck the officer with the hand-cuffs and then took to his heels. He was ordered to "stand" or be shot. Refusing to obey, Hubertus took out his shooting iron and fired away, hitting Shaw in the thigh, inflicting a flesh wound. The "skeddadler" halted, raised a flag of truce, and was escorted to the lock-up and Dr. Nye was called to examine the wound. The ball was not found, but the would was pronounced not a serious one. Shaw was arraigned before Police Justice Jones, for assaulting an officer, and held under $300 bail for his appearance before the Grand Jury, and in default thereof was committed to jail at Angelica, where he will undoubtedly learn something to his advantage. – *Wellsville Democrat.*

Notice.

We, the undersigned Physicians, of Coudersport, have determined upon a half-yearly settlement with all our patrons. All our accounts must be settled every six months to insure further treatment, as we will not treat those who do not comply with this rule. And farther, we will not treat (either or any of us) a person who will not settle with his physician according to the above rule. The settlement may be made by note, farm produce, cash or otherwise, as the parties may agree; *but the settlement must be made.* Immediate notice will be given to the members of the association, of any person refusing to settle in accordance with the above adopted rule.

A. French, Frank Buck, E. S. Mattison, C. W. Briesnick, C. S. French, E. H. Ashcraft.

The Potter Enterprise
Wednesday Evening, August 2, 1882 – Vol. IX, No. 12

- John Denhoff has taken unto himself a better half.

DIED.

CONE. – In Hebron, Pa., on Sunday, July 23, 1882, Mrs. Emma Cone, wife of Will Cone, and youngest daughter of Elijah Swift, in the twentieth year of her age.

One year ago the deceased became a happy bride, but O, how flitting are the joys of this world! She leaves a little daughter one week old, never to know a mother's love, a bereaved young husband, and loving relatives to mourn her untimely death. All of whom have the sympathy of the entire community in their loss of a loving wife, dutiful daughter and fond sister.

- Bark peeling is about over.

- Coudersport has two livery stables and is promised a third one.

- The busiest place in town these pleasant days is the croquet ground East of the Court House.

- A fourteen year old son of Henry Kimm, of Roulet, was shot last Monday while playing with a toy pistol. The pistol was loaded with a common cartridge and caused a severe wound. – *Port Allegany Reporter.*

- Have we a pound master, pound laws, &c., is getting to be a very common question. Cattle run the streets night and day and while people must put up with the latter, their gardens and lawns should be protected by a well enforced law at night. Mr. Poundmaster (if there is one), wake up.

- In our issue of the 13th inst., we recorded an accident happening to Geo. Bartlett, of this borough, in the bark woods. On Wednesday afternoon last Mr. Bartlett met with a more severe accident in the woods. Cutting down a large hemlock tree it lodged in a large soft maple, and in cutting down the soft maple the two trees became lodged in a large birch tree. In cutting the birch tree and when partly cut, it broke from the stump and Mr. Bartlett started to run supposing the tree would fall to the east the same direction the lodged trees had fallen, but instead fell to the north. Mr. Bartlett was caught in the mass of limbs and was made unconscious. The crash of the trees was heard in the village, and it was fully fifteen minutes before George was heard to hallo for help which was soon at hand. Mr. Bartlett was brought to his home, when it was ascertained that his right thigh bone was broken, his left limb badly bruised between the ankle and knee, and a severe cut near his right eye. Dr. Cobb was called and set the broken limb and dressed the wounds, and the unfortunate man was made as comfortable as possible. Mr. Bartlett is now on a fair road to complete recovery.
– *Ulysses Sentinel*.

- The County Commissioners have made a contract to introduce water from the Second St. main into the jail. The pipe will be run to the large tank now in the upper story of the jail, and from thence distributed to the different cells. New closets of improved style will be put in each cell. A new drain will extend from the jail to the river, into which the water from the roof will also be turned. The jail kitchen will be supplied from the water works. Examination proved to the Commissioners that something must be done, and that something at once. The old drain from the cells seems to have been stopped for some time, and is now filled with filth. The water as now used from the tank would not clean the drain, nor would it keep it clean, if taken up and put in proper shape. The stench from the drain was becoming intolerable in the cells, and must soon prove detrimental to the health of all in the building. This being the case the Commissioners have determined to remedy the evil, effectually is possible. It is believed that the drain pipe can be kept perfectly clean by using the water from the mains in the improved closets, to which will be added the water from the roof. The expense of this improvement will be $475, to which must be added the water rent. The amount of the latter we did not learn. We believe the Commissioners have made the right move this time.

- The world moves and the Coudersport & Port Allegany R.R. is gradually moving this way, notwithstanding several vexatious delays. The supervisors of Liberty township attempted to buck the engine off the track at Coleman's dugway. They held the fort for several days, assisted by quite a crowd of people. The railroad wanted the wagon road, and the supervisors were not satisfied with the road built in exchange over the hill. The rails were finally laid, under protest from the supervisors. At Clark's another obstruction was met in the person of Mrs. Clark who held the fence and grade for two days. Finally President Knox put in an appearance, and directed the workers to put down the ties, if the lady wished to stand on them let her stand; to put down the rails, back up the engine and put down more ties and rails, and back up again, but to be careful and not use unnecessary violence. The fence was torn down while the lady was leaning upon it, but she soon gave in to force of circumstances and retired in good order. She claims the deed to the property that point, and says the right of way was granted by others and not by her. She was informed that if the right of way was not valid the company would try and settle with her, if a settlement could not be agreed upon, appraisers would be appointed. Friday night the rails were down to the Burtville bridge and work was commenced on the structure and continued during Sunday. The construction train crossed Tuesday, and with good weather and good luck will boom into Roulet this week. Two large bridges remain to be built, some trestle work and a small amount of work along the grade. Mr. Blakeslee is now working over 150 men and expects to have the work completed on time, Sept. 1st. The depot at Roulet has been located and some arrangement will be made for its construction, this week.

Grand Jurors.

The following are the Grand Jurors, drawn for the September Term of Court at Coudersport, Sept. 18th, 1882:

L. B. Morley, Farmer, Allegany; Ezra Turner, Farmer, Ulysses; Watson Dyke, B'd'g house, Coudersport; Nelson Monroe, Farmer, Sweden; Henry Ingraham, Farmer, Eulalia; Bryan McGinnis, Farmer, Genesee; S. S. Carpenter, Farmer, Bingham; J. H. Harvey, Farmer, Sharon; James Moran, Farmer, Genesee; E. A. Monroe, Farmer, Hebron; J. H. Cole, Farmer, Clara; C. A. Voorhees, Farmer, Sharon; Hiram Smith, Farmer, West Branch; Nicholas Bloss, Farmer, Abbott; John Roberts, Farmer, Sweden; Wallace Mattison, Stage prop'r, Pike; Sterling Devans, Farmer, Homer; Hans Hanson, Farmer, Roulet; Gilbert Scoville, Farmer, Harrison; J. M. Holdridge, Farmer, Ulysses; Marcus Harvy, Farmer, Hebron; George Barbanks, Farmer, Sharon; T. E. Beirley, Farmer, Abbott, A. E. Martin, Farmer, Harrison.

Traverse Jurors.

Drawn for September Term, 1882:

Erastus Gurnsey, Farmer, Hector; Lyman Fesenden, Farmer, Oswayo; J. M. Walker, Farmer, Wharton; J. C. Burdick, Farmer, Bingham; Lester Shaw, Merchant, Hebron; Alvin Jordan, Farmer, Sylvania; L. H. Baily, Farmer, Sharon; C. E. Hosley, Farmer, Ulysses; E. F. Turk, Farmer, Pike; D. C. Chase, Farmer, Sharon; R. M. Post, Farmer, Hebron; M. H. Reynold, Machinist, Oswayo; O. G. Metzger, Lumberman, Coudersport; Thomas Moran, Farmer, Genesee; James Ives, Farmer, Pike; Robt. Smith, Farmer, Oswayo; J. W. Roby, Farmer, Hebron; John Brooks, Farmer, Wharton; L. C. Kilbourn, Farmer, Hector; N. W. Herring, Farmer, Sharon; Chester Stone, Farmer, Harrison; J. M. Hyde, Farmer, Sharon; Christian Broderson, Farmer, Abbott; Wm. Smith, Hotel

Keeper, Wharton; James Nelson, Farmer, Summit; G. W. Stevens, Farmer, Harrison; G. W. Yentzer, Farmer, Pleasant Valley; Curtis Kilbourn, Farmer, Hector, Charles Doud, Farmer, Harrison, W. A. Heath, Farmer, Ulysses; S. C. Hurd, Farmer, Genesee; Otis Weimer, Farmer, Pleasant Valley; W. B. Genung, Farmer, Harrison; John Johnson, Farmer, Summit; James VanCuren, Farmer, Sharon; Norman Keach, Farmer, Genesee.

The Potter Enterprise
Wednesday Evening, August 9, 1882 – Vol. IX, No. 13

- Dr. C. S. French rejoices in the advent of a son, at his domicile.

- Maggie, aged about 13 years, daughter of John Metzger, of Coudersport, was buried on Friday last.

- Mrs. John K. Burt, one of the old citizens of Roulet township, was buried on Monday last.

- Delos Genung, of Lewisville, has received a back pension of $1,250.

- There was a pleasant re-union of the brothers and sisters of the Larrabee family, after a separation of about thirty years, at the residence of Postmaster Larrabee, in this village, on Thursday, the 27th of July last. There were present two sisters, Mrs. C. E. Burdick, of Wilman, Minnesota, Mrs. Lorenzo Wilson, of Whitesville, N.Y., and four brothers, D. C. Larrabee, of Coudersport, M. M. Larrabee, Emporium, M. V. Larrabee, Roulet, C. A. Larrabee, Port Allegany. It was a happy occasion, in which old times were talked over, and former scenes and incidents related. – *Port Allegany Reporter*.

- On Monday morning Amos Burbank fell from the barn of Mr. Rockefellow on which he was at work injuring him so badly that it was thought at first he could not recover but it is thought at this date that he may get well. He was at work alone on the roof when it seemed he slipped and fell to the scaffold but with such force that he was unable to get hold of it, and went from there to the ground, about twenty-five feet further striking on his side in the road. Mr. Rockefellow's boy saw him and thought he was killed, but ran for his father, who soon reached the spot and with the aid of a neighbor removed the wounded man to his house. Dr.'s Remington and Place were called, but say that it is impossible to tell at present what the injuries may be. – *Palladium*.

- Quite a little stir was occasioned on Wednesday in the lower end of town, caused by Fred Lord eloping with another man's wife at Oswayo and bringing her to this place. The injured husband followed, and when he arrived here he saw his wife and paramour riding up Kansas street together, whereupon he hallooed for them to stop, but instead, the woman put the whip to the horse. The husband followed in hot pursuit, overtook the pair and jumped into the vehicle, when they all returned to the Oswayo house. He pleaded with his truant wife to return home with him, but she would not. Bed time came and the outraged husband retired, after which his *Lord*-ship and the fair one left for parts unknown. The eloping parties are first cousins, and it is said "the end is not yet." – *Duke Centre News*.

- Decatur Francis met with a severe accident at Oleona, on Friday, the 21st inst. A hemlock log became lodged and upon loosening it it started down the hill striking Mr. Francis, knocking him some thirty feet. Mr. Francis' left leg was broken just above the ankle, and his right ankle dislocated. Dr. Meine, of Germania, was called and set the broken limb and Mr. Francis, at last account, was on the gain. – *Sentinel*.

The Potter Enterprise
Wednesday Evening, August 16, 1882 – Vol. IX, No. 14

- Born – To Mr. and Mrs. J. L. Knox, Thursday last, a son.

Millport. Mr. and Mrs. Geo. Varney have a little son.

- Mr. John VanBuskirk, of Keating Summit, while engaged in peeling on Colwell's job Monday forenoon last, met with quite a serious accident. In falling a large hemlock tree it lodged on a small bush, uprooting it. Seeing his dangerous position, Mr. VanBuskirk sought to escape, but was unable to do so. He was overtaken by the tree, a limb of which struck him on the left shoulder from the rear, causing a fracture of the shoulder blade and also a severe bruise upon the head and arm. He was cared for by Dr. Otto, and the injury, though severe, is not supposed to be fatal. – *Reporter*.

The Potter Enterprise
Wednesday Evening, August 23, 1882 – Vol. IX, No. 15

Sartwell Creek. Miss Mina Lehman had a little girls' birthday party, recently. They reported a good time.

- Mr. Dunham, of Sharon, died last week.

- Merrett Lyon, aged 28 years, formerly a resident of Sweden, died at North Warren, Pa., August 28th, 1882, and was buried in Coudersport beside his parents, on Wednesday last. Funeral next Sunday, the 27th inst., at 2:00 p.m., at the Bird school house.

- Merrit J. Lyon, formerly of Sweden, was buried in the Coudersport cemetery last Wednesday. Last winter he was taken to Warren insane asylum, but the physicians there could not help him. It is said he died of voluntary starvation, refusing to take food. Before the malady showed itself, he was a bright business-like young man.

C & P. A. R. R.

Last Sunday contractor Blakeslee put down three-fourths of a mile of iron on Coudersport & Port Allegany Railroad. It is expected that the rails will be down to the state road bridge to-day, six miles from Coudersport.

Next Sunday will bring them to the bridge, at the foot of the Taggart dugway, a little over two miles from this place. All the culverts are in below the bridge, and the gangs of men are distributing the ties. Piles are now being driven for the bridge. A dozen or more of the piles delivered for the bridge have been rejected and new ones will have to be procured, which may delay the bridge a little. It is expected, however, that it will be ready for the timbers by Sunday night. From three to four days will be required to erect the bridge and put it in shape for the running of trains.

Two weeks from to-day with favorable weather, and no mishaps, ought to put the construction train into Coudersport. Even now the whistle of the engine can be heard here, if the wind happens to be blowing up the valley at the time.

The depot at this place is being lathed and plastered. That artist of the trowel, Horton, is doing the job in good order.

Dan Vanwegen has taken the contract for erecting an engine house, a little south of the depot, 32 x 50 feet, 14 foot posts, walls and roof to be packed with tan bark.

The Potter Enterprise
Wednesday Evening, August 30, 1882 – Vol. IX, No. 16

Roulet. Born to Mr. and Mrs. J. V. Weimer, a son.

Whites Corners. Born – On the 20th inst., to Mr. and Mrs. A. A. Ross, a daughter.

MARRIED.

BUNNELL – HABOR. – In St. Paul's Church, Wellsboro, Pa., Aug. 16, 1882, by the rector, Rev. Chas. Breck, D.D., Mr. Deck Bunnell, of Wellsboro, and Miss Mary Habor, of Germania, Pa.

OWEN – HOSLEY. – At Ulysses, Pa., on August 27th, 1882, by Rev. T. L. Perry, Mr. A. H. Owen, to Miss Eve Hosley, both of Ulysses, Pa.

Roulet. Died, in Roulet, Aug. 4th, 1882, Orvalla, wife of J. K. Burt, aged 63 years, 7 months and 9 days. Death has come into one of our families, and in a few days wrought a work which months and years cannot repair; made heart wounds which no lapse of time can heal. Unstayed by prayers and tears, he has performed his task, and hurried a kind sister, an affectionate wife and devoted mother down into the long, unbroken silence of the tomb. Of all the losses which we are called to sustain, few are more sad than the decease of the mother of a large family. When such departs, the tenderest feelings are stirred, and the deepest emotions of sorrow overflow the soul.

"Yet again we hope to meet thee,
When the day of life is fled,
Then in heaven with joy to greet thee,
Where no farewell tear is shed."

- Billy Smith, the aged Englishman, for some time past living with W. J. Brown, of Millport, died Sunday evening last. After eating a hearty supper, he appeared as well as usual, but was taken with a fit or heart disease a short time after, falling out of his chair, and before he could be helped up was dead.

- Merrit Gridley of Lewisville has purchased the privilege of an eating house, selling cigars, etc., on the Fair Grounds, paying therefor $50.

- The track layers on the Coudersport & Port Allegany R.R. reached Fred Schaudenberger's lane last-night, Monday. Bad weather has delayed them some. The bridge will not be reached before Wednesday noon.

Teachers' Institute.

The Teachers' Institute of Potter county was held at Lewisville, beginning Aug. 21. The instructors present during the week were Hon. Henry Houck, Deputy State Sup't, and Miss L. E. Patridge, of Philadelphia. Miss Lettie Palmer gave instruction in penmanship. The singing was under the charge of Mrs. H. A. Lewis, one period each day was given to discussions by the teachers of some subject connected with school work.

The following is the list of members who attended:

Ulysses – Prof. Cobb, Mrs. Cobb, Ella Crowell, Minnie Bartlett, Jesie W. Lewis, Mary Potter, Adda Worden, J. B. Wagoner, A. H. Bice, W. F. Kelts, C. L. Farnsworth, W. C. Allen, Agnes Farnsworth, A. J. Evans, Flora Cady, Imogene Drake, Ella Worden, Kate Bassett, C. M. Stillman, Flora Stillman, Carrie Stillman, Minnie Cushing, Mary Daniels, Kate Burt, Ella Allen, Arthur Drake, Cora Williams, Erastus Monroe, Clara Hosley, Addie Douglass, Mark Harvey, Alice Gridley, Kate Gee, Lizzie B. Tansom, A. W. Gee, A. V. Howe, C. L. Gridley, John Chappell, Addie Scott, Art Burt, Carrie Carey, J. W. Ferris, Inez Ferris, Addie Gibson, Nelia Francis, Ella Clark, Hattie Loucks, Kate Brown, Mrs. C. A. Lewis, Ione Brigham.

Coudersport. – J. R. Groves, Elbert Greenman, Thurlow Greenman, I. P. Collins, Mrs. Delia Collins, Lavina Dingee, Mary Aylesworth, Rosa Crane, O. L. Hall, Luzerna Edgecomb, Lydia Crosby, Libbie Crosby, May Rossman, Mary Teuscher, Belle Haskell, L. A. Hollenbeck, J. B. Colcord, W. W. Harvey, Mrs. Harvey, A. F. Hollenbeck.

Roulet. – Edith Pomeroy, Clistia Kimm.

Ellisburg. – Nettie Bishop, Carrie Bishop, Lottie Webster, Allie Hendrix, Josie Reynolds, Ida Arnold, H. H. Hall, Ira Bishop.

Raymond. – Lettie Benton, Lettie Palmer, W. W. Collins, Josie Smith.

Millport. – Nellie Vanderhoef.
Andrews Settlement. – Henry Kies.
Harrison Valley. – D. D. Chapin, Belle Williams, Ellen White, Emma L. Adams, Hattie Kelts, Eliza Kelts.
North Bingham. – Mary Clark, Grace Lewis, Minnie Ensworth, Lavina Hart, Delwin Hart, Elmina Howe, Daniel Howe, Thera Howe, Carrie Grover.
Genesee Fork. – Bettie Race, Orisa Hurd, Hannah Hurd, Jennie Bacon.
Sweden. – Lena Jackson, Mary Jackson, Cora Miller, Nettie Miller, E. C. Franke.
Clara. – Helen Brooks.
Pike Mills. – Carrie Ansley.
Gold. – Cora Langdon.
Brookland. – Nellie Reynolds, Nettie Reynolds, Estella Witter.
East Hebron. – Electa Greenman, J. M. McKee.
Stone Dam. – Kate Doyle, Little Doyle, Maggie Doyle.
Corning, N.Y. – Annie Jones.
Lawrenceville. – Lydia Buckbee.
Gaines. – Nett Rexford.
Marshfield. – Rena Bernauer.
Spring Mills. – Josie Holbert, W. F. Owens.
Whitesville. – Myra E. Harris, Nancy Wilson.
Hector. – O. A. Kilbourne.
Sunderlinville. – Florence Carriel, Susie Wilkinson, Hattie Embre.
Mills. – Ettie Harrison.
Whites Corners. – Addie White.
Westfield. – R. W. Swetland, Cora Close, Mari Close.
Bingham Centre. – Mary Ransom.
Colesburg. – Delmar Nelson.
West Bingham. – Myra E. Abbott, Anna Robbins.
West Pike. – Orpha Ives.
Williston. – Lottie Weimer.
Smethport. – A. W. Sullivan.
Trowbridge. – Frances Hinman.
Cross Fork. – Helen Gibson.

Monday P.M.

The institute was called to order by the County Sup't, Miss Anna Buckbee. After singing by the Lewisville choir, Prof. Cobb was called upon for an address. He spoke briefly of the object of institutes, and commended some of the new features which it was proposed to introduce. Miss Helen Brooks, of Clara, delivered a fitting response.

Miss L. E. Patridge was introduced and spoke on the subject of Primary Teaching. A little child coming into the school room is in the most impressionable period of his life. Teachers must regard the pupil as of a three fold nature – mental, moral and physical. The moral and physical are often neglected. The great object of the teacher should be character building, - and not the imparting of a given amount of knowledge. The best the teacher can do is to supply the child's mind with the means of growth. It is the teacher that makes the school. Fine buildings and expensive apparatus are not essential to success.

The exercises on Monday evening consisted of readings by Miss W. C. Wickham, of New York. Miss Wickham is a reader of unusual ability, and the audience were well pleased with the evening entertainment. The selections read were, "An Order for a Picture," "A Young Lady's Meditations in Church," "The Story of the Little Hatchet," "The Fall of Pemberton Mills, "The Story of the Great Beef Contract," "The Bells of Limerick," and a "Woman's Conversation Through a Telephone."

Tuesday Morning.

Devotional exercises were conducted by Rev. Tansom.

Hon. Henry Houck was then introduced. He said: I had determined to visit this year every county in the state in which I have not before attended an Institute. I sometimes hear persons ask what good institutes do. To answer this, I will simply ask. "Would you be willing to go back to the state of affairs twenty-five years ago." I have never attended an institute at which I did not learn something. Teachers must organize, and work together. Mr. Houck then took up the subject of spelling. We do not accomplish satisfactory results in teaching spelling. If I were to give out a list of hard words in ordinary use, you would miss 33 per cent of them. One reason we fail is that the books are not properly arranged. One defect in teaching spelling by dictation is that sufficient attention isn't given to misspelled words.

Mr. Houck called upon several teachers to give their methods of correcting misspelled words.

Prof. Cobb: I teach spelling mainly by the oral method.

Miss Doyle: I write the misspelled words upon the board, and have each pupil copy only those he has missed.

Mr. Houck: Most rules for spelling are not of much use. Here is one good one with reference towards ending in *cious* or *cuous*. Words that relate to matter end *cuou*, words that do not in *cious*.

Miss Patridge gave a drill upon the consonant sounds of the language, and then spoke on Primary reading. Her plan was to exclude the text book entirely during the first stages of instruction. Bring some object before the class and talk with the pupils about it. Write the name upon the board repeatedly. Do not *print* it.

The remainder of the session was devoted to a discussion of the advantages of written work and oral.

The subject was opened by Mr. I. P. Collins, Horace Hall and Wagoner participated in the discussion.

Tuesday P.M.

Miss Palmer spoke on the subject of writing. Teach the principles of the letter thoroughly. Have pupils measure the letters and learn to criticise their own work. I would not set copies in books, but would use the board.

Mr. Hall: I have met with success by combining drawing with penmanship.

Mr. Houck gave the following common errors in teaching:

1. Too much Arithmetic; too little language.

2. Too long lessons, with non-essentials.
3. Teachers do not show their pupils how to study.
4. Teachers do not require proper attention during recitation.
5. Scholars do too little *hard word*.

Primary reading: Miss Patridge. All after study depends on how the child learns to read. The following principles should condition primary teaching:
1. Things before words.
2. Thought before expression.

In teaching a little child to read pursue the following order.
1. Stimulate thought of child.
2. Oral expression from child.
3. Written expression by teachers.
4. Reading of this by child.

The Sup't then announced the following committee on resolutions: R. W. Swetland, Allie Hendryx, Elmina Howe, H. H. Hall and O. A. Kilbourne.

Tuesday Evening.

Hon. Henry Houck lectured upon the subject, "What we Owe the Children." Mr. Houck is a forcible speaker and was heartily applauded.

(Concluded next week.)

The Potter Enterprise
Wednesday Evening, September 6, 1882 – Vol. IX, No. 17

Railroad.

The bridge builders completed the railroad bridge at the Taggart dugway last Saturday evening. Monday morning the track layers commenced the laying of the iron on the bridge and notwithstanding the storm when quitting time came had reached halfway through the cut at the Mehring bank.

The iron and spikes are mostly at the bridge and the ties are only three miles below, so that everything is handy. The distance yet to be ironed is about a mile and half, which ought to be completed by Thursday night. The culverts are all in and the road is ballasted up to the bridge below the Taggart dugway. As yet no switches have been put in. The road will not be completed before the 15th although it is likely that trains will be running before that time. Just as soon as the last two miles can be ballasted.

Last week a car load of freight was hauled up to the end of the iron. The loading was for the Corner Store. The goods were dumped off side of the track and from there hauled up by teams.

- V. M. Stannard, of Genesee Forks, formerly constable of Genesee township, now a Justice of the Peace, was brought to Coudersport on Monday. Mr. Stannard is Financial Reporter of Genesee Forks Lodge K. of H., and as such has handled the funds of the Lodge. It is charged that he has appropriated the money of the lodge, and forged receipts from the Grand Treasurer. At the proper time we may say more about this case. Mr. Stannard failed to secure bail and was locked up.

The Potter Enterprise
Wednesday Evening, September 13, 1882 – Vol. IX, No. 18

- Miss Nora Nichols, assisted by a score of little ones, celebrated her sixth birthday, Saturday afternoon.

Railroad.

On Thursday afternoon the construction train of the Coudersport & Port Allegany Railroad backed up to the Coudersport Depot and the Engine took a drink from the Coudersport Water Works. Coudersport is at last united with the outside world. It was the day long looked for by our citizens and a day which promises better things for this section of the county.

Nearly half the town was out to see the rails laid and the iron horse move in. Everybody was in the best of spirits – the spirit of good feeling. There was a total absence of the spirits that inebriates.

The depot is well under way and will be completed according to contract, by the 15th. It is a credit to the company and the town. Work is progressing on the turn-table. The engine house has been commenced. The general impression is that the road will be able to run regular trains by the first of next week.

Saturday The Ark sent out the first load of freight – baled wood – on flat cars. About forty "D.H.'s" went along to see that it went through all right. The party found the road remarkably smooth for a new road. Good time was made when running, but the stops were numerous on account of the surfacers. A stop of half an hour was made to take water, the supply being drawn from a small stream, by a chain pump. Below Roulet the bars had to be let down in several places. For some time past there has been but little running on the lower end, and farmers had put up fences to keep cattle out of the fields.

The road is being fenced the whole length with barbed wire and better facilities will be had for the water supply.

As we have said before, it will be the best narrow gauge in the country when fully completed. As far as it goes everything is first class. The officers of the road and contractor Blakeslee have every reason to be proud of it. The company has about forty cars on hand including one passenger coach. The latter is a beauty.

The return trip was very pleasant. The train brought freight for several of our merchants and the household goods of Superintendent McClure, and also those of the Section Master, who moved into the house formerly occupied by James Turner. Several lady passengers were on the return trip. Everybody was pleased and pronounce the Coudersport and Port Allegany Railroad the Boss.

> **NEW STORE!**
> **C. M. HERRINGTON,**
> SWEDEN, PA.
> A full line of Dry Goods, Provisions, Boots and Shoes, Hardware, &c. All kinds of produce taken in exchange. Goods sold as low as the lowest and as good as the best.

The Potter Enterprise
Wednesday Evening, September 20, 1882 – Vol. IX, No. 19

Bingham. D. T. Hauber had to be hooped to keep him from bursting with joy, and all because it was a bouncing boy.

Costelloville. E. O. Austin did not hoist his sign for the "Freeman Run House" in vain. There was a traveler stopped there the other day, and engaged board until twenty-one years of age. – It's a boy.

MARRIED.

BURLESON – BARTHOLOMEW – At the residence of A. N. Lillibridge, Sept. 17th, by Rev. O. C. Hill, Mr. H. H. Burleson, and Miss Della Bartholomew, both of Roulet.

STONE – REISSMAN – At the bride's home, on the 18th inst., Mr. Howard Stone, of Eulalia, to Miss Katie A., daughter of C. Reissman, of Coudersport.

WOOD – STEARNS. – In Bingham, Sept. 10th, by J. D. Carpenter, Esq., F. E. Wood, of Millport, Pa., and Mira Stearns, of Greenwood, Steuben Co., N.Y.

GARDNER – JUDD. – At the residence of the bride's parents, Emporium, Pa., on Wednesday evening, Sept. 6th, 1882, by Rev. W. J. Judd, of Binghamton, N.Y., Mr. James T. Gardner, Supt. of B. N. Y. & P. R. R., to Miss Nellie R. Judd, of Emporium.

The wedding was the grandest affair, of the kind, that ever occurred in Emporium. The bridal presents were numerous and elegant, reaching a total value of over $1,500. Mr. Gardner presented an elegant piano; employees of the B., N. Y. & P. R. R. present a silver tea set, costing $500. Other presents from friends were numerous. The happy couple left, in a special car, for Buffalo and the far west. The bride is a native of Coudersport and has many friends here.

- John Wedsworth of Eulalia township was buried on Friday last. He was about 81 years of age and was one of the old citizens of Eulalia township. Mr. Wedsworth was a man without education – could neither read or write, but by industry and economy acquired considerable property. He always subscribed for newspapers and by hearing them read, kept posted on the news of the day, better than many who had far better opportunities. Mr. Wedsworth held a number of township offices, made a careful and faithful official.

Died.

A. G. Presho, August the 25, 1882. The deceased was born in Lenox, Berkshire county, Mass., Feb. 5th, 1827, came to Potter county in 1842, where he has lived since. The deceased experienced religion at the age of twenty-two and united with the Presbyterian church in which he has always lived a faithful member. He has always been a faithful worker in the Sabbath school. He has always been loved and respected in life, has left a wife and three children to mourn his great loss. In behalf of the bereaved friends we tender their thanks to the neighbors for their kindness to them in sickness and the honors paid to the deceased in his burial.

West Branch. Wm. S. Moore passed way, at three o'clock, on the morning of the 14th inst. His death cannot be anything but a relief. No possible view of the future can place him in a worse situation than he has been in for the last year or two. He died of a cancer, which commenced on the lip and eat his face away in a horrid manner, until death put an end to his sufferings. He was about sixty-three years of age.

- Mr. V. M. Stannard was brought to Coudersport last week charged with being a defaulter to the county as collector, in the sum of $250. Mr. Stannard has been collector of Genesee for several years and he and his friends claim that the trouble arises from negligence in collecting, that his books are correct, and that the full amount will be paid in full – most of which can and will be collected from the parties assessed. The matter is to be fully settled with the Commissioners this week Friday.

- In the case of V. M. Stannard, of Genesee Forks, charged with forgery, mention of which was made last week, a final examination was had before Miles White, Esq., on Saturday last. Several witnesses were examined, but nothing whatever of a criminal nature was shown, and Mr. Stannard was discharged.

- The Excelsior Cheese Factory, at White's Corners, has received, from April 3d to August 1st, 1882, 989,719 pounds of milk. Made from the same 99,100 pounds of cheese, which sold for $10,274.65. Netting patrons from 84 cents to $1.06 per cwt. for milk. The highest price received for cheese, 12cts., the lowest, 9-3/4 cts. No. Pounds milk for one pound cheese, from 9 6-10 to 10 24-100.

W. L. Warner, Treas.

Railroad Notes.

Considerably less than a mile of surfacing remains to be completed and Mr. Blakeslee expects to complete this part of the work by Wednesday night. The Directors will probably inspect the road this week.

The pit for the turntable at this place is dug, and the mason work, it is hoped, will be completed this week. At Port Allegany a track will be put down to the B. N. Y. & P. turntable for the present.

The new engine, from the Brooks Locomotive Works, Dunkirk, N.Y., will be on hand in a few days.

The side track at Coudersport is partially completed, and on Sunday last a number of cars were brought up from Port Allegany. There are now about twenty cars at this place.

The depot is finished and has been accepted. It is a goo one in every respect.

Dan Vanwegen is pushing the engine house along towards completion. The walls are now being filled with tan bark.

The stations on the road will be at Coudersport; at Lehman's, three miles from Coudersport; at the intersection of the road running to the pump station, a platform will be built and a flag station established, called Olmsted; at the intersection of the Freeman Run road, at Lyman Nelson's will be another flag station, called Nelson. Roulet and Burtville will be regular stations. Near the upper end of the Coleman dugway, will be a flag station, called Water station, and then Port Allegany. Olmsted station is located for the convenience of the pipe line officials, and at the earnest solicitation of the people in that neighborhood. Nelson is established for the convenience of the Freeman Run section. All trains will stop at flag stations to let off passengers or freight, or to receive passengers or freight when flagged.

The fare between Coudersport and Port Allegany will be sixty-five cents, if tickets are purchased at stations, if fare is paid on train, 75 cents.

For stations between, the fare will be at the rate of three and one-half cents per mile, if tickets are purchased at stations, paid on train will be a little more. Passengers from flag stations will only be charged three and one-half cents per mile, as no tickets will be sold at such stations, but tickets will be sold at regular stations to flag stations.

In our next issue we expect to announce that regular trains are running.

The Potter Enterprise
Wednesday Evening, September 27, 1882 – Vol. IX, No. 20

Costelloville. There is a great deal of sickness in this place. Several have died already. Mrs. David Jones departed this life on the 16th inst. She was an exemplary christian woman and will be deeply mourned for by her affectionate husband and children. They have the sympathy of all their friends.

Mr. Woolfinger buried his youngest daughter, Lena, aged 11 months, this afternoon, disease, whooping cough – which is very prevalent in Costelloville.

Death of John C. Bishop.

Very many of our readers will regret to learn of the sudden and unexpected death of John C. Bishop, of Allegany township. On Saturday afternoon last, he was in Coudersport in apparent good health, transacting business, but before reaching home was attacked with an apoletic fit and died in the evening. Last winter he had an attack of apoplexy but had become much improved in health, and although much of his former vigor had gone yet he had so improved that he bid fair to again become a vigorous man. Mr. Bishop came to Potter county about 40 years ago, and settled upon what was then a dense forest. By industry and hard labor and the assistance of his estimable wife he has cleared and improved one of the finest farms in this county, and secured to himself and family a comfortable maintenance. Ever since he first came to the county he has been one of the leading citizens of Allegany township, and there are but few men in Potter county the loss of which will be more widely felt or sincerely mourned than he.

- Last Fourth of July, fireworks to the amount of $100 was purchased, but not used on account of storm. The committee have decided to use them Wednesday evening, September 27th, second day of the Fair, and have given notice to that effect.

Court Minutes.

Court convened Sept. 18th, present S. F. Wilson and Associates Hammond and Chappell.

Constables of various towns made report.

Frand Cox vs Susanna Cox. Ransome Hinman and C. M. Allen appointed Commissioners to take testimony.

Comth. vs Mary Spencer, assault and battery, continued, bail $100.

Grand Jury called and sworn, Ezra Turner foreman, Isaac Kidney Constable.

Gustav Froebel, a native of Saxony, admitted to citizenship.

Comth. vs Z. Lawton and Williard Rodes, larceny, continued, bail $200.

A. B. Mann appointed guardian of Eddie Johnson.

Comth. vs Frank Ellis, continued, bail $200.

Frank Phelps appointed guardian of Mary Nelson, minor child of Jasper Nelson, dec'd.

On petition ordered that Harriet Reed be entitled to her own earnings, and clear from any contract or debts of her husband.

Mary D. Miner vs S. Miner, Samuel Beebe appointed Commissioner to take testimony.

Alma Brewster vs Geo. Brewster, sub. in divorce awarded.

E. O. Austin appointed guardian of Winnie Burt, minor child of Milford Burt, dec'd.

E. O. Austin appointed guardian of Lizzie Young, minor child of Robert K. Young, dec'd.

John M. Williams, administrator of Wm. McDougall dec'd vs W. L. Shattuck. Jury find for plff the land described to be released on the payment of $1,425.50; one-fourth in 9 mos. balance in three equal annual payments. Plff to have leave to issue writ of estrepment to prevent the removal of machinery or mill.

Comth. vs Gilbert Glover, bail forfeited and respited.

D. D. Ross vs Sarah A. Ross, decree in divorce from the bonds of matrimony.

Joel C. Witter vs Henry Witter, decree in divorce from the bonds of matrimony.

Comth. vs Willis Connable, selling liquor, nol pros, on payment of costs.

John Barr vs Hiram York, feigned issue and case to be placed at head of the ordered list.

Comth. vs W. H. Evans, selling liquor, discharged, no prosecutor appearing.

Comth. vs Luther Dingman, assault and battery, defendant discharged, but to pay costs within thirty days.

Estate of Hetty Scott, dec'd, D. C. Larrabee continued as Auditor.

Comth. vs J. A. Bogardis, larceny, not a true bill.

Comth. vs David Hammond, selling liquor, true bill.

Archy Campbell, a native of Ireland, admitted to citizenship.

L. H. Cobb appointed Auditor to pass upon exceptions filed and restate account of Albert Newman, guardian of minor children of James Scott, dec'd.

Comth. vs F. B. Prindle, larceny, a true bill.

Comth. vs H. J. Mills, obstructing a public highway, true bill, indictment quashed.

Comth. vs William Waters, Surety of the peace, bail $200 for appearance at next term, and to keep the peace, and to pay costs.

A. B. Mann appointed Auditor to report upon the advisability of administrator of estate of G. W. Presho, making a private sale of real estate.

Isaac Benson vs Portage twp, tax of ten mills ordered to pay debts.

Alice Johnson vs Geo C. Johnson, sub in divorce awarded.

F. W. Knox vs D. P. Reed, jury returns a verdict for deft.

John Brennan, a native of Ireland, admitted to citizenship.

Dennis O'Brien, a native of Ireland, admitted to citizenship.

Comth. vs Volney M. Stannard, forgery, Grand jury returns a true bill.

Sept. 20th, Grand jury report that outer walls of jail need repairing as pointing of said wall has crumbled out; some of upper cells need repairing to keep prisoners safely; out building in Court House square declared a public nuisance.

Comth. vs H. J. Mills, obstructing highway, bail forfeited and respited until next term.

John Ormerod appointed Auditor to distribute funds in hands of administrator of Jonathan McDonnell, dec'd.

Herman Schmidt, a native of Germany, admitted to citizenship.

Dr. E. S. Mattison, A. F. Hollenbeck and Frank Phelps appointed a commission in lunacy to enquire into case of Lydia M. Clark.

Veniries issued for 24 grand and 36 traverse jurors for next term of Court.

Estate of Wm. Shanley, administrator and bail discharged.

Mary Alderman vs Chauncey Alderman, sub in divorce awarded.

Sept. 21st, the several courts adjourned to meet Oct. 10, 1882, at ten o'clock p.m. The adjournment is for the purpose of determining residence of Lydia M. Clark.

Daniel Monroe, Sheriff of Potter county acknowledged deeds for lands sold at Sheriff's Sales as follows:

To E. J. Farnum, 80 acres in Hebron township, price $20, sold as the property of C. D. McKee.

To Wm. Cobb, 36.4 acres in Genesee township, price $305, sold as the property of Levi Keech.

To Bingham Estate, 102 acres in Hector township, price $25, sold as the property of Geo. Bartlett.

To Bingham Estate, 35.8 acres in Genesee township, price $25, sold as the property of Ashley Anderson.

To Bingham Estate, 53 acres in Hector township, price $25, sold as the property of Minerva Parish.

To Bingham Estate, 52 acres in Hector township, price $25, sold as the property of Henry Dalaba.

To Geo. W. Chisholm, 49.9 acres in Hector township, price $504.91, sold as the property of James Mallory.

E. Haskell, Treasurer of Potter county, acknowledged in open court 140 deeds for lands sold for taxes.

Trains Running.

On Monday President Knox and Directors Benson, Carey, Arnold and Benton, inspected the C. & P. A. R. R. and the road has been accepted, conditionally. Mr. Blakeslee still has some work to do to complete his contract.

The main track is in good shape and runs very smooth.

Superintendent McClure issued the following Monday evening:

Tuesday, Sept. 26, the first passenger train will leave Coudersport, on N.Y. time, at 9 a.m., stop at all stations, if flagged. Return train will leave Port Allegany at 2:45 p.m. and stop at all stations. Wednesday and Thursday, Sept. 27th and 28th, No. 1 will leave Coudersport 7:20 a.m. Arrive at Port Allegany at 8:40. No. 2 will leave Port Allegany at 12:25 p.m. Arriving at Coudersport at 1:40 p.m. No. 3 will leave Coudersport at 5 and arrive at Port Allegany at 6 p.m. and will return to Coudersport same evening and stop at all stations. Regular Time Table on Friday.

The Potter Enterprise
Wednesday Evening, October 4, 1882 – Vol. IX, No. 21

- On Thursday morning last, Mr. Harry Scoville, of Rixford, and Miss Milla Armstrong, of Coudersport, were united in matrimony, at the residence of W. B. Gordnier. A host of friends unite in wishing the happy couple long and happy lives.

Married.

SCOVILLE – ARMSTRONG – At the house of W. B. Gordnier, in Coudersport, Pa., Sept. 28th, 1882, by Rev. C. Dillenbeck, Harry A. Scoville, of Rixford, Pa., and Milla Armstrong, of Coudersport.

FANCIS – REYNOLDS – At the bride's parents, on Monday, Sept. 26th, by the Rector of All Saints Chapel, Brookland, Pa., Mr. Henry E. Fancis, and Miss Eleanor E. Reynolds, both of Ulysses township, Potter Co., Pa.

Allegany. By the death of J. C. Bishop, a gloom is cast over the community, and a loss is felt by all, in the many ways he was of use among us, both as friend and neighbor. He and A. G. Presho were both Justices of the Peace, and both have been removed by death, leaving that office vacant in Allegany township.

SHOT AND KILLED.
Geo. Chisholm Shoots Thomas Watrous, of Hector.

For some time past, Mr. Geo. Chisholm and a neighbor, Wm. Watrous, living in the Southern part of Hector township, in what is called Rock Spring Valley, have not been on good terms. At the last term of court, Mr. Watrous was held to bail for appearance at next term and to keep the peace as to Chisholm.

Mr. Chisholm had some bark piled on the land of Watrous, and on Friday attempted to remove it, but was stopped by Mrs. Watrous, considerable of a quarrel ensued, but Chisholm finally left, without removing the bark. At this time only Mrs. Watrous was at home. Upon the return of Thomas Watrous, he soon was told of the trouble, and in his ante mortem statement he said he then went towards Chisholm's house, encountering a brother with a wagon who turned around and went with him. Thomas called Chisholm out, and told him he must not attempt to remove the bark in the absence of the elder Watrous. Chisholm then used language calculated to anger a man, if any thing would, and Watrous retorted by inviting him into the road to settle matters. Chisholm stepped into the road, drew a revolver of 32 calibre, walked up with it presented toward the breast of Watrous. Watrous grabbed the hand holding the revolver, and intended taking Chisholm by the collar, but the revolver was fired and being depressed, the ball struck Watrous in the lower part of the stomach, lodging near the back bone. His brother then picked him up, put him in the wagon, assisted by others and took him home. A post mortem examination was held by Dr. Bottom and others. The above version of the case we have from a gentleman living in the immediate vicinity, of the parties.

Watrous died on Sunday, about 11 o'clock. We are informed that Chisholm gave himself up and claimed that the shooting was done in self defense – that Watrous attacked him.

We called upon Mr. Chisholm, Tuesday morning, but he very sensibly declined to say any thing about the affray, and we did not question him. He did say that he had no idea of shooting Watrous when the quarrel occurred, that he had always tried to avoid the trouble he had with the elder Watrous, and had done his best to live in peace with his neighbors and uphold morality, and the good of the neighborhood, and says that he had suffered persecution at the hands of Watrous.

- About a year ago Geo. Melzer was indicted by the Grand jury of this county on a charge of larceny, for robbing Mr. Whitney, of Freeman Run, and D. Hall, of Homer. As he had left the county a bench warrant was placed in the hands of Sheriff Monroe. The result, last Sunday evening Sheriff Monroe turned the key of the Coudersport jail on Melzer. The Sheriff has made a faithful and continuous hunt, carrying on the game in such a manner that he finally got to exchanging letters with Melzer, (under an assumed name), and tried to get him back into this county. Finally Melzer was taken ill and ceased to write. The Sheriff began to think the game might be up, if matters were not hurried, and he then procured a requisition which was forwarded to the Sheriff of Tioga county, N.Y., and Melzer was lodged in the Owego jail, and as stated above, Monroe lodged him in our jail Sunday last. The whole story of tracing Melzer, shows fine detective ability. It was worked down fine. We are not at liberty to give particulars, as it might advertise parties who would rather have nothing said about the matter.

BANK OF
COUDERSPORT
W. K. JONES, BANKER,
SUCCESSOR TO
ARCH F. JONES & SON, BANKERS.
Coudersport, Penn'a.
DEPOSITS RECEIVED.
PROMPT REMITTANCE MADE
ON COLLECTIONS.
DRAFTS SOLD ON
NEW YORK, PHILADELPHIA
And all principal points in Europe
and the British Isles.
OFFICE HOURS FROM 9 A.M. TO 4 P.M.

Coudersport & Port Allegany Railroad		
On and after Friday, September 29, 1882, trains on the C & P A R R will run as follows:		
WESTWARD TRAINS.		
Leave Coudersport	7:10 a.m.	4:00 p.m.
Leave Hammonds +	7:45	4:05
Leave Olmsted +	7:55	4:11
Leave Nelsons +	8:04	4:23
Leave Roulette	8:19	4:39
Leave Pomeroy Bridge	8:23	4:44
Leave Burtville	8:33	4:55
Leave Silver Spring +	8:40	5:00
Arrive Port Allegany	9:00	5:20
EASTWARD TRAINS.		
Leave Port Allegany	12:20 p.m.	6:05 p.m.
Leave Silver Spring +	12:38	6:23
Leave Burtville	12:45	6:30
Leave Pomeroy Bridge	12:55	6:40
Leave Roulette	1:00	6:44
Leave Nelsons +	1:15	7:00
Leave Olmsted +	1:25	7:15
Leave Hammonds +	1:35	7:24
Arrive Coudersport	1:40	7:30
Trains are run on New York time. "+" Trains stop upon signal only.		
Train No. 1 connects with the Trains FOR Smethport, Bradford, Olean and Buffalo, also for Train for Emporium and the west.		
Train No. 2 connects with Train FROM Buffalo, Olean, Bradford and Smethport.		
Train No. 3 connects with Train FOR Emporium and the east.		
Train No. 4 connects with Train FROM Buffalo, Olean, Bradford and Smethport.		
B. A. McCLURE, Supt.		

The Potter Enterprise
Wednesday Evening, October 11, 1882 – Vol. IX, No. 22

MARRIED.

THOMPSON – DYKE. – In Coudersport, Oct. 4th, by Rev. Leavenworth, W. W. Thompson, and Miss Eva Dyke, both of Coudersport.

COSTELLO – GILLON. – At the residence of the bride's parents, in Coudersport, Pa., on Thursday, Oct. 5th, 1882, by Rev. J. S. Madigan, Mr. T. J. Costello, of Carrolton, N.Y., and Miss M. E. Gillon, of Coudersport, Pa.

The Enterprise printers return thanks for kind remembrances, and unite in wishing happiness to the happy couple.

WILLIAMS – HURLBUT. – In Harrison Valley, Sept. 30th, 1882, by Rev. S. L. Bovier, F. L. Williams, of Wharton, Pa., and Anna Bell Hurlbut, of Harrison Valley, Pa.

BAKER – DENISON. – At the residence of the bride's parents in Sherburne, Chenango county, N.Y., by the Rev. G. R. Burnside, Charles H. Baker, of Ulysses, Pa., and Miss Hattie Denison, of Sherburne, N.Y., Sept. 31st, 1882.

Eleven Mile. The thirty-fifth wedding anniversary of Mr. and Mrs. B. F. Lyman was made the occasion last Saturday of a surprise visit from many of their friends and neighbors. The company came prepared with the where-with-all for supper, and after pledging anew the old time vows, the happy pair sat down to the table well loaded with the usual feast of such occasion, and as the guests departed it was discovered they had left a lot of nice presents and money, in remembrance of the occasion. The original marriage notice reads:

MARRIED.

By Rev. O. Hopson, Sept. 29th, 1847, B. F. Lyman and Miss Sophia Wood, at Fairhaven, Vermont.

DIED.

OLMSTED. – At his home in Bennettsville, Chenango Co., N.Y., on Monday, Oct. 1st, 1882, of Typhoid Fever, Daniel Olmsted, in the eighty-fourth year of his age.

CRUM. – In West Bingham, Oct. 1st, 1882, of typhoid fever, Clark L. Crum, aged 30 years.

- Daniel Olmsted, father of A. G. and H. J. Olmsted, was buried at Ulysses, last week.

- On Monday last an accident occurred at Hammond's tannery, which for a time was feared would prove fatal to Fred Hoffner. Mr. Hoffner was assisting in repairing a barn that had been moved, while at work some of the heavy timber fell upon his back, crushing him to the ground. One leg was broken in two places, and the other once. It was at first reported that his back was broken, but such did not prove to be the case. He lay in a critical condition two or three days, and the physicians reported that he could not recover. Reaction finally set in and at last reports the injured man was improving. He is not out of danger by any means, but there is a hope of his ultimate recovery.

- On Sunday ex-Sheriff H. T. Reynolds lodged Michael Peryitt in our county jail, on a charge of larceny. The story as told us is about as follows: "On Tuesday last Peryitt hired a team and platform wagon, at a livery stable at Babb's Creek, Tioga county. The team he drove to Gaines and traded to Charles Hurlburt for an old horse, some poor notes, and a few dollars in cash. The old horse he left in a pasture. From Gaines he went to Pike Mills, and on the fifth hired a horse, harness, buggy, etc., of B. D. Ellis, to drive to Brookland. Not returning in a reasonable time Mr. Ellis commenced making inquiries, and as a result took out a warrant before Thomas Hull, Esq., for the arrest of Peryitt, putting it in the hands of H. T. Reynolds. Peryitt drove to Brookland, and at Hull's store purchased crackers, cheese, tobacco, etc., of Hank, and offered to trade more if he would take one of the notes received at Gaines. This gave Reynolds a good knowledge of the man, and he started in pursuit, tracing him to Coudersport, where he took supper and left in the night. From L. H. King it was learned that Peryitt had been at Sharon Centre, and from that point traveled up the Oswayo. A telegram was sent to Wellsville and Reynolds followed getting trace of his man beyond Oswayo. When he reached Wellsville he found Peryitt had been arrested and the property secured. He then brought Peryitt to this place, the prisoner coming without a requisition, of his own free will, thus saving time and some trouble. An examination was had Monday morning before Miles White, Esq., on the charge of stealing the Ellis property and the prisoner was locked up to await the action of the Grand Jury, next December.

The Potter Enterprise
Wednesday Evening, October 18, 1882 – Vol. IX, No. 23

- Frank Niles, of Eulalia, and Miss Carrie Clark were married at Emporium on Wednesday last.

DIED.

SLOAT. – At the house of W. Langdon on the Eleven Mile, Oct. 10th, 1882, Mrs. Dillie Sloat, of Millport, aged about thirty-three years.

She leaves a husband and two little girls, who have the sympathy of the entire community.

"Weep not dear husband, I am with thee still.

I am your angel, who was your bride, And now, though dead, I never have died."

- Mr. C. O. Brown has taken the job of getting in 2,000,000 feet of hemlock logs on Pine Creek, in the Pike Mills neighborhood, next winter, for Messrs. Colton & Canfield. We understand Mr. Canfield expects to get about 8,000,000 of hemlock into the two branches of Pine Creek next winter.

Adjourned Court.

Oct. 10 – Present S. F. Wilson, presiding associate N. C. Hammond.

In the matter of sale of Real Estate of Corlis E., Arthur R., Nellie L., Effie and Cora Buck. D. C. Larrabee appointed auditor to inquire into facts. Frank Buck appointed guardian of Nellie, Effie, Cora and Arthur Buck, minors. C. E. Baker appointed guardian of Corlis Buck.

D. C. Larrabee appointed auditor to investigate the facts in case of application of A. Bishop, guardian of Cora Howard, minor, for the sale of real estate.

In the matter of Lydia M. Clark, a lunatic, Wharton township certified at the legal settlement of said Lydia M. Clark. Court order that Lydia M. Clark be sent to the State Hospital, at Warren, Pa.

In the matter of the estate of Frederick Harrison, minor, rule on S. K. Stevens, guardian, to file an account on or before Dec. 11, 1882, or show cause why an attachment should not issue. Returnable next term.

Perry Devall, appointed overseer of the poor of Wharton township.

Sarah Quick, by her next friend, vs Jonathan Quick; proclamation ordered.

Samuel Thompson vs Eulalia township, special tax of ten mills ordered.

Inquest on the body of Thomas Waters presented and approved by the court.

Ester Baker, by her next friend, vs J. S. Baker; A. F. Hollenbeck appointed commissioner to take testimony.

The Potter Enterprise
Wednesday Evening, October 25, 1882 – Vol. IX, No. 24

Allegany. The fifteenth marriage anniversary of Mr. and Mrs. M. A. Veeley occurred on Oct. 13th. It was remembered by their friends and neighbors, in a joyous social gathering of fifty or more in number. They were the recipients of numerous presents.

West Branch. Last Sunday Mrs. M. V. Prouty, of Pike, was up here with five of her children, on a visit at her father's, S. M. Conable. While going home in the afternoon, one of the clevis pins worked out and let the whiffletree drop down against the legs of one of the horses, which caused the team to become unmanageable. Mrs. Prouty and the children were thrown from the wagon and all of them were more or less injured, except one of the little girls. One of the little boys, Jesse, was so badly injured that he died the following Tuesday, and was buried here Wednesday, in the West Branch Cemetery.

- Smith's Hotel at Harrison Valley had a narrow escape from fire last Thursday night. Fire broke out in the roof from a defective flue, at a late hour, but was discovered by one of the inmates who was suffering from phthisic and could not sleep. The fire was soon subdued. In a few minutes more the fire would have been beyond control, and the hotel property would have been destroyed.

- Last Monday afternoon as George Hurlburt, of Harrison Valley, was driving a drove of cattle along the west end of the river bridge in this borough, he struck a fractious steer over the head with a stick when the stick broke, one piece flying in his face lacerating the lid and completely destroying the right eye. Dr. Masten attended the unfortunate man. – *Free Press*.

Coudersport Chapter No. 263, R. A. M.

Tuesday, Oct. 17th, marks a red letter day in the advancement of Free Masonry in this section. On that day Coudersport Chapter No. 263, Royal Arch Masons was constituted by D.D.G.H.P., Joseph H. Simonds, of Bradford, assisted by Companions from Bradford, Olean, Emporium, Smethport, Port Allegany and other places.

The Grand Chapter opened at 2:30 p.m., with the following officers: Joseph H. Simonds, M.E.Gr.H.P.; Geo. Metzger, M.E.Gr.K.; P. A. McDonald, M.E.Gr.S.; E. B. Dolley, M.E.Gr.T.; J. C. Backus, M.E.Gr.Sec.; Victor Gretter, G.Chap.; H. C. Rockwell, G.C.H.; Geo. M. Smith, G.P.S.; Chas. Barrett, G.R.A.C.; J. P. Folt, G.M.3dV.; Carlton N. Bard, G.M.2dV.;' John D. Logan, G.M.1stV.; O. L. Snyder, G.S.M.C.; W. F. Lloyd, G.J.M.C.; E. P. Dalrymple, G.P.; Anson Taylor, G.T.; Wm. H. Clark, Grand Marshal.

The following is a partial list of the Companions present. Several names we were unable to obtain:

Bradford: J. H. Simonds, W. D. Gallup, H. Trumbower, G. W. Ashdown, Victor Gretter, G. B. Doerfus, Walter Grubb, M. Getty, T. L. Sartwell, W. H. Clark, L. E. Fuller, H. L. McCoy, A. Taylor.

Port Allegany: C. H. Moore, N. R. Bard, P. A. McDonald, H. J. Barrett, C. M. Barrett, D. Martin, Miles Irons, Geo. N. Barrett, E. B. Dolley, E. R. Bard, E. P. Dalrymple, O. L. Snyder.

Eldred: D. C. Young.

Emporium: J. P. Felt, John D. Logan, H. C. Rockwell, Geo. Metzger, Wm. F. Lloyd.

Smethport: C. S. King, J. C. Backus, G. M. Smith.

Oswayo: J. C. Wilkinson.

Olean: S. E. Rowley, Dr. L. F. Moore.

Coudersport: B. A. McClure.

Buffalo: Mr. Haviland.

After the organization of the Grand Chapter M.E.G.H.P. Joseph H. Simonds proceeded to constitute Coudersport Chapter, No. 263, R.A.M., in ample form, assisted by the companions present, and installed Lewis W. Crawford, M.E.H.P.; D. C. Larrabee, King; W. K. Jones, Scribe; and David White, Treasurer, of the new Chapter.

After the afternoon session the companions assembled in the dining room adjoining the Hall, and partook of an excellent supper prepared by J. M. Covey, of the Nichols House.

In the evening the Chapter again assembled and the work of the several degrees were fully exemplified by D.D.G.H.P. Joseph H. Simonds. Remarks were made by several of the visitors, and at a late hour the meeting closed, with expressions of good wishes on all sides.

The following are the officers of Coudersport Chapter for the balance of the Masonic year:

L. W. Crawford, H.P.; D. C. Larrabee, King; W. K. Jones, Scribe; David White, Treasurer; W. W. Thompson, Capt. II; J. L. Knox, R.A. Capt.; C. A. Stebbins, P. Soj.; R. L. White, M.1stV.; W. J. Lewis, M.2ndV.; A. Sidney Lyman, M.3dV.; W. J. Brown, Pur.

The members of Coudersport Chapter return their thanks to all visiting companions for their presence and assistance and trust that their visit to

Coudersport will ever be remembered with pleasure and will be pleased to again greet them in the Chapter Hall of No. 263.

The new Chapter starts out under very flattering prospects, and we have no doubt success will attend this new move of the craft.

The Potter Enterprise
Wednesday Evening, November 1, 1882 – Vol. IX, No. 25

- Born – To Mr. and Mrs. Charles Stoneham, of Hebron, Saturday last, a daughter; weight 10 ½ pounds.

MARRIED.

NICHOLS – McGREGOR – At J. McGregor's Thursday, Oct. 19th, 1882, by Rev. Rhinevault, Mr. Frankie Nichols and Miss Anna McGregor, both of Sharon.

WHITTAKER – PERRY – At the home of Mr. Whittaker in Eulalia, on the 25, by Rev. A. Cone, Mr. Thomas Whittaker, of Eulalia, to Miss Jemima Perry, of Bethel, Sullivan Co., N.Y.

Whites Corners. Mrs. Colston, living near this place, was buried on the 25th inst.

- Mr. Hoffner who was injured at the tannery some weeks since, and who has been reported as recovering, is now reported as failing, and but little hopes are entertained of his recovery.

- A dozen houses could be rented within twenty-four hours in Coudersport, if they could be found. Not a single house is empty, and several not fit to be classed as dwellings are occupied. Many who would make Coudersport their home are kept away by reason of no place to live in.

- Last week those of our merchants who depend on gas for light were left in the darkness. There was a great hunting for old lamps, lanterns and candles, and a more disgusted lot it would be hard to find. Investigation showed that a rat had gotten into the air pump, and been caught in the wire cord holding the weight, throwing it out of the pulley. After much trouble and two evenings of darkness the evil was remedied, and peace reigns again.

Mr. Editor:

Whence did Eulalia township derive its name? The term Eulalia is evidently compounded of two Greek words "Eu" good and "lalia" speech or report. Will some of your readers inform us why this was at the first township of good report making it worthy of the name! May it not have been thus named because of the wide bottom lands that were formed here? In these the early settlers could readily find a home and see a prospect of fruitful fields. Or was this the name of some ancient Goddess whose title our first settlers applied to their township?

Potter County, Pennsylvania Potpourri – Volume I
1880 through 1884

There must have been some special occasion for this Greek name to this particular township. What was that occasion? C.

- Potter county is making steady and sure gains in wealth and population. The Coudersport, North Wharton, Harrison Valley, and Pike Mills tanneries alone have added greatly to the population, by employees of the tanneries, bark peelers, who have moved in, and those employed in cutting and getting out the logs. Each tannery has built up quite a village, made up almost entirely of persons employed in and about the establishments. Besides the vast sums spent in buildings and machinery, must be counted the increased value of hemlock lands. The bark alone will now bring more than the land and timber together would bring a few years ago. But Potter county is improving very fast in the farming districts. Good farm buildings are the rule, and good teams, good wagons, etc., show that the farming community are, as a rule, prosperous. Potter county is indeed improving.

- Miss Kate Doyle recently left Genesee for the purpose of teaching school in Dakota, where she is to receive $60 per month. This deprives Potter county of one of her best teachers. In Genesee, where she has taught, the citizens offered to raise enough by subscription to make her salary $30 per month and board, if she would stay, but believing that her health would be benefitted by a change of climate, as well as her purse, she removed to Dakota. She has two sisters, teachers, Miss Lillie, who has been teaching at Shongo, and Miss Maggie, at Eleven Mile, both are first class teachers.

- O. J. Rees met with a runaway accident last Saturday. He was on his way home this side of Cherry Springs, with a single rig. In this buggy, partly on the seat he had a big buck. A jolt caused the deer to slide forward breaking the dash and throwing it against the heels of the horse, which started on a jump tipping the carriage over and throwing both Orlando and the deer out. Orlando was dragged several rods receiving cuts and bruises about the head and face, but nothing of a serious nature. Finally one of his lines broke and the horse was turned into the woods and stopped. Orlando has but one hand, but a horse has got to be lively that gets away from him.

- For some time past Sheriff Monroe has held a bench warrant for David Hammond, of West Branch, indicted for selling liquor, contrary to laws made and provided. Dave has made himself rather scarce of late, living most of the time in York state. Last week Monroe met him by the merest accident at Lewisville. Dan arrested him of course, Hammond offered no resistance but asked to see the warrant, and as the Sheriff took the warrant from his pocket , Hammond took for the woods. It was a beautiful race, but the Sheriff showed want of proper training and Hammond gradually drew to the front distancing his competitor, and taking the heat. Monroe had no revolver with him, or the tale might have had a different ending. If Hammond does not keep out of Potter county, Monroe will turn the key on him some fine day. He wants him bad and when Monroe wants a man bad he is going to get him.

One day later – Sunday night, Sheriff Monroe was on the road nearly all night looking for Hammond but failed to find him, although he got very close. Monday Mr. Hammond delivered himself up and gave bail for his appearance at the next term of Court.

- Dr. Frank Buck meet with an accident last Tuesday which kept him indoors for several days and from which he has not yet fully recovered. He was driving up the Sinnemahoning and part way up the hill, by the side of the road, W. B. Rees was reading a newspaper, and resting. As the Doctor came in sight, the wind caught one corner of the paper causing it to flutter in such a way as to frighten the Doctor's horse, which whirled about like a flash throwing the Doctor over the bank upon his head and shoulders. The horse ran to the foot of the hill, receiving a few scratches. The buggy had a thill, cross bar and whiffletree broke, three sides of the box smashed and both axles sprung. Mr. Buck was taken to the residence of his sister, Mrs. Banks, and medical aid summoned. We are glad to state that the Doctor is able to be out again, though walking very deliberately with the aid of a cane. He is yet very sore and lame.

The Potter Enterprise
Wednesday Evening, November 8, 1882 – Vol. IX, No. 26

- Luther Seibert is happy all over, and clear through – a son was born to him last week, weight 3 ½ pounds.

- Cyrenus Rennells steps a little higher and the sunshine seems brighter than of yore, all on accounts of a ten pound girl baby.

Keating. Born, Oct. 26th, to Mr. and Mrs. James Micheltree, a son. Nov. 2nd, to Mr. and Mrs. Josiah Hackett, a son.

- Frank Jones, of Auburn, N.Y., brother of C. S. Jones, died at the residence of the latter in Coudersport on Wednesday, Nov. 8th. His remains were taken to Owego, N.Y., for burial. The remains were escorted to the train by a delegation of masons, of which order the deceased was a member.

Sudden Death.

A very sudden death occurred at the residence of I. V. Reed, of Pleasant Valley. On the morning of Oct. 21, 1882, Mrs. Stout of Centralia, Illinois, accompanied by her son Clarance, an assistant Engineer in the railroad office at Centralia and Cairo, for the past six years. Mr. Stout on account of over work accepted a leave of absence for a few weeks, and a pass over the different railroads from Cairo to Friendship, N.Y., the former home of his Mother. On nearing Olean, Mrs. Stout concluded to first visit her sister, Mrs. I. V. Reed, of Pleasant Valley. Clarance seemed to be improving and wrote to his old home that he would soon be able to return and resume his duties. The day before his death he was about the farm feeling well and in the morning his mother went to his room to call him to breakfast, but found him sleeping soundly, returning a short time afterwards she discovered that he was breathing hard. She called some of the family and as they came in, seemed to breathe easier, and while they stood in the room thinking that he was as well as usual, and resting better, he passed from life to death. His age was 23 years.

DIED.

LYMAN. – At Eleven Mile, Pa., Oct. 26th, 1882, Rachel Taggart, wife of A. S. Lyman, aged 43 years.

Very suddenly this loved and cherished wife, fond mother, and faithful friend was snatched from the clinging arms that all vainly sought to stay ___ upward flight. She had every quality of mind and heart that is amiable and endearing, ever forgetful of self, her willing hands and cheery tones made her home the dearest spot on earth to all its inmates, and a most-pleasant-resting place for her many friends, truly, "The Gospel of a life like hers is more than books or scrolls."

On the 28th of October her funeral was largely attended from the M.E. church at Oswayo, A. W. Estes Post, G.A.R., served as a guard of honor, gently bearing to their resting-place the remains of one, who in life had taken an active interest in their welfare. Showing thus their grateful appreciation of the same. The services were conducted, and words of comfort spoken by Rev. N. North from Rev. 21-4. Though the shadow of great sorrow hangs over the stricken ones she has left, we feel she is safe on that nightless, tearless shore.

"Our cherished one, whose smiles
    Made brighter summer hours,
Amid the frosts of autumn time
    Has left us with the flowers.
No paling of the cheek of bloom
    Forewarned us of decay;
No shadow from the Silent Land
    Fell 'round our darling's way.
The light of her sweet life went down
    As sinks behind the hill,
The glory of a setting star,
    Clear, suddenly, and still.
Fold her O, Father! In thine arms
    And let her henceforth be
A messenger of love between
    Our human hearts, and Thee."

- The first snow of the season, just a few flakes, fell election day. Last year the first snow was on the 4th of November.

- A subscriber informs us that Eulalia township was named after Eulalia Lyman, the first white female child born in the county. Eulalia Lyman was named after Eulalia Keating, daughter of Mr. Keating, patentee of large quantities of land in Potter county.

Burglary in Coudersport.

On Sunday night last thieves entered the store of C. H. Armstrong, by removing the rod from the cellar window. They then passed up the cellar stairs and upon leaving opened the back door from the inside. The thieves drilled the front of the safe, a Mosler & Bahman, and with powder blew off the door.

The thieves secured about $100 in cash and carried off a number of valuable papers, notes, deeds, insurance policies, etc. From the store money drawer, several dollars in small change was taken. They left one three-cent piece and a two-cent piece in the drawer. This is a custom with burglars, we are informed, as they consider it unlucky to take the last cent.

The thieves entered the engine house of the C. & P. A. R. R. and stole the hand car, with which they left town. The car was found off the track near Coleman's. The car with two men upon it was seen just at break of day, at Burtville, but it was not light enough to distinguish faces or clothes. Search was made near where the car was found but no signs of the thieves or papers was found, and at this time everything is shrouded in mystery.

Burglary at Lewisville.

On Friday night last the Postoffice building was burglarized by three individuals. The thieves gained admission by removing a light of glass. After gaining admission the thieves drilled the Postoffice safe and succeeded in blowing it open, and then secured about $100 in Postage Stamps, and seven or eight dollars in money.

To deaden the sound the thieves covered the safe with a carpet and an overcoat which they found in the store. These caught fire and a hole was burned in the floor. The inside of the store was considerably blackened by the smoke from the powder used.

After leaving the store the burglars stole a team and wagon from Eugene Leet. The rig was left about a mile outside of Wellsville, where the parties were seen and a description of them obtained.

Near Bolivar the thieves were cornered in a piece of woods, but managed to elude their pursuers. It is reported that they have since been arrested at Bradford.

The Potter Enterprise
Wednesday Evening, November 15, 1882 – Vol. IX, No. 27

- Henry Fessenden has withdrawn from the dray business, for a short time, and is now engaged in "tending" a bouncing girl baby, born Tuesday morning, Nov. 14th, 1882.

Potter County, Pennsylvania Potpourri – Volume I
1880 through 1884

MARRIED.

ABBOTT – ABBOTT – At Loucks Mills, Hector, Pa., Nov. 5th, 1882, by Wm. J. Loucks, Justice of the Peace, Mr. Clark Abbott and Mrs. Caroline Abbott, both of Hector, Pa.

HODSKIN – GOODSELL – On the 9th inst., at A. A. Hodskin's, in Coudersport, by Rev. A. Cone, Knapp R. Hodskin to Miss Martha L. Goodsell, all of Coudersport.

BEEBE – DOWNS – By Rev. J. L. Swain at his residence, in Raymond, Oct. 21st, 1882, Mr. John Beebe, of Oswayo, to Miss Lenie Downs, of Genesee.

WESCOTT – GILLILAND – By Rev. J. L. Swain, at his residence, in Raymond, Mr. Wescott and Miss Jennie Gilliland, both of Genesee.

Obituary.

The Hon. Frank L. Jones died at the residence of his brother, Charles S. Jones, in Coudersport, Potter county, Pa., on yesterday afternoon, Nov. 8th, 1882.

Mr. Jones was born at Lisle, Broome county, in 1822, having attained the age of sixty years at the time of his death. He was the son of Levi Jones, a prominent citizen of his town, who filled for several years, under the old judiciary system, the office of Associate Judge of Broome county. The son came to Owego in 1839 and engaged as a clerk in the store of Allen & Storrs, Dr. Allen and A. P. Storrs constituting the firm. In 1844 or thereabouts, he was sent to Sheshequin, Pa., by this firm to take charge of their lumber business in that vicinity, remaining there until 1847 when he went to Coudersport and engaged in business for himself. It was at that latter place that he married his first wife, an estimable woman, who died ten or twelve years ago in this village. In 1850 while residing in Coudersport, he was elected Sheriff of Potter county and served a term acceptably in that office. In 1855 he returned to Owego and became a partner with Storrs & Chatfield in the hardware business, continuing with them for several years. In 1860 he served for a few months as sheriff of this county by appointment of Gov. Morgan to fill a vacancy caused by removal. In 1865 the insurance firm of Jones & Stebbins was formed, which continued until dissolved on the appointment of Mr. Jones to the office of Agent and Warden of Auburn prison in 1880, which office he resigned a few days previous to his death, having become incapacitated by ill health for the performance of its duties. He also filled the office of Postmaster for over two terms under the administration of Presidents Grant and Hayes, very acceptably to the citizens of Owego, having been the immediate predecessor of our present worthy postmaster, Mr. D. M. Pitcher.

Mr. Jones was a man of remarkable business capacity, faithful to every trust of man of rare intelligence, a good citizen, of kindly disposition, generous to a fault, a true friend and a devoted husband and father. He was a prominent and consistent member of the Congregational church, exemplifying the teachings of its scriptural tenets in his walk and conversation.

A few years ago he married for his second wife Miss Hannah C. Curtis, a lady of rare attainments and excellence, daughter of Luke Curtis, of Maine,

Broome county, who survives him, together with a daughter by his first wife, Miss Anna Jones, and a little daughter and son, the former six and the latter two years old, by his second wife, to mourn his loss.

The remains of the deceased were brought to Owego last night on No. 12, for interment in the family lot in Evergreen Cemetery. – *Owego, N.Y. Blade*, Nov. 9th.

– We have received a line from Leroy Lyman, of Roulet, dated "Camp in the Woods, 28 miles from Mantistique, and 24 miles from Lake Superior, Schoolcraft Co., Mich., Nov. 2d." He states that it took him eight days to reach the "Camp" and then he was sick eight days more. A. H. Wood, of Painted Post, was already in camp, S. P. Pomeroy accompanied Mr. Lyman. Milo Lyman reached the camp the week before the note was written. The party had already killed forty-one deer, two bears, one coon, one mink, and pheasants and ducks too numerous to mention.

Wanted.
Fifty men to work in the woods. Good wages paid.
Albert Lyman
Coudersport, Pa.

The Potter Enterprise
Wednesday Evening, November 22, 1882 – Vol. IX, No. 28

MARRIED.

BUTTON – O'BRIEN. – At Louck's Mills, Nov. 11th, 1882, by Wm. J. Loucks, Esq., Mr. Willis Button, of Hector, Pa., to Miss Ella O'Brien, of Osceola, Tioga Co., Pa.

– Monday two more inmates were added to the county jail list, both insane. Luther Neother of Roulet had been at work for Dr. Ellison cutting logs, acted strange and finally became violent. Monday he walked his cell screaming at the top of his voice. Monday morning Miss Frable wandered about town, visited the school, and carried off dinner pails and baskets, went into the Corner Store, picked up a large plaster bust used for displaying goods and dashed it upon the walk, breaking it into small fragments. After dinner she walked into D. C. Larrabee's yard and took an umbrella from the porch, when called upon to return it she at first payed no attention. The second call she returned and attempted to break the umbrella over the head of Mr. Larrabee, and also attempted to strike him with a heavy tumbler taken from the school house. She tore his watch chain from his vest and retained it until locked in the jail. She became very violent and noisy, but was finally lodged in the jail, although it required two good strong men to get her there. Miss Frable has had spells of insanity before, but never so violent.

Potter County, Pennsylvania Potpourri – Volume I
1880 through 1884

The Potter Enterprise
Wednesday Evening, November 29, 1882 – Vol. IX, No. 29

West Branch. John Persing has husked two hundred bushels of ears of corn this fall. He was ninety-three years old the fourth day of last October.

- Luther Neother was removed to the Warren Insane Asylum last Wednesday by Sheriff Monroe. Neother was so violent that it was found necessary to strap his arms down and use every precaution to prevent his doing injury to himself and others.

- For several days past C. L. Peck has been soliciting subscriptions for a proposed telephone line from Coudersport, via Sweden, Brookland, Gold, Lewisville, and Mills to Harrison Valley to connect with the Cowanesque line. He has been very successful and has secured sufficient pledges from Coudersport and Brookland to insure the completion of the line, provided the other stations subscribe their quota. The line will cost from $1,200 to $1,400. It would prove of great convenience to the business men along the line, and ought to pay a good profit on the money invested.

- The people of Harrison Valley are taking active measures to secure the right of way for Magee's Railroad from Westfield to their place. Many have donated it and quite a large portion of the amount necessary to pay for what is not given has already been raised. Hamilton White, Frank Dodge and some others, through whose farms it passes, have given the right of way, and they together with J. W. Stevens, Geo. Stevens and other business men there, have taken hold of the project with energy. With such men in charge it will be done. Magee has promised to build the road as soon as practicable if the right of way can be secured. We have no doubt that the cars will be running to Harrison Valley before the close of next summer. – *Sentinel.*

- The man who was injured at the Tannery several weeks ago by the falling of some barn timbers has been removed to his home in Portville, and bids fair to live many years. His case is a singular one and shows what a man can endure and live. Both limbs were broken, and at first it was reported that his back was also broken. The latter was not the case, although the injuries were so severe that the lower part of his body was paralyzed for several weeks. A spot on his back as large as a man's hand sloughed off until the bone was visible. His back pained him so that he had to be moved often, and his prevented the bones of one leg from uniting, and formed a false joint. When sufficiently recovered to stand the operation this defect can, in a measure, be remedied by the surgeons. In the other leg the bones united making a sound member. When first injured his case was reported hopeless, and it was thought he could live but a few hours at most. The broken limbs were not set for several days until he rallied from the shock. He then appeared to improve until the sloughing near the back bone occurred. He then seemed to fail gradually, and for two weeks his death was looked for at any hour, but his time had not come, and in spite of injuries and the opinions of the physicians, he bids fair to become quite a man again.

NOTICE.

WHEREAS my wife, Lizzie Smith, has left my bed and board without just cause or provocation, I hereby forbid all persons trusting or harboring her on my account, as I will pay no debts or her contracting unless compelled by law.

Richard Smith
Coudersport, Pa., Nov. 24th, 1882

The Potter Enterprise
Wednesday Evening, December 6, 1882 – Vol. IX, No. 30

Whites Corners. Some excitement was occasioned in this place last week by the sudden death of Miss Ella Cummings living near Harrison Valley. She was well to all appearance till Friday evening, when she was taken ill and died immediately.

- A very sudden death occurred at Harrison last Friday. Miss Ellen Cummings, a young lady nineteen years of age, was in a healthy state, went out to catch some fowls, slipped and fell, walked into the house and said she thought she had broken her back, fell upon her face and died instantly. She was working for a Mr. James Kettle, at the time. A great many reports are afloat but investigation so far proves that a blood vessel was broken and it caused her death at once. She was buried at Whites Corners last Sunday. An inquest would have settled a great many disputed arguments. – *Free Press*.

- Joseph Crane, of Coudersport, aged about 19 years, was buried on Thanksgiving day. He was a very quiet, industrious young man, well liked by all his acquaintances. Erysipelas caused his death.

- The Froebel girl who as locked up as insane was released last week, but again becoming violent it was found necessary to confine her in the jail again. She will, doubtless, be sent to the Warren insane asylum.

- Sheriff Monroe has eight regular boarders, Seeley serving out his sentence; Chisholm charged with murder; Peryitt ,stealing a horse; Prosser, stealing money, watch, etc.; Mezler, stealing money, etc.; Miss Froebel, insane; Myron and Harriet Halstead, cruelty to a child. There is yet room for more in the jail.

New Saw Mill.

D. W. Vanwegen, Wilbur Quimby and Truman Quimby are making arrangements to put up a first-class mill between this place and Colcord's – just outside the borough limits. The land has been secured from the Keating Estate and work will commence at once. The machinery has already been purchased. The boiler is sixty horse power, engine 40 horse power. A switch will run from the Coudersport & Port Allegany R.R. to the mill so that the lumber can be shipped without hauling on wagons or sleighs. The logs on the "Eulalia Farm" will be put in at the new mill by Benjamin Rennells, at once, and it will not be many weeks until the whistle of the new mill is heard and lumber will soon be dropping from the saw.

Locked up for Cruelty.

On Monday L. B. Cole, Constable of Coudersport, arrested Myron and Harriet Halstead, of Ulysses township, charged with cruelty to an infant child. An examination was had before Miles White, Esq., and mainly on the evidence of the defence they were held to bail in the sum of $200, for lack of which they were locked up.

The child in question is aged about six years, the child of Halstead by a former wife from whom he separated. When about one year old it had scarlet fever from which it has never fully recovered. Constable Cole found the child in a cold chamber, sleeping on a little hay covered with rags, with part of an old horse blanket for cover. A pan of old crusts of bread was beside this excuse for a bed.

It is charged that the child has been cruelly beaten and misused, and reports are to the effect that the defendants were driven from York State on this account.

Telephone Company.

The Potter County Telephone Company (limited) was organized at the office of Benson & Peck, in Coudersport, on Saturday afternoon last.

The following are the officers and managers:

C. L. Peck, chairman, Coudersport; Wm. Dent, Treasurer; Thomas G. Hull, Secretary, Brookland; J. W. Stevens, Harrison Valley; E. U. Eaton, Lewisville; Amos Raymond, Gold; D. F. Glassmire, Sr., Coudersport.

The object of the organization is the building, maintaining and working a telephone line from Coudersport to Harrison Valley, and such other points in Potter county as may hereafter be determined upon.

The managers were authorized to construct the line from Coudersport via Lymansville, Raymond, Gold, Brookland, Lewisville and Mills to Harrison Valley, upon the most feasible route, as they shall determine.

The capital stock of the company is $1,500, divided into shares of $25 each, and has all been subscribed. At Harrison Valley the line will be connected by switch with the Cowanesque line.

The managers have levied an assessment of 25 per cent on each share, and intend pushing the line through without delay.

The Potter Enterprise
Wednesday Evening, December 13, 1882 – Vol. IX, No. 31

Roulet. Born to Mr. and Mrs. John Tenbrook, a little daughter.

Costelloville. A pleasant little wedding took place at the house of C. C. Reese on Thanksgiving Day, uniting Miss Lillie Reese of this place and Mr. Monte Edwards, of Emporium, in the bonds of Holy matrimony, by the Rev. Holland. May all their clouds have silver lining.

- The remains of Mrs. Rennells, mother of Benjamin Rennells, of Coudersport, were brought from Bradford county to this place, for burial, Monday afternoon. The deceased was well known in this section, having lived here many years. Her age was 83 years.

Freeman Run. On Thanksgiving day the remains of Joseph Crane, of Coudersport, were brought here for burial. This is the third one of Mr. Crane's family that has been buried here within a few years. The family have the sympathy of the entire neighborhood.

Assessor's Statement.

Statement of Farm Products and Manufactures of Oswayo township, for the year 1882:

FARM PRODUCTS AND STOCK.	
QUANTITY.	$ VALUE.
704 Bushels Wheat	880
14000 Bushels Oats	7,000
2850 Bushels Buckwheat	1,710
10098 Bushels Potatoes	5,049
2303 Bushels Corn (in ear)	921
3000 Bushels Apples	1,500
117 Bushels Rye	117
90 Bushels Peas	90
127 Bushels Millet	100
2000 Tons Hay	16,000
5774 Pounds of Wool	1,905
33075 Pounds of Butter	8,268
250 Lambs sold	750
1350 Store Sheep	4,050
200 Hogs and Shoates	2,500
171 Horses, 4 yrs and over	17,100
38 Horses less than 4 years	3,660
220 Cows, 4 years and over	6,600
470 Neat Cattle, less than 4 yrs.	7,050
20 Oxen, 4 years and over	1,500
Total Value,	$86,750
MANUFACTURES, &C.	
4,000,000 Hemlock Shingles	6,666

1,300,000 ft. Hemlock Lumber	6,500
2,000,000 ft. Hemlock Logs sold	5,000
2,000,000 ft. Pine logs cut and taken from the township	30,000
Total Value,	$48,166
TANNERY.	
6000 Tons Bark, cost	30,000
1,000,000 Lbs. Leather made	150,000
No. Taxables	275
No. Dogs	86
A. S. Lyman, Assessor.	

The Potter Enterprise
Wednesday Evening, December 20, 1882 – Vol. IX, No. 32

- It is a girl and Nelt Chaffe is happy.

MARRIED.

LEACH – EVANS. – In Hector, Dec. 3d, 1882, Mr. Alpheus Leach, of Hector, and Miss Emma Evans, of Spring Mills, N.Y.

CRANMER – GRIDLEY. – At Brookland, on the 25th of Nov., by the Rector of All-Saints church, Mr. Elmer Cranmer and Miss Angie Gridley.

BEGELL – LARRABEE. – At the house of the bride's parents, on the 12th inst., by Rev. A. Cone, B. F. Begell, of Harrison Valley, to Miss Lottie E., daughter of M. V. Larrabee, of Roulet.

JOHN S. ROSS,

Of Coudersport, died at Jersey Shore, on Thursday afternoon last, Dec. 14th, and was buried in Eulalia Cemetery on Sunday.

Mr. Ross was taken ill Tuesday morning with chronic inflammation of the stomach, complicated with spinal congestion. A physician was called Wednesday morning. At times he suffered great pain, but his end came peacefully, without a struggle. Early in the afternoon of Thursday he was about the room feeling better. He retired to his bed and while an attendant was rubbing his hands, death came so quietly that the attendant was unaware of its approach, until the spirit had fled. The remains were brought to Coudersport, and on Sunday last followed to the grave by a large number of relatives and friends. The funeral services were held by Rev. O. M. Leggett, assisted by Rev.'s Craw and Cone.

John S. Ross was born in Coudersport and has always resided here. He has never been what is called strong and rugged, and for a number of years his health has been poor. As a boy he was studious and in after years was a great reader, and remembered what he read. On matters pertaining to Potter county, very few could as readily answer questions as to lines, dates, elevations and matters of interest, usually to be found in books of reference, or by long search through records and documents, as we have reason to know, having often called upon him for information, when other sources failed to give us the facts. In this respect John was often called a walking encyclopedia.

John was a good surveyor and at the death of his father, a few years since, he took charge of the estate. By careful management and good judgment, he has since kept it in good shape, and in a profitable condition. In his dealings with his fellow man he was strictly honest and upright. John Ross never wronged a man knowingly or took advantage of a man's poverty or circumstances to drive a hard bargain. His word given was never forgotten and was considered as sacred as a bond. To all he was courteous and kind – always a gentleman.

About twelve years ago he was united in marriage to Miss Lydia Colegrove, of McKean county, who survives to mourn the loss of a kind, loving husband. Mr. Ross, had he lived, would have been 35 years of age next month. Peace to his ashes.

Court Minutes.

Court convened Dec. 11th, present H. W. Williams, President Judge, and Associates Hammond and Chappel.

Constables of different townships appeared and made returns.

A. B. Mann appointed guardian of Ally Johnson, minor child of Washington Johnson, late of Roulet township, dec'd.

Grand Jury called and sworn. Ed Fickler appointed foreman. Grand Jury discharged Dec. 14th.

Com'th vs Wm. Rhodes and Jael Lawton. Wm. Rhodes held to bail in sum of $100.

Patrick Fitzsimmons, a native of Ireland, admitted to citizenship.

Adelbert G. Lyman adopted by R. A. Moon.

Chas. Willing et al vs Nellie Curan, now Nellie Russel. Jury find for pl'ff, the land described to be released on payment of $639.52 within 30 days.

N. B. Smiley admitted to practice in the several courts of Potter county.

Charles Willing, et al vs N. W. Keech, et al. Jury find for pl'ff the land described to be released on payment of $415.62 within 30 days.

Com'th vs Geo W. Melzer, larceny, plead guilty. Sentenced to restore the property taken, if not already restored, pay a fine of $100 to the Commonwealth the costs of prosecution, and undergo imprisonment, at hard labor, in the Penitentiary, for the Western District, of the State, for the term of one year and ten calendar months.

Com'th vs Henry Grodevant, assault and battery, not a true bill, prosecutor O. W. Strong to pay costs.

Com'th vs David Hammond, selling liquor, plead guilty, sentenced to pay a fine of $50 and costs.

Virgil Spencer vs Ida Spencer, divorce granted.

F. L. Cox vs Susanna Cox, divorce granted.

W. B. Gordnier vs G. W. Snyder and S. W. Baker, settled as per writing filed.

Com'th vs Wm. Waters, bail forfeited and respited to next term.
Mary D. Miner vs S. R. Miner, divorce granted.
C. P. Kilbourne appointed Constable of Hector township.
Com'th vs George W. Chisholm, murder, true bill, case continued.
W. B. Chapman admitted to practice in the several courts of Potter county.
F. L. Mascho vs Enos Adams and W. J. Dickens, E. Hyde appointed auditor to distribute funds arising from Sheriff's Sale.
Com'th vs Michael Peryitt, larceny. Jury return a verdict of guilty. Sentenced to restore the stolen property, if not already restored, pay a fine of $1, costs of prosecution and undergo imprisonment in the Western Penitentiary for the term of two years and eight calendar months.
Merrick Jackson and O. J. Jackson vs Sylvania township, verdict for pl'ff in sum of $160.10 and costs. This suit was for damages. The plaintiffs, about a year ago, met with an accident on the dugway at the mouth of the East Fork, whereby one horse was killed and other damages sustained. This judgment should make supervisors more careful to keep roads in good repair. Mr. Jackson's costs, aside from Lawyer's fees, amount to over $100. The township's costs will be as much more and with attorney fees must swell the sum to about $500.
Com'th vs Gilbert Glover, assault and battery, defendant and bail discharged.
Com'th vs Matthew Prosser, larceny, plead guilty, bail $300 for appearance at next term.
Com'th vs H. J. Mills, nuisance, true bill, guilty, bail for appearance at next term, $200. This is known as the Sharon dog suit. It is claimed the defendant kept too many dogs; that they were cross, and interfered with the happiness of the neighborhood, and the sheep, chickens, &c., of the neighbors. The evidence indicated that Mills had somewhere in the neighborhood of eighteen dogs. The costs he had to pay in this case, aside from his attorney fees, amounted to $130.18. Expensive dogs.
Henry King admitted to practice in the several courts of Potter county.
Francis Presho, by her next friend, vs Lyman C. Presho, A. F. Hollenbeck appointed commissioner to take testimony.
Alice C. Johnson, by her next friend, vs Geo C. Johnson, Sheriff to make proclamation.
Rose L. Morse vs James Morse, G. W. Pearsall appointed commissioner to take testimony.
Com'th vs Charles Seeley, attempting to shoot a person, nol pros.
Com'th vs Charles Seeley, obstructing an officer, nol pros.
Lena Froebel, declared a lunatic. Hebron township certified as residence of same and ordered that she be removed to the Warren Insane Asylum.
Com'th vs Frank Ellis, assault and battery, def't and bail discharged.
Com'th vs Myron Halsted, cruelty to children. Jury return a verdict of guilty. This is the case mentioned in our columns a short time since, from Ulysses township. The defendant was sentenced to pay a fine of $1 to the

Commonwealth, pay costs of prosecution and undergo imprisonment in the Western Penitentiary for one year and six calendar months.

In the matter of the iron bridge over Oswayo Creek at Shingle House. Grand Jury report the bridge as necessary and the cost greater than is reasonable for the township to bear. The township has built very fine stone abutments and the county is to pay for putting up the iron bridge, and making the same passable, at a cost of $1,000.

Com'th vs Rufus Howland, keeping a gambling house, continued.

B. W. Green admitted to practice in the several courts of Potter county.

Com'th vs Michael Peryitt, ordered that sum of $25 be paid to D. B. Ellis for arresting Peryitt, committed for larceny.

An adjourned court will be held in the Prothonotary's office Jan. 5th, 1883, at 10 o'clock a.m., to hear case in orphans court, ordered that Jury wheel be filled with 400 names for ensuing year. Veniries ordered for twenty-four grand and forty-eight traverse jurors for March Term, 1883.

Dan Baker appointed auditor to settle with Prothonotary, Clerk of courts and Register and Recorder.

Com'th vs Harriet Halstead, bail $100 for appearance at next term.

Com'th vs Wm. Mulkin, obtaining money under false pretences, nol pros.

Com'th vs Thomas Lawton, assault and battery, nol pros.

Pike Poor District vs Sweden Poor District residence of pauper, Dell Dunbar, a child, certified to Pike Poor District, and ordered that said District pay Sweden poor district $101.75 expended for reasonable relief and support of said pauper.

L. B. Seibert admitted to practice in several courts of Potter county.

John R. Millard vs Mary E. Millard, divorce granted.

Elizabeth Place vs S. C. Place, divorce granted.

Dan'l Smith vs the J.S.P.C. & B.R.R., appeal from award of viewers, settled. The company to pay Smith $200, put in crossings, guards, fences, &c. and maintain same.

Eunice Brown vs Albert J. Brown, B. C. Rude, of Wellsville, and S. W. Smith, of Port Allegany, appointed commissioners to take testimony.

Grand Jury returned W. T. Hosley, Amos Veely and Geo W. Boyer for unlawfully engaging in games of hazard for money.

Grand Jury report jail in good condition but recommend that the jail yard wall be repainted.

Estate of Wm. Ellis, A. F. Hollenbeck appointed auditor to distribute funds in hands of administrator.

Petition of Caroline E. Neefe for separate estate granted.

Estella Baker vs John S. Baker, divorce granted.

Daniel Monroe acknowledged the following deeds for property sold at Sheriff Sales:

To J. W. Stevens for 83.1 acres in Harrison twp., sold as the property of Samuel Metcalf, for $15.

To J. F. Carling, C. P. Kilbourne and Curtis Kilbourne for 2 ½ acres in Hector, sold as property of Enos Evans, W. I. Dickens and T. J. Surdam for $669.

Potter County, Pennsylvania Potpourri – Volume I
1880 through 1884

To F. E. Neefe, for ½ acre in Coudersport, sold as property of D. B. Neefe for $25.

To Luther W. Green for 110 acres in Allegany, sold as property of ----- for $110.

Dec. 16 – Ordered that a special court be held on the second Monday in March for the trial of civil causes, and that thirty causes be put down for trial, and that Veniries be issued for 36 traverse jurors for said special term. Sheriff allowed two assistants in conveying persons to Penitentiary.

Allegany Statistics.

	1878	1879	1880	1882
Horses, working	165	170	154	165
Oxen	30	28	28	25
Cows	425	434	488	406
Colts, 3 years	16	13	21	15
Colts, 2 years	18	17	15	16
Colts, 1 year	22	16	17	11
Colts, Suckling	15	17	18	16
Heifers milking, 3 years	92	145	118	81
Heifers milking, 2 years	45	65	46	37
Heifers not milking, 3 yrs		2	3	8
Heifers not milking, 2 yrs		42	45	18
Steers, 3 years		20	14	4
Steers, 2 years	74	16	19	12
Yearlings	199	226	243	113
Calves	294	351	232	276
Sheep	930	1226	1619	1756
Shoats to winter	144	93	114	132
Winter wheat, Bushels	1352	1281	601	1166
Spring wheat, Bushels	1673	997	336	182
Corn in ear, Bushels	4732	5244	4200	2230
Buckwheat, Bushels	2405	3425	2751	2861
Oats, Bushels	20486	20574	19248	21159
Millet, Bushels	461	1074	1380	1528
Rye, Bushels	149	23	233	81
Peas, Bushels	368	140	191	115
Beans, Bushels	91	125	84	36
Potatoes, Bushels	8129	4703	11081	9512
Apples, Bushels	1682	9293	7692	4426
Pork killed, Lbs	35306	41254	37932	38178
Butter, Lbs	55298	59647	60784	39714
Cheese, Lbs	62000	45995	18960	40000
Maple Sugar, Lbs	21135	30488	19465	31185

Wool, Lbs	3610	4084	5182	5761 ½
Acres winter wheat sown	116	52	56	60 ¼
Bushels winter wheat	220	90	104	94
Acres Rye sown	19	22	7 ½	2
Bushels rye	30	34	9 ½	2
Swarms of Bees wintered		78	66	65
No. young swarms		118	103	76
Am't honey taken		684	795	655
Charles Coats, Assessor Allegany Township				

The Potter Enterprise
Wednesday Evening, December 27, 1882 – Vol. IX, No. 33

Costelloville. Mr. Sam Haskins did nothing last week but receive congratulations on his girl.

MARRIED.

COX – SMITH – At the Methodist Parsonage, in Lewisville, Wednesday evening, Dec. 13th, 1882, by Rev. W. C. Tansom, Mr. F. L. Cox, and Mrs. Satilla Smith, both of Lewisville.

HANN – HARRIS – At Lewisville, Dec. 17th, 1882, by Rev. Tansom, Mr. Frank Hann, and Miss Emma Harris, both of Genesee Forks, Pa.

Freeman Run. Mrs. A. E. Williams, of Keating Summit, died last week, leaving a babe but two weeks old. The remains were taken to New York state for burial.

- At the last term of Court, I. F. Carling, C. P. Kilbourne and Curtis Kilbourne purchased at Sheriff's Sale, two and one-half acres of land in Sunderlinville, together with the steam saw mill thereon, sold as the property of Enos Evans, W. I. Dickens and T. J. Surdam. The new purchasers at once commenced putting the mill in shape for cutting out lumber. Wednesday evening after supper one of the employees was at the mill and found it safe, and everything apparently secure. About midnight the mill was discovered to be in flames, and soon burned to the ground. The machinery was damaged, and part of it ruined. We have not learned whether or not the mill will be rebuilt. The fire is believed to have been the work of an incendiary.

No Paper Next Week.

The time for the Publisher's annual bear hunt is at hand, and in consequence thereof, and according to our usual custom, there will be no paper next week. The office will be open, and all demands for job printing promptly executed.

Officers Elected.

The following were elected officers of Coudersport Lodge, K. of H., last Thursday evening:

C. L. Peck, D.; Eugene Baker, V.D.; D. W. Vanwegen, A.D.; W. K. Jones, Treasurer; F. J. Norton, F.R.; W. C. Rennells, R.; N. M. Glassmire, Chap.; W. W. Thompson, Guide; A. S. Olmsted, Guard; Charles Reissman, Sentinel. Representative to Grand Lodge, W. K. Jones; alternate, C. L. Peck.

The Hunters.

Over fifty deer and deer saddles were brought into town last week. A party from near Ceres brought in twenty, killed on the East Fork, another party brought in eighteen, others sent in by stage and other conveyances bring the number to over fifty. More deer have been killed this season than in the three seasons preceding. The slaughter must make deer comparatively scarce for a year or two to come.

Last week Aaron Robinson killed four large deer on the Sinnemahoning, among the number being one of those rare specimens known as a white deer. This one was a buck, about three years old, almost white, a little of the blue coat being mixed with the white. Unfortunately this deer had lost his horns. The last cold snap took off the antlers from the bucks and they will go unadorned until next season's growth starts.

Christmas morning Earle Crane had business on the hill south-east of town. Hearing a hound he walked to the brow of the hill, and a little distance below saw a large fox followed by a dog, the fox was tired, and a buck shot through one fore leg impeded his travel somewhat. Crane had no gun, and as the dog did not seem inclined to pick up the fox, he started in pursuit down the hill, the fox leading, the dog a good second and Crane working his way to the front in good style. It was a beautiful race – no put up job, before Mill Creek was reached the dog was left behind and the pace becoming too hot for the fox he took refuge under a log, where Crane finished him with a club, winning the race and brush in the unprecedented time of --- the judge, James Pearsall, got excited and forgot to keep time.

Last week two young fellows from Yorkstate, making Cherry Springs their headquarters, killed two deer and a small bear. For sheer good luck they are ahead of the bear. They had followed some deer until nightfall, compelled them to give up the chase. The next morning they started after the same deer and followed them several miles, finally giving up the chase, returning on their back track, they found where a young bear had been following in their tracks, finally turning off up the hillside, following the track for a quarter of a mile brought them to a stub where the tracks ceased and where the bear had gone to rest. The stub was a large one, they had no axe, but fortunately did have matches. A fire at the base of the stub was soon compelled bruin to climb out at the top where a Winchester ball compelled him to drop to the ground, a distance some thirty feet, a dead bear.

Recently a big bear from either Clinton or Cameron county put in an appearance on Cowley having been chased there by hunters. Cowley Run hunters followed him to Reed's Run in Roulet. Here Laroy Lyman, the famous hunter of the Northern Tier, with several companions took after bruin, never to give up until the death of the bear dropped the curtain. For four days and a half they followed the trail, over hill and down dale, through swamps and almost impenetrable laurel patches where it seemed impossible for a rabbit to get through, they ploughed their way through the snows. On the Hamilton, in McKean county, bruin was brought to bay. Four balls from a 45:75 Winchester wound up the hunt. The bear was a very large one and quite fat.

The Potter Enterprise
Wednesday Evening, January 10, 1883 – Vol. IX, No. 34

West Homer. Two of Homer's young people have commenced 1883 with happy hearts and bright anticipations of the future. Mr. John Quimby was united in marriage to Miss Lydia Crosby, by Rev. W. S. Holland, on Jan. 1st.

MARRIED.

LEHMAN – BREMER. – In Port Allegany, Jan. 1st, 1883, by C. E. Wright, Esq., at the residence of the officiating officer, Mr. Jacob Lehman, of Eulalia, and Miss Elizabeth Bremer, of the same place.

FELTWELL – BARCLAY. – In Sylvania township, on Saturday, Dec. 30th, 1882, by J. M. Rees, Esq., Mr. Joseph Feltwell, of Little Marsh, Tioga Co., Pa., to Miss Amanda S. Barclay, of Wharton, Potter Co., Pa.

QUIMBY – CROSBY. – At the residence of the bride's parents, in Homer, Pa., Jan. 1st, 1883, by Rev. W. S. Holland, Mr. John A. Quimby, and Miss Lydia C. Crosby.

ASHCRAFT – JONES. – At the home of the bride's parents, Corning, N.Y., Dec. 26th, 1882, E. H. Ashcraft, M.D., and Miss Anna L. Jones, by Rev. Fuller.

SMITH – CHESBRO. – On Monday, Jan. 8th, 1883, at the home of the bride's brother, Mr. Warren C. Chesbro, by the Rector of Christ Church, Coudersport, Mr. Edgarton John Smith, of Scranton, to Miss Hattie L. Chesbro, of Homer township, Pa.

DIED.

ROONEY – In Genesee, December 14th, 1882, John Rooney, aged 91 years.

John Rooney was a native of Letrim county, Ireland. He settled with his family on the Sherwood farm the first of November, 1856, where he has lived up to his death.

LOCKWOOD – In Eulalia, Jan. 6th, Benjamin Lockwood, aged 22 years.

He was at work at a log slide, was struck by the log, thrown some distance and one limb was badly mangled. He lived a few hours. He leaves a young wife to whom he was married about two months since.

Killed.

An accident occurred at the lumber job on the Cole lot near Nelson Clark's, in Eulalia township, last Friday, which resulted in the death of Benjamin

Lockwood. A log was partially out of the ground slide, and Mr. Lockwood attempted to put it back in. He was on the lower side of the log, when it suddenly started, throwing him some distance and crushing one leg from his foot to his hip. He never rallied from the shock and on Saturday died, notwithstanding Drs. Ellison and Ashcraft rendered all assistance possible. The deceased leaves a wife to whom he had been married about three months.

G. A. R. No. 204.

The following officers of A. F. Jones Post, of Coudersport, were publicly installed by Com. A. S. Lyman, of Post 125, Saturday evening, Jan. 6.: J. M. Covey, Com.; C. J. Marble, S.V.C.; John Metzger, J.V.C.; C. N. Barret, Adjt.; Geo. N. Tuttle, Q.M.; Albert Colcord, O.D.; Geo. Mitchell, O.G.; A. D. Colcord, Chaplain; Hiram Baker, Q.M.S.

The Post has a membership of 69 at last muster.

Officers Elected.

The following officers were installed for the ensuing year, at the last meeting of Eulalia Lodge, No. 342 F. & A. M.: C. A. Stebbins, W.M.; W. K. Jones, S.W.; N. A. Pinney, J.W.; N. H. Goodsell, Sec.; Almeron Nelson, Treas.; D. C. Larrabee, Chap.; D. F. Glassmire, Jr., S.D.; W. I. Lewis, J.D.; S. A. Phillips, S.M.C.; L. F. Andrews, J.M.C.; Benjamin Dennis, Pur.; James L. Knox, Guide; Benjamin Rennells, Tiler.

E. A. U. No. 294.

The following named officers, of Coudersport Union No. 294, were installed, for the ensuing term, on Tuesday evening, Jan. 2d, 1883:

C. J. Marble, Chancelor; Mrs. C. J. Marble, Advocate; Geo. N. Tuttle, Pres.; Albert Colcord, Vice Pres.; A. C. Millard, Sec'y; W. A. Abson, Acct.; R. M. Post, Treas.; A. D. Colcord, Chaplain; Jno. Bacon, Auxillery; L. R. Bliss, Warden; O. B. Vanwegen, Sentinel; Horace Toombs, Watchman.

The Union has a membership of sixty-four.

Court Minutes.

Adjourned Court, Jan. 5th, 1883. Hon. A. G. Olmsted, Additional Law Judge, Presiding; present Associate Judge Hammond.

Alma Brewster vs Geo. Brewster. Rule on respondent to show cause why he should not pay the reasonable expenses of the libellant and such allowances as the Court may direct for her support during pendency of proceedings.

John Reed declared a lunatic and ordered that he be removed to the Warren Insane Asylum.

Administratrix of Augustus Streeter ordered to sell real estate.

Sarah A. Quick vs Jonathan Quick. Divorce awarded.

- James McNulty recently cut, skidded and banked at Ellison's pond a cherry log 18 feet in length, sound and clear, which scales 1550 feet. This log was cut on the Bingham lands and was all there was in the tree. J. W. Allen sealed the log and pronounces it the finest and largest cherry he has ever seen, in this or any other county. The estimated weight of the log is 10,850 pounds, and it is worth about $150.

G. A. R., Oswayo.

At the annual election of officers for A. W. Estes Post G. A. R. the following were chosen:

A. S. Lyman, Commander; J. B. Stewart, S.V. Commander; W. L. Shattuck, J.V. Commander; Geo. F. Roulee, Quartermaster; Robt. Densmore, Surgeon; Wm. Fessenden, Chaplain; John Davis, Officer of the Day; V. R. Kenyon, Officer of the Guard.

The Commander has appointed J. C. Wilkinson, Adjutant.

Installation services will take place Jan. 13th, 1883, and will be open to the public, who are invited to attend.

- There are millions of feet of hard-wood timber going to waste every year in this county. While the tanneries are consuming thousands of acres of land annually, the hard-wood is left standing or is consumed by forest fires. It seems to us that this section of the country now offers – with its improved railroad facilities – the best of inducements for practical men to locate here and engage in the manufacture of such articles as will work up the beech, birch, ash, maple and oak timber which is so plentiful and cheap. Factories for turning out all kinds of wooden-ware, hubs, handles, furniture and other articles literally too numerous to mention would undoubtedly yield good dividends. We predict that the day is not far distant when the eyes of capitalists will turn upon our hard-wood forests, and then the timber will be utilized. But it might be worked up by our own citizens, much to the benefit of their own pockets, without waiting for the capitalists to come and reap the harvest.

The Potter Enterprise
Wednesday Evening, January 17, 1883 – Vol. IX, No. 35

West Homer. Miss Hattie Chesbro was very abruptly snatched from our midst by a gentleman from Scranton. We have no idea how long he has had her in view, but this is certain he was not long getting away with her when he once got possession. We are sorry to lose Hattie for she was one of our best. May her days of married life be long, with just enough shadow to temper the glare of the sun.

Also on New Year's day Mr. John Quimby and Miss Lydia Crosby were married by Rev. W. Holland. Wilbur are you asleep and dreaming? Are you now aware that you are like

"The last rose of summer, left blooming alone,
   It's lovely companions faded and gone."
Why what would you do, suppose some one
   Should come and take Libbie from you?
Hold down your head and blush with shame,

And die with old age, without wife or fame.

MARRIED.

LOUCKS – PLAGEMAN – At the residence of the bride's mother, in Kibbeville, by Rev. T. L. Perry, Mr. W. M. Loucks to Miss Carrie L. Plageman, on Jan. 7th, 1883.

West Branch. Last Monday morning, the 8th inst., a man by the name of Isaac West was killed while working on the slide, on the Charlie Brown lumber job at Pike Mills. A small log jumped out of the slide and struck him on the side of the face and broke his neck, he was about 20 feet from the slide on the upper side. Mr. West had a wife but no children; she left their home that morning on a visit to friends in Delmar, Tioga Co., Pa. Mr. West was taken to Wellsboro for burial.

The Potter Enterprise
Wednesday Evening, January 24, 1883 – Vol. IX, No. 36

MARRIED.
GLASSMIRE – SMITH. – In Coudersport, Jan. 18th, at the residence of Mrs. A. F. Jones, by Rev. A. Cone, Mr. D. F. Glassmire and Miss M. A. Smith, all of Coudersport.

- Albert Goodsell died in Coudersport, Monday night, in the 61st year of his age. Mr. Goodsell was one of the early settlers in Coudersport, carrying on the business of gunsmith. He was a good workman, and a good citizen, kind hearted, and a good neighbor. For many years he has been a member of the Baptist church in this place, and has done all in his power for the success of the organization. Mr. Goodsell will be missed in Coudersport.

Roulet. Benj. Card died at Smethport, last Monday; his remains were brought home and interred in Card Creek cemetery Friday.

Costelloville. Mr. Ephram Reed, aged sixty-nine, died of typhoid fever on the evening of the 17th, after an illness of six weeks.

DIED.
CARD – In Smethport, Pa., Jan. 16th, Benjamin Card, of Roulet, aged fifty-nine years and eleven months.

GOODSELL – At his residence in Coudersport, Jan. 23d, 1883, Albert B. Goodsell, aged sixty years, nine months and five days.

- The narrow gauge is located from Gaines to Crippen's dugway on the West Branch. Monday morning the corps started in at the Red school house, to survey from the West Branch to the East Fork. There is little doubt the road will be built next season.

List of Grand Jurors for March Term 1883.

B. F. Bishop, Farmer, Genesee; Wescott Burlingame, Farmer, Wharton; Lyman Burt, Farmer, Roulet; J. F. Carlin, Farmer, Hector; H. W. Dingee, Lumberman, Keating; Andrew Erway, Farmer, Harrison; George Fowler, Farmer, West Branch; John Freeman, Farmer, Sweden; L. L. Holcomb, Laborer, Sweden; N. W. Hubbard, Farmer, Harrison; Almond Lehman, Laborer, Hector; Peter Leonard, Cheese maker, Harrison; George Lane, Laborer, Sharon; Don Manning, Blacksmith, Roulet; F. B. Nelson, Farmer, Eulalia; J. W. Neefe, Farmer, Sweden; Ezekel Rooks, Farmer, Harrison; T. B. Rees, Mechanic, Eulalia; W. B. Rees, Merchant, Coudersport; George Sutton, Farmer, Pike; Wm. Snyder, Farmer, Sweden; Eugene Weed, Farmer, Wharton; Rodney White, Merchant, Roulet; Ed Wheaton, Farmer, Hector.

List of Traverse Jurors for March Term 1883.

FIRST WEEK.

J. L. Allen, Farmer, Clara; G. W. Bennett, Farmer, Ulysses; Arthur Barclay, Farmer, Wharton; W. J. Brown, Farmer, Sharon; E. M. Bishop, Laborer, Hebron; Seth Briggs, Farmer, Wharton; Ambrose Ball, Farmer, Hebron; A. Bisbee, Laborer, West Branch; Anthony Cochran, Farmer, Genesee; W. H. Crosby, Farmer, Homer; John Collar, Farmer, Genesee; George Clark, Farmer, Sylvania; S. E. Crittenden, Farmer, Oswayo; Edwin Dodd, Farmer, Sweden; J. H. Dexter, Farmer, Oswayo; Henry Dyer, Farmer, Stewardson; Page Groesbeck, Farmer, Roulet; John Gordnier, Farmer, Homer; Geo. Greengrass, Laborer, Hector; Elymus Hackett, Mechanic, Lewisville; Thos. J. Hull, Farmer, Ulysses; E. E. Kelley, Farmer, Allegany; C. H. Kilbourn, Laborer, Hector; L. B. Lewis, Farmer, Bingham; C. H. Loucks, Farmer, Hector; E. D. Leet, Farmer, Ulysses; Robert McDowell, Farmer, Pleasant Valley; Asal Marble, Farmer, Harrison; Wm. Mattison, Farmer, Sharon; C. C. Nelson, Farmer, Sweden; Seymour Norton, Laborer, Coudersport; Albert Parker, Farmer, Hector; Henry Rogers, Farmer, Allegany; L. F. Rice, Farmer, West Branch; Burt Reed, Farmer, Roulet; Eli Rees, Farmer, Sylvania; W. H. Rexford, Farmer, Sharon; J. B. Stewart, Farmer, Oswayo; Coleman Smith, Laborer, Oswayo; Wm. Stevens, Laborer, Sharon; Wm. W. Trask, Farmer, West Branch; Wm. Willkinson, Farmer, Hector; F. D. Weimer, Farmer, Clara; E. S. Worden, Farmer, Hector; Frank Welton, Farmer, Wharton; R. H. Young, Farmer, Ulysses; M. J. Young, Farmer, Portage; John Zingerle, Farmer, West Branch.

SECOND WEEK.

Henry Berfield, Jr., Farmer, Wharton; C. E. Burt, Merchant, Lewisville; O. L. Blackman, Farmer, Pike; B. F. Berfield, Farmer, Wharton; T. J. Burdick, Laborer, Sharon; J. L. Collins, Farmer, Allegany; A. H. Coe, Laborer, Hebron; Abe Chase, Farmer, Sweden; Willis Conable, Farmer, West Branch; J. M. Dodge, Farmer, Harrison; J. M. Davis, Farmer, Harrison; C. A. Estes, Farmer, Oswayo; Amisa Ellis, Farmer, Genesee; John Earle, Farmer, Eulalia; E. H. Estes, Farmer, Genesee; L. C. Forsythe, Laborer, Roulet; M. P. Flynn, Farmer, Hector; Allen Frink, Farmer, Hebron; A. L. Harvey, Farmer, Ulysses; Frank Heath, Laborer, Ulysses; E. P. Johnson, Farmer, Ulysses; Allen Kennada, Farmer, Harrison; Henry Moore, Farmer, Wharton; Wesley Morley, Farmer,

Potter County, Pennsylvania Potpourri – Volume I
1880 through 1884

Allegany; A. D. Nelson, Farmer, Wharton; W. A. Nichols, Farmer, Sharon; B. F. Nichols, Farmer, Sharon; F. P. Nichols, Farmer, Sharon; L. M. Quimby, Farmer, Homer; R. N. Rice, Farmer, Oswayo; A. T. Smith, Blacksmith, Oswayo; A. G. Stewart, Farmer, Sharon; Lemuel Sherman, Farmer, Pike; Nelson Vaninwegen, Farmer, Hebron; Isaac Wheeler, Laborer, Sylvania; O. R. Webb, Farmer, Roulet.

The Potter Enterprise
Wednesday Evening, January 31, 1883 – Vol. IX, No. 37

- Sheriff Monroe had the misfortune to lose a fine revolver last week. He had orders to move some bark up Teed Hollow, in Hector township, and as some threats had been made that the bark should not be moved he took a "persuader" along and he thinks he lost it in or near Water's dooryard. The bark in question is same that was the immediate cause of the death of young Waters and the imprisonment of Chisholm, now in jail charged with murder. The particulars of which were given at the time.

The Potter Enterprise
Wednesday Evening, February 7, 1883 – Vol. IX, No. 38

- Ed. Greisel, of South Hill, was married to Miss Dell Dingman, of Coudersport, last Wednesday evening. Yes, boys, it's true, Ed has really got the matrimonial halter slipped over his neck, now he has to begin to think up excuses, why he was out late, you know, do not envy him.

MARRIED.

PHILLIPS – LARRABEE – At the residence of the bride's parents, in Coudersport, February 3d, 1883, by Rev. A. A. Craw, Mr. Samuel A. Phillips and Miss Carrie M. Larrabee, both of Coudersport.

GREISEL – DINGMAN – In Coudersport, January 31st, 1883, at the residence of the bride's parents, by Rev. A. A. Craw, Mr. Edward Greisel and Miss Dell Deingman, both of Coudersport.

WILSON – GOODSELL – At the residence of the bride's mother in Coudersport, Jan. 26th, 1883, by Rev. A. A. Craw, Mr. Wm. H. Wilson, of Springfield, Mass., and Miss Minnie E. Goodsell, of Coudersport, Pa.

LUNN – BAHAM – Jan. 28th, 1883, in Sharon Township, by G. W. Pearsall, Esq., Mr. Fred Lunn, of Shingle House, Pa., and Miss Helen Baham, of Andover, N.Y.

- Mr. and Mrs. D. C. Larrabee celebrated their Silver Wedding last Friday evening in the presence of a large number of relatives and friends.

- Leroy Harris, who lives near Millport, met with an accident on Andrews' lumber job, Dingman Run, last Friday. He was engaged putting logs into the trail when a log got the start of him, striking his left leg, breaking the point of the left ankle joint on the inside and rupturing some of the tendons, making very painful would. Dr. Ashcraft rendered surgical aid.

- The rain and warm atmosphere of Saturday and Saturday night raised the water in the river. The ice was loosened partially, and was helped by men considerably. Part of it went out of Mill Creek taking N. H. Goodsell's dam with it, and became jammed from Braitling's to the Main St. bridge, flooding the lots south of Water St. The water surrounded Basset's and Neefe's dwellings. Neefe's shop had several inches of water over the floor. All cellars in that neighborhood were well filled. Elder Leavenworth was compelled to remove his horses as the water flowed through his barn. Braitling was in a like fix. The cold air of Sunday shut down the flow of water, or much damage would have been done.

- The dwelling of John Klein, Eulalia Township, burned to the ground last week. The fire caught from the pipe, we believe. The inmates attempted to save the house, but the fire had gained too much headway. Nearly all the furniture, clothing, &c., burned. The house was a good one and well furnished. Loss about $1500, with no insurance.

Telephone Line.

The Potter County Telephone line has been sold. The New York and Pennsylvania Co., controlling the Bell Telephone in this section, refused to furnish instruments to the home company, although a sub-agent had promised to. The N. &. & P. Co. agree to purchase the line, paying first cost after the poles are set. They are to give the old Co. $500 in tickets at 20 per cent discount, balance cash. All tickets not used in two years to be redeemed. Offices to be established as contemplated by the home company. The N. Y. & P. Co. say they will put up the wire before the 1st of April, make connections with Elmira, N.Y., and extend this line to Bradford.

The Potter Enterprise
Wednesday Evening, February 14, 1883 – Vol. IX, No. 39

- C. G. Rukgaber of Germania, and Miss Anna Hazelbarth, of Cedar Run, were married at Germania, on the 3rd.

MARRIED.

McDOWELL – COLEMAN. – At the residence of the bride's parents, on Tuesday, Feb. 6th, 1883, by the Rev. O. C. Hills, Mr. E. T. McDowell, of Burtville, Potter Co., Pa., and Miss Mary A. Coleman, of Port Allegany.

Sartwell Creek. Mr. Eldin McDowell, formerly of this place, and Miss Mary Coleman, of Port Allegany, also Mr. William McIntosh, of Erie Co., Pa., and Miss Jennie McDowell, were united in the bonds of matrimony, Feb. 6th.

- Mrs. Tuttle, of Maryland, mother of George Tuttle, of Coudersport, is dead.

Sartwell Creek. Death has again entered our community and taken one from our midst. Mr. Reuben Card, after an illness of about four days, suffering untold agonies, with that dreaded disease erysipelas, passed from this earth of sickness and sorrows. He has left a vacant place in this neighborhood which none can fill.

The Potter Enterprise
Wednesday Evening, February 21, 1883 – Vol. IX, No. 40

MARRIED.

PERRY – ATHERTON – At Ulysses, Pa., Feb. 11th, 1883, by A. Carpenter, Esq., Mr. Willis Perry, of Allegheny Co., N.Y., and Mrs. Katie Atherton, of Genesee Forks, Pa.

Bingham. Several deaths have occurred, notably among others were those of Mr. Peter Chase, of Whitesville, N.Y., Mr. James Statham, North Fork, Pa., Mrs. A. P. Kibbe, N. Bingham, Pa., and Mrs. Brown of Bingham Centre, Pa.

JUSTICES' COURT.
Death Caused by Neglect – Assault and Battery – Selling Liquor Without a License.

On Tuesday afternoon last Constable Cole brought before Miles White, Esq., D. P. Reed, his wife Mrs. Hattie Reed, and Willis Reed, son of the two former, and Wm. Blarigan, of Roulet, charged on the oath of Albert Sherwood and William Gleason, with the murder and killing by neglect and ill treatment, of Mrs. Alleck Reed, the mother of Daniel Reed, and grandmother of Willis Reed, for whose support the Reed's were responsible.

Until last fall the Reed's resided in Roulet township, and until the building of the railroad the deceased Mrs. Reed had a very comfortable room, and there is nothing to show that she was not well cared for. During the building of the railroad the Reed's boarded a number of the laborers and to make room, partitioned off a part of a back porch for the old lady. It is said the partition was of rough boards and not battened. In this place she was kept until in December. Mr. Reed was than at Keating Summit. Before going there he tried to bargain with Blarigan for the care and keeping of his mother, but failed to make a bargain.

The family wishing to move to Keating Summit, Mrs. Hattie Reed and the son Willis did make a bargain with Blarigan, that he should take care of the old lady, for four dollars per week.

Blarigan's house is simply a board shanty, 12x16 feet, in which resided himself, wife and three children, and to the objection of want of room it was agreed to build an addition to the house which was done. The room built on was of rough boards, battened, the floor of shingle boards, ice and snow were on the boards, inside, when it was built, and remained there at the time the old lady died, December 16th. This room had an outside door but no door connecting it with the other part of the house, and there was no stove in this room. In this place the old lady, who had reached the advanced age of ninety-four years, and was helpless, was kept until the time of her death.

The day before her death two women, witnesses in the case, called to see the old lady and found her in this room, the ice still remaining on the boards, the old lady's hair frozen to the pillow supporting her head and the quilts on the bed frozen together. They took her out of doors and carried her around and into the room occupied by the Blarigan family. As soon as the invalid began to get warm she fainted away. The quilts and bedding were dried and warmed and she was again taken back to the cold room, from which she had been taken, and left alone.

Some time during the night the angel of death, more merciful than man, released the spirit from its tenement of clay, and relieved from earthly suffering the aged mother, who should have received the tenderest care instead of the cruel treatment she was subjected to.

When the body was prepared for the last sad rites on earth the limbs were found frozen to the knees. The son attended the funeral but did not complain of the treatment his mother had received, and now says he did not know what quarters she had been furnished with. He certainly knew that Blarigan with his small shanty house had not the accommodations necessary for a helpless old lady of 94 years, and deserves the severest censure for not seeing that her last days were made as comfortable as possible.

The Reed's waived a hearing and gave bail in the sum of $500 for appearance at Court. Blarigan had a hearing and was held in the same sum for appearance at next term.

ASSAULT AND BATTERY.

Thursday evening Esquire White had an assault and battery case. During the afternoon, James Loughery and Amos Veeley had a quarrel, and we believe, came to blows. Veeley finally went to District attorney Cobb's office and while there Loughery came in and borrowed a dollar of Cobb. He made some remarks to Veeley, and a fight ensued. The combatants were separated, but soon got together again, while yet in Cobb's office, and Veeley was so seriously pounded that he could not appear on the streets next day. Loughery was arrested for assault and battery and held to bail.

WHISKEY CASES.

Saturday Esquire White had before him Harrison Koon, George Ward, Robert Niles and James Johnson, charged with selling liquor contrary to the statutes made and provided. Robert Niles and Harrison Koon had an examination and were held to bail for appearance at next term of Court. Johnson and Ward waived examination and gave bail.

MORE OF THE SAME.

On Monday John Krusen was brought before Esquire Rees charged with selling beverages of too intoxicating a nature to come within the limits of the Potter county law. He waived an examination and gave bail.

Potter County, Pennsylvania Potpourri – Volume I
1880 through 1884

Amos Veeley was the next call of his Honor, on a similar charge as above. No prosecutor appearing, the defendant was discharged, and Court adjourned till next time. And thus ends a week's work in the Justices' Court of Coudersport.

A correspondent of the Emporium *Independent*, writing from the Forest House, under date of February 11th, says: Last Wednesday four men and teams started from one of the jobs above Emporium for Potter County, stopping at one or more of your hotels to drink and replenish their bottles. Three came through all right to Avery's, but the fourth, who was driving Mr. Williams' team, lost consciousness down by the Salt Works, and was found late in the evening near Dennis Hall's, so drunk and so near frozen to death that he did not know who he was or where he wanted to go. Next morning he discovered he was minus team, whip, blankets, gum coat, cap and his overcoat torn half off of him, and he had no idea how it all happened. Going on to Mr. Williams' he found the team had ran home and stood out all that freezing night and were thoroughly chilled. Comment is needless.

- Last week Dr. Mattison removed from the hand of a daughter of Albert Colcord, of Homer, a piece of a needle which had been in the hand over three years. The girl got the needle in her hand by falling on the floor. The point and eye broke off leaving the middle, nearly an inch long, which could not be removed, when surgical aid was called on account of swelling. The piece removed was badly corroded.

The Potter Enterprise
Wednesday Evening, February 28, 1883 – Vol. IX, No. 41

MARRIED.

HEAD – QUIMBY – At the residence of the bride's grandfather in Homer, Pa., Feb. 22d, by Rev. A. A. Craw, Mr. Charles M. Head, of Oswayo, Pa., to Miss Flora A. Quimby, of Homer, Pa.

Millport. Letters from Sedgwick City, Kansas, report the death by diphtheria, of Nellie, oldest daughter of Charles Barnes, formerly of this place.

Whites Corners. Mr. James Statham died very suddenly a few days ago.

Carson Holsted.

Many have wished to hear about the present condition of the boy, whose father was sent to prison for neglect and abuse. All will remember the wretched condition of the child at the preliminary examination last November. On Saturday last I visited him, at Mr. Estes' in Oswayo. I found him walking about the house spry and active. His health is almost wholly restored. He talks fluently and can sing some pieces quite well. His eye is bright and clear. Though Mrs. Estes has had the care of him only nine weeks and had to teach him as she would an infant, he shows an aptness to learn and a readiness to obey that are commendable. Those who rescued him from his wretched condition, under his father, and have cared for him so tenderly, deserve great commendation. He has truly a good home.

A. Cone.

TOWNSHIP ELECTIONS.
The Result in the Various Townships Last Tuesday.
ABBOTT.

Constable – Louis Hoppe; Assessor – Louis Hoppe; Clerk – Fred Woelfel; Treasurer – Fred Bodler; Overseer of Poor – Anton Kilbeck; Supervisor – Henry Zoerb; Auditor – Otto Paul; School Directors – Marcus Handwerk, Edward Wenzel; Inspectors – William Sandbach, Otto Braun; Judge – Christian Broderson.

ALLEGANY.

Justice – Frank Bishop, 82, L. B. Morley, 79; Supervisor – D. H. Veeley; Constable – Isaac Kidney; Assessor – Chas. Coats; Treasurer – James Currier; Clerk – L. Heggie; Auditor – Charles Nelson, 67, Eli Nelson, 55; School Directors – M. A. Veeley, 69, E. Kelley, 4. I. D. School Directors – Charles Nelson, 3 yrs, Samuel Atkinson, 3 yrs, J. R. Bird, 2 yrs; Judge – E. J. Kies; Inspectors – Wilbur Slaughter, Charles Nelson; Overseer of Poor – John Mattison, 33, Horace Peet, 40.

BINGHAM.

Justice – A. A. Johnson; Supervisor – E. B. Lewis, Z. O. Bacon; Constable – M. N. Babcock; Assessor – D. Worden; Treasurer – A. N. Clark; Clerk – L. B. Lewis; Auditor – N. J. Peck; School Directors – J. C. Hawley, 71, A. H. Briggs, 83, L. J. Thompson, 69, Abel Bishop, 69; Judge – B. R. Grover; Inspectors – E. L. Monroe, John Holbert; Overseer of Poor – John Henry, 76, J. E. Harvey, 69, A. C. Crum, 68, D. T. Hanber, 77.

COUDERSPORT.

Burgess – F. W. Knox; Council – P. A. Stebbins, C. S. Jones; School Directors – C. A. Stebbins, W. F. Yunge; Justice – Dan Baker; High Constable – E. D. Lewis; Constable – L. B. Cole; Auditor – H. J. Olmsted; Assessor – Z. J. Thompson; Inspectors – A. F. Hollenbeck, Ed Fickler; Judge – N. H. Goodsell; Overseer of Poor – W. W. Thompson.

CLARA.

Assessor – F. P. Brooks; Supervisor – Timothy Glines; Treasurer – Florentine Stevens; Clerk – Jas. H. Cole; Auditor – W. A. Cole; School Directors – Ellen A. Glines, Helen D. Brooks, Anson Chapman; Judge – Jesse Morey; Inspector – Ezra Bessey, C. S. McDonald; Constable – G. R. Fosmer; Oversee of Poor – A. J. Fosmer.

EULALIA.

Supervisor – Joseph Guenter; Justice – Franklin Phelps; School Directors – E. M. Baker, 3 yrs, C. C. Breunle, 3 yrs, J. D. Earle, 2 yrs; Assessor – Mason Nelson; Constable – J. D. Earle; Judge – J. M. Spafford; Inspector – E. N. Woodcock; Overseer of Poor – C. Stearns, 32, J. M. Spafford, 67; Treasurer –

Potter County, Pennsylvania Potpourri – Volume I
1880 through 1884

Jacob Klein; Auditor – G. W. Snyder, 66, B. G. Clark, 33; Clerk – Jacob Lehman.

GENESEE.

Justice – J. J. Waterman, 74, Pat Roach, 44; Supervisor – N. Keech, 30, Willard Hickox, 77; Auditor – John McGinnis; Judge – Josiah Webster; Inspectors – John Hart, John Collins; Assessor – Ira Easton; Overseer of Poor – John Carney; Constable – W. W. Atherton; Clerk – C. W. Parker; Treasurer – S. G. Rooney; School Directors – N. Chapman, 63, H. H. Hall, 56.

HARRISON.

Supervisor – M. N. Brooks, 76, S. C. Lewis, 71; Constable – B. H. Harrison; Overseer of Poor – S. K. Stevens; School Directors – G. W. Stevens, 64, Geo. Whitman, 114, S. K. Stevens, 77, A. E. Holcomb, 63, Frank Hand, 48; Treasurer – J. A. Nealey; Assessor – C. H. Doud; Judge – J. A. Nealy; Auditor – D. D. Chapin; Inspector – D. D. Chapin, S. N. Stone; Clerk – J. W. Stevens.

HECTOR.

Constable – C. P. Kilbourne; Supervisor – J. M. Swimlar; Overseer of Poor – J. M. Swimlar; Auditor – J. S. Reynolds; Judge – W. D. Redner; Assessor – D. A. Abbey; Treasurer – A. Wilbur; Clerk – A. D. Redner; Inspectors – D. A. Sunderlin; M. A. Leonard; School Directors – J. W. Lewis, 52, A. M. Metcalf, 56, Amos Northrop, 36, Joseph Brooks, 25.

HOMER.

Supervisor – H. M. Case; Auditor – James Wallace; School Directors – W. C. Chesbro; Walter Edgcomb; Treasurer – P. McKinney; Clerk – W. A. Crosby; Constable – Eli Glaspy; Inspectors – John ___, John Gordnier; Judge – G. F. Younglove; Overseer of Poor – W. Clesa; Justice – J. McCann; Assessor – James Bundy.

HEBRON.

Justice – S. Greenman, 39, F. W. Lane, 19; Supervisor – R. Stearns, 38, Wm. Reynolds, 22; Constable – E. D. Clare, 36, A. C. Castle, 24; Assessor – W. C. Reynolds, 39, Myron Estes, 21; Treasurer – W. W. Dwight; Clerk – John Schollard; Auditor – C. A. Estes, 36, R. Swift, 24; School Directors – W. L. Campbell, 39, C. W. Gorham, 59, Olin Bly, 23; Judge – A. Ball; Inspectors – D. B. Lowrey, Wm. Clare; Overseer of Poor – E. H. Bishop.

LEWISVILLE.

Burgess – G. C. Marion; Council – C. M. Allen, G. H. Cobb, C. E. Burt, E. Blackman, James Nickerson, E. Rathbone; School Directors – F. M. Bronson, H. A. Gridley; Overseers of Poor – W. A. Bishop, 74, C. E. Baker, 75; Judge – M. D. Drake; Inspectors – C. T. Freeman, E. A. Burt; Auditor – C. A. Lewis; Constable – Fred Baker; Assessor – W. M. Hosley; High Constable – E. A. Hovey.

OSWAYO.

Treasurer – Arthur G. Wells; Supervisor – Thomas Coyle; Overseer of Poor – L. D. Estes; Justice – Samuel Beebe; Clerk – D. M. Wheeler; Assessor – G. F. Rowley; Constable – E. D. Rice; School Directors – A. S. Lyman, J. H. Dexter, N. H. Rice; Auditor – T. J. Farnham; Judge – Allen Hammond; Inspectors – D. M. Wheeler, John Morley.

PIKE.

Supervisor – J. S. Phenix; Auditor – G. W. Sutton; School Directors – J. Ives, 28, Deloss Sutton, 20, Ed Swartwood, 19; Clerk – F. A. Brown; Treasurer – S. J. Acker; Constable – E. H. Haxton; Assessor – Deloss Sutton; Overseer of Poor – O. L. Blackman; Inspectors – O. C. Flynn, G. T. Foster; Judge – O. L. Blackman.

KEATING.

Supervisor – Casper Hoffmeister; Constable – J. M. Younglove; Assessor – John E. Earl; Treasurer – J. W. Dingee, 19, Geo. C. Lewis, 19; Auditor – A. Bulaskia (to fill vacancy), Austin Crosby (full term); Clerk – D. C. Rum; Overseer of Poor – C. Hoffmeister, 2 yrs, 24, A. E. Nelson, 2 yrs, 19, C. Hoffmeister, 1 yr, 15, C. Dingee, 1 yr, 15; Inspectors – E. Prouty, Z. L. Moody; School Directors – A. Bulaskia, 39, Oscar Andrews, 37, Ed Fourness, 18, J. W. Dingee, 13; Judge – Oscar Andrews.

PLEASANT VALLEY.

Judge – J. C. Fessenden; Inspectors – Earnest Keeler, C. P. Reed; Constable – D. F. Yentzer; Supervisors – Philander Reed, H. D. North; Clerk – J. L. Yentzer; Treasurer – I. V. Reed; Assessor – Robert McDowell; Auditor – Otis Weimer; Overseer of Poor – B. A. Haynes, 19, Ansel Joseph 20; School Directors – Earnest Lamp, 37, H. D. North, 34, Chas. Haynes, 25.

PORTAGE.

Supervisor – M. M. Hackett; Oversee of Poor - ___ ___; School Directors – F. N. White, E. O. Austin; Auditors – L. D. Ripple; J. M. Conrad; Inspectors – C. Morris, C. D. Austin; Judge – M. J. Young; Constable – O. M. Card; Clerk – S. B. Haskins; Treasurer – Frank Austin; Assessor – C. A. Lamont.

ROULET.

Supervisor – Henry Kimm; Constable – Alonzo Morey; Treasurer – John V. Weimer; School Directors – Christopher Knowlton, Wm. Earnst; Town Clerk – Henry Teuscher; Assessor – O. R. Webb; Auditor – Jasper Card; Judge – D. W. Reed; Overseer of Poor – Henry Kimm; Inspectors – J. J. Carey, D. F. Manning.

SHARON.

Justice – Dana Drake; Supervisor – A. F. Smith; Constable – J. C. Bump; Assessor – N. C. Newton; Treasurer – Jacob Failing; Clerk – Fred N. Newton; Auditor – M. A. Nichols; School Directors – Adelbert Deremer, S. H. Manley; Judge – James Dickinson; Inspectors – E. A. Perkins, Charles Warner; Overseer of Poor – G. W. Hall.

SUMMIT.

Justice – Merrick Jackson; Supervisor – Henry Reed; Clerk – C. H. Ruscher; Treasurer – Merrick Jackson; Constable – John Wallace; Auditor – James Blauvelt; Judge – James Nelson; Assessor – Lester Watson; Inspectors – Byron Bassett, Miles Blauvelt; School Directors – O. G. Jackson, James Nelson.

SYLVANIA.

Justice – J. W. Thorn; Constable – George C. Colegrove; Supervisor – George Clark; Overseer of Poor – George Clark; Treasurer – George C. Rees; Clerk – A. J. Haskins; Auditor – J. M. Rees; School Directors – W. B. Pierce,

Leroy Haskins; Judge – Isaac Wheeler; Inspectors – Pardon Haskins, James Rees; Assessor – Alvin Jordan.

STEWARDSON.

Treasurer – G. W. Slarrow; Clerk – Martin Jeorg; Justice – Martin Jeorg; Constable – James Impson; Supervisor – Reuben Hess; School Directors – Willard Andresen, 2, Wesley Allen, 14; Auditor – John Vannatta; Assessor – Martin Jeorg; Judge – G. W. Slarrow; Inspectors – Martin Jeorg, Wesley Allen; Collector – James Impson.

SWEDEN.

Supervisor – M. E. White, 50, A. W. Rossman, 66; School Directors – Wm. Snyder, 70, Henry Tauscher, 75; Auditor – C. C. Chase, 77, C. D. Corsaw, 32; Overseer of Poor – H. J. Neefe; Constable – S. O. Dodd; Judge – A. Chase; Inspectors – M. O. Harris, J. S. Bird; Assessor – C. M. Herrington; Treasurer – J. W. Neefe; In favor of stock running large, 43, against stock running at large, 39.

ULYSSES.

Supervisors – W. J. Grover, Miles Dykeman; Assessor – G. W. Bennett; Constable – E. B. Monroe; Treasurer – A. Burt; Clerk – H. T. Reynolds; Judge – A. Burt; Inspectors – M. S. Crum, E. H. Bassett; Auditors – Wm. Dent, M. S. Harvey; School Directors – Charles Ross, H. T. Reynolds; Overseer of Poor – W. J. Grover.

WEST BRANCH.

Supervisor – B. F. Burrows; Clerk – A. Bisbee; Assessor – J. M. Connable; Overseer of Poor – C. Rukgaber; Treasurer – G. W. Fowler; Constable – Fred Burrows; Auditors – C. Hehl, 3 yrs, J. S. Slocum, 1 yr; Judge – N. K. Prouty; Inspectors – F. Stritz, F. Stuart; School Directors – G. W. Fowler, 3 yrs, 36, W. Deisroth, 3 yrs, 41, A. P. Logue, 1 yr, 63.

WHARTON.

Constable – Orrin Courtright; Justice – B. F. Berfield; Treasurer – W. G. Wilbur; Overseers of Poor – Seth Briggs, Perry Devol; School Directors – G. A. Logue, 3 yrs, A. J. Bailey, 3 yrs, W. G. Wilbur, 2 yrs; Clerk – W. H. Parmenter; Auditor – Allen Jordan; Assessor – J. B. Burlingame; Inspectors – J. M. Walker, J. M. Devoll; Supervisor – A. D. Nelson, 17, Jesse Carman, 31; Judge – S. F. Horton.

The Potter Enterprise
Wednesday Evening, March 7, 1883 – Vol. IX, No. 42

DIED.

BROWN – At Millport, Pa., March 1st, 1883, Edgar C., only son of Herbert and Nettie Brown, aged 1 year, one week, and 3 days.

"We watched him breathing through the night,
His breathing soft and low,
As in his heart the wave of life,
Kept heaving to and fro.
So silently we seemed to speak,

So slowly moved about,
As we had lent him but half our powers,
To eke his living out.
Our very hopes belied our fears,
Our fear our hopes belied –
We thought him dying when he slept,
And sleeping when he died.
For when the moon came dim and sad,
And chill with early showers,
His quiet eyelids closed – he had
Another morn than ours."

The Potter Enterprise
Wednesday Evening, March 14, 1883 – Vol. IX, No. 43

West Pike. – Mr. Sinette is a happy man. It is a little daughter that gladdens his home.

MARRIED.

HOLLENBECK – JACKSON – At the residence of the bride's parents, March 10th, by Rev. A. A. Craw, Mr. L. A. Hollenbeck, of Coudersport, and Miss Emelina Jackson, of Sweden.

Genesee Forks. Notwithstanding the inclemency of the weather, a company of 51 or 52 friends from this place and Ellisburg, relatives from York's Corners assembled at Norman Chapman's March 10th to celebrate their fifteenth anniversary of their wedding day. It proved a complete surprise to them, but was none the less enjoyable. Some presents were given, a bounteous repast was served, which with meeting old acquaintances, and pleasant conversation, the afternoon passed only too quickly. We wish Mr. and Mrs. Chapman many happy returns of the day.

DIED.

SNYDER – In Sweden, March 4th, Mary Ann Shay, wife of Daniel Snyder, aged 68 years.

CHAFFE – In Coudersport, March 10th, Etta, infant daughter of Charles and Hattie Chaffe, aged three months.

Roulette. Miss Rose Card, of Sartwell Creek, died of scarlet fever, the 28th ult.

Costelloville. Death visited us again last week and claimed the only child of Mr. and Mrs. S. B. Haskins, also an infant child of Mr. and Mrs. Sol Dale.

Allegany. The funeral services of Mrs. Calvin Ford was held at the Judd school house last Saturday, five children are left motherless, a home without a wife and mother, and a vacant place in the neighborhood not easily filled.

- At the election of Directors in Genesee Independent School District, held March 3d, Bryan McGinnis and Patrick Roach were selected.

TRIED FOR MURDER!
COMMONWEALTH VS. GEORGE CHISHOLM!
SYNOPSIS OF THE EVIDENCE AS BROUGHT OUT AT THE TRIAL

Monday court was called by Judge Olmsted and some routine business transacted. The attorneys for Chisholm asked leave to make application for continuance Tuesday morning.

Tuesday morning the court room was packed with people. The attorneys again asked for more time. Judge Williams, on the bench, granted them until noon. At noon the request for continuance was refused, and attachments for witnesses were issued, both for the defence and the commonwealth.

Most of our readers are acquainted with the particulars of this case. In September last, in the township of Hector, Thomas Waters received a pistol shot from a weapon in the hands of George Chisholm, which caused his death a few days thereafter. At that time we gave full particulars as we picked them up from parties, having some knowledge of the affair and at this time we do not propose to give a rehash of the story, but will try and give the evidence as brought out in court, and our readers can form their own opinions and ___ them best, and most equitable.

Court called shortly after two o'clock p.m. and a few minutes later Sheriff Monroe appeared with Mr. Chisholm who took a seat back of his attorneys, after shaking hands with a few acquaintances and bowing to others.

The prisoner's complexion showed the bleaching effect of his confinement in jail, but a short time in the court-room brought color to his face again. The room was intolerably close and warm. Chisholm was neatly dressed in a suit of black, evidently new, and he had somewhat of a ministerial appearance, we believe that was his profession at one time. Over all he wore a black cape, of the style fashionable for gentlemen some years ago. He appeared calm and his nerves were very steady for a man about to be tried for his life.

District Attorney Cobb read the indictment, to which the prisoner, in a low tone of voice plead "not guilty."

The impaneling of a Jury commenced at once. C. H. Loucks, of Hector, was the first man called, and was objected to by the defence for cause; Wm. Stevens, of Sharon, was the second and a preemptory challenge from the commonwealth relieved him of further trouble. In the following order the entire list was gone through, with results:

3 L. F. Rice, West Branch, peremptory challenge by defence.
4 Henry Rogers, Allegany, directed to stand aside and await further proceedings.
5 Page Goesbeck, Roulet, was the first Juror selected and sworn.
6 Henry Dwire, Stewardson, passed same as No. 4.
7 Burt Reed, Roulet, rejected by the com'th.
8 Wm. W. Trask, West Branch, rejected by defence.
9 A. Bisbee, West Branch, rejected by com'th.

10 E. M. Bishop, Hebron, passed.
11 Arthur Barclay, Wharton, not in attendance, and name taken from box.
12 W. H. Rexford, Sylvania, passed.
13 Frank Welton, Wharton, rejected by def't.
14 Eli Rees, Sylvania, same.
15 Rob't McDowell, Roulet, same.
16 Anthony Cochran, Genesee, had not heard of the case and had read nothing of it, the first man of the kind found, but not the last, passed.
17 Wm. Mattison, Sharon, so far as reading or hearing of the case, a full partner of No. 16, was excused by the court.
18 W. J. Brown, Sharon, rejected by the def't.
19 John Gordnier, Homer, same.
20 Seymour Norton, Coudersport, made No. 2 in the Jury box.
21 E. E. Kelly, Allegany, accepted.
22 Asal Marble, Harrison, not in attendance.
23 Thomas G. Hull, Ulysses, rejected by def't.
24 S. E. Crittenden, Oswayo, rejected by com'th.
25 L. B. Lewis, Bingham, accepted.
26 Wm. Wilkinson, Hector, passed.
27 Coleman Smith, Oswayo, accepted.
28 R. H. Young, Ulysses, rejected by defence.
29 Geo. Clark, Sylvania, same.
30 J. B. Stewart, Oswayo, accepted.
31 E. D. Leet, Ulysses, accepted.
32 Geo. Greengrass, Hector, passed.
33 J. L. Allen, Clara, had conscientious scruples against capital punishment, and was excused.
34 Elymus Hackett, Lewisville, had conscientious scruples, but not strong enough to be rejected, and he was passed.
35 E. S. Worden, Hector, rejected by def't.
36 C. H, Kilbourne, Hector, accepted.
37 Seth Briggs, Wharton, rejected by def't.
38 M. J. Young, Portage, passed.
39 Edwin Dodd, Sweden, rejected by def't.
40 F. D. Weimer, Clara, accepted.
41 C. C. Nelson, Sweden, passed.
42 John Collar, Genesee, rejected by def't.
43 John Zingerle, West Branch, rejected by def't.
44 Jas. H. Dexter, Oswayo, accepted.
45 Albert Parker, Hector, passed.
46 G. W. Bennett, Ulysses, accepted.
47 Ambrose Ball, Hebron, evidently bound not to serve and was rejected by com'th.
48 W. H. Crosby, Homer, the last name in the box, was accepted as the 12th Juryman.

The Jury as completed is as follows:

Potter County, Pennsylvania Potpourri – Volume I
1880 through 1884

Page Groesbeck, Seymour Norton, E. E. Kelly, L. B. Lewis, Coleman Smith, J. B. Stewart, E. D. Leet, C. H. Kilbourne, F. D. Weimer, James H. Dexter, G. W. Bennett, W. H. Crosby. They are classed as to occupation farmers, 9; laborers, 3.
    J. C. Cavanaugh and Erastus Lewis were sworn as tip staffs to attend Jury.
    WEDNESDAY MORNING 9 A.M.
    Court room full; a large number of ladies in attendance. Case opened briefly by Edson Hyde, Esq., Dr. A. L. Bottom called and sworn, lived at Westfield, am a physician and surgeon; was called to treat Thos. Waters at his father's house, in Hector twp., Friday, 3 or 4 o'clock p.m.; found him on the bed suffering from a gun shot wound; wound in left side about 1 ¼ inch above joint of hip bone and inside, direction of wound backward and downward; probed the wound slightly; gave him opiates hypodermically to relive intense pains; gave him quieting powders, gave him morphine, he was laboring under depression from shock to nervous system caused by injury; stayed about one hour, visited him next day in company with Dr. Humphrey, of Osceola as counsel; some symptoms of fatal termination. He was not then in a dying condition in my judgment, did not think he would recover; saw him again at post mortem examination, Sunday a little before dark. Dr. Pritchard, of Harrison Valley, assisted at post mortem examination; found that the course of the ball was downward, inward and backward, lodged in front of lower portion of backbone, passed through abdominal walls, membraneous lining through small intestine and muscles examined heart and lungs, found them in a healthy condition; believe his death resulted from the gun shot wound. The wound was necessarily fatal; bullet identified by witness.
    CROSS EXAMINED – First at the house of Waters on Friday night; nothing in line of course of ball to deflect; angle of probe would indicate the line of pistol, course of ball angled downward about 45 degrees, or a little less, directions of wound indicated that party shot stood at side, and not in front of party shooting and pistol held at about an angle of 45 degrees; used about ½ grain of morphine at first dose hypodermically; doses left from ½ to ¼ grain, probably ½ dozen or more; directed that he should take powder in from 4 to 6 hours to control pain. From the nature of wound the patient would not necessarily come to a comatose state, but was likely to have faculties impaired just before death. Deceased was about 5 ft. 10 inches in height, weight 150 to 160 pounds and a vigorous young man.
    Dr. Pritchard called and sworn. Reside at Harrison Valley; am a physician and surgeon; assisted Dr. Bottom in post mortem examination at house of Waters, on the body of Thomas Waters; was there before Dr. Bottom some time, do not remember just what time commenced; body was bloated and was yet warm (wound and course of ball, evidence about same as Dr. Bottom). Identified ball found in body, organs of body in normal condition; death was caused by gun shot wound.
    CROSS EXAMINATION – Did not see patient in life; he was a strong and well developed young man; downward, angle of wound between 25 and 45 degrees, pistol must been held at considerable of an angle; ball passed only

through soft tissues and course was almost straight; ball must have been fired a little from left side.

Mrs. Beulah Works called and sworn. Reside in Hector, in the neighborhood of Chisholm's; saw Thomas Waters at Chisholm's on the 29th of September; Thos. came up to gate, in front of house, Chisholm was out after a load of wood; Thomas called Chisholm out, said he wanted to talk to him; I was before front door; door was open; Thos. Waters said Mr. C. will you please come out, I want to talk with you; did not hear Chisholm's reply; Thomas then said "I don't care to;" Chisholm came in and laid down wood, said "some of you put it in the stove" and then walked in the other room – sitting room. He pushed sitting room door shut; was in the sitting room but a short time, came through the room and went out the front door and went down to the gate where Thomas stood. Thomas says, Mr. Chisholm was you the man who chopped into the line fence or struck an axe into it. Mr. Chisholm bowed, did not hear him say anything. Thomas called Mr. Chisholm a son of a bitch; Mr. Chisholm stood as if talking, moving his head; did not hear that Mr. Chisholm said anything. Thomas says "a bastardly son of a bitch, eh? That's what you are." Mr. Chisholm had his hand in his right coat pocket made a motion, and Tommy said, don't show that, Tommy says you dare not lay aside the revolver and call me that, if he did he said he would whip him, or something else "if I am man enough." Mr. Chisholm put his left hand on gate to open it, drew the revolver and walked out of the gate, walked up in front of Tommy drawing the revolver up even with Tommy's breast. Tommy says "Mr. Chisholm don't shoot," making motion to push revolver down; heard report of revolver; as revolver went off Tommy said again "don't shoot." Tommy went from the gate before he was shot, walking backward, Chisholm following. Chisholm carried revolver by his side till he got where Tommy stood; Tommy retreated 10 to 14 feet before the revolver was fired. Have pointed out to Mr. Hyde, Mr. Rees and others where shooting took place. Tommy fell back to the ground when shot; Chisholm stood and looked at him, revolver still in hand; did not undertake to help him up. Tommy got up and fell again, got up again and took hold of Chisholm. Mr. Chisholm drew the revolver again ___ you want another one?" the pistol pointing toward Tommy. Tommy fell again, tried to get up again, when his brother James Waters came down the road. James put him on the wagon and took him home; James helped him to the wagon, Mr. Chisholm did not assist. As I went out the gate I said to Mr. Chisholm, "you are a murderer, if that man dies," he said "he did" I said "he didn't," Mrs. Chisholm said "yes, he did," repeated it twice. Mr. Chisholm said "you do not know what I have suffered from that family this summer;" I told him "I was sorry I was there," he said "you were sent here a purpose," once he said he wished it had not happened.

CROSS EXAMINATION – I live about a mile from Chisholm's; do not know in what direction; do not know points compass, road runs south-west, about one mile from my house to Chisholm's rode up with James Waters that day on a bark rack, Thomas passed along a short time before James passed my house. I asked to ride; got off at Chisholm's; found Mr. and Mrs. Chisholm and daughter in the house, took a seat in front of the door which was open; it was about five o'clock in the afternoon. The house is as far from the street as about two-thirds across the court room (about 40 feet). My sight is good, hearing good, had been at Chisholm's about five minutes when Thomas Waters came to the gate; Mr. Chisholm was in the room; had no special conversation with Mr. Chisholm. Mr. Chisholm soon went out into the woodshed; cannot describe clothes, do not know whether he had a hat or coat on. Thomas said at the gate, "Mr. Chisholm will you please come out here, I want to talk with you," did not understand reply; heard Thomas say "I don't care to," do not know what that was in answer to. They did not act as though they were made at the gate at first; saw no indications of anger when Thomas called Chisholm "a son of a bitch." Council for defence requested witness to repeat the evidence given on direct examination from the time Thomas called Chisholm a bastardly son of a bitch (repeated very close). Cross examined as to evidence given at Harrison Valley, in September; do not think Thomas had hold of Chisholm when the pistol went off. Do not think that I said the first word I said after the shot was fired, that I expected it would end in murder. Lena (Mrs. Chisholm's daughter) sat near the window, facing the road; told Mr. Chisholm I would have to take my oath to the occurrence; am friendly with the Waters family; was equally friendly with the Chisholm's.

Re-direct, had been invited by Mr. Chisholm to call but a short time previous; had an errand there that day.

James Waters called and sworn. Am a brother of Thomas Waters, deceased, of Hector; was near Chisholm's when the difficulty occurred; was seventeen rods about Chisholm's house setting on my wagon. First saw my brother coming down the road, he walked to Chisholm's gate and said he wanted to see him; Chisholm was out after wood; Chisholm asked him to come in; Thomas declined; saw Chisholm come out the front door; about four or five rods from door to gage. Mr. Chisholm came to gate; Thomas asked him if he had been cutting through fence? Did not hear reply; told him he wanted him to keep off until the old man (Mr. Waters, Sr.) came home or he would put him off; Chisholm said you little bastard son-of-a-bitch you can't do any thing; Thomas said you come out and try it, Chisholm stepped to gate and pulled out the revolver; Thomas told him to put it up, he did not want anything like that here; the pistol was pointing at my brother's breast; brother put out his hand to put it aside, pressing it down, the pistol cracked and Thomas fell; I ran down and asked "what does this mean?" brother says "he has shot me and given me a good one;" put my arms around my brother and carried him to the wagon and took him home. Mr. Chisholm said nothing while I was there; Chisholm made no move to examine injury; from Chisholm's to Water's home about one-fourth mile; Chisholm did not offer to assist in removing my brother; got home about five o'clock; went five or six miles after a doctor; Thomas died Sunday morning.

CROSS EXAMINATION – Brother younger than I am, he was 23 years past; we had been to Westfield that day; I stopped when I met my brother coming from home towards Chisholm's, and waited there, first heard my brother say, "Mr. Chisholm I would like to see you," "all right, come in, won't you?"

Mr. Chisholm said; my brother did not ask him to come out into the road at that time (examined as to evidence given at preliminary hearing) both my brother and Mr. Chisholm was in the house from two to five minutes; think Chisholm had no coat on at a wood pile; my brother told him if he caught him on the land he would ___ wanted him to understand it, next heard my brother say if he would come out into the road and say so he would thump him if he was big enough; told him or dared him out two or three times, Chisholm then came out of the gate drawing his revolver at the same time, letting it hang down by his side; as Chisholm came through the gate my brother backed up fourteen feet, Chisholm following him up; think my brother shoved the arm holding the revolver down, before it went off; could see a man going from Chisholm's door to the gate, all the way, from where I was; the spot where my brother lay was fourteen feet from the gate-way and nearly in the beaten road; have stated all I heard my brother say; my brother did say "he has shot me and given me a good one, but it is all right he will pay for this;" Mr. Chisholm and I had no conversation; did not see Thomas take Chisholm by the collar; brother did not stop where I met him and passed but a word with him as he passed on; I had no reason for stopping in the road, at that time; it was about 5 minutes from the time I stopped until the crack of the pistol; actions were hasty; don't think my brother was angry at first; did state at Harrison Valley that when the two were in the road that they worked toward each other, but thought I had corrected it; I have been acquainted with Chisholm about three years; there had been some unfriendly feeling between us; there was no unfriendly feeling on my part at the time this occurred; called him a son of a bitch, at Harrison Valley on first examination; have been on good terms with Chisholm since living there; did not on or about September 1st, 1882, say that I would give $5 to have that son of a bitch licked (referring to Chisholm) and pay the costs; did not swear at Chisholm in September last, and slap his face.

David Widger called and sworn. Live in Harrison Valley, know Chisholm, saw Chisholm between five and six o'clock at his house the night of the occurrence; Chisholm said he had shot Thomas Waters, said he had nothing against him and that he was not the man he ought to have shot; advised him to give himself up; went with him to Westfield; when most there he said he wanted to see Mr. Strang; Mr. Stranng is a lawyer; went to see Strang; told Strang he came for council; said he had shot Thomas Waters; Strang said if he had shot Waters he could do nothing for him. He said Waters had took hold of him and shook him around and he shot him.

CROSS EXAMINATION – Was on friendly terms with the Chisholm's. He said he had shot Thomas Waters, was sorry he had done it, and would rather have given a thousand dollars or something of that sort if the accident had not happened; will not say that I was not under the influence of spirits that day; think I did have something that day. Question – Did Chisholm say, Thomas took hold of him, shook him about and he shot him under excitement. No. Sir. Was sworn at Harrison Valley; may have testified at Harrison "I said, George that is not the man you ought to have shot, and he said no that is not the man I ought to have shot." Chisholm expressed no vindictive feelings against Waters at any time during our conversation. I know H. S. Tuttle, did not tell Tuttle that I knew enough to clear Chisholm; did not say that I knew all their plans and threats, and was in the ring.

H. Harrison. – Live at Harrison Valley, was constable in September last, arrested Mr. Chisholm. Revolver, a 32 Smith & Wesson, single action, produced and identified as one received of Mrs. Chisholm on Monday, October 2d.

Wm. Hurlburt. – Live in Harrison, know Chisholm, he told me he had trouble with the Waters' and if any of them laid hands on him he would shoot them, as he was afraid of his life, at times; said he had a revolver.

CROSS EXAMINED – Told me this in the road near the hotel at Harrison Valley, understood if they laid hands on him he would defend himself.

Wm. Trim. – Live at Westfield, heard Chisholm say he was going to get the bark if he had to do it at the muzzle of his revolver; was referring to Wm. Waters (stricken out); saw Chisholm have a revolver previous to the shooting at Sept. court.

George Lane. – Live at Westfield; revolver produced; sold George Chisholm such a revolver May 29th, last.

Charles Proctor. – Reside in Brookfield, was staying at Chisholm's in May last; was with him when he purchased a revolver, similar to one produced; said he bought the revolver to defend himself; said he was afraid of his life, this was on Chisholm's land, and he exhibited the revolver at the time.

Mrs. Nancy Waters. – Am the mother of Thomas Waters; he was brought home about five o'clock Saturday night; he put his arms around my neck and asked if father was coming home at night; said he should stay but a little time; said his time was short; said this just daylight Sunday ___ time.

S. K. Stevens. – In September last resided in Harrison, seven or eight miles from Waters'; was at Waters the morning Thomas died, when I went in he said his affidavit could not be taken too soon; the statement was then taken by me, and reduced to writing; statement was taken about daylight (statement identified and marked exhibit 1); his mind seemed to be clear, but he was weak.

Julian Gill. – Was at Waters when messenger went after men to take statement; Thomas said they could not do it too soon, this was Sunday morning.

Flora Waters. – Am a sister of Thomas Waters deceased; first saw him after he was shot when he was carried into the house Saturday night near midnight; he said he did not think he was going to last very long.

Dr. Bottom recalled. – Told Thomas Waters of his condition; that he would probably die; when first saw him Waters made a statement, before it was executed he was informed that he would probably die (statement identified, and marked as exhibit No. 2); Recross statement taken about 2 o'clock Saturday; Thomas Waters was not questioned, made it himself. At that time his mind was clear; do not think he was told that *all* hope was gone.

Susan Waters. – Thomas Waters was my brother-in-law; he said Saturday night "they don't give me very much hope"; Sunday morning said they could not take his testimony too soon.

Potter County, Pennsylvania Potpourri – Volume I
1880 through 1884

Edson Hyde. – Was present when statement of Thomas Waters was taken; Thomas Waters was sworn before S. K. Stevens, J.P. I reduced the statement to writing as given (exhibit No. 1, 2d statement identified).

CROSS EXAMINED – Learned that he had made a written statement, on Saturday, which was used at preliminary examination.

Com'th offer exhibit No. 1, 2d statement as evidence; defence object to certain portions of statement as irrelevant, and not admissible, objection sustained, and balance of statement read in evidence.

EXHIBIT No. 1.
DYING DECLARATION OF THOMAS WATERS.
Taken at the house of William Waters, October 1st, A.D. 1882:

Thomas Waters, being duly sworn, according to law, deposeth and saith: My name is Thomas Waters, aged 24 years, the 9th day of next March; I reside with my parents, William Waters and Nancy Waters, in Hector township, Potter county, Penn'a. On the 29th day of September, A.D., 1882, I was wounded by a pistol ball, and having been informed that the nature of the wound is such that it will probably prove fatal and that it may result in death at any moment, I make the statement with a full knowledge of my condition. About six o'clock on the 29th day of September, 1882, I wend down to George Chisholm's and told him I would like to talk with him; Chisholm came out to the fence; I told him he must not cut another hole through the line fence while my father was gone, if he did I would kick his ribs in. He said, "Thomas Waters, you will get sick of that work, you dirty low-lived son-of-a-bitch." I told him he dare not come out into the road and tell me that, if he did I would cuff his ears if I was man enough. He came through the gate, turned partly around and shut the gate, then turned around again and pointed his revolver at me; he drew the revolver out of his pocket as he came through the gate. I told him to put that up he did not want to use any such thing as that here, but he pointed it at me. I tried to get hold of the revolver but could not. I pushed his arm away and reached to get hold of his collar and he shot me. I did not go toward Chisholm at all, but he came toward me with the revolver pointed at me. When he shot me I fell and I do not recollect what happened after that till my brother James put me on the wagon. Chisholm called me a bastard and a son-of-a-bitch. That is what he said. I did not at any time go towards Chisholm or offer to touch him, only as he came into the road and came at me. [I did not have any intention of hurting Chisholm when I went there, but I was mad because he cut the hole through the fence and misused my mother, but I would not have touched Chisholm if he had not come at me with the revolver.] I made a statement to the doctor yesterday but was in great pain and do not know as I stated it fully but I have endeavored to do so now, as I remember it. This is all I think of that happened. I desire Andrew Mallory to sign my name for me as I am too weak.

his
THOMAS X WATERS
mark

Signed in presence of S. K. Stevens and E. Hyde.
Sworn and subscribed before S. K. Stevens, J.P., Oct. 1st, 1882.

The above statement was read and signed in presence of the following persons who certify the above to be correct and true according to Thomas Waters statement.

Andrew Mallory,
Flora Waters,
Nancy Waters,
Susan Waters,
James Waters,
M. F. Neiley,
G. B. Glover,
J. H. Gill

(The portion enclosed in brackets was thrown out and not read before the Jury. – Ed.)

Commonwealth rest; defence calls for re-cross examination James Waters; Known M. L. Foster, he was at my house on Oct. 1; he was at my father's house that day; did not say to him that I could not see them at the gate or when the shot was fired; did not say I could not hear what Chisholm said.

Mrs. Work re-cross – Reside at Harrison Valley; did not say that Tommy had hold of his arm when the shot was fired; talked some with James of what occurred at the gate on our way to the preliminary hearing; sat three feet back of the door; have been to Chisholm's before this occurrence; was there last before berrying time.

Defence opened by John Ormerod, Esq., Exhibit No. 2 offered in evidence.

EXHIBIT No. 2,

Hector, Sept. 30, 1882.

Anti Mortem Statement of Thomas Waters:

I am 23 years of age. I went to the house of George Chisholm on Friday evening, about six o'clock, to tell him he must not come across the line on father's land while he was absent. My father's name is William Waters. I told him (Chisholm) that if he did I would kick his ribs in. He said, "Thomas, you will get sick of that work." He called me a "dirty low-lived son-of-a-bitch." I said "if you will come through the gate and call me that I will cuff your ears if I am man enough." He then took out of his pocket his revolver, opened the gate and came out swung around and pointed his revolver at me, when I reached and grabbed him by the coat collar, after I failed to secure his pistol. As soon as I took him by the collar he fired the pistol and I fell to the ground.

Thomas Waters.
Per Andrew Mallory.

I make this statement with the knowledge that the wound may prove fatal.

Witnesses present:

W. F. Humphrey, M.D.,
A. L. Bottom, M.D.,
A. B. VanGorder,
Sylvester Gill,
M. G. Bowman,
Mary Neeley,

J.H. Gill.

Mrs. Mina Schoonover. – In September last lived in Hector, in sight of Chisholm'' house; on the 29th of Sept. saw Thomas Waters going up the road toward the bark, between five and six o'clock; when driving up the road his sister Flora was with him; the bark road is a little below where I live, on the opposite side. Question: What did his sister say to him as he started up the road? Objected to as incompetent and immaterial. Objection sustained; saw Thomas when he came back; in ten or fifteen minutes saw him again; saw him again in about half an hour on the bark wagon with James, going towards his father's house; Thomas was sitting on the spring board seat; James appeared to be holding him and driving the team; myself and husband went up to Waters; got there as soon as the wagon and James and my husband carried Thomas in; heard Thomas make a statement of how the affair occurred; "Thomas said he went down and called Chisholm out; said Chisholm called him some names; said if he would come into the road and call him that he would fix him or whip him; said Mr. Chisholm came through the gate and he collared him, he jerked him or got him partly down; not certain what; Chisholm said if he did not let him alone he would shoot him; Chisholm drew his revolver; he caught his arm and tried to take it away from him and he shot."

CROSS EXAMINATION – Bark road perhaps 25 rods below my house, when I heard the conversation between Thomas and Flora; they were about four rods apart; Thomas going up the bark road; saw Thomas when he came back, but do not know whether I stood in the door or was at work about the house; VanGorder and Widger went with us to Chisholm's; Thomas was taken in the room and the family came in, stayed a few moments and the family went out; do not think they came in again within fifteen minutes; I was at the preliminary hearing; did not testify there.

RE-DIRECT – Think James had gone for a doctor when Thomas made a statement of occurrence. When Thomas left to go up the bark road, Flora said," Thomas, he isn't there," the answer was "Well, I am going to see;" my house is on an elevation above the land; I have told all the conversation I heard between Thomas and Flora.

RE-CROSS EXAMINED – Do not think I said, in the presence of Mr. and Mrs. VanGorder, that I knew nothing about this affair.

Joel Schoonover. – Lived in Hector township, Sept. 29th; saw James Waters when he went home with Thomas; saw them below my house while on our way to Chisholm's; had heard a shot down towards Chisholm's; went home with Waters; VanGorder and Widger were on the wagon when I met it, James Waters driving, Thomas sitting on spring board seat; helped carry Thomas in and laid him on the bed; the women folks were around the house. Thomas said he went down, called Chisholm out. Chisholm called him a son-of-a-bitch; told him if he would come out into the road and call him that he would lick him. Chisholm came through the gate, took him by the collar. Chisholm said if he did not let him alone he would shoot him; grasped him by the arm to take it (the pistol) away from him and Chisholm shot. This was said in presence of myself and wife only. Saw Flora Waters go towards home that evening before I saw James and

Thomas perhaps half an hour previous; Flora was driving the old man Waters' team; Thomas Waters would weigh about 160 pounds about 5 ½ feet in height; saw Thomas a few minutes before I saw him and James; after he had been to the bark Thomas, in presence of VanGorder, and myself after VanGorder had said, "Tommy, they did not get the bark," said "he knew it, he had just been up." He asked where Chisholm was. I said he had gone home about noon; Thomas said it was a good thing he did not find him there. Tommy then went toward Chisholm's; at this time we were thirty rods above the bark road.

CROSS EXAMINATION – Diagram, showing Chisholm's, the bark road, location of road, &c., in and around where the tragedy occurred, showed witness and recognized as substantially correct. At the time of conversation with Tommy was twelve or fifteen rods from my house. When I heard the shot I was near Widger's; VanGorder was there. It was from 60 to 80 rods from Chisholms. After hearing the shot we started down the road, I to my house, they down toward Chisholm's. From my house to Chisholm's, by the road, is about 80 rods. At the house I examined Thomas, at his request, as he said he thought he was bleeding. No one present except my wife. Thomas seemed to be suffering some; was not then bleeding; the members of the family were in and out frequently, asking him how he felt; he complained of pain in side and leg. Think I did not hear any of the family ask him how it happened; remained at Waters' until about 9 o'clock p.m. A few days after the occurrence told Mrs. Chisholm what Tommy told me at the house. My wife was present. Next told Mr. Cory, this was the day I was subpoenaed, about two weeks ago.

Miss Lena Chisholm. – Am a daughter of George Chisholm; was home 29th of Sept.; saw Thomas Waters drive by that day, Flora Waters was with him; they were going toward home, this was between four and five o'clock; I was near the front door peeling apples; saw James Waters drive up the road, after Thomas perhaps five minutes afterward; Mrs. Works was with James; Mrs. Works came to our house; first saw Tommy again at the upper gate post; at this time my father was out the back door after wood; heard Tommy ask pa to come to the road, that was the first I heard; my father answered "won't you come in?" no, don't care to come in, come down; father said I'll take in my wood and get my hat; came in with the wood and went into the other room and got his hat, do not know if he shut the door or not; the door would swing to till it struck the latch of its own accord; he went to the front door and asked Tommy to come in; don't think Tommy made any answer; father then walked to the road, and leaned upon the lower gate post; they are large posts, about as high as my head; Tommy was leaning against the upper post; the gate was hung with strap and weight; First heard Tommy say I understand you have been up after the bark; "yes I have been up there"; Tommy said it was a damn good thing I wasn't there or you would have got a ball hole through you, if you ever go there again I'll fix you, and if you ain't a damn coward you'll step through the gate now, and I'll fix or lick you, you damn false liar; father then said I don't fight with dogs and beasts; Thomas said I know you have got a revolver, for you drew it on mother to-day, but I ain't afraid of that, you damn coward, just come through the gate; father said I am not afraid to come through the gate, but I am not coming through to fight; Tommy said then if you are not a damn cowardly bastard you'll step through the gate, Tommy was angry; father stepped through the gate, opened the gate with his right hand, stepped through and down, letting the gate swing partly to, holding it with his right hand; did not at that time have a pistol in his hand; Tommy rolled his sleeves up and grabbed pa; pa went to step back through the gate, and he grabbed him by the collar by both hands and jerked him around several times nearly jerking him down, jerked him one way and the other; father said "hold on Tommy, stand back," a number of times; don't know how many; when Tommy was up and pa down the street, Tommy said shoot and be damned; I then saw the revolver in pa's hand, this was the first I saw it; at same time Thomas grabbed his hand; first saw revolver at his side, then heard the report; Thomas dropped on left knee, got up and grabbed pa and said "Jesus"; pa pushed him with his hand, he then fell down, helped himself up by taking hold of pa; heard nothing said then; Thomas walked a few steps up the road, and met James; James asked what is the trouble? Thomas said "he has got one into me, it is a good one, but it is all right," James looked at pa very angry; Thomas said again "'t is all right, Jim, it is all right;" James unbuttoned his clothes and asked where it was; Thomas said "let's go home, it bleeds like hell;" James asked if he could walk he said yes, James assisted him to walk; father did not at any time point his pistol at Tommy and ask "do you want another?" When father started for the road I was going from sitting room to the kitchen; was on the steps at the time of the shooting; Mrs. Works ran down the steps and said "she had seen enough, I expected this, I must go home;" all went down to the gate; Mrs. Works said, Mr. Chisholm you are a cold blooded murderer, and I shall swear against you; Chisholm replied, "why Mrs. Works," she said he only took hold of your wrist to take the revolver away;" "Mrs. Works didn't you see him collar me?" she replied "I did not;" she said to me "Lena won't you go home with me" do not remember that she said anything else except she had got to be a witness; the box and accouterments of the pistol were kept in the kitchen, the room Mrs. Works and the rest of us were in that day; my father kept the pistol in this box in the kitchen when he did not have it with him; when he came out of the sitting room he had his hat in his hand, do not know which hand; saw Mr. Widger when he came to our house that night; he had been drinking, so that it bothered him to get up the steps; Mr. Widger said to father "George, Tom is not the man you ought to have shot;" when he first came to the house. The witness then testified to her father wearing a truss for years on account of a breach and that when the prisoner was going to Westfield, he put on his truss. It is her belief that he did not have it on at the time of the affray; testified that Widger said to Mrs. Chisholm that he had given Tuttle permission to tell what he had heard the night before.

CROSS EXAMINED – Have not detailed words used by Thomas in full; do not remember all he said, he used words I never heard before; do not remember hearing father say one word to Thomas or James after the shooting.

RE-DIRECT – Father said he was sick that day and had been abed nearly all the afternoon.

Mrs. Schoonover re-called – Saw Widger shortly after Thomas was shot, I called him considerably intoxicated.

Mrs. M. J. Griswold. – Live in Leavenworth, Kansas; am a sister of def't; he is about 57 years of age.

Fayette Lewis. – Live at Lewisville; am a surveyor; in February last made a survey of the locality of the occurrence taking levels, &c., draft produced and identified; details of survey, &c. explained and distances given; stated that experiments were made by placing a box 2 ft. 9 in. high in the road, estimating depth of snow under the box 6 in., and parties passed from Chisholm's house to this gate, while others stood on the box to see if parties could be seen all the way from the house to and at the gate the box said to have been placed at the point where James Waters' wagon stood when Thomas Waters was killed; witness standing in gate could not see a man on the box in the road, and part of way from gate to house along the path, could not see man on the box.

Seth Lewis. – Stated that he was on the ground about two weeks after Thomas was shot, examined surroundings; all fence, from the gate to the creek, was six rails high; [said to be in the line of vision from gate to place where James was at time of the shooting.] At the time of survey, at highest point, one _____ judgment, taking the rail off lowered the fence ten inches; detailed experiments same as Fayette Lewis.

Seth Lewis re-called. – The place shown me by Lena Chisholm, as the place where Thomas fell, was about eight feet from the gate, angling down the road and was, in my judgment, same place shown me when the survey was taken. Examined as to the testimony at the preliminary examination. Mrs. Works testified that Tommy had hold of Chisholm when the shot was fired and that Tommy previously stepped toward Chisholm. James Waters swore at preliminary hearing, "I did not see him point the revolver at my brother, only heard the crack," and "I stopped and wanted to hear what was the rumpus." [Referring to stopping his team after meeting Tommy.] Swore that Thomas walked to the wagon with his help.

CROSS-EXAMINED – Have been employed as council for defence since Sept. 30th.

A. D. Cory. – Testified that he assisted Fayette Lewis in making survey of the location of the shooting and surroundings. In experimenting, as to line of vision from place, where James stopped to path from house to gate, could see person only part of the way. From the gate to where a man could be seen, breast high, toward the road was ten feet. Examined as to testimony of Mrs. Works, Widger and James Waters, at Harrison Valley. James swore that, with his assistance, Thomas walked to the wagon.

CROSS-EXAMINED – Was acting for defence at preliminary hearing. Did not take notes of evidence. Upon cross examination did not James say "Chisholm pointed his revolver at Tommy as he came into the road but I did not see the revolver when it cracked?" Answer, No. Commonwealth present paper containing notes of evidence, containing the answer denied, which the witness recognized as his writing. Then explained that he did take some notes, but had forgotten, did not take all, only sketches; and that was minutes of direct examination for the purpose of cross examination.

Perry Brigham testified about the same as previous witness as to diagram, measurements and experiments. At location of affray, by getting out of the road [at the place where James Waters stopped] two feet, could just see an arm of a man standing at point where Tommy fell, according to diagram made by Fayette Lewis. Common height of wagon to top of bolster is 2 ft 9 in. to 2 ft 10 in; a man six feet tall on spring board seat to bark rack, his head would be from six to seven feet above the ground. Standing on the box that day my head was nine feet from the ground.

CROSS-EXAMINED – Standing on the box could see a man standing ten feet outside of gate.

H. A. Gridley testified substantially as given before, by others, in relation to diagram, measurements, &c.

Dr. Ashcraft testified to making examination, about ten days since, and that Chisholm had a breach, mild type of hernia, was not wearing a properly fitted truss.

I. C. Thompson. – Live at the mouth of Potter Brook, about two miles from Chisholm's. Testimony relating principally to diagram and experiments, about same as others.

James Metcalf. – James pointed out to me the day Thomas died, the spot where Thomas was shot. He said "near that low spot." This spot was three and one-half steps from the fence.

CROSS-EXAMINED – This depression is perhaps one foot or a foot and one-half across.

M. L. Foster. – Know Mrs. Works; she said to Wm. Fuller, in my presence, that "Tommy fell six or eight feet from the gate;" heard James Waters say, On Oct. 1st, that he "could not see them at the gate, and only a portion of Tommy when he was shot;" said he "could not hear a word Chisholm said but could only guess from replies made by Tommy;" helped measure Tommy for coffin measured six feet.

CROSS-EXAMINED – Was retained by Mr. Chisholm about one year ago as attorney in civil cases. James made his statements at his father's house, in answer to various questions.

H. S. Tuttle. – Was riding home with James Waters and Mr. VanGorder at one time, when James said, as we passed Chisholm's, "there is a son-of-a-bitch I would like to see licked." Mr. VanGorder said, so would I. James said to VanGorder, "if you will lick him till he can't get off the bed for six weeks I'll give you $5 and pay all expenses." Widger told me he knew enough to clear Chisholm; this was about a month after the affray. He said, I know all their plans and threats, I have been in the ring. Suppose I should swear that Tommy said that day "I will go down and call Chisholm out and if he don't come out I'll go under his bed for him and cut his g-d d---d throat.

CROSS-EXAMINED – The time I came up with James and VanGorder was a year ago last fall, just at dusk. Do not know that Chisholm was in New York at that time. First told of this on Saturday or Monday last, and told it to Mr.

Larrabee; do not remember telling it to any one else before; I was subpoenaed about two weeks ago; have been a witness twice for defendant before to-day.

J. W. Allen. – Know Chisholm; advised Chisholm to buy a pistol, in Feb. 1882, I think; at Sept. term of Court saw James put his hand roughly on the shoulder of Chisholm, and speak roughly in relation to bark.

Fayette Lewis. – A man at the point where James' wagon was would have to be about forty-eight inches higher to see the same point at the gate, with the rails on at the highest place in the fence, as now visible with the rails off, supposing the rails removed to have raised the fence ten inches.

H. Pride, I. C. Thompson, C. P. Kilbourne and others testified to good reputation of Chisholm as a peaceable citizen.

Map of location of affray and surroundings, made by Fayette Lewis, explained by him.

Defendant Rests.

A. B. VanGorder – In rebuttal – Was with Mr. Schoonover at his house the day of the shooting; went towards Waters' to near Widger's house; talked there with Widger perhaps an hour; while there Miss Flora Waters went by driving team; heard the shot, was near Widger's house then; first I saw of Thomas Waters was near bark road with James after the shooting; Mr. Widger, Schoonover and I were together; did not call Widger drunk; Thomas had no conversation with any of us; we went to Waters'; I helped put out the team; came back to the house within about five minutes; saw Mr. and Mrs. Schoonover coming from Waters' house; did not see Schoonover again while I was at the house which was about half an hour.

CROSS-EXAMINED – Mr. Widger that afternoon had been drinking; had seen him two or three times that day; had drank with him; I had been drinking was not very much intoxicated; we, James and I, took the team about fifteen rods, unhitched them, put one in the barn and returned to the house, walking fast; have had difficulty with Mr. Chisholm; heard Schoonover say that he knew nothing of the affair.

Mrs. Susan Waters. – From James Waters' to William Waters' is from 12 to 15 rods; I went to Wm. Waters' in from five to ten minutes after James came out, after carrying Tommy in; Mr. and Mrs. Schoonover were at that time coming from the door toward the road; Thomas did not talk when I went into the house, to amount to anything.

Flora Waters testified to going after water when Thomas was first brought in; Tommy was not left alone by the family at this time; did not hear Tommy talk any; went about fifteen rods after the water.

Mrs. Nancy Waters. – Went into the room when Thomas was carried in; was not out of the room while Mr. and Mrs. Schoonover were present; Thomas did not make any statement whatever while the Schoonovers were there; Thomas suffered some and kept his eyes closed and did not seem to notice anything.

Mr. Widger. – Was with Schoonover the day of the shooting about 4 o'clock; was with him half an hour, VanGorder was there also; while we were together Thomas did not come up the road to where we were and have conversation with any of us.

O. J. Rees, Surveyor, testified to measurements, directions, &c., of the surroundings of the place of the affray. From Schoonover's house to the bridge in a straight line a little over twenty rods; from house to road twelve rods.

E. Hyde. – Appeared before the committing magistrate and reduced the statement of James Waters to writing. On cross examination he did not say that he could not see the pistol; went to Chisholm's premises to make observation March 2d, 1883, from the gate to house &c., and from the gate to where James said his team was. There was a wagon there, James Waters setting on a buckboard seat, when I was in the gate could just see his hat; about three feet from gate, inside, could see the board James sat on, one step farther toward house could see road team and wagon; five or six feet outside of gate could see his hat same as while in the gate; at eight feet could see his waist, one step farther could see his horses. From place, pointed out to me by James, where Thomas fell, could see wagon and road plain; place pointed out was about two feet from wagon track; S. K. Stevens, H. N. Stone, O. J. Rees, Geo. Ross, H. H. Cobb, James Metcalf, James Waters, Mrs. Works and a man living in Chisholm's house were present at this time; Mrs. Works pointed out place, about six inches from where James pointed it out as the place were Thomas fell 14 feet, from fence, from gate 15 feet 6 inches.

CROSS-EXAMINED – James as sitting about eight feet high; view from the gate was obstructed, so could see but top of head; I was on the board and saw James in the gate; will not say that at any point from gate to house one would not be obscured; think perhaps two feet out of the gate one would be obscured; think that with Chisholm at one gate post and Thomas Waters at the other could not see their bodies; from two feet inside to eight feet outside could not see a man's hands if down by his side; on the morning before Thomas died the spot was shown me where Thomas was shot and was substantially as shown me by James; it was out and above the gate.

S. K. Stevens – testified, corroborating, substantially, that of E. Hyde, as to observation and lines of vision, &c.

H. N. Stone – Testimony corroborative, substantially, that of Stevens and Hyde as to measurements and observations.

James Metcalf – Corroborating Stevens, Stone and Hyde as to observations. The place, pointed out as the place where Thomas fall, at this time, was not the place pointed out to me shortly after the death of Thomas, by James Waters.

Mr. VanGorder – Contradicted the evidence of Tuttle, as to James Waters' offer of $5 &c., to have Chisholm whipped.

James Mallory – Know Chisholm, have worked with him; he is a stout man.

Adney Thorp – Consider him a strong man at a lift; have worked with him some.

Edward Flewellen – Consider him a vigorous man.

Commonwealth finished and Court adjourned until Saturday morning.

The argument for the Commonwealth was opened by Isaac Benson, who spoke for an hour and a half. He was followed by D. C. Larrabee for the defence, continuing until noon. In the afternoon Mr. Bemis spoke two hours and a half for the defence and then M. F. Elliott closed for the prosecution. The pleas

were able and exhaustive, and injenious, weaving theories, apparently positive. The case was fought from the beginning to end carefully and for all there was in it, and no stone was left unturned. The charge of Judge Williams was short, clear and to the point, and impartial. At a little after six o'clock the jury retired to make up their verdict. After and absence of about three hours the jury returned to the Court room and rendered a verdict of
GUILTY OF VOLUNTARY MANSLAUGHTER
and the trial of George W. Chisholm came to a close.

During the trial the prisoner's wife, daughter, two sisters and a brother occupied seats at his side, and cheered him with their presence. The prisoner was cool throughout, exhibiting nervousness only when the pleas of the Commonwealth were extraordinarily severe upon his conduct and actions.

Tuesday morning, Chisholm was brought into Court. He was accompanied by his wife. District Attorney Cobb moved for sentence. A plea for mercy was made by D. C. Larrabee, counsel for defendant.

Chisholm was then asked if he had anything to say. He arose and made quite a long address, in which he said that he had never had more than a dozen words, and these mere words of courtesy with Tom Waters. He said he had had trouble with the old man Waters in relation to the bark, and that he had not been fairly treated by him. Of the occurrence at the gate, he told substantially the same story as Lena Chisholm, but not at as great length. The shooting he does know how it was done, that Tom had him by the wrist at the time. He carried the revolver openly as a means of defence and to intimidate parties from assailing him. Carried it at all times.

He did not find fault with his Attorneys, the Court, Jury or Commonwealth, although he thought he had not received justice. He had thought that he would be cleared. He appealed to the Court for mercy on his own account and for the sake of his family.

Judge Williams made a few remarks to the prisoner and then
SENTENCED
him to undergo imprisonment in the penitentiary for a period of four years; pay a fine of $1 to the Commonwealth; costs of prosecution and to stand committed until sentence is complied with. Imprisonment to the computed from time of sentence.

The prisoner was perfectly cool, as he had been during most of the trial.

Court Minutes.

In the matter of the alleged lunacy of John Reed, Dr. Frank Buck, C. L. Peck and J. L. Knox appointed commissioners to take testimony. Sheriff directed to remove John Reed to asylum, county to pay costs.

Estate of Augustus Stroele, administrator ordered to sell real estate.
Sarah A. Quick vs. Jonathan B. Quick, decree in divorce awarded.
Isaac Benson vs Keating township, a special tax of 10 mills to be levied.
Consider Stearns appointed overseer of poor of Eulalia township.
Grand Jury called and sworn, R. L. White, Foreman, L. B. Cole, Constable, to attend Grand Jury.

Com'th vs James Johnson, same vs Robert Niles, same vs Harrison Koon, same vs John Ward. Prosecutor, Amos Veeley, allowed to withdraw, and J. M. Hamilton substituted.

Com'th vs Williard Rhodes, larceny, discharged.

M. E. Olmsted vs Homer township, special tax of ten mills ordered.

In the matter of Lydia Clark, a lunatic, George Clark and Nathan D. Ayers ordered to be at one half the expense of maintenance and the poor district of Wharton one half.

A. B. Mann appointed guardian of Eva Neill.

Geo. C. Lewis appointed treasurer of Keating township.

Joseph Fries, a citizen of Switzerland, admitted to citizenship.

H. C. Dornan admitted to practice in several courts of Potter county.

Mrs. Orel V. Corsaw appointed Stenographer of the several courts of Potter county.

Com'th vs Mathew Prosser, larceny, bail $200 for appearance.

Com'th vs Charles Shaw, def't and bail discharged, no prosecutor appearing.

Com'th vs Esther E. Shay, fornication, true bill.

Com'th vs Rob't Niles, selling liquor, true bill.

Com'th vs Amos Veeley, selling liquor, true bill.

In the matter of petition for a public road from Dan Baker's farm in Bingham township to Charles Crowell's in Ulysses. Report set aside and new view appointed as follows: O. J. Rees, Consider Stearns and G. W. Bennett.

Com'th vs N. E. Weed, larceny, *nol pros* entered.

Francis Presho vs Lyman C. Presho, decree in divorce.

Com'th vs Horace Nelson, continued.

Com'th vs L. C. King, selling liquor, continued.

Com'th vs C. G. Watkins, selling liquor, true bill, plead guilty, sentenced to pay a fine of $100, and costs or prosecution.

Com'th vs Charles Marvin, bigamy, true bill.

Com'th vs Lucy Harvey, larceny, true bill, by agreement, def't to pay costs and useless other proof be found the case not to be prosecuted.

Com'th vs H. J. Mills, keeping vicious dogs, sentenced to pay a fine of $1 and costs.

Free Will Baptist church of West Pike incorporated.

Com'th vs E. McGonigal, selling liquor, true bill, continued.

Com'th vs J. M. McGonigal, selling liquor on Sunday, not a true bill.

E. A. Whitney appointed clerk of Keating township.

Com'th vs John Krusen, selling liquor, plead guilty.

Com'th vs Clark Judd, selling liquor, true bill, continued.

Com'th vs E. McGonigal, selling liquor to minors, true bill, continued.

Com'th vs James Loughery, assault and battery, continued.

Com'th vs H. J. Mills, obstructing highway, true bill.

Com'th vs George Clark, forgery, true bill.

Com'th vs Fred Devanport, selling liquor, true bill.

Com'th vs John Ward, selling liquor, true bill.

Com'th vs James Johnson, selling liquor, not a true bill, Co. for costs.

Potter County, Pennsylvania Potpourri – Volume I
1880 through 1884

Com'th vs D. P. Reed, voluntary manslaughter, not a true bill.

Com'th vs D. P. Reed, Harriet Reed, and Willis Reed, involuntary manslaughter, true bill.

Com'th vs Robert Haskins, larceny, nol pros entered.

Com'th vs P. D. Hawley, selling liquor, plead guilty.

Sheriff Monroe appeared in court and acknowledged the following deeds for lands sold at Sheriff's Sales:

To Walter Wells for ¼ acre in Oswayo, for $5, sold as property of M. H. and E. J. Reynolds.

Geo. Fox, M.D. for 156.5 acres in Hebron, for $25, sold as property of G. W. Varney.

Bingham Estate for 119.8 acres in Hector, for $25, sold as property of Benj. Ferris.

John Ormerod for 75 acres in Summit, for $5, sold as property of G. W. Brewster.

John Ormerod for 53 acres in Summit, for $15, sold as property of G. W. Brewster.

A. G. Olmsted for 52.2 acres in Genesee, for $395, sold as property of James C. Burdick.

- The trial of Chisholm last week excited more interest than any suit ever before tried in Potter county, if the crowds in attendance was any indication of public interest. During the whole time of the trial the court room was packed full, and Saturday standing room was at a premium.

- Mike Veeley of Allegany recently set a steel trap for foxes and on visiting it a few days since was surprised to find that he had captured not a fox but a fine specimen of the white headed eagle. The bird was caught by one foot and aside from bruising the flesh a little was not injured in the least. The spread of the eagle's wings is six feet and four inches. S. P. Olmsted is now the possessor of this fine specimen. The bird seems to be doing well, and on Saturday was able to eat its rations, consisting of two pounds of beef steak.

- The case of the commonwealth vs Marvin, charged with bigamy, on trial Saturday evening, is one of the queer ones. It seems Marvin and wife No. 1 in New York entered into an agreement to live as man and wife so long and no longer than was agreeable. Five children were born to them. Finally Marvin went to Brookland and while there took Miss Shay to Wellsville, and on their return they claimed to have been married. Both women were in court as witnesses for the defence, and Marvin and No. 2 were very affectionate, doing considerable hugging and not a little kissing, when they met in the court room. No. 1 standing by apparently an uninterested spectator. According to law Marvin could not be tried for bigamy in this State but the Jury concluded he was guilty enough to stand the costs. An indictment has been found against Marvin for adultery.

- It is reported that the Jury in the Chisholm case stood on first ballot, 2 for acquittal, 1 for manslaughter, 9 for murder in first degree. That Bemis received $500 for his services in the trial. That Chisholm is far from being satisfied. That the Jury fees last week, traverse and Grand, amounted to over $1,100. That the entire costs the county will have to pay on account of this trial will foot up about $1,300.

- The residence of B. A. McClure was the scene of what bid fair at one time to be a very serious accident on Saturday. The girl doing house work, whose name we did not learn, had just put some coal in the stove and turned away when she discovered that the back of her dress was on fire. She gave a scream which brought Mr. and Mrs. McClure to the spot. By this time the flames were above here head. Mr. McClure quickly pulled off his coat and with it attempted to smother the flames, while Mrs. McClure was throwing water upon the girl. Mrs. McClure's dress also caught fire. Mac himself was burned about the hands, and for a time it was the liveliest house in town. Fortunately the flames were soon subdued and no one was dangerously burned. The girl's outer clothing nearly all burned off and she was somewhat injured, but nothing of a serious nature.

- E. A. Austin, Justice of the Peace, sent to prisoners to Sheriff Monroe Monday. John Cummings, on a charge of selling liquor, and John McQuay, charged with an attempt to commit a rape on the person of Triphene Hallock, on the 6th of March.

The Potter Enterprise
Wednesday Evening, March 21, 1883 – Vol. IX, No. 44

- The happiest man in Coudersport last week was Watson T. Dike. A girl baby weighing 9 pounds.

Freeman Run. Married March 6th, at the residence of C. W. Dingee, by the Rev. W. S. Holland, Mr. Newell Pangburn and Miss Rena Bennet. Much joy and happiness is the wish of their many friends.

MARRIED.
HODGE – CHRISTEY. – In Wellsville March 12, 1883, by F. W. Beecher, Mr. Harlo H. Hodge and Miss Mary E. Christey, both of Oswayo, Pa.

COX – PLAGEMAN. – In Lewisville, Sunday evening, March 11th, 1883, by Rev. Thos. L. Perry, Mr. John Cox, of Elmira, N.Y., and Miss Mary Plageman, of Ulysses, Pa.

WALLACE – HILL. – In Lymansville March 18th, 1883, by Frank Phelps, Esq., Joseph J. Wallace, of Elmira, N.Y., and Miss Marion Hill, of Lymansville, Pa.

DIED.

HURD – At St. Croix Co., Wis., Feb. 16, 1883, of Rheumatic fever, Granvel Hurd, formerly of Genesee township, Potter Co., Pa., aged 58.

CARNAHAN. – In Los Angelos, Calif., March 7th, 1883, of Pulmonary consumption, Mrs. Kate Bird Carnahan, aged 28 years.

- Mrs. Charlotte Press of this place died very suddenly Tuesday morning while sitting at the breakfast table. Mrs. Rose Press had prepared her breakfast and stepped out of the room, returning found her hands down by her side and head on the table, dead. – *Palladium.*

- Matthias Smith of Coudersport was killed by the cars at Renovo, Wednesday evening last. Mr. Smith had been selling baskets, and in passing the rail road yard stepped to one side to get out of the way of a passing train, when he was struck by a locomotive, and instantly killed. Four locomotives passed over him, grinding his remains into an unrecognizable mass. About eighteen dollars in silver was found along the track where the accident occurred. He is supposed to have had about $70 in money, having sold most of his baskets. It is thought he had paper money, which was destroyed by the locomotives. His remains were brought to Coudersport on Friday and from here taken to the Catholic cemetery in Genesee for burial. Mr. Smith has long been a resident of Coudersport, following his business, that of making baskets. He leaves a wife and two daughters, Mrs. John Pearsall and Mrs. Valentine Kline, to mourn his loss. Mr. Smith was a peaceable, industrious citizen, aged about 60 years.

- In our Court Minutes last week, for George Clark, indicted for forgery, read JAMES CLARK.

- Forty-nine years ago to-day, March 20th, the great wind blow occurred in this section, by which hundreds of acres of timber was blown down. The effect is yet to be seen on the hill near Lyman Nelson's, about Lymansville and in Sweden. In many places very little timber except fire cherry, has replaced the timber then destroyed.

- We understand that work on the extension of the C. C. & A. Railway from Westfield to Harrison Valley is to be commenced soon, and that within ninety days cars will be running to the latter named place. Whether the road is to be built to Olean this season or not is not known to a certainty, but knowing ones are inclined to believe that it will. With the completion of the road to Harrison Valley two-thirds of the passenger and freight traffic of Potter county will come over this road. – *Knoxville Courier.*

Court Minutes – Continued from last week.

Com vs C. G. Watkins, selling liquor; sentenced to pay a fine of $100 and cost of prosecution.

Com vs John Krusen, selling liquor; sentenced to pay a fine of $100 and cost of prosecution.

Willard King vs Charlotte King; Court award a writ to make pertition whereby said property shall be set out in severalty.

Bingham Estate vs Chester Gill; jury find for plaintiff the land described in writ.

Veniries issued for 24 Grand and 36 Traverse Jurors for June Term.

J. W. Stevens vs Frank Dodge et al; ordered that the estrepment in this case be dissolved upon the filing of a bond for $1,000.

License issued to L. D. Estes.

Com vs Wm. Blarigan; involuntary manslaughter; defendant discharged.

H. H. Nye vs Herbert Johnson; settled.

J. M. Spafford vs C. L. Ayers, et al; verdict for plaintiff in sum of $237.60.

Alice C. Johnson vs George C. Johnson; divorce granted.

Benjamin Genter and Raimond Bendell, natives of Germany, admitted to citizenship.

Estate of Hiram H. Chesbro; Mrs. Elmina Chesbro appointed administrator.

Wm. Ansley vs Pike township; special tax of five mills ordered.

Estate of Moses Hacket; leave granted to pay money into Orphans Court.

L. H. Cobb, assignee, vs Henry Grodevant; verdict for plaintiff in the sum of $100.

Dan'l Clark vs Sala Stevens et al; verdict for plaintiff in the sum of $1,993.60.

Wm. Perkins vs Richard Shay; verdict for defendant.

W. H. Millard granted a license to peddle.

Ransome Burt vs Mary Reer; verdict for plaintiff in the sum of $100. Rule to show cause why new trial should not be granted, returnable next term.

G. W. G. Judd vs D. J. Smith; verdict for plaintiff in sum of $48.06.

Maria J. Jones vs Sylvania township; special tax of five mill ordered.

M. E. Olmsted vs Summit township; special tax of five mill ordered.

Seth Connable vs West Branch township; special tax of ten mills ordered.

Sam'l Beebe appointed clerk of Oswayo township.

In the matter of R. L. Nichols, assignee of W. L. Starkweather; prothonotary to give notice that account will be presented at June Term for confirmation.

Geo. Trask vs H. J. Mills; verdict for plaintiff in sum of seven dollars.

Petition of Rose C. Avery for separate estate granted.

Clark Trask vs H. J. Mills; verdict for plaintiff in sum of ten dollars.

Appointment of A. B. Mann as guardian of Eva Neill, annulled.

Lizzie Smith vs R. Smith; *alias sub* in divorce issued.

D. C. Larrabee appointed auditor to restate account of Margaret O'Donnell, administratrix.

Estate of Henry Reynolds; administrator and bail discharged.

Elizabeth Reed vs Levi Reed; *alias sub* in divorce awarded.

Com vs Robt Niles; sentenced to pay a fine of $100 and costs of prosecution.

M. L. GRIDLEY,
NEW FLOUR and FEED STORE,
COUDERSPORT, AP.,
FLOUR, FEED,
COARSE AND FINE MEAL,
Constantly on Hand. Prices VERY LOW.
Grain of all kinds taken in exchange.
In the building recently known as King's
Hotel, Main Street.

On Hand at G. H. Grabe's
Successor to GRABE BROS.
With a Full Line of

FURNITURE !

For the Spring Trade,
Consisting of Walnut, Ash and Softwood Chamber Suits,
Bedsteads, Common and Fancy,
Wash Stands and Parlor Stands, Extension and Breakfast Tables,
Woven Wire Mattrasses and Spring Beds.
Upholstered Goods and Mattrasses, Cain and Wood Seat Chairs,
Cain and Wood Seat Rockers, Picture Frames, Mouldings and Mirrors.
Which Will be Sold as Cheap as the Cheapest.
Repairing and New Work Made to Order on Short Notice.
UNDERTAKING!
Cloth Covered Caskets, Wood Finished Burial Cases, Ladies, Gents
and Child's Robes, Trimming of all kinds constantly on hand at
G. H. GRABE'S
Maine Street,   COUDERSPORT, PA.

The Potter Enterprise
Wednesday Evening, March 28, 1883 – Vol. IX, No. 45

- On Monday of last week Joe Lester, of Eulalia, was made happy – a ten pound boy. The day following John Marvin stepped to the front and announced a 9 ½ pound girl.

- L. D. Horton is still stepping around quite lively, and the boys are smoking good cigars at his expense. A nine pound boy causes the rejoicing.

MARRIED.

HARRIS – PRESHO. – In Sweden, March 18th, 1883, by H. S. Lent, Esq., Mr. O. E. Harris and Francis Presho, all of Sweden township.

Raymond. Joseph Phillips died at Gold on Thursday last.

Hebron. Mrs. Frank Gale died Friday, the 16th inst., after an illness of one week only. She leaves a husband and three children to mourn her loss.

Millport. We are sorry to announce the death of Champion Munger of this place, who was buried on the 20th inst. He leaves many mourning friends, and his widowed mother has the sympathy of all in her affliction.

Millport. Mrs. Kemp of the Eleven Mile was also buried on the 23rd. Her death caused a great shock in the neighborhood, and much sympathy is felt for the husband, who is left with four small children, the youngest but a few days old.

Clara. To-day Champ. Munger of Millport was buried here. He leaves a wife, and many relatives and friends to mourn his loss. He was attended in his sickness by Dr. Remington of Shingle House, he had an attack of Erysipelas, but died, I understand, from some lung disorder.

Eleven Mile. Death, whose harvest is reaped at all seasons, and consists of people of all ages and classes, has been active. Yesterday Mrs. Kemp, wife of Welcome Kemp, was buried at the cemetery here. Four motherless babes are left without her brooding care. At the same hour at Oswayo Mrs. Franklin Gale, Sr., was laid in the place appointed for all to lie, and one week ago to-day her son's wife was buried, she too left four children of tender years to the care of her bereaved husband.

Eleven Mile. On the 9th inst., Philemon C. Lovell was buried from the church at Oswayo. His obsequeies were attended by Gardner Post G.A.R. of Bolivar, N.Y., Estes Post of Oswayo and Barnes Post of Sharon. Rev. N. North preached a beautiful sermon on the occasion, and the body was buried with the use of burial service of the G.A.R. So we see that no exemption is made from the stroke of the Destroyer. Much illness exists from a distemper or cold that prevails very extensively hereabouts.

- Tuesday afternoon of last week the farm house of David White, about five miles from Coudersport, in Sweden twp., was burned to the ground with most of its contents. It seems that Mr. White was at home alone, and after building a good fire in the stove, went to the barn to do his chores, and on returning sometime after, found the house in flames, and too late to save much. The house was built about twelve years ago, and cost about $2000. It was furnished in a substantial manner, and the total loss will reach $3000 at least. There were another family living in the house at the time, but they were also away from home. Insurance $1500. – *Journal*.

WHO COMMITTED THE MURDER?
A Dead Potter County Convict Said to Have Been Guilty of a Murder for Which Silas Gray is Now Under Sentence of Death. The Story Told by John Pettys.

Silas Gray has been convicted of murdering Mrs. McCready, and is now in Greensburg, Westmoreland county, under sentence to be hanged on the 24th of May next.

Now Hiram Bowermaster, of Cumberland county, comes to the front and tells a story, which he claims was told him by John Pettys, a Potter county convict, which if true should relieve the neck of Gray from the halter.

Bowermaster says that in the Fall of 1879 or 1880, he is not positive as to the year, he was a fellow prisoner with Jack Pettys in the Western Penitentiary, working in the wire and link shop upon machines next to each other, and that he often wrote letters for Pettys and other prisoners. Silas Gray was confined in the Penitentiary, at the same time for horse stealing.

"Sometime in the latter part of 1879 or '80, I am not positive which year, anyhow about a month or so before Christmas we heard that an officer had come down from Westmoreland county to have Silas Gray detained on a charge of murdering a Mrs. McCready. I had just written a letter for Jacky Pettys and we were sitting in his cell, looking out on the Ohio river. It was in the resting time in the middle of the day. The letter was to two people who he said were his cousins, John and Mary Easton, of Shingle House, Potter county. Jack Pettys said to me: 'Hiram, I wonder what they would do with me if they knew that I took that woman across the mountain myself and made away with her?'

"I said: 'They would hang you, I suppose, if they had the evidence.'

"I asked him if he had made away with her in the mountains. He said 'No, along the water.'

"After that he talked with me in this same way almost every day until Christmas. He never told me any more than that and never said how or why he killed the woman, but said always that it was along the water, out somewhere in Indiana or Westmoreland county. He also talked to Frank May, a man from Tyrone, who was in the same prison and carried the wire into the shop where Jack and I worked. He talked to him so much about it that Frank said to me one day that he was tired of Jack's talk about killing that woman. It seemed to prey on Jack's mind so that he couldn't help talking about it. On Christmas night, or about that time, Jack Pettys hanged himself in his cell. He did not tell me he was going to do it, but the evening before as I was passing his cell, he reached me out his onions and said 'Take these, Hiram, I won't want any more onions.' He had taken the horn he used at his machine into his cell, stuck it into a hole above the door and making a rope out of his towel, hanged himself with it. I told McKean, the deputy warden in charge of our prison, that I believed Jack Pettys hanged himself because he killed Mrs. McCready, but I wasn't called before the coroner. I refused to be one of his pall bearers and threw away the onions because I thought they might bring me bad luck.

"I don't know Silas Gray. I never saw him. But from what Jack Pettys told me I think he is an innocent man hung. The people around here don't know I was ever in the Westmoreland Penitentiary, and it will kind of give me away, but I will go with you to the squire and swear to this."

A dispatch from Pittsburg to the Harrisburg *Patriot* says: That the officers of the Penitentiary stated that the deputy warden to whom Bowermaster claims to have told that Jack Pettys hanged himself because he murdered Mrs. McCready has removed to Missouri. McIlvain, one of the keepers, stated that shortly before his death Pettys came to him several times and asked him what the law could do with a man for a crime committed a good many years ago. McIlvain told him the statute of limitation would protect a man after a certain period of time had elapsed, except in a case of murder. Pettys murmured or grunted something to himself and said nothing further. He repeated his question on several occasions. McIlvain also says if Pettys would have revealed his secret to any one it would probably be to Bowermaster, for they were more intimate than any two men in the prison. Pettys was sent down from Potter county to serve a term of twenty-six months for horse stealing. He had only sixty-two days to serve when he committed suicide. A convict named McCullough, still in the Penitentiary, says he is willing to make affidavit that Dickson the chief witness against Silas Gray, threatened that he would get even with him (Gray) for some old grudge he bore him. The woman, Mrs. McCready, disappeared mysteriously about seven years ago. She was a friendless creature and nobody made much search for her. In 1879 this convict Dickson revealed what he claimed a confession of Silas Gray to the effect that he had murdered the woman and thrown her body in the Kiskiminetas river. A boy who was fishing hooked up a shawl out of the river which was identified as hers and on this and Dickson's testimony, supported by circumstantial evidence, Gray was convicted.

Some of our readers will remember John Pettys. At the March term of our court in 1878, he was charged with larceny, having broken into a house, in Sharon township, and stole a clock and some other articles of small value. Pettys plead guilty to the charge, and he was sentenced to twenty-six months in the Penitentiary. Pettys was taken to Pittsburg by John M. Covey, who was then Sheriff. To Covey he owned that he had been a hard case, and said that forty years before he had been a member of a gang engaged in stealing horses, whose headquarters were on the Pine Creek. He told him that at the head of a left hand hollow on the Nine Mile was a cave, concealed, where horses were kept, until pursuit was over, and they could be disposed of safely. Pettys was about sixty years of age.

The Potter Enterprise
Wednesday Evening, April 4, 1883 – Vol. IX, No. 46

Allegany. Another couple have joined the matrimonial number, Geo. Collins and Miss Monroe. May peace and prosperity attend them.

- For half a century the Postoffice at Roulette, Potter Co., has been in the hands of the Lymans – father and sons. This is a long term, but the Messrs. Lyman have made a good record for themselves in official capacity. – *Reporter*.

- Dennis Hall, of Potter county, was coming to Emporium with a load of hay and stopped at Nelson Sizer's at Sizerville to feed his horses and get dinner, leaving the wagon side of the road near the railroad crossing. In a short space of time the hay was discovered to be on fire, and it is supposed to have caught from a spark from a passing engine. The wagon was saved by tipping off the hay and removing the vehicle from danger. The hay-rack was considerably scorched, and Mr. Hall lost, in addition to his hay, a number of bags, his horse blanket and overcoat. – *Cameron Press*.

John's Dogs.

Last week John Ormerod, Esq., purchased a dog – a female dog, black-and-tan rat-terrier, answering to the name of Fanny. We are thus particular about describing the dog, in the hope that it may serve John a good turn some time in the future. But John bought the dog, and doubtless paid for it. At any rate he fully realizes that he owns a dog. A few days since Fanny eloped, absconded, left, vamoosed the ranche, absquatulated, &c., (an ordinary dog would simply have run away but this is an extraordinary dog). John enquired of everybody he met if they had seen a dog – his dog, and finally he learned of a dog similar to his dog, accompanying a boy along the road towards Lymansville. John gets a horse and buggy and starts off in hot pursuit, and they cry "Have you seen a little black-and-tan dog?" echoed and re-echoed along the valley, from the Keystone Mill to David White's, and from David White's to Lewis Lyman's and a mile back in the woods. The last mile was made on foot – horse supposed to have been tired out. John was, after tramping through the snow. But perseverance brought its reward, and John returned with the dog, and he wasn't just exactly happy either. Peace now reigns on Fifth Street, and until the dog is lost again John can be found at his office, during business hours, ready to attend to clients, discourse on dogs or lick any man that coaxes away his dog – all in good shape too.

The Potter Enterprise
Wednesday Evening, April 11, 1883 – Vol. IX, No. 47

MARRIED.

MANNING – LYMAN. – At the residence of the bride's parents, in Roulet, on Saturday, March 31st, 1883, Mr. Mark Manning, of Port Allegany, and Miss Chloe Lyman, of Roulet.

KELSA – STACKEN. – At the residence of Mr. Augustus Voss, Eulalia, on Thursday, April 5th, by the Rector of Christ Church, Coudersport, Mr. John Kelsa and Christine C. Stacken, both of Potter Co., Pa.

NOTICE.

Whereas my wife, Mary Brine has left my bed and board without just cause or provocation, I hereby forbid any person harboring or trusting her on my account as I will pay no debt of her contracting unless compelled by law.

John K. Brine,
Roulet, Pa., April 2d, 1883.

The Potter Enterprise
Wednesday Evening, April 18, 1883 – Vol. IX, No. 48

Hebron. Mr. and Mrs. Dunbar have a fine baby boy.

MARRIED.

WILCOX – BROOKS. – At the residence of the bride's parents in Clara, April 7, 1883, by J. L. Allen, Mr. A. J. Wilcox, of Wellsville, N.Y., and Miss Helen D. Brooks, of Clara, Pa. "May they live long and prosper."

White's Corners. Mrs. John Snyder was buried at this place a few days ago.

DIED.

DINGMAN. – Arthur S., infant son of Wm. Dingman, of Coudersport, died on Saturday last.

GALE. – At Oswayo, March 21st, 1883, of paralysis of the throat, Mrs. Almyra Gale, wife of Franklin Gale, Sr., in the 75th year of her age.

DENNIS. – April 5th, 1883, at the residence of her son, Charles P. Dennis, in Harrison Township, Mrs. Sally Dennis, in the 87th year of her age.

Fire at Wharton.

On Friday evening last the store building at Wharton was discovered to be on fire and in a short time it burned to the ground. The building was occupied by J. M. Spafford, of Lymansville, and Frank Williams, of Wharton, dealers in merchandise, and the dwelling part of the store by Frank Williams and family. The fire caught in the upper part of the building and was not discovered until the burning coals fell through the floor. There had been no fire in the upper rooms for several days. It is believed the fire originated from a defective pipe – the cause of eight out of ten fires.

Upon the alarm of fire a number of men from near the mill went to the scene to render all assistance possible, but very little of the household property was saved. A few hundred dollars worth of goods were carried out. The store probably contained from two to three thousand dollars worth of goods, on which there was an insurance of $1000 in the agency of Lucien Bird, of Pennfield. Loss on household goods about $500, insured in the North America by A. B. Mann, of Coudersport, for $300. The building was owned by Samuel C. Georgia, and cost when built over $3000. It was well put up of good pine timber. It was insured in the London Assurance Corporation, by L. B. Cole, of Coudersport, for $550.

The Potter Enterprise
Wednesday Evening, April 25, 1883 – Vol. IX, No. 49

Sartwell Creek. Arthur Witter can hold his head as high as any one now. It is a boy.

Allegany. The young gent that demanded board at M. A. Veeley's a few weeks since is well pleased with the place and seems determined to stay.

MARRIED.
GLASPY – HALL. – At the residence of John Baker, in Sylvania, April 11, 1883, by Rev. W. Stuart Holland, Mr. Edward Glaspy and Mrs. Cartha C. Hall.

The Case of Silas Gray.
Before the Pardon board on Tuesday of last week the case of Silas Gray was heard, and the story told of Pettys, the deceased Potter county convict, has saved one man from stretching hemp.

Ex-Lieutenant Governor John W. Latta appeared for Silas Gray, the Westmoreland county murderer. Mr. Latta said that he was surprised that the board did not commute Grays sentence at the last meeting, but since that time certain parties, by letter and affidavit, had cast additional doubt upon the guilt of Gray. He then proceeded to read the affidavits of Bowermaster and others who had been in the Western penitentiary with Jack Pettys and had heard him at different times, especially after the retainer had been lodged for him in the McCready case, say that he had killed the woman and describe the manner of her death. He held that although the men who furnished the affidavits were not of the best class of people, yet they were the equals if not the superiors of Gibson upon whose testimony alone Gray was convicted. In the affidavit of James C. Brown, ____ Gibson said Gray was innocent, but he would swear it upon him because Pettys and himself belonged to the same gang of horse thieves. It further says that Pettys said he had killed other people, but the only one he was sorry for was the Westmoreland county woman. The other affidavits read tended to show that Pettys was in constant dread of being hanged and frequently talked of suicide. A letter ready by Mr. Latta from H. S. Milleiten, a present inmate of the penitentiary, states that he asked Pettys if he knew of the murder. Pettys replied, "a damn sight more than is good for me." He then told several of the men how he had killed the woman. Milleisen says he couldn't testify at the inquest of Pettys because the warden prevented him.

The speaker stated that he believed it was Gray's boastful manner more than anything else that caused his present situation; that Gray wanted to represent himself a greater criminal than he really was.

Mr. Peebles spoke also in behalf of the condemned. He said that nearly all the people of Westmoreland county felt that Gray was innocent and to hang him would tend to effect the administration of justice in cases of a like character in the future. The board recommended the commutation.

- The telephone poles are now all set and the line will be in operation in about two weeks.

- Several private telephone lines will doubtless be erected in Coudersport soon. D. C. Larrabee is to have one from his office to his residence, and others are thinking the matter over seriously.

The Potter Enterprise
Wednesday Evening, May 2, 1883 – Vol. IX, No. 50

- A nine and one-half pound girl at the residence of George Ross, last Sunday morning, made George think he weighed a ton.

MARRIED.

GIBSON – BAILEY. – At the Baptist parsonage in Lewisville, by Rev. T. L. Perry, April 14th, 1883, Mr. Robert Gibson to Miss Thedocia Bailey, both of Hector, Pa.

SLINGERLAND – HURD. – By Rev. J. L. Swain, at his residence, April 59th, Mr. Elmer Ellsworth Slingerland, of Allegany, to Miss Effie D. Hurd, of Genesee.

Notice.

Whereas my wife Belle Sprigg has left my bed and board without just cause or provocation, I do hereby warn all persons against trusting or harboring her on my account, as I will pay no debts of her contracting after this date, unless compelled by law.

Charles Sprigg,
Coudersport, Pa., April 30th, 1883.

Potter County, Pennsylvania Potpourri – Volume I
1880 through 1884

The Potter Enterprise
Wednesday Evening, May 9, 1883 – Vol. X, No. 1

West Homer and North Eulalia. Don't you know what Joe Coddington is smiling about? Why, his last *boy* is a girl, about a week old, *that's why*.

Keating. Born April 24 to Mr. and Mrs. Joseph Codington, a daughter.

West Homer and North Eulalia. The ladies of our place were invited at the house of our new neighbor, Mr. Cameron, to celebrate the seventeenth birthday of his daughter, Miss Dell, the afternoon was passed away very pleasantly, and amid the gossip and laughter, that is usual with a company of ladies (especially if Miss Libbie is among them) a quilt was taken from the frame and BOUND, and after partaking of a *delicious* supper the more *sedate* ladies returned to their respective homes, leaving the young and hopeful to trip the light fantastic toe till – they ought to have been home.

West Homer and North Eulalia. Mr. Andy Holt, of Homer, and Miss Mary Gifford, of Eulalia, were married April 29th, by O. L. Hall, Esq. Now girls as *Andy* is no more in the market, you will be obliged to turn your tearful eyes in another direction. *You surely have our deepest sympathy.*

MARRIED.
KILBOURNE – BRUSE. – May 2d, 1883, by C. P. Kilbourne, Esquire, Maj. John M. Kilbourne, of West Pike, and Mrs. Oreelia Bruse, of Hector, Pa., late of Horseheads, N.Y.

Allegany. The past two weeks have been noted for wedding anniversaries. April 27th, a surprise party of about thirty young people gathered at the residence of W. P. Cool, in remembrance of their first year of wedded life. A pleasant evening of enjoyment, with nothing to mar but the darkness in returning home.

Saturday afternoon and evening, May 5th, the 20th anniversary of Mr. and Mrs. Peter Green was celebrated by the gathering together of nearly a hundred friends from this town and other places. The presents were of various kinds and nice, dress goods, linens, laces, china, glass, majolica, &c. The tables were spread with a bounteous supply of good things to eat, which was partaken of by all. Everything passed gayly till the late hours, when the friends took their departure, wishing Peter and Mary many happy returns, &c.

Death of an Old Citizen.
Mr. Samuel Pollard died at his residence on Cross Fork, April 18th, after a week of severe pain and sickness. Mr. Pollard was one of the earliest settlers on Cross Fork, and was a kind neighbor respected by all who knew him. He left a wife, six sons and three daughters and a large circle of friends to mourn his loss. His remains were buried in the Cross Fork cemetery. Funeral services were conducted by Rev. S. P. Glass.

Potter County, Pennsylvania Potpourri – Volume I
1880 through 1884

List of Grand Jurors for June Term 1883.

John Absom, Mechanic, Coudersport; E. H. Bassett, Tanner, Ulysses; Samuel Beebe, Agent, Oswayo; George A. Bliss, Farmer, Clara; A. F. Dodge, Farmer, Harrison; Sylvenus A. Harris, Laborer, Bingham; C. C. Haskins, Farmer, Harrison; George Head, Farmer, Oswayo; Alfred Herring, Farmer, Sharon; O. W. Hickox, Farmer, Genesee; James Hill, Farmer, Genesee; Samuel Haskins, Grocer, Portage; Martin Joerg, Farmer, Stewardson; J. W. Kemp, Farmer, Sharon; Leroy Lyman, Farmer, Roulet; Lyman C. Perry, Farmer, Ulysses; J. M. Rees, Farmer, Sylvania; Wm. H. Rounsville, Mechanic, Coudersport; Florentine Stevens, Farmer, Sharon; Winfield Scott, Farmer, Hector; John Strait, Farmer, Hector.

List of Traverse Jurors for June Term 1883.

F. P. Austin, Farmer, Portage; S. J. Acker, Farmer, Pike; W. W. Arnold, Farmer, Genesee; John Bolich, Farmer, Abbott; Charles Baker, Mechanic, Lewisville; Wm. Boyington, Hotel Keeper, Roulet; Belden Burt, Lumberman, Roulet; Ira Bishop, Farmer, Allegany; W. C. Chesebro, Farmer, Homer; Arthur Cook, Farmer, Oswayo; Elmer Deming, Farmer, Pleasant Valley; Amos Dennis, Farmer, Bingham; J. B. Davidson, Laborer, Roulet; J. D. Elliott, Farmer, Sharon; G. M. Estes, Farmer, Hebron; Rodney Fessenden, Farmer, Roulet; James Glaspy, Farmer, Sylvania; Caleb L. Gridley, Farmer, Ulysses; Wm. J. Grovey, Farmer, Ulysses; Wm. Hazen, Farmer, Roulet; Curtis Howard, Farmer, Harrison; Frank Hand, Farmer, Harrison; Samuel Jones, Farmer, Sharon; V. R. Kenyon, Farmer, Oswayo; Charles Knickerbacker, Farmer, Summit; H. C. Kilbourn, Farmer, Hector; Jasper Lloyd, Farmer, Pike; John Lockwood, Farmer, Oswayo; Miles Marsh, Farmer, Roulet; Henry Menge, Farmer, Abbott; Luther Perkins, Farmer, Allegany; C. M. Stillman, Mechanic, Lewisville; John Schaar, Farmer, West Branch; Chauncey Tucker, Farmer, Allegany; A. B. Whipple, Farmer, Allegany.

The Potter Enterprise
Wednesday Evening, May 16, 1883 – Vol. X, No. 2

MARRIED.

BURT – HANSON. – In Roulet, Pa., May 9th, 1883, at the residence of the bride's parents, by Rev. Bennit, Mr. Calvin Burt and Miss Annie Hanson.

DIED.

MOREY. – In Roulet, Pa., May 8th, after a short illness, Johnnie Morey, aged 15 years.

"We shall sleep but not forever, There will be a glorious dawn.
We shall meet to part no more, On the resurrection morn."

- Gaylord Colvin, at one time a resident of Bingham Township, died at his home in Osceola, Tioga county, last Tuesday. Mr. Colvin was Commissioner of Potter county three years, and Associate Judge for ten years.

Potter County, Pennsylvania Potpourri – Volume I
1880 through 1884

- During a recent thunder storm lightning struck the barn of Mr. F. Steadman, of Bingham, killing a valuable bull chained to one of the posts of the barn frame. Although the bolt passed down a post where a quantity of straw was stored, the barn was not fired. The storm was a very severe one.

Papers Found.

On Sunday night, the 5th of last November, burglars entered the store of C. H. Armstrong in Coudersport, broke open the safe and carried off about $100 in money, and a large number of valuable papers, notes, deeds, receipts, insurance policies, &c. The thieves left town on a hand car which was abandoned near Coleman's. Nothing has since been heard of the burglars, and until Saturday morning last the papers were still missing. About 5 o'clock Saturday morning, Will Abson was passing in front of F. W. Knox's barn; at one end of the bridge going into the barn he saw a paper bearing the name "C. H. Armstrong," which he picked up and in doing which he discovered other loose papers, evidently scratched out from under the bridge by hens. Further search revealed two drawers taken from Mr. Armstrong's safe last November, full of papers. Will immediately carried the papers to Mr. Armstrong's house, and we warrant a more welcome caller has not been inside the gate in many a long day.

Examinations showed that all the missing notes and papers of value difficult to replace were safe, a very few were slightly stained. One of the boxes was as bright as if it had never been taken from the safe, on the other one the veneering had loosened. The first impression was that the papers had been put where they were found recently. Mr. Armstrong looked the matter up and found that the boxes had been placed under a wide board where it was perfectly dry. One paper was found that had fallen from the box, partly covered with litter and hay seed, mouldy and rotten, and the general belief now is that the papers had lain concealed under the bridge since November. The find is a valuable one for Mr. Armstrong.

R. R.

Potter county gets more wind and less work in railroad matters than any other county in the State. It used to be all wind, but now there is a slight improvement. The B. N. Y. & P. cut across one corner years ago; last fall the Coudersport and Port Allegany was built; Magee is now shoving his broad gauge through to Harrison Valley, and then we strike the wind work, unless the Wellsville, Coudersport & Pine Creek be counted as a worker. This road drags and wheezes, but may yet reach somewhere. It will never reach Coudersport, if we may judge from present indications. Charters cover every important section of the county, Pike Mills gets at least half a dozen, Coudersport four or five, Lewisville two or three, and Brookland about the same, and other sections are not left out in the cold. The last charter calls for a road from Gaines to Coudersport. This is understood to be part of the Addison & North Pennsylvania road. If built it will be built at once, and if dropped it will be dropped quickly. Platt and his associates go ahead or go backward, but do not stand still. Should this road be built it means farewell to the East Fork line. To-day, Tuesday, a meeting is to be held at Gaines, in the interest of this last charter, and next week we hope to be able to give something more positive.

The Potter Enterprise
Wednesday Evening, May 23, 1883 – Vol. X, No. 3

Hebron. A fine boy baby has found a home with Mr. and Mrs. J. S. Barnes.

MARRIED.

STONE – BURT. – At the residence of bride's parents, in Lewisville, May 11th, 1883, by Rev. J. L. Davis, of Kendall Creek, Pa., Mr. John F. Stone and Miss Kate L. Burt, both of Lewisville.

- By a private dispatch received here on Monday afternoon, dated New Orleans, May 21st, we learn of the sudden death in that city of Charles F. Huntington, formerly of Coudersport.

Genesee Forks. Death again has entered our midst. This time the reaper's sickle has cut down an aged one, who has withstood the blasts of many winters. Mrs. Catharine Billings, aged about 75 years, died May 15th. She was one of the early settlers of this place, endured many hardships and trials, but now the cares of life for her are o'er. She peacefully rests, these words come forcibly to my mind as one after another passes away. "Are you ready, are you ready, should the Lord call to-day?"

Whites Corners. Mrs. H. Stebbins died very suddenly on Monday last with apoplexy. Her daughter, Mrs. Hurlburt, intends to keep house for her father and brother in the future.

Saw Mill Burned.

Keating Summit has again lost one of her saw mills. On the morning of Sunday, May 20th, about 2 o'clock, fire was discovered in the mill owned by Mr. Avery, and before any one could reach the mill it was seemingly all on fire on the inside, and in about one hour the mill, five loaded cars and considerable lumber piled on the platform was a mass of ruins. We understand that Mr. Avery's loss will be very heavy as he had a very small insurance, only about $500.

The Potter Enterprise
Wednesday Evening, May 30, 1883 – Vol. X, No. 4

- Born – To Mr. and Mrs. I. C. Staysa on Friday last a daughter. Weight 12 ½(?) pounds.

Charles F. Huntington.

On Monday of last week a dispatch was received here that Charles F. Huntington had died that morning in New Orleans. Charlie studied law with District Attorney Cobb, and was admitted to the Potter county Bar. He then removed to Hastings, Nebraska, where he soon gained many friends and a prominent position at the bar. Although but twenty-eight years of age he was last fall a prominent candidate for the important office of Judge, in his county. He was beaten for the nomination by a small majority. Some of the associated Press dispatches state that he came to his death from chloral administered by himself for that purpose, and that the cause was business difficulties connected with his Nebraska practice. This latter statement may be cleared up when his business is settled. That he committed suicide there seems to be no reason to doubt from the information so far furnished by dispatches. Mr. Huntington was a member of Coudersport Lodge, Knight's of Honor, in good standing. His insurance certificate was assigned to Mrs. Isabella Ross, who will doubtless receive the amount, $2,000, as soon as the proof of death is forwarded and the necessary formalities gone through with. The remains of Mr. Huntington were buried at Spring Mills, N.Y., on Friday last.

- Our streets at night present the appearance of a city. The bark peelers are out in force, swelling the crowd to circus-day proportions.

- The Catholics of this section are moving right along in the matter of building a church, and it looks now as if they would have a place to hold services in before the snow flies. Many years ago the Keating estate donated the square south of Hodskin's for this purpose, and recently subscribed $250 for the building which has been increased by the subscriptions of others to about $1000. A day's work would probably add $500 more. It is proposed to erect a structure 30 x 60, at a cost of about $2,000. The plan would be similar to the church at Port Allegany.

Bernie Nott.

Many of our readers have been acquainted with B. C. Nott, who resided at the Forest House off and on for two or three years, acting as clerk at the hotel, station agent, &c. He afterwards came to Coudersport, accepting a position in Thompson's drug store, where he made many friends. At times there appeared to be something wrong with him, and on this account he was discharged. Mr. Thompson first thought he was drinking, afterwards that he was using some drug. Nott went to Springville, and then to Olean, where he was clerk in a hotel. Here he acted so strange, talking about robberies, &c., that he was inuring the business of the house, and he was discharged. He then came to Coudersport. It soon became evident that his mind was badly affected, and he was sent to Mr. Nott, of Holland, N.Y., whose adopted son he was. Not improving any he was soon sent to an asylum. Bernie Nott was a bright young man of good business qualifications. It is hoped that proper treatment may restore his reason.

The Potter Enterprise
Wednesday Evening, June 6, 1883 – Vol. X, No. 5

MARRIED.

BRIESENICK – JOHNSON – At Olmsted Station, Potter county, Pa., June 4th, 1883, by Rev. W. S. Holland, Chas. W. Briesenick, M.D., of North Wharton, Pa., and Miss Anna M. Johnston, of Coudersport, Pa.

FESSENDEN – MERWIN – At Oswayo, Pa., May 27th, 1883, by A. S. Lyman, J.P., William Fessenden, of Oswayo, and Mrs. Eliza Merwin, of Ulysses.

- Fred. Rukgaber, of the Westfield *Free Press* was married at Elmira, N.Y., last Tuesday, to Miss Sophia Bowers. We congratulate Fred and wish him and his bride long and prosperous lives. The wedding tour ended with a visit to the parents of Mr. Rukgaber, Mr. and Mrs. Christian Rukgaber, at Germania, where there was a family reunion and festivities reigned with good wishes and hearty welcome.

DIED.

RAYMOND. – In Sweden, June 1st, 1883, Lorimela S., wife of the late W. S. Raymond, aged 73 years, 7 months and 18 days. She died as she has lived, trusting in her Saviour.

Roulet. The remains of Mrs. Julia Thompson, who died in Hebron, was interred in the Sartwell Creek Cemetery, on Tuesday last.

- Our West Branch Correspondent writes us that Erastus Crippen has been restored to the pension rolls with an increase of pension, by act of Congress, he draws on his first voucher over $1,600, and $30 per month from the 3d of March.

- Already there is complaint of flower stealing at the cemetery. Flowers planted by loving hands are picked and often pulled up by visitors. Even women grown have been seen to go from grave to grave and rob them of the floral offerings of friends. It hardly seems possible that any one can be so devoid of feeling as to rob a grave of the flowers put there by bereaved friends, but such is the case. We believe there is a heavy penalty fixed by law for such vandalism, and it is one that should be enforced to its extreme limit and the person taking the matter in hand will confer a great benefit of the community at large by thus protecting the graves and perhaps a lasting benefit on the thieves by teaching them that there are some things sacred from which they must keep their hands. This same despoiling of graves occurs every summer and it is high time a stop is put to it.

- A few days ago M. L. Gridley found a large rat in one of his rooms in his feed store. He closed every avenue of escape, and called in assistance to despatch the rodent. Jule Hodskin was one of the assistants. In company with the big rat was another one though much smaller, and the presence of this last one was unknown to the rat slayers. With sticks and clubs the slaughter of the old rat was accomplished, and the boys had lots of fun. Suddenly Jule grabbed the slack of his pants, pretty well up under his coat-tail, and yelled like a circus Indian, and the war dance began. For a few minutes it was lively work during the excitement of the battle the little rat had crawled up inside of Jule's pants, and the discovery of his presence was the cause of Jule's circus troubles. He finally squeezed the life out of the rat, but the look of disgust clung to his face for two days, and he'll not go into another rat killing match until he has a certain knowledge that no young rats can crawl up his pants.

- A gang of laborers were put at work last week on the line of the New York and North Pennsylvania railway, the route of which extends from Coudersport to Gaines, connecting with the A. & N. P. railway. The men were at work in Potter county, when an injunction was served on them by the State Line, Brookland and Pine Creek Railway Company, and all work was suspended. The last named Company proposed to build a narrow-gauge railroad from Wellsville to Manchester to connect with the Pine Creek Railway, and on Wednesday last its officers sent a party of workmen to Gaines and began grading about a mile above that place. But turn-about is fair play, and the New York and North Pennsylvania Company promptly served an injunction on their rivals Thursday morning. While these rival railroads stand with locked horns waiting for the courts to decide on the merits of their case, the Jersey Shore, Pine Creek and Buffalo Railway Company holds the right of way for a standard gauge railway from Manchester to Coudersport. It looks very much as if there would be a railway of some sort up Pine Creek very soon, if the spirit of rivalry and number schemes on foot have anything to do with it. The argument of the injunction cases was set down for yesterday at this borough, and several gentlemen interested in the roads attended at that time; but the cases were continued to the 11th of June at Coudersport. – *Wellsboro Agitator.*

- An accident occurred at Ellison's saw mill on Monday, quite serious and it may prove fatal to Alfred Taylor, recently of Emporium. A slab caught on the large circular saw and was thrown with great violence striking young Taylor in the stomach, causing a very bad rupture, and probably other serious injuries.

- At Costello's tannery, at North Wharton, on Monday last, a German fell over back from the running plank into a hot leach. His feet hung to the plank and he kept his head from the hot liquor. From his knees to his neck he was badly scalded. It is not believed that he can recover. His name we did not learn.

Officers.
The officers of A. F. Jones Post, G. A. R., for 1883, are:
J. M. Covey, P.C.; C. J. Marble, S.V.C.; John Metzger, J.V.C.; C. N. Barrett, Adjutant; G. N. Tuttle, Q.M.; Dr. Frank Buck, Surgeon; A. D. Colcord, Chap.; Albert Colcord, O.D.; John Dolway, O.G.; John Earle, S.M.; H. Baker, Q.S.

Meetings on 1st Friday and 3d Saturday evenings of each month.

The Potter Enterprise
Wednesday Evening, June 13, 1883 – Vol. X, No. 6

West Homer – South Eulalia. Born – To the wife of Wm. Dennis, a son, June 4th. What is remarkable about this child is it has ten grandparents.

DIED.

THOMPSON – Crandall Hill, May 28th, after a short illness, Julia, wife of Burt Thompson, aged 16 years and 11 months.

And now they tell me you are dead;
   Oh! Julia, Julia, can it be,
Your weary bark has stranded
   On the shores of the eternity?
Full soon, full soon, the flowers bloomed
   That were grown to grace your sleep;
And now the stars above your grave,
   Will their loving vigils keep.

West Branch. Mrs. May Campbell died yesterday afternoon, June 7, a the residence of her parents. She was the daughter of Erastus Crippen, she leaves a babe not yet three months old. May was not quite sixteen years old, but was a large, robust looking person; she attended the Decoration ceremony at Wellsboro, on the 30th of May, and took a cold that soon terminated her short life. She was attended by Dr. Reynolds of Sunderlinville and Dr. Meine of Germania. They called the disease rheumatism.

- Ralzy Steadman, an old and respected citizen of Harrison, died yesterday morning at the house of his son, L. Steadman, at the advanced age of 85 years. Mr. Steadman was a pioneer settler of Potter county; having resided in Harrison township for about fifty years, and during the long period he has uniformly enjoyed the esteem and respect of his fellow citizens. He leaves three sons and two daughters to mourn his loss. – *Westfield Free Press.*

Up in Potter.

A trip to Coudersport, over the C. & P. A. narrow gauge, takes one back several years to the time when brakemen wore thick gloves and swung all over the car platform, at the approach to every station, in their endeavor to bring the train to a stop; and the contrast is so great that one cannot but notice it. To step off from a B. N. Y. & P. train where all the employees are togged out as nicely as a parlor car conductor, and don't have any more work to do, and then watch the running of a road that has not reached the air and vacuum brake era, the change is very noticeable. But the little road has done and is doing much toward building up the country through which it passes; a section though settled three-quarters of a century ago, in spots to-day, has much the appearance of the newer settlements in the northern tier. And the railroad is doing it all. Mills and other industries are scattered on every side and the whole region has taken on a new look, more especially in and around the borough of Coudersport. This is one of the prettiest villages to be found in Northern Pennsylvania, and has been seventy years in building. There are few traces to be seen of the great fire which occurred on the afternoon of May 18, 1880, and which destroyed the business portion of the town. But it was a blessing, for now solid brick blocks, in most instances, occupy the site of the old tinder boxes. The jail and the bank are built of stone. One is intended to keep people from breaking out and the other from breaking in. Mr. Monroe, the Sheriff, and Mr. Jones, the banker, both enjoy a good business, but the latter gives better satisfaction to his customers and holds their patronage longer. There are two newspapers published here, but the preceding subject has nothing to do with this, they never conflict. The Journal is the old paper and was established in '48. It is now being published by Edwin Haskill who was first connected with it in '52. He has been out of the harness for twenty years. The Enterprise, by W. W. Thompson, is the other paper, and like its aged neighbor is a first class production. The other industries are five saw mills, two grist mills, two tanneries, one carding mill, and a foundry. Of lawyers and physicians there are enough. It is said that twenty-five buildings are being erected. There is much talk about new railroads. The Corning & Cowanesque is now running from Lawrenceville to Westfield, a distance of twenty-five miles. It is being built to Harrison Valley, six miles farther, and surveyors are extending the line to Coudersport. There is also talk of extending the narrow gauge, which runs from Addison, N.Y. to Gaines, Tioga county, and connecting it with the C. & P. A., but that doesn't seem at all probable for it is an Erie feeder, while the Corning road is a N.Y.C. institution and the C. & P. A. right of way was obtained through its officers. The outlook for Coudersport is certainly very bright, but before the town can improve to any extent, the fabulous prices at which land is held must be knocked down. A good hotel building is needed very much, but a desirable site cannot be had at less than $100 per foot front. The Nichols House is being conducted in good style, but Mr. Covey, the proprietor, needs more room and a better building. – *Eldred Eagle*.

The Potter Enterprise
Wednesday Evening, June 20, 1883 – Vol. X, No. 7

Clara. Burt Campbell and wife rejoice over a bran new baby boy.

Clara. Wedding cards were received by many friends here from Mr. and Mrs. T. A. McMahon, of Martinez, Cal. Mrs. McMahon, *nee* Martha R. Chase, was a Potter county girl and has the congratulations of many warm friends from here.

MARRIED.

LYMAN – DICKINSON – On June 9th, 1883, at the M. E. Parsonage, Lyndville, N.Y., by Rev. G. E. Ackerman (the bride's brother) A. S. Lyman, of Oswayo, Pa., and Mary A. Dickinson, of Bath, N.Y.

REYMER – YENTZER – At the residence of the bride, in Roulet, Pa., on June 13th, 1883, by Rev. W. A. Bennett, Mr. Isrial Reymer, of Rock City, Ill., and Miss Lena Yentzer, of Roulet, Potter county, Pa.

Court Minutes.

Court convened June 11, H. W. Williams, president judge, presiding. Present associates Hammond and Lewis.

Constables of the several townships made returns.

Thomas Kelley, Thomas Gorman and Frederick Schwab admitted to citizenship.

Comth vs E. E. Wood, nol pros.

Grand jury called and sworn; Samuel Bebee foreman, Louis Hoppe constable to attend same. Grand jury discharged June 13.

A. L. Harvey appointed guardian of Ernest Chase and Hattie L. Chase.

Leave granted to send up a new indictment in comth vs D. P. Reed, Harriet and Willis Reed.

Ordered by court that hereafter constables be selected from the different townships in alphabetical order to attend grand jury, commencing with Abbot for present term.

In matter of Carl Seibenheimer, a lunatic, prothonotary to give notice that account will be presented at next term of court.

Thos. Leary vs Allen Jordan, defendant to pay half of yearly rental fixed by jury of inquisition to J. L. Barclay.

John Taubert appointed treasurer of Homer twp.

A. B. Mann appointed auditor to report upon the expediency of authorizing E. O. Austin, guardian, to sell real estate of Rob't K. Young, dec'd, at private sale; also same in case of Winfred Burt, dec'd.

Merrick Jackson vs Sylvania twp, mandatory writ ordered.

In matter of alleged lunacy of G. W. Daniels, a resident of Bingham, E. W. Chapell appointed committee, notice to be given alleged lunatic and his wife.

Charles L. Hackett, Minnie E. Hackett and Munson B. Hackett adopted by F. M. Younglove.

James Impsom qualified as constable of Stewardson twp.

John R. Nicklaus, a native of Switzerland, admitted to citizenship.

Esther L. Burrows appointed guardian of Ida Dingman, minor child of Nancy Ann Dingman, dec'd, of West Branch. A. B. Mann appointed auditor to report as to advisability of selling real estate at private sale.

A. B. Mann appointed auditor to report on advisability of selling at private sale real estate of C. Burrows, minor.

O. M. Card appointed supervisor of Portage twp.

L. A. Hollenbeck admitted to practice in several courts of Potter county.

Keziah Frazier vs John Frazier, alias sub in divorce awarded.

Comth vs John Cummings, selling liquor, true bill.

Comth vs Charles Button and John Pickett, larceny, true bill, bail forfeited and respited.

Comth vs Clark Judd, selling liquor, guilty. Continued to next term.

Comth vs J. O. Edgcomb, selling liquor, guilty, fined $100 and costs.

J. W. Stevens vs Harrison twp, special tax of six mills ordered.

L. D. Ripple appointed guardian of Margaret Gallagher and to give bond in the sum of $2,000.

Comth vs D. P. Hawley, selling liquor, sentenced to pay a fine of $100 and costs.

Comth vs Edward McGonigal, selling liquor, fine of $100 and costs.

Comth vs D. P., Harriet and Willis Reed, involuntary manslaughter, bail $200 for appearance at next term.

Comth vs E. A. Graves, contempt of court, sentenced to pay costs. Same vs Charles Warner and George Humphrey, same as above.

Comth vs Fred Davenport, selling liquor, fine $100 and costs.

Comth vs John Ward, selling liquor, plead guilty, bail $200 for appearance at next term.

Comth vs Amos Velie, selling liquor, fine $100 and costs.

Comth vs L. C. King, selling liquor, bail $200 for appearance at next term.

Comth vs E. McGonigal, selling liquor to minors, continued.

Bryan McGinnis appointed overseer of poor of Genesee twp.

Comth vs W. B. Perkins, settled, def't to pay record costs.

Comth vs Charles Marvin, indictment quashed, leave granted to send up new indictment.

Comth vs Esther Shay, fornication, bail $100 for appearance at next term.

Comth vs John Cummings, selling liquor, fine $1 and costs and to undergo imprisonment in county jail for a period of sixty days.

Comth vs Harrison Koon, selling liquor. Def't discharged.

Comth vs Mrs. Thomas Glover, larceny, true bill, def't discharged on motion of district attorney.

Comth vs H. J. Mills, obstructing highway, indictment quashed.

Rob't Church vs Frank Morey, jury find property belonged to defendant and the value thereof was $75.

Comth vs John Nesbit, assault and battery, not a true bill; same vs same, not a true bill; county to pay costs in both cases.

Comth vs John M'Quay, assault and battery with an attempt to commit a rape, not a true bill; county to pay costs.

Comth vs Charles Marvin, fornication, true bill.

Comth vs John Crusen, selling liquor, defendant discharged from prison by consent of District Attorney.

Comth vs Lucinda Seals and Florentine Stevens, adultery, nol pros to enter on payment of costs.

Comth vs L. C. King, selling liquor, plead guilty, bail $200 for appearance at next term.

Comth vs Rob't Niles, selling liquor, discharged from prison by consent of District Attorney.

Wm. Rotsell vs D. Rotsell, divorce granted.

Comth vs Charles Marvin, fornication, not guilty.

Comth vs Julius Prindle, assault and battery, nol pros on payment of costs.

License granted to L. C. King to peddle.

Luke G. Crandall vs Emma Crandall, A. B. Mann appointed auditor to distribute funds arising from Sheriff sale.

Tubbs for use vs Geo. W. Chisholm, A. B. Mann appointed commissioner to take testimony.

Thomas Abbott vs Mary Abbott, A. B. Mann appointed commissioner to take testimony.

Henry C. James vs Alsada James, A. B. Mann appointed commissioner to take testimony.

John P. Miller vs L. C. Bruce, jury find for plaintiff in sum of sixty dollars.

H. H. Dent for use vs Jackson township, tax of five mills ordered.

John Henry vs Bingham township, tax of five mills ordered.

F. M. Reynolds vs Allegany township, tax of five mills ordered.

W. P. Metcalf and J. W. Stevens appointed guardians of Cora B. and Perry Rumsey, bond $2,000.

Comth vs Mathew Prosser, larceny, defendant discharged.

Veniries to issue for 24 grand and 36 traverse jurors for September term.

Lizzie Smith vs R. Smith, H. C. Dornan appointed commissioner to take testimony.

Elizabeth Reed vs Levi Reed, H. C. Dornan appointed commissioner to take testimony.

Elvina C. Baker appointed guardian of Frank C. Baker, minor child of George L. Baker, bond $1,200.

Comth vs John Darcy, surety of the peace, defendant to pay one half the costs and prosecutor, Mrs. Lewis, the other half.

Estate of Sobieski Ross, J. C. Johnson appointed auditor to restate the account of W. K. Jones.

J. L. Knox appointed auditor to distribute funds arising from sale of real estate of Washington Johnson, deceased.

Virginia Quinett vs Edwin Quinett, record amended by substituting desertion.

Estate of Garret Fosmer, H. C. Dornan appointed auditor.

Thos. J. Abbott vs Mary Abbott, divorce granted.

H. C. James vs Alsada James, divorce granted.

Adjourned Term of Court, for argument of certain cases, &c., will be held on the second day of July.

Daniel Monroe, Sheriff of Potter county, acknowledged the following deeds:

To. J. W. Stevens for 30 acres in Harrison, sold as property of W. H. Jones, for $20.

To Henry Ingraham for 177 acres in Roulet, sold as property of J. J. Carey, for $25.

To John Parkhurst and E. L. Pattison for 25 acres in Abbott, sold as property of M. Gutgsell, for $26.
To Mary J. Griswold for 100 acres in Hector, sold as property of Geo. W. Chisholm, for $1,376.
To E. M. Johnston, executor, for 12 tracts in Oswayo, sold as property of M. H. Johnston, for $120.
To Bingham Estate for 121.6 acres in Hector, sold as property of John Strait, for $25.
To A. G. Olmsted and I. Benson for 150 acres in Sweden, sold as property of Cyrenus S. Jones, for $100.
To Bingham Estate for 53.2 acres in Hector, sold as property of L. J. Lovell, for $12.
To Bingham Estate for 106 acres in Oswayo and Genesee, sold as property of John O'Donnell (south), for $25.

The Potter Enterprise
Wednesday Evening, June 27, 1883 – Vol. X, No. 8

Colesburg. On the 16th inst., Mr. and Mrs. Eli Nelson celebrated their eighteenth anniversary with a variety wedding. There were about ninety guests and they presented Mr. and Mrs. Nelson with many very beautiful presents as a token of their kind regards.

- Last week Tuesday, Tony Bendell, of Coudersport, a lad ten or a dozen years of age, was taken ill, and presented an appearance of poisoning. For several hours his life was despaired of, but he finally recovered. Some of the boys who had been playing with him said he had eaten some red berries. The red berries were supposed to have been laurel buds, as his case presented symptoms of laurel poisoning. On Sunday the boy was again taken ill in a similar manner, now believed to be a worm fit, and on Monday forenoon death came to his relief. Everything possible was done for the boy but without avail. Tony was an only child, bright and active.

DIED.

TRACEY – In Hebron, June 20th, 1883, Susan, wife of J. P. Tracey, aged 54 years.

Borough Council.

At the meeting the Borough Council on Thursday evening last, D. F. Glassmire, street commissioner, was directed to give the owners of the Metzger & Stevens mill, at East and Fifth street, ten days notice to remove lumber and logs from the streets, and to remove additions to the mill projecting into the streets, and if not moved within the time specified, then the street commissioner is to remove the same and collect the expenses from the mill owners.

Robert Mann appointed pound master.
Z. J. Thompson appointed fire marshal.

Crossing ordered on north side of Fourth street across East street.

Permission given M. L. Gridley to put in hay scales. Same not to interfere with travel or use of street.

Charles Kernan directed to estimate cost of removing sound portion of Second street bridge and erecting same at Seventh street, and to report to council.

The Potter Enterprise
Wednesday Evening, July 4, 1883 – Vol. X, No. 9

No Paper Next Week.

No paper will be issued from this office next week. The office will be open every day for the transaction of business or execution of job work.

OFFICIAL DIRECTORY.

PROTHONOTARY – W. A. Crosby.
REGISTER AND RECORDER – E. D. Lewis.
TREASURER – Edwin Haskell.
SHERIFF – Daniel Monroe.
DISTRICT ATTORNEY – L. H. Cobb.
COUNTY COMMISSIONERS – F. A. Nelson, Burt Oleson, A. H. Spencer.
COUNTY CLERK – William Harvey.
AUDITORS – Thomas Coulston, Dan Baker, L. D. Rippel.
COUNTY SUPERINTENDENT – Anna Buckbee.
COUNTY SURVEYOR – Fayette Lewis.
COUNTY CORONER – Dr. Frank Buck.
JUDICIARY – PRESIDENT JUDGE – H. W. Williams; ADDITIONAL LAW JUDGE – Arthur G. Olmsted.
ASSOCIATE JUDGES – N. C. Hammond, Burton Lewis.
TIME OF HOLDING COURT – First Monday in March, Second Monday in June, Third Monday in September and the Second Monday in December.

Coudersport Boro.

BURGESS – F. W. Knox.
COUNCIL – C. H. Armstrong, M. L. Gridley, P. A. Stebbins, Jr., O. H. Crosby, D. C. Larrabee, D. F. Glassmire.
CLERK – A. B. Mann.
TREASURER – C. S. Jones.
OVERSEERS OF THE POOR – C. S. Jones, R. L. Nichols.
CONSTABLE – L. B. Cole.
HIGH CONSTABLE – E. Crane.
JUSTICES OF THE PEACE – O. J. Rees, Miles White.
SCHOOL DIRECTORS – D. C. Larrabee, President; H. J. Olmsted, O. H. Crosby, William Shear, W. B. Gordnier, Arthur B. Mann.

Coudersport Church Directory.

PRESBYTERIAN – Corner of Main and Fourth streets. Rev. A. Cone, pastor. Services every Sunday at 10:30 a.m. and 7:30 p.m. Sunday School at 12 m. Prayer meetings Thursday evenings.

METHODIST EPISCOPAL – Third street, between Main and East streets, Rev. A. A. Craw, Pastor, services every Sunday At 10:30 a.m. and 7:30 p.m.

BAPTIST – Market Street, south side of the river, Rev. Leavenworth, Pastor, services each Sabbath, morning And evening.

EPISCOPAL – Rev. Wm. Marshall. Services in K. of H. Hall; Services every Sunday (except last Sunday of month) at 10:30 a.m. and 7:45 p.m. Sunday-School at 12 m.

BUSINESS DIRECTORY.
ATTORNEYS.
F. W. KNOX & SON,
ATTORNEYS-AT-LAW, will attend the several Courts of Potter, McKean and Cameron counties. Office corner of Main and First Sts., COUDERSPORT, PA.
A. B. MANN,   JNO. ORMEROD.
MANN & ORMEROD,
ATTORNEYS-AT-LAW, Coudersport, Potter Co., Pa., will attend to business in Cameron, McKean, Tioga and Potter counties.
D. C. LARRABEE,   W. I. LEWIS.
LARRABEE & LEWIS,
ATTORNEYS-AT-LAW, Will attend to business in the several Courts of this District. Office opposite the Court House, Coudersport, Penn'a.
C. L. PECK,
ATTORNEY-AT-LAW, with power to retain M. F. Elliott to assist in the trial of causes. Collections promptly attended to. Office, corner Main and Second Street, second floor, Coudersport, Pa.
A. F. HOLLENBECK,
ATTORNEY-AT-LAW, Coudersport, Penn'a. Office, at Benson's Law Office, Second street. All business promptly attended to.
E. HYDE,
ATTORNEY AND COUNSELOR AT LAW, Main street, Ulysses, Pa. Collections and Legal business promptly attended to. Will also prosecute claims for pension and bounty.

PHYSICIANS.

F. BUCK, M.D.
OFFICE AND RESIDENCE OVER REES' Drug Store. All calls attended with promptness.

MRS. DR. L. A. BROOKS.
PHYSICIAN, Roulet, Pa., will attend all professional calls promptly.

DR. CHARLIE FRENCH.
GENERAL PRACTICIONER. Special attention given to night calls. Consultation with his father, Dr. A. French, without extra charge whenever necessary.

E. S. MATTISON, M.D.
OFFICE Opera House, Second Floor, Front, Main street, Coudersport, Pa. Office hours, 9 to 12 a.m. and 1 to 4 p.m. Night calls at his residence, West street. All calls promptly attended.

DENTISTRY.

S. A. PHILLIPS,   R. S. WREAN.

DRS. PHILLIPS & WREAN.
DENTISTS. Office over the Postoffice, Coudersport, Pa. Gas given when desired. Filling and orders for plates promptly attended to, cheaper than the cheapest. Parties wishing work done at their homes can be accommodated by sending a postal to S. A. Phillips, Coudersport, Pa.

HOTELS.

AMERICAN HOUSE.
NEAR THE DEPOT, Coudersport, Pa. Fred Devanport, Proprietor. New House and new furniture throughout. Good Stabling.

NICHOLS HOUSE.
J. M. COVEY, PRO., COUDERSPORT, PA. This house has been repaired and refitted. Good Sample Rooms for Agents. Good Stabling. *FREE BUS to and from all trains. Passengers carried to any part of town, at reasonable rates.*

HARRISON VALLEY HOUSE.
WM. M. SMITH, Proprietor, Harrison Valley, Pa. This is a new house, newly furnished and first-class in every particular. Good stabling attached.

SURVEYING.
ORLANDO J. REES,
SURVEYOR and CONVEYANCER, Coudersport, Pa. Orders from any part of the county for surveying or conveyancing will receive prompt attention.

W. A. CROSBY,
SURVEYOR, CONVEYANCER and DRAUGHTSMAN, Prothonotary's office, Court House, Coudersport, Pa. Business promptly attend to in any part of the county.

GROCERIES.
C. H. ARMSTRONG,
DEALER in Groceries, Provisions, Crockery, Glassware, Woodenware, Boots and Shoes. Second Street, nearly opposite the Court House, Coudersport, Pa.

TAILORING.
S. VANWINKLE.
TAILOR. Shop over Greisell's Harness Shop, Main street, Coudersport. Making and Cutting in the latest styles and best manner, and at reasonable rates.

PRINTING.
W. W. THOMPSON.
PUBLISHER AND JOB PRINTER, Enterprise Office, Second and West Street, Coudersport, Pa. A full line of Envelopes, Letter Heads, Bill Heads, Statements, Plain and Ornamented Cards, constantly on hand. Blanks of all kinds on hand or printed to order.

BOOTS AND SHOES.
K. ZIMMERMAN,
DEALER in Boots and Shoes, Upper Leather of all kinds, linings, Sole leather, and findings of all kinds. A complete stock of Shoemakers' supplies. Boots and Shoes, of best make, on hand. Repairing promptly attended to. Store on Main Street, below Second, Coudersport, Pa.

BLACKSMITHING.
MAT. M'GOEY.
BLACKSMITHS, corner of West and Second Streets, Coudersport, Pa. Horse shoeing, Carriage Ironing and Custom work in all its branches.

COOPER.
CHRISTIAN ZIMMERMAN,
COOPER, Butter Tubs, Barrels, Churns, Sap Pails, Etc., made to order. Repairing will receive prompt attention. Prices Low. Shop on Second Street, above the Keystone Mill, Coudersport, Pa.

MILLWRIGHT AND BUILDER.
D. W. VANWEGEN.
MILLWRIGHT AND MECHANICAL ENGINEER. Millwrighting in all its branches, mills built or repaired in any section. Special attention given to setting engines. Plans and Specifications made on application. Satisfaction guaranteed. Address, at Coudersport, Pa.

JOSEPH FORSTER
CARRIAGE AND WAGONMAKER, Coudersport, Pa. Shop on Alley, near Perkins' Blacksmith Shop. New work to order. Special attention to repairing of all kinds. None but the best of materials used. Satisfaction guaranteed as to quality of work and timber.

STOP HIM!
If you have any Whitewashing or Paper Hanging to do.
Selected line right from Elmira for ceilings. House and Sign painting will receive special attention. First-class work guaranteed.

JOHN B. PEARSALL,
Coudersport, Pa.

BANK OF COUDERSPORT.
W. K. JONES, BANKER,
SUCCESSOR TO
ARCH F. JONES & SON, BANKERS.
Coudersport, Penn'a.
DEPOSITS RECEIVED.
PROMPT REMITTANCE MADE ON COLLECTIONS.
DRAFTS SOLD ON
NEW YORK, PHILADELPHIA
and all principal points in Europe and the British Isles.
OFFICE HOURS FROM 9 A.M. TO 4 P.M.

> **FIRE, LIFE, AND ACCIDENT**
> **INSURANCE AGENCY**
> **OF**
> **L. B. COLE & SON,**
> **Coudersport, Pa.**
> Policies written in Reliable Companies at the standard rates. Will visit any part of Potter county on request. All business intrusted to us will receive
> PROMPT ATTENTION.
> Office, Up Stairs, in P. A. Stebbins, Jr., & Bro's Store Building.
> **Coudersport, Pa.**

> **MANN'S INSURANCE AGENCY,**
> **COUDERSPORT, PA.**
> **Twenty Millions of Dollars Represented.**
> **The Best and Strongest Companies.**
> The Insurance Company of North America, of Philadelphia, OLDEST STOCK COMPANY IN AMERICA.
> The Pennsylvania Fire Insurance Company of Philadelphia.
> The Fire Association of Philadelphia.
> The Commonwealth Insurance Company, of Boston, Mass.
> The Fire Insurance Association (Limited) of London, England.
> The Connecticut Mutual Life Insurance Company, of Hartford, Conn.
> The Travelers' Accident Insurance Company, of Hartford, Conn.
> **WHEN YOU WANT**
> **INSURANCE!**
> Go to **MANN**. When you want to join some subscription agency, go to some stranger of whom you know nothing.

- It is Ed. Cornell who is receiving congratulations now. A fine healthy girl warms his heart and makes music in his home.

- Frank Stevens has already commenced his Fourth of July Celebration. A fine girl baby at his house this morning is what mixed him on dates.

MARRIED.

COLGROVE – BENTON – By Rev. J. L. Swain at his residence in Allegany, June 10th, 1883, Mr. Warren L. Colgrove, of Sharon Centre, to Mrs. Lettie L. Benton, of Allegany.

Potter County, Pennsylvania Potpourri – Volume I
1880 through 1884

Tony Bendell.

There has been a great deal of conjecture, and diversity of opinion, concerning the cause of death of Tony Bendell, a lad of ten years who died a few days ago in convulsions, supposed to ensue from worms, or something he had eaten.

Notwithstanding the *Journal*, in concluding the paragraph on his death, gave the physicians the credit of not knowing the cause of death, after an autopsy. We gather from the physicians themselves, that he died from inflammation of the brain and spinal cord.

It seems that this is the fourth child Mr. Bendell has lost in convulsions. It is no reasonable to believe that each death ensued from worms or something eaten.

Tony had several attacks in a milder form for two or three years past, and had been growing worse, until about two weeks ago, when he had an attack accompanied with paralysis of one side.

A physician was called and all was done that could be and at the end of nearly ten hours of violent spasms, he became easier and after a day or two he was out again.

On the following Sunday he went with his parents a distance of three miles on foot to visit a friend, when he was taken again with convulsions, this time accompanied with high fever, and unmistakable symptoms of inflammation of the brain, and died the following day at noon.

A *post mortem* was held by Drs. French, Ashcraft and Stebbins which resulted as above stated. No derangement of the stomach or bowels were found.

There seems to have been a hereditary predisposition to nervous disorders among these children, by peculiar make up of nervous system and combination of temperaments.

Great sympathy is felt for the bereaved parents in the loss of their only remaining child, who was an unusually bright and engaging boy.

- Six weeks ago Henderson Corsaw, of Sweden, weighed about 130 pounds; last week he weighed a little over 230 pounds. It is said that he has Bright's disease.

- Keron Hanlon will in a short time open a meat market at Coudersport. The people of that village will be supplied with the best the market affords, as Mr. Hanlon thoroughly understands how to run a first-class meat market. – *Port Allegany Reporter.*

- The Episcopal Church Society have about $1,100 on hand with which they intend to commence the erection of a church building, on Main street, corner of Sixth, on the lot presented the church for that purpose, by Miss Kate Dent, of Brookland.

- There was a lively time at the residence of C. A. Stebbins last Tuesday. Charley's bird dog had not been well for a day or two. Supposed to have a touch of distemper. Tuesday it was in the house, frothing at the mouth and exhibiting other symptoms of hydrophobia. Charley got the children into a room, closed the door and with gun in hand attempted to drive the dog out of doors. He finally succeeded but the dog showed fight, snapping and biting at everything in his way. Ten feet from the door was far enough and a charge of shot ended the life of the dog. Charley has no doubt the dog was suffering from hydrophobia.

Adultery, Paris Green, Murder, &c.?

On the 25th of October, 1878, on the Billy Lewis road, between the Turnpike and the Denton Hill road, a little five year old child of Mr. and Mrs. John Schall was lost in the woods, and although hundreds of men searched the woods for several days no trace of the child was found, and the matter still remains a mystery. Last week the matter was again brought to public notice.

To begin the present story properly we will commence at the marriage of John Nesbitt and Mrs. Rose Braitling, a year or more ago. The Nesbitt place is located about a mile from the Schall place, and was occupied by Nesbitt at the time the child disappeared. On this place Nesbitt and his wife lived together until recently, when from some cause she left and went to keeping house for Mr. Grodevant, on the Lymansville road.

The story goes that a week ago last Saturday night, Mr. Gibson, living with Nesbitt, called at Grodevant's and during his visit have his host a drink of whiskey, which Grodevant drank, but that given Mrs. Nesbitt was put in a cup and set aside out of sight. Some time during the night, it is said, Nesbitt opened a window in Grodevant's house and found Grodevant and Mrs. Nesbitt occupying the same bed. He did not rave, but said he had got all the evidence he wanted, and left.

The next morning physicians were called to see Grodevant, who claimed to have been poisoned. Paris Green was found in the cup alleged to have been set aside. Grodevant's case did not present strong symptoms of Paris Green poisoning, and he soon recovered. Talk of warrants for adultery and attempt at poison flew thick and fast and we believe were actually issued in the former case. It was charged that Nesbitt mixed the whiskey and poison which Gibson delivered. Gibson himself says it was a fair article of liquor, of which he drank with Grodevant, and from which he felt no ill effects.

Thursday morning Mrs. Nesbitt made oath, on which a search warrant was issued, that she believed the Schall child was killed by John Nesbitt and buried under one of two stumps on the Nesbitt farm. This information she claimed to have obtained from Nesbitt's talking in his sleep, and she said that when she charged him with it afterward he did not deny it but said if she ever "blowed" he would "put her under the other one," (a stump standing near).

Thursday afternoon Sheriff Monroe, accompanied by Mrs. Nesbitt and a dozen or more men, repaired to the Nesbitt farm. Here Mrs. N. pointed out a stump which she said was the one, the second stump having been turned back since she married Nesbitt. The stump in question was that of a large hemlock tree which had been turned over by the wind, afterwards sawed off and the stump turned back. With block and tackle the stump was again turned over and a thorough search made, but no remains were found. A small stump near was served in the same manner, with a like result. While the posse were at work Mr.

Nesbitt arrived from town where he had been on business, and he rendered assistance and furnished tools.

The parties most interested, Mr. and Mrs. Nesbitt, passed a good many hard words, Mrs. N. reiterating her statement that Nesbitt talked in his sleep of killing the child and burying it under the stump which had been sawed off and turned back. When asked for the motive, she said it was because Schall was jealous of Mrs. Schall and Nesbitt and the object was the separating of the Schall family. Nesbitt denied any knowledge of the lost child's whereabouts or its fate, and invited the Sheriff to pull every stump on the farm and make such other search as he desired. The stumps pulled had no remains under them, and they had certainly not been tampered with for a year or more.

This story of Nesbitt's talking in his sleep of the lost child is not an entirely new one. A similar one was told to the District Attorney several months ago by Mrs. Nesbitt in company with a man who had worked for Nesbitt.

It is reported that Thursday night Nesbitt visited Grodevant's and a settlement of existing difficulties effected, and all proposed prosecutions dropped.

- High School at Shingle House – The school directors at a meeting last week decided to build a new school house near the road that leads to the Sunny Side on the land of Geo. Nichols if it could be obtained and throw up the Nichols school house and the one here and as they are both nearly worthless and build a good two department school house and try and have nine months school a year. This plan ought to be encouraged by every one in the town as it would save the hiring of one teacher and would give more money for the hiring of a teacher and provide a place where our children could be educated at home in the higher branches and would induce others from a distance to patronize our school. It should be made as good a school at there is in the county. – *Palladium*.

Grand Celebration and Picnic at North Wharton, Pa., July 4, 1883.

Base ball match; foot races, sack race, wheelbarrow race, etc.; platform dance afternoon and evening; first-class music; dinner and refreshments served on the picnic grounds; grand display of fireworks, at a cost of $100.00. Balloon ascension, discharging at various elevations, continuous streams of meteors, bombs, variegated showers, gold rain, etc.

The Potter Enterprise
Wednesday Evening, July 18, 1883 – Vol. X, No. 10

- Charley Welton blushes and smiles as he receives the congratulations of his numerous friends. A bouncing boy Tuesday.

MARRIED.

McMULLER – BENNETT – At Lewisville, Pa., July 5th, 1883, by Rev. Thos. L. Perry, Mr. Matthew McMuller, of Wellsville, N.Y., to Miss Annie L. Bennett, of West Pike, Pa.

HOOVER – PERRY – At the residence of the bride's parents, July 5th, 1883, by Rev. T. L. Perry, Mr. Alexander P. Hoover, of Summit City, Pa., to Miss Estella A. Perry, of Lewisville, Pa.

Eleven Mile. Last Tuesday, the 10th, Mrs. Joseph Elliott was buried at the Oswayo Centre cemetery. An Adventist improved the opportunity to again expound his wisdom for the enlightenment(?) of the congregation. It must have been tedious for the mothers of the numerous babies and small children present to sit for an hour and a half under such powerful demonstration from both children and speaker. The deceased left a husband and four small children, the youngest a babe of four weeks.

Eleven Mile. On June 25th, Hiram Goodale was buried in the same cemetery. He left a wife and two small children in quite limited circumstances. He was an industrious, peaceable citizen and neighbor.

- A white mink was killed in the lower part of town Sunday.

The Potter Enterprise
Wednesday Evening, July 25, 1883 – Vol. X, No. 11

West Homer and South Hill. The ladies of our place were invited to celebrate the birth days of Charles Furgeson and daughter, on the 11th of July. Well we all gathered together with one accord at his house and partook of a delicious supper. Among the rest was Edith Lathrop, and we were all pleased to see her out once more. Mr. Charles Knickerbocker, of Ayers Hill, was also present. We think these little afternoon gatherings a great help to the sociability of the neighborhood.

West Pike. Miss Laura Bennett is no more. She passed from the stage of action as a single lady, a few days since, and has launched her bark on the matrimonial sea. May happiness attend her.

MARRIED.

PLANTS – JAMES – At the residence of Miss Mariah Coates, in Allegany, June 30th, 1883, by L. B. Morley, J.P., Mr. Reuben C. Plants to Mrs. Alsada James, all of Allegany.

SNYDER – STEADMAN – At the Fassett House, Wellsville, July 15th, by Rev. A. Colt, Mr. Otis H. Snyder and Miss Maggie C. Steadman, both of Harrison, Pa.

KIES – BISHOP – At the residence of the bride's brother, B. F. Bishop, on Sunday, June 15th, by Rev. N. North, Mr. Henry Kies and Miss Carrie E. Bishop, both of Allegany, Potter county, Pa.

- Miss Ellen J. Tassel, of Hebron, died July 11th, 1883, aged 26 years, 8 months and 11 days. A good christian lady, died in peace.

West Homer and South Hill. We are sorry to hear of the death of Mrs. John Brownlee of North Wharton. She died of Cancer, has had all done for her that kindness or money could do, having visited Rome, N.Y., three times but of no avail. She has been a great but very patient sufferer. She yielded submissively to God's will. We extend our greatest sympathy to the bereaved family.

- The white mink killed at the lower end of town last week was, doubtless, John Covey's pink eyed, straw colored ferret which escaped from his cellar a few days previous.

- Geo. Lewis met with a surprise while working at D. C. Larrabee's last Saturday. He was smoking a cigar and got his face over a gasoline barrel which still contained a very small amount of the liquid. There was a flash and a blaze, of short duration, but sufficiently long enough to burn his hands, neck and face quite severely.

Summer Races.

Are announced to come off on the Coudersport Driving Park, Thursday, August 2d. Four races are announced: Three minute class; three year old running race; 2:50 class and free for all running race. Purses, $50 for each race, divided. Entries, ten per cent. of purse and close August 1st, at 9 p.m. Races called at 1 o'clock p.m. Admission to the grounds, 50 cents; carriages free. Enough good horses are already promised to make a fine day of sport. Old Hartland and two of his colts will be on hand for the running races. Four races for one afternoon, will make a warm afternoon work.

- The deputy U. S. Marshal visited Coudersport last Monday and arrested Amos Veelie and L. C. King, on the charge of selling liquor without a United States license. We understand the parties propose to give bail.

- The house of George McGowan, of Lymansville, was burned to the ground last Monday night. The fire was discovered by some of the neighbors about midnight and the alarm was promptly given. A large number of the neighbors responded, but the fire had gained such headway that it was impossible to save the building or remove any great amount of the contents. The fire, apparently, originated in the kitchen but there had been no fire in that part since the noon previous. There was no insurance. At the time of the fire Mr. and Mrs. McGowan were away from home, attending a party on South Hill.

The Potter Enterprise
Wednesday Evening, August 1, 1883 – Vol. X, No. 12

Whites Corners. Amanzo J. McCutcheon and Miss Lucretia Wallace were married on July 1st. We wish them much joy.

- Joseph Butler, for many years a resident of Sweden township, was buried on Saturday last. His death was caused by a cancer on his tongue. For a long time he has been a great sufferer and for some time unable to eat solid food, and this forced starvation wasted his frame until he was nothing but a skeleton.

Democratic County Convention.

The Democratic Convention met in the Court House on Thursday last and was called to order by Wm. Dent, chairman of the County Committee.

James Nelson was selected as Chairman of the Convention, and C. L. Peck and Ira Easton, secretaries.

A committee of six were appointed to confer with a like committee from the Greenback Convention, then in session at G. A. R. hall, to see if a Union ticket could be agreed upon.

Wm. Dent was appointed Delegate to the State Convention, with power to appoint substitute.

The committee having returned reported that if the Democrats would endorse Leroy Allen, of Clara, for Sheriff, the Greenbackers would endorse the Democratic nominees for Treasurer and District Attorney. The proposition was agreed to.

Charles Coats and S. B. Haskins were named for Treasurer. Mr. Haskins was nominated on first ballot.

For District Attorney H. C. Dornan and Edson Hyde were named. Mr. Dornan was nominated on first ballot.

The County Committee is to consist of one from each township or borough. The following are the appointments as far as made:

Charles Coats, Allegany; Henry Theis, Abbott; L. B. Lewis, Bingham; O. H. Crosby, Coudersport; Ira Easton, Genesee; John W. Lewis, Hector; E. A. Burt, Lewisville; Ed. McGonigal, Oswayo; S. B. Haskins, Portage; J. B. Davidson, Roulet; Jacob Failing, Sharon; C. M. Herrington, Sweden; A. J. Burleson, Sylvania; Wm. Dent, Ulysses.

Samuel Haskins, a resident of North Wharton, a Potter county boy, well qualified for the position of Treasurer. When still a boy he received injuries to one limb from which he has never recovered, and which unfits him for manual labor. By his own exertion he received a good education, teaching school and saving his means carefully, expending the same in attending school and procuring books. He has filled various township offices and has always left a clean record. Once before he has been nominated for a county office, that of Register and Recorder. He was defeated, but his vote was far ahead of his ticket. The run he made then was one to be proud of. Mr. Haskins is every way competent for the office for which he has been nominated and a vote for him is a vote for a self made young man, who deserves as well at the hands of his fellow citizens.

H. C. Dornan was born in Schuylkill county, received a collegiate education and studied law with Hon. James Campbell, an eminent Philadelphia lawyer. He was admitted to the bar in 1874, and shortly after removed to McKean county, where he has, until his removal to Coudersport, practiced his profession, and where for three years he acted as assistant District Attorney, during the pressure of criminal business consequent upon the oil excitement. The experience of those three years peculiarly fits him for the position for which he is a candidate. Ex-District Attorney, S. W. Smith, of McKean, speaks very highly of Mr. Dornan as an assistant and of his legal qualifications. Mr. Dornan is the right man for District Attorney.

J. L. Allen, of Clara, is one of the well known citizens of Potter county, a farmer who has followed the business successfully. For many year he has been Justice of the Peace in his township, being re-elected term after term, showing that his neighbors, who know him best, consider him a man of good judgment, and one in whose judgment they are willing to trust. Mr. Allen did not ask for the nomination, but the nomination sought him, and he accepted. We believe no one can say aught against Mr. Allen or his qualifications for the office of Sheriff.

Hair Weaving of all kinds, waves or switches, - roots of the hair turned up. Orders filled promptly.
Call on Mrs. E. Aylesworth.

New Meat Market.
K. Hanlon has opened a new Meat Market, in the Carey building south of the Main street bridge, and has stocked it with the choicest fresh and salt meats, fish, vegetables, &c. He proposes to keep a first class market, always well stocked. Call in and see.

Drs. Phillips & Wrean,
DENTISTS,
COUDERSPORT, POTTER CO., PENN'A.

We use the Best of Material, and Warrant all of our work. Look at the following prices:

We extract the teeth and make a double set for	$20.00
Single set,	10.00
Partial plate for four teeth,	6.00
Ordinary Gold Fillings,	1.50
Diamond Cement Fillings,	.75
Amalgam Fillings,	.75
Extracting Teeth, each	.25
Gas, for Extracting Teeth without pain,	1.00

Parties wishing work done at their homes will please drop us a postal card at Coudersport, PA.

S. A. Phillips can be found at the home office, in Coudersport, at all times.

DR. R. S. WREAN

Will visit the following places regularly every three weeks, commencing July 30th, 1883:

Shingle House,	Monday
Oswayo,	Tuesday
Ellisburg,	Wednesday
Whitesville,	Thursday
Harrison Valley,	Friday

The following week, commencing August 6th, 1883:

Ulysses,	Monday
Pike Mills,	Tuesday
Gaines,	Wednesday
Germania,	Thursday
Oleona,	Friday

The following week, commencing July 23d, 1883:

Costelloville,	Monday
Forest House,	Tuesday
Emporium,	Wednesday and Thursday
Port Allegany,	Friday
Roulet,	Saturday

The Potter Enterprise
Wednesday Evening, August 8, 1883 – Vol. X, No. 13

- John Ormerod was called to Canada last week by a telegram announcing the death of his father.

DIED.

CHAMBERLAIN – In Hebron, Potter Co., Pa, July 27th, 1883, Solomon Chamberlain, aged sixty-three years.

SCHADENBERGER – In Eulalia, August 2d, 1883, Walter C., son of Mr. and Mrs. Christian Schadenberger, aged nine years, ten months and six days.

Hebron. Yesterday a play was enacted in town. It was announced in the morning as a tragedy; perhaps it was, but everybody laughed and I thought it was a comedy. The particulars I can gather are as follows: Jeff. Burdic and wife have been working this summer for Leroy Witter. It seems that Mrs. B. had decided not to live with her husband longer. But Jeff. took it to heart seriously. He announced to all the neighbors as he journeyed toward Oswayo that he wished to bid them a long farewell as he was about to poison himself. Word came, in the afternoon, that he had really taken poison, and some of the neighbors going into Jim Moyer's found him apparently suffering much. About five o'clock Mr. Witter and Mrs. B. went up to view the remains; but it seems Jeff. recovered sufficiently to start off in the buggy with them, and when opposite Henry Lamberton's he was seen (by some who had heard the loud voices in altercation and rushed out) to jump out and run around on the other side of the buggy and strike Witter several times over the head with a stick he had in his hand, upon which "the woman in the case" seized the lines and drove rapidly away. It seems that Jeff. was enraged with jealousy of Mrs. B. and had taken this way to avenge himself. He started for Esq. Estes saying he should give himself up. The finale is yet to come but will, no doubt, be very thrilling. The suicide however miscarried as it appears; at least the subject seemed quite lively last night.

The Potter Enterprise
Wednesday Evening, August 15, 1883 – Vol. X, No. 14

- Born, to Mr. and Mrs. Charles Freck, on Friday last, a daughter.

Raymond. It is reported that Mr. Burton Fassit sleeps good now, has slept good just one week. He was fearful it would be a girl; but it is a boy, a nine pounder. His other children are girls.

DIED.

JOHNSON – At her home in Ulysses, Aug. 3d, 1883, after a long and painful illness, Mrs. Julia E. Johnson, in the 74th year of her age.

CUTLER – At his home in Lewisville, Aug. 5th, 1883, of jaundice, W. J. Cutler in the 70th year of his age.

$2,000.

Some months since Charles F. Huntington died in New Orleans. He was a member of Coudersport Lodge Knights of Honor, in good standing, having kept up all assessments since leaving Coudersport. Proof of death and other papers necessary were forwarded to the Supreme Lodge as soon as they could be properly made out or secured, but having to procure evidence from New Orleans, it required some considerable time. But it was all accomplished finally and last week Mr. Huntington's executor, Mrs. I. Ross, received a check for $2,000, the amount of the policy or insurance certificate, held by Mr. Huntington in the Knights of Honor. Mr. Huntington, since becoming a member of the order, had been called upon to pay less than sixty assessments of one dollar each. This is the first death among the members of Coudersport Lodge since its organization.

- The Catholic pic-nic last Wednesday was a grand success. A large crowd was present, including many from Port Allegany, Turtlepoint and Smethport. It was the largest pic-nic party ever seen in Coudersport. The best of order prevailed. Not a drunken person seen on the grounds, which is astonishing considering the number of persons present. It was well managed, and those having it in charge are deserving of great credit. Five hundred and sixty-five dollars was added to the Church fund by the pic-nic. About six hundred dollars had been subscribed previously. We understand the Smethport Church owes the Coudersport Church fund two hundred and fifty, and the lot, a full square, is a present from the Keatings. It looks now as if the committee had a sufficient amount secured to warrant them in moving right along.

- Late Tuesday night or early Wednesday morning an attempt was made to enter the dwelling house of L. C. Kinner at Shingle House, but the intruders disturbed Mr. Kinner's dog and left without accomplishing their purpose. The burglar then went to Kinner's store, and by means of a ladder entered the upper rooms occupied by John A. Gray, where they appropriated a gold watch and chain, from Mr. Gray's vest, and would probably have relieved him of other property had he not awakened. The burglar made haste to leave, jumping from the window to the awning and from thence to the ground and escaped. No trace has yet been found of the thief. Mr. Kinner had, at his house, considerable money, and no doubt the thief was aware of this fact.

- A charter was issued Friday to the Pine Creek and Susquehanna Railway Company, the line of which will commence at Pike Mills, Potter county, running to Westport, Clinton county, following the Pine Creek and branches and the Valley of Kettle Creek and branches from Pike Mills to Westport. Said railway shall have a gauge not exceeding three feet. The principal office is located at Elkland, Tioga county, and the treasurer for the first year is Mr. C. Sheldon, of New York city. The capital stock is $400,000. The president is C. L. Pattison, of Elkland, Tioga county. The directors are Edgar Munson, D. H. Merriman, Williamsport; Mrs. C. Platt, New York; Charles L. Pattison, Elkland; W. E.

Potter County, Pennsylvania Potpourri – Volume I
1880 through 1884

Womelsdorff, R. H. Wombaugh, Coudersport; Giles Roberts, Knoxville; William H. Fuller, Westfield; William C. Sheldon, New York; S. E. Jones, Henry Baldwin, Addison, N.Y.; George H. Blanchard, New York. The distance of the new road will be forty miles.

Arrested for Burglary.

In November last the store of C. H. Armstrong, in Coudersport, was entered by burglars, the safe blown open and contents carried off. Last Spring two drawers containing papers taken from the safe were found under the bridge of F. W. Knox's barn. From that time until last Saturday evening the matter has received but little public attention.

On Saturday evening a warrant was issued by Miles White, Esq., for the arrest of L. D. Card, on the charge of being concerned in the robbery of Armstrong's store. Card was in town Saturday but hired a rig of James Johnston and left before the warrant was issued. He returned Sunday evening and was promptly arrested by constables Lewis and Cole. Monday Card waived an examination.

Some time after the papers were found last Spring, in looking them over Mr. Armstrong found a small scrap of paper, one side of which was printed, on the other was a due bill given by Birney Clark, of Eulalia, to L. D. Card. Mr. Armstrong had never had the order in his possession, so it must have gotten in the papers after the robbery. Mr. Clark was interviewed, said he had given the due bill to Card, had since paid the debt but when he asked Card to return the due bill was informed that it was lost or had been mislaid in his trunk. Several times he told Clark the same story, the last time on Saturday of last week. This was considered sufficient to warrant legal proceedings which have been commenced as stated above. The due bill was dated the same day that the robbery occurred at night.

Some time after the robbery, this due bill was placed in the hands of Abram Jones as security and afterwards returned to Card. This fact proves the papers were not placed under the bridge at the time of the robbery. It is quite probable that they were not under the bridge any great length of time before they were found. Card's story about the due bill, that it was lost, &c., looks a little strange, and it now looks dark for him. He claims however that he can prove an alibi, and show conclusively that he had nothing to do with the burglary. Only one side of the story is now in possession of the public. It is to be hoped the young man can show that he is innocent of the charge. He has a right to be heard, at least.

ROBBERY AT LEWISVILLE.
Over $200 Taken and Two Safes Damaged.

Last Friday night or Saturday morning, burglars entered the store of Geo. Cobb and Willard Cutler's hardware store in Lewisville.

Cobb's store was evidently the first one visited. The combination knob of the safe was broken in and the lock destroyed so that the bolts were drawn. About $164 in money was taken. Cobb's safe is reported "a burglar proof" and was guarded by a savage bull dog, but neither was proof against the burglars of

Friday night. Saturday morning the dog met Cobb at the door wagging his tail, and evidently pleased to meet his master.

At Cutler's the same game was tried on the safe, but it did not work and they were compelled to drill the safe and use powder. The safe was badly damaged and the burglars secured about forty dollars. They might have saved themselves much hard labor, if they had tried to open the door by turning the bolt knob, as the safe was not locked. They evidently left Cutler's in a hurry as they did not take their tools with them.

The burglars are supposed to be two men who came to Dimon's Hotel Thursday and who stayed there until Friday, when they had an early supper, paid their bill and departed, saying they were going to walk to Coudersport. The larger of the two men did not leave his room at Dimon's during their stay except to take his meals. The smaller one was seen on the streets several times. The following description is given of them.

The smaller of the two is about five feet, six inches in height; slender, black hair a trifle wavy, black or very dark blue eyes, moustache not very heavy, but very black, wore a navy blue shirt, dark clothes, shoes considerably worn, braided straw hat, speckled or spotted, age about 25 or 26 years.

The larger one had a smooth face, sandy complexion, light hair, blue eyes and a very large and prominent nose. Age about forty years.

Two men, one large and the other small, was seen about a mile out of Lewisville, on the road to Brookland, about daylight. Since that time nothing has been heard of them, although a prompt pursuit was made.

The Potter Enterprise
Wednesday Evening, August 22, 1883 – Vol. X, No. 15

- Born – In Coudersport, Thursday morning last, to Mr. and Mrs. D. W. Vanwegen, a daughter.

- And now it is Wm. Koehler, of Sweden, and George Mitchell, of Summit, who are putting on airs. A bouncing boy in the family of each is the cause.

- L. D. Card is out on bail in the sum of $600. His father and brother signed the bail bond.

Jury List – September Term, 1883.
TRAVERSE JURORS.

Abbott – Marcus Handwerk, Lewis Hagerman, Jacob Ohweiler, George Scheultheis; Allegany – Sam'l Atkinson, F. S. Conable, Henry Haskell; Bingham – Joseph Coulston, W. J. Clark, Elymus Monroe, W. G. Raymond; Clara – Jeff Burdick; Coudersport – N. M. Glassmire, D. W. Vanwegen; Genesee – Wm. Hill, Frank Hendryx; Hebron – W. M. Earl, Wm. Greenman; Harrison – J. Metcalf; Lewisville – Fred Allen, A. E. Baker; Pike – F. A. Brown; Roulet – A. W. Johnson, S. B. Pomeroy; Sharon – A. J. Barnes, G. C. Lyon, Geo. W. Prince; Sweden – S. O. Dodd; Summit – Merrick Jackson; Sylvania –

Potter County, Pennsylvania Potpourri – Volume I
1880 through 1884

W. B. Pierce, Wm. Putnam; Stewardson – Wm. Robinson; Ulysses – W. E. Turner; West Branch – John Kherle Jr., Jacob Zengerle; Wharton – W. G. Wilbur.

GRAND JURORS.

Abbott – John Hug; Allegany – Wm. S. Ford, D. L. Raymond; Bingham – Lewis C. Baker, Wm. Ensworth, George Kibbe, L. G. Monroe; Coudersport – A. S. Olmsted, Wm. F. Yunge; Genesee – James Gilliland, George W. Hackett; Hector – W. W. Bailey, T. J. Surdam; Homer – H. M. Case, Harrison Edgcomb, G. F. Younglove; Harrison – Benj. Johnson, G. R. Smith; Hebron – L. D. Reynolds; Pleasant Valley – Philander Reed, Jr.; Sharon – Dana Drake, Proctor Lunn, R. McDonald; Ulysses – Charles Crowell.

Charter Notice.

Notice is hereby given that application will be made on Tuesday of September Term of Court of Potter county, in Coudersport, for the purpose of obtaining a Charter for incorporation of the First Seventh Day Baptist Church of Shingle House, Pa. A corporation formed for the support of public worship according to the faith, usage and practice of the Seventh Day Baptist Church. Signed by Edson Warner, J. J. Kenyon, B. O. Burdick.

Shingle House, Pa. Aug. 20, 1883.

A Rare Chance.

The undersigned offers for sale his two stores with stock and fixtures, or without stock if desired, also, house and lot. Buildings nearly new and well located, doing a business of thirty-five thousand dollars a year. Reasons for selling, poor health of family and self.

L. C. Kinner.

Shingle House, Pa., Aug. 10, 1883.

NEW GROCERY!
NEW STOCK,   FRESH GOODS
ABRAM JONES,
(Nearly opposite the depot,) Coudersport, Pa., has filled his new store with a choice stock of
GROCERIES AND PROVISIONS.
Everything in the Grocery or Provision line
CHEAPER THAN THE CHEAPEST.
Quality and Prices tell.
It will pay you to call and see.

The Potter Enterprise
Wednesday Evening, August 29, 1883 – Vol. X, No. 16

- Born – In Hebron, Aug. 24th, to Mr. and Mrs. John Schollard, a daughter. Weight 9 ½ pounds.

DIED.

CONABLE – In West Branch, Aug. 27, 1883, Anna May, infant twin daughter of Mr. and Mrs. Willis Conable, aged 3 months and 8 days.

KILLED BY LIGHTNING.
Dennis Maginnis of Genesee Instantly Killed.

On Thursday last Dennis, eldest son of Bryan Maginnis, of Genesee township, was killed by lightning. In company with two younger brothers, Frank and James, he was at work on the Welch farm, about three miles from the Maginnis homestead. At noon the boys went into a milk house to eat their dinner. While in there a thunder storm came up and lightning struck the milk house. The shock rendered the younger boys insensible. One of them upon recovering consciousness put his hand upon Dennis and spoke to him but received no answer. He was leaning against a post, in an upright position, dead. The lightning had passed down the post striking Dennis in the side, tearing one leg of his pantaloons and ripping his boot. The shock killed him so quickly that he still remained standing. One of the younger brothers was burned on one arm and the other on one leg. As soon as sufficiently recovered one of the boys walked and crawled to the nearest house, about half a mile for help.

On Saturday Dennis was buried. His remains were followed to the grave by almost the entire neighborhood – eighty-five carriages were in the procession.

The deceased was only twenty years of age, a very steady, industrious young man and a general favorite with all who knew him. The bereaved family have the sympathy of all in their sad affliction.

Obituary.

It is our mournful duty to record the death of an estimable woman, Mary Ann, wife of L. H. Dolley, of Port Allegany. Mrs. Dolley had been a sufferer for a number of years, and it was hoped by her friends that a change of climate would be of benefit to her. In company with her husband and some friends, Mrs. Dolley started for a transcontinental trip a few weeks ago. Proposing to visit at the homes of her husband's relatives in California and Oregon. To reach the home of the first brother it was necessary to add a stage journey of seventy-five miles to the thousands of miles of railway passage, and the exertion proved too much for the frail constitution of the feeble lady. After a sudden and brief attack of her long standing difficulty, a disease of the stomach, the spirit of Mrs. Dolley bade adieu to its mortal tenement upon the 14th day of August. The subject of this sketch was the daughter of Michael Snyder, of Sweden township. She was a woman of strong sympathies, and the finer attributes of heart and soul, cherished by all who knew her. The mourning over her sudden death is heartfelt and sincere. She will be missed at the hearth stone and in the social circle. The sympathies of the entire community is with the bereaved husband and relatives.

Obituary.

Passed to the higher life, in Oswayo, August 10th, 1883, Mrs. Fannie Louise, wife of Joel H. Beebe and daughter of George W. and Ellen Tyler, aged 22 years. The deceased left a little son only a few hours old, who will never know a mother's love. Also a large circle of relatives and friends to mourn her sudden and untimely end. The blow falls heavily upon the young husband, with whom she had passed a little more than four years of uninterrupted happiness. And also upon the parents who, a little more than two years ago, were called to mourn the loss of their eldest daughter and now their second and last daughter is taken from them. The memory of her sweet disposition and many amiable qualities will ever remain as a comfort to her friends, and the flowers she has cultivated and the many little fancy ornaments she had made will speak continually to the mother's heart in silent tones words of love and comfort.

She met the death angel with a smile that left its impress upon her earthly features till she was buried from our sight forever.

- A very singular accident occurred at Metzger's mill Monday. Cephus Niles was standing at the side of the circular saw. When the engine started the saw caught in the leg of his pants at the back of one knee and threw him clear over the saw on the carriage. His pantaloon leg was cut from the knee to the foot, but there was not a scratch on the leg. The fall on the carriage made him feel a little sore, but nothing of a serious nature. His escape was a remarkable one.

The Potter Enterprise
Wednesday Evening, September 5, 1883 – Vol. X, No. 17

Costelloville. The young people of Costelloville spent an enjoyable evening at the house of Thomas Moran, on the 29th inst., celebrating Miss Mary's birth-day. There were some forty present, each bringing a token of remembrance, and at twelve p.m., the table, which was spread to receive the presents, became loaded with jewelry, silver ware, dry goods, &c. Ice cream and other refreshments were served at an early hour, and, by the aid of good music, we tripped the light fantastic until two a.m.; then went to our respective homes well pleased with the evening which went so rapidly, and also with Mr. Moran and family's kind hospitality.

Raymond. On the 25th of August, Mr. Levi Moore's 72nd birth day, of which he was reminded the day before by a surprise visit from his family relations, children, grand-children, nephews, nieces and at least one grand-niece, also his family connections. Some forty-five birth-days Mr. Moore has had in this place. His health seems better than it was some years ago. The object of the visit was substantial tokens of regard, and it was a success. May the couple see many more such days.

MARRIED.

ROGERS – DOERNER – In Coudersport, at the residence of the bride's parents, on Tuesday, September 4th, by Rev. A. Cone, Mr. Jesse W. Rogers to Miss L. Amelia Doerner, all of Coudersport.

The printers were kindly remembered, and good wishes follow the happy pair. They left on the morning train for a tour in New York. The bride was, for a year and a half, a compositor in the Enterprise office, always faithful, kind and pleasant and if the good wishes of this office will secure happiness, her married life will be a long and happy one, free from trails or afflictions. May peace, happiness and prosperity attend them.

CARPENTER – SMITH – At the parsonage, in Raymond, on August 25th, 1883, by Rev. J. L. Swain, Mr. Theodore Carpenter, of Ulysses, to Miss Josephine Smith, of Raymond.

MALTBY – GOSS – At St. Marys, Aug. 7th, 1883, C. W. Maltby, of Roulet, and Miss Ettie Goss, of First Fork.

LOGUE – WHITE – At Wharton, Pa., by B. F. Berfield, Esq., Alexander Logue, of Wharton, and Mrs. White of Whites Corners, Pa.

- Henry Taubert, of Homer, died on Thursday, August 30th, 1883, aged 60 years.

- Mr. E. Terwilliger, of East Hebron, was buried on Thursday last. For several years he has been an invalid, a portion of the time helpless, suffering from inflammatory rheumatism.

Bingham. Burton Henoy, aged about ten years, died so suddenly of typhoid fever that some of the neighbors hardly knew that he was dangerously ill, before he was dead. He had been staying, for a few weeks, at the widow Grovers. He was buried Aug. 26th, at North Bingham, without a funeral. The doctor, when first called to see him, pronounced the case hopeless.

- In making a flying switch last Thursday, a box car on the C. & P. A. was thrown off the track, delaying the noon train about an hour. This is the first car that has ever been run off the track since the building of the road, which speaks well for those in charge, showing that they have been very careful.

- A Camp of the Sons of Veterans is about to be established at Oswayo. A. S. Lyman, Commander of A. W. Estes Post G. A. R. has been detailed to organize it, and expects to muster the new camp about September 15th. It will be named Camp Leroy West and be in the bounds of the Division of Western Pennsylvania which is under command of Col. Seiforth, of Pittsburgh.

- The water company should hurry up a little. West street has been torn up for two weeks and the work is not completed yet. The company has the right to lay its pipe in the street but the people have some rights too, and the company should respect those rights, in being as expeditious as possible.

K. HANLON
CARY BUILDING,
MAIN STREET, NEAR RIVER BRIDGE,
COUDERSPORT, PA.
Keeps constantly on hand
the Finest Quality of
FRESH AND SALT MEATS, FISH, &C., &C..
Also, all kinds of
VEGETABLES AND FRUITS,
AT LOW PRICES. CALL AND SEE.

The Potter Enterprise
Wednesday Evening, September 12, 1883 – Vol. X, No. 18

- In June last Wm. Howard, a member of Genesee Forks Lodge K. of H. died. About two weeks since his widow received a check for $2,000 from the Grand Lodge.

- On Monday, Mrs. James Johnston received a dispatch that her brother, Merville Calkins, was not expected to live but a few days at most. For some years Merville has lived in Minnesota; before going west he worked at the printing business in the Journal and Enterprise offices.

The New Deer Law.
The Lock Haven Journal gives the following as the correct law for regulating the hunting of deer, passed June 29th, 1883:

"The act prohibits the killing of deer except between October 1st and December 15th, next following, and also prohibits any person from having in his possession and offering for sale or transport any wild deer or fresh venison except between the 1st day of October and the 30th day of November next following.

The killing of spotted fawn at any time is unlawful.

The running of dogs is prohibited, and a fine of $50 is imposed upon any person who shall kill a deer which has been chased into the water by dogs.

To have the fresh skin of a deer or fawn in possession is made an offence, punishable the same as having fresh venison in possession out of season.

Dogs pursuing wild deer may be killed by any person, and constables or other town officers may kill any dog that habitually pursues deer. The owner of such dog is made liable to a penalty of $10 for each deer killed by his dog.

All acts or parts of acts which are inconsistent with the foregoing provisions are repealed."

Potter County, Pennsylvania Potpourri – Volume I
1880 through 1884

The Potter Enterprise
Wednesday Evening, September 19, 1883 – Vol. X, No. 19

Hebron. Born – To Myron and Belle Howard, Sept. 2d, 1883, a boy, weight 9 ½ pounds.

- On Saturday last the remains of Mrs. Marry Dolley were brought to this place from California, where she died last month. Funeral services were held in Sweden, her old home, and her remains consigned to the home cemetery.

Hebron. Ed. Terwillegar, after eight years of terrible suffering, has passed on to the better land, where he no doubt has found the "spiritual body" spoken of by Paul; with no more suffering and sorrow. How blessed must be the change. The remains were taken to Sharon for interment.

- For the first time in nearly two years, the Potter county jail is empty. This item is for Monday morning of September court. Before the week is over there may be half a dozen prisoners.

Poor House.

The county commissioners will submit to a vote, this fall, the question of purchasing a poor farm. They have the refusal of the Consider Stearns farm, in Eulalia, containing 104 acres, nearly all improved; $4,000 is the price asked for the farm. We invite correspondence for publication, on this question. It is one of great interest to the people and taxpayers and the matter should receive more than a passing notice. Let us have the opinion of the people.

Blacksmith Shop at Millport.
The old patrons of the Millport blacksmith shop are notified that it is again running with a first class blacksmith in charge. All are invited to call and give him a trial.
W. J. Brown, Prop'r.

The Potter Enterprise
Wednesday Evening, September 26, 1883 – Vol. X, No. 20

DIED.

HARRIS – At his home in Keating, Pa., after a lingering illness, on Friday, September 21, 1883, Mr. Pliny Harris, aged 71 years and 3 months.

Freeman Run. Again death has entered our neighborhood and taken one of our oldest and most respected citizens, Mr. Pliny Harris, who has been sick for a long time, died on the evening of the 21st of September, 1883, aged a little over seventy-one years. His sickness and death was a calm and peaceful one. During his sickness not a murmur or dissatisfied word was heard; he was perfectly satisfied with all that was done for him. He was a good neighbor, a kind husband and father. There is not another in the neighborhood who would be more missed than he will be. Among those who will miss Mr. Harris none will miss him more than the little children of this place as he always had a kind word and pleasant smile for each one of them and even during his sickness he seemed always glad to have them call to see him. Mr. Harris was a strictly temperament man and by his death the cause of temperance has lost a firm friend. On Sunday his burial service was conducted by the Rev. Wm. Marshall, of Coudersport, which was Mr. Harris' request. At the grave, the children and young people of the neighborhood marched around the grave each throwing in a bunch of flowers, thus showing their respect for the dead.

- Judge Williams presided at the trial of the case of Hunt vs. Weightman, last week, on account of Judge Olmsted having been engaged in the case as counsel before his election to the office of Judge. The case was over a quantity of timber on Kettle Creek, which had been cut, valued at about $20,000; and the matter hinged on warrant lines. The jury were sent out Saturday before noon, and were discharged Sunday morning being unable to agree.

- The only important criminal case decided last week was that of Reeds, charged with involuntary manslaughter. The main facts in the case we gave in the Enterprise last winter as found at the preliminary hearing and were brought out by the death of the mother of Dan'l Reed. This old lady was 94 years of age, childish or insane. Reed being about to leave Roulet, hired a man named Blarigan to take care of the old lady. He and a son of Dan Reed built a shanty next to Blarigan's house, and in this the old lady lived for or five days and died. There was no fire in the shanty occupied by Mrs. Reed, and no door or window connecting it with the living rooms of Blarigan. The jury evidently believed the Reeds "half-guilty" as they brought in a verdict of not guilty as charged, but put the costs on the defendants. The Commonwealth costs foots up nearly $400.

- A very distressing accident happened in Lewisville last Monday, by which Perry Brigham was seriously injured. He was running the slitting saw in his mill, ripping up hard lumber, and when the piece on which he was engaged was nearly finished his hand was within six inches of the saw. Just at this time as he was pushing quite hard, his foot slipped on a wet edging which had fallen under his feet and his right hand was thrown upon the saw. It cut between the first and second fingers of the right hand, running back about the whole length of the hand, cutting the thumb and fore finger nearly off. It would have entirely severed them but for the plank on which his hand rested being thick so that not enough of the saw came above it to entirely cut through the hand. This is the same hand that was mutilated by a circular saw eleven years ago this summer.

Mr. Brigham has managed to do a great deal of work with his crippled hand heretofore but we fear now it will become entirely useless to him. – *Sentinel.*

Court Minutes.

Court convened Sept. 17th, A. G. Olmsted presiding, Hammond and Lewis, associates.

Bernard Biggins admitted to citizenship.

Comth vs Esther E. Shay, fornication, *nol pros* on payment of costs.

Dana Drake sworn as foreman of Grand Jury and T. F. Kidney of Allegany Constable to attend them.

Keziah Frazier vs John Frazier, D. W. Haven appointed commissioner to take testimony. Sheriff to make proclamation.

And now, to wit, Sept. 17, 1883, this being the first term held by the Court in and for the County of Potter, after the passage of the Act of Aug. 7, 1883, it is ordered by the Court, that the regular terms of Court for the county of Potter, shall be held on the first Monday of June, third Monday of September and the second Monday of December, of each year, and each term to continue one week. This order to be published in the Potter Journal and the Potter Enterprise at least 30 days before the time fixed for holding said Court. By the Court.

Comth vs D. P. Reed and Willis Reed, involuntary manslaughter, jury find a verdict of not guilty, but that defendants pay the costs.

Estate of Maggie Gallagher, minor child of Robt. K. Young, A. B. Mann appointed auditor to report on application of L. D. Ripple to sell real estate.

J. M. Kilbourne appointed overseer of the poor for Pike township.

Comth vs Jeff Burdic, surety of the peace. Bail $50.00 for appearance at next term.

Minnie Seibenheimer adopted by John and M. Keschoweck and to assume the name of the adopted parents.

Comth vs Abram Salomon, assault and battery with intent to have unlawful carnal knowledge of female. True bill, bail $500 for appearance at next term.

Comth vs George Nickerson, May E. Edgar and Abigale Nickerson, unlawful assembly and assault, true bill, bail $200 for appearance at next term.

Comth vs August Froebel, pointing a gun, true bill.

Comth vs Andrew Wagner, perjury, true bill.

Comth vs Lorenzo Wagner, perjury, true bill.

Comth vs J. W. Allen, false pretence, true bill, bail $200.

On motion D. W. Baldwin of Tioga admitted to practice in the several courts of Potter county.

Ralph Niles, a lunatic, ordered to be removed to State Lunatic Hospital at Warren. Eulalia township certified as his place of legal settlement.

Harry Parsons of Williamsport admitted to practice in the several courts of Potter county.

Comth vs Frank Goodwin, selling liquor, true bill.

Comth vs Geo. W. Parker, surety of the peace, defendant and bail discharged.

Comth vs David Kibbee, perjury, true bill.

Comth vs Edward McGonigal, selling liquor, plead guilty, bail $200 for appearance at next term.

Comth vs Anna Bendell, malicious mischief, not a true bill, prosecutor Peter Halleuer to pay the costs.

Comth vs George Sherwood, perjury, true bill.

E. D. Wolcott and N. C. Newton administrators, acknowledged deed to Jacob Failing for 50 and 22 acres respectively in Sharon twp.

V. Robinson vs H. E. Robinson, sub in divorce awarded.

Charles McConnell vs Susan A. McConnell, sub in divorce awarded.

Levi G. Stillman vs Mary J. Stillman, H. A. Gridley of Lewisville and Nicholas Wall of Hammersley Fork appointed commissioners to take testimony.

Poor House question ordered to be submitted to vote of the people of Potter county.

Comth vs E. McGonigall, selling liquor to minors, plead guilty, bail $200 for appearance at next term.

Comth vs James Clark, forgery, true bill.

Comth vs John Nesbit, assault and battery, not a true bill, prosecutor W. H. Grodevant to pay the costs.

Comth vs Rosanna Nesbit, adultery, not a true bill, prosecutor John Nesbit to pay costs.

Dan'l Monroe, sheriff of Potter county, acknowledged deeds for property sold at Sheriff's sale to:

Ralph Nelson for 43.8 acres in Genesee for $18; sold as property of Wm. Henry Terwilliger.

Trustees Bingham Estate 65.5 acres in Hector for $25; sold as property of John G. Gill.

A. Sidney Lyman 65 acres in Oswayo for $25; sold as property of James H. Leach.

Richard Gallagher, a native of Ireland, admitted to citizenship.

Sept. 21 – Hon W. H. Williams presiding.

Jasper Card appointed guardian of Mable Card.

Comth vs Lorenzo D. Card, breaking and entering a store with intent to commit a felony. True bill, bail $500 for appearance at next term.

Comth vs L. D. Card, larceny, true bill, bail $500.

J. M. Bassett appointed guardian of Josephine Adams.

Comth vs Wm. Crawford, *nol pros.*

Comth vs Jas. H. Wright and Geo. W. Pearsall, conspiracy, not a true bill, prosecutor Geo. W. King to pay the costs.

Same vs same, same as above.

Comth vs W. H. Grodevant, fornication, not a true bill, prosecutor John Nesbitt to pay the costs.

Comth vs Geo. W. Sherwood, sentenced to pay costs.

Comth vs Martin VanLiew, surety of the peace, prosecutor David Kibbee sentenced to pay the costs.

Elizabeth Reed vs Levi P. Reed, divorce granted.

In the matter of the inquiry concerning the advisability of asking the county to assist in building the iron bridge on Second street, Coudersport, the grand jury report in their opinion, "the aid asked for by said borough is not needed."

The Grand Jury recommend that the jail roof be painted, inside and outside walls painted, and other repairs. They also recommend the construction of a fire proof vault in the Commissioners' office.

Thomas Perry, a native of England, admitted to citizenship.

Henry Bartlett, a native of England, admitted to citizenship.

Comth vs L. C. King, selling liquor, sentenced to pay a fine of $100 and costs of prosecution.

Comth vs Clark Judd, selling liquor, sentenced to pay a fine of $100 and costs of prosecution.

Comth vs John Ward, selling liquor, sentenced to pay a fine of $100 and cost of prosecution.

L. D. Wagner vs J. W. Allen, rule to show cause why def't shall not be allowed to enter an appeal from the decision of Frank Phelps, J.P., continued to next term.

Veniries ordered for 24 Grand and 36 Traverse jurors for Dec. term.

Comth vs Thomas Garrity, selling liquor, defendant discharged.

A. B. Mann appointed auditor to restate account of David Hammond, administrator of estate of Polly Ann VanHuysen.

Virginnia Quinnette vs Edwin Quinnette, divorce granted.

John H. Hunt vs Wm. Weightman, F. W. Benedict, administrator etc. of E. L. Piper dec'd. Jury failed to agree and were discharged.

The Potter Enterprise
Wednesday Evening, October 3, 1883 – Vol. X, No. 21

Allegany. Two weddings of late. A. Atkins and N. Cool have each taken companions for life. May they find more sunshine than shadow, and likewise may prosperity attend them.

- From all we can learn, the vote on the poor house question will be quite different from what the vote was when the question was submitted a few years ago. It was then defeated. Less than 300 favoring and over 1700 voting against it. Several towns have paid out in costs, in law suits, more than their share for the farm and buildings.

Correction.

In the court proceedings, last week, appear "Comth vs J. W. Allen, false pretences, bail $200." It should have read "G. W. Allen."

Potter County, Pennsylvania Potpourri – Volume I
1880 through 1884

The Potter Enterprise
Wednesday Evening, October 10, 1883 – Vol. X, No. 22

MARRIED.

BOOTH – CHAMBERLIN – At the Presbyterian Parsonage, Coudersport, Oct. 7th, 1883, by Rev. A. Cone, Mr. John Booth, of Talimage, McKean county, to Miss Martha E. Chamberlin, of Hebron, Potter Co.

- Joshua Jackson, an old and respected citizen of Sweden, was buried on Saturday last.

- A county house will reduce the number of paupers and save innumerable law suits between townships.

- The Encampment of Grand Army Posts, on the Fair Grounds last week, was a success notwithstanding the short time for preparation and difficulties to contend with. About 500 people were on the ground each day. One hundred and fifty of the boys in blue from Barnes, Lewis, Estes and Jones Posts were present. A pole and flag was raised, speeches were made by Messrs. Kilbourne, Austin, Bridges and others. Dancing was indulged in during the afternoon. The soldier's dinner was a picnic dinner consisting of all the delicacies of the season. Maj. Kilbourne was elected chairman and J. M. Covey secretary. A resolution was passed that each Post appoint one representative and one alternate, the representatives to appoint time and place of next meeting, and give three months notice.

PREMIUMS AWARDED AT THE FAIR.
Class I – Horses.

H. T. Reynolds, Brookland, brood mare 2d premium; suckling colt, 90 days old, second premium.

S. Thompson, Coudersport, farm and road team, 2d p.

C. Cook, North Bingham, 2 year old colt, 1s tp.

F. A. Nelson, Coudersport, brood mare, 1st p.; 2 year old colt, 2d p; 1 year old colt, 1st p; suckling colt, 1st p.

David Raymond, Raymond, farm and road team, 1st p.

E. A. Cottrell, Andover, N.Y., Norman Percheon stallion, 1st p; ditto 2 year old 1st p.

J. J. Downey, Ulysses, Clydesdale stallion, over 3 y o, 1st p; ditto s c, 1st p.

J. P. Lehman, Coudersport, y c, 2d p.

A. R. Moore, Raymond, 3 y o c, 2d p.

J. W. Allen, Coudersport, stallion, 1st p.

L. J. Skinner, Potter Brook, stallion, 2d p.

Geo. Forsyth, Whitesville, N.Y., 2 y o g, 1st p.

Henry Gridley, Ulysses, matched driving colts, 1st p.

M. L. Gridley, Coudersport, 3 y o trotting breed, 1st p.

Class II – Cattle – Division A.

Leroy Lyman, Roulet, Holstein bull, 1st p.

W. J. Harris, Coudersport, b c, 2d p.
Wm. Neefe, Colesburg, b c, 1st p; h c, 2d p.
Nelson Woodcock, Colesburg, cow, 2d p.
G. F. White, Coudersport, y b, Durham 1st p.
F. Phelps, Lymansville, cow, 1st p.
Earl Crane, Coudersport, cow, half y o b, Alderney, 1st p; heifer, 2d p.
W. Benson, Sweden, 5 y heifers and 4 2d p; bull c, 1st p.
J. W. Allen, Coudersport, Alderney cow, 1st p.
J. L. Allen, Clara, s h Durham b, 1st p.
G. W. Stillman, Hebron, y b, Holstein, 1st p.
H. Schilberger, Coudersport, y h, 1st p.
T. Carpenter, Gold, calf, 1st p.
Chas. Hosley, Ulysses, Ayrshire bull, 3 y o and 6 Ayreshire h's, 1st p.

Class II – Cattle – Division B.

A. C. Palmateer, Coudersport, yoke oxen, 1st p.
Arthur Gordnier, Coudersport, y 2 y o steers, 1st p.
O. M. Kelley, Coudersport, y o, 2d p.
Albert Lyman, Coudersport, y 4 y o oxen, 1st p.

Class III – Sheep.

E. M. Bishop, Hebron, 6 Paxton lambs, 1st p.
W. J. Harris, Coudersport, Merino buck lambs and half Merino lambs, 1st p.
S. L. Burdick, Colesburg, Shropshiredown buck and 2 ewes, 1st p; buck lamb, 2d p.
J. P. Lehman, Coudersport, y b, 2d p; 3 y o b, 1st p.
W. B. Gordnier, Coudersport, 5 Southdown ewes and 5 bucks, 2d p; 1 Southdown b 1 y o, 3d p.
L. W. Lyman, Coudersport, 3 y o b, 1st p; 2 ewes, 2d p.

Class IV – Hogs.

W. Benson, Coudersport, Berkshire boar, 1st p.
D. White, Coudersport, yearling sow, 1st p.

Class V – Poultry.

E. M. Bishop, Hebron, poultry display, 1st p.
Amos Colcord, Coudersport, pair turkeys, 1st p.
D. White, Coudersport, best display of young ducks, 1st p.
J. Simons, Coudersport, pair white Bramah fouls and pair geese, 1st p; pair turkeys and ducks, 2d p.

Class VI – Dairy.

O. M. Kelly, Coudersport, tub butter and roll, 2d p.
E. M. Bishop, Coudersport, factory cheese, 1st p.
Wm. Neefe, Colesburg, tub butter and roll, 1st p.
S. W. Baker, Coudersport, r'l but'r 3d p.
Amos Colcord, d-m cheese, 1st p.

Class VII – Grain.

Leroy Lyman, Roulet, winter wheat, spring wheat and beans, 1st p; peas, 2d p.
B. F. Babcock, Coudersport, corn, 2d p.

Potter County, Pennsylvania Potpourri – Volume I
1880 through 1884

O. M. Kelley, Coudersport, beans, 2d p.
Amos Colcord, Coudersport, sample corn and 7 var beans, 3d p.
John Gordnier, Coudersport, oats, 2d p; buckwheat, 3d p.
J. P. Lehman, Coudersport, b w, 2d p.
Hiram Lent, Coudersport, oats 3d p.

Class VIII – Fruit.

Leroy Lyman, Roulet, apples, 1st p.
B. F. Babcock, Coudersport, sample apples, 1st p.
W. W. Gridley, Ulysses, fall pears, 3d p.
D. L. Raymond, fall pears, 1st p.
M. V. Larrabee, Roulet, var pears, 2d p.
A. Rounsville, Coudersport, var apples 17 kinds, 3d p.
J. Simons, Coudersport, Russian apples 2d p.
H. Schildberger, variety of apples, 2d p.

Class IX – Vegetables.

B. F. Babcock, Coudersport, 2 pumpkins, 3d p; 2 kind potatoes, 2d p; onions, 1st p.
O. M. Kelley, pumpkins, 2d p.
Amos Colcord, Coudersport, 12 carrots and peppers, 2d p; pop corn, 3d p.
J. P. Lehman, Coudersport, 3 pumpkins, 1st p.
Mrs. D. Monroe, Coudersport, onions, 2d p.
J. Simons, Coudersport, turnips, 3d p.
Mrs. H. Schildberger, Coudersport, onions, bundle oyster plants, carrots, caraway seed, beet seed, horse radish, 3d p; cabbage, basket vegetables, turnips, 2d p; cauliflower, bus turnips, 1st p.

Class X – Agricultural Implements.

S. W. Baker, Coudersport, potato digger, diploma.
W. B. Gordiner, Coudersport, Royce reaper, sulkey rake with seeder, Eureka mower, Rawson mower, clipper plow, Whitesville side hill plow and iron beam plow, drill, harrow and seeder, road scraper, cultivator, dip.

Class XI – Mechanical Department.

A. F. Raymond, Gold, double open buggy, double covered buggy, American sewing machine, Campbell churn, reciprocating dash, dip.
R. J. Mott, Port Allegany, light single harness, dip.
Albert Lyman, Coudersport, platform wagon, dip.
J. Miller, Ulysses, specimen blacksmithing, dip.
J. W. Allen, Coudersport, platform wagon, dip.

Class XII – Domestic Manufactures.

O. M. Kelley, Coudersport, 1 pr woolen stockings, 2d p.
David Raymond, rag carpet, 1st p.
M. W. Gridley, buckskin gloves and mittens, 1st p.
S. W. Baker, woolen mittens, 2d p; woolen stockings, 1st p.
Mrs. Jerome Knickerbocker, Coudersport, rag carpet, 2d p.
Mrs. Rachael Hess, Cross Fork, patchwork quilt, 2d p.
Mrs. F. A. Nelson, patchwork calico quilt, 2d p; pieced quilt, 1st p.
Leroy Lyman, patchwork quilt, 3d p.

Laura Monroe, pieced quilt, 3d p.
Mrs. Clara Tombs, patchwork quilt, 1ˢᵗ p.
Mrs. D. Baker, pair woolen stockings, 1ˢᵗ p.
Mrs. J. Nichols, rag stair carpet, 1ˢᵗ p.
Wm. Dingman, skein stocking yard, pair woolen mittens and blankets, 1ˢᵗ p.
Class XIII – Culinary Articles.
David Raymond, maple syrup, crab apple jelly, tomato pickles, crab apple pickles, 1ˢᵗ p.
Leroy Lyman, honey, 2d p.
Josh Willen, honey, 1ˢᵗ p.
S. W. Baker, sugar cookies, 1ˢᵗ p.
Mrs. Dan Monroe, var can'd fruit, 1ˢᵗ p.
Mrs. D. Baker, loaf corn bread, 2d p; plate sugar cookies, 3d p; soft cookies, 1ˢᵗ p.
Mrs. J. Nichols, loaf corn and graham bread, 1ˢᵗ p; sugar cookies, 2d p.
Hiram Lent, canned fruit, 2d p.
Class XIV – Division A – Embroidery and Fancy Work.
Thomas Rees, patch work "sunshine and shadow," 1ˢᵗ p.
Laura Monroe, macrama lambrequin, 1ˢᵗ p.
Mrs. Jerome Knickerbocker, foot rest, wersted, 1ˢᵗ p.
May Blackman, Port Allegany, silk embroidered sofa pillow, 1ˢᵗ p; dito pin cushion, plush stitchery embroidery, chenille dito, dito handkershief, 2d p; crazy afghan, 1ˢᵗ p.
Mrs. J. W. Allen, silk worsted sofa pillow, 3d p; silk sofa pillow, 2d p.
Mrs. K. R. Hodsin, table scarf, 2d p; beaded lace, 1ˢᵗ p.
Raymond & Taggart, exhibition of millinery, 1ˢᵗ p.
Carrie White, embroidered dress, 1ˢᵗ p, dito lamberquin, 2d p.
Mrs. Jennie Nichols, scrap bag, 1ˢᵗ p; sofa pillow, 2d p.
Mrs. Carrie Phillips, sofa pillow, silk Japanese work and embroidered apron, 1ˢᵗ p.
Mrs. W. I Lewis, hand painted cushion, 3d p; satin cushion, hand made lace cover, hand painted toilet bottles, tidy spatter work, 1ˢᵗ p.
Mrs. B. A. McClure, embroidered table spread, 1ˢᵗ p.
Class XV – Division A – Flowers.
Leroy Lyman, flowers, 2d p.
Mrs. H. Schildberger, boquet of parlor flowers, 1ˢᵗ p.
Mrs. A. Rounsville, lilly (parlor), 1ˢᵗ p.
Class XV – Division B – Art.
L. R. Bliss, two frames of photographs, two large ink pictures, one oil painting, 1ˢᵗ p.
Mrs. W. I. Lewis, oil painting, trout piece, 1ˢᵗ p; dito bird, 2d p.
Mrs. J. M. Spafford, specimen of painting, ocean moss, 1ˢᵗ p.

- Last Friday night a tramp entered an unoccupied bed room in the house of N. J. Pangburn, at the Forest House, and occupied the bed till morning. After Mr. Pangburn had gone to his work he came out and demanded his breakfast and what money there was in the house. While he was eating breakfast, Mrs. Pangburn slipped out and called her husband, but before he could reach the house, the tramp had ransacked it taking a pocket book and a revolver. Pangburn spent some time hunting for the tramp with his rifle. During his absence the tramp returned and, with the revolver stolen from the house in the morning, threatened Mrs. P. She screamed and the tramp left, dropping the revolver in the yard and was not again seen. He is described as about five feet ten inches tall, heavy dark beard, slightly gray, dark hair and eyes, dark complexion, badly pock-marked, walks a little lame; had on a dark suit of clothes badly soiled.

POTTER COUNTY PENSIONERS.

We have received from E. G. Rathbone, of the Pension Bureau, the list of pensioners on the roll Jan. 1st, 1883. Many have been added since and others increased. The list, as published, for Potter County, is as follows:

	Andrews Settlement.	
	Cause.	Monthly Rate.
Henry C. James	Gunshot wound left hand	$2
	Bingham Centre.	
Clark J. Woods	Gunshot wound right arm	18
Levi B. Lewis	None given	12
Geo. H. Shutt	Gunshot wound right side, left hip, left shoulder	15
DeWalt Shutt	None given	7
Catherine L. Kile	Widow	8
	Brookland.	
Henry T. Reynolds	Not given	8 ½
	Burtville.	
Lewis C. Burdic	Gunshot wound right thigh	4
Wait C. Simons	Wound left thigh	18
Phebe B. Slade	Mother	8
	Clara.	
Wm. A. Cole	Dis of abdominal viscera	6
Joseph Lawton	Gunshot wound right foot	4
Burr S. Wakely	Dis of lungs	6
Joseph Fepender	Disability	8
Perry Wilcox		6
Mary A. Elliott	Mother	8
Minerva Fosmer	Widow 1812	8

Coudersport.

Samuel Hull	Catarrh	10
Hiram H. Chesbro	Disability	31 ¼
James Johnston	Gunshot wound left forearm	4
John Mead	Gunshot wound left shoulder	4
Edward F__	[newspaper folded]	
George M. Parker	Loss index finger	2
George W. Mitchell	Not given	6
James Wallace	Chronic diarrhea & scurvy	12
Lyman Toombs	Disability	4
John T. Smith	Total deafness one ear	12
Wm. W. Brown	Disability	18
Alanson L. Baker	Gunshot wound left side head	10
Wm. C. Bridge	Gunshot wound right hand	2
Chauncy R. Byam	Rheumatism	4
George S. Baldwin	Shell wound left hip	8
John L. Wallace	Gunshot wound head	2
Leonard C. King	Disability	4
William Dingman	Disability	3
Wm. T. Hosley	Dis of lungs	6
Charles U. Ruscher	Not given	18
Adam Hartwick	Chronic rheumatism	4
John D. Earl	Frozen feet	18
F. B. McNamara	Debility	6
Philander McKinney	Dis spine	18
Henry W. Grodevant	Disability	18
George C. Lewis	Chronic rheumatism	10
Joseph J. Carey	Gunshot wound scalp & shoulder and foot	16
Ruth Gibbs	Widow 1812	8
Lavina Lewis	Widow	8
Diana Burton	Widow	8
Jane Cannon	Widow	8
Lavena H. Chesbro	Mother	8
Ida A. Fisk	Mother	8
Orange W. Strong	Father	8
Sally Foster	Widow	8

East Hebron.

Leonard Davis	Disability	8
J. E. Terwilliger	Gunshot wound left arm	15
Henry Sherwood	Rheumatism and dis of abdominal viscera	12
Stephen VanGilder	Dis lungs	14
John Goodenough	Gunshot wound left thigh	4
Charles D. McKee	Gunshot wound left shoulder	4

Adolphus Castle	Disability	14
Elizabeth Weltch	Mother	8
Lucy Luce	Widow	8
	East Sharon.	
O. Burdick Barber	Var veins right leg	12
David McNamire	Not given	18
John A. McNamire	Dis heart	18
Aurelia Crawford	Widow	8
	Eleven Mile.	
Frederick S. Gillett	Gunshot wound right side	6
John Morley	Dis right eye	6
James H. Leach	Rheumatism	8
	Ellisburg.	
Henry Terwilliger	Disability	18
Benjamin F. Bishop	Gunshot wound left thigh	8
Asa Downs	Injury right shoulder	12
Robert F. Harris	Disability	18
Norman Chapman	Disability	5 1/3
Daniel Reeder	Not given	24
Samuel J. McConnell	Gunshot wound left forearm	2
Sarah J. Thompson	Widow	8
John Holland		8
Albert Slingerland	Gunshot wound hand	8
Lucy Seely	Mother	8
Mahala Lathrop	Mother	8
	Forest House.	
Jacob Reed	Dis of heart	8
Lewis Hummel	Disability	6
Charles A. Butler	Would left hip	5 1/3
	Genesee Fork.	
Jerome J. Waterman	Disability	6
George Barlow	Epileptic fits	18
Isaac Hodgins	Injury to abdomen	6
Byron Basett	Gunshot wound left leg	8
Isaac Dawley	Gunshot wound of body	24
Patrick Kain	Disability	8
George A. Leach	Dis heart	6
John A. Keech		8
Bridget Clancey	Widow	8
Mary Williams	Mother	8

Germania.

Frederick Schroder	Not given	8
George M. Rexford	Not given	24
Christian Rukgaber	Dis of lungs	18
Carl Leibenhuhuer	Injury abdomen	4
Albert DePlaque	Not given	17
John Traton	Injury to abdomen	12
Catharine Braun	Widow	20
Salome Hagemann	Mother	8

Gold.

Wm. R. Clark	Rheumatism	6

Harrison Valley.

Wesley Humbert	Disability	8
Nyrum Haskin	Gunshot wound right side	4
Isaac Hurlburt	Disability	3
Newton U. Hubbard	Dis of kidneys	8
Wm. R. Howland	Gunshot wound left side	18
James Maricle	Gunshot wound left leg	4
Fanton L. Northrup	Gunshot wound right foot	8
Elias Bullock	Dis stomach & bowels	8
Edwin L. Jones	Chronic diarrhea	12
Charles A. Jones	Disease	8
Wm. H. Stone	Disability	18
Jason W. Stevens	Disability	4
Chas. E. Hunter	Loss right thumb	4
Chester L. Stone	Not given	18
Lewis Briggs	Gunshot wound right foot	8
Dexter P. Burley	Var veins left leg	8
Norman Buck	Disability	18
Calvin Dibble	Disability	10
Chas. H. Doud	Gunshot wound left foot	-
John Fletcher	Gunshot wound left thigh	-
Angeline Cummings	Widow	8
Catherine Thompson	Mother	8
Ruth Persing	Mother	8
Sarah Phillips	Widow	8
Rosalinda Hurlburt	Widow	8
Catherine Keneda	Widow	8
Amy Wetenhall	Widow 1812	8
Silas Fox	Survivor 1812	8

Hebron.

Lewis Hall	Disease of heart	18
John R. Millard	Not given	4

Potter County, Pennsylvania Potpourri – Volume I
1880 through 1884

	Hector.	
Levi J. Quant	Shell wound right thigh	2
Sally Douglass	Survivor 1812	8
	Kettle Creek.	
Geo. Scheultheis	Dis of eyes	10
	Keating Summit.	
Allen W. Williams	Gunshot wound wrist	4
	Lewisville.	
Irving B. Miner	Chronic rheumatism	4
	Millport.	
Wellman P. Nichols	Not given	18
Nathan W. Herring	Dis kidneys	8
Rinaldo D. McDonald	Dis of lungs	6
Lewis I. Carpenter	Disability	24
John R. West	Disease of heart	18
Ruth Hay	Widow	8
	Mills.	
John N. Tompkins	Dis heart	10
John J. Jones	Loss part of thumb & injury index finger right hand	4
Emily M. Tompkins	Widow	8
	North Bingham.	
Ezra L. Fuller	Dis abdominal viscera	12
Louisa Clark	Widow 1812	8
Susannah Robbins	Widow 1812	8
	North Fork.	
Swinton Ludington	Loss part of 2 __ & 1 fingers right hand	6
	North Wharton.	
Clark A. Lamont	Gunshot wound left arm & shoulder & right hand	6
Leroy Haskins	Disability	12
	Oswayo.	
Francis W. Lovell	Gunshot wound head	12
Alfred V. Higley	Gunshot wound left ankle	6
Philo Stonemetz	Disability	10
Geo. M. Estes	Sunstroke	4

Name	Condition	Value
Thomas Crittenden	Dis kidneys	18
Jas. H. Stilson	Disability	18
Jas. T. Lockwood	Gunshot wound right hip	6
Philemon C. Lovell	Gunshot wound thighs	12
A. Sidney Lyman	Dis heart	12
Squire Estes	Dropsey	24
Chas. E. Estes	Disability	12
G. W. Bradley	Shell wound left shoulder	6
Lorenzo D. Estes	Disability	4
Dennis Goodenough	Epilepsy	12
Waterbury Miller	Chronic diarrhea	18
Geo. Brizze	Gunshot wound right leg	14
Wm. H. Lewis	Injury right side	8
Chauncy Shryver	Loss right fore finger	2
Henry S. Miller	Gunshot wound left hand	8
Wm. Fessenden	Dis abdominal viscera	8
Van Ransaler Kenyon	Chronic bronchitis	2
Jerome B. Stewart	Chronic rheumatism	6
Girden R. ___	[newspaper folded]	
Jas. M. Buchanan	Disability	16
Luther Brizzee	Paralysis	50
John C. Wilkinson	Chronic rheumatism	4
Rosetta Carpenter	Widow	8
Ruth Cole	Mother	8
Permelia Higley	Widow	8
Mary Ann West	Widow	8
Mary J. Hatch	Widow	8
Laura Kenyon	Mother	8
Louisa Moore	Survivor 1812	8
Mary F. Phillips	Widow	8

Pike Mills.

Name	Condition	Value
John Q. Merrick	Dis of spine	8
John M. Kilbourne	Disability	25
Baker D. Ellis	Disability	5

Raymond's.

Name	Condition	Value
Edward D. Carr	Chronic diarrhea	6
Simon Byam	Chronic rheumatism	12
Boyer A. Whipple	Gunshot wound right thigh	6
Samuel W. Hopkins	Injury right forearm	6
Edward E. Kelly	Gunshot wound left shoulder	12
Wm. B. Palmer	Not given	2
Daniel Fuller	Loss both arms	72
Alonzo E. Wright	Disability	4
Lenora M. Presho	Widow	12

Mary Bunnell	Mother	8
Daniel Raymond	Survivor 1812	8
	Roulette.	
Wm. H. Hazen	Dis kidneys	8
Benj. A. Green	Rheumatism	4
Charles H. Barr	Gunshot wound left hip	14
Mary Fisher	Mother	8
Truman Willoughby	Father	8
Susan Bar	Widow	8
Mariah Burt	Widow	8
Eliza A. Thompson	Widow	8
Laura Pomeroy	Widow	8
Susan Barr	Survivor 1812	8
	Sharon Centre.	
John V. Brown	Disability	2 ¾
	Shingle House.	
Jas. Sherwood	Gunshot wound face	10
Amos E. Burbank	Disability	8
Levi C. Kinner	Disability	18
Levi H. Kinney	Dis abdominal viscera	20
John S. Pearsall	Injury right ankle	8
Thos. H. Appleby	Bed sore right hip	4
James Thomas	Disability	24
Wm. Sherwood	Gunshot wound right knee	12
Joseph Kerr	Gunshot wound left shoulder	8
Nancy M Joy	Mother	8
E. T. Blanchard	Widow	10
Charlotte Press	Mother	8
Ruth Rockafeller	Mother	8
Abzina Brightman	Mother	8
Emily Corwine	Mother	8
	Turner Creek.	
Am. H. Wheaton	Drrh gunshot wound arm	10
	Sunderlinville.	
Hiram G. Moore	Not given	24
John T. Morton	Not given	10
Ai Robins	Dis heart	8
Cornelius H. Loucks	Disability	24
George L. Plank	Not given	12

Ulysses.

Name	Condition	
Henry C. Hosly	Injury to abdomen	12
Ephraim T. Worden	Gunshot wound head	12
Edwin H. Bassett	Chronic diarrhea	4
John J. Baldwin	Debility	6
Alonzo Disbrow	Rheumatism	12
Frank Wagoner	Disability	8
Jas. C. Wright	Disability	2
George J. Whiteman	Disability	24
Alonzo G. Stewart	Shell wound left shoulder	10
Levi J. Thompson	Not given	24
Almeron H. Perry	Dis of liver	8
Lyman E. Perry	Not given	7
W. W. Farnsworth	Not given	4
Lewis E. Carpenter	Gunshot wound right leg	4
Wm. O'Neill	Dis eyes	12
Joseph B. Johnson	Dis heart	8
Vine Johnson	Partial deafness	13
Elias P. Johnson	Disability	6
James H. Jennings	Disability	24
Abiram D. Galutia	Disability	4
Wm. H. Gee	Gunshot wound right hip	6
Chas. W. Gridley	Disability	18
Delos Genung	Gunshot wound left ankle	6
Wm. J. Grover	Chronic pleurisy	4
Edson Hyde	Gunshot wound left forearm	24
Albert L. Harvey	Disability	8
Jacob T. Hovey	Disability	14
David W. Rathbun	Not given	6
Albert L. Rennells	Not given	24
Robt. Rowley	Chronic diarrhea	8
John W. Lewis	Injury to abdomen	4
Albert C. Evans	Gunshot wound left leg	4
Wm. Daniels	Disability	8
Martha L. Harris	Widow	8
Harriet Perry	Widow	8
Louisa Brigham	Mother	8
Betsey Blackman	Mother	8
Susanna Close	Widow	8
Sarah J. Edmendorf	Widow 1812	8
Angeline Hosley	do	8
Julia E. Johnson	do	8
Louisa Chilson	Mother	8

West Bingham.

Name	Condition	
Wm. Henry Millard	Chronic diarrhea	10

Sarah Hallock	Widow 1812	8
Charity E. Wilson	*West Branch.* Widow	8
	West Pike.	
Monroe G. Wheaton	Disability	6
Orman Blackman	Disability	8
Bradley B. Wetmore	Disability	5 1/3
Susan Rogers	Widow	8
	Wharton.	
Allen Jordan	Disability	8
Charles L. Ayers	Lumbago debil &c.	6
	Whites Corners.	
Caleb A. Palmatier	Gunshot wound left knee	8
Wilbert Simmons	Loss right index finger	2
Polly Lilly	Widow	8
Catherine A. Cady	Widow	8
Lucy R. Greely	Widow	8
Nancy Caston	Mother	8
Wm. J. Latta	Survivor 1812	8

The Potter Enterprise
Wednesday Evening, October 17, 1883 – Vol. X, No. 23

- By reason of an irregularity in the application made to the Court of Common Pleas to submit the question of a county poor house to the voters of Potter county, the matter cannot be voted on at the election in November, but will have to be deferred to the time of township elections in February next. Therefore there will be no vote taken on the subject at the coming election.

Arrested at Last.

Frank Goodwin, late of Shingle House, being subpoenaed to appear at the county court to testify in a liquor suit, arrived with alacrity at the county seat. But upon his arrival his ardor received a sudden cooling as he discovered that w warrant had been issued for his arrest, for violation of the U.S. liquor laws. Thinking the atmosphere of Coudersport too warm for him, Goodwin pulled out in the cool hours of the night, for the vast wilderness of the Sinnemahoning, casting anchor on Deering Run. But Uncle Sam knew even Deering Run, and sent one of his deputy marshals, who gently took Mr. Goodwin in his wake and landed him within the gray stone walls of the Hotel de Monroe. Mr. Goodwin confidentially told the officials, who came in contact with him, that he had smuggled whiskey from Canada; and had sold whiskey from Maine to Potter county, and had never been apprehended for it, and that when he succeeded in escaping from the minions of the law, he would sell whiskey in Potter county for two years. When the officer returned for his prisoner, Goodwin had exchanged his light shoes for a pair of heavy ones with short spikes in them for climbing the hills. Evidently with the intention of escaping from the officer while enroute to Tioga. But a set of steel jewelry bent upon his wrists and another set on his ankles with one fastened to the foot bar of the buggy took the conceit out of him, and thus Mr. Goodwin went to the arms of his Uncle Sam.

The Potter Enterprise
Wednesday Evening, October 24, 1883 – Vol. X, No. 24

- Frank Niles, of Niles Hill, is the happy father of a ten pound girl.

West Homer and South Eulalia. Mrs. Mary Crosby is now very sick. She is being treated by Dr. Mattison. Her fifty-fifth birthday was celebrated the 30th of September by her children and grand children. She knew nothing of it, until they came, bringing in the nicely dressed chickens, with other goodies. After partaking of a bountiful repast they presented her with a beautiful cashmere dress. Would that more mothers could be treated thus.

MARRIED.

HASKINS – REED – At Keating Summit, October 17th, 1883, by Rev. Wm. Stewart Holland, Mr. Orlando B. Haskins, of Sylvania, and Miss Ella J. Reed, of Summit township.

- On Monday last at John Brisbeau's lumber camp, on Darien Run, Mr. Cubb of Eleven Mile was almost instantly killed. With others he was skidding logs on the side hill. Mr. Cubb caught a "back cant" and was thrown over the log; the log struck him on his breast. He lived but a very few minutes. The remains were taken through Coudersport on Tuesday, enroute for his former home.

DIED.

VANWEGEN – At North Wharton, on the 7th of October, 1883, Ethel, only child of Albert and Florence Vanwegen, aged five months.

- A petition is being circulated among the poor masters of the county asking that the poor house question be submitted to the voters at the February election. It requires the petition of two-thirds of the poor masters of the county before the Court can order an election.

The Potter Enterprise
Wednesday Evening, October 31, 1883 – Vol. X, No. 25

MARRIED.

GUENTHER – BRENULE – At the home of the bride, Oct. 18th, by Rev. A. A. Craw, Mr. Gustave Guenther to Miss Dora Brenule, all of Eulalia, Pa.

WATSON – REED – At the M.E. Parsonage, Coudersport, Oct. 20th, by Rev. A. A. Craw, Mr. Martin Watson to Miss Rosymon Reed, both of Summit, Pa.

EVERETT – CLARK – At the house of Mrs. Everett, in Coudersport, Oct. 21st, by Rev. A. A. Craw, Mr. James Everett, of Coudersport, to Miss Luella Clark, of Oswayo.

STEVENS – ARMSTRONG – At the home of the bride's parents, in Coudersport, Oct. 24th, by Rev. A. A. Craw, Mr. Edward C. Stevens, of Ceres, N.Y., to Miss Amy Armstrong.

DIED.

FLYNN – In Hector, Oct. 19th, Hattie, wife of M. P. Flynn, aged 23 years and 10 months.

- Diphtheria is raging on the East Fork of the Sinnemahoning in a very malignant form. Seventeen cases have already been reported, and in John Williams' family four deaths have occurred within ten days.

- Mrs. Dehn, of Roulet, died a few days since in Yorkstate, while on a visit to friends.

- It is reported that Mrs. Kinney, wife of Capt. L. H. Kinney, of Sharon, died last week in Michigan.

- John Kelly, at Hammond's Tannery, died very suddenly Wednesday morning. He was at work Tuesday. Wednesday morning his children were sent to school, as usual, although he was complaining some, it was not thought he was dangerously ill. Before ten o'clock he was a corpse. His trouble is supposed to have originated from a fever sore.

- On Wednesday morning about four o'clock, Mr. E. Drew, aged about fifty years, died at the residence of Harlow Dingee, in Coudersport. For twenty-five years Drew has had no permanent home. He traveled the country selling essences and light Yankee notions. He was a very singular being, hump backed, and otherwise deformed. His back, breast, limbs and arms were covered with tumors or bunches from the size of a pea to that of a hen's egg. He claimed he was born with these bunches upon him and that his mother was similarly afflicted. He presented a truly wonderful appearance. Last March he was brought here during Court week, as he said, to testify in a law suit, of which he knew nothing, but who brought him he either could not or would not tell. Since then he has been boarded by Mr. Dingee at the expense of the borough of Coudersport. It is said that Drew has relatives living at or near Rochester, N.Y., but their names are not known here.

- The *Palladium* says: "As Charles Woodkirk was passing the house of Samuel White on the Plank above East Sharon he stopped his team to let a team pass then started on, not noticing any children, but while he was stopped the youngest boy of Samuel White, a boy about six years of age, had climbed on the hind wheel and as the wagon started it threw him over on the ground killing him instantly. The funeral was held Monday last.

A Sad and Fatal Accident.

On the night of the 22d inst., E. O. Austin, Esq., was notified that a man had been killed that day at John Brisbois' logging camp on Darien Run, in Sylvania, and requested to make a view of the case. On making the view, he found it so manifestly a blameless accident as to be unnecessary to summons a jury.

John Hubbs, while engaged with a number of other men in skidding logs, attempted to hold one with his cant hook from the back side. Getting to high a hold he was thrown upon and over the log, stumbled and fell across the skid, when the log rolled over and lay upon him until rolled off by his comrades. The whole scene occupied but a moments time, and John died in a few minutes.

Mr. Hubbs was about nineteen years old, of a splendid physice, amiable disposition and a universal favorite with all. He was an orphan, raised in the --- Catholic Asylum, New York, and was adopted by, and lived with, Thomas O'Donnell, of Genesee.

Mr. Brisbois deserves and receives the thanks of his men for his care in fitting the remains for burial and sending them to Genesee.

On the same day a Mr. Thomas, of Sylvania, was injured in a similar way, but there is hopes of his recovery.

- Last Tuesday evening Mr. Sylvester Greenman, of Hebron township, lodged Dudley Douglass in the county jail, on a charge of larceny. Douglass is charged with stealing a whip, buffalo robe and other articles from the barn of Mr. Greenman, and twenty bushels of oats of Mr. McKee. The property was found in the possession of Douglass, on the farm of George Snyder where he had stopped and engaged to work. Dudley also had in his possession a new wagon, leased from Oscar Nelson, of Lymansville. When arrested he wanted to settle but Mr. Greenman is not of the compromise kind, and intends to let the Court do the settling.

The Potter Enterprise
Wednesday Evening, November 7, 1883 – Vol. X, No. 26

West Homer and South Eulalia. "Lady Moon came down last night" or rather Sunday morning October 28th, and presented Mr. and Mrs. John Gordenier with a young daughter. We do not wonder now that Mr. Gordenier puts on style, why shouldn't he? And now we know why Arthur does not want to go to school this winter, he had rather stay at home and rock little sister.

MARRIED.

ESTES – STILLSON – In Clara, by J. L. Allen, J.P., Albertie B. Estes to May L. Stillson, all of Oswayo, Pa.

CLUGSTON – CARD – At the home of the bride, in Wharton, Nov. 5th, by J. W. Thorne, J. P., Mr. Howard S. Clugston, of Franklin county, Pa., to Mrs. Julia A. Card.

- George Leibe, of Wellsboro, died very suddenly last Saturday. He was a very worthy young man, and a brother of Mrs. N. M. Glassmire, of Coudersport.

- On the 28th of October at Monterey, Mich., Mrs. L. H. Kinney, of Sharon, died. Some four weeks previous Mrs. Kinney left Sharon to visit her old home two weeks later she was stricken with paralysis, from the effects of which she finally died. Mrs. Kinney was a most excellent woman, beloved and respected by all who knew her, and her death is a sad blow to her husband. Many friends in Potter county extend to him their sympathy in his great bereavement.

- In Coudersport last Tuesday 100 votes were polled. A glance over the registry lists shows 38 voters in the boro absent, sick or not voting. These 38 are actual voters in the boro. This would shod that we have 228 actual voters, and as the usual estimate is five inhabitants to each vote would indicate that the population of Coudersport is very close to 1140. Call it an even thousand and Coudersport then shows a gain of 323 inhabitants since the census was taken in 1880.

The Potter Enterprise
Wednesday Evening, November 14, 1883 – Vol. X, No. 27

- Mrs. Reuben Post, of Hebron, was buried on Tuesday.

Cheese.

Statistics of the Genesee Fork Cheese Manufacture for the year ending September the 1st, 1883. Factory opened May 7th, and closed Sept. 31st.

Total amount of milk, booked 426,003 lbs.
Deduct 1222 lbs. from above amount. Watered milk.
Total amount of cheese manufactured, 44373.25 lbs.
Receipts of cheese estimated from the various prices of sales made during season, $4431.315.
Average price per lb. cheese, $9.0998.
Average rate of milk per lb. cheese, 9.57 lbs.
Cheese makers commission for manufacturing, $554.66.
Commission for hauling cheese to Wellsville, $61.07.
Commission for hauling milk to factory .64 per cent of patrons $147.08.
Commission for figuring dividends, $11.00.
Greatest number of patrons in dividends, 7.
Average per cent of patronage, 21.66.
Total amount to patrons, less com., $3657.49.
Average per cent to patrons, figured from average per cent patronage, $168.859.

The number of cows for the supply of milk has not been ascertained. The probability is that they are as few in number as could be selected elsewhere in the county for the supply of milk as above tabled.

Jurors for December Term.
GRAND JURORS.

Abbott – Eberhard Gnau; Bingham – W. J. Arnold; Coudersport – R. L. Nichols, F. M. Stevens; Genesee – Thomas Caller, Ira Easton; Harrison – Edward Angood, T. P. Badgero, Hiram Courtright; Hebron – George P. Kenyon; Keating – Marion Younglove; Oswayo – Thomas Crittenden, J. L. Fessenden, A. A. Goff, George M. Tyler; Pike – M. V. Prouty, H. M. Tice; Pleasant Valley – Wilson McDowell; Portage – George F. Smith; Roulet – Isaac Lyman; Sharon – Charles Cole, Wm. Hyatt, F. N. Newton; Sweden – Edwin Lyman.

TRAVERSE JURORS.

Abbott – Charles Meissner, John Noelk; Allegany – E. L. Heggie, M. A. Veelie; Bingham – Charles Grover, Orlando Hubbard, J. C. Hawley, Amos Johnson; Coudersport – J. R. Groves, N. A. Pinney, W. C. Rennells, P. A. Stebbins; Eulalia – Amos Colcord, J. M. Spafford; Genesee – Norman Chapman; Harrison – Martin English, H. P. Metcalf, S. K. Stevens; Hebron – Morris Lent; Hector – J. S. Little; Keating – Robert Clinton, G. C. Lewis; Oswayo – C. N. Brown, Walter Wells; Pike – J. F. Lossey; Pleasant Valley – Frank Judkins, Otis Weimer; Sharon – Frank Farley, Wm. Mulkin, Calvin Perry; Stewardson – Decatur Francis; Sylvania – Columbus Rees; Ulysses – G. W. Burt, J. S. Hopkins, F. A. Raymond; West Branch – L. Z. Crippen.

– The County Commissioners on Thursday, in accordance with the recommendation of the Grand Jury of Sept. term, made a contract with the Hall Safe & Lock Co., of Cincinnati, O., to furnish and put up fire proof vaults for the records of the Com's and Trea's office. The vaults will be of iron and concrete, warranted fire proof in every respect and to cost $2800. This is an improvement very much needed. The records of the Com's and Treas. Office have now no protection in case of fire, the loss of which could not be repaired and would occasion endless litigation. – *Journal.*

The Potter Enterprise
Wednesday Evening, November 21, 1883 – Vol. X, No. 28

DIED.

MATTISON – In Hebron, Nov. 20, Ruby, daughter of Dr. E. S. Mattison, aged 3 years, 3 mos.

– Last Saturday a message by telephone was received at this place, asking Coroner Buck to come to Hector township and hold an inquest. Dr. Buck was out of town, and did not return until Monday, too late to attend this call. We have been unable to get particulars, but it is reported that a woman named Stiles was found dead in bed, with an infant nearly frozen by her side. Malpractice or neglect is rumored to have been the cause of her death. We hope to be able to give full particulars in our next. There seems to be a mystery about the matter which needs clearing up.

Under Lock and Key.

On Tuesday Sheriff Monroe turned the key on James Clark, formerly of this county, and now Jim is a steady boarder at the expense of the county.

Four years ago last June Clark offered for sale two notes of seventy-five and two hundred and fifty dollars respectively, signed by John Eldridge of Tioga county. Eldridge is said to be worth from ten to twenty thousand dollars, and the notes were disposed of to Amos Veelie of Coudersport, and Wm. W. M'Dougall, then of Bradford. The notes were dated Dec. 8, 1878, and were due nine months from date.

When the notes became due and payment was asked for, Eldridge pronounced them forgeries. The matter dragged along for some time, and finally Eldridge had the judgments opened, on his oath that the notes were forged.

At the last June term of Court, we believe, the Grand Jury found a true bill against Clark for forgery.

A requisition was obtained, and a week ago last Monday Sheriff Monroe started for Chippewa Falls, Wisconsin. Upon presenting the proper papers the sheriff of Chippewa county proceeded to Cadoutt, about twelve miles distant, arrested Clark and turned him over to Sheriff Monroe, by whom he was brought to Coudersport.

Since going West Clark had married a widow lady, had secured a nice little farm, with considerable personal property about him, and was living in comfortable circumstances.

He was considerably surprised at being arrested, but keeps a "stiff upper lip" and says he will come out all right. He says he received a paper containing the Court proceedings, showing that he was indicted.

Clark claims that he can prove that the notes were signed by John Eldridge, and are not forgeries. If he does he will make it hot for Mr. Eldridge. If Eldridge proves they are forgeries, he will make it hot for Clark. December Court will probably settle the matter.

Wanted!

I want One Hundred and Fifty Thousand feet of Maple logs to be delivered at the mill at Coudersport. Also will pay Highest Cash Price for Cherry, Ash, Chestnut and Basswood logs. Call on or address D. W. Vanwegen, Coudersport, Pa.

The Potter Enterprise
Wednesday Evening, November 28, 1883 – Vol. X, No. 29

Roulet. Born to Mr. and Mrs. John Knowlton, a little son and daughter.

MARRIED.

WILLIAMS – STILLMAN – At the residence of L. R. Burdick by Elder G. P. Kenyon, Mr. Allen E. Williams of Keating, Pa., and Miss Ida E. Stillman of Hebron, Pa.

- Diphtheria on the East Fork has caused the death of five children in the family of John Williams, one for Zeb. Williams, two for Moses Williams. In other families the disease is still raging.

Found Dead in Bed.

Last Friday, as Dan Stevens was passing the house of Erastus Styles, about two miles from Sunderlinville, he saw a light burning in the house at 9:30 a.m.; he stopped his team, went to the house and found the door fastened, which he broke open and saw Mrs. Styles lying dead in her bed, with a child nearly two years old lying across her breast. The child, which was nearly frozen, was immediately cared for, and steps were taken to procure and doctor and coroner or justice. No Justice could be brought until quite late the next day. It was first thought that she had been murdered, although the coroner's jury decided that Mrs. Styles came to her death through her own instrumentality. There was no evidence to show that any person had entered the house previous to her being a corpse and all the evidence showed that in her attempt to sacrifice the life of an unborn child she met her death. The autopsy was held by Dr. Masten of this place, before Justice Gridley, of Ulysses.

Mr. Styles was engaged in a lumber job on Pine Creek, to which he started about one week previous to this sad call. Mrs. Styles was about twenty-one years old. – *Westfield Free Press.*

- By a recent order of the Telephone Company, the following places have been connected with Coudersport: Lawrenceville, Greenwood, Hornellsville, Whitesville, Andover, Wellsville, Corning, Horseheads, Elmira, Watkins, Bath, Owego and several others. For particulars inquire at the Nichols House. Five minutes conversation with any of the above points from 30 to 35 cents.

- James Cavanaugh met with a singular accident one day last week. He was driving a colt and the animal took it into his head to kick. The colt was not shod, and the sharp edge of the hoof struck Mr. Cavanaugh's hand in which he held the whip. The flesh on his forefinger was torn from the bone making a very ragged and painful wound.

- For some time past Sheriff Monroe has allowed the prisoners in jail the privilege of the corridor. None of them were supposed to be at all dangerous or inclined to take advantage of the kindness shown them. Goodwin and Douglass now occupy one of the strong cells, and will no more roam the corridor. These two intended to leave the jail, while the Sheriff was off after James Clark. The plan was to knock Mrs. Monroe over, when breakfast was brought in, and make a skip for the woods. The plan was not carried out because Douglass did not get some money he was expecting. It is safe to say that it has been indefinitely postponed.

Grossly Deceived.

The G. A. R. at Portville is said to have been badly deceived a short time ago. The story goes that the Commander of the Post received a letter from Sharon Centre, Pa., from a woman purporting to be a daughter of Dr. Porter, who was formerly a member of Wessells Post, stating that her father was dead and requesting them to come there and conduct the funeral service, which would take place Sunday the 11th instant. The Post mustered about fifteen members and drove through the mud to Sharon Centre only to find that Dr. Porter had been dead and buried two weeks, having died at Warren, Pa. It seems that the daughter, none too intelligent herself, and a still more unbalanced step son, had arranged the plan to get the remains from Warren and hold the last sad rites over him at Sharon Centre, under the auspices of the Post; but their financial condition made such a plan impossible. Hence nothing remained but for the Post to return, which they did in not the most amiable of moods, if we are correctly informed. – *Olean Times.*

The Potter Enterprise
Wednesday Evening, December 5, 1883 – Vol. X, No. 30

Whites Corners. D. Hart, of Bingham, and Jennie White, of this place, were married on the eighth inst.

MARRIED.

HEATH – NEEFE – In Coudersport, December 3d, 1883, by Rev. W. B. Leavenworth, Mr. James Heath, of Liberty, McKean county, and Miss Maria Story Neefe, of Allegany, Potter county, Pa.

Silver Wedding.

On Saturday evening last, Dec. 1st, a large number of friends gathered at the home of Mr. and Mrs. O. H. Crosby in Coudersport, the occasion being the 25th anniversary of the wedding of Mr. and Mrs. Crosby.

The evening was spent in social enjoyment, and kind wishes for those who for 25 years have been joined in happy wedlock were showered on them thick and fast. Refreshments were served, and at a late hour the guests returned to their homes, leaving as tokens of their kind regard a beautiful Silver, Gold Lined Tea Set. Silver Cake Basket, Silver Butter Dish, Jelly Spoon, Flower Vase of Silver and Crystal and numerous other and beautiful articles. We trust the bride and groom will live to enjoy and celebrate their Golden Wedding.

- Programme for local Institute to be held at the upper School house, on the Eleven Mile, Oswayo, Dec. 8th: Morning session, 10:00; Opening Remarks, Maggie Doyle; Response, A. S. Lyman; Song, May Rowley; Class drill in Reading, Lettie B. Colegrove; Select Reading, Maggie Maginnis; Essay, Addie Douglass. Afternoon Session, 1:30. Song, Ella Morse; Discount Class Drill, Edith Haskell; Recitation, Villa Rathbun; Methods in Spelling, Orisa Hurd; Essay, Adrian Gardner; Results of Primary Writing, H. H. Hall; Recitation, Nett Bishop; Diacritical Marks, Anna Buckbee. Evening Session, 7:30. Song, H. H. Hall; Select Reading, Marinthe Goodsell; Address, Jerome Dodge; Busy work for pupils, Lillie Doyle.

The Potter Enterprise
Wednesday Evening, December 12, 1883 – Vol. X, No. 31

MARRIED.

CORSAW – RISCHEL – In Sweden, Dec. 10th, 1883, by H. S. Lent, Esq., Chester Corsaw, of Sweden, and Miss Jennie Rischel, of Smethport.

MORLEY – ROGERS – In Raymond, Dec. 2d, 1883, by Rev. J. L. Swain, Mr. Jasper W. Morley and Miss Elvira L. Rogers, both of Gold.

ZACHARIAS – KLESA – At the home of the bride's father, in Homer township, on Thanksgiving day, Nov. 29th, 1883, by Rev. Wm. Marshall, Mr. Clayton A. Zacharias, of Coudersport, and Miss Anna Klesa.

GROSS – PLAGUEMAN – In Ulysses, Dec. 9th, 1883, by A. Carpenter, Esq., Mr. Michael Gross, of Canton, Branch county, Mich., to Miss Rocena Plaugeman, of Ulysses, Pa.

Roulet. The tin wedding of Mr. and Mrs. A. V. Lyman was celebrated the evening of the 27th ult., a goodly number of their friends were present, and presented them with several useful presents, among which was a hanging lamp and an arm chair.

- The little daughter of Frederick Devanport died on Tuesday.

Andrews Settlement. Yesterday the relatives, friends and neighbors attended the funeral of Mrs. Curtis who died on the eighth, the funeral was held at the residence, and conducted by Rev. Tupper, the Methodist minister in charge here.

- Dudley Douglass, arrested for stealing in Hebron township, failed to report at the opening of court. He owned four or five hundred dollars worth of property. His bail was reduced to $200, and his property given as security for the bail. He told a fellow prisoner that if he was bailed, it was with the understanding that he should or would leave the county. This would be a good thing for him for it would save him a trip down the river, it would be a good thing for his bail as they would secure double the amount of the bail. If it is true as reported, it ought not to be allowed.

Potter County, Pennsylvania Potpourri – Volume I
1880 through 1884

Over 1,000.

Z. J. Thompson, borough assessor, in making the assessment, just completed, also made a census of the borough. His list foots up 1,016 inhabitants, big and little; this does not include families or persons who are here temporarily as contractors and jobbers, but simply those who call this their home. Of those who are here temporarily there are from fifty to one hundred persons. The increase of population for the past three years is a healthy growth and a permanent one. The number of taxables in the borough foot up 329; horses, over four years old, 76; cows, 59; dogs, 30.

Officers Elected.

At its last meeting A. F. Jones Post, G. A. R., the following officers were elected for the ensuing year:

J. M. Covey, P.C.; C. J. Marble, S.V.C.; W. H. Hazen, J.V.C.; John D. Earl, Adjutant; George N. Tuttle, Q.M.; Dr. Frank Buck, Surgeon; A. D. Colcord, Chaplain; Albert Colcord, O.D.; John B. Dolway, O.G.; J. V. Weimer, Q.M.S.; C. N. Barrett, George N. Tuttle, Delegates to Department Encampment. Hiram Bridges, Alternate.

Allegany Statistics.

	1880	1882	1883
Horses Working	154	165	172
Oxen	28	25	30
Cows	488	466	428
Dogs	76	73	62
Colts, 3 years	24	15	13
Colts, 2 years	15	16	6
Colts, 1 year	17	11	16
Colts, suckling	13	16	21
Heifers, milking 3 years	118	81	88
Heifers, milking 2 years	46	37	33
Heifers, not milking 3 years	3	8	21
Heifers, not milking 2 years	45	18	19
Steers, 3 years	14	4	13
Steers, 2 years	19	12	112
Yearlings	243	113	165
Calves	232	276	325
Sheep	1619	1750	1820
Shoats to winter	114	132	123
Winter wheat bus.	604	1166	427
Spring wheat bus.	336	182	119
Corn in ear bus.	4200	2230	75
Buckwheat bus.	2751	2861	2824
Oats bus.	19248	21189	26928
Millet bus.	1380	1528	731
Rye bus.	233	81	40

Peas bus.	194	115	662
Beans bus.	84	36	1
Potatoes bus.	11081	9512	15297
Apples bus.	7602	4426	1422
Turnips, bus.	827	11157	552
Tons of hay	2043	2754	2873
Pork killed, lbs.	37932	38178	36439
Butter, lbs.	60784	59714	63171
Cheese, lbs.	48960	4000	51826
Maple sugar, lbs.	19465	31185	18273
Wool, lbs.	5482	5762 ½	6298
Swarms of bees wnt'rd	56	65	46
No. young swarms	103	76	45
Amt honey from same	795	655	577

Charles Coats, Assessor.

The Potter Enterprise
Wednesday Evening, December 19, 1883 – Vol. X, No. 32

- Mike Holland, Engineer on the C. & P. A., is the happy father of a bouncing girl baby.

DIED.

PROUTY – In West Branch, Pa., Dec. 12th, 1883, Myrtle, daughter of Mr. and Mrs. M. V. Prouty, aged three years, eight months and 26 days.

HASKINS – In North Wharton, Nov. 10th, 1883, Edith, only daughter of Orange and Kate Haskins, aged ten months and seven days.

Oh how we miss the darling
For you was so dear to us
But we must check our teardrops
For we know thou art sleeping
With the angels.
Sleep little baby sleep
Not in thy cradle bed
Not on they mother's breast
But with the bright angels.

Court Minutes.

Court convened Dec. 10th, Hon. A. G. Olmsted presiding, Hammond and Lewis associates.

Grand Jury called and sworn. R. L. Nichols foreman; R. H. Howe, deputy constable of Bingham, constable to attend same. Grand Jury discharged Dec. 14th.

Fox Estate vs E. Wheeler, et al; jury find for plaintiff land described to be released upon payment of $1493.83, one half in 30 days and one half in six months.

W. H. Rounsevill appointed appraiser of estate of John Kelly, deceased.

Fox Estate vs. Ira P. Grover; jury find for plaintiff land described to be released on payment of $1336.40; one-half in 30 days, balance in 6 months.

R. L. Nichols vs Hellen P. Blanchard; jury find for plaintiff land described to be released on payment of $238.81 within 20 days.

Martha L. Hodskin, on petition, declared a *feme sole trader*.

Abram Chase appointed Treasurer of Sweden township.

Mary Baker, wife of Curtis Baker, granted separate estate &c.

L. U. Snead appointed guardian of Leah O. and Mary O. Snead.

Frederick Jordan adopted by M. A. Harvey.

G. McCalmont, of McKean county, admitted to practice in the several Courts of Potter county.

McKinny Erway appointed constable of Harrison township.

Ordered that an election, for the purpose of fixing place for holding elections, be held in Genesee township, Feb. 19th, 1883.

Frank A. Fitch appointed guardian of Ida Luella Petrie.

Mary Ann Burns adopted by B. L. and Almira Easton.

Genesee Poor District vs James Burns and Felix Burns; rule on defendants to show cause why they should not support Ann Burns their mother.

M. J. Colcord, member of the McKean county Bar, admitted to practice in the several Courts of Potter county.

Ordered that the jury wheel be filled with 400 names for ensuing year. Veniries ordered for 24 grand and 36 traverse jurors for March term.

In the matter of the alleged lunacy of Rosina Easton; Seth Lewis appointed commissioner.

Dan Baker appointed auditor to settle with the Prothonotary and Register and Recorder.

Dec. 15th John Ormerod, District Attorney elect, came into Court and was duly sworn.

L. E. Halsey, administrator vs David Wambold; continued.

J. W. Allen vs L. D. Wagner; certiorara discontinued.

Elijah Hill, declared a lunatic and ordered to be removed to Warren Insane Asylum. Oswayo township certified as his legal residence.

On petition of two-thirds of the Overseers of the Poor of Potter county, the Court directed that an election be held Feb. 19th, 1884, to decide the question of Commissioners purchasing a farm for poor purposes.

A. B. Mann appointed auditor to restate account of Dewitt Hammond administrator of estate of Polly Ann VanHusen.

Ordered that Charles Stoneham, lunatic, be committed to Warren Insane Asylum and Hebron township be certified as his legal residence.

A. B. Mann appointed auditor to distribute funds in hands of executor of Anthony Jones.

Daniel Monroe, High Sheriff of Potter county, acknowledged the following deeds:

To S. M. Fox and Geo. Fox, executors, for 33 acres in Harrison, for $25.00; sold as property of Chas. Outman.

To W. K. Jones, executor, for 24 acres in Coudersport, for $25.00; sold at property of Henry Dingman.
W. R. Howland vs Susan Howland; divorce granted.
Henrietta Staudefield vs Henry Staudefield; divorce granted.
Mary A. Ackerman vs Sam'l Ackerman; sub in divorce awarded.
Cora Burrows vs Seeley F. Burrows; sub in divorce awarded.
Wm. Morey vs Maria Morey; sub in divorce awarded.
Luke G. Crandall vs Emma Crandall; divorce awarded.
Levi G. Stillman vs Mary J. Stillman; divorced granted.
John Hosmer vs Julia Hosmer; J. L. Knox appointed commissioner to take testimony.
Josephene Drake vs Fred N. Drake; J. M. Kilbourne appointed commissioner to take testimony.
Alma Brewster vs George Brewster; libel in divorce, verdict for the libelant.
Nancy Miller vs R. E. Miller; Martin Dodge, of Harrison, Pa., and Reuben Vosburg, of Dresden, N.Y., appointed commissioners to take testimony.
Matilda Hill vs Myron J. Hill; sub in divorce awarded.
Rosena Nesbit vs John Nesbit; divorce granted.
Commonwealth vs James Clark, forgery; under charge of the Court, the jury returned a verdict of not guilty.
Com vs S. J. Burrows, desertion; defendant and bail discharged.
Com vs George Nickerson, A. Nickerson and E. Edgar; continued.
Same vs Jacob Reed, larceny, *nol pros.*
Same vs Abram Solomon, assault and battery &c.; not guilty, county to pay costs.
Same vs Dudley Douglass, larceny; true bill, bail forfeited and respited until next term.
Same vs P. Kirk, statutory burglary; not guilty.
Same vs Edward McGonigal, selling liquor to minors; continued.
Same vs same; continued.
Same vs Andrew J. Wagner, perjury; continued.
Same vs O. W. Strong, selling liquor; true bill.
Same vs David Cornelius, selling liquor; true bill.
Same vs Stephen Horton, selling liquor; true bill.
Same vs Elmer Aylesworth, selling liquor; true bill, continued.
Same vs L. D. Wagner, perjury; continued.
Same vs Nathan Babcock, perjury; not a true bill.
Same vs W. F. Clark, larceny; not a true bill.
Same vs Geo. Mahon, larceny; *nol pros* on payment of costs.
Same vs Lorenzo D. Card, larceny; not guilty.
Same vs Geo. Sherwood, perjury; *nol pros* on payment of costs.
Same vs David Kibbee, perjury; *nol pros* on payment of costs.
Same vs Charles Vanoux, selling liquor; true bill, bench warrant ordered.
Same vs Willard Nelson, selling liquor; true bill.
Same vs John Rooney and Ann Clark, assault and battery &c.; John Rooney plead guilty, fined $10 and costs.

Same vs James Ryan, fornication and bastardy; true bill, continued.

Same vs August Froebel, pointing a gun; not guilty, defendant to pay half the costs and prosecutor, Mahlon Peterson, one half.

Same vs D. P. Reed and Willis Reed, involuntary manslaughter; continued.

Same vs. Lorenzo D. Card, breaking and entering a store; *nol pros* entered.

Same vs Peleg Burdic, selling liquor; true bill, continued.

Same vs C. H. Breisenick, selling liquor; true bill, continued.

Same vs Frank Berfield, selling liquor; true bill, bench warrant ordered.

Same vs Burt Rees, selling liquor; not a true bill, county to pay costs.

Same vs John Dorsey, selling liquor; not a true bill, county to pay costs.

Same vs Frank McGinnis, selling liquor; not a true bill, county to pay costs.

Same vs Jeff Burdic, selling liquor; bail forfeited and respited until next term.

Same vs C. N. Brown, selling liquor; continued.

- Last week the Grand Jury had their hands full, most of their business being to inquire into alleged violations of the liquor law. The move last week was not made by the temperance people, but in most of the cases, if we are correctly informed, on complaint of Frank Goodwin, now serving out sentence for violation of the liquor law, and John Ward, recently discharged from jail, where he was confined for a similar offence. Among those complained of was W. B. Rees, druggist. The grand jury ignored the bill in this case. Mr. Rees has been very careful in handling liquor, and his prosecution was the result of spite; it is a pity the complainant did not have the costs to pay. Before court Goodwin sent letters to various parties in different sections of the county demanding money as the price of not complaining of the parties for violation of the liquor law; in some cases demanding only ten dollars in others as high as fifty. Suits for attempt at black-mail are threatened and ought to be carried out. For the whiskey seller we have no sympathy, but for citizens who have not violated the law to be hauled up before the grand jury and published as whiskey sellers, is altogether wrong, and the parties engaged in such business deserve punishment.

Statistics of Genesee Township, 1883.

Horses over 4 years	185
Colts over 3 years	13
Colts over 2 years	11
Colts over 1 year	6
Colts sucking	21
Cows	332
3 year olds	65
2 year olds	60
1 year olds	326
Calves	347
Sheep	2700
Oxen	49
Hogs to winter	163

Dogs	87
Hay, tons	2036
Oats, bu.	22275
Buckwheat, bu.	2509
Wheat, bu.	238
Corn in ear, bu.	200
Barley, bu.	103
Potatoes, bu.	24532
Butter, lb.	28627

A quantity of the milk sent to factory.

Ira E. Easton, Assessor.

The Potter Enterprise
Wednesday Evening, December 26, 1883 – Vol. X, No. 33

- No paper will be issued from this office next week. The office will be open every day and orders for job work will be filled promptly.

MARRIED.

GRABE – RINK – In St. Johnsonville, N.Y., Dec. 20th, 1883, by Rev. Cook, Theodore Grabe, of Coudersport, and Miss Mary L. Rink, of St. Johnsonville. N.Y.

- Isaiah Sutton, for many years a prominent citizen of Sunderlinville, was buried in Pike township last Sunday.

- W. W. Thompson and wife left Coudersport this (Wednesday) morning for Hillsdale, Mich., to attend the funeral of Mrs. Thompson's uncle, Dr. Frank French, who died on Christmas. The deceased was a brother of Dr. A. French, of this place.

Demands Satisfaction.

Under date of Dec. 20th Frank Goodwin writes us that we must take back what we said about his writing letters to parties demanding money, or they would be prosecuted for selling whiskey. Goodwin says he "never wrote the first letter," and "there was letters wrote out of here to that effect, but I didn't write them and I do not wish to be accused for other peoples doings." We do not wish to accuse Goodwin of anything he is not guilty of and are very glad to give him an opportunity to deny the charge. Somebody did write such letters and we understood they were signed by Goodwin, and we are not sure now that Goodwin's name is not at the bottom of some of them, although Goodwin may not have signed them himself. We have a letter postmarked Nov. 11th, written to the Enterprise for publication, which states "we intend to bring them (Oleona and Germania) into the limits of Potter county and in the borough of Coudersport and have them naturalized and have them know that they are in the

United States, and we don't intend to slight them any more so we invite them to attend the next Court and give an account of their stewardship.

Sign the Bengal Tiger, Frank Goodwin.

The two letters are, evidently, not the same hand writing, and it is possible other letters have been sent out signed the same way.

The Potter Enterprise
Wednesday Evening, January 9, 1884 – Vol. X, No. 34

- Herbert Brown, of Millport, could not wait until New Year's Eve to hang up his stocking, so he hung it up Sunday night and got a ten pound boy.

MARRIED.

HORTON – WYKOFF – At the house of M. F. Wykoff, Dec. 20th, 1883, by Perry Duval, Esq., Mr. Stephen Horton, of Wharton, Pa., and Mrs. C. E. Wykoff, of Grove, Pa.

LEWIS – ROBBINS – At the Methodist parsonage, in Lewisville, Dec. 24th, 1883, by Rev. W. Miller, Mr. Geo. D. Lewis, of Willing, N.Y., and Miss Sarah A. Robbins, of Bingham, Pa.

HOOKER – BLOSS – At the bride's home in Ulysses, Dec. 19th, 1883, by Rev. W. Miller, Mr. J. H. Hooker and Miss Olive Bloss.

JOHNSON – IVES – At the residence of the bride's parents in Ulysses, Dec. 25th, 1883, by Rev. T. L. Perry, Mr. L. B. Johnson, of Harrison, to Miss S. E. Ives, of Ulysses.

HELENBROOK – ROBBINS – At the home of the bride's parents, in Harrison, Dec. 29th, 1883, by Rev. A. S. Gould, Mr. Willie H. Helenbrook, of Olean, and Miss Rosie V. Robbins, of Mills, Pa.

STONE – HORNSBY – At the home of the bride's parents in Whites Corners, Dec. 30th, 1883, by Rev. A. S. Gould, Mr. Lafayette Stone and Miss Faith Hornsby, both of Whites Corners, Pa.

GRIFFITH – LEECH – At the Baptist parsonage, Jan. 1st, 1884, by Rev. T. L. Perry, Mr. L. D. Griffith and Miss A. S. Leech, both of Genesee.

- Reuben Clark, aged 95 years, died in Hebron on the 30th ult. Mr. Clark was, probably, the oldest person in Potter county, and was one of the first settlers in this section.

- On Monday Mrs. J. M. Covey was called to Broome county, N.Y., by a telegram that her mother had been fatally injured by a running away of a horse.

- F. B. McNamara, Sr., was held to bail on Saturday for assault and battery on Mrs. F. B. McNamara, Jr.

- Sheriff Monroe has removed his family and household goods to Bingham township. Dan is now a farmer on the Samuel Monroe farm. In his new vocation we wish him abundant success. As Sheriff of Potter county he leaves the office with more friends than when he entered upon the discharge of his official duties. His business has never been neglected, for friend or foe and no one has been pushed to the wall until absolutely necessary. Kind hearted to a fault, if possible, he has always done all in his power to assist those in distress, and few have the opportunity to do as many acts of kindness as a sheriff. Those compelled to board with him were well treated and well fed and left the jail firm friends to Mr. Monroe. Dan's record as sheriff for the past three years is one that he may well feel proud of. Potter county never had a better kinder hearted official than Daniel Monroe.

Officers Elected.

At a meeting of Coudersport Lodge, K. of H., on Friday evening last, the following officers were elected for the ensuing year:

D. W. Vanwegen, Dictator; W. W. Thompson, Vice Dictator; Charles Reissman, Assistant Dictator; I. P. Collins, Reporter; F. J. Norton, Financial Reporter; P. A. Stebbins, Treasurer; J. L. Knox, Chaplain; W. C. Rennells, Guardian; W. B. Rees, Guide; W. K. Jones, Sentinel; Dr. E. H. Ashcraft, Medical Examiner; W. K. Jones, J. M. Covey and N. M. Glassmire, Trustees.

The following are the officers elected by Coudersport Chapter, R.A.M., for the ensuing year:

D. C. Larrabee, H.P.; W. W. Thompson, King; C. A. Stebbins, Scribe; W. J. Brown, Treasurer; N. H. Goodsell, Sec.

A full list of the officers will be published as the appointments are made.

The following are the officers of Lewisville Lodge, F. & A. M., for the ensuing year:

Geo. C. Marion, W.M.; F. M. Bronson, S.W.; L. C. Perry, J.W.; H. K. Lane, Treas.; D. E. Hosley, S.D.; C. W. Bailey, J.D.; E. A. Burt, S.M.C.; E. A. Hovey, J.M.C.; W. T. Hosley, Pur.; A. A. Johnson, Chaplain; Charles Erlbeck, Tiler; Seth Lewis, Secretary.

- Voters should bear in mind that the question of the poor house is to be voted on at the coming February election, and look into the matter carefully. It is a question of considerable importance and each one should vote intelligently on the question.

Masonic Reception.

Thursday, December 27th, was a red letter day in the Coudersport Masonic Calendar. In the afternoon the Craft met to install the officers of Eulalia Lodge, No. 342, for the ensuing year. It was expected that D.D.G.M. Charles L. Wheeler, of Bradford, would be present, but at a late hour a telegram was received announcing that important business prevented his leaving home.

The following officers were installed:

W. K. Jones, W.M.; Norman A. Pinney, S.W.; James L. Knox, J.W.; Almeron Nelson, Treas.; N. H. Goodsell, Sec.

In the evening came the reception and dance of Eulalia Lodge and Coudersport Chapter.

The dancing was in the Opera House, which was beautifully festooned, wreathed and trimmed with emblems in evergreens and flowers. Ninety-eight couple were in attendance and until a late hour in the morning enjoyed themselves. Everything passed off pleasantly without hitch or jar. The music by the Randolph Band was the best ever offered in this place.

The Supper in the Masonic Dining Rooms, above the Opera House, was a credit to W. T. Dike, who had sole charge. The tables were neat and tasty and the supply of provisions ample and very fine including fruits &c.

The lodge and reception rooms were thrown open to the guests and those not inclined to dance, here found a very pleasant place to chat, and amuse themselves and each other.

Altogether the reception was a success.

NOTICE.

By the existing ordinances of the Borough of Coudersport, cattle are not permitted to be at large in the streets of said borough between December 1st and April 1st. Persons interested will please take notice.

By order of the town council.

Arthur B. Mann, Clerk.

AT THE ARK
Furs Wanted
BEAR, MINK, FOX, OTTER, MUSKRAT,
SKUNK, RACCOON, MARTIN, DEEER
AND HOUSE CAT (BLACK)
E. N. STEBBINS.

The Potter Enterprise
Wednesday Evening, January 16, 1884 – Vol. X, No. 35

- There was recently born to Mr. and Mrs. John Sullivan, of North Wharton, a child weighing twenty-two pounds. The sex of this immense youngster we did not learn.

Whites Corners. Mr. John Waters died at his residence, on December 30th, 1883, very suddenly. Mr. Waters was very much liked as a neighbor and will be much missed.

- Mrs. Lewis W. Lyman, of Sweden, was buried on Monday last. For a long time she has been a patient sufferer. She will be sadly missed, not alone by relatives, but by all who knew her.

- Last week we made mention of F. B. McNamara, Sr., having been arrested for beating his daughter-in-law. Mr. M. tells quite a different story from the woman, and from his story the beating was pretty much all on one side, and he got the worst of it in attempting to get away from the woman.

- Below we give the full list of officers of Eulalia Lodge, No. 342, F. & A. M., for the ensuing year.
W. K. Jones, W.M.; Norman A. Pinney, S.W.; James L. Knox, J.W.; Almeron Nelson, Treas.; N. H. Goodsell, Sec'y; D. C. Larrabee, Chap.; B. W. Dennis, Guide; S. A. Phillips, S.D.; Willis I. Lewis, J.D.; Henry Carsten, S.M.C.; J. M. Covey, J.M.C.; D. W. Vanwegen, Pur.; M. S. Winfield, Tyler.

The Potter Enterprise
Wednesday Evening, January 23, 1884 – Vol. X, No. 36

- Chas. Reining and wife have an addition to their family in the shape of a nice girl. It was born on the 22d inst.

- Aunt "Jane" is happy now because Mr. and Mrs. William Clear has a nice 9 ½ pound girl – born Jan. 19th.

MARRIED.
HALL – PHILLIPS – At the residence of the bride, near Gold, Dec. 29, 1883, Mr. Joel P. Hall, of Ulysses, to Mrs. Mary C. Phillips, by Rev. Swain.

DIED.
HASKINS – At East Homer, Dec. 13, 1883, Clemet, youngest son of William and Kate Haskins, aged one year, eleven months and twenty-five days.

- Sheriff Worden is being well supplied with boarders. Last week brought him three. James Mallory, of Hector, for cutting timber on land owned by another; John Ferguson, of Pleasant Valley, charged with appropriating an axe without rendering any equivalent and without the consent of the owner thereof, and Ryan Miller, of Pike Township, charged with indecent exposure of his person and assault on Eva Reed, aged ten years. The offence was committed on January 14th.

The Potter Enterprise
Wednesday Evening, January 30, 1884 – Vol. X, No. 37

- Born, in Coudersport, on Thursday last, to Mr. and Mrs. J. L. Haughenberry, a daughter, weight 9 ½ pounds.

- On Friday last John Cavanaugh, of Roulet, was lodged in jail, as a lunatic.

- Underneath the "beautiful snow" lies rubbish and filth enough to spread disease and death in many families, unless great care is exercised at the break up.

- There seems to be an impression in some parts of the county that if the coming vote should be in favor of a Poorhouse the Commissioners will buy the Stearns' farm. This is a mistake. At the time the move was first started they did make a contract for that farm, but it was thrown up when they found they had started wrong. Under the law they cannot purchase or make any selection until after the election, and have no particular farm in view now.

- On Saturday afternoon, John Cavanaugh, lunatic, now in jail, made a desperate effort to commit suicide. He selected a protruding catch on one of the doors, and rushed across the corridor to butt his head against the catch. Fortunately he struck it so that it made a glancing blow and a long cut over the top of his head was the result. Had he struck it square it would have killed him instantly. Dr. Mattison rendered medical aid. Cavanaugh has been removed to Warren.

Poor House Question.

Every reader of the county newspapers has doubtless observed the election notice of Daniel Monroe, Sheriff, announcing to the voters of Potter County that an election will be held February 19th, 1884, for the purpose of settling the question whether the people are in favor of continuing the present plan of supporting the unfortunate poor, or whether they will authorize the County Commissioners to purchase real estate, erect thereon suitable buildings, provide tools, and furnish employment and relief to the destitute poor of the county, as provided by Act of Assembly of June 4, 1879.

With your permission, Mr. Editor, and believing this to be a very important matter, one that should be carefully and candidly investigated before casting a vote, the following facts and conclusions are respectfully submitted:

1st. Would it be economy to provide one suitable place to care for and support the indigent poor of the county?

2d. Can such poor persons be better cared for in a properly managed county poor house, than is or can be provided for them under the system of each Township keeping and maintaining the poor?

For the year 1882 the poor taxes levied, collected and applied to this object in the several townships and boroughs was as follows:

Abbott	$187.87
Allegany	255.67
Bingham	256.83
Coudersport	437.11
Eulalia	880.52
Genesee	420.20
Harrison	572.69
Hebron	509.29
Hector	1,123.98
Homer	132.63
Lewisville	75.50
Pike	176.16
Pleasant Valley	49.02
Roulet	210.83
Sharon	217.60
Sweden	562.30

Sylvania	265.43
Total,	6,333.66

The year 1882 is taken because a greater number of townships and boroughs had made returns to the Commissioners. The amount of Poor Tax returned up to this time for 1883 from the several townships and boroughs is $5,381.69, and it will be observed that in the list there are several leading townships that I could find no returns on file, but I learn on inquiry, most of them are nevertheless paying poor tax. As near as I am able to learn, about 45 persons have been fed, clothed and cared for, during the last two years, in the county. Allowing that no debts are made above the taxes collected, it costs the tax payers very near $150 per year for the support of each pauper, and I know many of the boroughs and townships are now badly in debt and so many poor persons calling for help, that the overseers of the district, at the end of the year, find their money gone, and claims unpaid. The county is now paying for the various townships to the Warren Insane Asylum for the care and support of the Potter county insane $1,200 per year. The charges are $3.00 per week, and it is safe to say that if the county of Potter had a suitable Poor House, all that are not violently insane, could and would be transferred from the Warren Asylum to the poor house. I have in my mind many persons that are in the madhouse at Warren, that it would be far better for them and a great deal cheaper if they could have a home in a well kept county house. Every taxpayer knows that all the bills paid by the county commissioners to the asylum, are charged over to the township or borough, that is so unfortunate as to have a person there, and just now the commissioners are threatening suits against several townships and boroughs because they are so unhappily situated, that the poor fund is all paid out to keep and maintain the paupers at home. And there is still another large item of expenses that arises between the townships, and our courts are full of these cases, to settle the residence of the pauper. Many of the cases have been very expensive. With a county house these cases would not arise.

The most important question for tax-payers to consider in this connection is, can, after a suitable farm and building has been purchased, a poor person be fed and cared for at a less sum than it costs now. I have no doubt if the Commissioners do their duty honestly and fairly to the people, and purchase a good vegetable and grass farm, the poor can be well subsisted and have warm, comfortable rooms and beds for $1.50 per week; all farm labor will, in raising vegetables and care of the cows, be carried on by the inmates. This is the universal practice in managing the poor house farm in the other counties where established. More next week.

F. W. Knox.

GET THE BEST!
For Sale in Every City and Town in the United States.
AND BY
H. J. OLMSTED & SONS,
COUDERSPORT, PA.

The Potter Enterprise
Wednesday Evening, February 6, 1884 – Vol. X, No. 38

MARRIED.

OSTRANDER – MANN – At the residence of the bride's parents, in Coudersport, on Feb. 2d, 1884, by Rev. A. A. Craw, Mr. Geo. Ostrander to Miss Eva L. Mann.

- Mrs. Ellison, wife of Dr. O. T. Ellison, of Coudersport, died on Sunday morning last.

DIED.

HENDRYX – At his residence in Ellisburg, on Thursday, Jan. 31st, 1884, Mr. H. Hendryx, aged 61 years.

Mr. Editor:

I saw in your paper an article from F. W. Knox. Would it be policy to build a poor house? Now, Mr. Editor, if the tax-payer, in this county, will inform himself he will answer, No. Firstly, because public institutions are run too extravigantly. Second, because it costs more to take care of the poor in a county house than at home. My friend took the year 1882 for example. We will take the same year and the auditor's report of Tioga county for ours. Below we give the report:

Paid to O. D. Bly, Superintendent of poor house,	$800.00
Extra hire on farm and in house	784.64
Clothing, provisions, Dr. bills, &c., for poor house	<u>10554.56</u>
	$12139.20

Now you see that it costs Tioga county a little over $200 per year, the average number being about sixty inmates. My friend says it costs about $150 to take care of the poor at home. Then what is the use of paying $1,584.64 for a superintendent and hire on a farm.

My friend says that all litigation between townships will stop when the county house is established. Now this is a mistake, each pauper must have a residence in some town just the same as the insane. The county pays for farm buildings, superintendent &c. Each town has to pay for its own poor. Will make an estimate of farm buildings.

Martin Lewis, Ulysses, Pa.

County Poor House.

Editor Enterprise:

It will be remembered, in last week's communication, that the amount of poor tax, as returned to the office of the Commissioners for 1882, was $6,333.66. The townships that had not made returns were Ulysses, West Branch, Wharton, Portage, Oswayo, Keating, Clara and Stewardson. Most of these townships, I learn, are collecting poor taxes and applying the same for the support of the unfortunate poor. Allowing that these townships are collecting a five mill tax for poor purposes the aggregated amount collected from the citizens of Potter county will exceed $9,300. And I find for 1883, so far as the townships have made returns, far exceeds the amount levied in 1882. For example, Eulalia collected in 1882, $880.52; in '83, $1,191.57. Bingham in '82, $256.83; in '83, $344.62. Coudersport '82, $437.11; in '83, $594.91. Pleasant Valley '82, $49.02; in '83, $183.17. It will be seen the increase is very great and it is equally evident that the paupers are increasing in the same proportion or the taxes would not be levied and collected.

From the foregoing it will be seen if the same ratio of increase of poor taxes in all the townships and boroughs, is maintained, full $10,000 has been collected in 1883. Every reading and reflecting voter knows that forty-five paupers can be fed, clothed and properly cared for, under one roof, far cheaper than they can be as now provided for . In a county house would be one kitchen, one fire for cooking, one dining room and eat from one table. As now practiced these forty-five persons are in thirty to thirty-five families and no one wants them and can not keep them as cheaply in this way.

In Crawford county the Commissioner's clerk, under date of Jan. 30th, 1884, says, "Our poor house averages 100 paupers; costs $10,000 which includes removal of paupers, salaries of all officers and hired labor and repairs of buildings. In this county we would not know how to get along without a poor house." O. H. Hollister, Clerk.

From Chester Co., the Commissioner's Clerk reports as follows, after stating that the annexed annual statement had been sent: "You will see all the expenses of running our alms house (poor house), the average cost per week about one dollar each. There is a farm of about 365 acres. The alms house was built in 1855 and will accommodate about 400. We have a building for contagious diseases. If we had no liquor selling in our county, would not cost us near so much." Jas. T. Hill, Clerk.

Here is Crawford county with one hundred paupers, costing no more than it costs us to feed and clothe half that number; and Chester county, because of the large number of inmates, are able to maintain them at one dollar per week.

The fact that every county in the State that has adopted the county poor house plan, never change and never want to change to the old way again is to my mind, conclusive evidence, that Potter county should, at this time, adopt the same cheap and excellent system of caring for her needy poor.

Since my communication appeared in last week's Enterprise, many persons have called on me. Nearly all were in favor of the change, but sought information as to the locality of the poor house farm. To all, I said emphatically, this was a matter of no account to the tax payers of the county. There are excellent locations in every township in the county, in fact the act of 1879, section 2, says, "The Commissioners of each county are authorized and empowered to select and purchase real estate, *within said district*, erect thereon buildings &c.," and the 3d section of same act says, "the Commissioners *shall not purchase* until recommended so to do by petition and votes." In other words, the voters of the county must first pass upon the question of "for" or "against" poor house. If, at the coming election, the majority of the votes should be "for poor house," I can see how it is of vital importance, that the County Commissioners purchase a farm well adapted to the purpose, good vegetable and grass soil, easily worked, plenty of good running water and an abundance of timber for fuel, and it is no matter whether it is in Roulet, Oswayo, Eulalia, Ulysses or Harrison or any other township or whether it is located on main highway or cross road, if the important requisits of good, easily worked soil, with water and timber are the constituant parts of the proposed farm. And I am certain every voter of the county would say, if a farm on some accessible cross road, with equal advantages for the purpose, could be purchased at less price, there make the location. At least two of your Commissioners are good farmers and can make a good selection if they will do so for the benefit of the people of the county. But if they should be so unmindful of their duty in this regard and be controlled by some political or personal friend, their political doom would be forever sealed. It is, I am glad to say, believed they will all do their duty without fear or favor and wil take a wide range for examination. Next Summer, when

Potter County, Pennsylvania Potpourri – Volume I
1880 through 1884

crops are growing, would be the time, provided the voters, on the 19th inst., grant the permit. Will treat second proposition next week.

F. W. Knox.

List of Grand Jurors for March Term 1884.

Rosco Andrews, Farmer, Allegany; M. W. Bailey, Farmer, Hector; A. J. Brizzee, Farmer, Oswayo; John Bodler, Shoemaker, Abbott; Joseph Brooks, Farmer, Hector; G. P. Bailey, Farmer, Hector; D. E. Crandall, Farmer, Pike; B. F. Dickens, Farmer, Hector; V. E. Freeman, Farmer, Ulysses; W. E. Gilbert, Farmer, Harrison; Elba D. Holmes, Farmer, Sharon; Geo. W. Humphrey, Farmer, Sharon; L. C. Kinner, Merchant, Sharon; Daniel Neefe, Wagon Maker, Coudersport; Emel Peltz, Farmer, Abbott; Calvin Palmer, Farmer, Allegany; M. A. Surdam, Farmer, Hector; W. G. Sutherland, Farmer, Sharon; William Suhr, Farmer, Ulysses; Wm. Smith, Landlord, Harrison; Avery Smith, Farmer, Harrison; Charles Warner, Farmer, Sharon; Josiah Webster, Farmer, Genesee; James White, Miller, Coudersport.

TRAVERSE JURORS.

C. M. Allen, Jeweler, Lewisville; Giles Allard, Farmer, Eulalia; C. H. Barnes, Farmer, Sharon; Christian Broderson, Teacher, Abbott; C. C. Breunle, Farmer, Eulalia; Henry Bach, Sr., Farmer, Abbott; Asahel Christman, Farmer, Clara; Stephen Carman, Farmer, Wharton; John Cavanaugh, Farmer, Roulet; Erastus Crippen, Farmer, West Branch; Alfred Cool, Farmer, Allegany; Abel Clark, Farmer, Hebron; Albert Colcord, Farmer, Eulalia; William Coyle, Farmer, Oswayo; S. W. Cushing, Farmer, Ulysses; Michael Dehn, Farmer, Roulet; H. S. Densmore, Farmer, Allegany; W. H. Dingee, Farmer, Keating; Wm. Fourness, Farmer, Eulalia; Dennis Hall, Farmer, Keating; S. P. Hemphill, Farmer, Hebron; Carlos Hackett, Farmer, Harrison; Mark S. Harvey, Farmer, Ulysses; G. W. Johnson, Farmer, Clara; James Lockwood, Farmer, Oswayo; George Lane, Farmer, Sharon; B. F. Langdon, Farmer, Allegany; A. C. Millard, Mechanic, Coudersport; H. J. Neefe, Farmer, Sweden; J. W. Roby, Farmer, Hebron; Luke Scott, Farmer, Hector; C. D. Tubbs, Farmer, Hector; Samuel White, Farmer, Sharon; Monroe Wheaton, Farmer, Hector; Abram Walker, Farmer, Oswayo.

The Potter Enterprise
Wednesday Evening, February 13, 1884 – Vol. X, No. 39

Poor House Question.

Ed. Enterprise: As a large number of the persons that are assisted and cared for by public charity are imbecile or weak minded, one place for them and one humane and kind hearted superintendent to have full charge over them, to direct their labor when able to work, a well organized county poor house would be the best possible place for them. The unfortunate poor who become the wards of public charity deserve and should receive that kind of treatment that becomes a christian people; and if they can be better cared for in the way proposed, it is a humane duty which we owe to our race. My former letters show that the people of this county are and have been paying large sums of money yearly for this charitable object, and if this fund so collected by tax can better the condition of these persons, by placing them under the care of a well qualified superintendent and under one roof, and will cost less money, why the opposition?

The Act of 1879 heretofore referred to, places the poor and destitute of the county under the charge of the county commissioners and Sec. 12 of the Act provides that the commissioners "shall meet at least one a month at the poor house, visit the apartments, inspect the management of the work upon and about the real estate. See that the poor are properly treated, hear all complaints and cause all grievances that may happen by neglect to be redressed." Here is an imperative duty to be performed by three leading county officers; they must every month visit the poor and inspect the apartments and hear complaints. Who inspects the apartments where they are now kept? The old law imposes no such duty on overseers and it is never done.

I see one or two persons in the *Sentinel* are having the night-mare on account of a "county debt" now existing. If they had looked at the annual statement of the commissioners in the same paper they were writing for, they would never have called public attention to the subject. The auditors report as follows:

Liability of Co. on bonds	$11000
Due Co. on special tax from unseated lands of 1882-3 and in hands of collectors	7530
Leaving Co. debt	3470

The unseated taxes for 1882-3 will be paid by June next and the small amount in collectors hands will be handed in by that time. And I am informed a special Tax is now levied for 1884 sufficient to cancel all county debts. No county poor tax could be assessed before next year, then all county debts would be provided for. Most of the districts are now assessing and collecting a ten mills tax for poor purposes. If the same was assessed and collected in all the boroughs and townships it would yield a poor fund of about $15,000 for 1885. This sum would purchase a good farm; erect good buildings of sufficient size to answer the purpose at this time, and in my judgment keep every pauper that would be sent there, and after that a four or five mill tax would be maple to maintain the poor and pay the salary of the superintendent and all medical bills. The commissioners under the law appoint one competent person as superintendent and make an agreement with some physician to visit the poor house when any of the inmates need his care, at so much a call. These are all the officials that can be appointed under the law.

Any persons who are hesitating and doubting as to their duty in this matter, I ask as a special favor that they read and carefully consider the articles in last weeks Journal, on the same subject.

I rather like a controversy with a sharp, intelligent, truthful person; one, when he quotes from the public records and documents, honestly states the matter as he finds it; but how is it with Martin Lewis, whose false statement appeared in the Enterprise and *Sentinel* last week, relating to the Poor House expenses of Tioga county for 1882, and I sincerely regret that young Mr. Lewis should be so unmindful of his honor when writing for public information. He ought to remember that other persons may perchance have the commissioners financial statement of Tioga county for 1882. Below are items from the much talked of Auditors Report of Tioga county.

Relief of poor outside poor house $6117.42; Clothing, provisions, etc., for poor house, $4437.14; O. D. Bly, superintendent of poor house, $800.00; Labor in poor house and on farm, $784.64. All that can be charged to yearly expenses of poor house are the last three items, making the sum of $6021.78. Mr. L. says there are sixty inmates, although the statement makes no showing on this subject, but he may be correct. If the inmates are sixty, then it cost about $100.00 per year, for clothing and finding each pauper, and in this is included salary of superintendent and labor, (one-half less than stated by L.).

Relief of poor outside of poor house is where the county commissioners under the old law rendered assistance to poor people in cases of sickness or injury, and the report does not show the number of families or persons that received partial aid for long or short time, at their homes, and were never in the poor house as inmates, and can not be charged to the expense of the poor house. There may have been fifty or one hundred families found in distress, and relieved by a separate fund, and this is what the auditors say concerning the outside relief; and in the very report from which Mr. Lewis obtained his figures, we find the following: "Many will perhaps be surprised at the increased expenses during the past year for the relief of the poor outside the county house, cases of misfortune and necessity, and others in which the commissioners have no discretion and which cannot be avoided, are constantly springing up. The relief in most cases is only temporary and can be supplied cheaper in this way than by removing to the poor house. *** The auditors are satisfied however that the present board of commissioners are entitled to credit for carefulness and good judgment in disbursing the county fund." Signed by E. A. Bryden, Eugene Beauge, L. K. King, Auditors.

All the evidence that has been received from every and all quarters clearly and unmistakably show that in a well managed county poor house, the poor can be cared for far better and very much cheaper than in the old way. The farm and property owners of this county are now allowing poor taxes to be assessed and collected out of them, yearly, full $9000 to $10000 to find and clothe about forty-five persons. Tioga county finds and clothes, as Mr. Lewis says, sixty inmates, that costs $6021.78. What further or more conclusive evidence can be presented for the tax paying people of Potter county, that it will be economy to vote For Poor House.

F. W. Knox.

Ed. Enterprise: Noticing that the "Poor House Question" is being somewhat agitated through your columns, permit me to add a little to suggestions already made, also to correct an error into which my friend Lewis seems to have fallen, as to questions of residence and contest among townships. Under the old law his statement would be correct, but under Acts of 1877 and 1879 the county becomes one common poor district and the expense of the support of the poor is paid from a county fund; this necessarily does away with litigation between townships in settling questions of settlement, and the expense of such litigation. I am not informed as to the exact number of paupers in the poor house of Tioga county, but the superintendent, Mr. O. D. Bly, in a personal conversation with me recently, informed me that since he had been the superintendent of the institution (which is I believe for the last four years) the actual cost of supporting each pauper, including the salary of the superintendent and directors or overseers of the poor and all incidental expenses was less than $1.25 per week each, the extra expense shown by auditors report arises from what is known as "outside help" and in all cases is less than $1.25 per week per person or cheaper than they can be kept at poor house. I have for the last week been in Tioga county and talked with well informed men upon the subject and they all informed me that any system looking to a return to the old plan would, on a vote be defeated ten to one, that the working of the present system was perfectly satisfactory to the people at large.

Another important fact is elicited from the figures Mr. Lewis has taken the pains to obtain. Tioga has a population of about 50,000 – Potter at the last census had something over 13000 now probably 15000, we have rarely less than 45 to 50 subjects of town charge while Mr. Lewis says that Tioga with a population of almost four times that of Potter, and a county where intoxicating drinks being publicly and freely sold and which would tend to increase pauperism has only an average of sixty paupers. The estimate for Tioga is too small by probably twenty, or an average of eighty paupers, but even that is over fifty per cent smaller than Potter. The explanation is this, a large per cent of the persons who under the present system are town charges and who residing at their own homes or that of friends can be supported at township expense but who are in reality able to care for themselves, will make the extra effort necessary to earn their own living, rather than suffer what they regard as the disgrace of going to the poor house. This is the experience of all counties where the poor are cared for at county expense. Overseers cannot always tell who are the proper subjects for assistance and rather than subject themselves to the charge of being heartless and negligent, permit themselves to be imposed upon. Under the poor house system the three commissioners do the work now done by over fifty men in the county, thus saving a large amount of labor and expense.

The farm if purchased at a fair price is not likely to depreciate in value and at any time will be worth the amount paid for it. If the experience of other counties, as shown by letter of Mr. Knox of last week, can be taken as a guide, it is easy to see that the saving in expense will in a very few years build a first class poor house and be saving of several thousands of dollars each year to the tax-payers of Potter county. Under our present system many of our poor are shamefully ill treated and neglected and their support is merely a means of speculation; at a poor house they are well cared for, and as a humane measure the poor house method is far preferable to the present one.

Potter County, Pennsylvania Potpourri – Volume I
1880 through 1884

I regard this as an important question for our county, and a somewhat careful examination of the subject has satisfied me that either from a financial or humane stand point the interest of our county is *for* a County Poor House.

C. L. Peck.

Commissioner's Office,
Coudersport, Feb. 11, 1884.

Editor Enterprise:

I have been asked by many interested on both sides of the Poor House question to publish the following figures. Will you please to find room for them this week:

Total amount of poor tax levied for 1883 in Potter, $7086.86; number of paupers, Nov. 1st, 1883, was 50; average cost per week, $2.72. This includes all who would go to the poor house and many who could probably be maintained outside at a less cost to the county. I also give figures from other counties, showing the average cost per week of those kept in the poor house all the time, and including all expenses to the county, salaries of officers, Doctor bills, clothing, fuel, &c. Chester Co., $1.07; Bradford, $1.50; Crawford, $1.94; Schuykill, $1.10; Allegany, N.Y., $1.25. I might give many more but these are fair examples, showing the lowest and the highest I have heard from.

W. W. Harvey, Comm'rs Clerk.

The Potter Enterprise
Wednesday Evening, February 20, 1884 – Vol. X, No. 40

MARRIED.

GRAHAM – YENTZER – At Coudersport, Pa., February 2d, by Miles White, Esq., James Graham and Malinda Yentzer, both of Lymansville.

Whites Corners. Samuel Robinson, one of the old settlers of the town, was buried at this place on the 14th inst.

Joseph Mann.

On Monday last, at one o'clock p.m., Joseph Mann, of Coudersport, passed from this life. On the Tuesday previous Judge Mann was taken with a chill, which soon developed into typhoid pneumonia, resulting in death as stated above. Mr. Mann was born at London Grove, Chester county, Pa., October 8th, 1810. Most of his life has been spent in Potter county in active business pursuits which yielded him a competency for his old age. For many years he engaged in the mercantile and lumber business in Sharon, removing from there to Coudersport nearly twenty years ago to engage in the mercantile business here. About twelve years ago he retired from active business. He has always been a prominent business man, an active citizen and a good neighbor, always pleasant, cheerful and kind. He will be missed by old and young, and all will unite in saying that a good man has gone to rest.

Tuesday's Election.
COUDERSPORT.

Burgess – J. W. Allen; Council – W. K. Jones, J. L. Knox; School Directors – A. B. Mann, O. H. Crosby; Constable – J. L. Haughenberry; High Constable – H. T. Nelson; Overseer of the Poor – A. F. Hollenbeck; Assessor – Z. J. Thompson; Auditor – W. C. Rennells; Judge of Election – C. H. Armstrong; Inspectors – Wm. Metzger, W. W. Harvey; For the Poor House, 120; Against the Poor House, 17.

EULALIA.

Supervisor – J. P. Lehman; Assessor – C. F. Breunle, 43, Jacob Lehman, 43; Inspectors – Wm. Fourness, P. C. Hall; Judge – A. D. Colcord; Constable – J. D. Earle; Overseers of the Poor – C. Stearns, 80, J. M. Spafford, 41, Stephen Burr, 46; Treasurer – Dallas Benson; Clerk – Jacob Lehman; Auditor – J. M. Spafford, 43, O. M. Kelly, 42; School Directors – Samuel Thompson, 3 years, 86, Henry Ingraham, 3 years, 38, Jacob Klein, 3 years, 48, Sherman Baker, 2 years, 44, J. M. Spafford, 2 years, 41; For Poor House, 68; Against Poor House, 18.

POOR HOUSE.

The Poor House is beaten three to one. The following is the vote as received up to noon to-day:

	For	Against
Coudersport,	120	17
Allegany,	21	108
Homer,	-	41
Oswayo,	46	64
Roulet,	23	126
Hebron,	37	79
Eulalia,	68	18
Ulysses,	11	114
Sweden,	-	50 maj.
Harrison,	27	157
Lewisville,		94 maj.

Bingham only two votes in favor of Poor House. Full returns next week.

The Potter Enterprise
Wednesday Evening, February 27, 1884 – Vol. X, No. 41

- Lawyer Scoville was setting up the cigars last week. An eleven pound boy at his house is the cause of his present happiness.

MARRIED.

MORLEY – RAYMOND – On Wednesday, February 13th, 1884, by Rev. J. L. Swain, Mr. C. H. Morley to Miss E. R. Raymond, eldest daughter of Mr. David Raymond, all of Gold.

DIED.

CRITTENDEN – At Oswayo, Pa., January 21st, 1884, of Scarletine, Clarence, oldest son of Edgar and Ida Crittenden, aged five years, four months and eleven days.

We miss his bright face in our circle of love,
We miss the good cheer of his voice,
We miss him below – but angels above
To crown him a welcome – rejoice.
Mourn not for the child, from they tenderness riven,
Ere stain on its purity fell,
To they questioning heart, lo ___ answer from Heaven,
"Is it well with the child?" It is well.

Poor House Vote.

Below we give the full vote on the Poor House question, with the exception of West Branch, which township made no return to the Commissioners.

District.	For.	Against.
Abbott,	4	82
Allegany,	21	108
Bingham,	1	174
Clara,	1	49
Coudersport,	120	17
Eulalia,	68	18
Genesee,	6	164
Harrison,	34	152
Hebron,	37	79
Hector,	43	42
Homer,	-	41
Keating,	3	41
Lewisville,	1	95
Oswayo,	46	64
Pike,	1	53
Pleasant Valley,	-	44
Portage,	4	22
Roulet,	23	126
Sharon,	9	177
Stewardson,	3	18
Summit,	-	34
Sweden,	3	61
Sylvania,	27	14
Ulysses,	11	114
West Branch,		
Wharton,	7	43
Total,	473	1802

Majority against Poor House, 1329

ELECTION.
ABBOTT.
Constable – Peter Zepp; Assessor – Peter Zepp; Supervisor – Eberhart Gnau; Town Clerk – Fred Woelful; Treasurer – Paul Milde; Auditor – Christian Broderson; School Directors – T. Bailey, Henry Theis; Inspectors of Election – Henry Menge, Otto Braun; Judge of Election – Louis Hoppe; Overseer of Poor – Franz Willetta.

ALLEGANY.
Supervisor – A. B. Whipple, E. J. Kies; Constable – I. F. Kidney; Assessor – C. Coats; Treasurer – J. C. Cavanaugh; Town Clerk – W. W. Scoville; School Directors – B. F. Langdon, I. Stryker; Judge of Election – A. C. Scoville; Inspectors of Election – C. Palmiter, B. Glase; Auditor – Ira Bishop; Overseer of Poor – James Currier; Woodville Independent District School Directors – C. Coats, G. Bird, C. Lasher.

BINGHAM.
Supervisor – T. E. Gridley; Constable – Frank Lewis; Assessor – E. D. Wheaton; Treasurer – A. N. Clark; Town Clerk – L. B. Lewis; Auditor – R. H. Howe, 3 yrs, J. Daniels, 2 yrs; School Directors – A. A. Johnson, John Holburt; Judge of Election – James Briggs; Inspectors of Election – C. W. Burt, Frank McConn; Overseer of Poor – T. E. Gridley.

CLARA.
Constable – William Morey; Supervisor – Jacob Cole; Auditor – O. E. Corsaw; Town Clerk – J. H. Cole; School Directors – Dan Hacket, F. D. Weimer; Judge of Election – J. M. Tyler; Inspector of Election – Lester Burton, John Tauscher; Town Treasurer – B. S. Wakely; Assessor – R. B. Cole.

COUDERSPORT.
Burgess – J. W. Allen; Councilmen – James L. Knox, W. K. Jones; School Directors – Arthur B. Mann, O. H. Crosby; Constable – J. L. Haughenberry; High Constable – H. T. Nelson; Overseer of Poor – A. F. Hollenbeck; Assessor – Z. J. Thompson; Auditor – W. C. Rennells; Judge of Election – C. H. Armstrong; Inspector of Election – W. W. Harvey, W. M. Metzger.

EULALIA.
Supervisor – John P. Lehman; School Directors – Sam Thompson, Jacob Klein (3 yrs), Sherman Baker (2 yrs); Overseer of Poor – C. Stearns; Clerk – Jacob Lehman; Treasurer – Dallas Benson; Constable – John D. Earl; Auditor – J. M. Spafford; Assessor – C. F. Breunle, Jacob Lehman, tied; Judge of Election – A. D. Colcord; Inspector of Election – Wm. Fourness, P. C. Hall.

GENESEE.
Justice of the Peace – J. J. Ryon; Constable – Pat Stephens; Judge of Election – Dennis Kane; Assessor – Pat Hart; Inspectors of Election – J. Dolly, H. L. Moran; Supervisor – Bryan Maginnis; Town Treasurer – James Moran; Auditor – John Coulston; Town Clerk – Charles Parker; Overseer of Poor – Bryen Moran; School Directors – J. A. Keach, A. D. Stephens.

HARRISON.
Supervisors – H. N. Stone, S. C. Lewis; Constable – McKinney Erway; Assessor – C. H. Doud; Town Treasurer – J. A. Neely; Town Clerk – J. W.

Stevens; Auditor – H. O. Chapin; School Directors – Edwin Stathan, J. J. Jones; Judge of Election – J. A. Neely; Inspectors of Election – A. A. Swetland, T. F. Holcomb; Overseer of Poor – A. F. Dodge.

HEBRON.

Justice of the Peace – Square Estes; Supervisor – A. Ball; Constable – Ed Clair; Town Clerk – John Schollard; School Directors – William Clair, I. H. Dingman; Overseer of Poor – J. C. Hallett; Judge of Election – D. B. Lowery; Inspectors of Election – Isaac Whitam, E. E. Swift; Auditor – Orin Bly; Treasurer – W. W. Dwight; Assessor – A. C. Castle.

HECTOR.

Constable – C. P. Kilbourn; Supervisor – J. W. Lewis; Assessor – J. M. Swimlar; Auditor – D. W. Havens; Treasurer – J. L. Havens; Town Clerk – C. E. Dimon; Overseer of the Poor – J. W. Lewis; Judge of Election – J. A. Leonard; Inspectors of Election – D. A. Sunderlin, Lon Kilbourn; School Directors – T. V. Barker, L. J. Earl.

HOMER.

Supervisor – J. B. Bundy; Auditor – T. N. Quimby; School Directors – D. C. White, J. P. Gates; Town Treasurer – John Tauburt; Town Clerk – W. H. Crosby; Constable – Eli Glaspy; Inspectors of Election – R. A. Parson, John Gordnier; Judge of Election – G. F. Younglove; Assessor – O. H. Crosby; Justice of the Peace – Geo. White.

KEATING.

Justice of the Peace – G. C. Lewis; Supervisor – C. W. Dingee; Constable – D. C. Rima; Town Clerk – H. A. Avery; Treasurer – J. W. Dingee; Assessor – M. N. Hall; Auditor – W. H. Dingee; Poor Master – H. Bridges; School Directors – Frank Kline, E. A. Whitney; Judge of Election – T. Glover; Inspectors of Election – J. E. Earl, F. L. Monday.

LEWISVILLE BORO.

Burgess – W. T. Hosley; Council – A. D. Corey, E. Hyde, H. C Hosley, H. K. Lane, H. A. Gridley, Geo. A. Farnsworth; School Directors – C. A. Lewis, C. M. Allen, Geo. C. Marion; Auditor – Jno. F. Stone; Assessor – Wm. Millard; Constable – M. D. Drake; High Constable – Fred Baker; Overseer of Poor – E. A. Burt; Judge of Election – D. A. Corey; Inspectors of Election – Wm. M. Hosley, A. L. Burt.

OSWAYO.

Justice of Peace – Edward Fergason; Supervisor – S. E. Crittenden; Constable – E. D. Rice; Assessor – Fred S. Rozell; Town Treasurer – A. G. Wells; Town Clerk – Tie between Sam'l Beebe and A. W. Carmer; Auditor – Jas. Lockwood; School Directors – Dean Hosley, 2 yrs, Bealy Kemp, 3 yrs, E. Delamatter, 3 yrs; Judge of Election – C. J. Tubbs; Overseer of Poor – O. M. Kemp; Inspectors of Election – J. B. Stewart, T. J. Farnum.

PIKE.

Supervisor – Ira Wariner; Treasurer – H. Tice; Town Clerk – F. A. Brown; Judge of Election – J. F. Foster; Inspectors of Election – W. W. Marion, J. S. Phenix; Constable – D. E. Crandall; Auditor – C. A. Brown; Assessor – R. L.

Clark; Overseer of Poor – S. J. Foster, J. M. Kilbourn; School Directors – J. Q. Merrick, A. Lambert.

PLEASANT VALLEY.

Judge of Election – J. C. Fessenden; Inspectors of Election – Earnest Keeler, Chas. Haynes; Constable – D. P. Yentzer; Supervisor – Earnest Lampe; Town Treasurer – J. V. Reid; Assessor – C. P. Reid; Auditor – N. D. Fessenden; Town Clerk – D. L. Yentzer; School Directors – D. L. Yentzer, W. T. Haynes; Overseer of Poor – Israel Burt.

PORTAGE.

Constable – J. E. Brownlee; Supervisor – D. A. Everett; Overseer of Poor – D. A. Everett; Town Clerk – Wm. Brownlee; Town Treasurer – M. J. Young; Auditor – Jacob Peet; Assessor – Hugh Young; Inspectors of Election – T. W. Brownlee, J. M. Conrad; Judge of Election – C. D. Austin; School Directors – T. W. Brownlee, Jno. Brownlee.

ROULET.

Supervisor – Miles Marsh; Town Treasurer – J. V. Weimer; Town Clerk – A. W. Johnson; School Directors – M. V. Larrabee, A. H. Morey; Overseer of Poor – J. J. Carey; Judge of Election – W. S. Brine; Inspectors of Election – Henry Tauscher, N. French; Assessor – O. R. Webb; Auditor – J. R. Fessenden; Constable – G. L. Yentzer.

SHARON.

Justice of the Peace – Chas. Cole; Constable – J. C. Bump; Supervisor – W. G. Sutherland; Assessor – N. C. Newton; Treasurer – Jacob Failing; Town Clerk – F. N. Newton; Auditor – L. C. Kinner; School Directors – S. J. White, Ed Warner; Judge of Election – S. B. Drake; Inspectors of Election – Ira Bixby, Truman Barns; Overseer of Poor – O. Mills.

SWEDEN.

Supervisor – C. F. Neefe; Constable – S. O. Dodd; Assessor – C. M. Herrington; Town Treasurer – A. Chase; Town Clerk – J. W. Neefe; Auditor – David Wambold; School Directors – Geo. Tuttle, A. W. Rossman; Judge of Election – Hoxie Roberts; Inspectors of Election – Jno. Freeman, Wm. Snyder; Poor Master – Johnson Chase.

STEWARDSON.

Judge of Election – G. W. Slarrow; Inspectors of Election – Ole Olson, Wesley Allen, Martin Joerg, tied; Supervisor – James Impson; Auditor – W. F. McCoy, G. W. Slarrow, tie; Assessor – Martin Joerg; Constable – Isaac Pollard; Treasurer – Wesley Allen, Henry Andresen, tied; Town Clerk – Martin Joerg; School Directors – Ole Olson, Isaac Pollard, Washington Campbell, M. F. McCoy; Overseer of Poor – Henry Andresen.

SUMMIT.

Supervisor – Daniel Burger; Treasurer – Merrick Jackson; Town Clerk – C. H. Ruscher; Constable – Jno. Wallace; Auditor – W. B. Jackson; Assessor – Lester Watson; School Directors – C. H. Ruscher, Joseph Watson; Judge of Election – A. D. Ayers; Inspectors of Election – Geo. Morton, Erastus Burger.

Potter County, Pennsylvania Potpourri – Volume I
1880 through 1884

SYLVANIA.

Supervisor – James Logue; Constable – B. R. Whitcomb; Assessor – Isaac Wheeler; Town Clerk – A. J. Haskins; School Directors – Thomas Moran, Henry Wheeler; Town Treasurer – G. C. Rees; Auditor – A. J. Burlison; Judge of Election – James Rees; Inspector of Election – Leroy Haskins, Henry Wheeler; Overseer of Poor – Pardon Haskins.

ULYSSES.

Constable – E. B. Monroe; Treasurer – A. Burt; Auditor – Wm. Suhr; Assessor – Henry Bartlett; Supervisor – Miles Dykeman; Poor Master – Miles Dikeman; Inspector of Election – C. H. Turner, Jacob Clark; Judge of Election – A. Burt; School Directors – C. H. Gridley, Wm. Clark; Town Clerk – H. T. Reynolds.

WEST BRANCH.

Supervisor – Chas. Traub; Town Clerk – A. Bisbee; Assessor – S. M. Conable; Overseer of Poor – Chas. Prouty; Town Treasurer – G. W. Fowler; Auditor – L. F. Rice; Justice of Peace – A. Bisbee; Constable – F. Burrows; Judge of Election – N. K. Prouty; Inspectors of Election – F. Streitz, J. W. Crippen; School Directors – Eli Main, Sidney Burrows.

WHARTON.

Constable – J. M. Walker; Treasurer – Sol. Ross, H. Nelson; School Directors – M. T. Seibert, A. D. Nelson, H. Nelson to fill vacancy; Supervisor – H. Bailey; Poormaster – Samuel Card; Justice of the Peace – Seth Briggs; Auditor – C. A. Miller; Judge of Election – S. F. Horton; Inspectors of Election – G. D. Walker, S. L. Carman; Assessor – S. L. Carman; Clerk – W. H. Palmeter.

The Potter Enterprise
Wednesday Evening, March 5, 1884 – Vol. X, No. 42

– Andrew Luce and E. P. Turck have each a new boy, and C. A. Turck is the happy possessor of another girl.

MARRIED.

BICKFORD – RANDALL – At the residence of L. R. Burdick, by Elder G. P. Kenyon, Mr. George E. Bickford and Miss Edith M. Randall, all of Hebron, Pa.

The Potter Enterprise
Wednesday Evening, March 12, 1884 – Vol. X, No. 43

Whites Corners. A. P. Elder is the man that steps high at present. It is a boy, weighing eight pounds.

MARRIED.

GUNTHER – ZIMMERMAN – At Coudersport, on March 10th, 1884, by the Rector of Christ Church, Mr. Benjamin Gunther, of Eulalia, and Miss Annie Zimmerman, of Coudersport.

WILLIAMS – LANGDON – At the residence of the Rev. J. L. Swain, in Allegany, on March 8th, 1884, by Rev. Swain, Mr. Ardell Williams and Miss Cora E. Langdon, all of Allegany, Pa.

DIED.

ARMSTRONG – Mrs. James Armstrong, oldest daughter of the late H. H. Hendryx, aged 38 years. She was buried on Sunday, March 2d, 1884, just four weeks after her father.

- McKinster, for whose arrest the Court authorized the Commissioners to offer a reward of $300, is the young man who assaulted a school teacher, some time ago, in Sharon township.

- The case of D. L. Wagoner, charged with perjury, attracted a great deal of interest. The case grew out of a note which the young man refused to pay claiming he was not of age when the paper was signed. The young man's parents swore that the boy was not of age. To combat this, others were brought to swear to the contrary, including neighbors, the doctor who was present at the young man's birth, and the proof of an application signed by him for membership in the Equitable Aid Union and a great mass of other testimony, sufficient to convince the jury.

PUBLIC SALE.

I will sell at Public Venue on Thursday, March 20th, 1884, at 10 o'clock, a.m., on the farm lately occupied by R. V. Post, deceased, in Hebron Township, Seven Cows, a Span of Horses, two Lumber Wagons, two Buggies, a set of Bob Sleds, a Mowing Machine, Horse Rake, three Drags, two Plows, Grain Cradle, Scythes and Snaths, and numerous other articles of use upon a farm.

Terms: - Bids of $10 and under, Cash. Over $10 reasonable time will be given on good security.

Daniel Clark
March 10, 1884.

Court Minutes.

Court convened March 3d; Hon. H. W. Williams, presiding; present Associates Hammond and Lewis.

Constables of different townships made returns.

Commonwealth vs Stephen Horton, selling liquor; not a true bill, defendant to pay costs.

Com'th vs Geo. McKewen. Nol pros.

Constables of the different townships qualified.

J. S. Hull appointed commissioner of East Fork Road District.

W. I. Lewis appointed auditor to distribute funds in hands of administrator of John Dawley, deceased.

Grand Jury called and sworn. Josiah Webster, foreman; constable of Clara to wait on same.

Estate of Edward A. and C. A. Freeman, advisability of sale referred to A. B. Mann.

W. A. Gardner appointed guardian of C. A. Freeman.

W. A. Gardner appointed guardian of Wm. A. Gardner and Mary E. Gardner.

Com'th vs James Ryan, fornication and bastardy; defendant discharged.

J. E. Whittaker, for use vs Geo. J. and Josephine Brooks; sheriff to sell property unless deft, give receipted bond.

Com'th vs C. H. Breisenick, selling liquor; sentenced to pay a fine of $100 and costs of prosecution.

Sheriff Worden directed to make deed to Amelia Willets for land purchased by her at Sheriff's sale, June 15, 1883.

Chas. Meine vs Wm. Campbell and George Slarrow; jury find for plaintiff the land described to be released on payment of $611, with costs &c., to be paid within 30 days.

J. Q. Merrick appointed auditor of Pike township.

Com'th vs Frank Goodwin, selling liquor; bail $200 for appearance at next term of court.

Returns of poor house election computed; for poor house, 474 votes; against poor house, 1,891.

J. E. Brownlee appointed supervisor of Portage township.

Estate of Mary A. Bailey; Chas. W. Bailey appointed trustee in place of W. B. Jennings.

Com'th vs Ryan Miller, open lewdness; true bill, nol pros.

Same vs same, assault and battery; plead guilty, sentenced to pay a fine of $50, pay costs and undergo imprisonment in the county jail for a period of six calendar months.

Wesly Allen appointed treasurer of Stewardson township.

Com'th vs O. W. Strong, selling liquor; not guilty, prosecutors Frank Goodwin and John Ward to pay the costs.

Com'th vs Peleg Burdick, selling liquor; plead guilty, bail in sum of $200 for appearance at next term.

Carrie M. Burns adopted by Maxwell and Martha L. Williams.

Glenn Hornsby adopted by Ansel P. and Flora Erway.

Com'th vs Jefferson Burdick, surety of the peace; discharged.

Com'th vs Edward McGonigall, selling liquor; bail for appearance at next term in sum of $200.

Com'th vs Chauncey Brown, selling liquor; not a true bill, county to pay costs.

Com'th vs L. D. Wagner, perjury; guilty, sentenced to pay a fine of $100, cost of prosecution and undergo imprisonment in the Western Penitentiary for a term of three years and one calendar month.

Com'th vs Frank B. McNamara, assault and battery; plead guilty, bail $100 for appearance at next term of court.
Com'th vs Porter Clark, rape; true bill, bail $700 for appearance at next term of court.
Com'th vs Alexander McKinster, assault and battery with intent to commit rape; true bill.
Com'th vs Richard Kilduff, pointing a gun; true bill, bail forfeited.
Com'th vs Wm. Rounseville, rape; true bill, $600 bail for appearance at next term.
Com'th vs John Vergason, larceny; true bill, bail $100 for appearance at next term.
Perry Devoll appointed overseer of the poor of Wharton township.
W. W. Smith appointed clerk of Oswayo township.
Com'th vs Geo. Nickerson; bail $100 for appearance at next term.
M. E. Olmsted vs Homer township; tax of two mills ordered to pay debts.
A. G. Olmsted vs Stewardson township; tax of ten mill ordered.
Josephine Drake vs Fred N. Drake; divorce granted.
Com'th vs D. P. Reed, involuntary manslaughter; discharged.
Com'th vs Elmer Aylesworth, selling liquor; not guilty.
Com'th vs C. M. Brown, selling liquor; discharged.
Geo. Ross and Russel Niles, witnesses, not appearing when called, fined $10 and costs.
Com'th vs Willard Nelson, selling liquor; nol pros on payment of costs.
Tax of two mils ordered in Roulet township to pay debts.
John Horner vs Julia Horner; decree of divorce.
Com'th vs H. S. Tuttle, surety of the peace; defendant discharged.
P. C. Hall appointed overseer of poor in Eulalia twp.
J. W. Dingee vs Miles White; jury find for plaintiff in sum of one dollar and costs.
Com'th vs M. Pritchard, selling liquor; true bill, bail $200 for appearance next term.
Com'th vs Wm. Gilbert, selling liquor; not a true bill, county to pay costs.
County Commissioners authorized to offer a reward of $300 for the arrest of Alexander McKinster.
Ellen Miller vs R. E. Miller; divorce granted.
Com'th vs A. J. Wagoner, perjury; bail $500 for appearance at next term.
Com'th vs August Froebel, surety of the peace; bail $100 for appearance at next term.
G. M. Wetzel vs Miles White; jury fail to agree, discharged.
Tax of ten mills ordered in Keating twp to pay debts.
L. E. Hosley vs David Wambold; jury find for deft.
Com'th vs Richard Howland, surety of the peace; defendant to pay half the costs and prosecutor the other half.
March 8th, ordered that venires issue for 24 grand and 48 traverse jurors for court to be held second Monday in June also 36 traverse jurors for adjourned term of Court of Common Pleas to be held the 4th Monday in May 1884.

Ellen Miller vs R. E. Miller; Charles Hoyt appointed commissioner to take testimony.

Keziah Frasior vs John Frasior; J. T. Green appointed commissioner to take testimony.

E. S. Worden, High Sheriff of Potter county, acknowledged deeds as follows, for property sold at Sheriff sale:

To R. & J. Doty for 25 acres in Sharon, sold as the property of Wm. Mulkin, for $50.

To Trustees of Bingham Estate for 58 acres in Summit, sold as the property of John Schall, for $25.

To C. L. Burdick for 62 acres in Sharon, sold as the property of H. S. Burdick, for $20.

To F. W. Knox for 98 acres in Sweden, sold as the property of Johnson Chase, for $305.

To N. B. Adams for 50 acres in Genesee, sold as the property of W. A. Lochry, for $60.

To Dennis Maginnis for 50 acres in Genesee, sold as the property of Thos. Maginnis, for $425.

Wm. Cobb for 13 acres in Bingham, sold as the property of John W. Miller, for $25.

To Amelia Willets for 85 acres in Sweden, sold as the property of A. T. Herrington, for $25.

The Potter Enterprise
Wednesday Evening, March 19, 1884 – Vol. X, No. 44

Millport. Miss Fannie Brown, of Millport, and Mr. Eugene Drake, of Sunnyside, were united in marriage. We wish them all happiness in life.

- A few of the friends and relatives of Mr. and Mrs. Jerome Knickerbocker, of Lymansville, gave them a surprise on their fifteenth anniversary, and as a token of respect gave them a hanging lamp and some other things. After partaking of a bountiful repast they returned to their homes feeling they all had a good time.

Millport. The death of Dillie, wife of James Munger, of this place, caused a feeling of sadness throughout the neighborhood. She had made many friends and she will be missed by old and young. Her husband has the heartfelt sympathy of all. There have been a few cases of diphtheria. Mrs. Munger is supposed to have died with this disease.

- In the Court Minutes of last week one paragraph should have read, Com'th vs August Froebel, surety of the peace, *Plaintiff* held to bail. Froebel had already paid his share of the costs and the case was called up to compel the plaintiff, Mr. Peterson, to pay his share of the costs.

FIFTY YEARS AGO.

On the 20th of March, 1834, the great wind blow passed through this county. Starting South-west of Lymansville, sweeping and tearing down the timber in its course until it reached the little place called Lymansville, where there were fifty-three people, old and young, destroying every building in its course. Some were swept clear from their foundations, and others were held by their large stone chimneys, but these were badly wrecked. The water was blown from the mill-pond and carried eighty rods, old logs were taken from their beds and moved before the wind. The gale only lasted about one minute.

When the force of the wind had subsided we picked ourselves out of the rubbish and looked about to see who was hurt. We found that out of all the people in the place only one had been severely injured, Nelson Wood had a leg broken, others were bruised more or less but no others so serious. The gale kept its course North of East, sweeping the forest before it from one half to three-fourths of a mile wide, through Sweden, Allegany, Ulysses, Bingham and Harrison Townships. Palings and painted clapboards were carried from this place to Troups Creek, in the state of New York. The wind did but little damage after it left this place, except to tear down fences as the whole distance was but very thinly settled.

It will be fifty years the 20th of this month, at 4 o'clock p.m., since the wind blow at Lymansville, and there are only three besides myself left in the place who were here at that time – Nelson and Calintha Wood, and Mason Nelson.

Almeron Nelson.

LOOK HERE!
Now is the time to prepare for
SPRING PAPERING!
If you are in need of
DECORATING,
OR PLAIN PAPERING,
CALCIMINING, &C.,
Call on or address the undersigned.
ALL WORK GUARANTEED.
T. J. GILBERT,
Coudersport, Pa.

The Potter Enterprise
Wednesday Evening, March 26, 1884 – Vol. X, No. 45

MARRIED.

SCOTT – AYLESWORTH – At the house of Mrs. T. Ives, in Coudersport, on the 24th inst., by Rev. A. Cone, Mr. Luke Scott, of Hector, to Mrs. Mary Aylesworth, of Coudersport.

Notice.

All persons are hereby warned not to purchase two notes, signed by me, given to Laderna Reynolds, one for $6 and one for $74, dated June 18th, 1883; both notes are endorsed by Frederick Coats. The notes were obtained by fraud and I will not pay them unless compelled by law.

Simon Byam
Raymond, Pa., March 21, 1884.

Statistics,

Relating to Potter county, taken from the annual report of the department of Public Instruction, year ending June 1, 1883:

Grounds of sufficient size,	81
Grounds suitably improved,	2
No. of Houses in the county,	137
No. frame,	136
No. log,	1
No. built during the year,	4
No. unfit for use,	44
No. badly ventilated,	137
No. without suitable privy,	47
No. of first class school houses,	3
No. with suitable furniture,	33
No. with injurious furniture,	97
No. supplied during the year,	4
No. well supplied with apparatus,	0
No. without apparatus worth mentioning,	123
No. in which apparatus was increased during the year,	10
No. of graded schools,	4
No. graded during the year,	0
No. graded schools necessary,	3
No. schools well classified,	49
No. in which books are uniform,	61
No. in which the bible is read,	76
No. in which drawing is taught,	22
No. in which vocal music is taught,	24
No. in which higher branches are taught,	15
No. of public examinations,	25
No. of Directors present,	24
No. receiving provisional certificates,	141
No. receiving professional,	3
No. of applicants rejected,	39
Average grade of certificate	2.05
No. of male teachers employed,	44
No. of female teachers employed,	180
Average age of teachers,	22
No. who have had no experience,	37

No. who have taught less than one year	47
No. who have taught more than five years,	31
No. who intend making teaching a permanent business,	56
No. who have attended a State Normal School,	27
No. who have graduated from a State Normal School,	23
No. who have read books on teaching,	69
No. who hold professional certificates,	11
No. who hold permanent certificates,	5
No. of visits to schools by County Superintendent,	273
No. schools not visited,	0
No. Directors present,	54
No. Patrons present,	31
No. schools regularly visited by patrons,	36
No. of local institutes held,	11
No. of districts in the county,	29
No. of school directors,	174
Total number of permanent certificates granted to teachers in Potter county,	15
Average length of terms in months for entire county,	5.85
Average salary of males per month,	$25.03
Average salary of females,	$19.38
No. of male pupils enrolled,	1868
No. of female pupils enrolled,	1810
Average number attending school,	2366
Cost per month,	$0.99
Amount of tax levied for school and building purposes,	$21,288.18
State appropriation,	$3,034.52
Total receipts,	$31.037.09
Total expenditures,	$26,123.53

We publish the above report in response to numerous requests to do so.

The Potter Enterprise
Wednesday Evening, April 2, 1884 – Vol. X, No. 46

Roulet. Born – To Mr. and Mrs. John Tenbrock, a little son.

MARRIED.

CONLEY – CHESTAIN – At the residence of the bride's parents, in Roulet, on March 29th, 1884, by Rev. A. Brooks, Mr. George Conley to Miss Lizzie Chestain, all of Roulet.

A large company of invited guests assembled to witness the "launching on the Matrimonial Sea." Many and sincere were the congratulations offered to the pretty bride and smiling groom, together with many beautiful presents. May they "live long and prosper."

Hebron. On March 3d the friends of "Aunt Maria" Stillman and husband gave them a joyful surprise. It was their fortieth marriage anniversary. About sixty friends assembled bringing a sumptuous dinner and presents valued at over fifty dollars. "Aunt Maria" as everybody calls her, was overwhelmed with astonishment to think of anybody else doing for her, she having been so much in the habit of doing for others. She has always worked hard, and has raised five children, not her own, beside caring for an invalid husband. Even now she has taken to her heart and home a little motherless babe, and spite of the privations and seeming hardships of life, persists in considering it a blessing. May her days be long upon the earth, and may many, seeing her good works and the beauty and simplicity of her happy life, go and do likewise.

- Mr. and Mrs. Wm. Quimby, after a residence of over thirty years in Potter, intend moving to Oregon. They will leave in about three weeks. Potter will lose and Oregon gain by this move. We wish our friends abundant success in their new home.

- A new post office has been established in Pleasant Valley township, called Pleasant Valley, with Pulaski Reed as Postmaster. The new office will be a great convenience to many, and the new postmaster will be found very obliging. It is a good thing all around.

Notice.

The following "notice" appeared in the Shingle House *Palladium*. We have no doubt it will have the desired effect: -

" I hear by Forbid enny one taking Selah A. Porter or note or corlecting one of them for he is not capable of doing business At all in enny Shape and all that owes him call at Sarah Porter and Pay and Save coust there are a few that has run the length of their chain and he is just about crasy and all those that has got enney of these Brooms that belongs to F. J. Hay will save cost to leave them at the Post office at Mill Port for him I hereby understand that Selah A. Porter fell when he was A small Boy fell from the chamber down by the door and was Picked up for dead and it hurt his Senses So he is not what he ought to be. There fore I do not wont you to trust him or cheat him or at all and his helth is not good for he has Spells of when he is A walking A long that he falls down in the road and are picked up for dead and he will no dout bee A town charge and his mother clothes him last fall he worked that it come to 15 dol and he was fool with Some keys and Cheates him out of his work and his mother told the Man to not let him have them but in reply he did not care who had them so he got his Pay for them and So he cared the keys till now and hade the stove to use A little while and in have it the his Sone in law took the Boy crover and conversion leved on all of A nothers Man brooms and his own Save and Poot him in Prison and got A Shame of it and then let him out and to fether his beed Scart him and he got one 10 dol note and one 40 dol note o deth where is they Sting o grave Victory Short nottice to all. Sarah Porter.

Potter County, Pennsylvania Potpourri – Volume I
1880 through 1884

The Potter Enterprise
Wednesday Evening, April 9, 1884 – Vol. X, No. 46

- K. Zimmerman is the happy man this time. It is a boy. Heretofore Karl's boys have all been girls. Consequently this last addition to his family is doubly welcome.

- A surprise party was given Dr. A. French on Tuesday, his seventy-sixth birthday.

MARRIED.

JONES – BECKWITH. – At the Free Baptist parsonage, in Port Allegany, by Rev. O. C. Hills, March 29th, 1884, Mr. Robert C. Jones, of Bolivar, N.Y., and Miss Hattie Beckwith, of Pleasant Valley, Pa.

- On Friday last Ransome Page, aged twenty-three years, died at the boarding house of Leonard Davis in Coudersport. Mr. Page had worked in this section, off and on, for two or three years. In January last he was taken sick at Mr. Davis' where he was well cared for by Mr. Davis and his family assisted by the boarders. On Monday Mr. Page was thrown upon the town, as he had no money and it was believed he could live but a short time. Mr. Davis had done all in his power for the unfortunate man, and did not feel able to stand the expense of his burial. The remains of Page were sent to his parents in Scio, N.Y. A brother of the deceased has promised to settle all bills incurred in the case.

- Log drivers on Pine Creek get from $3.50 to $4.00 per day.

- On Monday last a row occurred at or near Wm. Sherwood's, in Roulet, between a half breed Indian named Charles Hall, on the one side and Sherwood and Smith on the other. The half breed is said to have been more than half full of hard cider, and as ugly as he was full. He finally attacked Sherwood with a knife, and Sherwood met him about half way with a revolver. The ball struck the red man on the top and back part of his head making a flesh wound, but not serious. A warrant was issued for the Indian and most of Tuesday afternoon Constable Haughenberry and Deputy Sheriff Brightman hunted the swamp south of Coudersport in pursuit of Hall who was last seen in that locality. In the afternoon Constable Haughenberry arrested Hall in Homer Township and lodged him in jail to await examination to-day. Hall tells a very different story from Sherwood. He admits quarreling with Smith but says Sherwood shot him before he had made any attack upon him. The wound received by Hall is slight and the fact that it is across the back of the head would lead one to infer that he was not going for Sherwood with a knife very ferociously unless he is inclined to a sidewise gait.

- Saturday evening last, about eight o'clock, the cry of fire startled our citizens, and started a stampede. The fire was in Mrs. M. W. Mann's house. Mrs. Mann went to the room occupied by M. S. Thompson's nieces, and either knocked a lamp over or it exploded. The burning oil caught along the casing and floor and but for prompt help, a disastrous fire would have resulted. It was some time before the fire was completely extinguished as it worked its way between the walls where it was difficult to get at. The children lost nearly all their clothes. Carpets were damaged, and the woodwork badly charred. The loss is covered by insurance. In attempting to smother the flames Mrs. Mann had her hands burned, but not seriously.

The Potter Enterprise
Wednesday Evening, April 16, 1884 – Vol. X, No. 48

Freeman Run. "Nice weather?" said one of the neighbors to G. R. Reed last Sunday. Riley took off his cap, put it under his arm, scratched his head and replied, "Nice! Well, yes, we think so, it's a girl!"

Andrews Settlement. Clara Furman has changed her name to Haskell and her residence to Colesburg. May joy, peace and happiness be hers.

MARRIED.

BRIGGS – HOWE – At the residence of the bride's father in Bingham, Pa., on April 3d, 1884, by Rev. A. H. Briggs, Mr. M. W. Briggs and Miss E. J. Howe, all of Bingham, Pa.

WELCH – PLANK – In Sunderlinville, April 3d, 1884, by Rev. S. L. Bovier, Wm. B. Welch, of Westfield, and Fannie P. Plank, of Sunderlinville.

Andrews Settlement. We have had sickness and death in our midst during the winter. A little child of Wm. Dennis died with pneumonia.

DIED.

BRIDGES – At her home in Keating, April 14th, 1884, Miss Laurie Bridges after a long and painful illness.

He giveth his beloved sleep.

BRIDGES – In St. Mary's, April 15th, 1884, of Consumption, Herman Bridges, aged about 30 years. The deceased was a son of H. Bridges of Freeman Run.

Republican County Convention.

The republican county convention assembled in the Court House, Thursday afternoon. The attendance was rather slim. Delegates or substitutes were present from Bingham, Clara, Coudersport, Genesee, Harrison, Lewisville, Oswayo, Roulet, Stewardson and Sharon, and appointments were made for Allegany, Eulalia, Sylvania and Ulysses.

The convention was called to order by D. C. Larrabee; Burt Oleson was made Chairman, D. C. Larrabee and Geo. W. Dodge Secretaries.

J. H. Chase was elected Representative delegate to the State convention.

George W. Dodge, A. B. Mann and Walter Wells were appointed conferees for congressional delegates to Chicago.

Charles Ross of Tioga was recommended as Senatorial delegate, and W. I. Lewis and R. L. White were appointed conferees.

A resolution was passed declaring for Blaine and Lincoln for President and Vice President, and directing conferees to vote for delegates to the National convention who will support them.

In the ballot for Presidential choice, D. C. Larrabee, of Coudersport, stated that his preference was Blaine, but many of his constituents were for Edmunds, he therefore cast two votes for Blaine and Lincoln and two for Edmunds and Lincoln.

John Earle cast the three votes of Eulalia for Logan, with Blaine for Vice President.

Walter Wells cast the five votes of Oswayo for Edmunds, with Blaine for Vice President.

All the other towns represented were scored as solid for Blaine and Lincoln.

The Potter Enterprise
Wednesday Evening, April 23, 1884 – Vol. X, No. 49

South Coudersport. Born, to Mr. and Mrs. G. H. Grabe, on Thursday, the 17th inst., a son.

MARRIED.

CAVANAUGH – ARMSTRONG – In Coudersport, April 20th, 1884, by Frank Phelps, Esq., Mr. James Cavanaugh and Mrs. Ann Armstrong, all of Coudersport.

CROSBY – DEREMER – At Ceres, April 18th, Mr. Walter Crosby, of Cuba, N.Y., and Miss Fannie Deremer, of East Sharon, Pa.

Freeman Run. Once more this little neighborhood has been called upon to mourn and sympathize with those whom death has afflicted. On Monday morning, the 14th, all were grieved to hear of the death of Laurie Bridges, who had been sick with inflammatory rheumatism. Tuesday afternoon came a message, from St. Mary's, telling of the death of her oldest brother, Herman, who had been sick for some time with consumption, the funeral, which had been appointed for Wednesday, was postponed until the next day, to give them time to bring the body of her brother home. The funeral was largely attended on Thursday; the services being conducted by Rev. A. A. Craw. As there was no visible sign of decay, it was concluded only to bury the remains of the son; so strange had been the death of Laurie, so unexpected, that a faint hope was entertained, by some, that life was not extinct. Her remains were kept until Sunday, lacking less than twenty-four hours of being a week from the time she died. Even then the remains looked perfectly natural; that it seemed more like a peaceful sleep than like death. Laurie was one who had many friends, a true christian girl. What more could be said of her.

Herman Bridges was formerly a resident of this place. He leaves a young wife to whom he had been married only about nine months. The family have the sympathy of their many friends in this, their double bereavement.

The Potter Enterprise
Wednesday Evening, April 30, 1884 – Vol. X, No. 50

Obituary.

Once more we have been called upon to mourn and sympathise with those whom death has afflicted. On Friday, April 25th, a dispatch informed us of the death of our friend and relative, Henderson Corsaw, the oldest son of Mr. and Mrs. C. L. Corsaw, of Sweden, Potter county, Pa., and although the blow was not an unexpected one, it was nevertheless a severe one. He had been afflicted for nearly a year with Bright's disease, and although his sufferings were long and severe, he bore up under them with remarkable patience until April 24th, 1884, when death came to his relief.

Mr. Corsaw was forty-one years of age with good business qualifications, a dutiful son and the ever true and loving husband of a tender and affectionate wife, with whom he had lived happily for eleven years. He was a man whose genial qualities and manly bearing won for himself a large circle of friends.

One year ago we saw him, as it were, but yesterday, full of life and bright anticipations, with fair prospects to attain to the allotted time of man. But, how frail is the stream of life? Yesterday he was; to-day he is not. His lips are silent, his eyes are closed in death, we shall feel the warm clasp of his more than friendly hand no more. He leaves an affectionate wife, a kind father and mother, and five brothers to mourn his loss, and who have the sympathy of a large circle of friends.

The last sad rights were performed on Saturday, April 26th, 1884, from the residence of his parents.

DIED.

DINGEE – On Freeman Run, on the 24th inst., Jewell Dingee, son of Eleazer Dingee, aged about 18 years.

- Thirty-five years ago Roulet had the largest and best built school house in the county. Many a person now past middle life was educated in the old red school house and enjoyed many seasons of play on the spacious green lawn. From the time of its erection it served the people well for funerals, religious and political meetings, annual elections were held here also. The dear old red school house is doomed – the good people of this day have grown proud, and are now completing one of the handsomest of school buildings; sightly to look at, spacious room, large windows, handsome tower, and ornament to the place. And near by a large fine church building is nearly completed. Truly the people of Roulet are progressive and more than liberal to reach down deep enough in their pockets to build two so fine public buildings in one year. Money well expended.

- Drunkenness is becoming altogether too common on our streets. It may be impossible to prevent drinking, but there is surely a way to prevent the parties from making a disgusting appearance on the street – for any great length of time.

FOREST FIRES.
Three Families Rendered Homeless by the Flames.

Monday last was a bad day for forest fires, and all day long the air was full of smoke and charred leaves from fires on Fishing Creek, where a considerable amount of timber, fences, &c., were destroyed. Near the head of the stream, the fire destroyed the dwelling house, furniture and clothing of Otis Lyman and family, leaving them destitute. The particulars we have not been able to gain.

A fire was also raging around Liberty on the B., N. Y. & P., in the bark slashings, and it was with great difficulty that the buildings at that point were saved.

The wind blew a hurricane, and through the dead hemlock tops where the bark had been peeled and logs removed the flames rushed over the mountains. Near the Forest House, scattered through the woods were several thousand cords of wood. Mr. Briggs alone having about two thousand cords. This only fed the flames. From the top of the hill, east of the Forest House road, large brands of fire were carried by the wind to the opposite hillside into the slashing of Dennis Hall. Mr. and Mrs. Hall did not even have time to secure their clothing ere their property burned almost immediately and they had to flee for their lives. One hundred cords of wood in the middle of a large field did not escape and a wheatfield in many places was run over by the fire. Afterward the fire burned down the hillside and destroyed the house and contents belonging to Perry Everett. Mr. Hall had an insurance, through the agency of L. B. Cole, of $1,000 – not one half his loss. Tuesday morning he was engaged hauling lumber for a new house, full of courage and pluck that will yet make him a comfortable home.

List of Traverse Jurors for the Adjourned
Court the 4th Monday of May, 1884.

A. C. Allis – Farmer – Allegany; Charles M. Burt – Farmer – Bingham; John Baldwin – Farmer – Hector; J. W. Beebe – Laborer – Oswayo; John Brooks – Farmer – Wharton; T. W. Brownlee – Farmer – Portage; D. A. Corey – Harness Maker – Lewisville; M. J. Conrad – Mechanic – Portage; F. A. Crowell – Farmer – Ulysses; O. H. Crosby – Farmer – Homer; Austin Crosby – Farmer – Keating; Jerome Dodge – Farmer – Sharon; John Flynn – Clerk – Sylvania; John Glaspy – Farmer – Sylvania; James Gibson – Farmer – Ulysses; Wilson Gee – Farmer – Bingham; Allen Hammond – Farmer – Oswayo; James Hawthorn – Farmer – Abbott; John Henley, Jr. – Farmer – Sharon; Willard Hickox – Farmer – Genesee; C. A. Lewis – Merchant – Lewisville; Morris Jordan – Farmer – Wharton; O. G. Metzger – Lumberman – Coudersport; W. F. Nobles – Farmer – Bingham; Loren Prince – Farmer – Sharon; W. R. Prouty – Farmer – West Branch; Henry Ruscher – Farmer – Summit; Israel Reed – Farmer – Pleasant Valley; Horace Stillman – Farmer – Ulysses; Jacob Snyder – Farmer – Sweden;

Potter County, Pennsylvania Potpourri – Volume I
1880 through 1884

J. B. Sweeten – Farmer – Sharon; Frank Stewart – Farmer – West Branch; W. J. Thomas – Farmer – Sharon; Allen Torrey – Farmer – Sharon; Chas. Welton – Stage Driver – Coudersport; D. Worden – Farmer – Bingham.

The Potter Enterprise
Wednesday Evening, May 7, 1884 – Vol. XI, No. 1

MARRIED.

BRIDGE – PEARSOLL – At the residence of W. B. Brightman, Coudersport, on Saturday, May 3d, 1884, by Miles White, Esq., Mr. Madison J. Bridge, of Ceres, Pa., and Miss Dora Pearsoll, of Shingle House.

- Kate, daughter of Sol. Ross, of East Fork, died of diphtheria, last week.

- On the 28th of April, in Bingham township, Marian Monroe, wife of ex-commissioner Samuel Monroe, passed from this life, at the age of sixty-four years. The deceased had been in poor health for a long time and her death was not unexpected. She was a woman beloved by all who knew her.

Obituary.

Williston, Potter Co., April 28, 1884.
WEIMER – Mrs. Laura Weimer died, April 19th, 1884.

She was a daughter of Burrel Lyman, known to the older residents of this region, and a sister of Leroy Lyman. She was born in 1826, in Roulet, Potter county, Pa., and married to George Weimer, 1842. They celebrated the forty-first anniversary of their marriage last Thanksgiving day. Their wedded life has been singularly characterized by mutual confidence and an agreement.

Mrs. Weimer was the mother of eleven children, nine of whom are living, three sons and six daughters. There are also eleven grandchildren living. Her death occurred at her home in Pleasant Valley, on the farm where she had spent her whole married life. Death resulted from heart disease. As a wise counsellor and affectionate wife and mother she was dearly beloved and will be sadly missed. Society has also lost a valued member.

We now come to speak of her christian experience – a thing of greater moment to her than all things else. About thirty-four years ago she was led to consider her soul, its condition and turn to Christ, in whom she found forgiveness, rest and peace. Since that time her life has been filled to a large degree with a consciousness of the Saviour's abiding presence. During these many years she has been enabled to say, with great confidence, "I know that my Redeemer lives." As the end approached she seemed to gird herself for the conflict with the promises of God, and to enter into the enjoyment of "the victory which overcometh the world – our faith." The greatest desire of her heart for the loved one she was leaving, was that they all might become savingly acquainted with Christ. May her fondest hopes be realized, so shall there be at last a glorious reunion in heaven. The last words she uttered were to her brother concerning her hopes and anticipations.

The bereaved family have the kind wishes and sympathy of their many friends. The funeral, which was largely attended, took place at the residence of the deceased April 21st, at one o'clock p.m. An appropriate sermon was preached, by Rev. N. Hart, from Rev. 7:13-17; "Blessed are the dead which die in the Lord."

- A few days ago on the head of Reed Run, Leroy Lyman killed a very large bear. Bruin was quite fat and was the best furred of any bear Mr. Lyman has killed in a long time. Mr. Lyman says this bear was from Michigan – came from there last fall and was on his return when overtaken with death.

Fires and Wind.

Last Friday, in the forenoon, was a gentle reminder of the cyclones we read about in the west. We believe we never knew of the wind blowing so hard, for so many hours in this section. Fences were blown down and on the hills, timber was falling every few minutes. A big Balm-of-Gilead tree fell on Z. J. Thompson's house, and in getting it off more valuable trees were injured. Loss not very heavy, scare immense.

On Fishing Creek the fires raged, doing great damage as will be seen by our correspondence from that section.

Below town fires were in the woods causing a great deal of nervousness on the part of the citizens of the town, but the damage was slight. The scaffolding of the Catholic church was blown down.

In Hector the barn of Mrs. Adeline Lewis was burned. Barn and contents insured by L. B. Cole for $250.

On the Sinnemahoning the entire population had to fight fire. In the bark slashings the fires were terrible. Much valuable timber was killed. At one time the dry house and bark pile at Costello's tannery were on fire, but the company has a fire engine and among the employees a well drilled fire company, and their property was saved. Brisboi's camp was deserted, but did not burn. In moving out of camp some one broke into a trunk from the camp and stole two gold watches and two gold rings belong to Brisboi; $127 in money in the trunk was not found by the thieves. A number of sheep belonging to Jefferson Hewitt and James Rees were smothered to death by the smoke. Fences were destroyed, but forunately _____.

At Sterling Run, Cameron county, the tannery was saved by great effort, but a dozen or more houses were burned leaving many families homeless.

The Potter Enterprise
Wednesday Evening, May 14, 1884 – Vol. XI, No. 2

- Horace G. Yeomans died at Hindsville, Madison county, Arkansas, May 1st, 1884, aged 28 years, 11 months and 21 days. Mr. Yeomans has lived in Arkansas for over two years, going there for his health, being troubled with weak lungs, but to no purpose, as consumption finally set in and caused his death. He was a very steady, industrious young many, with very many friends wherever he was known.

Suicide.

Mige Burt, of Burtville, who has been living alone at the above place, since his wife parted from him a few weeks ago, was found dead in his bed by school children last Thursday morning. When found he had the appearance of being dead for several days, as decomposition was fast taking place. Blood was on the face and pillow, the eyes were protruding from the sockets and his face was black and swollen, and presented a horrible appearance. An inquest was held which resulted in a verdict that he came to his death by poison administered by himself. On investigation arsenic was found in a package in his vest pocket.

Burt had not lived happily with his wife and her friends induced her to remove to Waverly, N.Y. Written notices were posted threatening revenge on the parties who had induced his wife to leave. Recently the building of one of the parties burned and suspicion fell upon Burt as the incendiary. Detectives were put on his track. They discovered papers, written by Burt, and the writing corresponded so exactly that they were about to arrest him when he committed suicide. The deceased was of rather weak mind, as his actions indicate.

Ellisburg. Again we stand in the solemn and mysterious presence of death. Again we ask ourselves the old, but ever recurring question "If a man die; shall he live again?" And as we gaze on the material part of what was Thomas Gilliland, Sr., or as he was affectionately called "Uncle Tommie,"

"Our love does dream, our faith does trust
(Since He who knows our needs is just)
That somehow, somewhere meet we must."

The subject of this sketch was born at Danville, Northumberland county, Pa., in 1796. His father was drowned in the Susquehanna, and his mother, soon marrying again, he was thrown upon the world at a very early age. He lived with his grandfather in Maryland a few years, but joining a family who were going to Ontario county, N.Y., he found himself, at the age of twelve, friendless and alone among strangers. He shared the fate of most orphans, finding, by bitter experience, that "the tender mercies of the wicked are cruel." But having a splendid constitution he grew to manhood. In 1819 he married Jane Carson near Geneva, N.Y., here two children were born to them. But resolving to make Allegany county their home they started in midwinter to make the journey with oxen; but here the saddest event of a long life occurred. Little Emeline, their oldest child, fell from the front of the sleigh and was crushed to death with the runner. After residing a few years at Cuba he removed to this county, in 1848, and has since that time been a useful and respected citizen. Last Sunday morning he passed peacefully away, but he has left us a rich and grand legacy in the example of a useful, industrious life, together with an unspotted social reputation.

- The Wellsboro *Gazette* says: The McKean county paupers, who have heretofore been supported by a system of outdoor relief in each township, threaten to leave the county rather than enter the new almshouse. That proves conclusively that the almshouse is a good thing for the county. Potter county refused to build a poor-house, and now it will have the inestimable privilege of supporting the McKean county aristocrats, who are too poor to live unaided and too proud to go to the county house.

Notice.

Whereas my wife, C. E. Horton, having left my bed and board without just cause or provocation, I hereby forbid anyone trusting or harboring her on my account as I will pay no bills of her contracting unless compelled by law.

Stephen Horton.
Wharton, Pa., May 13, 1884.

The Potter Enterprise
Wednesday Evening, May 21, 1884 – Vol. XI, No. 3

Ellisburg. And now Gran. Hurd can be seen whittling a basswood stick and making mental calculation of how much it will cost to buy "the boy" boots until he is twenty-one.

- Wilbur Quimby got the start of the boys last week. He very quietly left town and when he returned brought with him his bride, Mary Glavin, of Smethport. His many friends congratulate him and with the twain a world of happiness just as heartily as though they had known all about it beforehand.

The Potter Enterprise
Wednesday Evening, May 28, 1884 – Vol. XI, No. 4

Ellisburg. And now Charles Pye is whitling the stick and wondering about the boots, "It's a boy."

Keating. *Sonrise* occurred at the house of A. H. Crosby, some time since, though not recorded in your valuable journal. "How old is he?" asks the admiring visitor. "O, he'll be a year old next April." reply the proud and happy parents.

- The school directors in a meeting a few weeks ago decided to give one thousand dollars toward a school building at this place and bought the ground on George Nichol's place, near A. A. Mulkin's. The inhabitants here have subscribed about three hundred dollars and should raise enough to put up a good building that will accommodate the people for years, and with at least two departments and recitation rooms. – *Shingle House Palladium*.

- For the past two years, or more, Oscar Goodwin, of Maine, has made this section his home. Part of the time he has sold sewing machines and all the time passed himself off as a single man. A short time ago a wife, left by him back in the Pine Tree State, made it too warm for him here by writing letters, and he left very suddenly for the west. Some time ago a young man named Mercer, from Maine, came here as a friend of Goodwin and the two made arrangements together for going West. On Thursday last H. T. Nelson met these two parties on the train at Eldred and with them a young girl from Coudersport. His suspicions were aroused, and he telegraphed the father of the girl, that she was on the train in company with Goodwin and Mercer. Her parents were very much surprised. She had left on the 5:30 train to visit relatives a short distance out of town, with the consent of her parents, but had gone by her stopping place, and met Mercer and Goodwin. Her father started in pursuit of the runaway and met her returning home from Olean. She exhibits a marriage certificate signed by an Olean clergyman, that she and Mercer were married on Thursday and on the very next train she returned home, and is now at home. She is not yet sixteen years of age, and now very much regrets her foolish, romantic action of last Thursday. The influence of Goodwin, who had boarded with her parents for a long time, and a friend of Goodwin's, added to that of her now husband, Mercer, induced her to take the step. We have not given the name of the young girl because we do not wish to advertise her foolishness. In this section, and where the facts have been distorted, we trust this will stop the false reports, as the truth is sad enough.

Shooting Scrape.

Last Friday evening a shooting scrape occurred on Second street, near the east line of the borough. John Grom held the pistol and a neighbor, Mr. Hoffman, was the person fired at. Fortunately the ball did no harm. A spring of water on the hillside runs through Grom's land and empties into a trough, by the road. Several families obtain their supply of water at the trough and it was over this water the parties were quarreling when the shot was fired. The parties had not been on good terms for some time previous. Grom was arrested Saturday morning. He refused to make any defense and declined to give bail. He was then locked up in jail, but a few hours seclusion brought him to his senses and he gave bail for his appearance at the next term of Court.

The Potter Enterprise
Wednesday Evening, June 4, 1884 – Vol. XI, No. 5

MARRIED.

THOMPSON – ARNOLD – At Ulysses, Pa., by Rev. S. W. Cole, Mr. Grant Thompson and Miss Ida Arnold, all of Ellisburg, Pa.

Roulet. The funeral of H. T. Barr, who died the 13th ult., was largely attended. He was buried under the auspices of the G. A. R., members of the A. F. Jones Post, officiated.

Potter County, Pennsylvania Potpourri – Volume I
1880 through 1884

Decoration.

Decoration Day opened with about as discouraging prospects as one could imagine. A heavy freeze followed by four hours of snow made anything but a pleasant outlook. However the afternoon was pleasant, and while the morning's unfavorable weather kept many away, still there was a good crowd in town. The Soldier's Monument was handsomely decorated with evergreens and flowers. At 1:30 p.m., A. F. Jones Post G. A. R., headed by the Coudersport Cornet Band, marched to the monument and held the services prescribed by the ritual of that order, after which they marched to the court room which was already well filled. The meeting was called to order by Hon. D. C. Larrabee. After prayer by Rev. A. Cone, singing by the choir, and music by the band, H. C. Dornan, the speaker of the day, gave a very interesting address, suitable to the occasion.

The Post marched to the cemetery, followed by a large number of citizens and decorated the graves of the soldiers.

The Potter Enterprise
Wednesday Evening, June 11, 1884 – Vol. XI, No. 6

- Daniel W. Goodsell, of Hornby, Steuben county, N.Y., father of N. H. Goodsell, of Coudersport, died on Tuesday, June 3d, at the advanced age of ninety-six years and twenty days. For several years the deceased had been an invalid, attended by his aged wife who survives him. He had lived more than the allotted age of man and was prepared and ready to meet his maker.

DIED.

HAMEL – In Keating township, Potter county, Pa., on June 9th, 1884, Fred, only son of F. J. and K. M. Hamel, aged 14 years and 19 days.

- The heaviest thunder storm of the season visited this section Monday evening. For an hour and a half the rains descended in torrents accompanied by lightning and heavy thunder. The streets were flooded, running over the sidewalks in many places. Many cellars were flooded and gardens were badly washed. An open window in the second story of the corner store made work for the boys for a few minutes, fortunately it was discovered in time to save the goods from a wetting. A leak in the roof of the Seibert building let in a large quantity of water upon the books and papers of L. B. Cole, insurance agent, doing considerable damage. At Lymansville lightning struck the dwelling house of Mort Benson. The fluid struck the chimney and passed down to the cellar, shattering things somewhat. Fortunately there was no one in the house at the time. The building did not take fire. The Hydorne school house was struck by lightning and considerably shattered. Two sheep and a lamb near the school house were killed.

Attempt at Suicide.

John Grom, of Coudersport, took a large dose of ladanum last Sunday night. Dr. Buck was called and by prompt work relieved Grom of the poison. Recently Grom was arrested for shooting at a neighbor, and his troubles have so preyed upon his mind that he took this course to seek relief. He will not try it again right away.

THE NEW OIL FIELD.
Oil Here and There in Potter County, Especially There.

At last after years of weary waiting, heartsick from hope deferred, Potter county comes to the front as an oil producer, present and prospective. Sharon township is at the head, but this section may soon enter the race for first place.

The first producer in Potter is the well on the Prince farm in Sharon, about one mile south of the State line, and about two miles north of Shingle House. This well was shot on Saturday last, and soon commenced flowing. On Sunday the well was cased and packed. Considerable oil flowed, a portion of which was saved. From six o'clock Sunday evening until six o'clock Monday morning, the well put eighteen barrels of oil in the tank, by actual measurement. The citizens of that section are wild with excitement, and have cause to be. Oil speculators and not a few sharks are overrunning that section. Land is changing ownership in very many instances, at good prices. Other wells will be put down at once, and it looks now as if Sharon would be a very lively township before Fall.

The Nelson Station Well, five miles west of Coudersport, has been treated to a heavy shot. In this well twenty-eight feet of fine sand was found. The shot opened it up so that oil flowed in, filling the well to a depth of sixty feet, on Sunday.

The bailer was run on Sunday last, and came up full of oil. The owners do not claim much for this well, but are now sure that a pool or belt exists somewhere in this section. The Dingman Run well it is expected will throw some light on the subject. On Monday a line was lowered into the hole. It indicated two hundred feet of oil. Carefully handled the well would make about a three barrel producer. So the managers say.

The Dingman Run well, which has been at a stand still since the explosion of the boiler used for drilling, is to be pushed ahead at once. The boiler and engine from the Nelson Station well was removed to this well, or rather will be. They started with it Monday and when a short distance from the well the load tipped over. With good luck the drill will start to-day. Mr. Watson thinks another hundred feet will complete the well.

The Potter Enterprise
Wednesday Evening, June 18, 1884 – Vol. XI, No. 7

MARRIED.

YEOMANS – LEE. – In Columbus, O., at Wesley Chapel, June 7th, by Rev. C. H. Bitler, W. C. Yeomans, of Coudersport, Pa., and Miss Mary Lee, of Columbus.

NELSON – EVANS. – At the church of the Redeemer, Addison, N.Y., June 12th, by Rev. F. F. Rice, assisted by Rev. Cowan, Charles Nelson, of Coudersport, and Miss Mary Evans, of Addison, N.Y.

Freeman Run. The friends of Mr. and Mrs. A. H. Crosby gave them a surprise party last week, on the 10th anniversary of their marriage, bringing them many nice and useful presents of tin.

DIED.

DEXTER. – Oswayo township, Potter Co., Pa., June 13th, 1884, Lucy Maria, wife of William Dexter, in the 63d year of her age.

Freeman Run. The funeral of Fritz Hammel who died Monday was held Wednesday at the Klien house. Fritz was a bright promising lad, besides being an only son. The services were conducted by the Rev. Mr. Marshall, of Coudersport.

D. F. Glassmire, Sr.

On Monday night June 16th, Mr. D. F. Glassmire, Sr., passed from this life, in the 64th year of his age. He was born in Reading, Penn'a, but for over thirty years has been a resident of this county, and for nearly 29 years a resident of Coudersport. For many years he was landlord of the Coudersport Hotel in which capacity he was known to the majority of the people of Potter county, and since that time has always been in active business of some kind. Always stirring and energetic. Although over sixty years of age, he appeared strong and active, and as full of energy as ever. His last work was the building of the skating rink and hall in which he displayed the push that characterized his earlier years. He has done much to improve Coudersport, and his death will be a loss to the community. In all public improvements he was interested, and his money was as ready as his words. His business life was successful, not at all times, but as a whole. Several weeks since he contracted a very hard cold, and on Wednesday of last week was obliged to take to his bed. The cold developed into pneumonia and its course was short. This, Wednesday, afternoon the remains will be laid to rest in the Coudersport Cemetery, followed to the grave by mourning relatives and sorrowing friends, from the little children who were always treated to a Christmas ride by Mr. Glassmire, to his business friends and acquaintances. Coudersport has indeed met with a sad loss.

JULY 4TH 1884.
A Big Celebration at Coudersport.

We are very glad to announce that the committee on the Fourth of July celebration are progressing finely with the arrangements and a big celebration is assured. Hon. W. W. Brown, of Bradford, and others are expected to deliver addresses. Hon. Wm. Shear will read the Declaration of Independence. Hon. D. C. Larrabee, President of the Day.

The Grand Army Posts of Potter county hold their annual re-union on the 3rd and 4th, and will assist in the celebration. The Posts will give an exhibition drill, under the command of Major Kilbourne, Marshal of the day. There will be the usual laughter provoking races, a dance afternoon and evening; music by the Coudersport Cornet Band and the Oswayo Drum Corps. $300 worth of fire works in the evening and a world of fun all day. The entire programme is not yet made out, but all may rest assured that this celebration will be the best ever seen in Potter county. The finance committee have already secured a large fund for this purpose and more has been promised. It will be a success. The C. & P. A. Railroad will run special trains at reduced rates. See posters and small bills.

- Mrs. Geo. W. Sheldon, of Crandall Hill, met with a severe accident near the reservoir of the Coudersport Water Company. She was in the wagon driving the horse, her husband and child walking. About the steepest part of the hill the wagon struck a stone and in cramping the wagon it was thrown over the dug way, with the horse. Mrs. Sheldon stopped about 30 feet from the road, down a sharp incline and was quite badly bruised, and also received a scalp wound from striking a rock. The lady weighs over three hundred pounds, and the wonder is she was not more seriously injured. Dr. Charles French rendered medical assistance.

Church Dedication.

The dedication services of the new M. E. church at Sweden Valley will be held on Friday, June 20th, 1884. At 11 o'clock a.m., preaching by Rev. O. S. Chamberlain, P.E., of Olean Dist. At 12:30, pic-nic in grove. At 2 p.m., preaching by Rev. D. W. C. Huntington, D.D., of Bradford. A cordial invitation is extended to all. Come with loads, your teams will be cared for and you shall be fed both in body and mind.

By order of Committee.

Court Minutes.

Court called June 9, 1884. Hon. A. G. Olmsted presiding; present associates Hammond and Lewis.

Grand Jury called and sworn. A. A. Swetland, foreman. J. L. Haughenberry constable to attend Grand Jury.

N. T. Arnold admitted to practice in the several courts of Potter county.

James Calgan appointed constable of Sylvania township.

In the matter of final account of Josiah Berfield, guardian of James E. Berfield, J. L. Knox appointed auditor.

Comth vs Andrew Wagner, perjury, plead guilty. Bail $600 for appearance at next term.

M. E. Olmsted vs Homer twp, tax of ten mills ordered instead of two mills.

Ann Burns vs James Burns, alias sub in divorce awarded.

James Clark for use of Wm. M'Dougall vs John Eldridge, verdict for def't.

Estate of Polly Ann VanHusen, additional exceptions filed.

Sam'l Angood appointed deputy constable of Roulet township.

H. H. Dent, for use, vs Jackson twp, tax of ten mills ordered to pay debts.

H. J. Olmsted vs Eulalia twp, special tax of five mills ordered.

Fred Bodler vs Abbot twp, special tax of five mills ordered.

Comth vs Geo. Nickerson, bail $100 for appearance at next term.

John Henry vs Bingham twp, special tax of four mills ordered.

L. M. Fox and Geo. Fox executors, vs Alvin P. Lewis, jury find for pl'ff the land described to be released on the payment of $1890.94 and costs, as follows: $500 in 30 days, half the balance in one year and the balance in two years.

Same vs Joseph Stone and James A. R. Greenman, terre tenant. Jury find for pl'ff the land described to be released upon the payment of $666.03 with interest and cost within 60 days.

Same vs H. L. Merrick, Lester W. Merrick and David Grover, terre tenant, jury find for pl'ff the land described to be released upon the payment of $1,668.51 with interest and costs within 60 days.

P. A. Stebbins and Mary E. Stebbins exr's vs Abiel Sheldon et al, jury find for pl'ff the land described to be released upon the payment of $226.22 with costs and interest within 30 days.

A. B. Mann appointed commissioner to enquire into the alleged lunacy of John Cavanaugh and report thereon.

In the matter of the estate of Lettie Ellis and Henry Ellis, minor children of Wm. Ellis, A. B. Mann appointed auditor to decide upon the advisability of making private sale of real estate.

Comth vs Wm. Rounseville, rape, not guilty.

Comth vs A. C. Peasly, larceny, true bill, nol pros entered, de'ft and bail discharged.

Comth vs Wm. Shingler, perjury, continued, bail $200.

Comth vs Porter H. Clark, rape, bail $1200 for appearance at next term.

Comth vs Edward M'Gonigal, selling liquor, bail $200 for appearance at next term.

Comth vs Peleg Burdic, selling liquor, bail $200 for appearance at next term.

Comth vs Francis Maginnis, disorderly house, not a true bill, county to pay costs.

Comth vs Patrick Carey, disorderly house, not a true bill, county to pay costs.

Rodney Smith appointed Overseer of the Poor of Pleasant Valley twp.

Comth vs J. H. Wetzel, assault and battery, discharged, no prosecutor appearing.

Comth vs M. Pritchard, selling liquor, nol pros entered.

C. E. Burt, guardian of Satie Bennett, minor child of A. Bennett deceased, acknowledged deed to W. T. Hosley also deed to Wm. Daniels.

Patrick Mitchel, a native of Ireland, admitted to citizenship.

Estate of S. Taylor, exceptions having been filed to the account of L. H. Rush, adm'r, H. A. Scoville appointed auditor in this case.

Emily W. Blanchard vs Freeman R. Blanchard, decree of divorce from the bonds of matrimony awarded.

Marian Wallace vs Joseph J. Wallace, sub in divorce awarded.

Comth vs John Grom, shooting with intent to kill, true bill, jury return a verdict of not guilty.

Comth vs Francis Maginnis, selling liquor, true bill.

Patrick Carey, selling liquor, true bill, bail $200 for appearance at next term.

Comth vs Ernest Acker, Mayhem, true bill, jury find de'ft not guilty.

Comth vs C. O. Brown, selling liquor, not a true bill, county to pay costs.

Comth vs Ernest F. Acker and Grant G. Acker, aggravated assault and battery, true bill, nol pros entered and defendants discharged.

Vernia Robinson vs H. E. Robinson, divorce decreed.

Comth vs Richard Kilduff, pointing a gun, bail $200 for appearance at next term.

Geo. W. Prince appointed guardian of Susan M. Prince.

James Impson appointed constable of Stewardson township.

Lorinda Packard et al vs Aaron Robinson, ordered that summons be published.

Anna Burns by her next friend vs James A. Burns, H. A. Gridley appointed commissioner to take testimony. Sheriff to make proclamation.

Mary A. Dougherty vs D. Dougherty, A. B. Mann appointed commissioner to take testimony.

Eliza M. Haskins vs J. F. Haskins, A. B. Mann appointed com'r to take testimony, divorce awarded.

J. F. Williams, adm'r, vs Geo. W. and Elmer E. Bradley. Geo. W. Bradley appointed guardian of E. E. Bradley, ad liberati.

Estate of Eva Niell, late of Buffalo, dec'd, W. I. Lewis appointed auditor to distribute funds in hands of adm'r.

Henry Harris appointed supervisor of Keating township to fill vacancy caused by death of Casper Hoffmeister.

Geo. W. King vs Geo. W. Pearsall, continued, action amended.

Peter Halleuer vs Raymond Bendell, judge of nol pros entered.

S. M. Conable vs Sabra Ann Conable, sub in divorce awarded.

G. W. Berfield vs Irene Berfield, sub in divorce awarded.

Eulalia twp vs A. W. Cameron, verdict for defendant.

E. S. Worden, High Sheriff of Potter county, acknowledged following deeds for property sold at Sheriff Sale:

To A. B. Mann for 13 acres in Coudersport, sold as property of John E. Monroe, $20.

To Francis P. Nichols, 1 acre in Sharon, sold as property of Nichols and Harvey for $100.

To Bingham Estate for 50 acres in Hector, sold as property of Ambros K. Wood for $50.

J. W. Stevens vs Harrison twp, tax of six mills ordered.

Comth vs W. C. Sherwood, assault and battery, deft and bail discharged, no prosecutor appearing.

Comth vs Aaron J. Hall, assault and battery, deft and bail discharged, no prosecutor appearing.

Comth vs C. Vergason, recognizance forfeited.

Veniries ordered for forty-eight traverse and twenty-four grand jurors for September Term.

Mary A. Ackerman vs Samuel Ackerman, alias sub in divorce, C. H. Cole appointed commissioner to take testimony.

Court of Common Pleas, Quarter Sessions and Orphan's Court adjourned until Saturday, June 21st, at 3 o'clock p.m.

The Potter Enterprise
Wednesday Evening, June 25, 1884 – Vol. XI, No. 8

- Born. – To Mr. and Mrs. Fenton _dith, Lyman's Mill, June 21, a son.

- On Thursday morning last Frank M. Stevens died at Colton, California, in the 32d year of his age. About two months ago Frank left Coudersport in search of health. For a short time he thought California air would cure him, and he seemed much better, but diarhoea set it, caused either by the change or the last stage of his disease, and death relieved poor Frank of his sufferings. Frank was well known to everybody in this section. For a long time he was clerk in the Postoffice. Last winter he was employed in the Bank. Several years ago he served an apprentice-ship in the *Journal* becoming a very good printer. Wherever he was employed he gave satisfaction. He was active, careful, and strictly honest. He has been failing for years and spent one winter South, which seemed to benefit him. Last winter physicians of note told him that he could live but a short time in this climate, but that if he would go to Southern California they thought he would surely recover. It was certain death to remain here, and death, as it has proved, was to meet him at the end of his journey across the continent. His disease was a solidifying of the lungs. He leaves a mother, sister, brother, wife and two children. Frank had an insurance of $1,000 in Connecticut Mutual.

SUICIDE.
Joseph Kline, of Eulalia, Shoots Himself With a Gun.

On Sunday afternoon Joseph Kline, of Eulalia township, committed suicide by shooting himself with a shot gun loaded with buck shot. The deceased was aged 82 years, of German birth, and had been a resident of Eulalia for many years. From the facts brought out by the Coroner's Inquest, we have gleaned the following.

For some years Mr. Kline has lived with his son, on a farm back of Lyman Nelson's. Last Sunday morning all the family except the wife of the deceased went to Roulet, on a visit. A little before noon Mrs. Kline went to Mrs. Brehmer's a mile or two distant, leaving her husband engaged in reading his Bible and hymn book. She was gone until three o'clock. She was seen passing Lyman Nelson's, both going and coming. When she returned home she found Mr. Kline on the kitchen floor, his clothes on fire, and blood spattered over the floor. She put the fire out, and went to Lyman Nelson's for help.

Examination indicated that Mr. Kline had loaded a shot gun which usually hung upon the wall, but was not loaded, with powder and buck-shot. A portion of the ammunition was found on the table, as he left it after using it. He then placed the breech against the base-board and fired the gun with a stick. The charge entered his side making a wound two inches across, a few of the shot passed entirely through him, and lodged in the rafters and floor above. His clothes were set on fire by the burning powder, and the body as considerably burned. Death must have been instantaneous. Mrs. Kline testified "that the deceased was 82 years of age last May; he said to me a few days ago that his feet began to swell and he was afraid he would have to suffer a great deal, he never said anything to me about committing suicide. After he heard that Grom had tried to commit suicide, he said to me that if he did not die soon he would end his death himself." Mrs. Lyman Nelson testified to hearing a gun about 3 o'clock in the afternoon, some little time before she saw Mrs. Kline returning home.

All the witnesses testified that so far as they knew there was no family troubles. The Coroner's Jury rendered the following verdict:
COMMONWEALTH OF PENN'A }
POTTER COUNTY. } ss:

An inquisition indented and taken at Eulalia township, in the County of Potter, Penn'a, the 22d day of June, A.D. 1884, before me Frank Buck, Coroner of the county aforesaid, upon the view of the body of Joseph Kline, farmer then and there lying dead, upon the oaths of W. I. Lewis, W. B. Brightman, D. W. Vanwegen, C. A. Stebbins, D. F. Glassmire, Joseph Forster, good and lawful men of the county aforesaid, who being duly sworn to inquire on the part of the Commonwealth, when, where, and how the said Joseph Kline came to his death, do say upon their respective oaths, that at three o'clock p.m., on the 22d day of June, A.D. 1884, at Eulalia Township, in said county, the said Joseph Kline came to his death by a gun shot wound received in the breast, the said gun being in his own hands and discharged by himself.

In witness whereof, we have hereunto set our hands and seals, this 22d day of June 1884.

Frank Buck, Coroner.
W. I. Lewis,
D. F. Glassmire,
D. W. Vanwegen,
W. B. Brightman,
C. A. Stebbins,
Jos. E. Forster.

The Coroner's Jury found the body lying in front of the stove and very near it, the gun lying back of him. The gun (a shot gun) had been loaded with No. 1 buck shot. The wound which caused death was in the right side between the fourth and fifth rib, coming out at the back just below the shoulder blade. The clothes were nearly burned off the body. Buck shot and marks of shot were found in the joist and floor nearly over where the deceased lay. The shot was nearly straight through him. A small stick was found near the body with which it is supposed he fired the gun.

Obituary.

This village was surprised on Tuesday morning June 17th by the sad news of the death of one our oldest and most enterprising citizens.

Daniel Fager Glassmire was born in Reading, Berks Co., Pa., July 19th, 1820. When a child he moved with his parents to Pottsville, Schuylkill county. At the age of fourteen he was apprenticed to Mr. Benjamin Haywood, a prominent member of the M.E. Church of Pottsville. He so distinguished himself in his occupation that at the age of 21 he was promoted to the position of foreman of the shop. In 1842 in the 22d year of his age he married Miss Caroline Mills, by whom he had four children, three of whom are citizens of this place. The fourth is deceased.

In 1851 he moved with his wife and the sons whom the Lord gave him in Pottsville to Potter county, and settled on what is called the Mills farm at Colesburg. There he remained two years making an aggressive warfare on the wilds of nature during which time he cleared a tract of land and built the Colesburg hotel, for the accommodation of travelers. In 1854 he moved to Coudersport and became proprietor of the Coudersport hotel. Since that time he has been a prominent and enterprising business man of this borough.

By economy, industry and good management he has acquired a competence, so that at the time of his death he had in his possession much valuable real estate of this place.

In 1880 he was called to pass through a sore bereavement – his wife who had been the companion of his toils for 38 years passed triumphantly to her eternal home, but in doing so she left a lonely place in his heart, which was also felt keenly in the church and community.

During a protracted meeting which was held a few days since in the M.E. church, he professed faith in Christ and united on probation with the church. Mr. Glassmire has gone to his reward – let us copy his virtues and throw the mantle of Christian charity over his faults.

A. A. Craw.

- The Driftwood *Gazette* relates the following narrow escape of a former Coudersport boy: James Cary, an employee at the depot, had a narrow escape from a fatal accident last Saturday evening. He was standing at the desk in the baggage room and stopped to get a check, which hung under the desk, and then stepped to the door. At the same time there was a man in the room with a Winchester rifle and he was taking empty cartridges from the gun. All at once bang went the gun and a bullet pierced the wall just where Mr. Cary had stood not ten seconds before. Had he been after a check at the time the gun was accidentally discharged he would certainly have been mortally wounded. It was a narrow escape, and one that Jim does not care to encounter again, and may be a lesson to the man, handling the gun, to not be so careless with firearms in the future.

- The Westfield *Free Press* says: The eyeglass and peanuts which were found in the possession of John Everitt and Henry Plank, of Sunderlinville, was simply the latch to thieves and burglars at Westfield.

It is strange but true that a next of burglars and thieves can reside in our midst, carry on their depredations for years, no doubt, and not even get caught. But, it must soon come out, sooner or later, although these parties were successful for some time yet the most simple article convicted them. John Everitt and Henry Plank, of Sunderlinville, were arrested and brought here, upon a charge of entering a barber shop and peanut store in this town, last Wednesday. It was learned that a Mr. Wm. Welch was connected with the same company and our constable brought him over, who confessed far more than had been laid against them. Several trips were made to Sunderlinville which brought forth almost a wagon load of all kinds of traps belonging to citizens of our town; such as cigars, razors, eye-glass, heel shaves, finger-ring, fish-pole, carpenter's tools, spirit levels, buggy seat cushion, &c.

Sherman & Krusen, S. B. Borden, James Butler, Ed. Close, F. D. McNaughton, I. Colbert, J. W. Smith and King Brothers are the parties who found some of their goods in the possession of these burglars. Tuesday and Friday were spent in looking up evidence and more goods, while on Saturday Everitt and Welch were called up before W. H. Parsons, for a hearing.

They waived an examination and were placed under bail of $500. As it was impossible to secure bail, Seth Tremain took them to jail at Wellsboro on Saturday afternoon. Henry Plank gave bail for his appearance before W. H. Parsons on Tuesday. Later, he was discharged, owing to not getting sufficient evidence to convict him.

Adjourned Court.

In the matter of the application of Mrs. Elmira S. Perkins for separate estate, ordered filed and recorded.

J. W. Dingee vs Miles White, motion for a new trial.

James B. Benson admitted to practice in the several courts of Potter county.

Court of Common Pleas, Quarter Sessions and Orphans Court adjourned to meet June 28th, 1884, at 2 o'clock.

The Potter Enterprise
Wednesday Evening, July 2, 1884 – Vol. XI, No. 9

No Paper Next Week.

No paper will be issued from this office next week. The office will be open for the transaction of business and orders for job work will receive prompt attention.

- Born. – To Mr. and Mrs. C. Mehring, Eulalia township, June 25th, a daughter.

DROWNED.
John Wedsworth, of Eulalia Township, Drowned in a Spring.

On Friday last John Wedsworth, of Eulalia township, aged about 42 years, was found drowned in the spring, at the Wedsworth homestead. The deceased was of weak mind and subject to fits, having them at times as often as two or three a week, at other times once in two or three months. On Wednesday last he had four.

Between twelve and one o'clock Mrs. Jane Wedsworth, his sister-in-law, saw him going to the spring for water. A few minutes afterwards, Mrs. Wedsworth thinks about five minutes, she went to the spring and found him leaning over the board, with his face and one arm in the water, dead. Assistance was called and the deceased was removed to the dwelling house. It is supposed that as he was leaning over to dip a pail of water, he was taken with a fit, and fell into the water and was drowned. He had fell in the spring before, and had to be helped as he could not get out alone owing to his want of strength.

Coroner Buck summoned the following Jury: W. B. Brightman, A. A. Allen, L. B. Cole, Geo. F. Ross, D. F. Glassmire and W. B. Rees.

After examining into the matter the Jury rendered a verdict that "John Wedsworth came to his death by accidental drowning, by falling into a spring of water, undoubtedly caused by his having a fit while getting a pail of water therefrom."

- B. W. Dennis, who left Coudersport some weeks since for California, arrived at Colton, before the death of F. M. Stevens. He says Frank received the best of care, and that everything possible was done to make his last days as easy as possible. Dennis has not been there long enough to know whether the climate was benefiting him much.

- Action should be taken by the people of this section to secure the passage of a law prohibiting the running of long logs in the Allegheny, unless the long logs are rafted. The Allegheny is too small a stream for long logs. It is a matter of interest to every person along the stream. In the Susquehanna all logs over 16 feet long must be rafted. At present the people have no rights the log drivers are bound to respect.

Prohibition Convention.

The prohibition home protection party, of Potter county, will hold a mass convention at Coudersport, on the 10th day of July, 1884.

Our principles are not unknown. We arraign the manufacture and sale of intoxicating liquors as the most complicated and infamous system of crime, ever fostered upon the earth.

We denounce the license system as twin sister to Moloch, and affirm that money paid to the government for protection to the liquor traffic is essentially the same as money paid for the privilege of assassinating our citizens, and to brand this bloody coin with the Name of the Lord is blasphemy.

Against this gigantic liquor crime we appeal to the most sacred trust of the American citizen – the ballot – and earnestly invite the men of Potter who are willing to espouse this righteous cause to meet with us in our convention. All women and minors willing to work with us will be welcomed to the labors and privitations of those who seek to help the world.

The W. C. T. Unions are solicited to send delegates to take part in our deliberations.

By order of the Chairman,
Mary E. H. Everitt.

Coudersport, June 16th, 1884.

FOURTH OF JULY.
Programme of the Celebration at Coudersport.

Hon. D. C. Larrabee, president of the day; Maj. J. M. Kilbourne, marshal; Hon. W. W. Brown, orator; Hon. Wm. Shear, reader; Rev. A. A. Craw, chaplain. Thirteen guns at sun-rise. At 10 o'clock the Band will escort visiting Posts, G. A. R. from the depot. At 10:30 procession forms, consisting of the Coudersport Hose Company and Fantastics, to be followed by a pig race – winner to keep the pig. Wheel-barrow race: $2.00 to 1st; $1.00 to 2nd; 50 cts to 3d. Sack race: $2 to 1st; $1 to 2d; 50 cts to 3d.

Two o'clock meeting on the court house square, to be called to order by president, prayer by chaplain and address by orator of the day; reading Declaration; music by band and choir during proceedings. Exhibition drill and parade by G. A. R. during afternoon; during morning exhibition roller skating at the rink; dance at Glassmire's hall afternoon and evening. Three hundred dollars worth of fire works at 8:30 p.m., a grand display, which all ought to see.

School House Repairing.

The school directors of Sweden will meet at the Neefe School House, on Saturday, July 12th, at one o'clock p.m., for the purpose of letting the job of repairing said school house. The repairs are a new roof, new floors, Verandah, &c., turning the building around and putting it upon a new wall. Job will be let to lowest and best bidder.

George Tuttle, Secretary
June 30th, 1884.

The Potter Enterprise
Wednesday Evening, July 16, 1884 – Vol. XI, No. 10

Fishing Creek. Mr. James Phenix and Miss Lydia Yentzer went to Oswayo the Fourth as two, and returned as one. May they enjoy a long and happy life is the wishes of their many friends.

MARRIED.

TEACHMAN – MONROE – At the Baptist Parsonage in Ulysses, by Rev. S. W. Cole, July 11, George E. Teachman and Laura Monroe. All of Bingham, Pa.

DARLING – TAUSCHER – In Sweden, June 29th, 1884, by the Rev. E. D. Carr, P. Sobieski Darling, of Coudersport, and Miss Mary L. Tauscher, of Sweden township.

OUTMAN – ROBBINS – At the M. E. parsonage in Harrison Valley, by Rev. A. S. Gould, June 28th, 1884, Mr. George Outman and Miss Hannah Robbins, all of Bingham, Pa.

HASSRICK – BROWN – In Roulet, July 2d, 1884, at the residence of the bride's parents, by Rev. A. Brooks, Mr. J. F. Hassrick, of Beaver Valley, Pa., and Miss Mary Brown, of Roulet.

SHERWOOD – ALLEN – At the residence of the bridegroom, in Genesee township, July $5t^{h,}$ 1884, by James I. Ryan, J.P., Mr. Amasa Sherwood and Mrs. Jane Allen, both of Genesee.

SCHWARTZENBACH – BRODERSON – At the residence of the bride's parents, in Germania, June 26th, 1884, by Henry Theis, Esq., Mr. Herman Schwartzenbach and Miss Anna Friedericke Magdalena Broderson, both of Germania.

DIED.

CHAMBERLAIN – In Oakland county, Mich., July 2d, 1884, of Paralysis, Mrs. Jane Reynolds, widow of Elisha Chamberlain, aged 87 years, 9 months and 17 days.

Cyclone.

On the fifty of July a small portion of Ohio was visited by a cyclone, destroying considerable property. The same day Cameron county was visited by a wind blow that demolished considerable timber.

A part of the same storm or its twin sister struck North Bingham the same day destroying timber, fences and buildings. J. L. Raymond at North Bingham had his house damaged, trees blown over, his barn was carried some little distance and utterly demolished, some of the pieces were carried over a quarter of a mile away. A horse in the barn at the time was not injured, but two buggies were wrecked. Others in Bingham suffered to a less extent.

The storm passed over into West Union destroying a number of buildings especially along "Squab Hollow." One house was turned completely bottom side up. A lady and her child were in the house at the time but neither were harmed. A Mr. Herrington living in Squab Hollow was severely injured, probably fatally by flying boards. His barn was wrecked and the house unroofed. Quite a number of cattle and sheep were killed.

July Fourth.

July 4th was a great day for Coudersport. The largest crowd ever seen in this town, and the very best of order. Drunkenness was not visible. The excursion train brought in eight car loads and every regular train including the night train brought a goodly number. The fantastics deserve mention, all the characters were good but Mr. Greenwood, with is 9 ½ foot genuine, non-painted white elephant, rather carried off the cookies. The Grand Army boys were out in force and assisted materially in the success of the day under command of Maj. Kilbourne and his aid, Capt. Reynolds, assisted by the officers of the different posts. The Sharon Post was armed. Too much praise cannot be given to the Boys in Blue. Owing to an accident on the P. & E. road, Hon. W. W. Brown was late in getting here, but the crowd was entertained by music, reading of the Declaration of Independence by Hon. Wm. Shear, excellent remarks by Major Kilbourne, D. C. Larrabee and H. C. Dornan. The address of Mr. Brown did not spoil by the delay and was listened to with great interest. The fireworks were the best ever seen in Coudersport. The Coudersport Cornet Band furnished good music and plenty of it. In the evening two dances kept the young folks busy, at the Rink and at Len Davis'. It was "a Grand Celebration."

The Potter Enterprise
Wednesday Evening, July 23, 1884 – Vol. XI, No. 11

- Born – To Mr. and Mrs. Leroy Herrington, in Sweden township, July 15th, an heir, weight nine pounds.

- Mrs. E. B. Williams, of Keating Summit, was buried in the Crandall Hill cemetery last week. The deceased was frightened by the wind blow on the Fourth of July and did not recover from the effects.

Sudden Death.

For some time past a German named Herman Hansen, formerly from Ohio, has been at work for Dr. O. T. Ellison, at his mill. Last Tuesday morning he was taken ill while going to the yard to milk some cows. Thursday afternoon Mr. Hansen died. He was 38 years of age.

During his illness he told a fellow workman that he had eaten a piece of cake at breakfast Tuesday that did not taste good, he thought there must have been heads of matches in it, and he believed he had been poisoned.

Under the circumstances, his friends thought it best to have a coroner's inquest held, and Coroner Buck was notified. The coroner summoned the following jury: W. R. Brightman, L. B. Cole, A. A. Allen, Luther Seibert, L. F. Andrews and W. W. Thompson. Friday morning Drs. Ellison and French held a post mortem examination. No traces of poison was found, and the Doctors testified that the deceased came to his death from acute inflammation of the bowels. The jury rendered a verdict in accordance with the evidence given by the Surgeons.

And thus another story of poisoning and crime is settled and the story stopped before any damage to character was sustained by any one.

Died.

In Colton, California, June 19th, 1884, Francis M. Stevens, of Coudersport, Pa. Born Sept. 9th, 1852, in Barrington, Yates county, N.Y. He came with his parents, at the age of six months, to Potter county, in which county he has lived, with the exception of a few months, until the time of his death.

Frank was well known all over the county, and had a host of friends. For years he was connected with the postoffice at Coudersport and the "Peoples Drug Store;" and lastly with the Bank of Coudersport. He was noted for his integrity and closeness to business accuracy. Some four years ago he was smitten by the terrible consumption, that carries so many to an early grave. Frank fought manfully with the fell disease, which never relinquishes its hold until it drove him to a distant State, and slew him there, over three thousand miles from home and relatives. But he found generous friends who soothed his last moments with tender hands. Frank's death bereaved a wife, and left fatherless two children. The entire community testified by its sadness, a sincere mourning for the departed.

The Potter Enterprise
Wednesday Evening, July 30, 1884 – Vol. XI, No. 12

Odin. Born – July 20th, to Mr. and Mrs. James Mitcheltree, a daughter.

- Mrs. Rennells, of Corning, N.Y., died last Friday evening, after a long illness. She was a sister of Mrs. A. A. Hodskins and Mrs. C. S. Jones, of this place, both of whom were with her. Mrs. C. S. Jones went to attend the funeral.

List of Grand Jurors Sept. Term, 1884.

H. Atherton – Farmer – Ulysses; H. Bartlett – Farmer – Ulysses; John S. Bump – Farmer – Sharon; B. F. Bishop – Farmer – Allegany; F. P. Brooks – Farmer – Clara; Joseph Daniels – Farmer – Bingham; John Freeman – Farmer – Sweden; Joseph Gilbert – Printer – Coudersport; Lucius Graves – Farmer – Sharon; Henry Gnau – Farmer – Abbott; Joseph Hull – Farmer – Eulalia; Henry Harris – Farmer – Keating; J. J. Jones – Farmer – Harrison; J. Keltz – Tanner – Harrison; O. H. P. Knickerbacker – Farmer – Stewardson; Alvin Lewis – Farmer – Bingham; Wm. F. McCoy – Farmer – Stewardson; S. P. Olmsted – Merchant – Coudersport; Jacob Rockefeller – Farmer – Sharon; Charles Rees – Farmer – Ulysses; Al Robbins – Farmer – Hector; J. W. Stevens – Merchant – Harrison; Frank Sherman – Farmer – Genesee; Henry Zoerb – Farmer – Abbott.

List of Traverse Jurors for Sept. Term, 1884.

O. E. Armstrong – Jeweler – Coudersport; John Abbott – Farmer – Roulet; Hiram Bridges – Farmer – Keating; Freeman Brizzee – Farmer – Oswayo; W. S. Brine – Brick Maker – Roulet; Horace Crocker – Farmer – Sharon; Clarence Corsaw – Farmer – Sweden; R. S. Carpenter – Farmer – Bingham; Joseph O'Donnell – Farmer – Genesee; Albert C. Evans – Farmer – Bingham; Levi Elliott – Merchant – Harrison; Michael Dwire – Farmer – Genesee; Adelbert Gale – Farmer – Allegany; Wm. Groesbeck – Farmer – Roulet; Frank Gale –

Potter County, Pennsylvania Potpourri – Volume I
1880 through 1884

Farmer – Hebron; Thomas Gilliland – Lumberman – Genesee; Hubbard Harrison – Farmer – Harrison; C. M. Herrington – Merchant – Sweden; Leroy Haskins – Farmer – Sylvania; J. L. Havens – Farmer – Hector; D. E. Hosley – Laborer – Lewisville; C. B. Lewis – Farmer – Bingham; Wm. Lewis – Farmer – Allegany; S. C. Lewis – Farmer – Harrison; Charles Mattison – Farmer – Sweden; Darius Moon – Farmer – Sharon; Bryan Maun – Farmer – Genesee; John Maginnis – Farmer – Genesee; James Nelson – Farmer – Summit; B. S. Potter – Farmer – Harrison; James Ryan – Farmer – Genesee; E. E. Swift – Farmer – Hebron; G. W. Stillman – Farmer – Hebron; Geo. W. Snyder – Farmer – Eulalia; W. W. Smith – Farmer – Oswayo; H. N. Stone – Farmer – Harrison; E. Spencer – Farmer – Bingham; Elijah Swift – Farmer – Hebron; Henry Theis – Merchant – Abbott; Willis Tauscher – Farmer – Roulet; Gottlieb Traub – Farmer – West Branch; C. H. Tauscher – Farmer – Sweden; Willis Weimer – Farmer – Pleasant Valley; A. D. Wolcott – Farmer – Sharon; D. M. Wheeler – Laborer – Oswayo; George Weimer – Farmer – Pleasant Valley; G. W. Witter – Farmer – Pleasant Valley; Charles Woodkirk – Farmer – Sharon.

The Potter Enterprise
Wednesday Evening, August 6, 1884 – Vol. XI, No. 13

MARRIED.

HAMILTON – GUSTIN – In Coudersport, August 4th, by Miles White, Esq., Albert Hamilton and Miss Hannah Gustin, all of Sharon.

HERSHBERGER – HUNGERFORD – In Coudersport, at the residence of the bride's mother, Aug. 5th, 1884, by Rev. C. H. Dodd, Mr. James A. Hershberger, of Bradford, and Miss Hattie Hungerford, of Coudersport.

- The clothing store of Levi Harris has been burglarized twice recently. The total losses, so far as known, are a gold ring, a few cigars and some silver change. How the burglars effected an entrance is not known.

- Milton Smith was before Miles White, Esq., Monday evening and gave bail in the sum of $400 for his appearance at court. The charge is that on Thursday Milton Smith and Wm. White drove some cattle from Roulet, belonging to Daniel Smith, to the Forest House and drove them down an old road on the east side of the railroad where they would get on the track. The cattle did get on the railroad and one cow, a two year old steer and a heifer were killed. White has not yet been arrested.

The Potter Enterprise
Wednesday Evening, August 13, 1884 – Vol. XI, No. 14

- Born – To Mr. and Mrs. Alva Taggart, August 9th, a daughter.

- Born – To Mr. and Mrs. Daniel Wells, of Allegany, Aug. 10th, a daughter. Weight nine pounds.

Potter County, Pennsylvania Potpourri – Volume I
1880 through 1884

Whites Corners. A great many marriages are taking place in and near this place. Charles Smith, of this place, was married to Miss May Cummings, of Harrison Valley; Elmer Downley, of West Union to Lucinda Harrington, and Miss Myra Harris to Thomas Quick, of Dennis Hill.

Whites Corners. Mrs. J. J. Smith, an old resident of this town, died at her home on Sunday July 27th. She was an obliging neighbor and was universally liked and respected. She leaves a large circle of friends to mourn their loss.

- Last week Mrs. John Rogers, of Raymond, received the sad news of the death of a sister, Mrs. Ichabod Culver, living in York State. She died suddenly of heart disease, July 28th, aged forty-eight years.

- Last week Mrs. F. B. McNamara, Jr., entered complaint before Miles White and Dan Baker, and asked for assistance from the Poor District of Coudersport. By order of the justices she was put upon the town. The overseers of the poor then had a warrant issued for her husband, for neglecting to support his family. Frank waived an examination, refused to give bail, and by order of Esq. White was lodged in Castle Worden, where he still remains.

DEMOCRATIC COUNTY CONVENTION.

The Democrats of Potter county and all persons therein opposed to Republican Rule are requested to meet at the usual places for holding Township and Borough elections in the respective townships and boroughs, on Tuesday, August 26th, 1884, between the hours of two and four o'clock p.m., to select delegates to represent them in a County Convention to be held at Coudersport, on Thursday, August 28th, at one o'clock p.m., to nominate candidates to be voted for county offices at the ensuing election, to select congressional and Senatorial conferees and to transact such other business as may property come before it. The members of the Vigilance Committees, hereafter named, are requested to be at the several places of holding elections in their respective townships and boroughs, promptly at two o'clock, on Tuesday, August 26th, to act as a board of election officers for the holding of the delegate election.

The several Townships and Boroughs are entitled to delegates as follows: Abbott 4, Allegany 3, Bingham 3, Clara 2, Coudersport 3, Eulalia 3, Genesee 4, Harrison 3, Hebron 2, Hector 2, Homer 2, Keating 2, Lewisville 2, Oswayo 3, Pike 2, Pleasant Valley 2, Portage 2, Roulet 4, Sharon 4, Sylvania 2, Sweden 4, Stewardson 2, Summit 2, Ulysses 4, West Branch 3, Wharton 3.

VIGILANCE COMMITTEE.

Abbott – Dr. Chas. Meine, Henry Gnau, August Voss.
Allegany – Chas. Coats, Isaac Striker, W. H. Scoville.
Bingham – Martin Babcock, Joel Raymond, Charles Grover.
Clara – C. W. Tauscher, Charles Tyler, Ira Fosmer.
Coudersport – W. F. Yunge, James L. Knox, J. L. Haughenberry.
Eulalia – Samuel Thompson, Dallas Benson, C. C. Breunle.
Genesee – John Hart, Amasa Ellis, J. J. Waterman.

Potter County, Pennsylvania Potpourri – Volume I
1880 through 1884

Harrison – Wm. Smith, Ham. White, Nelson Gill.
Hebron – Joseph Clear, Sr., Andrew Sandberg, Ed Meacham.
Hector – Nicholas Lambert, John W. Lewis, Rufus Corey.
Homer – Wm. White, John Gordnier, Wells Lathrop.
Keating – Thos. Glover, Joseph Coddington, Wm. Holland.
Lewisville – C. E. Burt, Geo. C. Marion, Fred Baker.
Oswayo – John Morley, George Rowley, Ed. McGonigall.
Pike – Thomas Harmon, R. L. Clark, O. Blackman.
Pleasant Valley – Robert McDowell, D. T. Yentzer.
Portage – Wm. Kaple, Charles Jacklin, Samuel Haskins.
Roulet – L. B. Burt, Jasper Card, J. R. Fessenden.
Sharon – Jacob Failing, A. M. Deremer, James Dickinson.
Sweden – Thomp. Chase, Charles Neefe, Milton White.
Stewardson – Wesley Allen, John D. Merranville.
Summit – Alonzo Reed, Hugh Haskins, James Nelson.
Sylvania – Pardon Haskins, Andrew Burleson, George Clark.
Ulysses – Charles Rees, Miles Dykeman, A. Carpenter.
West Branch – Gotleib Traub, Alphonso Burrows, John Klem.
Wharton – John Mahon, C. A. Miller, Stephen Horton.

William Dent, Chairman Co. Committee.

SCHOOL HOUSE LETTING.

The Coudersport School Board will receive proposals until noon of Saturday, 23d inst., for the erection of a School House on the East Fork. Specifications to be seen at the office of the undersigned. The board reserves the right to reject any and all bids.

Arthur B. Mann, Sec.
Coudersport, Pa., Aug. 6, 1884.

The Potter Enterprise
Wednesday Evening, August 20, 1884 – Vol. XI, No. 15

- Coudersport had an elopement last week. For some time past Bendell, the tailor, has had a young man in his employ. With this young man Mrs. B. eloped. Mr. Bendell commenced proceedings for a divorce, since which time his better half has returned. What the outcome will be remains to be seen.

The Potter Enterprise
Wednesday Evening, August 27, 1884 – Vol. XI, No. 16

DIED.

BAKER. – At Fishing Creek, Aug. 17, 1884, Mrs. Jerusha Amanda Baker, aged 25 years and 8 months.

- Laroy Lyman, of Roulet, starts for Michigan, on his annual hunt, early in September. Any hunter can obtain particulars by writing to Mr. Lyman.

- W. K. Jones evidently does not mean that thieves shall break through and steal the money deposited in the Bank of Coudersport. The walls of the vault are, we believe, four feet thick, the stones reaching clear across, laid in cement. He has recently replaced the fire proof door to the vault with one believed to be burglar proof from the Hall Lock and Safe Company. It is the finest vault door we have ever seen, and it has all the latest improvements. The first plate of the door is two inches thick of alternate layers of iron and steel. Inside the vault is a small safe for the protection of the currency, made of alternate layers of iron, soft steel and chilled steel. Thieves would have a hard time drilling or cutting open either the vault door or safe door within twelve hours working without a care for the noise they might make. The new vault door cost $800 beside the value of the fire proof door which the Company took in exchange.

- Luther Noether, of Roulette, who has been in the insane asylum at Warren, for nearly two years, has returned to his home perfectly cured. – *Reporter.*

Republican County Convention.

The republican county convention assembled in the Court House last Thursday and was called to order by Chairman Bennitt. Sol. Ross, of Wharton, was made Chairman of the convention, W. W. Harvey and D. D. Chapin secretaries.

Delegates were present from all the districts except Homer and Portage. Two residents of Homer were present and on motion allowed to act. One from Portage was admitted and allowed to cast two votes the district was entitled to.

W. W. Brown, of McKean, was recommended for Congressman, and D. C. Larrabee, of Coudersport, for State Senator, each with power to select their own conferees. For Representative the following were named: Elymus Hackett, of Genesee; Walter Wells, of Oswayo; Burt Oleson, of Stewardson. Four ballots were taken resulting in the nomination of Hackett. The ballots were as follows:

	1	2	3	4
Hackett,	38	39	39	46
Wells,	32	32	33	34
Oleson,	11	10	9	withd'n

For Prothonotary, W. A. Crosby, of Coudersport, and L. D. Ripple, of Portage, were named. Crosby was nominated on first ballot, receiving 66 votes. Ripple received 15 votes.

Erastus Lewis was nominated for Register and Recorder by acclamation.

The fight for county commissioner was a hot one and nineteen ballots were taken before it was finally settled. The following persons were named: Martin Dodge, Harrison; G. W. Bennitt, Lewisville; L. E. McCarn, Bingham; W. H. Matteson, Allegany; G. H. Lyon, Sharon; John Francis, Ulysses. Lyon was nominated on the first ballot, and Matteson on the 19th. The ballots were as follows:

	1	2	3	4	5	6	7	8	9	10
Dodge,	25	20	25	26	24	26	27	27	26	23
Bennitt,	23	7	W							

Potter County, Pennsylvania Potpourri – Volume I
1880 through 1884

McCarn,	17	10	8	W					
Matteson,	33	26	29	28	32	32	30	31	29	29
Lyon,	43								
Francis,	21	18	19	27	25	23	24	23	25	29
	11	12	13	14	15	16	17	18	19	
Dodge,	25	24	24	25	26	29	29	29	39	
Matteson,	29	29	29	29	29	29	29	33	42	
Francis,	27	28	28	27	26	23	23	18	-	

For county auditor the following were named: O. A. Kilbourne, Pike; P. W. Lawrence, Harrison; John Bodler, Abbott; H. A. Gridley, Lewisville; W. A. Grover, Ulysses.

H. A. Gridley was nominated on first ballot and P. W. Lawrence on the third. The vote was as follows:

	1	2	3
Kilbourne,	31	25	29
Lawrence,	36	33	49
Bodler,	26	12	W
Gridley,	44		
Grover,	21	10	W

On the first ballot for commissioner and auditor each delegate voted for two candidates.

The committee on resolutions, Seth Lewis, George Dodge, L. D. Estes, Geo. Colvin and Hiram Bailey, reported a set of resolutions of the stereotyped form which were adopted; the chairman of the convention and the candidates nominated were authorized to appoint a county committee, and the convention adjourned.

The Potter Enterprise
Wednesday Evening, September 3, 1884 – Vol. XI, No. 17

Clara. Mr. and Mrs. Gillian, who live on Mr. Fosmer's place, had the misfortune to lose a babe two months old, last week.

MARRIED.

SMILEY – LEWIS – At the residence of James Kibbe, in Ulysses, August 21, 1884, by A. Carpenter, Esq., Theodore Smiley, of Columbus, Ohio, and Mary Jane Lewis, of Ulysses.

DIED.

CLINTON – In Sylvania Township, August 31st, 1884, Lorisa, wife of George W. Clinton, aged 30 years and 15 days.

- Gone but not forgotten. Edward Bellus, the painter and paper hanger, who has been at work in Coudersport during the past season, is reported as being on an extended visit at Wellsville, N.Y. Nearly every business house on Main street wants to see him for sums due them, ranging from three to fifty dollars.

Democratic County Convention.

The Democratic County Convention assembled at the Court House on Thursday, August 28th, and was called to order by Chairman Dent.

Major J. M. Kilbourne was selected as Chairman of the Convention; Thos. G. Hull, of Brookland, and S. B. Haskins, of Sylvania, Secretaries; N. H. Rice of Oswayo, and John Abbott, of Roulet, Tellers.

The following delegates answered to the call of roll:

Abbott – Henry Theis, Fred Bodler, George Rexford, Fred Woelfel.
Allegany – W. H. Scoville, A. K. Weaver, Calvin Ford.
Bingham – John Raymond, J. C. Hawley, Thomas Coulston.
Coudersport – Miles White, Gus H. Grabe, T. J. Kannely.
Eulalia – Frank Phelps, F. Schadenberger, C. C. Breunle.
Genesee – Amasa Ellis, Ira Easton, John Simons, James Hill.
Hebron – Isaac Whittum.
Hector – John W. Lewis, Nicholas Lambert.
Homer – A. W. Lathrop, W. J. White.
Lewisville – George C. Marlon, W. F. Burt.
Oswayo – G. F. Rowlee, E. McGonigall, N. H. Rice.
Pike – John M. Kilbourne, C. H. Haxton, R. L. Clark.
Pleasant Valley – Robert McDowell, John McDowell.
Portage – S. B. Haskins, W. H. Chapel.
Roulet – J. R. Fessenden, Wm. Boyington, John Abbott, Sam'l Fergason.
Sharon – Jacob Failing, W. Hornsby, A. A. Mulkin, J. C. Bump.
Stewardson – Wesley Allen, Geo. W. Slarrow.
Sweden – J. W. Neefe, A. Rossman, C. Corsaw, Nelson Monroe.
Sylvania – G. C. Colegrove.
Ulysses – A. Carpenter, M. S. Crum, T. G. Hull, A. Raymond.

On motion the following committee on resolutions was appointed: Miles White, G. C. Marion, Thomas Coulston, George Rowlee and A. Carpenter.

For Representative Thomas Coulston and G. Raymond, both of Bingham, were named. Raymond was nominated on first ballot receiving 32 votes. Coulston received 23 votes.

C. E. Burt, of Lewisville, was nominated for Prothonotary by acclamation.

George Rexford, of Germania, was nominated for Register and Recorder by acclamation.

For County Commissioners the following were named: Bryan McGinnis, Genesee; C. M. Herrington, Sweden; F. A. Nelson, Allegany; J. B. Davidson, Roulet. McGinnis was nominated on third ballot, and Herrington on the seventh. The ballots were as follows:

	1	2	3	4	5	6	7
McGinnis,	24	28	30				
Herrington,	7	2	5	23	28	26	30
Nelson,	21	22	21	27	23	27	26

Potter County, Pennsylvania Potpourri – Volume I
1880 through 1884

Davidson, 4 4 - 6 5 3

For County Auditors Mason Nelson of Eulalia, and Jasper Card of Roulet were nominated by acclamation.

Miles White and W. W. Thompson were appointed Congressional Conferees, J. L. Knox and H. C. Dornan Senatorial Conferees, with power to appoint substitutes.

A resolution was passed authorizing the candidates nominated and the chairman of the convention to appoint the chairman of the county committee.

The following county committee was appointed by the delegates from the respective townships:

Abbott – Henry Theis.
Allegany – F. A. Nelson.
Bingham – J. C. Hawley.
Coudersport – Miles White.
Eulalia – Almeron Nelson.
Genesee – John Lewis.
Hebron – Isaac Whittum.
Hector – J. W. Lewis.
Homer – D. C. White.
Lewisville – E. A. Burt.
Oswayo – George F. Rowley.
Pike – Thomas Harmon.
Portage – Wm. Putnam.
Roulet – J. B. Davison.
Sharon – L. C. Kinner.
Stewardson – George Slarrow.
Sweden – J. W. Neefe.
Sylvania – G. C. Colegrove.
Ulysses – T. J. Carpenter.

The committee on resolutions reported the following which were unanimously adopted:

Resolved. That we, the delegates in convention assembled, representing the democracy of the county of Potter, hereby approve and adopt the platform of principles and the candidates, Grover Cleveland and Thomas A. Hendricks, for President and Vice President of the United States, placed thereon by the national democratic convention lately assembled at Chicago, and hereby pledge ourselves to work earnestly and zealously from this day to election to secure their triumphant election.

Resolved. That Robert E. Pattison, democratic governor of the Commonwealth, by his honest, careful and economical administration of the State affairs, and by his exemplary habits and christian character, has endeared himself to the people of the state of Pennsylvania.

Resolved. That the influential standing achieved by Hon. M. F. Elliott, as member at large in the house of representatives at Washington during the last session, has given great satisfaction to his numerous friends in all of the northern counties of the State, and we hereby recommend him as the democratic candidate in this congressional district, at the November election.

Resolved. That in the many pension laws introduced and passed by the democratic house in congress for the benefit of our soldiers who lost their health in fighting the battles of the Union, we recognize in the democratic party a most earnest friends of the soldier.

Resolved. That the candidates placed in nomination by this convention will receive our active co-operation and support, that all honorable means shall be used to secure their election.

The Potter Enterprise
Wednesday Evening, September 10, 1884 – Vol. XI, No. 18

Fishing Creek. Solon Scheaver says his clothes are all too small and that he will have to get No. 14 boots for it is a boy.

- About the first of August last, as many of our readers will remember, some cattle belonging to Daniel Smith, of Roulet, were driven to the Forest House where they were killed by the cars. The cattle were driven off by Milton Smith and Wm. White. The former was arrested and held to bail, White skipped over in New York State but was induced to return recently. On his return Wm. Sherwood was arrested for being concerned in the matter. An examination was had before Miles White Monday evening. White swore that Sherwood had agreed to give the two 55 cents to drive the cattle to the Forest House and said that if the cattle returned he would give them five dollars to drive the cattle "to Emporium or Hell." Sherwood was held to bail in the sum of $200 for his appearance at Court.

- Last Saturday night some miscreant visited the barn of Frank Phelps, in Lymansville, and cut a harness to pieces. The burs were removed from a lumber wagon and a platform. The strap on the neckyoke was cut, and the draw bolt on the lumber wagon was thrown into the woods near the barn. Some one ought to take a trip to Allegheny City for a year or two.

- Last week we mentioned the fact that Edward Bellus had left some of his creditors in the lurch. An attachment was put on his goods remaining in Coudersport. Bellus returned and had the attachment dissolved. Bellus, his son and Wm. Dingman were then arrested charged with conspiracy to defraud. An examination was had before Miles White and all the parties held to bail. Edward Bellus failed to find any one willing to go his security and he was lodged in jail.

The Potter Enterprise
Wednesday Evening, September 17, 1884 – Vol. XI, No. 19

- Horace Peet of Allegany is happy over a new born heir.

- Born – September 11th, at Olmsteds, to Mr. and Mrs. Albert Reed, a daughter, weight six pounds.

- Dan Glassmire is setting up the cigars to the boys this morning. A ten pound boy is the cause of his rejoicing.

MARRIED.
NELSON – MORGAN – At the M. E. Parsonage, in Coudersport, Sept. 4th, by Rev. A. A. Craw, Mr. Delmar Nelson and Miss Ocea Morgan, both of Allegany, Pa.

MATTISON – STRYKER – At the American Hotel, in Coudersport, Sept. 11th, by Rev. A. A. Craw, Mr. Wm. Mattison and Miss Marcia Stryker, both of Allegany, Pa.

HOWE – BRYANT – At the Nichols House in Coudersport, Pa., on Monday, Sept. 15th, 1884, by Rev. A. Cone, Mr. C. W. Howe, of Ulysses, to Miss Cora Bryant, of Oswayo.

GRAVES – LENT – At the residence of the bride's parents, in Hebron, Sept. 11th, 1884, by H. S. Lent, Esq., Mr. James L. Graves, of Willing, Allegany county, N.Y., to Miss Cora M. Lent, of Hebron, Pa.

South Coudersport. The infant child of John Golding died at the house of H. Schildberger last week. It was buried in the Coudersport cemetery.

The Potter Enterprise
Wednesday Evening, September 24, 1884 – Vol. XI, No. 20

- Miss Edna Haughenberry entertained a number of her young friends last Friday. It being her sixth birthday.

MARRIED.
RYCRAFT – WALES – At Keating Summit, Sept. 18th, 1884, by Rev. W. S. Holland, John H. Rycraft, of Canadea, N.Y., and Miss Cora B. Wales, of Freeman Run, Pa.

Odin. The infant child of George Wetsel, of Keating Summit, was buried here last Sunday.

- Last Tuesday morning about three o'clock Fred Woelfel's saw and grist mill, near Germania, was burned to the ground. A large quantity of lumber, including, probably, the finest stock of cherry in the county, also burned. The loss is very heavy, with no insurance.

Court Minutes.
Court convened September 15th, present a full bench.

F. B. Sherman appointed foreman of Grand Jury; J. D. Earle Constable in charge of same. Grand Jury discharged September 18th.

Commonwealth vs R. M. Post, Defendant discharged.

Comth vs Benjamin Green, assault and battery, deft discharged.

W. B. Brightman admitted to practice in the several courts of Potter county.

Comth vs A. J. Wagoner, perjury, bail $600 for appearance at next Term.

Geo. A. Barclay vs G. W. Huntley, et al, summons amended, damages claimed $3,000.

Comth vs P. C. Witter, maliciously leaving down fences, true bill, bail $100.

Comth vs Porter H. Clark, rape, jury failed to agree, bail $1,200 for appearance at next term.

Malinda C. Woodcock vs Lehman L. Woodcock, H. A. Gridley appointed commissioner to take testimony.

Marshall Stryker vs Mary E. Stryker, sub in divorce awarded.

Comth vs Patrick Carey, selling liquor, bail forfeited and respited.

In the matter of the alleged lunacy of Geo. C. Rossiter, M. Colcord appointed a commissioner to take testimony.

Comth vs Wm. Sherwood, malicious mischief, true bill, bail $400.

Comth vs Wm. Sherwood and Milton Smith, not a true bill, county to pay costs.

Comth vs Milton Smith, malicious mischief, true bill, continued.

Michael Slaven vs Alfred Costello & Co., summons amended and case continued.

T. A. Morrison, of McKean county bar, admitted to practice in several courts of Potter county.

Clara L. King vs Henry T. King, sub in divorce awarded.

Samuel Beebe appointed guardian of Fred and Jessie Prindle, minor children of Elizabeth Prindle, bail $500 in each.

Comth vs O. L. Hall, assault and battery, not a true bill, county to pay costs.

Mary Ann Dougherty vs Daniel Dougherty, divorce awarded.

Comth vs James Impson, Reuben Hess and Washington Campbell, nuisance &c., true bill, bail in each $100.

Comth vs Henry F. Moyer, fornication and bastardy, true bill, bail forfeited.

Comth vs Geo. Brizzee, assault and battery, true bill, bail $200.

Comth vs Ryan Miller, assault and battery, discharged from prison by order of court.

Annie Burns vs James A. Burns, divorce granted.

Comth vs Herman Froebel et al, larceny, plead guilty, bail $100 for appearance at next term.

Charles N. Kilbourne appointed guardian of Angelina, Eva and John Kilbourne, minor children of Esther Kilbourne, deceased, bonds $1,000.

Thomas Garrity, a native of Ireland, admitted to citizenship.

James McIntyre, a native of Ireland, admitted to citizenship.

Comth vs Kenrad Britling, pointing a gun, bail $250.

John M. Bruhn, a native of Germany, admitted to citizenship.

Comth vs Charles Cowburn, selling liquor, discharged.

Comth vs George Bellus and Wm. Dingman, conspiracy, nol pros, defts discharged.

Potter County, Pennsylvania Potpourri – Volume I
1880 through 1884

Comth vs W. T. Jones, selling liquor, not a true bill, county to pay costs.

Comth vs Daniel P. Reed, assault and battery, not a true bill, prosecutor to pay costs.

Comth vs George Hoffman, assault and battery, not a true bill, pl'ff to pay costs.

Ordered that the electors of Stewardson, on the 4th of November, vote upon the question of changing place of election to the public house of W. G. Elliott, near mouth of Cross Fork.

Ordered that the electors of Hector, on the 4th of November, vote upon the question of changing the place of election to the school house near S. H. Carr's.

May A. Ackerman vs Samuel Ackerman, Charles H. Cole appointed commissioner to take testimony.

Cora Burrows vs C. J. Burrows, A. B. Mann appointed commissioner to take testimony.

Sally J. Wetmore vs Nathan Wetmore, sub in divorce awarded.

Fred'k Mosier vs Johanna Mosier, sub in divorce awarded.

W. I. Lewis appointed auditor to distribute funds in hands of A. J. Barnes, administrator of estate of John Dawley, deceased.

S. H. Manley vs G. W. King et al, jury find for plaintiff in sum of $18.50 and costs.

Matilda Hill vs Myron F. Hill, divorce awarded.

Ruth E. Reaser vs Delos E. Reaser, divorce awarded.

John Brisbois, a native of Canada, admitted to citizenship.

Levi Harris, a native of Russia, admitted to citizenship.

John Moran, a native of Ireland, admitted to citizenship.

Comth vs Richard Kilduff, bail $100 for appearance at next term.

Comth vs Peleg Burdic, selling liquor, sentenced to pay a fine of $75 and costs.

Comth vs Frank McNamara, desertion, sentenced by the court to pay the sum of $3 per week to the overseers of the poor of Coudersport borough, for the support of his wife and children; bail for performance of same, $500, also to pay costs of prosecution, and to be committed to county jail until sentence is complied with.

F. N. Newton appointed auditor to distribute balance in hands of Laura Newton, admin'x of estate of B. F. Jones, deceased.

Joseph H. Hall vs John Brownlee and Thomas Brownlee, rule to show cause why venire should not be removed to Cameron county, returnable at next term.

Final account of Seth Lewis, assignee of Burtis & Potter, filed, to be presented for final confirmation Jan. 5th.

W. I. Lewis, H. C. Dornan and John Omerod appointed a committee to report upon the advisability of adopting the court rules of McKean county.

Ordered that the next term of court be fixed for the first Monday in January next, and that veniries be issued for 48 traverse and 24 grand jurors.

Dan Baker appointed auditor to settle with the Prothonotary and Register and Recorder.

Potter County, Pennsylvania Potpourri – Volume I
1880 through 1884

Comth vs Edward McGonigall, selling liquor, sentenced to pay a fine of $75 and costs.

E. S. Worden, Sheriff of Potter county, acknowledged deeds as follows:

To Clark W. Beach, for 25 acres in Hector, for $25, sold as property of Henry R. Hess.

To Bingham Estate, for 134 acres in Sweden, for $50, sold as property of L. A. Glase.

D. L. Raymond, Treasurer of Potter county, acknowledged about 140 deeds for lands sold as taxes.

The Potter Enterprise
Wednesday Evening, October 1, 1884 – Vol. XI, No. 21

Fishing Creek. The infant daughter of George Stillwell died on the 12th inst., aged four months and twelve days.

- Dr. A. French, of Coudersport, has just added one more to his list of over two thousand births during his practice of forty-six years in Potter county. This time it is to Mr. A. Sidney Lyman and wife and is a boy. Weight 10 ¼ pounds.

Forest House. There was a rather hasty wedding here the other day. The happy couple made arrangements with the Preacher to meet them at the station and perform the ceremony just before train time. The Rev. was a little behind time, and the train whistled when he arrived, but he was equal to the occasion and made them one and sent them on life's journey rejoicing. Mr. John Rycraft of this place and Miss Cora Wales of Freeman Run were the happy parties.

MARRIED.

McKEE – REYNOLDS – On Sept. 17th by and at the residence of Rev. J. L. Swain, Mr. George H. McKee, of Hebron, to Miss Junie A. Reynolds, of Allegany.

DIED.

GREEN – In Allegany, Sept. 23d, Mr. Clark Green, aged 77 years.

SNYDER – At his residence, on Ayers Hill, Sept. 18th, George W. Snyder, aged 48 years.

Mr. Snyder was born in Sparta, Livingston county, N.Y., and while yet a small boy, removed with his parents to Potter county, where he has since resided. George was always pleasant and he will be sadly missed by many friends in this section, where he has always lived, and where he was so well known. He leaves a wife and two small children to mourn their loss, and many more distant relatives and friends who will sadly miss him.

DODD – In Sweden, Pa., Sept. 27th, 1884, Mrs. Rebecca, wife of Sherman Dodd, aged 20 years.

Mrs. Dodd was born in East Wharton, Potter county, Dec. 30th, 1863, where she lived with her parents until about four years ago, at the age of sixteen, she was united in marriage with Mr. Sherman Dodd, of Sweden Valley, with whom she lived until her death.

About two years ago consumption marked her as a victim, and last Saturday, after a painful struggle, the disease won the victory and she passed peacefully to rest. Her funeral services were attended by a large assemblage of relatives and friends at the Sweden Valley M. E. church, on Sunday, Sept. 28th. Her remains were deposited in the Coudersport cemetery. She was much beloved and will be greatly missed.

- On Friday last a child of Chas. McCarty, aged about twenty months, was accidentally shot while sitting at the breakfast table. It seems that Mr. and Mrs. McCarty were, at the time, staying at James Reed's, in Summit, and on the morning in question Fred Rees, a lad about fourteen years old, went into the house and while there saw a shot gun which he took down and proceeded to load,, and in the operation, the gun, as usual, went off, the charge passing between McCarty and wife striking the child in the face and head. Dr. Buck was immediately summoned and, upon examination, found that three shot had penetrated the brain, and it was feared, at the time, that the child could not live, but at this writing, although one side is paralyzed, there is strong hopes of its recovery.

The Cyclone of Sunday Evening.

On Sunday last at about five o'clock p.m., a storm of a peculiar character visited this section.

About fifteen miles south of Bradford it appeared a black funnel shaped cloud moving with terrific force. The track of the storm was not more than five rods wide. But on either side for a half a mile in width, the country was strewn with huge hemlocks torn up by the roots and carried away. Debris of all kinds was scattered here and there.

At Alton, south of Bradford, it demolished seven houses; causing great peril to the inhabitants but killed no one. Several were seriously injured but none mortally wounded. It went towards Olean but did no serious injury in that region.

Another vein, not so destructive, came nearer to us. It unroofed the barn of Mr. A. Sherwood, of Eulalia, and did some other damage there. Then it laid low a piece of heavy timber on the height south of Coudersport. Then it struck the timber on the hill east of Lymansville. Next it unroofed the barn of C. M. Herrington, in Sweden. The path of this vein of wind was nearly due east.

But the Bradford cyclone did not cease its destructive work when it passed east of Olean. Though along its track was little more than a severe storm, it came down upon the little village of Shongo, N.Y., with all its force. The main part of the village was instantly a mass of ruins. Forty-two buildings, of all kinds, were destroyed together with all of their contents. The families are left in great need. Two persons were killed instantly and thirty-one others were injured, some fatally.

The injured ones were carried to the flouring mill, which remained intact. The physicians of Wellsville were sent for and hastened to the scene. All that could be done was willingly done to relieve the wounded.

The families were deprived of everything which their homes contained. They need shelter, bedding, clothing and food for the coming winter.

East of Shongo the storm seems to have ceased its havoc until it struck Wellsburg, east of Elmira. In that place it unroofed buildings, blew off chimneys, tore up shade and fruit trees and filled the streets with debris. Several persons were wounded by flying boards, but none killed.

This cyclone was the severest that has visited this region for many years. Outside of the narrow veins of the cyclone the rain fell in torrents. The hail fell in large quantities. The wind was in many places equivalent to a tornado.

THE COUNTY FAIR.
List of Premiums Awarded and to Whom.

On the whole the Fair Association was blessed with good weather, and a fair attendance so that the Society will be a little ahead this year.

The exhibit of stock was not as good as last year although there were many fine animals present.

The show of the agricultural implements, wagons, &c., was very good, but very little of it was entered for premiums as the only premium offered was a "diploma."

The fruit crop in Potter is very light and as a matter of course the display was light.

The ladies department was the best seen for years and was a credit to the fair sex.

Below we give a list of premiums awarded:

Class 1 – Horses.

First Premium – J. W. Allen, draft stallion, and trotting stallion, over 3 yrs; Walter Wells, stallion, 3 yr; F. A. Nelson, colt 3 yrs and sucking colt; Almeron Nelson, colt 2 yrs; B. Rennells, colt 1 yr; W. H. Neefe, pair draft horses; W. W. Benson, single carriage horse, brood mare and colt; L. L. Lay, horse or mare for speed; W. Snyder, farm and road team.

Second Premium – Geo. McGowan, draft stallion; B. Rennells, colt 2 yrs; M. O. Harris, colt 3 yrs; E. A. Wagner, single carriage horse; C. W. Gorham, farm and road team; F. A. Nelson, brood mare and colt.

Class 2 – Cattle.

First Premium – Sylvester Greenman, 3 yr old Holstein bull; C. W. Dingee, Aldemy bull 3 yrs; C. W. Gorham, Holstein and Durham bull, 2 yrs; J. W. Allen, Aldemy bull, 1 yr, Aldemy cow; M. O. Harris, grade Durham, 1 yr, grade Durham cow; W. W. Benson, bull calf; E. G. Crane, heifer, 2 yrs; F. H. Chappel, heifer Grade Durham, 1 yr; Mortimer Benson, yoke oxen; Arthur Gordnier, steers 3 yrs; Fordyce C. Gorham, steers 2 yrs.

Second Premium – S. W. Baker, grade Durham cow; E. G. Crane, grade Aldemy cow; Mrs. M. E. Barnes, grade Durham calf; Jerome Knickerbocker, yoke oxen; Nelson Woodcock, steers, 2 yrs.

Class 3 – Sheep.

First Premium – J. P. Lehman, Shropshire buck and pair of lambs; H. S. Lent, Cottswold; Almeron Nelson, merino; S. W. Baker, grade Cottswold and pair of ewes; M. O. Harris, buck lamb.

Second – M. O. Harris, lot of lambs; S. W. Baker, buck lamb.

Class 4 – Hogs.

First Premium – W. W. Benson, best sow; H. S. Lent, lot of pigs.

Second – H. S. Lent, sow.

Class 5 – Poultry.

First Premium – A. F. Hollenbeck, trio; Edward Gillon, coop.

Second – Mrs. M. A. Dingman, display; Mrs. S. A. Sechrest, trio.

Class 6 – Dairy.

First Premium – W. H. Neefe, tub, roll.

Second – O. M. Kelly, tub, roll.

Third – Sylvester Greenman, tub; Dallas Benson, roll.

Class 7 – Grain.

First Premium – H. and M. J. Young, acre of oats; Wm. Cunningham, ½ bu buckwheat; C. Schadenberger, acre of corn; Z. J. Thompson, sweet corn.

Class 8 – Fruit.

First Premium – Albert Colcord, display; P. A. Stebbins, winter apples; G. M. Butler, fall apples.

Second – A. H. Lewis, display.

Class 9 – Vegetables.

First Premium – Frank Stebbins, display; S. W. Baker, cabbage; H. S. Lent, beets, carrots; Mrs. W. I. Lewis, celery; Z. J. Thompson, ½ bu potatoes; C. Schadenberger, acre of potatoes; J. P. Lehman, bu onions, mammoth and yellow pumpkins, rutabagas; L. R. Toombs, turnips, squashes; J. W. Allen, parsnips.

Second – Mrs. J. W. Allen, display carrots, squashes; Dallas Benson, cabbage, beets; Wm. Bonnawits, ½ bu potatoes; F. S. Kirkpatrick, onions; O. M. Kelly, turnips; M. O. Harris, mammoth pumpkins; A. B. Peet, yellow pumpkins.

Class 10 – Agricultural Implements.

Diploma – L. W. Crawford, broad cast seeder, harvester and cultivator combined.

Mechanical.

Diploma – E. K. Potter, milk strainer; A. A. Allen, Domestic and New Home sewing machines; Wm. Dingman, whip lashes, whip stalks; C. H. Armstrong & Co., display of boots and shoes.

Class 12 – Domestic Manufacture.

First premium – Mrs. Geo. Nelson, rag carpet, stocking yarn; Mrs. Sarah Chase, woolen stockings; Mrs. M. A. Dingman, woolen mittens; Mrs. Wm. Cunningham, woolen sheets, ladies stockings; Mrs. W. W. Benson, pieced quilt; Mrs. F. A. Hammond, patchwork quilt; Mrs. F. A. Nelson, carpet coverlet; O. M. Kelly, woolen gloves; Odolph Menschal, quilt.

Second – Mrs. Lydia Adams, rag car-pieced quilt; S. W. Baker, stocking yarn, woolen stockings; M. A. Dingman, flannel sheets; B. A. McClure, patchwork quilt.

Culinary Articles.

First premium – Mrs. P. L. Boyington, wheat bread, biscuit; Wm. Cunningham, maple syrup, maple sugar; S. A. Sechrest, berry jelly, mixed pickles; C. A. Stebbins, greatest variety of canned fruit; M. Rounseville, canned corn, chowchow grapes.

Second – Mrs. O. A. Nelson, canned corn.

Embroidery, Fancy Work &c.

First premium – Mrs. F. A. Nelson, crochet tidy, embroidered tidy; S. V. Glassmire, hearth rug; M. Rounseville, hand knit woolen shawl; J. C. Green, knit edging; Mary A. Dingman, Afghan tidy; O. A. Nelson, wool java canvass tidy; Anna Reuning, knit tidy; W. W. Thompson, crochet shoulder cape, embroidered lambrequin, embroidered splasher; S. A. Phillips, cashmere shawl crochet border, table spread, fancy cushion; F. Hammond, crochet fascinator, apron, toilet set; August Gross, child's dress, child's jacket; E. W. Hamilton, canvass tidy, cotton tidy; Carrie White, stand spread, feather flowers, embroidered towels, pallet board; B. A. McClure, applique qork, lambrequin, plaque, clock cover, panel; Geo. Nelson, lamp mat; R. V. & I. Schadenberger, exhibit of millinery; P. A. Boyington, macrame.

Second – Mrs. L. G. Niver, crochet tidy, lambrequin; Geo. Nelson, knit edging; E. W. Hamilton, canvas tidy; Anna Reuning, knit tidy; Carrie White, fancy table spread; F. Hammond, stand spread, fancy curtain; W. W. Thompson, banner.

Flowers.

First premium – Mrs. G. V. Glassmire, flower ornament; B. A. McClure, house plants and flowers.

Second – Mrs. G. V. Glassmire, plants and flowers.

Art, &c.

First premium – Ezra Allen, insects of Potter county; Mrs. W. A. Crobsy, oil painting, landscape; E. A. Bliss, oil painting, general; Amy White, crayon portrait; L. R. Bliss, selection of photographs; L. A. Glase, architectural drawing; W. I. Lewis, mineral and geological specimens, trout flies; W. W. Thompson, bleached ferns.

Second – Mrs. W. W. Thompson, oil painting, general.

Stoves and Tin Ware.

Diploma – J. W. Prentis, steam cooker.

Persons not receiving their premiums in thirty days are requested to send postoffice address to W. K. Jones, treasurer, Coudersport, Pa.

Above report subject to correction of errors.

Arthur B. Mann, Secretary.

– A serious accident occurred at the Fair on Wednesday afternoon. Thomas Clarrendon, of Oswayo, gave an exhibition of bicycle riding, and made a trip around the track to see what time he could make. Just as he passed under the wire Hugh Burt, of Roulet, attempted to cross the track; a collision occurred and both men went to the ground. Mr. Clarrendon was severely hurt and for some time remained unconscious. He was removed to the residence of C. A. Stebbins, and a few days afterwards to Oswayo. He is improving but is still lame from injuries to his back. Last Spring he received a broken arm by a fall from a bicycle. Hugh Burt was severely bruised and had three ribs broken. He is getting along as well as could be expected.

The Potter Enterprise
Wednesday Evening, October 8, 1884 – Vol. XI, No. 22

West Homer. Born, on Sept. 26th, to Mr. and Mrs. O. L. Hall, a girl. On Oct. 5th, to Mr. and Mrs. Adam Hartwick, a boy.

Hammonds. Mr. Amel Karnickle was married to a lady, just over from Germany, on Saturday of last week, and after the wedding they had a nice little dance. Those that attended enjoyed it very much.

MARRIED.

HOLLY – LUNN – In Sharon, Sept. 28th, by Rev. H. P. Burdick, Alonzo A. Holly and Miss Hellen Lunn.

- The little daughter of Charles McCarty, who was accidentally shot, as reported in the Enterprise last week, is still alive and strong hopes are entertained of her recovery.

- James Fassett, an employee in the Harrison Valley tannery, had the misfortune to lose $180 last Thursday. He is a faithful, saving and dependent laborer. For fear that he might lose this money in his pocketbook he procured a pouch and fastened it around his neck, placed nine $20 bills in it and carried it that way for several days. On Thursday he discovered that he had neither the money nor pouch. A search was made in the tannery but no clue was found. – *Free Press*.

- The Court House is sadly in need of repairs. There are a number of windows broken, the steps have settled out of shape, the plastering in the court room is far from ornamental, up stairs the walls are covered with pencil and charcoal marks and sketches. It is a disgrace to the county. The court house presents a very dilapidated appearance. The Commissioners have done some good work, putting in fire-proof vaults, for instance, but they need to do more. The steps of the jail also need re-laying, and the pointing of the east wall is falling out. Gentlemen, the county expects that you will keep the county property from going to ruin. It is your duty and you know it. Why don't you attend to it?

The Potter Enterprise
Wednesday Evening, October 15, 1884 – Vol. XI, No. 23

- John Denhoff is setting up the cigars for the boys, and all on account of this new boy. Weight ten pounds.

Potter County, Pennsylvania Potpourri – Volume I
1880 through 1884

MARRIED.

DICKENS – BREESE – At the residence of the bride's mother, in West Pike, Pa., Oct. 1st, 1884, by J. M. Kilbourne, Esq., George Dickens, of Hector, and Miss Jessie Breeze, lately of Horseheads, N.Y.

MUNGER – SEALS – At the U. B. Parsonage, Millport, Pa., Oct. 6th, 1884, by Rev. E. L. Miller, Wm. R. Munger, of Millport, and Cinda L. Seals, of Clara.

RAMSEY – OLMSTED – At Brookland, Pa., by Thomas G. Hull, esq., Frank Ramsey, of Portville, Cattaraugus county, N.Y., to Mrs. Annis Olmsted, of North Fork, Pa.

FORSYTH – CARY – In Port Allegany, October 6th, by Rev. J. B. Wright, Leon L. Forsyth to Sarah A. Cary, both of Roulet.

- Ann C. Haven, wife of Samuel Haven, died at her home in Coudersport, on Friday morning last. Mrs. Haven was born in Albany, N.Y., Sept. 9th, 1819, and came to Coudersport in 1835, nearly fifty years ago. Forty-eight years ago she was united in marriage with Samuel Haven who survives her. Four children were born to them, all of whom are still living. For several years Mrs. Haven has suffered from a cancer which finally ended her days. One of the old citizens of Coudersport has passed away and one that will be missed, more perhaps, by the older people of the place than by the younger ones. The older ones knowing more of her kind acts, before illness called for care to her. Mrs. Haven was always ready to attend the sick and the afflicted, and her pleasant nature was as grateful to the sick as her kind ministrations.

- Lewis Yentzer, of Roulet, has harvested 445 bushels of buckwheat and 1,400 bushels of oats, getting his crops in before the rains of October. Mr. Yentzer, one day last week, dug sixty bushels of potatoes, not counting the little ones.

Potter County, Pennsylvania Potpourri – Volume I
1880 through 1884

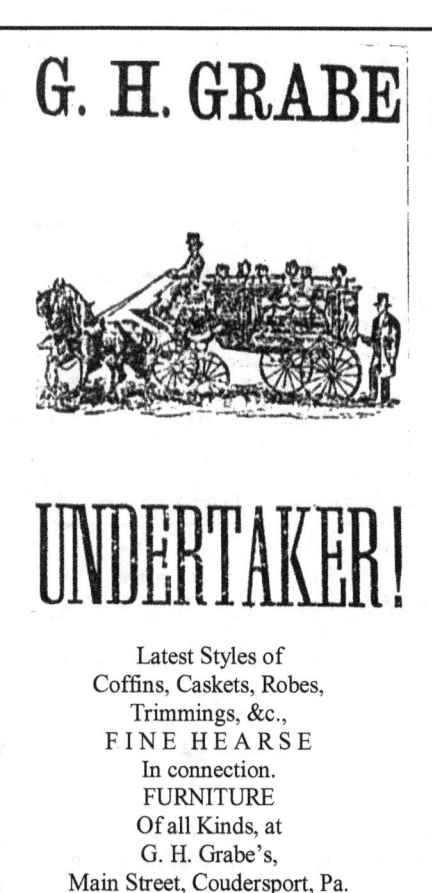

G. H. GRABE

UNDERTAKER!

Latest Styles of
Coffins, Caskets, Robes,
Trimmings, &c.,
FINE HEARSE
In connection.
FURNITURE
Of all Kinds, at
G. H. Grabe's,
Main Street, Coudersport, Pa.

The Potter Enterprise
Wednesday Evening, October 22, 1884 – Vol. XI, No. 24

- Born – To Mr. and Mrs. Lester Watson, of Ayer's Hill, October 21, a daughter.

White's Corners. Mr. John Riley and Miss Fannie Statham were married a short time ago. John has a housekeeper now.

Notice.

Whereas my wife Nancy Marble has left my bed and board without just cause or provocation, I hereby forbid anyone trusting or harboring her on my account, as I will pay no debts of her contracting unless compelled by law.

Aaron Marble.
Whites Corners, Pa., Oct. 16, 1884.

BAKERY!
ARTHUR BUCK, Proprietor.
At the old stand recently occupied by W. T. Dike.
Fresh Bread, Cakes, Rolls, Crackers
&c., constantly on hand.
OYSTERS!
First Class in any quantity. Also Served at the Bakery in all styles.
LUNCH ROOM!
Lunch Served at All Hours, with Tea or Coffee.

The Potter Enterprise
Wednesday Evening, October 29, 1884 – Vol. XI, No. 25

- Born – In Hebron, October 26, to Mr. and Mrs. Robert Booth, a son, weight ten pounds.

- Mr. John Calkins is happy over the arrival at his house on Saturday last of a little ten pounder.

Ellisburg. W. H. Lewis comes and marries Mary Plants Kelley and takes her to North Carolina and leaves one less chance for the young men.

MARRIED.
BALL – HIGLEY – In Hebron, Oct. 25th, 1884, by Sylvester Greenman, Esq., Mr. Lewis R. Ball and Miss M. Luella Higley, all of Hebron, Pa.
SHAY – LEACH – At the residence of Rev. J. L. Swain, Oct. 5th, 1884, by Rev. J. L. Swain, Michael J. Shay and Miss Hannah M. Leach.
LEWIS – KELLEY – At the residence of Marcus Webster, Oct. 26th, 1884, by Rev. J. L. Swain, Wm. H. H. Lewis and Mrs. Mary Kelley.

DIED.
GURNSEY – On Friday, October 10th, 1884, Mrs. Sarah Jane, wife of H. H. Gurnsey, aged 54 years.

- On Sunday last Harlan E. Brown died at Oswayo. He was taken sick about two weeks previous and for a time was reported dangerously ill, then came the news that he was better, to be followed Sunday by the news of his death. Harlan was in his 25th year. For some time he was a clerk in C. H. Armstrong's store, and for the past year was deputy postmaster and clerk for M. S. Thompson & Co. He was a young man of good habits, correct and prompt in all business matters, and made friends with all whom he met. We doubt if there was a young man in Coudersport with more friends and less enemies than Mr. Brown. He was a member of Eulalia Lodge No. 342 F. & A. M. About forty members of the craft followed the remains to their final resting place. From Coudersport about twenty masons were present. The solemn funeral service of the order was performed at the grave under the direction of W. K. Jones, W. M. of Eulalia Lodge. The display of flowers from friends of the deceased was large. The funeral was the largest ever seen in Oswayo. The memory of Harlan will long be cherished by his many friends here and at Oswayo.

The Potter Enterprise
Wednesday Evening, November 5, 1884 – Vol. XI, No. 26

MARRIED.

FINCH – FERNER – At the residence of the bride's father, on Freeman Run, Pa., Nov. 1st, 1884, by J. W. Thorne, esq., Albert E. Finch, of Addison, N.Y., and Miss Hittie E. Ferner, of Freeman Run.

West Homer. Tin wedding at the house of O. D. Crosby, the 29th inst., but on account of the rain but few were present.

DIED.

WYKOFF – At East Homer, Oct. 8, 1884, Charley, son of A. J. and Martha Wykoff. Aged 6 years, 4 months and 24 days.

- The friends of Mr. and Mrs. L. D. Horton, of Coudersport, will extend their sympathies to them at this time in their affliction. On Tuesday last their infant child died after a long illness.

- On Sunday last A. Bisbee, of West Branch, was laid to rest in the Crippen cemetery, West Branch township. Mr. Bisbee was one of the old citizens of the township and one of its most prominent men. For many years he has been clerk in the township and has held other important offices at the hands of his fellow citizens. The funeral services were conducted by the officers and members of Eulalia Lodge No. 342, A. & F. M., of which organization he was a member for many years.

Jury List – January Term, 1885.
GRAND JURORS.

Abbott – Henry Gressel; Allegany – Sanford Downs, O. S. Ford; Bingham – M. W. Briggs; Coudersport – H. J. Olmsted, Nelson Penny; Clara – J. C. Moffatt; Harrison – M. Pritchard; Hebron – W. L. Campbell, W. A. Earle, C. A.

Stilson; Hector – Jas. L. Douglas, J. W. Lewis, James Mallory; Lewisville – Charles Bailey, Geo. H. Cobb; Oswayo – Romeo Estes; Roulet – James Brooks, Fred Earnest; Sharon – Seth Drake, G. W. Dodge; Portage – D. A. Everett, L. D. Ripple; Ulysses – Alvin Johnson.

TRAVERSE JURORS.

Abbott – Geo. Rexford; Allegany – J. L. Cady, W. A. Gardner, W. H. Neefe; Bingham – I. P. Grover, J. H. Holbert, James Hamilton; Coudersport – I. P. Collins, J. L. Haughenberry, C. J. Marble; Clara – W. A. Cole; Eulalia – Wallace Abson, L. A. Glace; Genesee – Richard Ellis, Frank Ludden, Martin Moran; Harrison – D. P. Burley, Eli Bartoo, A. E. Holcomb, Chester Stone; Hebron – Edward Clair, Charles Davis, Henry Lamberton; Hector – R. S. Crippen, C. S. Rushmore; Keating – Charles Briggs, W. J. Templeton; Lewisville – E. R. Eddy; Oswayo – Albert Bryant, Alphonso Harris, F. W. Slaughter, A. G. Wells; Pike – Wallace Mattison; Pleasant Valley – John L. Yenzter; Roulet – Charles Maltby; Sharon – Wallace Burdick, Albert Mulkin, Horace Pearsall; Sweden – Clark Chase; Sylvania – A. J. Burleson, George Clinton, E. A. Jordan; Wharton – Ira Barclay, Orrin Courtright, J. M. Walker; West Branch – H. J. Deisroth, Oscar Fowler, Gustavus Gross.

Notice.

Whereas my wife, Francis Harris, has left my bed and board without just cause or provocation, I hereby forbid all persons trusting or harboring her on my account as I will pay no debts of her contracting after this date unless compelled by law.

O. E. Harris.

Sweden, Oct. 27th, 1884.

The Potter Enterprise
Wednesday Evening, November 12, 1884 – Vol. XI, No. 27

MARRIED.

GROM – LIMRINGER – At Lymansville, Pa., Nov. 1st, 1884, by Frank Phelps, Esq., Fred Grom and Eliza Limringer, all of Coudersport.

STILLMAN – WORDEN – Oct. 30th, 1884, at the residence of A. A. Howe in Lewisville, by Rev. W. Miller, Mr. C. M. Stillman and Miss Ella Worden, both of Lewisville.

WETMORE – SAUNDERS – In Roulet, Oct. 28th, 1884, by Elder J. G. Saunders, Loredo W. Wetmore, of Liberty, McKean county, and Miss Amy S. Saunders, of Roulet, Pa.

PRITCHARD – EVANS – At the M. E. parsonage in Nelson, Pa., Monday, Nov. 3, 1884, by Rev. J. Scoville, M. B. Pritchard, M.D., of Harrison Valley, Pa., and Miss Nettie L. Evans, of Lawrenceville, Pa.

> **CHAS. REISSMAN**
> Has added a New
> H E A R S E
> To his Undertaking Department and
> takes pride in announcing to his
> customers that he will serve
> with it, within the borough
> of Coudersport
> FREE OF CHARGE
> and only Moderate Charges will be
> made for drives in the country.
> He will, henceforth, keep a full and
> complete stock of
> Coffins, Caskets, Robes
> Etc., constantly on hand, and invites
> his friends to call and examine. His
> Furniture
> Stock is also more complete than ever
> before, and any one wishing to buy
> can positively save money by
> purchasing from him, as
> he sells
> TEN PER CENT. CHEAPER
> Than any dealer in neighboring towns.

The Potter Enterprise
Wednesday Evening, November 19, 1884 – Vol. XI, No. 28

Clara. Leon Tyler had a birthday party last week. Don't remember the date, anyway they played a play that Mr. Keller don't want to play any more.

MARRIED.

GURNSEY – SMITH – At the residence of the bride's parents, on Nov. 2d, 1884, by the Rev. E. D. Carr, Walter W. Gurnsey and Miss Satie E. Smith, both of Ulysses.

Hebron. I am sorry I did not get around to tell you about the silver wedding at Sylvester Greenman's. It was several weeks ago but it is talked about yet as one of *the* events of the year. About 150 guests were present and as they all came laden with some gift, their presence will be gratefully remembered. An elegant dinner was provided all went merry as a marriage bell.

- Mrs. Julia Hill died this week of cancer, at the home of her son, Nathan Hill. She was a great sufferer and at an advanced age, and must have considered it a joyful thing to lay down her worn out mortal body and put on that new one "not made with hands, eternal, and in the heavens."

- Mrs. Joseph Schwartzenbach, of Germania, was buried on Sunday last. For nearly a year she had been a great sufferer with dropsy. The funeral was the largest ever held in Germania, friends from far and near turning out to honor the memory of one who will long be remembered in Abbott township.

Arrested for Murder.

Some time ago an old man named Edward Hughes was shot and killed by his son Michael, near Pen Yan, Yates county, N.Y. The unnatural son waylaid his father and shot him seven times. The cries of the victim, for mercy, were heard for half a mile. The son took to the woods supposing that his father was dead, but the latter recovered sufficiently to tell the story. The object of the shooting was to get the old man's money and it is said to have been instigated by the boy's mother. For a short time a man has been at work in the woods in Pike township bearing the description of Michael Hughes. Papers were taken out for his arrest and S. A. Mundy arrested the man last week. The supposed Hughes had a seven shot revolver with him at the time, and the general belief is that the right man has been nabbed. A reward of $300 had been offered for Hughes.

BARBECUE!
Roast Ox at Coudersport.
Tuesday, Nov. 25th, '84

The Democrats of this section will celebrate the election of Cleveland and Hendricks, at Coudersport, on Tuesday afternoon, Nov. 25th. A. B. Crowell, of Ulysses, has contributed an ox which will be roasted and served at the Rink, at 3 o'clock p.m. Brief addresses will be delivered. At 6 o'clock p.m., torch light parade, with fire works. Music by the Coudersport Cornet Band. Everybody invited to participate. Be on hand at the dinner hour, 3 p.m., at the Rink. Everybody welcome, regardless of sex, age, color or politics. Come and see how it is done.

The citizens are requested to illuminate and decorate their dwellings and business places. There will be a dance at the rink in the evening.

Committee.

Notice.

Whereas my wife, Anna Bendell, has left my bed and board without just cause or provocation, I hereby forbid all persons trusting or harboring her on my account, as I will pay no debts of her contracting unless compelled by law.

Raymond Bendell.

Coudersport, Nov. 18, 1884.

Potter County, Pennsylvania Potpourri – Volume I
1880 through 1884

The Potter Enterprise
Wednesday Evening, November 26, 1884 – Vol. XI, No. 29

MARRIED.

LEHMAN – HAMEL – At the residence of the bride's parents, on Wednesday, Nov. 20, 1884, by Rev. J. W. Wright, Mr. Frederick Lehman and Miss Mary L. Hamel.

COREY – ROGERS – Nov. 19th, 1884, by Rev. J. L. Swain, at his residence, Mr. Anson L. Corey, of Wyoming, Ia., to Miss Mary A. Rogers, of Gold, Pa.

TENNANT – COLE – At the Baptist parsonage, Ulysses, Pa., on Thursday, Nov. 20th, 1884, by Rev. S. W. Cole, Mr. R. T. Tennant, Jr., of Preston, Wayne county, Pa., and Miss Minnie D. Cole, daughter of S. W. Cole, Ulysses, Pa.

DIED.

KENDIG – In Coudersport, Nov. 20th, 1884, the only son of D. E. and E. A. Kendig, aged 8 months and 20 days.

YENTZER – In Pleasant Valley, Nov. 17th, 1884, Mrs. Daniel Yentzer, in the 85th year of her age.

The deceased was one of the early settlers and experienced the privations and sufferings incident to a new country. When her family moved to the farm where she died everything was taken on a sled, there being no road on which a wagon could be used. But time brought the comforts of life and for many years she has had a pleasant home, and home comforts.

WORDEN – At Fertile, Iowa, Nov. 8th, 1884, Mary Peet, wife of David Worden.

Born Aug. 10th, 1807, at Elizabethtown, N.J., she came, with her parents and one younger brother, to Potter county, in the spring of 1811. They were the fourth family to settle in the county. In 1830 she experienced religion and joined the first Methodist class organized in the county, December 25th, 1842 she married David Worden, settling on Sartwell Creek, and moved in 1862 to Wisconsin, thence to Iowa. Husband, two sons and a daughter mourn her loss. Her daughter writes, "Mother has gone to rest, she died happy."

ROAST OX! A Cold Day, But a Warm Time!
A Big Gathering of the Faithful FROM FAR and NEAR.
A DAY LONG REMEMBERED. A Success In Every Particular!

Tuesday, the day appointed for the Democratic Ox Roast in Coudersport, opened cold and stormy, and the prospects for much of a gathering looked decidedly slim. About noon the people from outside the town began to arrive and before three o'clock, enough were present to satisfy anyone that there would be enough to make way with the roast.

Wm. Dent, of Brookland, came in with a six horse team and with him twenty-five voters of that section. Lewisville was well represented. Port Allegany's delegation numbered sixty or seventy, and Roulet and other stations increased the number to 150 or more. Other places sent more or less. Nearly a thousand people eat more or less at the Rink.

The Port Allegany Band was in attendance and assisted materially in rendering the occasion pleasant. Port Allegany may well be proud of this organization. They boys play well indeed and are improving. Neighboring towns must look to their laurels or "Port" will be at the head.

The Coudersport Band, also, furnished music, in their first-class style, and first rate quality. Coudersport is indeed proud of this organization.

Short addresses were delivered by Messrs. Peck, Knox, Benson and Dornan. The best of order prevailed and everybody seemed happy.

The committee on refreshments, furnished roast beef, bread and butter, coffee, crackers, pickles, gingerbread, &c., to all who came.

The steer was the contribution of A. B. Crowell, of Ulysses, and was as fine a one as could be found in this section.

The roasting was the work of Watson T. Dike. Too much credit cannot be given Watson. He prepared everything and attended to the work night and day.

He first prepared a deep pit, in this he burned over five cords of four foot wood giving him a bed of coals about three feet deep. To a strong pole the steer was fastened and Monday afternoon was hung over the coals. From this time until Tuesday noon it required constant attention, to keep it turning. A sheet iron cover was placed over the top leaving the ends open so that all ashes arising was carried off by the draft. It required over twenty pails of water for the basting material. When removed to the rink it was well cooked without being burned. None of it was wasted on account of the cooking. It was a first class job.

A. C. Perkins had charge of the cannon and awoke the echoes for one day at least.

The parade was the best ever seen in Coudersport. Torches, banners, transparencies and bonfires made the town red for once. One of the prominent features in the parade was a stuffed rooster, prepared for a republican parade when it was supposed Blaine would carry New York. It was kindly loaned by its owner.

Dan and Frank Neefe had charge of the fire works.

Among the houses and business places illuminated and decorated were the American Hotel, F. W. Knox's, E. N. Stebbins', Buck's bakery, Grabe's, Misses Schadenberger's, Miles White, Peck & Scovill's, Mrs. W. W. Thompson's, C. L. Peck's, J. L. Haughenberry's, Charley French's, W. T. Dike's, Luther Seibert's, C. W. Hungerford and others.

John Ward, John Pearsall, Ed Lyon, Wm. Boyer, and Vic Darling were assisted by a number of ladies and gentlemen in attending to the wants of the hungry.

One enthusiastic old democrat carried off a thigh bone of the steer. He said he had voted for many years only to be defeated. Now, in commemoration of the election of Cleveland, he was going to take that bone home, clean it, varnish it, and his wife should adorn it with ribbons, and it should hang on the wall where his children and his children's children could see it daily.

Potter County, Pennsylvania Potpourri – Volume I
1880 through 1884

The Potter Enterprise
Wednesday Evening, December 3, 1884 – Vol. XI, No. 30

- Born – To Mr. and Mrs. Thomas Simmons, of Eulalia township, Nov. 27th, a son.

Forest House. There was a wedding here the 27th. Mr. Mel. Hall and Miss Mary White were married, at the residence of the bride's parents, by Joseph Dingee, Esq.

Wedding.

Married, on Wednesday, December 3, at the residence of the bride's parents, by the Rector of Christ Church, James B. Benson, son of Isaac and Eugenia L. Benson, to Kittie J. Hodskin, daughter of Albert A. and Celina Hodskin, all of Coudersport.

It is superfluous for us to comment on the personal appearance of the happy pair, therefore we will briefly say that they more than justified the high enconiums of the assembled guests, who were chiefly personal friends of the contracting parties. The bride was very neatly attired in cream albatross and white brocade satin, with natural rose buds. Her traveling suit is of brown satin and brocade velvet, well suited for the purpose. After the wedding breakfast the happy pair set out by special train on their wedding tour, accompanied by friends to Port Allegany. They will visit New York, Philadelphia and Washington.

The presents were very numerous and costly. The following is a list in part: Cherry Music Cabinet, Mr. and Mrs. J. L. Knox; Cherry Stand, C. S. Jones; Silver Fruit Dish and dozen Silver Knives, Mrs. C. S. Jones; Silver Card Receiver and Pickle Castor, Mr. and Mrs. E. N. Stebbins; Pickle Castor, individual Salt and Pepper holders, Mr. and Mrs. C. A. Reynolds and K. S. Reynolds; Roger's Group "A Tap at the Window," Mr. and Mrs. J. C. Johnson; Fine Table Linen, Mr. and Mrs. P. A. Stebbins; Silver Cake Basket, Mr. and Mrs. C. A. Stebbins; Napkin Ring, Rathbone A. Knox; Embroidered Banner, Mrs. K. R. Hodskin; Perfume Castor, K. R. Hodskin; Pair Rose Blankets, J. D. Hodskin; Easy Chair, Mr. and Mrs. A. A. Hodskin; Perfume Candlestick, Miss Lulu Stebbins; Picture and frame, Mrs. C. V. Derland; Jewel Case, Mrs. H. S. Kidder; Glass fruit-dish, Mrs. H. Taubert; Tidy, Maggie Derock; Set toilet mats, Miss Lizzie Haxton; Toilet Case, Mr. and Mrs. F. W. Knox; Hand painted after dinner set, Mr. Abraham Stebbins and family; Gold watch and chain from the Groom; Check for $500.00, Mr. Isaac Benson; China cup and saucer, Mr. H. Taubert; &c., &c.

DIED.

EGGLESTON – In Burlingame, Kansas, of diphtheria, Altha, daughter of Delbert and Ettie Eggleston, aged two years, ten months and ten days.

- Last Saturday afternoon O. E. Harris, of Sweden, left his team in front of Thompson's grocery while he lifted a barrel into the wagon. As the barrel struck the wagon the team jumped and Mr. Harris was unable to reach the lines. In front of the Enterprise office the rear part of the wagon was left. The team then ran around the two squares, down West Street to Water and up Main Street, bringing up short against Wm. Thomas' dray, on the South side of the Corner Store, and within six rods of the spot where they started. Two bolts repaired all the damages.

- Hammond's tannery is now connected with Coudersport and the outside world by telegraph. A line has been put up from the tannery to the C. & P. A. depot at Coudersport where it connects with Sup't McClure's private line, which connects with the Western Union office and thus the outside towns and cities.

- The Court House at Coudersport, Pa., is in such a dirty, tumble-away-from-itself condition that vermin will no longer remain there, and Justice when she enters has to take out an accident policy. The foregoing we find in one of our exchanges. It isn't true. The Court House is not in a No. 1 order, neither is it falling down. We looked this morning to see. It does need repairs.

Some Game.

Laroy Lyman, of Roulette, Potter county, while out on a twenty day's hunt in Michigan recently, killed thirty deer, eight beavers, one lynx, one mink, one martin, two coons, one large grey eagle measuring seven feet from tip to tip, one raven, four skunks, five hedgehogs, twelve partridges and caught any amount of fish, such as bass, pickerel, perch, &c. This was all accomplished in twenty days. If you don't believe it try and beat it. – *McKean Miner.*

Over an Embankment.

An accident which resulted in the killing of a fine horse, the destruction of a buggy, and the probable death of one of the gentlemen in the buggy, occurred about two and a half miles from this place the forenoon of the 20th ult. Mr. O. H. Chace, a lumberman of East Fork, Potter county, and Jos. Laughlin of First Fork, were driving up the creek to the lumber camp, and reaching the point indicated, near the residence of Jacob Miller, where the embankment is some sixty feet high, the horse became frightened or was suddenly jerked by the reins to one side, when horse, buggy and occupants were precipitated to the bottom of the embankment, into the creek. The horse was killed by the fall. Mr. Chase is seriously injured internally and it is feared may die. We did not learn the extent of Mr. Laughlin's injuries, but understand he is pretty badly hurt. The road at this point is very narrow; teams and drivers have went over it before but never with such serious results. A broken jug, which evidently had been filled with whiskey, was picked up in the wreck. Whether the contents of this "black devil" had anything to do with the accident your correspondent saith not. – *Sinnemahoning Correspondent in Clinton Republican.*

> **WANTED!**
> We want to buy, in large quantities, Cherry, Ash, Black Birch, Hard Maple and Basswood Logs – to be cut 12, 14 and 16 feet, and nothing less than 12 inches at the small end, inside the bark, will be taken except at a reduced price. All logs to be subject to our inspection. We will buy cherry and ash logs or lumber at any point. Call on us before you sell. We will pay the highest cash price. All logs to be cut two inches longer than the lengths given.
> VanWegen & Quimby.
> Coudersport, Dec. 1, 1884.

The Potter Enterprise
Wednesday Evening, December 10, 1884 – Vol. XI, No. 31

- Mr. Lilly and Mrs. Vina Baker, both of Coudersport, were married on Wednesday of last week.

MARRIED.

KLESA – STACKEN – At the Sartwell house, Nov. 27, 1884, by the Rev. J. B. Wright, Mr. Frank Klesa, of Homer, Potter county, to Miss Mary C. Stacken, of Coudersport, Pa.

DIED.

WOOD – In Lymansville, Pa., Dec. 3d, 1884, at the residence of her daughter, Mrs. Adie Knickerbocker, Mrs. Betsey A. Taggart Wood, aged about sixty years.

- Last Friday evening David Brown died at the residence of Nelson Clark in Eulalia. Mr. Brown had been in poor health for some time, and was suffering with a severe cold. He was able to be about and at the time of his death was sitting in his chair. Brown had a good education, but something had turned his brain. He was never violent or dangerous, but on account of his insanity he was sent here by his people in Philadelphia. At Mr. Clark's he was well treated and kindly cared for. If his relatives had treated him half as well, we have no doubt he would have been alive to-day. A broken heart and spirit really caused David's death. He mourned for friends and his native home but was not permitted to visit them.

- Frank E. Bailey has purchased the Shingle House *Palladium* office, and that paper has ceased to exist. In its place has risen the *Signal*. It is smaller, neater, and better than its predecessor. Success to the *Signal*.

- This, Wednesday, morning before it was fairly light, Mr. Brennan, an employee at Hammond's tannery, fell into a vat of hot liquor. Both legs from the knees down were badly scalded, the skin hanging in shreds. Both arms and a spot on his back were in the same condition. About two weeks ago a Mr. Pierson had a similar accident at the same place. His limbs are in a bad condition yet and it will be some time before he can get about.

- The cherry lumber of Potter county is fast being marketed, and one of these days it will be a thing of the past. Even now the lumberman must go far back to the woods to secure his stock of this valuable wood. To-day cherry furniture is more popular than black walnut, and is fast crowding the latter out, as not being in fashion. When our cherry is gone the black birch will be nearly or quite as valuable. It is yearly coming more and more into use for furniture, and will be popular. With the proper finish it greatly resembles mahogany, and at a little distance only an expert can tell the difference. It does not work as easy as cherry, but must some day be substituted for this handsome wood. If you have a patch of nice black birch on your farm do not cut it down for wood. It will pay you better to sell the logs or keep it standing a few years.

Close Call!

About one o'clock Tuesday afternoon fire was discovered breaking out of the rear of the Methodist church, near the roof. It was not long until many willing hands were at work to save the structure and the adjoining property. The fire was burning slowly, the wind was from the opposite side. It had not burned through the roof so there was but little draft to force it. The bucket brigade was out in force and good service was done. Garden hose was stretched from H. J. Olmsted's, fully eleven rods off, attached to a garden hydrant, and soon a small but effective stream was turned on which soon deadened the fire. The damage to the church from fire is very little; a few clapboards burned and pieces of studding charred; water damaged the plastering and carpets. The fire caught from the chimney in the north-east corner of the building, and probably came from the fire in Rev. Wright's study. The fire must have been smouldering some time for there was very little fire in the study. The loss is fully covered by insurance.

This fire shows that the water works would be effective if given a fair show. We think some arrangements should be made with the water company and fire plugs put in. We have no doubt the company would be willing to supply water for fire purposes at a reasonable price, and no one has any doubt about the necessity of some better means for fighting fire in Coudersport. Had the church burned it would have been impossible to have saved a single building on the South side of the square, and the chances for those on North side would have been slim.

We believe Coudersport has a fire marshal. He should visit every house in town, examine the chimneys carefully and see that every means is adopted for the safety of the town from fire. A little care may save thousands of dollars.

Potter County, Pennsylvania Potpourri – Volume I
1880 through 1884

NOTICE.

Whereas my wife, Susan Carpenter, has left my bed and board without just cause or provocation, this is to forbid all persons trusting or harboring her on my account, as I shall pay no debts of her contracting after this date.

Robert Carpenter.

Oswayo, Oct. 28th, 1884.

The Potter Enterprise
Wednesday Evening, December 17, 1884 – Vol. XI, No. 32

MARRIED.

WAGONER – DIKEMAN – In Ulysses, Pa., Dec. 3d, 1884, by Rev. W. Miller, O. M. Wagoner and I. M. Dykeman.

There were over sixty friends and relatives present, and the presents were numerous and costly.

TOLAND – VAN HORN – In Allegany, Pa., December 4th, 1884, by Rev. J. L. Swain, Mr. George J. Toland, of Allegany, and Miss Emma R. Van Horn, of Sweden.

Obituary.

The announcement of the death of Mrs. Betsey A. Taggart Wood, which occurred last week, brings sorrow to the hearts of many in this community where the deceased has for many years resided, respected and beloved by a large circle of acquaintants and friends. She was a faithful, loving wife and mother, a kind, unselfish neighbor, and in her life and character, the beauties of the christian religion were fully exemplified. Her illness was of a lingering, wasting nature attended with continued suffering, which was borne with submission and a firm reliance on the promise of her Heavenly Father, "I will not leave your comfortless." Daughters, sisters, neighbors and friends, for whose comfort her willing hands never tired, will mourn for her, but our loss is her gain. In the name of the Lord, whom she trusted and loved, she has won the victory and passed through the gates into the city. We should not grieve, but remember with thankfullness her useful and beautiful life, and when the Master calls be ready to enjoy, with the departed, the rest prepared for the children of God in "green pastures beside the still waters." Mrs. Wood was buried in the cemetery, at Lymansville, beside her husband, Mr. Nathan Wood. A large number of relatives and friends followed the remains to the grave.

Statistics

Of Bingham township for the year 1884:

	3 yr	2 yr	1 yr	Under 1 yr
Cattle	214	222	240	397
Horses	22	21	19	20
Wheat, bushels		874		
		473		

Oats, bushels	40,298
Buckwheat, bushels	7,385
Corn, bushels	1,225
Millet, bushels	408
Barley, bushels	1,097
Peas, bushels	463
Potatoes, bushels	20,144
Apples, bushels	2,056
Beans, bushels	60
Rye, bushels	37
Bees, Swarms of	248
Sheep, number of	1,107
Hogs, number of	146
Assessable Property:	
Stags,	19
Oxen,	8
Bulls,	1
Cows,	698
Horses,	218
Mules,	6
Dogs,	111

The Potter Enterprise
Wednesday Evening, December 24, 1884 – Vol. XI, No. 33

- The thermometer, on Saturday last, went down, down, downie, down to 18° below zero, which is quite far enough to suit us.

NOTICE.

Notice is hereby given that application will be made to the Court of Common Pleas of Potter county, on the first day of January next term, for the incorporation of an association by the name of the Sweden Hill Cemetery Association. The character and object of said association being, a cemetery association for the maintenance of a burial ground in Sweden township, Potter county, Pa.

Benson & Dornan,
Attorneys for Applicants.

The Potter Enterprise
Wednesday Evening, December 31, 1884 – Vol. XI, No. 34

- Wm. Peck, father of C. L. Peck, Esq., was buried at Nelson, Tioga county, last week. The deceased was over seventy-two years of age and for the most of the time during the last forty-eight years had resided on the farm where he died.

DIED.

HALL – In Keating township, Potter county, Pa., on Friday, December 26th, 1884, Almond C. Hall, aged 21 years, one month and eight days.

- Lewisville Lodge No. 556, F. & A. M. will be under the following officers for the ensuing year: E. U. Eaton, W.M.; H. K. Lane, S.W.; A. Cady, J.W.; G. C. Marion, Treas.; Seth Lewis, Sec'y; J. O. Potter, S.D.; A. H. Lewis, J.D.; E. A. Burt, S.M.C.; C. W. Bailey, J.M.C.; F. M. Bronson, Pur.; A. A. Johnson, Chaplain; Chas. Erlbeck, Tyler.

To be continued...

Surname Index

Abbey 107 198 285
Abbot 73 188
Abbott 55 101 147 156
  194 198 239 261 330
  442 448
Absom 320
Abson 64 76 101 111 175
  275 321 464
Acker 286 320 432 433
Ackerman 328 386 433
  453
Adams 31 58 72 86 95
  113 136 239 269 359
  413 457
Alderman 159 174 224
  247
Alfred 169
Allaard 52
Allard 399
Allen 23 37 51 54 61 62
  63 67 74 87 92 94 98
  101 107 109 113 114
  133 138 157 159 172
  173 194 195 200 202
  205 210 224 238 246
  261 275 278 285 287
  290 303 316 344 345
  350 358 360 361 362
  363 364 376 385 399
  404 406 407 408 411
  438 440 441 445 448
  456 457 458
Allis 39 73 422
Allison 88
Amidon 142
Andresen 109 126 127
  134 195 201 287 408
Anderson 248
Andressen 37
Andrews 16 22 24 26 27
  50 90 91 93 101 115
  119 124 128 138 156
  157 170 183 191 229
  275 286 399 441
Angood 378 431
Ansley 37 86 87 239 310
Anton 16 24 25 27 92
Appleby 371
Armstrong 4 17 18 22 24
  26 27 29 30 33 49 50
  63 64 65 67 90 93 98
  101 120 124 128 135
  146 174 183 184 187
  192 248 260 321 332
  335 349 375 404 406
  410 420 442 457 463
Arnold 115 150 208 209

238 248 320 378 427
  431
Ashcraft 175 232 274 275
  302 338 390
Ashdown 255
Atherton 107 197 198
  222 281 285 442
Atkins 133 360
Atkinson 191 284 350
Atwater 159
Austin 19 63 95 96 108
  123 173 194 243 246
  286 308 320 328 361
  376 408
Avery 88 115 188 310
  322 407
Ayars 107 196
Ayers 52 78 101 109 115
  310 373 408
Aylesworth 66 67 93 136
  173 238 306 345 386
  412 414
Ayres 86 167 213
Babcock 86 106 115 156
  159 191 284 362 363
  386 444
Babicock 52
Bach 399
Backus 255
Bacon 57 136 151 191
  201 239 275 284
Badger 56
Badgero 73 107 378
Baham 279
Bailey 58 59 71 74 87
  106 130 160 197
  287 318 351 390 399
  406 409 411 447 464
  471 475
Baily 175 234
Baker 8 16 21 23 25 35
  36 38 41 51 58 62 63
  64 72 74 92 107 108
  129 137 147 148 156
  157 159 167 170 172
  175 178 188 190 192
  194 213 216 223 224
  252 253 254 268 270
  273 275 284 285 306
  317 320 325 330 332
  350 351 362 363 364
  366 385 404 406 407
  444 445 453 456 457
  471
Baldwin 127 170 349 358
  366 372 422
Ball 58 107 192 278 285

290 407 462
Banks 258
Bar 371
Barbanks 234
Barber 150 158 367
Barce 209
Barclay 58 87 101 131
  172 194 274 278 290
  452 464
Bard 255
Barker 166 407
Barlow 53 367
Barnes 51 73 111 147
  148 160 171 180 283
  312 322 350 361 399
  453 456
Barns 408
Barr 56 57 59 74 136 157
  160 172 247 371 427
Barret 275
Barrett 255 325 383
Barse 131 132 208
Bartholemew 124
Bartholomew 44 115 243
Bartlett 233 238 248 360
  409 442
Barto 107
Barton 81
Bartoo 96 115 464
Basett 367
Basset 45 73 280
Bassett 39 43 93 108 127
  199 223 238 286 287
  320 359 372
Bates 92
Beach 35 36 37 52 115
  136 454
Beatman 107 196
Beauge 401
Beckwith 108 114 136
  194 418
Beebe 99 108 112 127
  138 155 193 246 261
  285 310 320 328 353
  407 422 452
Beebee 31 39 99
Beecher 308
Begell 267
Beirley 234
Belanski 224
Bellus 447 450 452
Bemis 19 29 125 130 304
  308
Bendel 16 26 27 216
Bendell 176 310 331 338
  359 433 445 466
Benedict 360

Surname Index

Bennet 308
Bennett 6 115 127 278
  287 290 291 306 328
  342 432
Bennit 320
Bennitt 71 109 197 446
Benson 2 17 18 24 26 62
  63 65 73 88 92 96
  107 129 159 192 208
  209 213 217 247 248
  265 304 305 331 362
  404 406 428 437 444
  456 457 468 469 474
Benton 65 115 208 209
  238 248 337
Berfield 29 58 94 107
  109 127 136 167 188
  194 278 287 354 387
  431 433
Berger 127 131 177
Berick 113
Bernauer 239
Bessey 284
Bice 159 167 238
Bickford 409
Biggins 358
Billings 59 224 322
Bingham 310 330 331
  359 413 433 454
Bird 191 195 284 287
  317 406
Birdsall 88
Bisbee 66 101 109 198
  278 287 289 409 463
Bishop 62 63 64 65 73 90
  95 127 147 148 152
  156 192 194 201 238
  244 249 253 278 284
  285 290 320 343 362
  367 382 406 442
Bitler 429
Bixby 147 196 408
Black 169 177
Blackman 37 108 119
  127 196 278 285 286
  364 372 373 445
Blaine 420
Blakeslee 213 216 219
  244 248
Blanchard 147 189 349
  371 385 432
Blarigan 281 282 310 357
Blauvelt 89 160 196 286
Bliss 23 27 33 43 138
  177 179 275 320 364
  458
Bloss 234 389

Bly 107 192 285 397 402
  407
Boas 174
Bodler 19 73 106 197 284
  399 431 447 448
Bogardis 247
Bogardus 136 172
Boley 106
Bolich 88 167 320
Bonnawits 457
Bonnywitz 92
Booth 182 361 462
Borden 437
Bottom 249 291 295 297
Bovier 227 252 419
Bowermaster 313 314
  317
Bowers 324
Bowman 297
Bowtish 212
Box 225
Boyer 9 67 98 99 270 468
Boyington 65 73 320 448
  458
Bradford 109 197
Bradley 86 89 370 433
Brahmer 12 68 92 99 164
Braitling 339
Bratz 136 212
Braun 284 368 406
Bravo 78
Breck 237
Breese 460
Brehmer 17 24 26 33 95
  96 434
Breisenick 387 411
Bremer 274
Bremle 192
Brennan 247 472
Brenule 374
Breunle 61 107 127 163
  284 399 404 406 444
  448
Brewster 201 246 275
  307 386
Bridge 366 423
Bridges 52 108 159 193
  361 383 407 419 420
  421 442
Briesenick 324
Briesnick 232
Briggs 101 127 151 169
  191 192 278 284 287
  290 368 406 409 419
  422 463 464
Brigham 71 108 147 167
  238 302 357 358 372

Brightman 31 371 418
  423 435 438 441 452
Brine 19 25 124 195 213
  316 408 442
Brisbeau 374
Brisboi 424
Brisbois 376 453
Britling 452
Brizee 148
Brizze 370
Brizzee 159 201 370 399
  442 452
Brockway 202
Broderson 234 284 399
  406 440
Bronson 64 71 72 128
  179 285 390 475
Brook 94
Brooks 6 31 73 87 113
  128 190 212 234 239
  284 285 316 334 399
  411 416 422 440 442
  464
Brown 8 31 50 72 73 86
  88 104 108 111 113
  134 137 138 167 174
  195 196 200 238 253
  255 270 277 278 281
  286 287 290 317 350
  356 366 371 378 387
  389 390 407 411 412
  413 430 433 439 440
  441 446 462 463 471
Brownlee 73 87 108 159
  173 174 175 194 200
  201 224 343 408 411
  422 453
Bruce 330
Bruse 319
Bryant 451 464
Bryden 401
Buchanan 370
Buck 2 41 42 68 74 89 99
  111 159 171 179 191
  210 232 253 258 305
  325 332 334 368 378
  383 428 435 438 441
  455 462 468
Buckbee 31 176 178 239
  332 382
Bulaskia 286
Bullard 19
Bullock 368
Bump 59 134 197 286
  408 442 448
Bundy 107 127 193 407
Bunnell 237 371

478

Surname Index

Burbank 196 235 371
Burbanks 188
Burdett 108
Burdette 194
Burdic 38 59 91 92 107
   114 160 171 196 347
   358 365 387 432 453
Burdick 55 63 88 92 112
   133 167 180 188 234
   235 278 307 350 351
   362 380 411 413 464
Burger 408
Burleson 108 195 243
   344 445 464
Burley 368 464
Burlingame 278 287
Burlison 101 409
Burns 36 385 411 431
   433 452
Burnside 252
Burr 207 404
Burrett 173
Burrous 188
Burrows 109 126 129 176
   198 213 214 224 230
   287 328 386 409 445
   453
Burt 28 37 52 62 64 73
   74 99 101 106 108
   109 115 127 142 143
   150 167 176 188 193
   194 197 213 235 237
   238 278 285 287 310
   320 322 328 344 371
   378 390 406 407 408
   409 422 425 432 445
   448 449 458 459 475
Burtis 90 148 179
Burton 69 196 366 406
Butler 59 107 129 131
   136 147 152 158 172
   344 367 437 457
Butterfield 161
Butterworth 19 177
Button 150 158 262 329
Butts 196
Byam 93 229 366 370
   415
Cady 108 193 238 373
   464 475
Calgan 431
Calkins 68 91 99 355 462
Callaghan 138
Caller 378
Cameron 142 319 433
Cammell 200
Campbell 37 62 69 109
   188 195 229 247 285
   326 327 345 408 411
   452 463
Canfield 253
Cannon 60 131 136 158
   172 366
Card 31 109 121 138 156
   188 194 196 225 228
   277 281 286 288 328
   349 350 359 377 386
   387 409 445 449
Carey 44 86 113 131 132
   209 238 248 286 330
   366 408 432 452
Carlin 278
Carling 198 212 270 272
Carlton 255
Carman 87 287 399 409
Carmer 52 147 407
Carnahan 309
Carpenter 51 52 57 58 62
   69 81 83 101 109
   156 157 160 167 169
   178 191 197 200 204
   234 243 281 354 362
   369 370 372 382 442
   445 447 448 449 473
Carn 57
Carney 212 285
Carr 188 370 440 453
   465
Carriel 239
Carsaw 195 196
Carson 425
Carsten 221 392
Cary 131 208 436 460
Case 53 107 193 285 351
Casterline 94
Castle 285 367 407
Caston 373
Catlin 138
Caulkins 108
Cavanaugh 54 91 154 291
   380 393 394 399 406
   420 432
Cavenaugh 56
Chace 470
Chafee 188
Chaffe 288
Chaffee 199 267
Chamberlain 347 431 440
Chamberlin 361
Chambers 111
Chandler 69
Chapel 71 448
Chapin 50 64 65 167 197
   212 227 239 285 407
   446
Chapman 41 42 43 59 68
   84 85 86 87 99 198
   269 284 285 288 367
   378
Chappel 1 113 157 171
   178 200 202 268 328
   456
Chappell 167 238 246
Chase 1 19 37 67 109 113
   156 167 178 195 212
   234 278 281 287 327
   328 385 408 413 419
   445 457 464
Chatfield 261
Cheeseman 36
Chesbro 7 31 107 115
   147 159 190 193 274
   276 285 310 366
Chesebro 320
Chestain 416
Chestnut 151 152 158
Chilson 128 372
Chisholm 174 198 248
   249 264 269 279 289
   292 293 294 295 296
   298 299 300 301 302
   303 304 305 307 308
   330 331
Chriman 91
Christey 308
Christman 159 171 197
   399
Church 44 74 329
Clair 192 407 464
Clancey 58 60 115 367
Clare 285
Clark 36 37 52 57 58 59
   62 64 83 87 88 91 92
   93 101 106 107 108
   109 113 114 115 119
   136 157 158 159 161
   167 172 175 179 180
   190 191 192 195 197
   223 234 238 239 247
   253 254 255 274 278
   284 285 286 290 306
   309 310 349 350 359
   368 369 375 379 381
   386 389 399 406 408
   409 410 412 431 432
   445 448 452 471
Clarrendon 458
Clear 167 392 445
Clerk 138
Clesa 285
Cleveland 449 466 468

Surname Index

Clinton 36 101 202 231
   378 447 464
Close 239 372 437
Clugston 377
Coates 343
Coats 19 73 84 86 127
   156 170 191 229 272
   284 344 406 415 444
Cobb 16 25 26 27 31 37
   45 50 57 71 72 89 95
   110 138 151 157 171
   178 223 233 238 239
   240 247 248 282 285
   289 304 305 310 323
   332 349 413 464
Cochran 278 290
Coddington 319 445
Coddy 139
Coderman 37
Coe 92 278
Coffin 88 107 197
Coil 59
Coit 69
Colbert 437
Colcord 62 63 64 67 95
   96 97 107 161 171
   188 192 215 238 275
   283 325 362 363 378
   383 385 399 404 406
   452 457
Cole 11 16 22 24 25 26
   27 36 41 42 43 58 59
   61 74 87 91 95 96
   101 107 113 114 127
   128 137 155 157 160
   170 171 188 189 192
   196 212 219 221 224
   234 265 281 284 305
   317 332 337 349 365
   370 378 406 408 422
   424 427 428 433 438
   440 441 453 464 467
Colegrove 268 286 449
Coleman 92 233 280
Colgrove 188 222 337
   382 448
Coll 58
Collar 148 198 278 290
Collins 106 142 155 176
   191 216 238 240 278
   285 315 390 464
Colston 256
Colt 343
Colton 253
Colvin 52 188 192 200
   320 447
Colwell 37 54 154 236

Conable 77 122 141 254
   278 350 352 409 433
Cone 89 151 160 171 184
   199 214 218 232 256
   261 267 277 284 333
   354 361 428 451
Conklin 132
Conley 64 416
Connable 109 186 191
   198 224 247 287 310
Conrad 286 408 422
Cook 320 361 388
Cool 191 212 319 360
   399
Cooper 137 157
Corey 73 85 107 136 158
   167 173 407 422 445
   467
Cornelius 386
Cornell 50 65 188 337
Cornish 60
Corry 198
Corsaw 23 107 109 287
   306 338 382 406 421
   442 448
Cortwright 156
Corwine 196 371
Cory 224 301
Costello 39 162 185 202
   251 452
Costen 200
Cotter 46
Cottrell 361
Coulston 1 101 106 107
   149 156 157 178 332
   350 406 448
Courtright 194 287 378
   464
Covey 1 37 60 83 86 88
   101 120 124 160 171
   222 228 255 275 314
   325 327 334 343 361
   383 389 390 392
Cowan 429
Cowburn 452
Cox 246 268 272 308
Coyle 166 285 399
Crandall 108 130 196 330
   386 399 407
Crane 9 62 63 66 67 97
   98 192 216 220 238
   264 266 273 332 362
   456
Cranmer 267
Craw 267 279 283 288
   333 374 375 396 420
   436 439 451

Crawford 37 45 60 69 81
   167 173 195 212 255
   359 367 457
Cripen 107
Crippen 74 167 198 324
   326 378 399 409 464
Cristie 37
Crittenden 18 45 52 115
   161 278 290 370 378
   405 407
Crocker 160 171 442
Cronk 101
Crosby 1 29 30 38 42 43
   49 50 52 54 62 64 87
   88 91 93 107 108
   120 156 157 161 178
   184 192 193 238 274
   278 285 286 290 291
   332 335 344 374 381
   404 406 407 420 422
   426 430 446 458 463
Crowell 1 52 61 62 63 77
   147 156 238 306 351
   422 468
Crum 58 72 76 77 137
   170 252 284 287 448
Crusen 329
Cubb 374
Culver 444
Cummings 264 308 329
   368 444
Cunningham 188 457 458
Curan 268
Currier 213 284 406
Curtis 261 382
Cushing 53 59 71 108
   115 167 193 238 399
Cutler 137 174 200 347
   349 350
Daggett 193
Dalaba 248
Dale 288
Dallmage 138
Dalrymple 161 255
Danford 172
Daniels 52 71 102 106
   108 167 171 238 328
   372 406 432 442
Darcey 58
Darcy 330
Darling 440 468
Davenport 156 329
Davidge 158
Davidson 24 173 186 195
   208 320 344 448 449
Davis 138 148 152 156
   157 158 174 198 213

Surname Index

276 322 366 418 441 464
Davison 178 449
Dawley 73 196 367 411 453
Dean 59 137
Decker 134
Deisroth 109 198 287 464
Dehn 36 173 375 399
Delamatter 407
Delemater 213
Deming 108 320
Denhoff 34 221 224 232 459
Denison 252
Dennis 58 86 114 136 275 316 320 326 392 419 438
Densmore 276 399
Dent 62 70 114 147 156 157 186 265 287 330 338 344 431 445 448 467
DePlaque 368
Dereemer 156
Deremer 201 286 420 445
Derland 469
Derock 469
Dery 115
Devall 254
Devanport 109 194 306 334 382
Devans 234
Devens 52 193
Devol 287
Devoll 109 194 213 287 412
Dewaters 138
Dexter 31 53 88 278 285 290 291 430
Dibble 368
Dickens 269 270 272 399 460
Dickerson 73
Dickinson 89 160 196 286 328 445
Dickson 314
Dike 65 225 308 391 462 468
Dikeman 409 473
Dillenbeck 165 179 184 190 202 212 214 220 229 248
Dimon 38 107 127 188 198 407
Dingee 9 63 67 98 99 108 124 176 193 220 238

278 286 308 375 399 407 412 421 437 456 469
Dingman 9 49 51 63 73 99 107 129 167 247 279 316 328 364 366 386 407 450 452 457 458
Disbrow 372
Diven 150
Doane 17 18 25 27 28 32 126 128 141 176 177
Dodd 59 63 64 90 93 195 278 287 290 350 408 443 454 455
Dodge 11 29 52 101 105 107 109 115 127 170 188 196 197 263 278 310 320 382 386 407 419 420 422 446 447 464
Doerfus 255
Doerner 65 98 100 147 167 354
Dolley 57 255 352 356
Dolly 406
Dolway 325 383
Donovan 213
Dornan 306 330 344 345 428 441 449 453 468 474
Dorsey 88 387
Doty 114 170 413
Doud 235 285 368 406
Dougherty 433 452
Douglas 464
Douglass 73 101 107 188 198 201 228 238 369 376 381 382 386
Downey 361
Downley 444
Downs 62 261 367 463
Doyle 31 51 202 239 240 257 382
Drain 46
Drake 1 81 101 127 160 171 238 285 286 351 358 386 407 408 412 413 464
Drane 40 41 46 47 48
Drew 375
Drock 59
Dual 174
Duel 174
Dunbar 71 149 193 270 316
Dunford 159

Dunham 38 168 236
Dunn 114 176
Dusenberry 173
Duval 389
Dwight 52 60 92 176 224 285 407
Dwire 52 57 289 442
Dyer 278
Dyke 64 65 90 124 234 251
Dykeman 188 287 409 445
Earl 171 286 350 366 383 406 407
Earle 52 115 160 192 202 213 216 278 284 325 404 420 451 463
Earnest 464
Earnst 286
Easton 101 108 122 156 193 198 285 313 344 378 385 388 448
Eaton 7 115 167 171 179 193 218 220 265 475
Eckert 102
Eddy 464
Edgar 358 368
Edgcomb 2 107 160 192 285 329 351
Edgecomb 78 238
Edmendorf 372
Edmonds 94
Edmunds 420
Edwards 196 217 227 266
Eggleston 127 469
Elder 212 409
Elderkin 37
Eldridge 114 136 379 431
Elliot 213 216
Elliott 2 304 320 342 365 442 449 453
Ellis 92 141 147 173 189 200 223 246 253 269 270 278 370 432 444 448 464
Ellison 8 21 38 41 42 90 93 186 217 262 275 325 396 441
Ellsworth 37 137
Elwell 113
Embre 239
Emery 50 190
Emmerick 215
Emmerson 148
English 52 170 192 197 212 213 378
Ensworth 204 239 351

Surname Index

Erlbeck 72 108 179 193 390 475
Ernst 34 131
Erway 127 227 278 385 406 411
Estes 31 101 107 108 192 193 198 214 215 259 276 278 283 285 310 312 320 347 354 361 369 370 376 407 447 464
Estherson 91
Evans 114 131 191 238 247 267 270 272 372 429 442 464
Everett 108 194 375 408 422 464
Everitt 437 439
Failing 160 167 171 196 286 344 359 408 445 448
Fait 45
Fancis 248
Farley 378
Farnham 52 285
Farnsworth 72 87 108 188 193 238 372 407
Farnum 108 188 247 407
Farrell 174 200
Fassett 169 170 459
Fassit 347
Faust 216
Fay 114
Felt 255
Feltwell 274
Fengler 147
Fepender 365
Fergason 407 448
Ferguson 392
Ferner 463
Ferris 238 307
Fesenden 234
Fessenden 137 159 170 193 260 276 286 320 324 370 378 408 445 448
Fickler 49 62 64 192 222 268 284
Filmore 55 188
Finch 463
Findly 105
Fisher 102 175 371
Fisk 366
Fitch 385
Fitzgerald 45
Fitzsimmons 268
Fitz Stephens 19

Flashutz 160
Fleshuts 108
Fleshutz 108
Fletcher 368
Flewellen 304
Fling 70 128
Flinn 73 286
Flynn 278 375 422
Folt 255
Foote 137
Ford 92 106 127 191 214 288 351 448 463
Foreman 131 132
Forster 10 16 25 27 33 128 138 155 336 435
Forsythe 278 361 460
Fosmer 107 196 284 330 365 444 447
Foster 101 137 167 286 297 302 366 407 408
Fourness 192 286 399 404 406
Fowler 109 278 287 409 464
Fox 58 60 88 100 115 137 157 173 174 197 212 222 307 368 384 385 432
Frabel 59
Frable 262
Francis 52 101 109 197 198 201 236 238 378 446 447
Franke 239
Frasior 413
Frazier 328 358
Frech 222 347
Freeman 71 92 109 171 195 200 213 278 285 399 408 411 442
Fries 306
French 7 16 24 25 27 28 31 62 68 88 91 95 99 108 115 176 192 195 199 208 232 235 334 338 388 408 418 431 441 454 468
Frink 73 278
Froebel 246 264 269 358 387 412 413 452
Fronson 128
Frouk 34
Fuller 51 150 255 302 349 369 370
Fullerton 50
Fultz 7
Furgeson 342

Furman 7 133 178 419
Furness 156
Gale 32 60 70 196 312 316 442
Gallagher 329 358 359
Gallup 255
Galutia 372
Gamble 87 113
Gardner 74 87 106 137 191 243 382 411 464
Garfield 157
Garity 86 88
Garrett 165
Garrity 360 452
Gates 95 107 193 407
Gear 58 137
Gee 112 138 214 238 372 422
Genter 310
Genung 72 136 158 235 372
George 81
Georgia 317
Getty 255
Gibbs 32 366
Gibson 35 59 87 95 101 198 199 201 223 238 239 317 318 339 422
Gifford 188 319
Gilbert 101 168 188 197 399 412 414 442
Gill 147 202 295 297 310 359 445
Gillet 145
Gillett 196 367
Gillian 447
Gilliland 35 95 127 261 351 425 443
Gillon 9 67 68 98 99 216 222 251 457
Glace 3 37 64 120 192 217 464
Glasby 107
Glase 147 406 458
Glaspy 57 108 164 192 285 317 320 407 422
Glass 319
Glassmire 5 14 17 21 22 24 26 27 28 33 45 64 65 73 76 78 90 91 92 107 124 129 146 155 174 183 265 273 275 277 331 332 350 377 390 430 435 436 438 451 458
Glavin 426
Gleason 281

Surname Index

Glines 107 147 188 196
 284
Glober 193
Glover 58 174 189 193
 200 223 246 269 297
 329 407 445
Gnau 52 101 106 197 378
 406 442 444
Goesbeck 289
Golding 451
Goodale 342
Goodell 31
Goodenough 366 370
Goodnoe 115
Goodrich 201
Goodsel 54
Goodsell 63 64 65 69 91
 146 155 166 183 213
 261 275 277 279 280
 284 382 390 392 428
Goodwin 358 373 374
 381 387 388 389 411
 427
Goodyear 230
Goff 378
Goram 148
Gordenier 376
Gordiner 363
Gordinier 216
Gordnier 16 19 26 32 33
 49 62 68 69 73 92 98
 99 107 120 124 128
 184 188 248 268 278
 285 290 332 362 363
 407 445 456
Gordon 63
Gorg 37
Gorham 35 67 115 285
 456
Gorman 37 328
Goss 354
Gould 15 389 440
Grabe 119 177 213 229
 311 388 420 448 461
 468
Graham 58 88 114 158
 403
Grames 127 197
Grandier 87
Granes 214
Grant 138 261
Graves 133 160 329 442
 451
Gray 127 135 145 188
 313 314 317 318 348
Greely 373
Green 17 25 26 27 33 36

 52 58 77 89 107 111
 142 144 147 192 196
 222 270 271 319 371
 413 452 454 458
Greengrass 213 278 290
Greenman 1 31 64 65 66
 67 175 192 238 239
 285 350 376 432 456
 457 462 465
Greenwood 37 441
Greisel 279
Gressel 463
Gressell 106
Gretter 255
Gridley 2 29 30 49 50 62
 64 65 71 73 91 92
 108 109 124 148 193
 201 238 267 285 302
 311 320 324 332 359
 361 363 372 380 406
 407 409 433 447 452
Griesel 33 64 177
Griffith 389
Grisel 16 24 25 27
Griswold 301 331
Grodevant 36 57 268 310
 339 340 359 366
Groesbeck 278 291 442
Grom 64 99 114 167 216
 427 428 432 464
Grosbeck 108
Gross 59 88 114 116 127
 136 158 382 458 464
Grover 52 77 90 101 106
 114 119 127 142 157
 191 192 197 239 284
 287 372 378 385 432
 444 447 464
Grovers 354
Groves 6 68 238 378
Grovey 320
Grubb 255
Guenter 284
Guenther 374
Guernsey 19 137 190
Guinas 172
Guinnip 72 172
Gunther 410
Gurnsey 234 462 465
Gustin 443
Gutgsell 331
Habor 237
Hacket 188 310 406
Hackett 39 177 188 189
 258 278 286 290 328
 351 399 446
Hagerman 350

Hagemann 368
Hall 31 63 64 95 108 150
 152 159 176 193 238
 240 241 249 283 285
 286 315 317 319 368
 382 392 399 404 406
 407 412 418 422 433
 452 453 459 469 475
Hallauer 18 24 25 34
Halleuer 433
Hallet 168
Hallett 171 407
Hallock 160 308 373
Halsey 385
Halstead 264 265 270
Halsted 269
Ham 193
Hamel 428 467
Hamil 73
Hamilton 39 91 100 146
 306 443 458 464
Hamlin 208 209
Hammel 430
Hammond 1 52 65 113
 124 127 128 139 147
 157 177 178 188 193
 200 205 207 216 246
 247 252 253 257 258
 268 275 285 328 332
 358 360 384 385 410
 422 431 457 458 470
 472
Hanber 284
Hand 148 285 320
Handwerk 284 350
Handwork 37
Hanlon 338 345 355
Hann 272
Hannahs 158
Hannas 148 149
Hansen 441
Hanson 178 234 320
Hard 198
Harmon 445 449
Harriet 329
Harrigan 137
Harrington 91 444
Harris 46 74 78 108 109
 122 137 159 195 239
 272 279 287 312 320
 356 357 362 367 372
 433 442 443 444 453
 456 457 464 470
Harrison 59 115 127 136
 157 167 197 239 285
 295 443
Hart 199 239 285 381

Surname Index

406 424 444
Hartly 172
Harton 138
Hartwick 366 459
Harvey 31 63 73 95 96
  106 109 134 179 182
  191 234 238 278 284
  287 306 328 332 372
  385 399 403 404 406
  433 446
Harvy 234
Haskell 9 106 141 178
  208 223 228 238 248
  332 350 382 419
Haskill 327
Haskin 368
Haskins 59 61 69 95 107
  108 109 142 147 195
  196 201 272 286 287
  288 307 320 344 369
  374 384 392 409 433
  443 445 448
Hassrick 440
Hatch 370
Hatfield 184
Hauber 191 192 243
Haughenberry 62 393 404
  406 418 431 444 451
  464 468
Haven 17 25 27 45 115
  129 154 157 198 224
  358 460
Havens 21 54 108 167
  197 198 407 443
Haviland 255
Hawkins 70
Hawks 147
Hawley 32 59 143 193
  284 307 329 378 448
  449
Hawthorn 422
Haxton 156 196 220 286
  448 469
Hay 60 88 94 369 417
Hayes 261
Haynes 17 26 37 43 86 89
  107 116 136 138 194
  286 408
Haywood 436
Hazelbarth 280
Hazen 142 195 208 320
  371 383
Head 73 101 108 193 283
  320
Healey 87
Healy 74 88 161
Heath 235 278 381

Heggie 64 106 175 191
  284 378
Hehl 109 287
Helenbrook 389
Helfrecht 52 197
Hemington 156
Hemphill 95 192 399
Henderson 71 72 190
Hendricks 449 466
Hendrickson 39
Hendrix 238
Hendryx 35 148 241 350
  396
Henley 59 93 422
Henoy 354
Henry 106 179 223 284
  330 431
Herring 13 58 87 147 234
  320 369
Herrington 109 195 287
  344 408 413 440 441
  443 448 455
Hershberger 443
Herzog 60 142
Heseltine 18 19
Hess 287 363 452 454
Heuter 60
Hewett 219
Hewitt 424
Hickok 87
Hickox 148 156 188 212
  285 320 422
Higley 116 369 370 462
Hill 52 133 136 192 198
  243 308 320 350 385
  386 398 448 453 465
Hilligas 224
Hills 280 418
Hinman 239 246
Hirsch 196 213
Hitchcock 59 160
Hizer 224
Hober 101 174
Hodecamp 201
Hodge 308
Hodgins 367
Hodsin 364
Hodskin 221 222 226 261
  324 385 469
Hodskins 442
Hoffman 219 427 453
Hoffmeister 286
Hoffner 252 256
Holbert 74 106 239 284
  464
Holburt 406
Holcomb 167 278 285

407 464
Holdridge 234
Holland 188 266 274 276
  308 317 324 367 374
  384 445 451
Hollenbeck 1 9 31 61 95
  111 127 135 159 201
  223 238 247 254 269
  270 284 288 328 333
  404 406 457
Holley 174
Hollister 398
Holly 459
Holmes 109 399
Holsted 283
Holt 173 200 319
Hooker 389
Hoover 134 342
Hopkins 71 114 136 158
  190 370 378
Hoppe 52 106 126 156
  197 284 328 406
Hopson 252
Horner 412
Hornsby 34 389 411 448
Horton 109 115 158 194
  237 287 312 386 389
  409 410 426 445 463
Hosley 50 52 57 60 65 74
  108 127 167 171 193
  227 234 237 238 270
  285 362 366 372 390
  407 412 432 443
Hosly 372
Hosmer 386
Houck 238 240 241
Hoven 195
Hovey 179 194 197 285
  372 390
Howard 60 158 159 253
  320 355 356
Howe 31 53 64 95 106
  136 159 167 191 193
  201 238 239 241 384
  406 419 451 464
Howell 91
Howland 199 270 368
  386 412
Hoyt 160 413
Hubbard 278 368 378
Hubbell 182
Hubbs 376
Hubertus 231
Hug 106 197 351
Hughes 15 138 466
Hull 62 120 133 139 142
  151 156 184 200 253

Surname Index

265 278 290 366 410
   442 448 460
Humbert 368
Hummel 367
Humphrey 291 297 329
   399
Hungerford 92 148 393
   443 468
Hunsicker 87 113
Hunt 87 112 161 357 360
Hunter 115 167 217 368
Huntingdon 73
Huntington 18 92 322
   323 348 431
Huntley 452
Hurd 36 95 101 107 112
   174 178 188 201 222
   223 228 235 239 309
   318 382 426
Hurlbert 58
Hurlburg 107
Hurlburt 194 222 252 254
   295 368
Hurlbut 252
Hyatt 157 378
Hyde 36 87 107 223 224
   234 269 291 292 296
   304 333 344 372 407
Hydorn 180 187
Hyler 55
Impsom 328
Impson 108 195 287 408
   433 452
Ingraham 40 44 46 47 49
   86 107 192 234 330
   404
Inson 219
Irons 255
Ives 30 54 64 65 72 154
   158 159 225 234 239
   286 389 414
Jacklin 212 445
Jackson 23 74 109 113
   137 138 163 166 167
   168 171 195 196 220
   239 269 286 288 328
   350 361 408
Jacobs 110 167 197
Jacobus 71 202
James 58 65 191 330 343
   365
Jenkins 173
Jennings 128 197 372 411
Jeorg 65 73 287
Jewell 44
Joerg 109 127 154 195
   320 408

Johnson 18 37 38 45 52
   89 91 106 121 148
   159 169 170 175 201
   202 219 224 225 235
   246 247 268 269 278
   282 284 306 310 324
   330 347 350 351 372
   378 389 390 399 406
   408 464 469 475
Johnston 21 62 66 67 68
   92 97 98 99 109 177
   179 331 355 366
Jones 7 11 16 17 18 22
   24 25 26 27 28 29 30
   31 32 33 37 49 54 55
   57 65 70 86 90 91 93
   95 100 105 107 113
   115 119 128 129 131
   132 137 138 146 148
   153 155 158 159 160
   161 168 171 175 176
   183 188 192 201 209
   214 215 218 221 223
   224 231 239 244 250
   255 258 261 262 273
   274 275 277 284 310
   320 327 330 331 332
   336 349 351 361 368
   369 383 385 386 390
   392 404 406 407 418
   427 428 442 446 453
   458 463 469
Jonson 172
Jordan 86 92 108 109 127
   137 158 168 172 194
   195 234 287 328 373
   385 422 464
Jorden 70
Jordon 73 114
Joseph 109 127 145 149
   194 286
Joy 371
Judd 34 54 138 154 165
   166 176 177 243 306
   310 329 360
Judkins 194 378
Junge 68 99
Kain 367
Kane 197 406
Kannely 448
Kaple 101 445
Karnickle 459
Keach 88 235 406
Kear 72
Keating 115 222 223 260
   323
Keech 248 268 285 367

Keeler 80 408
Keihle 24
Keim 138
Keeler 286
Keller 465
Kelley 17 24 26 90 106
   223 224 278 284 328
   362 363
Kelly 4 28 161 174 191
   196 201 212 217 290
   291 362 370 375 385
   404 457 462
Kelsa 316
Kelts 238 239
Keltz 442
Kemp 101 133 158 174
   188 193 200 312 320
   407
Kenada 368
Kendig 467
Kennada 278
Kenyon 58 114 127 136
   159 171 197 212 276
   320 351 370 378 380
   409
Kernan 7 17 92 98 111
   187 332
Kerr 371
Keschoweck 358
Kettle 264
Kherle 351
Kibbe 35 127 148 199
   281 351 447
Kibbee 158 358 359 386
Kidder 469
Kidney 106 191 246 284
   358 406
Kiehl 61
Kiehle 22 27 28
Kies 31 178 239 284 343
   406
Kilbeck 284
Kilbourn 167 196 234
   235 278 320 407 408
Kilbourne 3 107 147 148
   198 239 241 269 270
   272 285 290 291 303
   319 358 361 370 386
   430 439 441 447 448
   452 460
Kilduff 412 433 453
Kile 365
Kimball 101
Kimm 62 73 232 238 286
King 45 59 86 87 88 114
   115 116 136 144 166
   171 176 201 255 269

Surname Index

306 310 329 330 343
359 360 366 401 433
437 452 453
Kinner 87 145 348 351
371 399 408 449
Kinney 74 109 171 371
375 377
Kinny 130
Kirk 386
Kirkpatrick 457
Klein 28 99 108 160 165
192 193 280 285 404
406
Klem 445
Klemm 127 198 213
Klesa 382 471
Klien 430
Kline 24 27 160 166 309
407 434 435
Knapp 169
Knechtel 223
Knickerbacker 116 213
217 320 442
Knickerbocker 64 342
363 364 413 456 471
Knight 147
Knowlton 62 63 127 188
194 195 286 380
Knox 1 2 17 18 25 27 36
37 50 65 70 85 87 89
91 107 115 124 125
129 131 132 146 156
159 172 177 183 192
208 209 213 222 224
227 234 236 247 248
255 275 284 305 321
330 332 333 349 386
390 392 395 396 399
401 402 406 413 431
444 449 468 469
Koehler 350
Koon 167 282 306 329
Krusen 282 306 310 437
Kuhn 92
Lambert 158 174 196 408
445 448
Lamberton 347 464
Lamblin 152
Lamont 286 369
Lamonte 37
Lamp 108 286
Lampe 408
Landon 51
Lane 102 127 139 179
194 197 278 285 295
390 399 407 475
Langdon 92 197 239 253

399 406 410
Larkin 136 158 223 229
Larkins 199
Larrabee 1 6 9 17 22 24
27 28 33 36 37 49 54
58 59 62 65 66 67 88
92 97 101 107 128
139 153 154 158 176
177 201 235 247 253
255 262 267 275 279
303 304 305 310 318
332 333 343 363 390
392 408 419 420 428
430 439 441 446
Larrison 107 147 198 213
Lasher 406
Latham 190
Lathrop 107 188 193 342
367 445 448
Latta 116 317 318 373
Laughlin 470
Lawrence 213 447
Lawton 131 132 223 246
268 270 365
Lay 50 65 456
Leach 73 85 87 88 267
359 367 462
Leary 328
Leavenworth 215 251
280 333 381
LeCarn 212
Leddy 139
Lee 86 159 160 169 170
429
Leech 85 389
Leet 101 197 260 278
290 291
Leete 38
Leggett 267
Lehman 92 107 192 223
236 244 274 278 285
361 362 363 404 406
457 467
Leibe 377
Leibenhuhuer 368
Lenhart 168
Lent 61 62 74 101 102
107 127 151 174 188
192 223 312 363 364
378 382 451 457
Leonard 28 29 31 225
229 278 285 407
Lester 312
Lewis 9 19 34 49 52 62
64 68 86 88 90 99
106 107 108 111 114
127 134 136 147 159

167 170 172 173 174
178 179 188 191 193
197 198 201 202 212
223 229 238 239 255
275 278 284 285 286
290 291 301 302 303
306 328 332 333 343
344 349 358 361 364
365 366 370 372 378
384 385 389 390 392
397 401 402 406 407
410 411 420 422 424
431 432 433 435 442
443 445 446 447 448
449 453 457 458 462
464 475
Lillibridge 243
Lilly 373 471
Limringer 464
Lincoln 222 420
Litner 107
Little 52 107 198 378
Livermore 197
Lloyd 255 320
Locey 108 115 158 172
Lochry 413
Lockwood 108 213 274
275 320 370 399 407
Logan 255 420
Logue 109 287 354 409
Longee 122
Lord 235
Losey 136 137 196
Lossey 378
Loucks 116 198 238 261
262 277 278 289 371
Louge 210
Loughery 282 306
Lovel 17
Lovell 312 331 369 370
Loveridge 37 60
Lowell 37
Lowery 407
Lowrey 285
Luce 62 367 409
Ludden 464
Luddington 192
Ludington 369
Lunn 279 351 459
Luthner 138
Lyman 7 36 52 60 62 63
69 78 80 81 92 100
101 108 110 115 123
126 147 156 157 159
160 161 167 175 182
193 195 196 199 202
204 205 212 215 225

Surname Index

252 255 259 260 262
267 268 274 275 276
285 315 316 320 324
328 354 359 361 362
363 364 370 378 382
391 422 423 424 445
454 470
Lyon 18 26 54 55 109
128 155 160 223 236
350 446 447 468
Lyons 16
Macken 59 115 170
Madigan 251
Madison 147
Magee 321
Maginnis 36 352 382 406
413 432 443
Mahan 127 188
Maher 199
Mahon 222 386 445
Main 109 198 409
Malery 200
Mallory 223 248 297 304
392 464
Maltby 130 131 176 186
212 354 464
Manley 196 286 453
Mann 5 15 17 22 27 30
35 36 49 50 57 59 60
68 86 87 88 90 91 99
107 111 112 113 115
119 124 131 132 135
137 138 144 146 157
158 173 174 175 178
200 209 217 222 223
246 247 268 306 310
317 328 330 331 332
333 337 358 360 385
391 396 403 404 406
411 418 419 420 432
433 445 453 458
Manning 116 142 278
286 316
Marble 68 92 99 171 179
188 215 231 275 278
290 325 383 462 464
Maricle 368
Marion 72 81 157 171
179 285 390 407 445
448 475
Markham 108
Marlon 448
Marschner 63 64 65
Marsh 45 148 156 195
320 408
Marshall 69 125 149 214
215 333 357 382 430

Martin 52 107 127 129
196 234 255
Marvin 36 306 307 312
329 330
Mascho 200 222 269
Masten 254 380
Matteson 175 191 446
447
Mattison 2 17 25 26 41
42 56 92 106 121
142 149 157 175 232
234 247 278 283 284
290 334 374 378 443
451 464
Maun 443
May 313
Maynard 59
McAllister 88
McCalmont 385
McCann 285
McCarn 158 192 205 222
446 447
McCarty 196 455 459
McCaslin 128
McChesney 7
McClure 242 248 255
308 364 457 458 470
McConn 406
McConnell 359 367
McCormick 7 68 98 99
McCoy 109 255 408 442
McCready 313 314 317
McCullough 314
McCutcheon 344
McDermet 158
McDevit 59
McDonald 39 86 115 255
284 351 369
McDonnell 247
McDorman 81
McDormott 173
McDougall 138 175 246
379 431
McDowell 1 19 90 108
115 127 136 148 152
158 194 213 278 280
286 290 378 445 448
McEwen 60 88 115
McFall 201
McGinnis 60 101 107 142
156 234 285 289 329
387 448
McGoey 335
McGonigal 156 173 174
200 306 329 344 359
386 432
McGonigall 158 359 411

445 448 454
McGowan 192 343 344
456
McGregor 256
McGuey 168
McHale 107 115 158
McIlvain 314
McIntosh 280
McIntyre 181 182 452
McKean 314
McKee 107 147 188 192
239 247 366 376 454
McKewen 410
McKinney 54 192 193
285 366
McKinster 410 412
McMahon 327
McMuller 342
McNamara 4 158 199 366
389 391 412 444 453
McNamire 134 367
McNaughton 437
McNeil 39 173
McNess 58
McNulty 124 176 275
McQuay 308 329
McWasser 174
Meacham 445
Meachum 108
Mead 29 366
Mehring 64 65 107 223
241 437
Meine 1 139 157 178 197
204 236 326 411 444
Meissner 36 378
Mellon 88
Meltzer 158
Melzer 249 250 268
Menge 320 406
Menschal 457
Mercer 427
Merchant 46
Merranville 115 445
Merrick 19 86 108 192
196 370 408 411 432
Merrill 3 23 64 92 93 94
95 109 175 200
Merriman 348
Merwin 324
Metcalf 270 285 302 304
330 350 378
Metzgar 24 90 92 93 97
98 137
Metzger 22 67 68 98 99
142 143 176 215 216
234 235 255 275 325
331 353 404 406 422

487

Surname Index

Mezler 264
Micheltree 258
Milde 406
Millard 9 67 68 71 98 99
    270 275 310 368 372
    399 407
Milleisen 318
Milleiten 318
Millen 86 88
Miller 51 59 60 87 123
    159 172 173 195 198
    215 239 330 363 370
    386 389 392 399 409
    411 412 413 445 452
    460 464 470 473
Millon 72 88
Mills 222 247 269 306
    310 329 408 436
Miner 246 269 369
Mintayne 71
Mitchel 432
Mitchell 88 97 109 115
    275 350 366
Mitcheltree 442
Mix 222
Moffatt 463
Moffitt 50
Monday 407
Monroe 42 43 50 66 97
    102 108 109 116 129
    134 136 137 148 149
    150 151 159 167 174
    178 189 197 202 210
    212 224 234 238 247
    249 257 258 263 264
    270 279 284 287 289
    307 308 315 327 330
    332 339 350 351 359
    364 373 379 380 381
    385 389 390 394 409
    423 433 440 448
Moody 171 178 286
Moon 90 197 268 443
Moore 70 71 73 109 115
    123 223 224 244 255
    278 353 361 370 371
Moran 36 58 59 73 88
    107 158 159 188 223
    234 353 406 409 453
    464
Morey 196 286 320 329
    386 406 408
Morgan 261 451
Morley 106 148 156 157
    167 234 278 284 285
    343 367 382 404 445
Morrey 52 284

Morris 108 132 286
Morrison 452
Morse 269 382
Morton 109 371 408
Mortor 196
Moser 50
Mosier 453
Mott 363
Moyer 160 347 452
Mulford 19 127
Mulkin 87 270 378 413
    426 448 464
Mullen 139
Mundy 466
Munger 188 197 312 413
    460
Munson 108 180 348
Musto 137
Mustoe 123
Neal 71
Nealey 285
Nealy 285
Neefe 17 18 24 26 33 34
    68 73 99 109 141
    143 156 176 195 196
    216 217 270 271 278
    280 287 362 381 399
    408 445 448 449 456
    457 464 468
Neeley 297
Neely 406 407
Neffe 188
Neiley 297
Neill 306 310
Neiman 52
Nelson 9 24 62 63 65 66
    67 73 74 78 86 88 90
    92 94 95 97 107 115
    127 128 136 148 154
    156 157 158 167 173
    175 178 180 183 189
    190 191 192 194 196
    217 223 235 239 244
    246 275 278 279 284
    286 287 290 306 309
    331 332 344 359 361
    363 376 386 390 392
    404 406 409 412 414
    427 429 434 435 443
    448 449 451 456 457
    458
Neother 262 263
Nesbit 329 359 386
Nesbitt 399 340 359
Newcomb 224
Newman 35 36 247
Newton 19 31 61 73 105

109 134 137 147 197
219 286 359 378 408
453
Nichols 21 24 28 37 46
    50 51 52 64 65 87 90
    91 109 121 124 131
    132 134 135 138 147
    157 158 167 173 174
    188 192 197 200 201
    208 209 224 242 256
    279 286 310 332 334
    340 364 369 378 384
    385 426 433
Nickerson 108 194 285
    358 386 412 431
Nicklaus 36 328
Niell 433
Niles 17 24 26 49 92 98
    135 144 253 282 306
    310 330 353 358 374
    412
Niver 458
Noble 47
Nobles 41 46 47 422
Noelk 70 378
Noether 446
Norman 86
North 108 202 215 259
    286 343
Northrup 114 198 285
    368
Norton 7 9 17 18 25 27
    28 32 98 124 126
    128 141 176 177 182
    188 225 226 273 278
    290 291 390
Nott 323
Nye 39 57 59 93 232 310
O'Brien 247 262
O'Donald 52
O'Donnell 158 173 198
    310 331 376 442
O'Higley 86
O'Neill 372
Ohweiler 350
Oleson 73 178 332 419
    446
Olmsted 6 13 16 17 18
    22 24 26 27 28 30 33
    35 49 51 53 55 64 65
    69 85 88 91 107 113
    114 115 119 124 128
    131 132 137 139 146
    148 167 174 175 208
    209 223 227 252 273
    275 284 289 306 307
    310 331 332 341 351

Surname Index

358 384 396 412 431
442 460 463 472
Olney 107
Olson 195 408
Omerod 453
Opp 169 170
Ormerod 178 223 247
297 307 315 333 347
385
Osgood 74
Ostrander 396
Otto 236
Outman 107 385 440
Owen 42 43 110 164 165
177 237
Owens 150 239
Packard 433
Page 229 418
Palmateer 362
Palmatier 373
Palmer 95 238 240 370
399
Palmeter 409
Palmiter 406
Pangburn 308 364 365
Parish 248
Parker 52 73 85 107 156
198 278 285 290 358
366 406
Parkhurst 190 331
Parmenter 174 287
Parson 407
Parsons 358 437
Patridge 238 239 240 241
Patterson 38 86 114
Pattison 331 348 449
Paul 58 284
Pawson 31
Pearce 36
Pearsall 6 19 22 24 31 36
42 43 64 96 120 147
159 177 196 219 229
269 279 309 336 359
371 433 464 468
Pearsoll 1 27 28 40 178
423
Peasley 197
Peasly 432
Peck 2 23 34 50 74 95 96
146 150 152 156 183
192 263 265 273 284
305 333 403 468
Peebles 318
Peet 108 179 191 284 408
450 457
Peltz 197 399
Penny 463

Perins 26
Perkins 5 17 21 22 24 33
65 67 98 114 129
188 286 310 320 329
336 437 468
Perry 29 71 72 73 94 119
179 227 237 256 277
281 308 318 320 342
360 372 378 390
Persing 55 263 368
Peryitt 252 253 264 269
270
Peters 59 78
Peterson 93 143 173 387
413
Petlz 200
Petrie 40 41 44 45 46 47
49 385
Pettys 313 314 317 318
Phelps 77 156 246 247
284 308 360 362 420
448 450 464
Phenix 76 186 196 286
407 439
Phillips 4 16 24 25 34 62
90 124 177 183 275
279 312 334 346 364
368 370 392 458
Pickett 71 77 94 225 329
Pierce 17 24 26 28 60 64
90 166 286 351
Pierson 472
Piler 224
Pinneo 101
Pinney 148 183 275 378
390 392
Piper 360
Pitcher 261
Place 235 270
Plageman 277 308
Plagueman 382
Plank 198 371 419 437
Plants 343
Platt 321 348
Plum 155
Pollard 195 319 408
Pomeroy 115 170 195
238 262 350 371
Pomroy 167
Porter 202 224 381 417
Post 23 41 42 107 127
192 214 234 275 377
410 452
Potter 71 72 95 121 188
238 443 457 475
Pratt 231
Prentis 458

Prentiss 40 47
Presho 57 67 77 98 101
201 244 247 249 269
306 312 370
Press 196 309 371
Pride 303
Prince 197 231 350 422
429 433
Prindle 247 330 452
Pritchard 291 412 432
463 464
Proctor 295
Prosser 264 269 306 330
Prouty 108 109 127 196
198 213 254 286 287
378 384 409 422
Pursley 123
Putman 213
Putnam 87 159 351 449
Pye 88 426
Quant 369
Quick 201 224 254 275
305 444
Quimby 73 102 108 163
264 274 276 279 283
407 417 426 471
Quinett 330
Quinette 137
Quinnette 88 116 360
Race 59 107 239
Radde 113
Ramsey 460
Randall 88 409
Ransom 174 239
Ransome 201
Rathbone 59 73 127 192
285 365
Rathbun 161 372 382
Raub 9
Rausch 86
Rawson 138
Raymer 214
Raymond 35 51 57 59 74
127 153 167 172 173
175 182 187 191 217
265 324 350 351 361
363 364 371 378 404
440 444 448 454
Reamsch 93
Reaser 138 453
Reckhow 58
Redner 73 85 188 285
Reed 36 37 44 54 73 108
109 115 167 178 191
193 194 195 196 202
220 246 247 258 275
277 278 281 282 286

Surname Index

289 305 307 310 328
329 330 351 357 358
359 367 374 375 386
387 392 412 417 419
422 445 451 453 455
Reeder 367
Reer 86 114 310
Rees 1 3 10 17 18 19 22
24 26 28 32 42 43 49
51 52 54 55 60 74 96
108 128 142 143 146
147 155 158 159 164
170 175 177 195 216
223 229 257 258 274
278 282 286 287 290
292 304 306 320 332
335 364 378 387 390
409 424 438 442 445
455
Reese 266
Reeves 112
Reid 169 408
Reining 392
Reisman 21 175
Reissman 15 16 20 24 25
26 28 97 205 243
273 390 465
Reissmann 22 128
Remington 235 312
Remsch 223
Rennells 2 21 23 24 27 63
64 65 92 107 109
120 155 183 186 192
196 210 213 220 258
266 273 275 372 378
390 404 406 442 456
Reuning 458
Reves 60
Rexford 106 156 197 239
278 290 368 448 464
Reymer 328
Reynold 234
Reynolds 19 65 74 90
101 107 109 124 134
139 156 180 191 192
197 238 239 248 252
253 285 287 307 310
326 330 351 361 365
409 415 440 441 454
469
Rhinevault 256
Rhodes 160 268 306
Rice 39 95 101 109 138
156 167 193 198 278
279 285 289 407 409
429 448
Richardson 37

Rigney 199
Riley 199 419 461
Rima 407
Rinehuls 193
Rink 388
Rippel 332
Ripple 95 96 101 108 178
194 286 329 446 464
Rischel 382
Ritter 129
Rixford 137
Roach 87 107 198 285
289
Robbins 57 148 153 239
369 389 440 442
Roberts 74 109 167 208
234 349 408
Robins 371
Robinson 197 273 351
359 403 433
Roby 234 399
Rockafellow 371
Rockefeller 442
Rockefellow 235
Rockwell 255
Rodes 246
Roe 121 122
Roer 58
Rogers 107 116 188 191
278 289 354 373 382
444 467
Rohrbacher 138
Rooks 52 107 148 278
Rooney 58 86 136 157
168 201 224 274 285
386
Roony 158 173
Root 208 209
Rosa 115
Rose 63
Roselle 159 193
Ross 17 18 21 24 27 28
61 62 64 65 97 100
120 124 138 146 152
161 176 210 224 237
246 267 287 304 318
323 330 348 409 412
420 423 438 446
Rossiter 37 44 452
Rossman 156 157 238
287 408 448
Rotsell 330
Roulee 276
Rounds 138
Rounnsville 66
Rounsevill 385
Rounseville 99 137 141

164 216 412 432 458
Rounsville 64 97 192 320
363 364
Rouse 198
Rowell 53 201
Rowlee 161 193 199 448
Rowley 156 157 159 255
285 372 382 445 449
Roy 115
Rozell 407
Ruby 173
Rude 270
Rugg 223
Rukgaber 280 287 324
360
Rum 286
Rumpff 147
Rumsey 330
Ruscher 109 174 196 286
366 408 422
Rush 432
Rushmore 59 464
Russel 105 268
Russell 114
Rutherford 180 224
Ryan 101 198 212 387
411 440 443
Rycraft 451 454
Ryon 38 68 99 406
Sackett 64
Sackman 185
Sahr 188
Salomon 358
Sampson 108
Sandbach 52 106 197 284
Sandberg 445
Sanburg 188
Sanders 36 134
Sanderson 88
Sartwell 255
Saunders 92 170 212 464
Schadenberger 62 63 64
347 448 457 458 468
Schall 59 339 340 413
Schaar 320
Schaudenberger 64 215
238
Schauss 215
Scheaver 450
Scheibner 197
Scheultheis 350 369
Schilberger 362
Schildberger 63 64 65
364 451
Schildenberger 64
Schilderberger 146 177
Schmantz 106

Surname Index

Schmeitz 58
Schmidt 48 59 60 87 115
    136 247
Schneider 115
Schoemaker 198
Schollard 52 107 192 285
    352 407
Schoonover 57 298 301
    303
Schrader 223
Schroder 368
Schwab 91 328
Schwartzenbach 147 440
    466
Schwarzenbach 70
Scott 17 26 35 36 46 57
    60 87 88 201 222
    223 238 247 320 399
    414
Scovill 468
Scoville 51 191 234 248
    404 406 432 444 448
    464
Seals 329 460
Sechrest 457 458
Seeley 210 224 264 269
Seely 367
Seibenheimer 58 200 328
    358
Seibenhemer 60
Seibert 36 45 58 59 60 87
    115 184 258 270 409
    428 441 468
Seifert 93 222
Seiforth 354
Shanley 201 247
Sharier 198
Sharp 88
Shattuck 160 246 276
Shaw 231 232 234 306
Shay 288 306 310 329
    358 462
Shear 11 44 51 54 63 136
    157 179 183 223 332
    430 439 441
Sheat 107
Sheldon 179 348 349 431
    432
Sherman 19 167 279 437
    442 451
Sherwood 23 160 174
    210 223 224 281 359
    366 371 386 418 433
    440 450 452 455
Shields 73
Shingler 432
Shryver 370

Shutt 137 159 365
Sible 99
Siebenhahiner 37
Sikes 224
Simmons 373 469
Simonds 254 255
Simons 36 362 363 365
    448
Simpier 37
Simpson 208
Sinette 288
Sizer 315
Skinner 198 361
Slade 191 365
Slarrow 89 287 408 411
    448 449
Slaughter 143 284 464
Slaven 452
Slingerland 318 367
Sloan 173
Sloat 133 169 253
Slocum 229 287
Smiley 268 447
Smith 37 44 52 62 64 65
    73 76 90 101 105
    112 115 119 121 126
    132 138 147 158 161
    187 191 193 194 195
    197 200 201 219 223
    224 229 234 238 255
    264 270 272 274 277
    278 279 286 290 291
    309 310 330 334 345
    351 354 366 378 399
    412 418 432 437 443
    444 445 450 452 465
Snead 385
Snyder 18 36 53 109 195
    212 217 222 255 268
    278 285 287 288 316
    343 352 376 408 422
    443 454 456
Solomon 115 386
Spafford 7 101 107 113
    192 217 284 310 316
    364 378 404 406
Spargur 170
Spencer 73 106 115 127
    147 153 178 189 224
    246 268 332 443
Sprigg 318
Springer 223
Stacken 316 471
Stannard 107 138 241
    244 247
Starkweather 310
Statham 197 281 283 461

Stathan 407
Staudefield 386
Staysa 40 322
Steadman 321 326 343
Stearns 62 63 64 66 67
    101 133 192 216 243
    284 285 305 306 404
    406
Stebbins 12 14 15 16 17
    18 20 21 22 23 24 25
    26 28 29 30 33 49 54
    82 88 91 92 113 115
    124 128 131 139 146
    147 154 158 175 176
    183 192 208 217 218
    220 221 255 261 275
    284 322 332 337 338
    378 390 391 432 435
    457 458 468 469
Stedman 93
Stephens 46 192 406
Sterrett 1 86
Stetson 197
Steuart 123
Stevens 24 25 37 52 87
    93 107 115 123 129
    136 149 158 164 170
    197 222 227 229 235
    254 263 265 270 278
    284 285 289 295 296
    304 310 320 329 330
    331 337 368 375 378
    380 407 433 434 438
    442
Stevenson 17 26
Stewart 108 122 193 276
    278 279 290 291 370
    372 407 423
Stickles 182
Stiles 115 378
Stillman 31 89 95 96 127
    187 188 238 320 359
    362 380 386 417 422
    443 464
Stillson 32 376
Stilson 108 159 193 370
    464
Stillwell 454
Stone 107 197 202 234
    243 304 322 368 389
    406 407 432 443 464
Stoneham 256 385
Stonemetz 369
Storrs 44 47 261
Story 110 151 157 158
    173 200
Stout 258

491

Surname Index

Stoutenberg 216
Strait 213 320 331
Strang 92 170 294
Stratton 1 7 29 34 44 55
   73 80 89 92 110 119
   125 129 130 131 142
Streeter 37 137 275
Streitz 409
Striker 212 213 444
Stritz 198 287
Stroele 305
Strong 161 176 366 386
   411
Stryker 89 114 406 451
   452
Stuart 60 165 287
Stuckey 160
Styles 380
Suhr 109 197 399 409
Sullivan 194 195 213 239
   391
Sunderlin 285 407
Surdam 73 127 270 272
   351 399
Sutherland 196 399 408
Sutton 108 196 198 278
   286 388
Swain 57 77 178 191 261
   318 337 354 382 404
   410 462 467 473
Swarthout 69
Swartout 91
Swartwood 212 286
Sweeten 423
Swetland 2 67 90 92 93
   95 96 107 127 197
   239 241 407 431
Swift 73 107 127 188 285
   407 443
Swimlar 198 285 407
Sylvester 190
Taggart 161 175 212 230
   241 259 364 443 471
   473
Tansom 238 240 272
Tanson 225
Tapel 113
Tassel 343
Taubert 73 74 77 80 83
   86 107 193 328 354
   469
Tauburt 407
Tauscher 74 108 175 195
   213 217 287 406 408
   440 443 444
Taylor 35 170 255 432
Teachman 440

Teed 59
Templeton 464
Tenbrock 416
Tenbrook 155 265
Tennant 467
Terry 109 112
Terwillegar 356
Terwilliger 174 354 359
   366 367
Teuscher 115 216 238
   286
Thatcher 115 137 138
Theis 70 127 344 406 440
   443 448 449
Thetge 36
Thomas 371 376 423
Thompson 15 16 17 18
   20 21 22 24 25 26 27
   28 32 33 37 50 62 77
   78 81 82 93 95 107
   124 128 129 132 136
   150 154 157 167 176
   177 178 183 188 191
   192 209 251 254 255
   273 284 302 303 324
   326 327 331 335 361
   367 368 371 372 383
   388 390 404 406 419
   424 427 441 444 449
   457 458 463 468
Thorn 286
Thorne 377 463
Thorpe 304
Tice 108 138 156 196
   378 407
Tilburgh 110
Tingley 170
Toland 473
Toles 39
Tolls 224
Tombs 364
Tompkins 369
Tooker 36 60
Toombs 109 275 366 457
Torrey 197 423
Torsey 127
Townsend 37 224
Tracey 331
Tracy 151 167 173
Trask 58 115 220 278
   289 310
Traton 438
Traub 101 109 157 188
   409 443 445
Tremain 437
Trim 295
Trumbower 255

Tubbs 51 224 330 399
   407
Tucker 95 106 191 320
Tupper 382
Turck 86 89 220 409
Turk 234
Turner 63 88 91 93 112
   145 176 222 227 234
   246 351 409
Tuttle 48 58 68 71 159
   171 179 184 195 215
   275 281 295 302 304
   325 383 408 412 439
Tyler 52 73 107 171 183
   353 378 406 444 465
Underhill 170
VanAmmon 91
Vancise 134
VanBuskirk 236
VanCuren 235
VanDeboe 115
Vanderhoef 239
VanGelder 171
VanGilder 366
VanGorder 174 297 298
   299 302 303 304
VanHorn 37 115 128 473
VanHusen 385 431
VanHuysen 360
Vaninwegen 279
VanLiew 359
Vannatta 287
Vanoux 386
VanVorhees 172 173
VanWegen 62 63 64 91
   160 192 228 237 244
   264 273 275 336 350
   374 379 390 392 435
   471
VanWegin 142
VanWinkle 335
Varney 64 188 236 307
Vaughn 107 192
Veeley 170 225 254 282
   283 284
Veelie 131 343 378 379
Veeley 306 307 317
Veely 157 270
Veley 61 62 63 64 68 99
Velie 92 152 153 329
Vergason 159 172 193
   412 433
Verguson 62 193
Villetta 198
Vincent 174 196
Voorhees 52 109 134 234
Vosburg 386

Surname Index

Voss 70 106 143 316 444
Vroosman 28
Wagner 358 360 385 386
  411 431 456
Wagoner 29 91 137 193
  238 240 372 410 412
  452 473
Wakely 196 365 406
Walden 224
Wales 451 454
Walker 87 109 115 193
  194 234 287 399 409
  464
Wall 359
Wallace 101 105 193 196
  285 286 308 344 366
  408 432
Walley 73
Walter 138
Wambold 86 152 165 213
  385 408 412
Ward 58 87 137 174 194
  282 306 329 360 387
  411 468
Wariner 407
Warner 28 54 160 197
  212 213 226 286 351
  399 408
Warriner 154
Waterman 107 285 367
  444
Waters 107 114 198 224
  247 254 269 289 291
  292 293 294 295 296
  297 298 299 301 302
  303 304 305 391
Watkins 306 309
Watrous 249
Watson 38 73 109 136
  196 286 375 408 429
  461
Watts 38
Weaver 112 116 170 448
Webb 64 138 279 286
  408
Weber 63 64
Webster 77 95 101 238
  285 399 411 462
Wedsworth 243 438
Weed 278 306
Weidman 156
Weidrich 190
Weightman 357 360
Weimer 74 81 92 93 148
  194 195 202 235 237
  239 278 286 290 291
  378 383 406 408 423

443
Weiss 223
Welch 352 419 437
Wells 95 101 161 193
  197 212 285 307 378
  407 420 443 446 456
  464
Weltch 367
Welton 92 167 184 278
  290 342 423
Wenzel 284
Wescott 261
West 90 277 354 369 370
Westcott 55
Westerman 37 60
Westfall 115
Westgate 138
Weston 131 132
Wetenhall 368
Wetmore 373 453 464
Wetsel 451
Wetzel 412 432
Wheaton 73 85 108 147
  148 177 278 371 373
  399 406
Wheeler 108 153 198 279
  285 287 384 390 409
  443
Whipple 191 223 320 370
  406
Whitam 407
Whitcomb 409
Whitcome 164
White 3 9 17 22 24 26 28
  36 45 50 52 54 59 63
  66 67 68 73 91 92 97
  98 113 115 121 122
  126 127 150 151 155
  156 160 174 176 179
  180 192 195 197 212
  213 222 228 231 239
  244 253 255 263 265
  278 281 282 286 287
  305 313 315 332 349
  354 362 364 375 376
  381 399 403 407 408
  412 420 423 437 443
  444 445 448 449 450
  458 468 469
Whitehead 65
Whitehed 52
Whiteman 128 198 212
  372
Whitman 285
Whitmarsh 223
Whitney 108 200 229 249
  306 407

Whittaker 207 256 411
Whittum 107 448
Wickham 240
Widger 294 298 299 300
  301 302 303
Wilber 87 94 115 137
  159 167 198 224
Wilbur 107 109 194 285
  287 351
Wilcox 91 209 316 365
Wiley 62
Wilkinson 188 193 239
  255 276 278 290 370
Willen 364
Willetta 406
Willets 411 413
Williams 1 54 77 102 136
  138 154 157 178 193
  201 212 222 223 224
  238 239 246 252 268
  272 283 289 305 316
  328 332 357 359 367
  369 380 410 411 433
  441
Willing 116 268
Willoughby 80 81 371
Wilmoth 181 182
Wilouthby 108
Wilson 1 37 90 113 134
  172 178 200 235 239
  246 253 279 373
Wimmer 63
Winfield 392
Winters 219
Witter 9 151 167 216 223
  239 246 317 347 443
  452
Woelen 45
Woelfel 284 448 451
Woelful 406
Wolcott 196 359 443
Wolfanger 68
Wolfel 197
Wombaugh 349
Womelsdorf 111
Womelsdorff 349
Womlesdorff 149
Wood 29 57 83 90 182
  184 220 243 252 262
  328 414 433 471 473
Woodard 101
Woodcock 36 60 62 63
  64 86 88 90 114 190
  284 362 452 456
Woodkirk 375 443
Woodring 58 86
Woods 365

493

Surname Index

Woolcot 167
Woolfinger 244
Worden 36 101 106 107
    167 188 191 198 238
    278 284 290 372 392
    411 413 423 433 444
    454 464 467
Work 297
Works 37 292 299 300
    302 304
Wrean 334 346
Wright 51 156 157 196
    197 274 359 370 372
    460 467 471
Wygant 151
Wykoff 71 92 182 389
    463
Yale 123 161
Yates 68 99
Yaudes 200
Yentzer 36 37 74 92 108
    137 173 184 185 194
    200 201 212 214 229
    235 286 328 403 408
    439 445 460 464 467
Yeomans 107 424 429
York 136 157 247
Young 101 108 121 151
    154 155 194 246 255
    278 286 290 328 358
    408 457
Younglove 107 108 160
    167 173 193 285 286
    328 351 378 407
Yundt 174
Yunge 179 284 351 444
Zacharias 382
Zael 223
Zemper 57
Zengerle 93 197 351
Zepp 197 406
Zimmerman 4 17 21 25
    27 28 43 57 91 128
    177 335 336 410 418
Zingerle 278 290
Zinnert 91
Zirmart 198
Zoerb 284 442

www.ingramcontent.com/pod-product-compliance
Lightning Source LLC
Chambersburg PA
CBHW051333230426
43668CB00010B/1252